W9-BLU-207

SHERMAN

FIGHTING PROPHET

SHERMAN

FIGHTING PROPHET

BY LLOYD LEWIS

Konecky & Konecky
156 Fifth Avenue
New York, NY 10010

Reprinted by special arrangement by William S. Konecky Associates, Inc.

ISBN 0-914427-78-4

Printed in the United States of America

To Kathryn

CONTENTS

PART TWO: THE SUMMIT

PART THREE: THE PLATEAU

SHERMAN

FIGHTING PROPHET

FOREWORD

THE MOTTO OVER THE DOOR

CHRISTMAS was at hand, and the cadets of the Louisiana State Seminary of Learning and Military Academy had departed for their homes, all alight with the emotions of approaching vacation. Up the steps of the main building came a man with the United States mail. He passed in at a door over which stood a marble motto—"By the liberality of the General Government. The Union—*Esto Perpetua*."

Newspapers came to the private room of the superintendent, a tall, spare man red of hair, red of beard. The superintendent fixed his bright eyes upon words on a page—"South Carolina has seceded from the Union." The thing had been done at half-past one in the afternoon of December 20 in the year 1860. All at once William Tecumseh Sherman began to weep. He leaped to his feet and paced his office with the long, quick steps of a man who all his life would walk out his troubles—the swift steps of a soldier who must be marching, marching till a job was done.

He loved the South. Since his sixteenth year his closest male friends had been Southerners. Now that he was forty his Ohio boyhood seemed far away. Of the twenty-five years that had elapsed since he had left home practically all had been spent under the social influence of the South—four years in the United States Military Academy where Southern ideals ruled—six in the enamoring charm of Florida and South Carolina—four as the intimate of Southern-born army officers in California—two in army posts at St. Louis and New Orleans—six representing Missouri bankers—some scattering months in Kansas and Ohio—and now this last year as superintendent of an academy in Louisiana.

The South had put its stamp upon him. Outside the windows, carpenters even now were building him a home in which he had dreamed he would spend the rest of his life with his family. Across the South, his old army comrades were, he knew, preparing to follow South Carolina's lead. But Sherman could not go along. Something was holding him back —and it was not slavery, for he approved that. It was the sign over the door: "The Union—*Esto Perpetua*."

With the pacing superintendent in his room, this December day, was his professor of ancient languages, a Southerner to whom Sherman talked as if, indeed, this one individual were the whole South. "South Carolina," said the superintendent, "has precipitated war.

"If you leave the Union the North must fight you for its own preservation."

The South would drench the country in blood. Talking, marching, weeping . . .

"Oh, it is all folly, madness, a crime against civilization! . . . I must fight your people, whom I love best."

Southerners, he said, knew nothing of war's terrors. They did not understand that war meant months of suffering for every day of glorious fighting. Did they realize that more men would die of disease than of battle wounds? How could they fail to understand that in all history no nation of mere agriculturists had ever won against a nation of mechanics?

"You are bound to fail!"

Within three weeks the superintendent had resigned. To the Governor of Louisiana he said:

"I prefer to maintain my allegiance to the Constitution as long as a fragment of it survives."

The crisis had awakened the one religion that he, in seventy long years of life, would own—love of the Union, a faith given him in part by heredity but more by environment, the environment shaped for him by Thomas Ewing, sometimes known as the Bishop, the Salt-Boiler, Old Solitude, and the Nestor of the Ohio Bar.

PART ONE: THE CLIMB

1

THE BISHOP COMES UP THE RIVER

"DEATH bells."

The little boy whispered the words to himself as he stepped outside the picket gate and listened. He looked across the clearing, with its many stumps, to where the hazel thickets hid the feet of tall trees. The sound came from there—a faint silvery ringing which the old folks said was made by death bells, ghost voices calling truant children to destruction. Behind him, from among the log cabins that clustered about the blockhouse, there rose the friendly hum of a spinning-wheel . . . and the boy scampered back through the gate to safety.

Thomas Ewing, who had come with his parents into the wilderness of the Northwest Territory two years before, was not one, at the age of five, to suspect that his elders would throw false mystery about the janglings of distant cowbells. Inside his big head, so black with hair, ran solemn thoughts. Never would he be imagining things, but always putting two and two together. And a little later in that summer of 1794, the cowbells and the death bells came together in his mind.

Through the days of August his father and other men of the garrison showed him that they too were afraid to enter the hazel thickets. They stood in the clearing calling in vain for the cows to come home. Sometimes the animals could be heard lowing near the forest's edge, but they would not come near enough to be milked. The boy heard his elders say that Indians were in the woods and that it was dangerous for any white person to be abroad.

One old man of the garrison, however, announced that he must go on a pressing errand to the larger fort at Waterford, three miles through the wilderness. Every one of the thirty persons in the blockhouse begged him not to risk it. The little boy's father, George Ewing, lately an ensign in George Washington's army, argued with the old man, and when he saw that it was no use, said: "Well, then, bring me some turnip seed." Hours later, two booms came from the woods and the old man's son, sitting with his gun in his hand, leaped to his feet, crying: "That's the crack of Father's rifle!" and ran out. In fifteen minutes he was back saying that the Indians had lured his father into an ambuscade by tinkling a cowbell and had killed him. So cowbells and death bells were the same!

The next day the small boy stared at four men carrying the corpse home on a litter of poles. Through the green beech leaves that covered the body the scalped head of the dead man shone crimson. In the old gentleman's pocket were found Lieutenant Ewing's turnip seeds, wrapped in a rag.

The whole affair was a great thing for a boy to remember—and life in the blockhouse was exciting, too. One of the big boys read aloud from a book of songs about a woodsman named Robin Hood, and one song in particular, the tale of how Robin Hood tricked Aylmer the Bishop, stuck in Thomas Ewing's mind. "I had it at once by rote," he afterwards recalled, "and went about, a big-headed little wonder, reciting it. The young men gave me the sobriquet of 'the Bishop'—I wore a hunting-shirt which my brother George had outgrown which reached to my ankles and was the Bishop's cloak. I wore the sobriquet but not the cloak for more than twenty years."

For all the fun in the fort, the small Bishop was glad when his family left the garrison the following spring and moved to a cabin in a clearing across the woods. There was no more danger from Indians; everybody said so. A great soldier, Mad Anthony Wayne, had whipped the redskins in battle and brought peace to the Northwest Territory.

Once the Bishop's father kept him all night at an Indian camp, where after a bashful hour or two the white boy warmed toward the little savages and raced and wrestled with them happily. He could outrun them and throw them but they could climb trees much more rapidly than he. Coming to the wigwams for supper, he felt his stomach turn as he saw the red women cooking puppies in a pot. He sat outside in the firelight, a miserable little figure, while the others ate. By the embers, later that evening, he saw his father smoking tobacco with the young chief, White-Eyes, and he heard them talk about old times when both had fought against King George. Next day, going home, his father had told him that White-Eyes was a graduate of a college named Dartmouth and that even yet he read Greek books in the wilderness. Always the Bishop would remember White-Eyes's wife, a half-breed of fifteen, brown and beautiful in a black silk robe with silver brooches.

As the Indians grew friendly, so life became richer for the Olive Green Creek garrison in whose neighborhood the Ewings still lived.

For one thing, salt appeared in the food they ate. Ever since the first white men had come to this portion of the country, they had been forced to travel two hundred miles back across the Ohio River and the mountains to Chambersburg, Pennsylvania, for the salt which merchants would trade for ginseng and furs at the rate of from $5 to $8 a bushel. It was slow, hard work packing it home on horses. Somewhere in the neighboring woods the Indians had a salt spring, but no settler knew where it was. Now, however, with the end of the fighting, a strange Indian came out of the forest to say that he was a white man released from long captivity and that in return for shelter he would tell where the secret springs might be found. George Ewing, Jr., was one of the men who followed the guide into the forest to establish the camp where four men, working seven days and nights, could boil down six bushels of salt in their sugar-water pots.

Never would Thomas Ewing forget the "exquisite relish" that this salt brought to his food, and from the day when, as a boy of fourteen, he would first go to work for himself until his death he would keep his hand, one way or another, in the making of salt.

The year that he was six, 1795, the Bishop learned to read, his elder sister teaching him between her turns at the spinning-wheel. Watts's psalms and hymns, and Flavel's sermons he could not understand, but the stories in the Bible, for all their unpronounceable names, seemed as bright as the bonfires that boys were allowed to touch off when the men were clearing new ground. The Gospels in particular haunted the little Bishop. It was both puzzling and marvelous to read about the man who lived four different lives and was crucified each time; and it was disappointing to learn from one's father that they were only four different stories about the same life and the same crucifixion.

More books came into the youth's small hands in the autumn of 1797, when he was taken away to school. His father had put him in a canoe and paddled down the Muskingum and then a hundred miles up the Ohio to West Liberty in Virginia, where his Aunt Sarah Morgan lived and where he would spend the winter, a strange, serious scholar, unused to so many children. The schoolhouse lay two miles away through the forest—a distance that the Bishop and his cousin Ed trudged daily. Where Short Creek crossed their path Uncle Morgan took great pains to show the little boys how and where to hide from Indians if they should happen to see or hear the redskins passing. Although the Indians were no longer on the warpath, the white men thought it wise to avoid them. For all Thomas Ewing's scant eight years, he spelled down a class of boys of eighteen and twenty and read all the novels in his uncle's library. Unimaginative and practical, he earned a brisk switching from his Uncle Morgan because he lay long after dark beside a cemetery to see if the Welsh boys were right in saying that ghosts walked.

A few incidents like these he could remember in later years, but it was not until the spring of 1798 that his young mind started storing up things in detail. When school was out, his uncle brought him in a flatboat to the new clearing that Lieutenant Ewing had carved out of the beech and walnut forests in the Hockhocking Valley seventeen miles south of the blockhouse where the old man with the scalped head lay buried.

The wild plum trees were in bloom when the young Bishop came up the river on the banks of which he was to live for the remaining seventy-two years of his life. And even when he was famous and old—one of the foremost lawyers of the nation—he would sit in elegant New York hotels and complain because nothing tasted as sweet as the wild plums that he had gathered along the Great Hockhocking River when he was a boy. Service berries (people later called them June berries) were sweet too, in that early time, and the Bishop, with a spaniel as his sole companion, would scour the forest to mark those trees which would ripen first. All that summer of 1798 he watched his trees, only to discover when picking time came that a bear had already climbed the trunks, broken the limbs inward till they looked like the ribs of a folded umbrella, and stripped off the fruit. Later the boy learned to chop down trees to get at the berries and wild grapes and chestnuts. It was easier than climbing. Black haws were delicious, too—so delicious that before long they, like the wild plums, were gone from the country, destroyed by the settlers who had thought them inexhaustible. The Bishop learned to make tea from spicebush and sassafras roots and to trim the drink with maple sugar and cream. Wild strawberries were everywhere in early summer, their juice staining horses' legs scarlet to the knees.

By day pheasants drummed in the woods, by night wolves howled and panthers screamed like women. And by both day and night in the springtime and fall, wild geese swept overhead in great phalanxes against the sky or moon, making the air shudder with the beating of their wings.

With his sisters and brother so much older or younger than himself, the Bishop learned to rely upon the family dog for his chief playmate—and the dog preferred the more exciting company of that elder brother George who was a great hunter, shooting in one autumn and the following spring forty-seven bears. So said his younger sister Jane fifty years later, thinking back.

Jane remembered how she, as a toddler, had once followed the Bishop into the woods accompanied by the dog, which, taking it for granted that he should scare up a bear, did nose one out and bring it on the run toward the infants. Secure in his virtue, the dog harassed the bear until it was furious, and it came at the children mouth open.

"He was a red-eyed bear," said Jane—a description given bears in the springtime when they came out of their hibernation to blink in the sunlight and to view all nature with ill-temper. "We ran and I fell. Tom picked me up and kept behind me so that if the bear caught up to us I would have the best chance of reaching the house. We reached the clearing where our brother George had come up to find out why the dog was barking so. He shot over us and killed the bear."

For three years the Ewings lived in this clearing, cut off from intercourse with the world, their nearest neighbors fourteen miles away. More and more the Bishop turned to books, solemn thoughts, and his father's words. He heard his father tell with pride who his ancestors had been. There had been a great-great-grandfather who had been one of the Orangemen decorated by the English King William for gallantry at the Battle of the Boyne, and there had been a great-grandfather of Scotch blood, Thomas Ewing, who had left the north of Ireland for America in 1718, the time of the South Sea Bubble immigration, to become a Presbyterian deacon at Greenwich, New Jersey; and a grandfather Thomas Ewing also, who had been a Presbyterian elder. The Bishop learned that his father, George, had left his birthplace, Greenwich, because of tragic financial failure. When George Ewing had joined General Washington's army at the age of twenty-one, he had put his money, $8,000, in bonds, and when he emerged from the war six and one-half years later, the bonds, falling due, were paid in Continental money that was worth less than five cents on the dollar. So Lieutenant Ewing turned West, where some day when matters were straightened out veterans would receive the fat lands which the Congress had promised them.

Out beyond the Alleghenies, across the Ohio River, lay that immense sweep of forest which the Congress wished to use in paying its debt to soldiers. It had belonged to the King of England, clear to the Mississippi River and up to the Great Lakes, and George III, making peace after the American Revolution, had ceded it to the new United States. But the most powerful States in the Union had kept this land from the veterans, saying: "That Western territory belongs to us, not to the Confederated Government. Our original colony boundaries run west from the Atlantic seaboard to the Mississippi River or beyond." So Lieutenant Ewing and other veterans had waited while the greedy States held them from their reward.

The little Bishop, listening to settlers talking around the fireplace in

1798, would hear how the States had made life hard for pioneers as far back as 1776, when twenty-five thousand souls who had crossed the Appalachian Mountains to carve out homes around the headwaters of the Ohio River had been abused and mistreated by Pennsylvania and Virginia, both of which claimed the land. Often a settler paid taxes to both State governments and to escape the avaricious assessors, the twenty-five thousand settlers had asked the newly formed Continental Congress to make a State for them. Even if this dream did not come true, the central Government had at least shown signs of befriending them. By 1784 it had forced the rich States to take their hands off the fatter and wider lands lying just beyond the Ohio River—the Northwest Territory. Here and there States held small preserves with which to pay off certain allowable debts, but the great wilderness as a whole had been won for the people by the Government. For the first time there were Americans saying, "The Union, not any State, is our friend."

A small boy like Thomas Ewing, playing beside his father in stump-lined fields of the Northwest Territory, would hear how as far back as 1785 the Government had sent troops into the new country to clear out squatters; how it had sent surveyors to plat the land and one army after another to quiet the Indians. He heard how the Government had held on to the Northwest Territory even when as late as 1791 Congressmen were asking if it would not be best to forget the whole wilderness country, since the Indians were so bad, and make the Ohio River the northern boundary of the United States. They asked if Kentucky and Tennessee were not large enough to absorb all immigration that might come to it from the old States along the Atlantic. They pointed out the prosperity of the New England, New York, and Pennsylvania factory towns from which few persons were departing for the West; they showed that it was only from the temporarily unprosperous farming communities of Virginia and the South that young men were going into Kentucky and Tennessee.

Nevertheless the Federal powers had kept at their work, slowly conquering the Indians, and opening the Territory for settlement. The Government might be clumsy and try first one way of selling land, then another, but little by little it had made it possible for Revolutionary veterans and poor men generally to claim a home in the new country. And among the first immigrants to enter the Northwest Territory had been Lieutenant Ewing, who with his wife, Rachel Harris, and two children had been living on a farm at West Liberty, some forty miles west of the log town of Pittsburgh, in that narrow strip of Virginia which ran north between the Ohio River and Pennsylvania's western boundary. There his son Thomas had been born in 1789, on either the twenty-sixth or the twenty-eighth of December (no one could ever be sure which), and from there the family had, in 1792, crossed into the new territory to join the Olive Green Creek settlement on the Muskingum River.

By 1798, the year the little Bishop came home from school to find his family living in the valley of the Great Hockhocking River, the Northwest Territory had begun to grow. Since the previous year, white men had been paddling up the river in canoes between gigantic sycamores and had struck off to right and left to make homes for themselves in the walnut, hickory, and ash forests. So rich was the land that many a frontiersman, feeling prosperous, had quickly discarded his one-room log house for a double cabin, two buildings of logs connected by a roofed and floored space where the family might eat in the open air on pleasant days. Roofs were of oak staves, weighted down by rough timbers laid across them at right angles. Windows were of oiled paper; shutters were of thick lumber. Tables were split from logs, bedsteads were of poles interlaced with bark, bedclothes of bearskin and deerskin. Meat and vegetables dried on the rafters.

On the Ohio River was a big town, Marietta. Pittsburgh up the river could count fifteen hundred souls. Cincinnati had over a hundred cabins —Dayton, Cleaveland, Chillicothe and Detroit were growing. There were five thousand white males in the Territory, a legislature of twenty-two men had been formed and a twenty-seven-year-old lawyer, William Henry Harrison, elected to represent the people in the Congress. The Government had arranged for a path into the new country, promising Ebenezer Zane three grants of land if he would lay a wagon road from Wheeling, Virginia, to Limestone, Kentucky.

The Congress had befriended the Western settlers in the Ordinance of 1787, also guaranteeing them all the rights of citizens in the old States and more. They could not be tried except by jury, they should have schools, churches, no slave labor with which to compete, and be forever free from religious intolerance, which in some of the original States still withheld both the vote and certain public offices from free-thinkers, atheists, Jews, Roman Catholics, and men who did not believe in hell fire. It furthermore provided that the Northwest Territory and all States to be formed therefrom should "forever remain a part of the nation and that the compact could never be dissolved except by the common consent of its inhabitants and the people of the original States."

In this stipulation that the new Territory must forever remain in the United States there was a declaration of the permanency of the Union that was later omitted from the Constitution. Among the original States there might still thrive a belief that secession was legally permissible—but the Northwest as a whole would have no such notion.

It was a new world, indeed, that the Northwest Territory presented to Thomas Ewing in 1798 when he began to listen to his father talking of politics and government. Each of them, the small boy and the Northwest Territory, would mature in the creed that the Government must be thanked for life, liberty, and the pursuit of happiness. Freedom, wealth, the patents to their land, all came from the Federal power, not from the State. Soon enough the Territory would be dotted with men of all shades of political opinion, but the majority of the axmen would believe, as did the Bishop, that in the Union lay their strength.

This creed Thomas Ewing handed on, forty years later, to his foster son, a boy by the name of William Tecumseh Sherman.

2

KETTLE FIRES

THE year that the eight-year-old Bishop came to the Great Hockhocking Valley another boy with a large, heavy head was reciting Biblical verses to farm hands in Massachusetts. Too bashful to "speak pieces" in school, the youngster at sixteen found himself able to declaim at home in a voice so musical that the wheat-cutters would stop, sickle in hand, to listen. The time would come when Daniel Webster and Thomas Ewing would be bosom friends in Washington.

That same year a South Carolina boy of sixteen was learning a political creed that a little later on would make him the enemy of Thomas Ewing and Daniel Webster. John C. Calhoun was memorizing his father's motto, "That government is best which allows the largest amount of individual liberty compatible with the social order."

Across Kentucky that year, 1798, a youth of twenty-one was making political speeches in a voice that charmed his hearers almost out of their senses. Before many years, Henry Clay would number the Bishop as one of his most powerful political supporters.

In 1798 a tall, portly Indian was brooding, dreaming, in his wigwam by the White River in what would some day be the State of Indiana. He had been born thirty years before, one of triplets, to a Shawnee squaw on Mad River in that southeastern part of the Northwest Territory which his elders had ceded to the white men. That land must be reclaimed! Of what use was his proud name, Crouching Panther or Shooting Star—white men translated it both ways—of what use was it if he stood idle while the palefaces drove his people ever westward, corrupting chieftains with whisky and gold? In thirty years the Indian's name, Tecumseh, would be spoken often in the home that Thomas Ewing would build.

One day in 1798, as he read old newspapers on the cabin floor, Thomas Ewing found a puzzling thing—an article that exulted because so sterling a patriot as John Adams had "succeeded" General Washington as President. Anxiously the little boy ran to his father to ask him if he knew that General Washington was dead. In amazement he heard that the newspaper meant something else entirely. The Presidency wasn't an office that a man could hold for life, as a king held his; a President was elected every four years. General Washington had been elected twice and had refused to hold the post again, saying that it was not good for one man to have the power too long. The hero was still very much alive; thank God for it, too, since he could put down the rich men of the country, who still believed that the republic must sooner or later go back to the old form of monarchical government.

Young Thomas began to understand that the men of the Northwest Territory would never want a king.

At home the Bishop ate like an epicure. On the table that had been fashioned out of a walnut tree with an adze sat a pot of venison, bear meat, raccoon, or wild turkey where the family might attack it with sharpened sassafras sticks in lieu of forks. Mutton and beef the Ewings never tasted in those early years. Sheep and cattle, reproducing slowly, were sacred. Thomas Ewing always remembered the first time that he ate beef; it was tough and stringy compared with venison.

Once there was wild excitement among the children, who had grown more numerous with the onrush of settlers. Little Apphia Brown ate a love apple. Like the other youngsters, she had admired the pretty red fruit that hung on vines of the ornamental plant which foreigners had imported into the New World, but unlike the others she refused to remember that love apples were poison. All of a sudden one day she popped one into her mouth and swallowed it. Furiously the other children raced for help, screaming that Apphia was going to die. In after years Apphia was pointed out as the first person to eat a tomato in the valley of the Great Hockhocking.

From 1798 onward, the Bishop heard an ever-rising murmur of argument about something called States' rights. His father was a Federalist, one of those who wanted a strong central government and a powerful Constitution to rule the people. The boy was taught that men who voted to give the States greater powers were dangerous fellows. There was a noted quarrel about the Alien and Sedition Laws and the Kentucky Resolutions. His father's party had given President Adams power to imprison or drive out of the country persons who spoke or wrote against the Government.

The vice president, a red-headed, radical man named Thomas Jefferson, had secretly written an attack on these laws, urging people not to obey them, and telling States that it was their duty to resist unless they wanted to see man's sacred liberty stolen. Long evenings around the log fire young ears would hear the grown men disputing over the question, "Has a State the right to nullify a Federal law merely because it thinks the law unconstitutional?" In 1802 the boy listened to his father denouncing the Jeffersonians who, having captured the country, had drawn up for the new State of Ohio a constitution that had taken almost all powers away from the governor, and had limited the terms of judges to seven years—bold new strokes to keep executives and justices from ignoring the wishes of the common people.

It was in these listening hours beside the flaming walnut logs that Thomas Ewing learned the things that would make him in his own time the enemy of Jeffersonians and Nullifiers, and when the quarrel would go beyond words, he would send three sons and one foster son to fight with guns and swords against the States' rights doctrine that he had seen take root when he was a boy of eight.

More interesting than politics to the Bishop in 1799 were books, one in particular that he borrowed from Dr. Baker in Waterford, walking for it through the woods twenty miles and back with a spaniel for company. It was a translation of Virgil's Aeneid, and the little boy went stumbling on the lonely path home, lost in the stirring beauty of the pages. Even in his old age Thomas Ewing could begin, "Arms I sing and the man who first from Troy," and recite the lines seemingly without end.

The book—and the boy—were marvelous to Lieutenant Ewing's hired men on the farm. At noon, at evening, and on Sunday the youth would read Grecian adventures to them, and when he finished the love tale of Aeneas and Dido, he had to wait while the men debated. Some were outraged because Aeneas had jilted the queen, telling her that Jove had commanded him to leave her court. One frontiersman cried in heat, "He only told her a made-up story, just an excuse to get away. It was a damned shame after all the kindness she had done him!"

The Bishop began to be educated. Two schoolmasters passed his way, both Yale graduates, and one at least seeking in the wilderness escape from whisky's temptations. A certain Dr. Jones, graduate of Brown, dipsomaniac and eccentric woodsman, helped the scholar still more. Dr. Jones lived at the miller's near the mouth of Federal Creek, eight miles from the Ewing cabin, and whenever young Tom took grain to the mill he managed to wait around the place until the doctor returned from his hunting trips. Jones loved to take down one of his volumes of poetry and hand it to the boy to read aloud, while he himself, kicking off his wet moccasins, lay down on the floor with his feet to the fireplace and corrected the Bishop's pronunciation.

In the spring of 1803, ten or fifteen of the settlers living in the wide-flung community decided to raise a fund to buy a circulating library. Thirteen-year-old Thomas Ewing gave his entire wealth—ten raccoon skins—and watched it, with the rest of the pelts, grain, and cash, disappear as Samuel Brown, a neighbor, set off for Boston to make the purchase. And he was at the Brown home when Samuel returned, unloaded lumpy sacks from his horse, and emptied some seventy books on to the floor. It seemed to the youth that the treasures of the world lay before him, and for the next seven years he reveled in the pages, rereading the volumes and consuming the additional books that were added to the Coonskin Library from year to year.

And when, in 1803, Lieutenant Ewing moved his family to a small farm seven miles to the southeast on the road between Marietta and Chillicothe, Thomas Ewing was not sorry that he and his older brother were left behind on the old homestead to care for the live stock during the summer. He was still close to the Coonskin Library.

The more the Bishop read, the more he felt that his mind was standing still. Out beyond the forests another and fuller life was going on in a world whose news came to him from the lips of John Davis, the postboy. John came past the Ewing home once a week on his route between his home in Clarksburg, Virginia, and Chillicothe, Ohio, and in order to hear him talk the Ewings gave him free bed and board. On the nights that John was due Thomas would lie awake, listening for the post horn so that he might be up and ready to stable the rider's horse with all quickness. Rushing back to the kitchen, Thomas would sit and listen while Davis ate and talked.

Living as they did on the post road, the Ewings often took lodgers for the night, travelers to and from the bustling log town of Marietta. One of these strangers impressed Thomas Ewing particularly—an elegant gentleman who rode up to the youth and his father in the cornfield one evening and asked for quarters. At supper, around the fire, and at breakfast the next morning George Ewing treated the guest with such marked coolness that when the fellow had ridden away, Thomas asked what was wrong.

"That is Aaron Burr, who slew Alexander Hamilton," answered the father, his Federalist blood boiling at the sight of the man who in a duel had robbed the party of its leader. The son, then in his fifteenth or sixteenth year, understood soon afterward what Burr had been doing in the region. He had been living in the home of the Blennerhassetts on an island in the Ohio River near Marietta, plotting a Western empire. The beautiful wife of Blennerhassett was seen by the Bishop, too. Walking the streets of Marietta one day, the boy saw her ride into town on a shopping tour, a long ostrich plume on her hat, a scarlet riding-habit upon her slender body.

By the time he was nineteen, Thomas Ewing was famous in the lower Hockhocking Valley for two things, his ability to read and his Herculean strength. Six feet in height, powerful of shoulder, massive of head, he had the framework of a man who in maturity would weigh two hundred and sixty pounds. Legends had already begun to cluster about him as "the strong boy of the Valley."

Henry Stanbery, who as Thomas Ewing's partner in law and business in later years knew well the Bishop's history, told more concerning this period of the boy's youth:

> From the age of thirteen the life of Ewing was laborious. Then he became a substantial assistant to his father upon his farm and by-and-by he had the principal management of it. And as he grew older he had less time to read than when a boy. The little he had learned, however, but influenced him with a desire for learning more. The love of knowledge was the prevailing and all-absorbing passion of his soul. He felt that he had acquired all the knowledge within his reach, but this only taught him how little he knew. Poverty stared him in the face. The more he thought of his situation the more he despaired.
>
> Reflection at last ripened into actual suffering. But in the summer of 1808 [the Bishop's nineteenth year], he was awakened from this stupor by a youth nearly his own age whom his father had hired for a few months to assist him in farming and who had rambled about and seen much of the world. The narrations of this young man and many of his adventures awakened Ewing and as money was what he wanted—in order to obtain the means of pursuing his studies—he was induced to go with him to the Kanawha salines in Virginia. He obtained the consent of his father and left home early in August with his knapsack on his back.

The Kanawha salt wells were two hundred miles from home, a lonely mountain camp where only men of great strength could stand the grueling toil necessary to keep fires going night and day beneath the kettles in which salt water was boiled until it vanished in steam that left a thin white sift of precious mineral. The fire must be kept hot and the workman must cut his own cordwood from the forest near by.

Ewing, having walked to Marietta, caught a keel boat for Kanawha, worked his passage, and came to the camp with eagerness. Through the summer he toiled and at the beginning of winter he came home with $80—enough to finance him for a few months at least in the new college, Ohio University, that had been opened at Athens, not far from his father's house.

Tragedy, however, met him at the gate. His father, never a money-maker—"He read too many books to ever make money as a farmer," said his daughter Jane, years later—was in danger of losing his land from lack of payments, and the Bishop handed him the $80 and saw his hope for education postponed another year. With spring he was back at Kanawha and, knowing his trade far better now, could count $400 when winter came. Of this his father needed but $60, so that in December, 1809, the boy went to Athens and, as he described it, "spent three months there as a student by way of testing my capacity. I left the academy in the spring with a sufficiently high opinion of myself and returned to Kanawha to earn money for my education."

Six years followed one another in strenuous monotony—months, sometimes years, in a row were spent at the saltworks, where, in the words of C. B. Goddard, the intimate friend of his maturity, "he labored twenty hours out of the twenty-four and was often found during the four hours allotted to sleep, walking with open eyes, but still asleep, between the two rows of boiling salt kettles where a false step would probably have destroyed life."

Ewing let nothing swerve him from his goal. Soon after arriving at Kanawha he had settled upon a profession. Floating down to Marietta with a keel-boat load of salt, he had wandered about the city killing time and had come so to the courthouse, where lawyers were arguing a case. Fascinated by their oratory and ready wit, he had gone back to the saltworks with his future clear before him. He would study those subjects which would help him to become a lawyer.

Tremendous mental powers, slowly gathering force inside his massive skull, enabled him to master all available books on astronomy, navigation, surveying. At the age of twenty-three higher mathematics was simple for him. In ten days he conquered English grammar. The seventy-six rules in Adams's Latin Grammar he committed to memory in a single day. French he taught himself to read in fugitive moments among the kettles at Kanawha. To learn Latin was more difficult, for as he began to study, "the cold plague," akin to the influenza that would sweep America a century later, closed the college where he was making one of his three months' stays. Going home, he spread Virgil and a Latin dictionary on the hewn table before him and, timing himself by a watch, spent sixteen hours a day on his task until he had the sense of every sentence. "The first day I read sixty lines," he afterwards recalled; "the last day twelve hundred."

That he was missing something by so lonely and intensive a career dawned upon the big Bishop one day in 1812 when, coming home on a keel boat with $600 in Kanawha wages in his pocket, he met the granddaughter of Daniel Boone,

> a handsome, educated young lady who had somehow got the impression that I was a scholar and enticed me on the voyage to read novels and recite poetry to her. But my hands were chapped and black with toil—soap and water having no effect upon them—so that I hardly dared to offer them to help her out of the boat, and I took due care to hide them in her presence.

Ewing returned from this journey worn out with the saltworks grind and took to his bed. From the Coonskin Library came a strange book, "*Don Quixote,* which proved to be one of the best physicians that I ever called in. I laughed myself well in a short time."

There was an interlude from work when, in 1813, the English and Indians under General Proctor and Tecumseh swept down on Fort Meigs after their capture of Detroit. The Ewings, as old-time Federalists, did not approve of a war of invasion, but they did believe in defending their hearthstones, and the Bishop was one of five college students who rode out of town between rows of sweetly cheering females to join the militia that was forming near Athens. He was awkward trying to keep his horse, his borrowed sword, his seat, and the American flag under control, so that there was only relief in his heart when two days later the militia disbanded, having heard that the Indian "scare" was over. More serious than such interruptions as these were the long months that he must spend at the salt wells earning his college tuition.

In 1815 he made up his mind that he must leave the university and take up law. He was twenty-five; his youth was passing; he must collect money to finance the new endeavor. For three months he taught school at Gallipolis; he pocketed the salary, then rushed to the salines, where he earned $150 on piecework in four weeks of incredible toil. Hurrying to college for a last brushing-up, he was told by the board of trustees that they would waive his deficiency in Greek—the one subject that he had been too busy to tackle—and that they would examine him for honors, just as he stood.

Among the trustees who assembled on May 3, 1815, and gave Thomas Ewing the first Bachelor of Arts degree to be awarded in the Northwest Territory, was a certain lawyer for the Bishop to remember well and forever: Charles R. Sherman, a smiling, warm-hearted man who had come down from the intellectual capital of the valley, New Lancaster, up at the head of the Hockhocking River—a quick, brilliant fellow said to be the ablest lawyer in southeastern Ohio, a man of twenty-six who would watch over the hulking youth of twenty-five.

3

SHOOTING STAR

IT was inevitable that Thomas Ewing, aspiring to the law, should come to New Lancaster. Sitting in his father's cabin through May and June of 1815 with his university diploma in his pocket and Blackstone's *Commentaries* before him, he saw that opportunity would be brightest in the post-road town at the upper end of the Hockhocking Valley. Since 1799 immigrants from Pennsylvania and Virginia had been streaming into town over Zane's Road, many of them locating in and around the settlement, which the first wagoners, hailing from Lancaster, Pennsylvania, had named for their old home town. Swiss colonists and Germans had halted on lands near by, finding delight in the hills and bluffs that surrounded fertile woodland bottoms. To the north rose Standing Stone, a towering mesa, while to the south rolled the Kettle Hills, wild and rugged outcroppings of sandstone crowned with cedars.

Beside the town lay a pond—almost a lake—called Niebling's Pond now but originally so lined with wild fowl that the five hundred Wyandot Indians who camped there had named the place Cranetown. Several of the Wyandots were still living in the forests around the city, unable to leave the graves of their relatives, when Thomas Ewing rode into town late in July, 1815.

The Bishop looked at the place. For a Northwestern settlement it was progressive and cultured. It had been receiving mail once a week for sixteen years. Its eight hundred inhabitants—half of them Germans—lived in houses that were of brick as often as of logs. It had a sickle factory, four gristmills, and a powdermill and a factory for scutching flax were rising on the river rapids that came down from the Falls, six miles northwest of town. These falls which gave to the river the contour of a bottle had caused the Delaware Indians to name the stream Hockhocking, which in their language meant Bottle River.

Through New Lancaster poured white-topped wagons. The Northwest was filling rapidly, the majority of the immigrants coming from the North Atlantic States. In five years Ohio's population had risen from 230,000 to almost 400,000. Indiana Territory, to the west, had climbed from 24,000 people to 70,000 in that time and within a year would be a State. Kentucky, to the south, was old by comparison. It held 500,000 souls and was being deserted by young men who felt it to be overcrowded. They pushed into the black lands along the Illinois River. Missouri, Virginia, North Carolina, frightened at the numbers of their citizens who surged into the Northwest, considered passing laws against emigration. During the week of August 21, 1815, five American ports on the Atlantic received 1,500 persons from the British Isles; most of them struck off for the lands beyond the Ohio River.

Thomas Ewing saw plainly enough that a lawyer would prosper in a new land that had filled with a population so diverse. Legal details of landownership, wrangles over boundaries, disputes over titles, would be enough in themselves to keep a good barrister busy; then, too, there would be a fine criminal practice among frontiersmen who valued fist fights and liquor-drinking so highly. New Lancaster was the seat of the county, which, on account of its fertile acres, had been named Fairfield by the axmen of 1800. About the town there was the atmosphere of destiny: there was talk that New Lancaster would be the next State capital—indeed the town missed this honor by but one vote when the legislature decided to place the State government at Columbus instead of Chillicothe, where it had been located.

Without more ado, Ewing entered the office of Philemon Beecher, who had practiced law in New Lancaster since 1801 and was now the dean of the bar as well as a State legislator, a general in the militia, and rich enough to own a large brick house in the heart of the town. Thirteen months later the Bishop, having studied sixteen hours a day, was made a lawyer. To encourage the young man, Beecher asked him to help in a minor case or two, and praised his work in the court sessions that followed. The Bishop's reputation as a lawyer began, however, when Charles R. Sherman invited him to help prosecute a case of "wounding and trespass." It happened that Sherman's client was a prominent Methodist and when Ewing, conducting the argument in the presence of a courtroom full of the brethren, won his plea, the Methodists, powerful in the community, passed the word along that Ewing would do.

Judge Silas Wright, looking at the young lawyer, said, "His hat was so big that it would have fallen to the shoulders of most men and covered them like a tent." Other men said that he seemed never to have had a boyhood, so solemn was he in speech and manner. In court he spoke slowly and convincingly, appealing to the practical reasoning powers of his listeners. One of his admirers remarked, "His style seemed like that of a man who says, 'I am going to cut down that tree before dinner' and goes systematically about it."

For the next ten years Ewing was remarkably successful as a criminal lawyer, seven of these years being spent in frequent association with Sherman, who, though he never took the Bishop into open partnership, often took him along on trips through the northern counties, where Sherman had a commanding practice. Since Sherman was a distinguished man on circuits all the way from Marietta to Cincinnati and Detroit, his intimacy with Ewing added immeasurably to the new lawyer's prestige, a fact that Ewing recognized, saying in after years, "Though Sherman must have been well aware that I was to be his most formidable rival at the bar, he never failed when an opportunity offered to advance my reputation by commendation, countenance, and encouragement."

Traveling the circuit—or Stirrup Court, as it was called—Sherman and Ewing were as intimate as brothers. Through the woodland solitudes they rode their horses, overcoats and umbrellas strapped behind their saddles, leggings bound at the bottoms with string and spattered with mud. They shared rude beds, meals, and law cases. There was great benefit, too, for Ewing, so preoccupied and solemn a youth, in living with so social a being as Sherman. Transparently honest, sympathetic, quick to laugh, Charles Sherman was the equal in popularity of any barrister of the State, and when a little later he rose to sit in the Ohio Supreme Court, younger lawyers were warmed by the courtesy he paid them, listening to their arguments with an attention as fixed as that which he gave the mightiest of counsel.

In the taverns to which the lawyers and judges of the circuit adjourned after court, Sherman was more sociable than Ewing. The latter, in his old age, would recall one of his own experiences in the hostelries:

> Happening to have a case which required study, I was out in quest of authorities and as the fun grew fast and furious I returned with a law book under my arm. Dick Douglas, our wit par excellence, exclaimed as I entered the room, "Here comes the living embodiment of malice at the Common Law, a heart regardless of social duty and fatally bent on mischief." The mischief on which I was fatally bent, was a special plea or demurrer with which to defeat some good, jolly brother-lawyer's case.

By family tradition Charles Sherman was more inclined than Ewing to the law. The first of the Sherman line to establish himself in America had been a judge, Samuel Sherman, who had been born in Dedham County, England, in 1618, and who had come as a Puritan émigré to Connecticut in 1634, helping to found the town of Woodbury, which he represented in the colonial legislature and on the Supreme Judicial Tribunal. His son John, likewise a legislator, sat as a judge in Woodbury for forty-four years, and his grandson Daniel, born in 1721, was to be a judge for thirty-seven years and a legislator in sixty-five semi-annual assemblies. Daniel's son, Taylor Sherman, was probate judge in Norwalk, Connecticut, and a man judicious enough to be sent by his State into the Northwest Territory in 1805 to see that the Connecticut fire lands were legally and honestly sold. These lands had been reserved by Connecticut to be sold for the benefit of citizens whose property had been burned by the British during the Revolution, and Taylor Sherman, administering the sale, had bought a large tract for himself, thus establishing a small annual income, which his wife would need at his death in 1815. She was the daughter of the Rev. Anthony Stoddard of Woodbury, Connecticut, a divine who preached three times every Sunday and as often between times as his listeners would permit.

Charles R. Sherman, born in Norwalk, September 17, 1788, was the son of Taylor Sherman and as such destined for the bar. Following his graduation from Dartmouth College, Charles studied law in his father's office and was admitted to the bar in 1810. Marrying Mary Hoyt, a neighbor girl, that summer, he struck off alone for the fire lands, intending to build a home on his father's acres. The Indians, however, changed his plans. Since 1805 Tecumseh, abandoning his brooding dreams, had flared into action, stalking about the Mississippi Valley preaching organization to the red tribes. Peaceful confederation of all clans and unified refusal to cede further lands to the whites was his cry, but the savages had difficulty in understanding him and interpreted his cause only too often as license to kill white frontiersmen. Especially were the Indians troublesome along the Great Lakes, where the red blood ran hotter, and as late as 1810 northern Ohio was still theirs.

Shying off from such dangerous territory, Charles Sherman followed Zane's Road and so came to New Lancaster, whose unusual civilization in the wilderness delighted him. Opening a law office, he had at least one case by December, for on the tenth of that month he filed a petition against Jacob Boos and other overseers of the county poor to cause them to restore a mulatto child, Peggy by name, to its unwed mother, Fanny Mills. Law practice in the new town was promising enough to convince Sherman that New Lancaster must be his home and that winter he returned to Norwalk for his family. Not even the birth of a son, Charles, in that February of 1811 could alter his decision to hasten west. His wife did not flinch from the prospect of a thousand-mile horseback ride through the wilderness, although as the daughter of a wealthy burgher and as a graduate of a fashionable Female Seminary at Poughkeepsie, New York, she had been gently bred. When summer came, the young pair climbed into their saddles and, carrying the baby on a pillow that they handed back and forth, jogged the woodland miles to their new home. In Lancaster Sherman built a two-story frame house on Main Street, halfway up the hill that rose in the center of the town.

Quickly Charles Sherman established himself as a figure in the community. At the January term of court in 1812 he was appointed substitute county attorney when the regular incumbent, Slaughter, was unable to practice, and in April, when the call came to enlist volunteers for the war against the British and Indians, he was elected major and chief recruiting agent for the Fourth Regiment of Ohio militia. At twenty-four years of age he had become the chief patriotic speechmaker of the region, and although he did not accompany his regiment to Detroit, where it was tragically surrendered to the enemy by General Hull that August, he was recruiting men and directing commissary affairs until the end of the war.

Like all settlers in the Northwest, Sherman found his first years in the new land filled with talk about the Indian Tecumseh. The chieftain was at once the despair and the hope of white civilians from Pittsburgh to the Mississippi River. If he should decree war the danger was appalling, for he held the tribes from the Great Lakes to the Gulf of Mexico in obedience to his call. If, however, the Indian war should begin, Tecumseh was the white man's one hope that women and children and captives would escape massacre. Stately, serene, and humane, Shooting Star was recognized by all thoughtful settlers as a statesman rather than a savage. He could read and write, and kept a half-breed secretary, Billy Caldwell, chief of the Potawatamis, living in a cabin close to Fort Dearborn, where the Chicago River emptied into Lake Michigan. White men felt an irresistible admiration for the great chieftain who was attempting to hold his people's land by diplomacy rather than by bloodshed. And when war did come in 1812 with the redskins scalping and burning across the Northwest, legends of Tecumseh's magnanimity and mercy grew in the log cabins. He had struck up murderous tomahawks in time to spare lives, had denounced his British allies for inhumanity; and when he was killed at the Battle of the Thames in Canada, all through the United States there was genuine regret mixed with elation. To men like Charles Sherman there was nothing but shame in the reports that American soldiers, battle-crazed, had cut long strips of skin from Tecumseh's dead thighs so that they might have razor strops as souvenirs of victory.

When peace had come to the nation with the Indians' drifting farther west, Charles Sherman went back to law and success, but through his mind there still went thoughts of Tecumseh. He decided to name his next son after the red man, but when a baby boy arrived, in December, 1814, he found that his wife had already decided to name it for her brother James. The first-born had been named for her brother Charles; the second-born, a girl, had been named for herself; and the third must keep up the family tradition. Her husband must have taken private satisfaction in the thought that Mary had no more brothers. He would bide his time and wait for another boy. In February, 1816, there came a girl to be named Amelia, and on July 24, 1818, another girl, Julia Ann. Then on February 8, 1820, a boy at last, red of hair, redder of face, a fit one for the name Tecumseh, which meant Shooting Star.

4

TWO FAMILIES ON THE HILL

WHEN the news went over New Lancaster that Judge Sherman's wife had had another baby—her sixth—the neighbor women flocked in. Among them was a bride of nineteen, Mrs. Thomas Ewing, whom the Bishop had married a month before, and who now climbed the hill from her own more modest home in the lower town. As she stood beside the bed, looking at the tiny Tecumseh Sherman, Maria Boyle Ewing was beautiful enough to prove that the hulking, awkward Bishop had progressed in society as well as in the law. With her rose-colleen complexion and her cultured manners the girl had been the belle of New Lancaster, rivaled only by her younger sister Susan. They were the daughters of Hugh Boyle, Irish gentleman and clerk of the Fairfield County Court.

From County Donegal in Ireland Hugh Boyle had fled to America at eighteen years of age, forsaking the wealth of his gentleman father because of a disagreement with the British authorities. Arriving in Brownsville, Pennsylvania, in his hunt for work, he had married a certain Eleanor Gillespie against her father's wishes and had carried her away to the Western settlement at Chillicothe, where his two daughters were born—Maria arriving in January, 1801. The following year he had moved to New Lancaster, becoming county clerk in 1803. Family alliances added to his prominence, for when his wife's sister Susan came on from Brownsville for a visit, she had been wooed and won by Philemon Beecher. Eleanor Gillespie Boyle had died while her daughters were but children and her sister, the wife of Beecher, had taken her place as mother of the little girls, the two families living as one.

The elder of the girls, Maria, had been fourteen when Thomas Ewing had come to study law in her uncle Beecher's office, and in the five years that followed romance had been born. For a youth as poor as Ewing, marriage was a serious step. From his earnings he had still to help his father, who continued to read too much for the good of his farm land. The old gentleman had moved on to Indiana soon after Thomas went to New Lancaster.

As a devout Roman Catholic and one who had been proscribed for the wearing of the green, Hugh Boyle might have been expected to resist the union of his daughter with a Presbyterian and a descendant of Orangemen like the thirty-year-old Thomas Ewing, but in New Lancaster racial and religious lines were laxly drawn. Mixed marriages were common in that day across the whole expanse of the Western settlements. Germans, Irish, English, Scotch—Catholics, Protestants—all thrown together in the wilderness so very far away from Old World traditions, forgot ancient hatreds in their need for companionship. Maria Boyle and the Bishop were married on January 7, 1820, and went their separate religious ways without causing comment.

In that year of Thomas Ewing's marriage and the birth of Judge Sherman's sixth child, the thousand odd inhabitants of New Lancaster had but one church and one pastor—and the church did not belong to the preacher nor he to it. The little frame church had been built by the Catholics, Hugh Boyle among them, and its flock could only worship in it once a month when the hard-traveling Dominican priests came across the woods from St. Joseph's at Somerset, eighteen miles through the forests. Before the church had been erected, the priests had celebrated mass in the Boyle home.

New Lancaster's one resident clergyman was the Rev. John Wright, who since 1801 had preached in cabins about town or, more lately, in the courthouse. Pastor Wright it was who had baptized Charles Sherman's five older children as they came into the world and who now officiated over the new red-haired baby.

The boy was nicknamed Cump from the first—Tecumseh proving

too long a word for his three sisters and two brothers to pronounce. It was an affectionate nickname, as became a most affectionate family whose head, whenever he could be at home from his long circuit rides, would help with the children's clothes night and morning.

The red-headed baby did not arrive at a propitious moment. For three years poverty had troubled the family. In 1813, President James Madison had appointed Charles Sherman Collector of Internal Revenue for the Third Ohio District, and in this new office Sherman had sent deputies to collect taxes in six counties. Suddenly, in 1817, the Government announced that it would not accept the banknotes of the various local banks throughout the country and insisted upon receiving only gold or the paper of the United States Bank or its branches. Since the Northwest used local banknotes almost entirely, Sherman's deputies had been paid in that currency. He, as Collector, might have escaped the liability, for the Government habitually protected its honest Collectors against the failure of deputies. Sherman's accounts were correct to the penny, but he scorned to desert his men. Proudly he refused to make the necessary appeal to the Government for personal relief. Mortgaging his home and a large portion of his future earnings, he went to work to pay the indebtedness. Year in, year out, as long as he lived he labored so, doubtless strengthened for his task by the additional good repute that his act had brought him among his fellows.

Friendships, unusually intense, gravitated to him; men of consequence across the whole State gave him a fidelity that would outlast his life. There was Charles Hammond, for instance, a power in the State legislature and a leader of the Ohio bar; there was William Irvin, a lawyer who had married a half sister of Maria Boyle Ewing's mother from Brownsville, and who added strength to that remarkable coterie of city leaders which the Boyle-Beecher-Ewing-Sherman group established; and Henry Stanbery, who came to New Lancaster in 1824 as the partner of Thomas Ewing in law and later in a saltworks that Ewing—still drawn to salt as to the essence of life itself—had launched in his old home county Athens. And there was, of course, Ewing as the stanchest friend of all. With each year Ewing rose nearer and nearer to supremacy in the region. Serving equally well as a defender and as a special prosecutor, he acquired fame as a criminal lawyer. In 1819, when the authorities failed to halt the activities of a gang of counterfeiters in Sleepy Hollow—a retreat among the wild Kettle Hills south of town—Ewing organized a posse of riflemen, and one night smashed in doors and slugged desperadoes with his fists until they surrendered. Everywhere in southwestern Ohio Ewing was known to be strong in both body and head. Everybody, it seemed, knew the story of his early struggles for an education among the salt kettles of Kanawha, and "The Salt-Boiler" became his nickname.

As stout as the friendship of any such individual as Ewing was the support that the Masons of Lancaster gave Charles Sherman in his adversity. Sherman had been the highest of their officers when their local lodge was founded in 1820, and although the Boyle-Ewing clan was not of their membership, the order lived on such excellent terms with its neighbors that Sherman's Masonry was no barrier between himself and his Catholic friends or companions like Ewing who disapproved of all secret societies.

It was a kindly, thrifty town that the impoverished Charles Sherman and the latest Sherman baby looked upon in 1820—a town of two hundred houses, half of them brick, the other half frame (log houses had all but disappeared)—an important little town with a courthouse and a jail; a market house; two newspapers, one English, one German; and twelve stores, all of them "general," selling farm implements, saddles, whisky, groceries, patent medicines, clothing, harness, carpenters' tools, powder, shot, and dress-goods dyes. There were two tinners, a gunsmith, a silversmith, and a man who did nothing but make and repair spinning-wheels.

The town had no fire engine and would, indeed, have no conflagration until 1821, when a bolt of lightning would kill two oxen and set Peter Reber's gristmill ablaze. Thomas Ewing would have a fist fight, at this fire, with one Adam Weaver, disputing over the management of the bucket brigade that ran from a muddy pond to the blazing mill.

The first regular stagecoach line came to New Lancaster in the year that Tecumseh Sherman was born—the old pony-riders and wagon-drivers giving way to grand coaches with postboys listening as the cliffs of Standing Stone threw back the echoes of their horns. Communication with the outside world increased. Mail rates, however, were so high that even the richest New Lancastrians were economical about correspondence. For a letter that must go less than fifty miles, six and a quarter cents was charged; twelve and a half cents if it went farther than fifty and less than a hundred and fifty miles; eighteen and three-fourths cents for a hundred and fifty to three hundred miles; twenty-five cents would take it anywhere in the United States. The postmaster stamped the price on the envelope and either sender or receiver could pay the bill. Letters were written on three faces of a folded sheet, while the fourth formed the envelope and bore the address. Colored wax wafers sealed all communications.

In 1820 there came another touch of civilization to make men forget that it had been but three years since the last bear and the last panther had been killed within the city limits. A brick academy was erected to supplant the log schoolhouses, Thomas Ewing and Philemon Beecher footing much of the bill. From the farms of Fairfield County on all sides boys and girls rode in on horses to be educated. That year the county held sixteen thousand people.

If the red-haired baby could have understood the talk of his father and Thomas Ewing in that first year of his life, he would have heard much about the new battles in Congress over slavery. He would have known how the Compromise of 1820 had admitted Maine to the Union as a free State, Missouri as a slave State, and then stipulated that slavery be henceforth shut out from all the rest of the West above the line of Missouri's southern boundary. But in his cradle the baby could only sleep, eat, and sleep again.

When he was twenty months old, Cump had to forego the privilege of the youngest. He passed into the strict care of his grandmother while a new baby, Lampson, claimed the cradle and the soft admiration of the neighbor women.

Maria Ewing, coming up the hill to see this latest Sherman infant, carried a baby of her own, Philemon, born eleven months after Cump. A little later Maria Ewing would bear—and lose within a year—another son, George, whose death would decide her and her husband to move to the hill where the Shermans lived. Convinced that their home in the lower town was unhealthful, the Ewings bought the summit of the high ground, a lot half a block from the two-story brown frame house of the Shermans, and in 1826 erected upon it a brick mansion to which they kept making additions until 1831.

Babies came rapidly to the two neighboring homes. Maria Ewing, arriving on the hill with two—Philemon, six, and Eleanor, only a few months old—gave birth in the ten years that followed to four youngsters: Hugh Boyle, born October 31, 1826; Thomas, August 7, 1829; Charles, March 6, 1835; and Maria Theresa, May 2, 1837. In the smaller house Mary Sherman bore ten children: Mary Elizabeth, James, Amelia, Julia, Tecumseh, Lampson, John, Susan, Hoyt, and Fanny—a brood that, dating from the birth in Connecticut of the oldest boy, Charles Taylor, entered the world on an average of eighteen months apart.

Considering the intimacy of the two households, it was natural for the two herds of children to become as one, with each year producing some new toddler to join in their games. Cump Sherman found his chief playmate in Phil Ewing, with Lampson Sherman and Eleanor Ewing as hangers-on.

Whatever difference there was in the finances of the two families, with Ewing slowly forging ahead of Sherman in wealth, the degree was too slight for children to have taken any notice. In 1828—the year that he traveled to Washington to secure the right to practice before the Supreme Court—Ewing was still far from rich. "As to the piano," he wrote his wife, "I believe I cannot at present get it for you. I regret that I cannot, as you seem to desire it, but I have not now the money at hand to spare." It would be 1832 before he could find the $341 that the piano cost.

Both households lived well, for all the shortage of cash; both were noted for their sociability. Newspapers referred to the Sherman home as "the center of refined hospitality," a description probably accurate, since in all New Lancaster there was no other couple with the social and educational advantages of the Shermans—Charles with his Dartmouth training and Mary with her Poughkeepsie seminary "finishing." As a trustee of Ohio University, Charles was one of the intellectual prides of the town.

Prominent personages traveling Zane's Road made it a point to stop overnight in New Lancaster, whose hotels (seven in number) were among the best in the West, and it was at Charles Sherman's home that the social formalities of the place were extended to them. For instance, in 1825, Governor De Witt Clinton of New York and the elegant Duke of Saxe-Weimar, touring the country, were entertained there.

Also it was said that Mary Sherman's table, every day of the week, had room for more boys than had any other board in the village. In maturity Philemon Ewing would recall how often as a youngster he had sat down to dinner with Cump in the brown frame house. With her daughter Elizabeth and often her mother-in-law to help, Mrs. Sherman managed well. Occasionally—it could not have been often with so many babies on hand and on the way—she took long horseback trips with her husband on the circuit. Theirs was a rare affection, but one marked by long periods of separation after 1823, when the State legislature elected Charles a judge of the Ohio Supreme Court. Traveling in twos, the four judges toured the State on so far-flung and tediously traveled a circuit that their families saw comparatively little of them. One of the judges was old Jacob Burnet, with his hair still in a queue.

In the absence of Judge Sherman, his mother, Betsey Stoddard Sherman, took command. At the death of her husband, Judge Taylor Sherman, she had come West with her daughter Elizabeth to live close to her son. Elizabeth had soon married Jacob Parker, a youth who studied law in Charles Sherman's office, and had moved to Mansfield, between which and New Lancaster the old lady divided her time. Parker, who was an excellent land lawyer, stuttered so badly that he employed Sherman to represent him in jury cases. Old Mrs. Sherman was a stern and brisk woman who, as Cump described her sixty years afterward,

> . . . came down from Mansfield, three days' hard journey, to regulate the family of her son, whose gentle wife was as afraid of Grandma as any of us boys. She never spared the rod or broom, but she had more square, hard sense to the yard than any woman I ever saw. From her, Charles, John, and I inherit what little sense we possess.

Of evenings this grandmother told the children stories of the Revolutionary War. She remembered how the British and Tories had burned Connecticut towns.

Life in New Lancaster was good for a boy—good skating on Niebling's Pond, good hunting in the woods so close to town, and a good school in which to receive his first lessons. In after years, as a man who thought much about schools and education, Tecumseh Sherman would say that the Lancaster Academy was as good as any in Ohio. Built in 1820, it passed in 1825 into the hands of two remarkable brothers, Mark and Samuel Howe, who taught their pupils not only all the common branches of knowledge but Latin, Greek, and French as well. The academy was a progressive school in a country that to the self-satisfied East was still the wilderness. To its support Thomas Ewing and Judges Beecher, Sherman, and Irvin contributed—a private school, since there were no public schools in town until 1830.

More important than any schoolroom lessons to an impressionable boy was the talk of his parents and his parents' friends. Since the intellectual life of the town centered on "the Hill," the Sherman children heard good grammar; also they heard a never-ending flow of talk about national politics. The pioneers of the Northwest were amazing talkers. Men rose to fame and influence on their abilities as conversationalists. Oratory was the art most admired by the people. With newspapers few, new books scarce, and theatres entirely absent, story-tellers, spellbinders, folk-tale weavers, were popular. Preachers were attended as entertainers by the frontiersmen, who were—perhaps in the majority—freethinking and tinged with Jeffersonian skepticism. That lawyer or politician who could pour the most humor, philosophy, and poetry into his speeches or informal conversations was the idol of his community. Unknown to Cump Sherman, of course, a tall boy by the name of Lincoln was developing this pioneer art far away across the woods in Illinois.

Nearer at hand was the most renowned talker of the whole Northwest—that friend of Judge Sherman and Thomas Ewing, cello-voiced, witty Thomas Corwin. From the town of Lebanon, where Judge Sherman often sat and where Thomas Ewing often practiced, Tom Corwin came frequently to New Lancaster on legal, social, or political errands. Statecraft took him frequently to Washington too, and it was his habit to stop off for a visit with Sherman and Ewing, fellow Whigs. "Tom Corwin and my father were very friendly," Tecumseh Sherman would recall in manhood. "I knew him well, seeing him many times at Mr. Ewing's." No man can say how much Corwin influenced the bright, retentive mind of the boy. Certain it is that Cump, between the ages of six and sixteen, listened to him often, and certain it is that Corwin's flow of talk, endless for hours, impressed hard-headed adults of that time as perhaps did that of no other man.

And from somewhere—partly no doubt from his easy, brilliant father, partly from this magnetic visitor, who was the first of American stump speakers—Cump acquired powers of speech and expression that would make him in his fifties and sixties an extraordinary conversationalist, called by many observers the best in America. Like Corwin's, his talk would be endless, swift, animated, charming.

Tom Corwin was a pioneer boy from Turtle Creek Valley, having been brought at the age of four across to the Little Miami River country by his father. This was in 1798, the same year that little Bishop Ewing had come up the Great Hockhocking. As a stripling, Corwin had driven wagons of grain between Cincinnati and Lebanon, thus acquiring the nickname of the Wagon Boy, a title that stood him well with the Ohio voters as he fought his way up through the legislature to Congress, to the governorship, and on to the United States Senate and the Secretaryship of the Treasury.

Men, women, and children gravitated to him whenever he opened his mouth, be it in taverns, legislative halls, jolting stagecoaches, barrooms, churches, or in the White House at Washington. To illustrate his talk of simple things he would, without pause, draw upon Milton, Bacon, Bunyan, Shakespeare, but most of all upon the Bible, which he seemed to know backward. Racy, salty, sharp as a hunting-knife were his smiling satires against humbuggery and pomposity. The West loved him.

To amuse himself he would talk in imitation of the literary styles of the masters, impersonating the speech and ideas of Samuel Johnson for a time, then, without notice, switching to Gibbon, Voltaire, or Jeremiah. He could cite the philosophies of Napoleon on war, of Caesar on government, of William of Orange on freedom—and at the end of most allusions would hear his auditors roar with mirth. His swarthy face was like a great actor's, cultured, strong, mobile, picturing for onlookers every shade of mood in the stories that came from his lips.

In the years to come, Cump Sherman would learn on his own account how endless talk could hurt as well as help a man, but in his young days in Ohio no one could imagine such a thing as too much of Tom Corwin's speech. It would take time for Corwin's wit and sarcasm to create sufficient enemies to keep him from the thing he wanted, serious consideration as a candidate for the Presidency, a post to which his ability entitled him. The people of Buffalo, for instance, would never forgive Corwin for the ridicule he heaped upon their city one night during a speech at Syracuse. A delegation of his political opponents from Buffalo had come with banners and organized spleen to heckle him, and from their seats they yelled "Louder! Louder!" so often that at last they brought the meeting to confusion. They might have succeeded entirely if Corwin had not, all at once, thrown his hand aloft in menace and struck an attitude that awed his enemies. Solemnly and beautifully he said:

"When the Angel Gabriel shall stand with one foot on the land and one foot on the sea and with trumpet of doom shall proclaim that time shall be no more, some God-forsaken fool from Buffalo will stand up and cry 'Louder!'"

The bulk of the audience collapsed in laughter, the hecklers departed, Corwin returned to his speech, but he had made enemies. Throughout his life he would wound so many with his sarcasm that in his old age he would say to young men, "Never make people laugh. If you would succeed in life you must be solemn—solemn as an ass. All the great monuments are built over solemn asses." Once he said to Cump's brother John: "All that people who hear me will remember are only my jokes. Stay out of politics and attend to your law."

It was to Tom Corwin's town, Lebanon, that Cump Sherman saw his father start for a court session one day in 1829—a trip that the boy would always remember with a pang. June was in the air. The younger Sherman children sat in school, which in New Lancaster's enthusiasm for education held until the last of the month. Cump's oldest brother Taylor was away at Ohio University, and his next brother, James, who was fourteen, was clerking in a store at Cincinnati. His younger brother John at six was in the primary grade at the academy. At home were three infants: Susan, a little over three, Hoyt, aged eighteen months, and Fanny, six weeks.

A neighbor girl named Jane Sturgeon came hurrying to the school and whispered to the teacher, who called out the Sherman children and sent them home. There they were told by their grandmother that their father, off in Lebanon, was sick unto death. They saw their mother packing her things to go to him, then some hours later saw her return, white and faint, to be put to bed. At the town of Washington on the stage route, some one had come to the coach to tell her that it was no use to go farther, her husband was dead.

Father dead! The children could not understand it and discussed the matter gravely as they sat in the yard where their stern grandmother had told them to go and keep quiet. Soon the body arrived, their brother James with it. The little fellow had been summoned from Cincinnati and had come with an older cousin to be with his father at the last. Cump heard the neighbors come up with questions and repeat the answers to each other. Tom Corwin had been with Sherman at his death.

Judge Sherman had ridden from Cincinnati to Lebanon on a hot day, and had taken such a chill that he had had to adjourn court. Doctors had come rushing to the hotel. Persons of influence had collected, for the sick man was one of the most prominent figures in the State. Nothing, however, could be done, and on the sixth day of his illness the judge died. Cump heard it said that his father had died of the cholera, and saw it written so in the obituaries. Later the boy, with his zeal for realism and hard facts, would establish that the disease could not have been cholera, since that plague was not present in America in 1829. He reasoned that it must have been typhoid fever.

With Judge Sherman buried temporarily at Lebanon, his sons wondered what they could do. Pioneer boys, born of a race that could do and did do almost all things for itself, they proposed action; just what they could not determine. Little John was to grow up remembering:

"Many were the wise resolves, or rather the conceits, we discussed for 'helping mother.'"

5

THE REDHEAD CLIMBS THE HILL

THOMAS EWING sat in his brick mansion as June closed and thought of his dead friend—of all that he owed him, and of what the fatherless family would do now. The widow would have no more than four hundred dollars a year—a legacy from her father—and her mother-in-law received less than that from her husband's fire lands to the north. Judge Sherman's salary had been but twelve hundred dollars a year—the home was heavy with debt. Eleven children . . . ! Ewing talked to friends and relatives of the dead judge; they agreed to collect a fund for the lifting of the mortgage, and asked Ewing to handle the matter. His own donation was fifty dollars. With that settled, the Salt-Boiler waited for the widow to recover somewhat from her grief, then he went down the hill and explained to her how impossible it would be for her ever to feed and clothe all those boys.

"I want one of them," he said. "You must give me the brightest of the lot, and I will make a man of him."

"Take Cump, the red-haired one," said Elizabeth. "He's the smartest."

As her mother's household aide, Elizabeth was mature for her seventeen years, and Ewing accepted her recommendation. Tecumseh was called in from the street where he had been playing with the other children. He was told what had been decided, his few belongings were collected, and quickly he was gone—a tiny figure bobbing along beside the huge man, up the hill. It was only a few steps between the two houses, it was true, but nevertheless a long, long walk. "I took him home," said Ewing afterward, "and he was, thereafter, my boy."

In the large house Maria Ewing added Cump gladly to her brood. Philemon would be nine in November, Eleanor—called Ellen—would be five, and Hugh would be two in October; a fourth was expected in August.

For Cump the transfer was managed so deftly that it was, in his mind, little more than the switching of beds from one house to another. With Philemon he came and went in his own mother's house much as before, often eating meals there. For a time his brothers and sisters were still in the games. Toward his new father he speedily adopted the attitude of the Ewing children. Trained by Maria Ewing to hold their father in frank idolatry, the youngsters gave him an affection tinged with awe.

At forty Thomas Ewing was entering the fullness of his powers—a masterful, patient man whose prodigious memory and concentrated reading had made him one of the best-informed men of his time. Farmers sought his advice on agriculture, mechanics on machines, politicians on campaigns, prisoners and prosecutors on fine points of law—on real estate law his opinions were almost law itself. "Grandeur sat upon him," said Murat Halstead, the Cincinnati journalist. Some persons thought him proud, others that he was merely abstracted. Historians of Lancaster would describe him as one "who lived on an elevated plane and who was considered by some of his townsfolk unsocial, but when reached he was warm, cordial and sincere."

When Cump Sherman joined the family, the Salt-Boiler was not interested in politics. His one attempt to gain public office had met with defeat. In 1823 he had been a candidate for the legislature, but by refusing to endorse the demands of rich landowners for a revision of taxes he had lost their all-important support. Now law and business occupied his time. He rode various legal circuits and was often absent from home at saltworks that he was launching in Athens County. Yet so strong was his love of family that time and again he would ride his horse forty or fifty miles on week-ends, day and night, just to go to church with his wife and children on Sunday. To the children he was an overwhelming personality of grave tenderness—an affectionate Jehovah.

Thomas Ewing's attitude toward Judge Sherman's son was scrupulously just. He did not dream of taking the father's name from the boy by legal adoption; the child should be reared as Judge Sherman would have reared him, but he should be made to feel himself a Ewing as well. Family pride was tremendous in the Bishop. Of Cump's youth he would write in later years:

> There was nothing specially remarkable about him except that I never knew so young a boy who would do an errand so correctly and promptly as he did. He was transparently honest, faithful and reliable, studious and correct in habits. His progress in education was steady and substantial.

It would be the foster father's religion, Federalism, rather than the foster mother's religion, Roman Catholicism, that would sink into Cump's mind. Ewing, born a Presbyterian, attended the Catholic Church with his family, his bosom radiating a broad, easy respect for all creeds. If his family loved this particular faith, whose dogmas he could not accept in entirety, he was happy. He would encourage their church and give liberally to its upkeep. Cump in his maturity would summarize the religious difference between Thomas and Maria Ewing in these words:

Mrs. Ewing was so staunch to what she believed the true Faith that I am sure that though she loved her children better than herself, she would have seen them die with less pang than to depart from the "Faith." Mr. Ewing was a great big man, an intellectual giant, and looked down on religion as something domestic, something consoling that ought to be encouraged, and to him it made little difference whether the religion was Methodist, Presbyterian, Baptist or Catholic, provided the acts were half as good as their profession.

When priests from the monastery at Somerset visited his home once a month to remain a week instructing the children, Thomas Ewing welcomed them as readily as when they had come to baptize each newborn infant. Classes were held in an upstairs room, and it was there that, at the end of a session, the question of Cump Sherman's religion arose. Just as the priest was preparing to depart, some one said that Cumpy had never really been baptized. Maria Ewing promptly ran down the hill and put the question to Widow Sherman, who said that she had no objection to the priest's performing the ceremony. Maria returned. The front parlor, kept dark except for important occasions, was opened. The preliminary rites were held, then the priest asked the boy's name.

"Tecumseh."

"He must be named for a saint," said the priest, thinking no doubt how strange it was for a boy to be named after a red pagan. The clergyman opened a book and searched through it for a few moments. At length he announced, "Today is the feast of St. William, June 25; I'll name him William." And William it was, with Mrs. Ewing and Philemon as sponsors. For some reason, perhaps faulty memory, perhaps pride, Sherman would write fifty years later, "My father named me William Tecumseh Sherman." However, his signature on letters written before his baptism had been plain Tecumseh Sherman and after the event he began signing himself William Tecumseh or W.T.

That his mother, an Episcopalian attending a Presbyterian church and herself the widow of the founder of Masonry in New Lancaster, should so readily assent to her young son's baptism by a Roman Catholic priest, proved how slight was religious prejudice in the broad-minded atmosphere of Fairfield County in 1830. Zeal for religious dogmas was apt to wane, even among New England emigrants, after a few years of pioneer life. Families learning to rely upon their own strength and wits in the battle with the wilderness tended to become more independent of organized churches as well as of organized society. And in New Lancaster education, good manners, and tolerance had come with unusual promptness on the heels of the axmen.

With priests present only one week in every three, churchgoing was not a matter of rigor to the Ewing children. Then too, there were many Sundays in the summer when Cump and Phil would be far from any church, visiting the farm of Aunt Sarah Clark, some miles from town. This sister of Thomas Ewing had married Obadiah Clark in Athens County, and removed to Fairfield, where she had borne him eight children. To rear them had been difficult, for Uncle Obadiah had learned unthrifty habits as a fifer in the Revolutionary army, and Aunt Sarah had found it necessary to let her brother practically adopt three of her youngsters, Charles, Abigail, and Rachel. In return for this kindness and out of her own limitless love of children, Aunt Sarah welcomed the whole Lancaster contingent of youngsters to her farm in the summer time. Little Hugh, six years younger than Cump, remembered these visits:

> In a vale deep down in the "Kittle Hills" we passed happy days with her. Our first greetings over, we would rush for her Calamus bed, where we violently tore down the stalks and took the white, flesh-tinted roots to the rivulet to wash, eating them with a wild relish.

With the other boys, Cump hunted rabbits in the woods; they always carried large clubs with which to protect themselves against the horrible dangers of the hoop snake, which, although never caught in the act, was firmly believed to hiss at the sight of a boy, then catch its tail in its mouth and roll swiftly in pursuit of its victim. Always it was said to choose the smallest and fattest of the boys as its easiest and juiciest prey, and to time its revolutions artfully so as to sink its sharp poison-horn into the fugitive's rear. Cump's first acquaintance with military strategy was in the plan the boys devised for evading the snake should it ever appear. The scheme was for the pursued youth to run toward a tree, then to dodge aside and let the snake imbed its horn in the trunk, where it would perish miserably, unable to escape. "And the tree will wither and lose all its leaves in five minutes, the poison's *so* strong," said the boys.

For at least one whole summer Aunt Sarah entertained Cump and Phil on the farm, allowing them to raise and market watermelons. Long before daylight they would stow their melons among the butter, eggs, roasting ears, and squawking chickens in the hind end of the wagon and would snuggle down behind the end gate for the ride to New Lancaster's market house. It was exciting to roll away through the cool starlight, but when the driver reached his destination he usually found both boys asleep among the produce.

At other times Cump and Phil sat on hillsides speculating upon the commercial possibilities of the sumach that flamed scarlet about them. "Shoe-mack" or "shoe-make" they called it, after the fashion of the times, and, according to Hugh, they had heard his great-uncle, Judge Irvin, say that real Russia leather was dyed with the juice of this plant. To the Lancaster cobbler, Josey Work, Phil and Cump carried bundles of it, urging him to start a new industry. When he guffawed, "Take it to Russia," they kicked their bundles into the street and slunk away, nevertheless affecting to believe that when night came Josey would retrieve the sumach and use it as they had suggested. Hugh remembered, too, how Cump and Phil had been innocent enough to hang a cat nine times just to be sure it was dead.

Playing with his brothers and foster brothers, Cump was apparently happy and contented except for one great private worry—his red hair. In that day, as well as for some three generations to come, red hair was the object of juvenile derision. Proud and sensitive, Cump decided, with a love of action that would prove characteristic, to change its color. Commencing a series of experiments with available drugs and medicines, he finally produced a startling green effect that persisted until his hair had grown out once more. After that, Cump apparently gave small heed, in the next sixty-odd years of life, to his personal appearance or attire. Phil it was who evidently prompted him to extreme dislike of certain new trousers into which Mrs. Ewing, who made the children's clothing, one day fitted the two boys. They were soon discovered to have smeared the hated pants with pitch.

Philemon, although more delicately built than Cump, was the more aggressive. Once he took a great dislike to the schoolmaster who inducted the two youngsters into the mysteries of education. A gloomy fellow was this teacher, Williamson Wright, son of Parson Wright, and in the old red frame schoolhouse on East Main Street he preserved discipline by administering bread pills to insubordinate boys. Whispers had it that the doses were compounded of dough and dead flies in equal parts and when, out of school hours, street boys saw Master Wright at the windows of his home, they would say, "Look, he's catching flies!"

Outwardly, Cump was so gentle as to make his belligerent little brother John think him too easily imposed upon. All his life Cump's feelings would be easily wounded, and no matter how kind and just the Ewings might be to him, there must have been moments when the sight of the Ewing children heaping such open worship upon their successful father sent secret waves of misery through the red-haired Sherman boy—thoughts of his own beloved father's failure in money matters—thoughts of how he himself was living on the charity of neighbors.

His own brothers and sisters began to disappear from the games. Friends and relatives were taking them, one by one. Henry Stoddard, a cousin of their mother, took Taylor to live with him in Dayton while he finished college. Charles Hammond, the circuit-riding friend of Judge Sherman, and now owner of the *Cincinnati Gazette*, claimed seven-year-old Lampson. James had convinced every one that he could care for himself at his clerkship in Cincinnati. Elizabeth was "going with" William J. Reese, the rich young Philadelphia lawyer who had settled in New Lancaster two years before and become the social light of the younger set. Soon Cump heard that they were to be married, an accident on Mount Pleasant having brought the romance to a climax.

Elizabeth had gone for a walk with several other girls on Standing Stone and had by chance—of course—met there a party of young men, strolling too. Seeing young Reese among the boys, Elizabeth, in a coquettish fit, started to run, and in her blushing confusion fell over a precipice. Reese in desperate gallantry vaulted down to the ledge where she lay unconscious and carried her home, retaining secretly a torn fragment of her dress as a tender souvenir of the occasion. Naturally, they were soon married, and presently they were established as one of the town's most social couples.

By the spring of 1831 little John was gone too from the brown frame house. A cousin of his father's—also named John Sherman—had come to New Lancaster on his honeymoon for a visit and asked to be allowed to take nine-year-old John to live with him at Mount Vernon, fifty miles away. He promised to educate him until he had graduated from Kenyon College.

These departures made Cump more and more of a Ewing, and as he grew older it became apparent how all-powerful was the clan that he had joined, embracing as it did the rulers of New Lancaster's society and politics—the Ewings, the Beechers, the Gillespies, the Irvins, and the Stanberys. It was at Philemon Beecher's that the clan would gather on Sundays for dinner. And a remarkable sight it was to see them sitting there—remarkable, however provocative to a small boy like Cump Sherman, who kept peeking in at the door every few minutes to see if the old folks were not ready to depart and allow the children to rush to the "second table."

At the head of the table would sit Beecher, called the Black Prince—dean of the Fairfield County bar, Congressman from 1818 to 1825, and one-time general of militia. "I thought Napoleon a very small soldier compared with him," said Cump in later years. Near by sat Judge William W. Irvin, husband of Mrs. Beecher's half-sister Elizabeth. Irvin had served on the Ohio Supreme Court bench with Judge Sherman and in 1828 had defeated General Beecher for Congress—a political but not a social rupture.

Further down the table sat Beecher's two daughters with their lawyer husbands—Louise with Philadelphius Van Trump, Frances with Henry Stanbery, once a student in Thomas Ewing's office, and now his partner. Stanbery already showed the talent that would in time make him Attorney-General of the United States.

Present also was Hugh Boyle, Mrs. Beecher's brother-in-law, patriarchal with his thick white hair and baby-pink complexion, a gentleman of a school already ancient, clerk of the Fairfield County Court since 1803. After dinner Boyle would go walking with one of the little boys, allowing him to hold the forefinger of his left hand, in which he held his snuffbox. In his right hand the veteran beau waved a brown cane with an ivory knob, while on his head sat a great white beaver hat. He walked with his cutaway coat well open to display a bunch of seals dangling from his watch fob, and when the child at his side took wide steps crossing a street, he would say gravely—rolling his tobacco quid in his mouth—"Gentlemen, especially French gentlemen, always take short steps." Of his two daughters at the Beecher table, one, Susan, sat with her cultured husband from Philadelphia—Samuel Denman, a social ornament to the board.

And at the gathering was Thomas Ewing himself, the most powerful of the clan and in 1831 a Senator of the United States. The State Legislature had selected him as the outstanding Whig within their choice, an honor that intensified the worship of his children. "Of all the great men amongst whom my early days were cast," Cump said in his old age, "the noblest Roman of them all was Thomas Ewing. A better, nobler, more intellectual man never lived."

But even so august a man was not the center of the family clan. That dignitary was Mrs. Beecher—Great-aunt Susan to the boys—a personality indeed, with her crotchets, attractions, and endlessly brilliant conversation. Of days and evenings she wanted her relatives about her; of nights she wanted to be left alone to read religious books (she would open no others) until three o'clock in the morning. She enjoyed raising a vast commotion among her servants and farm tenants—all Negroes—when her hencoops or smokehouses showed sudden depletion, yet for all her stern questionings she was careful never to fix the guilt on any individual. It was the hubbub that she liked.

Usually in the evenings Maria Ewing, attended by Cump, Phil, or Hugh, visited Aunt Beecher, the youngsters carrying lanterns, since the town had no street lights. While the two women talked in the upstairs sitting-room, the boys cracked hickory nuts in the kitchen, listening to the tales of Darkey Jupiter, the houseman, or they slept uncomfortably on stiff horsehair sofas. At length Maria Ewing would call to them to prepare for the trip home. They would arise. The women would stand at the head of the stair winding up their conversation. What seemed like hours would pass before the boys would hear, "Well, good night!" Mrs. Ewing would descend to the middle landing, then Aunt Beecher would renew the talk and come down to the landing too. Slowly, and chattering on, the ladies would finally reach the foot of the stair, while the little boys draped themselves in dejection over chair backs. Time ground on. The talkers came to the front door; it opened leisurely and as the night air rushed in the boys would put on their caps and caper. Joy would be premature, for in the doorway the ladies would lock themselves with fresh topics of conversation. The boys would slump. "Well, good-by!" The boys lit lanterns and scuffled their feet. Mrs. Ewing would reach the porch. Now they were off! But Aunt Beecher would make a disgusting sally with last-minute memories, and on the veranda would talk for another eternity. Slowly the women would inch toward the steps. "Well, good night!" Unbelievably the end would come after all.

There were long trips for Cump when his own mother journeyed to Mansfield once a year to visit relatives. He remembered, years later:

> I had to drive her in an old "dandy" wagon. The distance was seventy-five miles. . . . We took three days and stopped at every house to gossip with the women folks and dispense medicines and syrups to the sick, for in those days all had the chills and ague.

Cump's education progressed. Even when absent at Washington, Thomas Ewing watched over details of the youngsters' schooling. On December 9, 1831, he sent a box of books and the following letter to Maria:

> Keep the children busy. Set out the large table and gather the whole concern around it—and the five, Phil, Cump, Ellen, Bub and let Tom have a place, too—let them all look at the pictures and let Phil and Cump take turns reading the stories for the general information of the company. The happiest evenings I ever recollect to have spent were in a poor log hut by my father's fireside, reading to my mother and sisters.
>
> To give them the proper effect you must become a hearer and seem interested in the stories and mingle an occasional expression of approbation and praise of the performance of the readers.
>
> I rely upon this system if fairly adopted and regularly attended to, more than anything else to guard the habits of those lads and keep them from falling into vicious practices. It may be somewhat irksome to you, but perseverance in it for a short time will make it much less so. . . . I am compelled by circumstances to leave the heavy charge to your unaided exertions. . . . Hold the sessions for half an hour or so in the evening. . . .
>
> And there is Cumpy too—he is disposed to be bashful, not quite at home.

Endeavor to inspire him with confidence and make him feel one of the family.

Constantly he enjoined Maria, "Tell the girls and Cump and Philemon that they must write every week." Even when the Senate recessed or adjourned, the demands of his law practice kept the Salt-Boiler away from New Lancaster much of the time. And when he was at home his habits of intensive study usually took him to his office in the evenings. This office was a two-story brick building that, after the fashion of lawyers, physicians, or wealthy farmers of the time, he had erected for himself in the sideyard. Neighbors peering at it late at night would say: "He's reading by *two* candles! Whoever heard of such extravagance?"

One winter night he arose from dinner saying that he would need Phil and Cump to sit in his office and tend the fire. In his presence the boys were always quiet and this time they were especially so, for earlier in the day they had purchased a new three-volume work, *The Spanish Cavalier*—in small red-leather volumes that they scanned in the firelight. The story was one of blood and thunder and the readers were lost in its terrors when Ewing raised his massive head to say, "Boys, get some wood." In the huge dark yard, with the woodpile at the other end of the lot, the boys found a path miles in length, with each mile beset by murderous Spaniards. They came panting back to the office with the cordwood, and although the firelight cheered them, they were not quite equal to further adventures with the Cavalier. Next day they asked the man at the bookstore if he wouldn't take back the books, which, since they were Senator Ewing's boys, he agreed to do, refunding the money.

Almost unbearable was the excitement when, in 1832, the Senator sent from Washington a miraculous instrument—a piano. With it Ewing sent a letter to Maria, announcing, "You must immediately commence learning—do not feel ashamed to take lessons." The dutiful wife obeyed.

When her husband was absent, Maria listened for the coachman's horn that announced the approach of the stage, rumbling over the turnpike. "Boys," she would call, "there's the stagecoach!" And they would tear down the hill to the general store, which, since there was no formal post office, kept pigeonholes for each family's letters. Upon one occasion when the storekeeper had reported nothing for the Ewings, Cump stretched himself on tiptoe, saying, "I think I see a letter there." The storekeeper in anger laid down the newspaper he was reading, arose as if to look again, but instead placed both hands suddenly upon the counter as if to vault the barrier and thrash the boy who disputed his word. In a flash Cump and Phil were gone.

Cump was developing a tendency to speak up on occasion. From his tenth year onward he heard, dimly, talk of politics as important men swarmed to see Senator Ewing. The old peril of States' rights was greater than when Thomas Ewing as a boy had heard it in his turn. Since 1827 South Carolina had been threatening to nullify a Federal law—"the tariff of abominations"—which, it said, favored New England manufacturers at the expense of Southern farmers. Carolina orators shouted that they were "chained to the car of Eastern factory owners." Senator Robert Y. Hayne, the South Carolina leader, was scheming to ally Western sentiment with the South; he said that the Eastern factory barons plotted to keep men from emigrating to the free lands of the West so that they would be forced to labor at small wages in New England.

It was to answer Hayne that Daniel Webster, spokesman of Ewing's party, the Whigs, inheritors of the Federalist tradition, rose in the Senate in 1830--swarthy Webster, "the divine Daniel," tipsy sometimes but with a dramatic eye and a thunder head that reminded observers of the old god Jove. Said Webster: The general Government has befriended Western settlers—it spent millions to extinguish Indian titles to the land; it sent armies to fight the Indians; it obtained Western land from the States; it negotiated the immense Louisiana Purchase in 1802, Florida in 1819; it has given Westerners opportunity to rise to wealth without competing with slave labor; it is putting through the Cumberland Road and canals to help the frontiersmen. Said Webster, warming to the music of his own voice: No State can ever nullify a Federal law; the Federal Government is not the creature of the States; does not the Constitution begin, "We, *the people*"? It does not begin, "We, *the States!*"

By December, 1832, Cump Sherman listened to Whigs praising their enemy Democrat, President Andrew Jackson, because he had told South Carolina there would be war if the Government was flouted. In the Southern stronghold, John C. Calhoun, successor to Hayne, pronounced it the right of every State to refuse obedience to Federal powers when it felt itself unjustly treated. Jackson, observing that "to say that any State may at pleasure secede from the Union is to say that the United States is not a nation," menaced South Carolina so fiercely that it temporarily abandoned its hopes of nullifying a Federal law. But if Senator Benton of Missouri was right in his observation, Calhoun was telling friends that the South could never be united against the North on tariff questions and that the basis of Southern independence must henceforth be slavery.

Regarding Thomas Ewing's word as law, Cump grew up in the older man's religion—the Union, the Constitution. Ewing was toiling powerfully in support of Webster's policies and had himself smashed at

Hayne's theories of State supremacy in a speech that the South Carolinian's biographer would declare to be an even stronger argument than that of Webster.

Cump was becoming a tall boy, quick to absorb the ideas of his elders. The autumn that he was fourteen and beginning to think shyly about girls, Ellen Ewing was ten—intense, intelligent, equally enthusiastic about her mother's church and her father's character, a warm-hearted little girl, devoted to her two big brothers, Phil and Cump.

6

WASHINGTON

THE red-haired boy at thirteen had grown so tall and so large for his age that Thomas and Maria Ewing realized that it was now time to plan for his future, just as for Philemon's.

As United States Senator, Ewing had at his disposal certain appointments to the United States Military Academy at West Point, and as a Whig and an intellectual aristocrat who knew the value of education, the Salt-Boiler did not share the distrust of the institution that ran through the midlands. In 1833 the Academy was but twenty-one years old, too young to have any traditions that might popularize it with distant democrats. Moreover, it was associated in the Western mind with the military profession, which was by no means helpful to it. Self-confident and independent, the pioneers, particularly of the Northwest, thought it all very well to cheer for those citizen soldiers who had gone out with their rifles to shoot redcoats from behind trees in the wars with England, but a professional soldier was something else—smacking too much of the Old World with its tyrannical wars. The best soldiers, they believed, were farmers who dropped the hoe and seized the rifle. Didn't their own success in the Indian wars prove it? Added to this early American tradition was the desire of the later immigrants to be free from conscription and standing armies. Many of the Irish, Scotch, English, and Germans who poured into America in the first half of the nineteenth century were fugitives from military impressment. The Napoleonic struggles had been one of the major causes for European emigration.

In the great forests of the West, a pioneer felt himself full of the Jeffersonian doctrine that the common man was superior to any king—

and that a school for training military officers belonged in a monarchy rather than in a republic. This spirit fermented steadily, and in the very year that Thomas Ewing was first thinking of sending young Sherman to West Point, the legislators of Tennessee passed resolutions in favor of abolishing the institution altogether. On November 26, 1833, they declared that:

> . . . a few young men, sons of distinguished and wealthy families, through the intervention of members of Congress, are educated at this institution at the expense of the great body of the American people which entitle them to privileges and elevate them above their fellow citizens who have not been so fortunate as to be educated under the patronage of this aristocratical institution.

And in the following March similar resolutions passed the legislature of Ohio, scoring West Point as "partial in its operations and wholly inconsistent with the spirit and genius of our liberal institutions." All across the country the sentiment grew, and on the first of March, 1837, resulted in the agreement of a special committee of nine Congressmen to do away with the Academy and substitute in its place a practice school for all soldiers. The decision was a blow at the British idea that an officer should be a gentleman and so apart from private soldiers—an idea that ran counter to the entire philosophy of the Jeffersonians whose French Republicanism had swept the American electorate. The special committee, however, was defeated by the vote of the House of Representatives when it was argued that the cost of educating, feeding, and clothing each of the two hundred and fifty cadets was only forty dollars per annum—a sum lower than that paid by students in the best nonmilitary colleges. To the accusation by the committee of nine that the institution was run for rich men's sons it was answered that the fault was not that of West Point but that of the Congressmen themselves, since each Representative had the appointment of one youth from his district. And when the committee of nine declared that it was useless to educate professional officers, since the militiamen would either refuse to enlist under them or if they did so would shoot the West-Pointers in the back at the first opportunity "and devolve the command upon some more congenial comrade," it was said in reply that nothing like that had happened in the War of 1812.

West Point was saved, but the opposition still thrived. In many congressional districts no young men of the required ages—sixteen to twenty-one—applied for examination, and Congressmen used their appointive power for political log-rolling with colleagues who had more applications than they could fill. It was not uncommon for a South Carolina boy, for instance, to enter the Academy as a citizen of the Ohio that he had never seen.

Senator Ewing planned an appointment for his wife's relative, William Irvin, son of the judge, when that youth reached the proper age in 1835. The following year either Cump or Philemon would be eligible. Ewing was thinking of them as early as 1833. Writing from Washington to Maria on December 22, he said:

> I want Phil to come down and stay with me the rest of the winter. He will be company for me and besides he will be really useful. Perhaps Cumpy would think himself slighted if he had not the offer coming, but Phil is so much more of a business lad in the capacity in which I want him that I would greatly prefer to have him here and you may tell Cumpy that I want him to learn fast that he may be ready to go to West Point or to college soon—and that I don't think Phil will be stout enough to go to West Point. Say nothing in a way that will mortify him—but try and prevent Cumpy getting the idea that he is less beloved by me.
>
> Kiss the little fellows for me.

The Senator's son Hugh, who was seven years of age when the discussion of West Point arose in the family, always remembered that the appointment had been definitely offered to Philemon and that Sherman received it when it was declined. "Philemon, his father being wealthy, said he had no wish to be educated at the Nation's expense," said Hugh. "And besides, he had aspirations to the priesthood, a more honorable profession than that of soldier." Another variant to the story was given by Philemon to his children in his later years. He told them that his father had offered him the appointment but that he hadn't wanted it. His eyes had been on the law, and as a consequence the cadetship had gone to Cump.

All that Sherman remembered was that he had been notified, prior to 1834, to prepare himself for the institution. He knew nothing about West Point except that it was very strict and that it led into the army. Toward militarism he had no special leaning. Much as he might admire General Beecher, he could have nothing but contempt for the militia that Beecher had commanded. All through his youth he had seen militiamen treat the profession of arms as a mere joke. Drill days were picnics—and nothing else. There were no standard muskets with which to drill. Uniforms were few, and such as existed were grotesquely assorted. Furthermore, there was no time to practice the manual of arms when so many watermelons waited in heaps to be slaughtered and when so much gingerbread stood on the tables under the trees, ready for the ravishers. Beeves were barbecued, foot races and horse races were run; it was the thing to get drunk and bet on wrestling matches. Fights raged in different parts of the grounds. The men were apt to cheer boisterously at the conclusion of the chaplain's prayer. On parade, officers were seen in ancient, ridiculous regimentals, carrying a sword in one hand and an umbrella in the other. Often as not, they bestrode fat farm mares whose colts tried to suck as the grand march progressed.

Other than hunting of game, there was nothing in young Sherman's youth to whet his appetite for arms. He enjoyed shooting rabbits and squirrels in the Kettle Hills. Hugh Ewing, who was the intimate of Cump's younger brother Hoyt, remembered how they teased Tecumpsey, as they called him, to let them accompany him on his expeditions. They even offered him the use of Hoyt's fat black dog, Coley Sherman, but Cump was adamant, sitting in Ewing's kitchen yard cleaning his gun and shaking his head No. The boys begged but, said Hugh,

> after it had become quite evident that our appeals to his natural affection, friendship and pity had been thrown away upon him, a revulsion of feeling came over us and we withdrew to the corner of the house, and with our retreat thus secured taunted him with appellations such as we deemed best calculated to harrow his feelings; chiefly relying, I remember, upon repeating with various inflections of voice indicative of depreciation and contempt the approbrious epithet of "Red-headed Woodpecker." Nothing however came of it—we neither succeeded in "gitting to go" nor in provoking an outburst of wrath. Our arrows glanced from a mail of real or assumed indifference, and calmly finishing his preparations, the Nimrod shouldered his gun and took to the woods alone.

Young Sherman's body, developing so rapidly, grew eager for action. A new bustle and pulse had come to New Lancaster just at the time when it would excite a boy of fourteen. That year the Cumberland Road had been pushing west from Maryland to Columbus, Ohio. Mercantile goods came rolling in from Baltimore, carried in long Conestoga wagons that looked like great sausages on wheels, and which were drawn by six or eight horses gayly decorated with colored gewgaws and bells. The road was full of traffic. And New Lancaster was seething with the internal-improvements enthusiasm that was sweeping the nation—the same excitement that was beginning to grip a lanky postmaster in New Salem, Illinois. As a member of the legislature Abraham Lincoln, between such times as creditors were not seizing his horses, was thinking of canals, even as the citizens of Ohio were thinking of them. New Lancaster was thrilled over the lateral waterway that would connect it with the Ohio Canal at a point eight miles above town, and it was as a rodman on surveying parties here that Tecumseh Sherman earned his first wages—fifty cents a day—in the autumn of 1834 and the spring of 1835.

That summer of 1835 his brother John came home from Mount Vernon, where his cousin's family had grown so large as to crowd him out. John was a bad boy, and had deviled one of Mount Vernon's schoolmasters, "Bunty" Lord, most unmercifully. Once John had persuaded some companions to help him carry a dead sheep into the schoolhouse after hours, and had placed it on "Bunty" Lord's chair, to be found in all its ghastliness in the morning. Upon its head John had fastened a Latin couplet of his own composition, calling attention to the worthiness of such a sacrifice to so poor a "Lord." Naturally John was detected through his handwriting, and expelled. He proved similarly incorrigible in New Lancaster, where from his mother's home he attended the school of Mark Howe. After one of John's impertinences, he was told by Howe to stand up and hold out his left hand for a rap from the ferule. John held out the hand, but before Howe could hit it, John swung his left fist full to the teacher's face.

"This," said John, telling the story a half century later, "created great excitement in the school, all the students being present, my brother Tecumseh among them. It was said at the time that the boys were disposed to take sides with me, but I saw no signs of it."

It was Mark Howe's brother, Sam, a teacher in the academy, who whipped John Sherman most frequently. Hugh Ewing saw such thrashings take place often:

> Sam kept bundles of sprouts, five to six feet in length, for whipping boys. John Sherman grew weary of being whipped and once rebelled, and when Howe came rushing at him, whip in hand, John hit him in the chest with an ink stand, soiling his linen. Howe proceeded to break whip after whip over John's back and legs until his arm grew weary. Philemon and John's brother, William, said at supper that night that John would be laid up for at least a week. But at dancing school, an hour after supper, there was John swinging down the center in high glee, arms and legs flying inelegantly right and left, his face beaming with excitement and pleasure.

In the year and a half that the two brothers were together at this period of their lives, they assumed the relationship that was to mark their intimacy for the next half century—John, the worldly practical friend who would always believe his brother too sensitive and kindly for his own protection—and who would later say:

> I had a good deal of intercourse with him, mainly in the way of advice on his part. At that time he was a steady student, quiet in his manners and easily moved by sympathy or affection. I was regarded as a wild, reckless lad, eager in controversy and ready to fight. No one could then anticipate that he was to be a great warrior and I a plodding lawyer and politician. I fired my first gun over his shoulder. He took me with him to carry the game, mostly squirrels and pigeons.

Cump's increasing habit of blurting out his opinions became more noticeable as he moved through his middle teens. His powers of penetration began to be noticed, too. Once he attended, with two friends, a tent show where Anderson, the Wizard of the North, puzzled the frontiersmen with feats of magic. Cump watched him shrewdly for a time and then began in a loud voice to explain to his companions how the tricks were done. His eye had seen through the magician's sleight of hand. People within sound of the boy's voice crowded to hear him expose the wizard, and altogether there was so much confusion that the performer became rattled and spoiled his show.

Sometimes Cump would be included in Maria Ewing's religious expeditions, when, filling the carriage with youngsters, with a coachman at the reins, she would take her brood eighteen miles to the Dominican church at Somerset for high mass. The pilgrimage would begin before sunrise and would end well after dark, when Maria helped her sleepy flock up the home steps once more. It was probably on one of these journeys that Cump saw for the first time a black-haired little Irish boy from Perry County—Philip H. Sheridan, whose father, an ardent Catholic, brought him to Somerset for religious instruction. The Ewings and Sheridans knew each other well. "Phil" was too young to have been an intimate of Cump Sherman, for he was born in 1831, but they stuck in each other's memory.

A decade and more would pass and this same Phil Sheridan would be thinking of West Point even as Sherman had been in 1835. One day in either 1847 or 1848, young Phil was brought to the monastery by his father for a serious talk with the priest. They entered the small brick house where Father Dominic Young received his parishioners. Father Joshua Young, another priest, famed for his ministerings about the region, was also present, and to the two clergymen the elder Sheridan poured out his troubles. It seemed that his son had received an appointment to the United States Military Academy and the parent wanted spiritual advice as to the propriety of accepting it. There was danger, he said, that the boy might lose his faith in that secular military school—a loss that would be a million-fold greater than any gain. West Point was rigidly Episcopalian. The discussion was long, and terminated when Father Joshua announced that the boy ought to stay among his friends in the Catholic community of Perry County and not, for any temporal advantage, go among unbelievers and perhaps lose his soul.

"But what shall I do with the boy?" asked the elder Sheridan in despair.

"Rather than send him to West Point," replied Father Joshua sternly "take him out into the back yard, behind the chicken coop, and cut his throat."

The Sheridans went home in deep thought. However, as Hugh Ewing told the story, "Sheridan thought this mode of disposing of Phil too drastic and, milder counsel prevailing, sent him to West Point."

Father Joshua Young, arriving in the region in 1839, had no chance to warn the Ewings against sending young Sherman to so dangerous a place as West Point. It was not the Senator's way to worry about religious fears and moreover it is not apparent that the Ewings ever thought of Cump as a Catholic in the full sense in which the other children embraced the faith. Maria had seen to it that the boy had the advantage of baptism and religious instruction, but she was evidently as careful not to force the youth into any new belief as her husband had been not to change his name. In the spring of 1836, the letter announcing Cump's appointment to the United States Military Academy arrived. In May the Senator wrote Maria from the capital:

> Tell Cumpy to pursue his studies manfully so that he may pass his examinations with honor. You will make arrangements to send him about the 1st of June and let him come by Washington, that I may see him. . . .
> P.S. It is advisable that Cumpy should bring with him as little citizen's clothes as possible, for all will have to be laid aside when he gets to West Point. They dress in uniform.

The May Day of departure came—the break-up of Cump's life in New Lancaster. Even the town itself would have changed before he returned: a canal would come through, population would increase, bustling, hustling merchants and factory men would pour in, the old charm would be gone, and the citizens in pride would be calling their town plain Lancaster, dropping the timid New that had preceded it.

Cump's boyhood was being broken off almost as abruptly as the coachman snapped his whip on top of the waiting stage. He said good-by to both his mothers standing there, and to all the Ewing-Sherman-Clark children with whom he had played. His brother John was soon to go to work as a surveyor's rodman; his crony Philemon would leave that autumn for Miami University. Ellen Ewing, now twelve, watched Cump climb into the coach. It was a brother who was leaving.

As he waved good-by he was remembered—"a tall, slim, loosely jointed boy with red hair, fair burned skin and piercing black eyes." Always there would be a dispute among his closest friends and relatives about the color of his eyes, some saying that they were dark blue, others black, others hazel, others brown—but all agreed that they were sharp and piercing. Perhaps their expression was so striking as to confuse observers as to their exact hue.

Facing the strange Eastern world, the boy rode off along the great National Road—chief East-West thoroughfare of the nation—three days and nights to Frederick, Maryland. Four horses drew the coach and they were changed every ten miles. Nine passengers could sit inside the coach and one might ride with the driver outside. On the roof rode the trunks and the freight. When the stage mired down, the passengers were expected to alight and pry out the wheels with fence rails while the coachman whipped his horses.

At Frederick, Cump debated. Two ways lay before him—the new-fangled steam railway to Baltimore or the two-horse hack direct to Washington. As became a shy and unassertive boy, "not having full faith in the novel and dangerous railroad," he took the hack. That night he reached Gadsby's Hotel in Washington, and in the morning hunted up Mr. Ewing, finding him "boarding with a mess of Senators at Mrs. Hill's and I transferred my trunk to the same place."

Cump at sixteen was able to understand something of Thomas Ewing's position at the capital. As a Senator, Ewing had fought for lower postal rates and for the final settlement of the Ohio boundaries, two strokes for the Northwest. And during one of his arguments in favor of extending aid to commerce on the Great Lakes he had earned the nickname Old Solitude. In denouncing a Democratic bill he had said, "If it prevails it will make the Great Lakes a solitude of waters." Daniel Webster in particular liked to tease Ewing about the title. When visiting at the Ewing home, "the divine Daniel" was seen by Thomas Ewing, Jr.—a small boy, peeping in at the dining-room door—to arise from the table and with his hands on his huge host's shoulders, exclaim:

> Oh, solitude, where are the charms,
> That sages have seen in thy face?
> Better dwell in the midst of alarms
> Than live in this horrible place.

Webster and Clay had, in Washington, intrusted to Ewing an important Whig duty, the exposure of Democratic corruption in the Post Office Department, a task that Ewing carried so deep into Jackson's spoils system that the Vice President, Martin Van Buren, admitted that "the Administration was damaged more in this quarter than in any others which were assailed by the Whigs." Van Buren thought Ewing "a most indefatigable agitator, possessed of highly respectable talents and capable of almost any extent of physical endurance." At the time that Cump visited Ewing at the national capital, the latter was preparing to fight the banking policy of President Jackson, a fight which would place him so high in Whig estimation that when, in 1840, the nation would turn to that party, the Salt-Boiler would be in line for great things.

Cump pressed his face against the White House fence for a solid hour to watch that violent old gentleman, President Jackson, pace the walk outside his mansion in "a cap and overcoat so full that his form seemed smaller than I had expected."

In Washington, a boy would hear little of the antislavery agitation that was rising in the North. Senators and Congressmen were generally of the belief that while slavery was an evil, nothing could be done about it. They tried to ignore the Abolitionists, who, led by William Lloyd Garrison, were pointing out that since Great Britain's emancipation of slaves in 1833, the South was the last civilized refuge of the "damning crime." In 1835 the South had taken to burning Garrison's paper, *The Liberator,* as well as hanging Garrison in effigy. Anti-Abolitionist mobs had beaten agitators in Philadelphia, Boston, and Utica, and each time they did it made converts for the antislavery cause. When howling throngs dragged Garrison, nearly nude, through the streets of Boston, a rich young aristocrat looked down from a window and resolved to turn his scorching eloquence thereafter upon slavery. He was Wendell Phillips. In 1836, John Greenleaf Whittier became Secretary of the American Anti-Slavery Society, the heat of his Quaker flame sending poems like flashes of fire about the North. William Ellery Channing, a scholarly Boston clergyman, abandoned his conservative past when Abolitionists were clubbed, and loosed his emotions in devastating books and sermons.

Southern slaveholders met this moral crusade with defiance. Each year more and more of them ceased to admit that slavery was an evil of which the white owner was as much a victim as the black subject. They began to defend it as "the cornerstone of our republican edifice." Their clergymen began to find justification for slavery in the Bible. In 1836 Senator Benton, slaveholding Senator from Missouri, declared the Union to be in more danger from Southern than from Northern extremists. Ex-President James Madison had observed two years earlier that the Southern demagogues were trying to solidify their section by pretending that the North held unconstitutional designs upon slave property.

The slave question, entering upon its last wordy phase, was deplored by Ewing, who disapproved petitions which begged Congress to abolish slavery in the District of Columbia, and was for quietude once the issue threatened to divide the Union. It was not that he disliked slavery less, but he loved the Union more.

Cump Sherman passed from Old Solitude's hands into the care of the United States Army, which was in itself as hostile as the South toward antislavery agitators, who would soon be crying that a Constitution that protected slavery was only "a league with death and a covenant with hell."

What the boy thought more about as he stopped in New York to visit the Hoyt relatives of his mother, was the theatre. One of his cousins, William Scott, "looked on me as an untamed animal just caught in the far West," but Cump recovered his spirits at the Park Theatre, where he saw his first professional dramatic performance. Back at home, he and Philemon had led the younger children in a series of private theatricals in empty storerooms; he had always hungered for shows and now he was face to face with the world of Edwin Forrest and Junius Brutus Booth, who were dominating the New York stage in the summer of 1836. He went up the Hudson to West Point with new melodies in his ears.

7

WEST POINT

AS Senator Ewing saw the boy depart, he wrote his wife, "I have great confidence that Cumpy will make a man that we shall be proud of. His opportunities will be very good if he improves them as he ought. He is a fine boy and deports himself well."

And as Cump walked into the strange Academy grounds, he found that Ewing's long arm was still around him. From among the sophisticated second-year men, came William Irvin ready to make life easy for his old playmate from Lancaster. By tradition, each new cadet must become errand-boy for some higher classman—a "plebe," short for plebeian. From among the 100 novitiates, Irvin chose Sherman, relieving the latter of much natural homesickness.

Among the dowdy buildings of stone and wood was one in which the newcomers registered—the Adjutant's office where reigned the handsome Lieutenant C. F. Smith, destined to remain for twenty-five years in Sherman's mind as the beau-ideal of a soldier.

The examination was simple; a boy must be at least sixteen, not over twenty-one, and have a command of reading, writing and simple arithmetic. Each youth had been advised in advance that "a knowledge of English grammar, geography and even of Latin is highly desirable and advantageous," but those subjects were not required as the lawmakers had felt that a standard any higher than the "Three R's" would "exclude many young men of worth whose early education has been neglected." It seemed that only an illiterate or a dunce could have failed to qualify, and Sherman, with his sound Lancastrian education, was soon able to notify Ewing that he had been successful. Relaying the news to Maria, Ewing allowed himself the luxury of referring to the boy's full name—

> Letters from William inform me he passed very easily though I think from the tone of his letters that he does not find the situation as comfortable as he expected. The cadets, it seems, live pretty roughly.

His examination over, Cump found himself enlisted for eight years' service—four at the Academy, then four more in the army. A Spartan régime stretched ahead. Barracks were small and bare, the furniture a cot and chair. Almost all the pay—twenty-eight dollars a month—was consumed in charges for food and clothing. The uniforms were uncomfortable, particularly the dress affair, a stiff gray coat with a short tail and standing collar and tight white trousers. The cap was of black felt with a round crown and a black pompon. Food was not of the rich variety that Cump had known in Lancaster.

For the first time in his life Cump learned that there was such a thing as caste. At home, where he had belonged to the aristocracy if such a distinction had indeed been recognized, everybody talked to everybody else. Here at the Academy, the officers did not speak to the boys and the older boys glared and shouted at the new plebes. There was some strange new force in the world—unreasoning authority! Nobody stopped to argue or to convince another person that a thing ought to be done. A command was given and it was obeyed; if it was not, punishment came swiftly.

Cadets scrambled out of bed at the blare of the bugle. They studied their books until breakfast at seven, recited or studied again from eight until one o'clock. Then they marched to dinner and back to their books, where they remained from two until four. Next came the drilling on the field, marching, handling muskets by command, until sunset, when the flag came down with ceremony. After supper, books must be studied until taps blew at ten. Between times roll calls and inspections and guard duty must be observed.

Young Sherman was fitted with fourteen other classmates into a section whose recitations lasted from an hour to an hour and a half, with students called to the front to demonstrate problems on the blackboard. By contrast with the discipline of Mark Howe, the new school was like a prison. No boy dared to talk back to a teacher in uniform. Where would his little brother John be if he should try his fisticuffs here? But except for the stiffness of discipline, there was nothing difficult for Cump in his new classes. Most of the subjects were not new to him, even if they were to the average cadet—algebra, geometry, French.

Before the year was out he would be studying trigonometry and hearing the second-year cadets talking of their calculus, surveying, geography, English grammar, topography, and drawing. The Academy curriculum was, as a whole, not far ahead of the better high schools of the East. Only in the fourth year would there be any classroom study of war. *The Nation* on December 28th, 1865, would say, in discussing the Academy of Sherman's time, that Yale and Harvard gave only one-third as much time to mathematics and yet carried a student as far in the first two years as West Point did in four. German, Latin and Greek were not on the Academy list. Jacob Dolson Cox, lawyer, general, statesman, educator, and diplomat, studied the Academy with an outsider's judicious eyes and concluded:

> The law forbade any entrance examination to West Point on subjects outside the usual work done in rural schools. Most cadets had had little preparatory education beyond that of the common country schools. Ulysses S. Grant (Class of 1843) said that he had never seen an algebra until after his appointment.
>
> Three years of study would put a cadet abreast of students entering college elsewhere and four years would carry them about as far as the end of the Freshman year in Yale, Harvard and Princeton. The West Point course covered two years' work in mathematics, one in physics and chemistry and one in construction of fortifications. This was the scientific part and the heaviest. A little English, mental philosophy, moral philosophy, elementary law, two years' study in French and one in Spanish. There was no instruction in strategy or grand tactics in military history or the art of war. The little book by Mahan on Outpost Duty was the only text-book on Theory outside engineering proper. At an earlier day the cadets had studied Jomini but it had been dropped.

In this last sentence Cox was particularly illuminating, for the military texts of Baron Jomini, once chief strategist for Napoleon, were almost like the Bible to student warriors in Europe. West Point taught the rudiments of artillery, infantry, and cavalry practice but did not attempt to teach strategy, as an art, to boys so young.

What it did teach them was obedience, regularity, reverence for authority. By example, stern command, and punishment it taught cadets the things that a gentleman and an officer did or did not do. It taught them honor—an officer's honor, a sort of a caste ritual: an officer did no manual labor, was above the soiling tricks of barter and trade; he did not tell lies or seek gain. He was above the tradesman class both in honesty and in manners. Into his soul the school tried to grind a trust in orthodoxy—orthodoxy in Christianity, in militarism, and in etiquette. Modeled on the British ideal, the Academy held high-church Episcopalian services each Sunday and commanded every boy, no matter what his faith, to attend. This had not been true from the first. The Academy itself had been backward and faltering between its creation by Congress in 1802 and the advent of Colonel Sylvanus Thayer as commandant in 1817. Thayer had lifted the curriculum and discipline out of the elementary grade, at least. And in 1825 the Academy had begun to take on the dignity of the aristocratic Episcopalian faith—traditional in the South, the established religion of several of the original colonies, the conventional religion of English patricians.

It was soon remarked how many of its graduates became clergymen. Among the most distinguished were Leonidas Polk, Bishop of Louisiana; Roswell Park, Class of '31, who had resigned to become a noted Episcopalian dominie and educator, and George Deshon, the Catholic prelate. West Point men found it easy to step from the profession of orthodox warrior to that of orthodox clergyman. Both faiths as taught at West Point were strict, formal; both bent the will of man to authority. "Duty and obedience" was the watchword of both. When Cump Sherman arrived at the Academy, critics of the place were sneering, "West Point's a great place to make preachers."

The Episcopal creed, as he heard it pronounced on Sundays between his sixteenth and twentieth years, was to touch young Sherman as little as had the Roman Catholicism in whose atmosphere he lived from the age of nine to that of sixteen. As soon as he left New Lancaster for West Point, the practice of any particular creed fell from him almost unnoticed and was never picked up again.

Cump Sherman had come from a liberal, democratic atmosphere into one that depended for its social character upon the South, whose boys came to West Point with characteristically better manners, greater assurance, and easier confidence than did the Western and Northern youths. Also they came in proportionately greater numbers. When the lists of graduates were scanned twenty-four years after Sherman's entrance, it was found that between 1802 and 1861 the Academy had held one cadet for every 5,757 persons in the Southern States and only one for every 8,330 Northerners.

Aristocratic in manner, in ideals, and in religion, the West Point that nursed William Tecumseh Sherman was similarly patrician in its attitude toward government and politics. Academy graduates emerged with a firm trust in things as they were—young reactionaries coming out of school with no divine nonsense about changing the world. Sons of low-church or churchless pioneers acquired in the school a new respect for the high church, and even the sons of Northern antislavery men came home to tell their fathers that the South knew best about matters of state.

The United States Army, like the civilians, had the view that men of the South, trained and educated to rule, were rightfully the leading statesmen of the nation. Sherman came under the influence of an army that had been from the first under Southern dominance. True, only nine of the eighteen men appointed to be Secretary of War had come from the South, but the Presidents, whose policies Cabinet members carried out had been chiefly Southern men. In 1836 the nation had spent thirty-nine of its forty-seven years under Presidents of Southern birth and ideals.

Naturally the West Point cadets were shaped toward the belief that so long as the public, that "great beast," as Alexander Hamilton had named it, must have its own government, Southern gentlemen had best administer its affairs. By tradition and training, Southern patricians felt themselves destined to hold the reins at Washington and to this ideal, which became orthodox by 1836, young Sherman was receptive. And although Cump's home training had been more Northern than Southern—Thomas Ewing was not one to let his section be trampled upon by another—the Senator was akin to the most influential Southerners in believing that intellect and education should rule. He shared their conservative beliefs about democracy, their distrust of the mob's passions. In philosophy and politics he was closely akin to General Winfield Scott, the Virginia gentleman who was the nation's military hero as well as model for schoolboys at West Point.

Old Solitude had no thought but that so tractable a boy as Cump would excel in a school where the premium was so high on obedience and conformity. What the Senator did not see was the immensity of the gulf that lay between his own world of logic, free speech, and easy, genial tranquillity and the West Point world of force. Cump had been docile under the Ewing discipline because his tender heart had responded to the reasoning and affection with which the Salt-Boiler and Maria handled their young. Just as the broad, tolerant influence of Thomas Ewing made young Sherman indifferent to the call of orthodox religion, so it made him unreceptive to the West Point valuations of etiquette and compulsion.

Now Cump found himself chained to a system that heaped demerits on the cadet whose shoes were improperly blackened, whose belt buckles carried a fleck of rust, whose room was not precisely swept, whose buttons failed to gleam brightly enough.

He learned that cadets might be the most brilliant of all their fellows in class and still find themselves expelled if their demerits in one year reached the fatal two-hundred mark. In his first letter to the Senator, the new cadet set down without comment the schedule of demerits by which a student's standing, when combined with classroom reports, was determined; one demerit for soiled clothing, three for absence from roll call, eight for absence from drill or parade. He made no complaint of the barren atmosphere of the living-quarters, merely asking Ewing to excuse his bad writing, since he was forced to write on a chair. Likewise he stated without comment that he had to walk guard eight hours out of the twenty-four. His realistic mind could not, however, forbear to point out to the Senator a slight hypocrisy on the part of his meticulous superiors:

> You mentioned that if I thought there would be no danger in having pocket money, you would send some. I thank you for the offer but I do not want any. However, it reminds me how expressly the appointment prohibited one from receiving money, but in truth there is a boy comes through encampment every evening with cakes and oranges and sells to the cadets in sight of the officers.

Sherman would say when, as a man, he looked back upon his cadet days:

> I was not considered a good soldier. I was not a Sunday-school cadet. I ranked 124 in the whole student body for good behavior. My average demerits, per annum, were about 150, which reduced my final class standing from Number 4 to Number 6.

Never could Sherman value the niceties of dress in the approved West Point manner. Deep in him had been planted the Western frontier trait of evaluating a man by what he said and did rather than by what he wore. Elegance of clothes or manner had been rather to the disadvantage of their wearer in the woodland regions and it was this carelessness that now kept Sherman from the standing to which his intellect alone would have raised him. His first realization of this fact must have come to him in June, 1837, when cadet standings were posted. On the Conduct Roll, which listed the entire student body of 211, he stood 124, with 109 black marks against his name. On the roll of his class he was Number 9 among the 76 cadets who had survived from the 100 who had entered in May, 1836. Judged on his academic record alone, he would have rated among the first five—honor men—of his class, but his errors in decorum had dragged him down.

By contrast, Cump's two cronies among his fellow-classmen, Stewart Van Vliet and George H. Thomas, were far superior, "Van" having but ten demerits and standing sixteenth on the Conduct Roll, while "Tom" with twenty "criminalities" held twenty-sixth place. On the Class Roll, the former stood Number Five, and the latter Number Twenty-six. Probably it was similarity of breeding that drew the three boys together. Van Vliet had been well reared in Vermont and Thomas had arrived with the stately manners of his landed Virginia family. That the Vermonter at twenty-one years of age and the Virginian at twenty should have taken the sixteen-year-old Ohio youth as their intimate was evidence that Sherman had matured early. Although in the succeeding three years Thomas would room with Van Vliet, it was Sherman who became his closest friend.

Dissimilarity of temperament and kinship of character doubtless attracted the two toward each other. Sherman was Anglo-Saxon, nervous, thin, quick, talkative; Thomas was Welsh and French Huguenot, grave, fat, slow, silent. Both were conspicuously honest and sensitive. As a small boy Thomas had felt the South wrong in denying education to slaves, and after school led his father's pickaninnies very stealthily to a grove where he taught them what he had learned during the day. Thirty-five years after their first meeting, Sherman described Thomas as

> my best friend . . . a high-toned, brave and peculiar Virginia gentleman. . . . When he made his decision, until the day of his death, he never flickered—never! He had extraordinary courage . . . and in his younger days displayed it in a negro insurrection which occurred in Virginia when the people were compelled to resort to block-houses for protection. It was necessary at one time to send a messenger from one point to another. George Thomas carried that message, though a mere lad, and for that brave act, General Jackson gave him his appointment as a cadet to the military academy.

As a plebe, Cump looked at the listing of the graduating class, finding among the first five one cadet to remember, the North Carolinian, Braxton Bragg. The caste system kept them apart, yet Bragg and Sherman were so akin that in another school they might have enjoyed the friendship that they would later develop. Both were tall, ungraceful in walk and gesture. Bragg was the more uncouth in manner; intelligence darted from both faces; Bragg was dark and heavy-browed and, like Sherman, spoke his mind freely, brusquely, without regard for consequences; "Bragg had unbending integrity," said his classmate Joseph Hooker. On the class record of the fourth-year men, Cump noted other names: Jubal A. Early of Virginia, Number 18; John Sedgwick of Connecticut, Number 24; and Hooker of Massachusetts, Number 29—

Joe Hooker, six feet tall, handsome with his heavy black hair and magnetic gray eyes, his bold, vivid manner of speaking, a magnificent figure of young Mars.

How had the third-year men come out? Where was Beauregard? Number 2! Pierre Gustave Toutant Beauregard, the olive-skinned, dreamy-eyed Creole from Louisiana, was another cadet who everybody said was to be a towering military figure. His bearing went with high rating. On the Conduct Roll he was tied for leadership, with no demerits whatsoever. Cadets said that he had been guilty of but three in his first year, only thirteen in his second. Now he was faultless. Below him among the forty-six men of that Class of 1838 came the name Irvin McDowell, a pudgy-faced boy born in Columbus, Ohio, but educated in France. Number 23 was McDowell, his standing dragged down by his 134 demerits. There was William Irvin of Lancaster, lower still with 179 demerits—another Western boy who could not properly value deportment.

Look at the next class, the sophomores, men of 1839! There was Henry Wager Halleck standing Number 5—solemn, pop-eyed old Halleck, rated by many as the brainiest student in school, perfect model of a cadet in studies and conduct. Where was Ord, Sherman's particular friend, Edward Otho Cresap Ord of Maryland? Only Number 21. Too bad, for Ord was a mathematical prodigy, a student among students. His conduct must have been bad? Yes, there it was—Number 193, only eighteen from the bottom. "A more unselfish and manly person never lived," Sherman would some day say of this cadet. And Canby? Edward Richard Sprigg Canby, the gentle Kentuckian—there he was, still further down, Number 33.

Cadets stared at the lists and some of them asked each other, "What would those lists mean if we had to go to war tomorrow?" They turned their backs on the lists, the seniors to graduate, the rest to prepare for the annual summer encampment, where they would learn to pitch tents, to shoot on the rifle range, to march and to ride over long sweeps of countryside.

With a sigh of relief and a rising sense of new-found superiority, Sherman and his classmates eyed the incoming plebes, and picked their errand boys. Among them Sherman would remember in later years a red-headed lad from Connecticut named Nathaniel Lyon; a slender, high-strung Ohioan, Don Carlos Buell; a Virginian, Robert Garnett; and a youth from Lancaster, Pennsylvania, John F. Reynolds, by name.

Summer encampment over, the cadets returned to another grinding year inside the Academy. That November an instructor in artillery classes, Lieutenant Robert Anderson of Kentucky, left for army-post service. He and Sherman would meet again.

Sherman became in his second year a better soldier, and when in April his grades were sent to Thomas Ewing, he was found to have only forty-eight demerits and to rank Number 7 in mathematics, Number 4 in French, and Number 1 in drawing. By June when the lists were posted he stood Number 6 in his class of 58 men and only Number 78 on the Conduct Roll, with a total of 66 demerits. Although he was still not considered a good soldier, he was improving.

When Cump arrived in New Lancaster on his first furlough that summer, Ellen Ewing, nearing fourteen, looked at her returning playmate to find that he had come back to her a man. She saw Cump come down off the stage, and when she was old, she would tell her children about that moment—how strong and straight he was, how clear-eyed and bright, how light of heart and how proud of his uniform.

That uniform! The first twinge of love?

8

ELLEN

FROM the day he had left home Sherman had found Ellen Ewing, as he told her father, "my best Lancaster correspondent." From her twelfth year onward the girl made her father's red-haired ward her special charge, sending him at first such gifts as pencils and maple sugar, then, as she grew older, knitting slippers for him. Ellen and John were the cadet's confidants and with them he kept up an intimate if spasmodic flow of letters, often, in Ellen's case, apologizing for delays of months between his writings.

During most of the winters Ellen was, like himself, in the East attending school. Eight months after Sherman had been sent to West Point, Thomas Ewing wrote his wife that he had arranged to send Ellen to Monsieur and Madame Picot's school in Philadelphia, "where the first ladies of that city are educated." Always Ewing distrusted the facilities of public schools, and in Ellen's case, he allowed Maria's zeal for religious training to divert the daughter from Picot's to the Roman Catholic Academy of the Visitation at Georgetown, District of Columbia.

In the summer Ellen was at home in Lancaster, ever strengthening her idolatry for that father who seemed to grow more wonderful as she grew older. Her health was none too good, a factor that may have heightened her appreciation for the Herculean parent. She was, however, intensely fond of her mother, and once when Cump wrote her that he despaired of receiving "that long wished for" letter from Maria, she rebuked him so sharply that, in August, 1839, he answered with profuse apologies:

> Very often I feel my insignificance and inability to repay the many kindnesses and favors received at her hands and those of her family. Time and absence serve to strengthen the claims and to increase my affection and love and gratitude to those who took me early under their care and conferred the same advantages as they did upon their own children. Although I have rarely spoken of it still I assure you that I have always felt sincerely and deeply grateful and hope that some event may occur to test it. Indeed I often feel that your father and mother have usurped the place which nature has allotted to parents alone and their children those of brothers and sisters with regard to myself.

These were the words of a boy a little bewildered by a new understanding of things that had been taken as a matter of course in earlier years—a boy not quite certain now whether he ought to be a Sherman or a Ewing. At nineteen he was old enough to understand matters that had been beyond him as a child, and in the new spirit of independence that West Point had awakened in him, he wrote on September 20, 1839, to his own mother, asking if she could spare him five dollars with which to "pay some little debts." To her he spoke frankly, "I do not wish to ever ask Mr. Ewing again for assistance and I have no doubt that by economy I can avoid doing so as after next June my pay will amount to upwards of $700 yearly."

Here, perhaps, was the shadow of that memory of his own father's debts—a Sherman speaking, anxious for independence. In a different tone he had written Maria Ewing five months after he had reached West Point in 1836. Fresh from her fireside, he had asked for some money with which to buy covering for his hands and ears during cold vigils on sentry duty. "You may think it strange," he had said, "that I should ask for money but in reality I would be the last person that would ask it unless it were absolutely necessary." In his correspondence with Ellen, however, Sherman was not given to debating long over family relationships. His letters were those of a boy interested in the daily life of the Academy and offering the pressure of studies as excuse for his own carelessness and negligence in writing.

Cump's vacation was divided between the Ewings and the Shermans. Maria Ewing had a new baby, born that May—Maria Theresa, called Sissie—for Cump to fondle affectionately. Thomas Ewing, his term as Senator concluded and a Democratic legislature choosing another for his seat, was again practicing law. The Abolitionists who were increasing so rapidly in Ohio were not Ewing men. They found Old Solitude too conservative. More to their taste were his political enemies, two law partners of Ashtabula, Joshua R. Giddings and Benjamin Wade, both men of strong frame and unappeasable appetite for badgering Southern fire-eaters. In the summer of 1838 Giddings was campaigning for Congress and Wade for the State Senate (in reality building fences for the United States Senate in the future) and around them were clustering the plaudits of antislavery farmers who of nights helped runaway slaves from station to station on the underground railway—solemnly breaking laws and fearing God.

Young Sherman, handsome and proud in his regimentals, looked upon "nigger-stealers" with the eye of an officer and a gentleman. They were cranks and dangerous agitators. Wherever he went on his horse-and-buggy trips with his mother and brothers across Ohio visiting relatives, he heard of the Abolitionists, yet gave them only contemptuous attention.

A languorous summer passed, and with autumn he was at West Point again, watching the plebes file into class. Among them was an Ohio boy, William Starke Rosecrans—Old Rosey, with a large red nose; an Alabama boy, James Longstreet; a hot-headed Mississippian, Earl Van Dorn; and an Illinois boy, John Pope, who would later on change the fashion in trousers for the cadets. Returning from furlough one autumn, Pope sauntered around the Academy in linen trousers with flies buttoning down the front instead of at the sides, as cadets had previously worn them. Major Delafield, the superintendent, staring at the invention, ordered it adopted by the whole student body, although his wife said that no boy dressed so outrageously should come to the superintendent's house for orders. The style, nevertheless, was set not only for West Point, but also for the whole army, which followed the Academy's lead in matters sartorial.

Sherman's own carelessness in dress and deportment had earned him 57 demerits by the time the lists were posted in midsummer, 1839, and had reduced him to Number 115 among the 231 cadets. Sixth position was all that he could achieve in class standing. Nevertheless, in three years he had come to like the life of a soldier, and to have no sympathy with William Irvin, who was graduating with the idea of resigning quickly in favor of the law. Cump wrote Ellen:

> No doubt you admire this choice, but to speak plainly and candidly, I would rather be a blacksmith. Indeed, the nearer we come to that dreadful epoch, graduation day, the higher opinion I conceive of the duties and life

of an officer of the United States Army, and the more confirmed in the wish of spending my life in the service of my country. Think of that!

As his fourth and final year began, Sherman looked down from his lofty height upon the immemorial gawks who slouched up for registration. Among them was a reluctant stripling who made timid insistence that the authorities had his name down wrong on the books. They had it written Ulysses S. Grant, whereas his name was Hiram Ulysses Grant. He'd like to have it right on the roll. But the registrars were military men, professional followers of written orders, and the Congressman who had sent in the name had written it Ulysses S.; and Ulysses S. it should remain until they received orders to the contrary. After a time the sturdy little cadet gave up, and became Ulysses S. or Uncle Sam Grant and finally, to the boys, just plain Sam—an unhappy youth who plodded out four years at the Academy, hoping always against hope that something would happen to close the place so that he might escape it without dishonor. In December of his first year when Congress, enjoying one of its periodic revulsions against professional militarism, debated the abolishment of the Academy, Grant read the papers with prayers on his lips.

The two Ohio boys, Sherman and Grant, passed the year with a great gulf between them—the chasm separating a fourth-year king and a first-year slave. Each was quick and intelligent in class, slouchy and untidy in dress; neither was military. Grant's unblacked boots and tarnished brass brought him 59 demerits in his first year and placed him 147th among the 223 cadets on the Conduct Roll; he was 144 among 219 in 1841, 157 among 217 in 1842, and 156 among 223 in 1843. These demerits forced his class standings down proportionately; his first year placed him Number 27 among 60 cadets; his second, 24 among 53; his third, 20 among 41, and his fourth, 21 among 39. Even so, his total black marks for his career were but 290 compared with Sherman's 380. In contrast to both of them was Sherman's friend George H. Thomas, who had only 87 black marks in his whole four years; and these came with a consistency that would characterize his character in adult life, 20 in the first year, 22 in the second, 24 in the third, and 21 in the last. Their friend Van Vliet would have only 10 in his first year and none in his three succeeding years; Halleck would have 16. Bragg 105 and Beauregard 14 in their entire student lives.

From the irksome detail of West Point etiquette the two Ohio boys, Grant and Sherman, found escape in varying ways—Grant in riding wild horses and Sherman in gregarious nocturnal pranks. Little Sam, growing more stoical as his course wound tediously to its end, delighted to put fiery horses over barriers that no other cadets in the history of the institution could conquer. All his life he would like to spend hours of friendly silence with horses.

Samuel G. French, a New Jersey cadet whose Quaker father rejoiced paradoxically to see him in a military school, always remembered Grant's stoicism in class. One day while awaiting the arrival of an instructor, Lieutenant Zealous B. Tower, a roomful of cadets examined an antique silver watch which one of them had brought from home—a huge heirloom four inches in diameter. When in repair it was said to strike the hours. Passing from hand to hand, it was in the possession of Sam Grant when Lieutenant Tower appeared. Grant, thrusting the watch into his bosom, found himself called, with three other cadets, to the blackboard to demonstrate mathematical problems, and while standing so, felt the ancient timepiece start to run. Handling had evidently loosened its works. All at once it began, most fiendishly, to strike the hours. The lieutenant ordered the door shut on the theory that the noise was coming from the hall. But the crazy gong kept booming and Tower began searching for the guilty cadet. Boys stiffened in their seats, grew red from suppressed laughter; hysteria hovered over the room as Tower's hunt went on. But Sam Grant, alone of them all, turned not a hair, nor blushed, nor ceased to write upon the blackboard—a Spartan boy with a wolf in his breast. While fury raged, he solved his problem, and by the time he was done the watch had subsided. He returned to his seat undetected.

Such self-control was never Cump Sherman's. Rosecrans perceived that he had no diplomacy, and remembered how sometimes, when called upon to recite, he would blurt out to the instructor:

"I can't do that, sir."

"Why not?"

"Well, to be frank, I haven't studied it."

Rosecrans saw the devil of independence rising in Sherman—the spirit that John had shown, but which would not take the form of John's fisticuffs. Cump was too sociable for that. His revolt was a mischievous defiance of oppressive rules. Rosecrans said:

> He was always ready for a lark and usually he had a grease spot on his pants from clandestine night feasts. He was the best hash-maker at West Point. Food at the table was cheap and poor and we stole boiled potatoes in handkerchiefs and thrust them under our vests; we poked butter into our gloves and fastened them with forks to the under side of the table until we could smuggle them out of the dining room as we departed. We stole bread and when we got together at night "Old Cump" would mix everything into hash, and cook it on a stew pan over the fire. We ate it hot on toasted bread. We told stories and at this, too, Sherman was the best. We would

all risk expulsion by going down to Benny Haven's [the historic tavern a mile away on the Hudson] at night to eat oysters.

Such adventures, particularly the trips to Benny Haven's, were risky, since to be caught wearing the civilian clothes donned for the journey meant expulsion.

Promotions in company organizations at the school went to the youths of the most military bearing and appearance and, said Sherman afterward, "at no time was I selected for any office, but remained a private throughout the whole four years." Grant once became a corporal, then a sergeant, but losing this post, he too remained until the end a private.

Leaders in Sherman's class, as graduation time came—the honor list—were, in order, Paul O. Hebert of Louisiana; C. P. Kingsbury of North Carolina; John McNutt of Ohio; William P. Jones of Washington; and William Gilliam of Indiana. Below them came the men of less promise, Sherman sixth, Van Vliet ninth, Thomas twelfth, Bushrod Johnson twenty-third. Again Sherman had missed the upper sphere and the seriousness of his failure lay in the fact that it brought him into conflict with Thomas Ewing's wishes. He wrote Ellen shortly before graduation:

I fear I have a difficult part to act for the next three years, because I am almost confident that your father's wishes and intentions will clash with my inclinations. In the first place, I think he wishes me to strive and graduate in the Engineer Corps. This I can't do. Next, to resign and become a civil engineer.

Only cadets with exceptional standing were permitted to choose the highly prized engineering corps, from which so many graduates stepped after a few years' experience into high-salaried posts on the public improvements that private capital and State subsidies were building over the nation. But Sherman, in his twentieth year, reasoned that the future was not bright in this direction; the States, he foresaw, would soon be so overburdened with debt that they must give up their roads and canals. Engineers, he said, were either overworked or entirely idle. He told John that he would be either a soldier or a farmer. "Should I resign, it would be to turn farmer, if ever I can raise enough money to buy a good farm in Iowa." Next to drawing, mineralogy and geology had been his best studies in the Academy.

The old Northwest was stirring in him—the Northwest where the farmer, free from haggling commerce and the dictates of superior officers, was the most independent of citizens. Cump urged John to get land in Ohio, Iowa, or Wisconsin. Nor was such advice unwise at the time, for John had lost his surveyor's job after the panic of 1837 and had since been idling and drinking in Lancaster. One day in the summer of 1839 he went home "very sick from drinking." There "my mother received me with much surprise and sorrow, but neither complained nor scolded and with the utmost kindness put me to bed and watched over and cared for me. . . . I then and there resolved never to be in such a condition again." He kept his resolution.

Now in 1840 John's brother Charles and his brother-in-law Reese were prodding him to study law, while Cump, by letter, objected:

> For my part it would be my last choice. Everybody studies law nowadays and to be a lawyer without being exceedingly eminent . . . is not a sufficient equivalent for the risks and immense study and labor. However, if you decide upon anything you should immediately commence to carry it into execution.

For himself, when his studies concluded and his commission as second lieutenant was handed him, Cump chose the artillery. That branch had a chance of seeing action in Florida, where the Seminole Indians were rampaging. He was to report to the Third Artillery at Governor's Island, New York Harbor, at the end of September. Meanwhile he would be free. He struck off for Lancaster—and Ellen.

Affection, edging toward love, had begun to speak out from his letters as early as November 1, 1839, when he had told her that it would be sacrilege for him to actually wear slippers which she had knit for him. At home, on his visit, he spent much time with her, and much with the two Ewing babies, Charles, aged five, and Sissie, the three-year-old, both of whom he often took on pony rides.

Phil was away studying law. Hugh and Tom seemed very young to Cump. Tom had a special playmate of his own, his mother's small relative from Brownsville, the son of her cousin Maria Gillespie, who had married a landed gentleman by the name of Ephraim Blaine. Tom's playmate was named James. Sherman said afterward:

> Being a commissioned officer at sixty-four dollars a month, I could hardly stoop to notice these lads, two cousins of about eleven years of age, as bright and handsome as ever were two thoroughbred colts in a blue grass pasture in Kentucky.

Little James G. Blaine liked nothing so well as to pay long visits to the Ewing home. In manhood he said, "I thought the world ought to feel obliged for permission to revolve around Lancaster." With Tom and Hugh he attended the school of an Englishman named Lyons, uncle to the British ambassador in Washington and a scholar whom three Lancaster families, the Ewings, Hunters, and Stanberys, had imported to tutor their children. With the Ewing brothers, young Blaine had once paid a visit to Columbus, Ohio, armed with a letter of introduction from Old Solitude to Colonel John Noble, proprietor of the leading hotel. Noble quartered the boys handsomely and at the end of several days saw them order their carriage to be brought around while Hugh stepped up to pay the bill.

"There is no bill," said Noble. "I couldn't charge Thomas Ewing's sons." Speechless with surprise, the boys retired to the piazza to collect their thoughts. Finally they approached Colonel Noble to say that if there was to be no charge they guessed they'd stay a little longer. Noble fell upon a sofa that shook with his mirth for some minutes thereafter.

With Tom and Hugh busy with their own friends, Cump stared at Lancaster, bidding farewell to his boyhood. His mother was modestly comfortable with her three youngest, Susan, Hoyt and Fanny, whom Cump scarcely knew. John was with Charles at Mansfield, studying law. His sister Amelia lived there too, the wife of Robert McComb, whom her uncle Parker had made his partner in a general store. Julia was also married, the bride of John Willock, who kept the general store in Lancaster. Old General Beecher was missing—dead for over a year, with his son Philemon, in a scarlet fever epidemic.

"What can I do for you?" Thomas Ewing had asked at his bedside.

"Open the west window and let me look at the green fields again," came the answer, and when Ewing parted the shutters, the Black Prince had looked long at the countryside that was his for almost as far as he could see. Then he had died. The first of the Northwestern pioneers were passing just as Cump Sherman came to manhood.

Cump saw little of Thomas Ewing during the summer. The Salt-Boiler was busy stumping the State with Tom Corwin, the Whig candidate for the governorship, and the two orators, fine foils for each other, were being followed in their tour by delighted farmers who, loading their families into conveyances with tents, for the nights, accompanied the speakers from barbecue to barbecue.

It was Sherman's fate, at the impressionable age of twenty, to march out of haughty, aristocratic West Point into the shambles of the most maudlin presidential campaign in American history—that of 1840. Scurrilous campaign songs, vilification, intoxication, gripped the West, which, revolting from the Democratic rule of Martin Van Buren and his New York politicians, was whooping for the Whig nominee, William Henry Harrison, one-time war hero at Tippecanoe, but now, at sixty-six, president of a county agricultural society near Cincinnati. To symbolize his frontier past, the Whigs were sending floats bearing miniature log cabins and barrels of hard cider everywhere, while orators screamed that "Matty Van, the Used-Up Man" ate roast beef from silver and gold dishes, whereas Old Tip ate cornbread. The Democrats, rivaling their enemies in distribution of liquor, jeered at Harrison as a weak-minded ancient who snoozed in a cabin, forever drunk on hard cider. The campaign was a colossal spree, with only a few speakers, such as Ewing, attempting to do anything but entertain the revelers. To add to the chaos, the Abolitionists had abandoned their policy of voting for those Whig or Democratic candidates who came nearest to sharing their views, and were placing their own ticket in the field. Before the campaign was done their membership, numbering now, in various societies, two hundred thousand men and women, split into two camps, one urging moral aloofness from politics, the other crying for direct action.

Sherman shrank from the shambles, a deep distrust of democracy growing within him. The campaign completed the aristocratic work of West Point. It was with relief, so far as Ohio was concerned, that he turned in September back to the life of a soldier. He told Ellen good-by. Love between them was ripening slowly, almost without recognition. None of the Ewing family could ever say when the bond between the boy and girl had ceased to be that of brother and sister and begun to be that of man and maid. The change came as easily as spring glided into summer each year in the Hockhocking Valley.

9

THE ENCHANTRESS, THE SOUTH

THE South began to weave its enchantments around Lieutenant Sherman in the autumn of 1840, when he joined the Third Artillery on the east coast of Florida. His company, A, was stationed at Fort Pierce and in the neighboring Indian River the twenty-year-old boy swam and fished in the clear warm water, speared sharks, trolled for redfish, or set nets for the green turtles which, when caught, were penned and fattened on mango leaves till ready for soup or steaks. Oysters delighted him as only they could delight a midlander. From neighboring posts—the regiment was scattered up and down the coast from St. Augustine to Key Biscayne—came boy lieutenants to visit him, Bragg, Ord, Thomas, Van Vliet.

Sherman saw slavery for the first time—owners leading back to South Carolina and Georgia blackamoors who had fled to the jungles of Florida and who had now been recovered. Not many of these did he see, however, for the success with which the blackamoors evaded capture in the swamps was one of the major reasons for the army's presence in Florida. Since colonial days slaves had found refuge—and often marriage—among the Seminole Indians, and the Government, attempting to halt the plantation owners' loss as well as to pacify its new tropical peninsula, had waged sporadic and unsuccessful warfare since 1821.

To Sherman, slavery seemed linked with his Government; it was an institution to defend. As for war, the campaign against the Seminoles was boresome. In past years there had been massacres and battles, but now the campaign consisted of nothing but minor expeditions into the forests to round up families of redskins. The Seminoles were difficult to capture, but their spirit was sure to die down as the white soldiers kept up a dogged system of raiding villages, burning cabins, destroying corn, and hacking pumpkins to bits. Sherman's first lesson in warfare was this: Destroy the enemy's supplies and you break his morale!

Other lieutenants had the good fortune to hear a musket fired; once Van Vliet shot an Indian, and once a sergeant brought home a scalp—a novelty so great that he got drunk in celebration—but Sherman smelled no powder. He was left behind on duty at the fort when his company had its single engagement, the firing of a few shots and the capture of thirty-four prisoners, mainly women and children. He was none too proud of the record as he wrote home:

> . . . one little girl with a ball through the back and coming out in the cheek scarcely utters a murmur; another woman, a buck-shot through and through, bears it with the fortitude of a veteran soldier. . . . You doubtless little sympathize with us in hunting and harassing a poor set of people.

Sherman's single adventure came when he was sent, with a squad of men, to capture the wily chief Cooacoochee, nicknamed Wild Cat. Stationing his men at the rear with orders to revenge his death if the Indians shot him down, Sherman rode directly up to the chieftain and his twelve warriors in their tropical village, and bluntly bade them surrender. Then, noting that the Indians' muskets were leaning against a tree, he engaged the chief in conversation while he stealthily motioned to the white soldiers to seize the weapons. Bringing the prisoners to the fort without difficulty, he observed, "It is absurd any longer to call it a war."

Thomas Ewing had small time to write Cump in these days. As

reward for his service in the campaign and in recognition of his ability in combating, as a Senator, the Democratic bank policy of President Jackson, he had been named Secretary of the Treasury in President Harrison's Cabinet. When after a month in office Harrison died, Ewing with almost all the other Secretaries could not agree with the financial policies of the new President, John Tyler, and in September, 1841, resigned. The Salt-Boiler returned to the private practice of law.

Sherman, his boyish nerves wearying of army-post tedium, wrote Ewing to discover if he could be transferred to the Western plains; he feared that the Third Artillery would be moved North and "stationed in the vicinity of some city, from which, God spare me." He developed a passion for collecting pets—a fawn, a pony, white rabbits, and tame pigeons. In his bedroom dwelt a tame crane and some crows, while in a corner one of many chickens brooded on eggs—"rather small matters for a man to deal with," Cump wrote Ellen, "but it is far better to spend time in trifles, such as these, than in drinking or gambling."

A year droned by, then on November 30, 1841, he received promotion to a first lieutenancy. Not only did it give to him eighteen months after graduation a rank that usually required some five to eight years' service, but it also situated him at an outpost—Picolata—twenty miles from St. Augustine, that beautiful and ancient Spanish town, where among the wealthy Southern planters who had migrated there for the climate he found gay society. The Spanish girls, he wrote Ellen, were very lovely, although ignorant, and had enticed some twenty officers into marriage.

Ellen flashed back a letter asking him why he did not leave the army and recommending religion to him. He replied that he was happy and contented in the army; he would be barehanded and unprepared if he left it to face the cold world. Every day, he said, he met men who had resigned their commissions to seek wealth, and all of them admitted the step to have been foolish. As to religion, he said that he had followed no particular creed since leaving home; he believed in the main doctrines of Christianity and "the purity of its morals" but he could "not attribute to minor points of doctrine or form the importance usually attached to them."

Southern society, where, as he observed, "the bright button was a passport at all times to the houses of the best," made much of the young officers. Sherman visited Mobile more than once, writing Ellen that "it would take a volume to name the ladies, their beauties and accomplishments" who had entertained him and his companions at balls, theatres, and art galleries. He told Ellen that he corresponded with a Brooklyn girl whose sister, Mrs. Bull, had entertained him in Mobile at her rosebowered home. Enamored of this life, Cump grew poetic in picturing for Ellen the roses creeping up latticed porticos, the arbors of shade trees, the soft glamour of the patrician South.

It was almost too good to be true when in June, 1842, he was ordered to that dream of any lieutenant's heart, Fort Moultrie, on Sullivan's Island, hard by Charleston, South Carolina, the social capital of the South. Existence at the fort was as leisurely as in the city, where the chivalry, snobbery, gallantry, culture, and indolence of the Southern civilization were at their peak. Here the fire-eaters of sectional fame were the fieriest, here the North was damned loudest for its sordid commercialism and for its "persecution" of the South on the high tariff and antislavery issues. In elegant homes, Sherman heard the gospel of disunion preached by eloquent gentlemen and lovely ladies. Echoes of Congressman Giddings's defiance of this civilization were still ringing. That Abolitionist enemy of Thomas Ewing was breaking the Northern political resolution to ignore the sarcasm and contempt that Southern extremists poured upon their sectional rivals, those boorish "mudsills" or "Yankee traders." Such statesmen as Ewing, who preached quietude for the sake of sectional peace, were in Giddings's vocabulary "doughfaces." Giddings would not hold his tongue, and he would belabor the slaveholders with the charge of moral decadence. When challenged to duels, he accepted, naming blacksnake whips and specifying that combatants be tied together by their left wrists for a finish fight. Since the weapons were outside the code, and Giddings a man of Herculean structure, no duels were fought with him. Northwestern pioneers might not, as a class, be yet ready to share Giddings's passion against slavery, but Whigs, Democrats and Free-Soilers alike, the masses rejoiced to see him deflate an aristocracy that scorned them.

To give intensity to the social disdain South Carolinians felt for the North, there was growing the bitter realization that the power of the South was waning. Twenty years earlier Charleston had stood sixth among American cities; now it was ninth, had actually lost population during the last decade, and would soon be passed by dozens of Northern cities that swelled with industry. Anthracite coal and machinery for working wood and iron had brought industrial revolution to the North, but not to the South, which was just beginning to awaken from the entrancing dream that the old beauty of life in the country—the traditional supremacy of the agrarian gentleman—would last forever. Southern realists were perceiving that as the plantations wore out under the nonrotation of cotton and tobacco crops, there would soon come a time when planters would have all the small farms bought up. Slavery demanded wider acres, new regions—Texas, perhaps. "Only one fifth of the white families of the South have any interest in slaves," the Abolitionists were saying. Wise Southerners knew that not twenty-five hundred families in the whole slave belt owned as many as a hundred slaves apiece. By 1850 the average acre tended by slaves would be worth $5.34, compared to the free-State value of $28.07.

In an atmosphere of social languor and political intensity, Lieutenant Sherman remained from his twenty-second to his twenty-seventh year, finding no quarrel with slavery and growing yearly more enamored of Southern culture. Amid the refinements of the homes on Sullivan's Island, where rich planters came in summer, the artist awakened in Sherman. Portfolios of prints, many oil paintings on the walls, talk of water colors, he met for the first time in his life. He bought an artist's equipment and without instruction started to paint. Drawing had been his best subject at West Point. Now he wrote Ellen:

> I have great love for painting and find that I am so fascinated that it amounts to pain to lay down the brush, placing me in doubt whether I had better stop it now before it swallows all attention.

His brushes were laid by, never to be taken up again, after the summer of 1843, when he came home to Lancaster on a three months' leave. Ellen was nineteen—and when he left they had an understanding as to their eventual marriage. When she first realized that the children were to be married, Maria Ewing objected, although when she thought about it, she realized that they really weren't related, of course. Little Sissie, aged six, was shocked at the news. "Why, they can't!" she exclaimed. It was hard for her to understand that Cump was not her real brother.

In love with Ellen though he might be, Cump had the normal young man's outlook on pretty girls in general. From Lancaster in October he wrote John of a slight adventure that had befallen him when a stage carrying him on a visit to relatives at Mount Vernon had broken down, causing the passengers, himself and "a pretty girl," to be transferred to a farm wagon and taken onward through a storm. "She had no umbrella—mine was small—the result was we rode in close proximity in an open road wagon in the hard rain over a detestable rough road." If propinquity led to greater adventures, Cump said nothing of it. Throughout his lifetime he would neither write nor talk of sex. Profanity would come easily to his lips when in masculine company, but women would be strikingly absent from his casual conversation—and even in his early twenties he was, as his regimental comrade Lieutenant Erasmus D. Keyes observed, "loquacious and communicative to an extraordinary degree."

How far had this tall red-haired youth of twenty-three gone with girls? Thomas Ewing, watching the boy who was to marry his daughter, must have asked himself such a question. Since he had been sixteen the active, affectionate youth had been in a world of army men who, as became their profession, took love as they found it. Scarlet women clustered around army posts—town girls cast bright glances at uniforms. Could this healthy, sensitive boy still be as pure as when he had come up the hill with his hand in that of the gigantic Salt-Boiler?

The second great love of Sherman's life came to him as he departed from the house in which he had just recognized his first. It was a river—the Mississippi! Returning to Charleston in November, 1843, by way of St. Louis and the majestic stream of which he had heard much but which he had never before seen, he was fascinated by the sight of so enormous a Father of Waters bearing traffic so thick. For six days he stayed in St. Louis, visiting West Point friends at the army post. "I then became impressed with St. Louis's great future," he said, noting that thirty-six steamers at one time crowded the wharves.

Away from the snow-covered North, down between the green banks of the Mississippi, through the iron-laced and filigreed streets of New Orleans, on among blooming roses to Fort Moultrie, he went, writing John that the sun was so bright "that I have almost renounced all allegiance to Ohio, although it contains all whom I love and regard as friends." Army duties took him to other portions of the warm Southland that winter. In February he was at Marietta, Georgia, from which he galloped to the top of the mountain towering above it, Kenesaw, and from the summit he stared eighteen miles across the rolling country to Allatoona Pass. Before he returned to Fort Moultrie in the spring, he knew the territory from Rome, Georgia, to Bellefonte, Alabama, and from Kenesaw Mountain to Augusta. The details of the ground were fixed in his memory on long horseback rides that he took alone. It was his habit, almost his passion, to study the slopes, curves, and stretches of the terrain—a habit born of a singular fondness for the earth.

His happiness and satisfaction with the army were now under fire, however. His prospective father-in-law wrote in February expressing the hope that the young lieutenant was studying for civil life. In June, 1844, Cump's original enlistment of eight years would terminate; was he preparing for something better than the slow progress of army promotions?

During his furlough, Cump had widened this breach between himself and Thomas Ewing by prompting Hugh, turning seventeen, to apply for West Point. He had even ridden with the youngster to the local Congressman to secure the appointment. The Salt-Boiler had objected strongly, but Hugh, the stormy one of the family, was present at the Academy when the plebes assembled in 1844. From Fort Moultrie Cump wrote Ellen concerning her father's wishes:

> He knows my perfect dependence and that were I to resign, I would have to depend upon some one till I could establish myself in the practice of some profession. Do you think I could do so? Certainly not, and should health be preserved to me, I shall never depend upon anybody, nay, even were he a brother. I would rather earn my living by the labor of my own hands. It would then be madness itself at this late date to commence something new.

Too late at twenty-four? Realist that he was, the boy must have known that in June the nation would be spotted with college graduates of that age, choosing professions. "Too late" was, more likely, his subterfuge to escape return to dependence. Once, however, he thought of surrendering to Ewing, and absented himself for a time from the elegant Charleston aristocrats in order to study that most hateful of subjects, law. He told Ellen of his work:

> I am endeavoring so to qualify myself that should you not like to encounter the vicissitudes that I am now liable to, I may be enabled to begin life anew in a totally different sphere. . . . Somehow or other I do not feel as though I would make a good lawyer, although I meet with but little difficulty in mastering the necessary book knowledge. Yet not being fitted for public speaking, and my education being such as to give me almost a contempt for the bombast and stuff that form the chief constituents of Modern Oratory, it would not seem that my prospects in that quarter were very brilliant.

Marriage was far in the distance, with his salary only seventy dollars a month and a portion of that sent home regularly to his mother. The widow, who had kept boarders and educated the three younger children, had told him that Susan would soon wed Thomas W. Bartley, a lawyer and merchant of Mansfield, and Cump wrote John, the new barrister, that their mother ought to move to that city and make her home with Charles, who had married and become legal representative of Eastern financial houses. "I never want her to take boarders again," he wrote John, and before the summer was over his plan had been accepted. At twenty-one ambitious John had become a Whig politician, delivering speeches for Henry Clay in his presidential contest with the Democrat James K. Polk. "What the devil are you doing?" wrote Cump. "Stump speaking? I really thought you were too decent for that, or at least had sufficient pride not to humble and cringe to beg for party or popular favor." To Ellen Cump wrote, "The people are fickle in the extreme, varying from one party to another without rhyme or reason."

Sherman moved in Charleston, the hotbed of political argument, without taking part in controversies. So pacific was he that in the autumn of 1844 he was sent to make peace among the squabbling officers of Company B at the Augusta arsenal, and at one Fourth of July celebration in Charleston he prevented a duel between Bragg and a certain journalist named Stewart. Bragg had resented the manner in which the rabid secessionist Stewart had spoken of his native North Carolina as "a strip of land lying between two States." Lieutenants Thomas and Bragg, although Southerners, were, like Sherman, pro-Union in the discussions of nullification and secession that were rising. Thomas the Virginian moved at Sherman's side like a noble St. Bernard dog, dependability evident in his every move. "Thomas's head," said Lieutenant Keyes, "was shaped like that of a Roman patrician. He was never ahead of time, never impatient, always serene and kept his appointments precisely." What Keyes noted most about Sherman was his general impatience of manner and his terse speech. Hearing Keyes once say to the company clerk, "Waterbury, conduct this quadruped to my dwelling," Sherman stepped up, saying, "Your style is too pompous. I'd have said, 'Waterbury, take this dog to my house.' "

Sherman became intimate with Captain Robert Anderson, his onetime instructor at West Point and now on duty at Moultrie. With this Kentucky-born officer he stood on the battlements and watched cotton ships from the North dump their ballasts of rock at a certain point in the shallows not far from them, across the water. Army engineers were building there a new fort to be named Sumter.

It was with another friend, Lieutenant John F. Reynolds, that Sherman was hunting deer on the estate of a host, Mr. James Poyas, the wealthy planter, when a fall dislocated his shoulder and gave him a furlough in Lancaster from January to March, and by the time he had returned his circle of friends had begun to break up. War was in the air. On the first of March, Congress had voted to annex Texas, and Mexico was certain to resent the rape. Sherman, surrounded by Southerners who strove for the annexation so that the slave States might have room for expansion, could not agree with the Northern Whigs who denounced the war. His own father's friend Senator Tom Corwin was pillorying Americans who defended the seizure of Texas on the ground that the nation needed more room. Said Corwin:

> If I were a Mexican I would tell you, "Have you not room in your own country to bury your dead men? If you come into mine, we will greet you with bloody hands and welcome you to hospitable graves."

Cump was writing John:

> As to Texas having been annexed for the sole purpose of extending slavery, I do not believe. Some politicians may do so, and abolitionists may act upon that decision and affect it.

He had become more Southern than Northern in his views.

For almost a year Sherman remained at his post, attending parties, taking long walks in the country alone, escorting Mrs. Anderson on shopping tours, sitting for hours in the Anderson home studying elegant books of engravings. Bragg, Thomas, and Reynolds had been sent to Texas, where General Zachary Taylor was mobilizing an army. Then in the spring of 1846 came the word that Taylor had crossed swords with the Mexicans. Bugles were calling. Recruiting was begun. By early May, Sherman was commanding a station for volunteers at Pittsburgh, then one at Zanesville, from which he made frequent trips over the thirty-six miles to Lancaster. But news of the American victories at Palo Alto and Resaca de la Palma on the eighth and ninth of May turned Sherman's head. "That I should be on recruiting service when my comrades are actually fighting is intolerable," he said. Leaping hurriedly at the chance to sail for California, which was also to be wrung from Mexico, he rushed his recruits—without any authority to do so—down to Cincinnati and delivered them to the Western recruiting superintendent, explaining that he had taken it for granted that the soldiers were wanted. For this he was reprimanded with curses; he had left his post without orders. Dismally he slunk back to Pittsburgh. There orders to hurry to New York for the California trip were waiting. Through the night he worked, completing his reports, and at dawn wrote Ellen farewell. He was off for the wars without seeing her. All he could leave her was his bookcase. He hoped she would give it a few caresses. In it she would find his papers for her to read and "to tell a tale for or against me." Only one memento he would take, a lock of her hair.

In the nick of time he caught the store ship *Lexington* and was off, with Ord for roommate, through warming seas, staring at pretty girls in Rio de Janeiro, sleeping to avoid seasickness while October lashed them with mountainous seas at Cape Horn, staring at new stars, the Southern Cross. They played cards "but never for money"; they looked in a cabin door to see Lieutenant Henry Wager Halleck, Old Brains, reading in his bunk. He was translating the French book by Baron Jomini, *The Political and Military Life of Napoleon.*. At thirty-one Halleck would be the author of *The Elements of Military Art and Science,* which would be a text for twenty years.

When the sun shone the lieutenants baited fishhooks with pork and angled for the sea birds that followed the ship. "The albatross," said

Sherman, "seems so perfectly indignant at being caught by stratagem. It stands upon the deck—surrounded by a singular race of wingless birds who are so cunning as to catch it."

Time hung heavy. Cump had given up tobacco; he explained to Ellen, "It hurt my chest." To her he sent his drawings of sights that attracted him; his letters were voluminous—one brusquely ridiculed missionaries whom he had seen in Valparaiso "sowing dissension among the so-called heathens." One hundred and ninety-eight days after leaving New York, the ship anchored in Monterey Bay—and California was at hand.

10

WITHOUT SMELLING GUNPOWDER

LIEUTENANT SHERMAN came ashore at Monterey with hopes of glory and adventure. Now at last after four and a half years of soldiering he might see a battle. The Californians, emulating the Texans, had revolted against Mexican rule a month before Sherman had set sail from New York. A United States fleet was on the Pacific and General Stephen W. Kearny had come overland with his dragoons, fixing the Stars and Stripes upon New Mexico in August, and was now clearing the country around Los Angeles. But in the three years that Sherman would spend in California he would hear no battle shots. The Mexicans, fading away among the hills, left the country to the political wranglings between the army under Kearny and the settlers under Colonel John C. Frémont, the explorer.

The three years would shape the young lieutenant for business, not war. As quartermaster of the forces that landed at Monterey he administered, with skill, the erection of sawmills, gristmills, and all the items of industry by which the post was made self-supporting. He showed talents at providing for men in his charge, buying horses for as low as four dollars each and beef at eight dollars a carcass. With other officers he kept the commissary supplied with wild fowl, deer, and elk. Kearny and his successor, Colonel R. B. Mason, noted the youth's executive ability, Mason making him his adjutant general and intimate.

More fruitful would be the admiration that one of Kearny's officers, Captain H. S. Turner, a Virginian, gave Sherman. When Kearny had brought his travel-frayed dragoons to Monterey, Sherman had taken two of the officers, Turner and Warner, to his headquarters and had given them new clothing. He refused payment and only at their insistence accepted the cost of the articles. So kindly and cheering was this talkative host that both newcomers were with him constantly through the winter and springtime and when Kearny, returning East in May, took his staff with him, Turner and Sherman had begun a lifetime friendship.

With Kearny's departure, Sherman found California increasingly boresome. He wrote Ellen that he hoped she would never see so depressing a land.

He thought Yerba Buena a "horrid place" when he saw it in July, '47—a village inhabited by some four hundred people, most of them natives from the Sandwich Islands. He scorned the suggestions of other officers that he buy lots there on speculation. The village would later be named San Francisco.

Ten months after arriving in California he wrote Ellen:

> I am so completely banished that I feel I am losing all hope, all elasticity of spirits. I feel ten years older than I did when I sailed.

And eighteen months after his arrival he wrote her:

> I have felt tempted to send my resignation to Washington, and I feel ashamed to wear epaulettes after having passed through a war without smelling gunpowder, but God knows I couldn't help it, so I'll let things pass.

In September, 1848, a few days after writing this letter, Sherman received a courier who had traveled overland with official word that the war with Mexico had ended in May. Reading of the promotions received by his friends in Mexico, Sherman thought of his one pathetic adventure in California—with ten men he had ridden into the town of Sonoma and arrested the illegally elected alcalde.

Here he was still a first lieutenant, while Bragg's handling of the Third Artillery guns in Mexico had won him a major's rank. The story was that General Zachary Taylor had won the Battle of Buena Vista by remarking, "A little more grape, Captain Bragg!" Reynolds had been promoted to a major's post at the same battle. Sam Grant had distinguished himself under fire and been made a first lieutenant. Robert E. Lee, of the West Point Class of 1829, was a colonel, Scott's chief engineer, and widely lauded. His classmate Joseph E. Johnston was a colonel, cited for gallantry. Albert Sidney Johnston, Class of 1826, was an inspector general. A dapper little Pennsylvanian, George B. McClellan, graduating six years behind Sherman, had fought so well that he was now a captain. A dour Virginian of McClellan's same class, Thomas Jonathan Jackson, was on equal terms with Sherman—a first lieutenant.

Even among his fellow exiles in California, Sherman was lagging. Joseph Folsom, his classmate at West Point, was a captain and Halleck, who had been made a captain in May, 1847, now served as a sort of secretary of state for the military governorship that Colonel Mason maintained.

The diversions of the regular Sunday night balls that Spanish families gave in Monterey gave Sherman only temporary relief from gloom. Years later, there would flourish a legend that Sherman had been deeply in love with a leading belle, Doña Maria Ygnacia Bonifacio. Gertrude Atherton, the novelist, visiting Doña Maria in the latter's old age, understood from younger people of the region that

> Sherman, when a young lieutenant, had loved her, and together they had planted a rose tree in her garden. He had loved her and ridden away but she had remained faithful to his memory and never married. . . . She told me that she had been so victimized by tourists, who snipped the branches from her rose tree and even wrenched the keys off the piano, that she had put a lock on the gate and admitted no one but her friends.

To her confidants Doña Maria declared that although she had known Sherman they had never been engaged and that he had never jilted her.

Once Sherman had some excitement in meeting a small, stooping, freckled, baby-blue-eyed mail-carrier in buckskins, who arrived with a pouch he had carried two thousand miles through plain and desert. He was Kit Carson, the scout whose exploits had been celebrated by Frémont's books. Sherman had met Frémont himself on diplomatic errands, had managed that prima-donna explorer smoothly, although secretly believing him to be full of pretensions and bombast.

One day in the spring of 1848 Colonel Mason called Sherman into his office and directed his attention to some yellow rocks on the table. Near by stood the two American settlers who had brought them to the army post.

"What is that?" Mason asked.

Sherman sent for an ax, beat the nugget flat, then said, "It is pure gold!" Mason handed him a letter. Captain Sutter, a landowner at Coloma on the American fork of the Sacramento River, forty miles away, had found the yellow pebbles while digging a race for a new sawmill, and now wanted to establish rights to a quarter-section. Mason told Sherman to answer the letter, advising Sutter that California was still under Mexican law and would be until the new owner, the United States, could set up civil government. Sutter subsequently lost his lands.

Mason thought little of the gold strike. Such tales had been current in the land for months, but by the end of the spring, in that year 1848, Sherman had become convinced that there must be something behind the increasing number of rumors that drifted down from Sutter's. He urged Mason to investigate. The Government at Washington should have a report. Mason gave him permission to visit Sutter's and soon Sherman was riding among four thousand excited men who stooped over their pans in the stream, gathering from thirty thousand to fifty thousand dollars' worth of yellow sand a day. He saw Mormons, Mexicans, settlers from all over the Western slope, rushing in. Hurrying back to headquarters, Sherman urged Mason to send a special courier to Washington. The lieutenant grasped the significance of a situation that to the brain of an old army man meant little more than another craze of the populace. Sherman wrote a report that Mason signed, packed three thousand dollars' worth of gold nuggets in a tea caddy, and sent the courier on his way. When President Polk, a little later, startled the world with his announcement of the California discovery, it was Sherman's words that he quoted, and when the great men of the nation and of foreign embassies came to the governmental desks to stare at the specimens, they looked at rocks that Sherman had collected.

The gold strike brought only wretchedness to Sherman at its beginning. Private soldiers, sneering at their pay of seven dollars a month, deserted to work in mines where twenty-five dollars a day was certain. Houses rented at five hundred dollars a month. Officers' salaries were no longer sufficient. Cump wrote John in August, 1848:

> None remain behind but we poor devils of officers who are restrained by honor—honor and poverty well mixed. I have never been so hard up in my life. . . . Colonel Mason is cooking his own meals.

To make matters worse, all of Sherman's savings of eight hundred dollars, which had been loaned the previous autumn, were swept away by the borrower's death. Sherman talked of resigning, but Mason persuaded him to remain, offering to allow him and Captain Warner to launch Warner's civilian clerk in a general store near Sutter's settlement. Sherman received fifteen hundred dollars from this venture. And when in February, 1849, official orders transferred him to San Francisco to act as adjutant general for the new commandant of the Department of California, Major General Persifer F. Smith, Sherman found that without the fifteen hundred dollars "I could not have lived through the winter." The muddy city, where "any room twenty-by-sixty feet would rent for $1,000 a month," repelled him. Like Mason and Smith, both of whom were Southerners, Sherman was disgusted with the crass commercialism and wealth hunger that were stampeding soldiers into desertion and servants into abrupt leave-takings. Once Sherman, with three other officers, pursued twenty-eight deserters through the night and although the men were armed, recaptured twenty-seven, Sherman bursting into a cabin alone with cocked musket to quell eighteen of them.

Sherman was, however, too good a business man, and too anxious to finance his long-postponed marriage, not to appreciate his opportunity in the gold fields. But he could only throttle his ambitions and stick to his post. Then, in the spring of 1849, luck suddenly came his way. From the East arrived Smith's regular adjutant general, Major Joseph Hooker. Sherman was automatically displaced, and although Smith made him his aide-de-camp, there was so little to do that the commandant suggested that he take a leave of absence and pick up some extra money. The kind old general gave the same permission to Lieutenant Ord, and the two youths, buying a horse, a wagon, and surveyors' tools, were quickly at work in different parts of the country, taking land as payment for their surveys. At the end of their sixty-day furlough, Sherman's share was six thousand dollars. Still, riches did not mean as much to him as did his place in the army. In the midst of his good fortune he read the official list of army promotions, noted that other officers had been advanced beyond him, and wrote a letter of resignation to Smith. His pride had been wounded:

> Self-respect compels me therefore to quit the profession which in time of war and trouble I have failed to merit, and accordingly through you I must respectfully tender my resignation . . .

If this resignation were accepted, Sherman would find himself where Thomas Ewing had long ago urged him to be, a civil engineer earning wealth in private life. Riches were now before him. But the resignation did not pass beyond Smith's hands. Returning to the post, Sherman withdrew the letter. Perhaps Smith's persuasions settled the matter. No one was ever told the reason. Sherman simply sank back into the dull routine of army-post life and remained there while the year 1849 passed.

When General Smith was replaced by General Riley, Sherman became merely the idle aide of an idle superior. Riley's staff officers now held the important posts, the only member of Smith's entourage to flourish being Captain Halleck who, still acting as secretary of state, was drawing up legal papers when California, at Riley's call, sent delegates to Monterey to draft a State constitution. Among the delegates, as

Smith's observer, sat Sherman, sniffing at politicians who connived "to secure the prizes of civil government."

Sherman saw California as the football of Free-Soilers and Slave-Staters. He understood how it had been kicked about in the last national campaign, from which General Zachary Taylor had emerged as President; how Congressman David Wilmot, proposing that slavery be excluded from the region, had widened the breach between North and South. Disputes over Oregon had been settled and now that the United States stretched from the Atlantic to the Pacific and from Canada to the Rio Grande, the Union was beginning to divide over the question of slavery or no slavery in the vast territories. Sherman read that Ohio, swelling with wrath against the slave-owners' insistence upon expansion, had elected an antislavery Democrat, Salmon P. Chase, to the United States Senate. In the Monterey convention he saw the Free-Soil forces triumphant. The issue seemed demagogic to him. He had only disgust for Frémont, the Free-Soil leader, as he returned from the convention to file his report with Smith.

At the post, Smith, like a delivering angel, handed him a paper. He was ordered to Washington as bearer of special dispatches!

Doubtlessly, the Salt-Boiler had been busy. Sherman's sponsor sat now among the mighty—Secretary of the Interior in President Taylor's Cabinet. As the friend of Webster and Clay—often called into legal consultation by the former—he had had great influence in the political campaigns of 1848, and when at the Whig nominating convention the delegates had chosen the Southerner Taylor as their candidate, a movement to name Ewing for the vice presidency had begun. But the Ohio delegation, which had been passionate for Henry Clay's presidential nomination, refused to be mollified. One of its members, L. D. Campbell, had cried, "Ohio wants no sugarplums!" and had killed the plan. It was Millard Fillmore who was named and who on Taylor's death was to become President. When the election of 1848 had returned the Whigs triumphant, John Sherman, at Mansfield, had begun angling for the district-attorneyship that his brother-in-law Thomas W. Bartley had held under the outgoing Democratic Administration. John asked Ewing for a recommendation and was angered when the Salt-Boiler declined on the ground that John was too young.

There was contrast between the Ewings and the Shermans who welcomed Cump back from California. Ellen, her mother, and the younger children were waiting for him when, after delivering his dispatches to General Scott in New York, Cump hastened to Washington. They welcomed him to a mansion Old Solitude had rented on Pennsylvania Avenue close to the White House. The family had grown up. Ellen was twenty-six, an old maid according to the social verdict of the time. For eight years she had waited for her lover, who came home once in two years, once in three years. Sissie, the youngest, was thirteen. Tom was attached to the White House staff, often acting as President Taylor's private secretary.

Greetings over, his baggage stowed in the room that was to be his, Cump saw Ewing in his office. The Salt-Boiler now weighed more than two hundred and fifty pounds and disliked to move from place to place. He said that if a man read intelligently and widely, travel was unnecessary. He had been one of the first persons in the East to catch the full significance of the gold strike in the report Cump had written and a month before the lieutenant's arrival had urged the nation not only to establish a mint in California but also to build a railroad across to the Pacific slope. Sherman had been thinking, too, of this national railroad and during the past year had sent surveyors into the Sierra Nevada Mountains to look for an eastward path. Ewing had trained Cump to think of the nation as a whole.

Sherman found Ewing a famous man. The United States Supreme Court had come to see Ewing's face as often as any lawyer's in the land. President Taylor had relied upon him for an important duty, the creation of a new Home Department, soon to be renamed the Department of the Interior, bringing under one head the hitherto scattered Land Office, Patent Office, and Bureau of Indian Affairs.

From the limelight in which the Ewings now lived, Sherman journeyed to visit his blood relatives; first, Elizabeth in Philadelphia. Her husband had failed in business and she had received from Cump in the past few years two hundred and fifty dollars. Four years earlier, Cump had urged his brother Hoyt to abandon his job as a typesetter and "improve his condition," and in that year he had given his brother James a hundred and thirty-five dollars with which to help set himself up in business at St. Louis. Visiting his mother at Mansfield, Cump was concerned because she was "dining out too much." His family must hold up its head. Taylor and John were doing well at the law and his sisters in Ohio were happy.

Cump returned to Washington. His wedding was set for romantic May Day. He roamed the city with Ellen or with army friends and sat long hours in the Senate gallery with Thomas Ewing, Jr., listening to the speeches.

He saw the three intellectual giants, Webster, Clay, and Calhoun, making their final appearances on the floor of the Senate that they had lifted to a distinction it had never attained before and which it would not attain in the eighty years that would follow their passing. All had been born while the guns of the Revolution were roaring and farmers were howling curses at redcoats. They had known Jefferson and Adams. They had seen the Union carried westward by men with long rifles over their shoulders and babies dangling out of the hind ends of covered wagons. They had seen the shadow of a black man settle over these Western lands, and quarrels rise and fall—each new quarrel louder and fiercer than the one before.

Three old men, demigods to their followers, two of them bent on sacrificing everything to the salvation of the sacred Union, one of them growing surer and surer that the only hope for his beloved South was in separation from the North. Each was qualified to have been President many times over, yet not one was tame enough to have been a successful candidate. All were growing old. Webster and Calhoun were sixty-eight; Clay was seventy-three. This session of Congress was to determine what the Union would do with the vast Western lands that war had added to the national domain, and the three ancient statesmen were needed. Clay came to speak with a cough softly tearing his chest. He tottered up the Capitol steps leaning on helpful arms, stopping every few steps to pant. Calhoun, wrapped in flannels, sat with that head like the skeleton of a lion erect, but with eyes half-closed, seeming to doze and dream while younger friends read his burning words to packed houses. Within a month he would be dead. Webster, for all the wine he had drunk, all his grief over the lost Presidency, was still strong. He studied from five to eleven each morning, practiced in the Supreme Court from eleven to three, and then went to the Senate to stay until ten at night. When he spoke his thunderous cadences, men said they seemed to see fire burn around his head.

In the winter of 1850 Sherman heard the three Titans sing their swan songs. He saw Clay, still striving to splice the parting sections of the Union, propose as his last conciliation the Omnibus Bill admitting California as a free State, spreading New Mexico's border to Utah and Wyoming without restriction against slavery, prohibiting the slave trade in the District of Columbia, and providing for a stricter fugitive-slave law. Calhoun was protesting that the North was growing in power while it restricted slave territory. Webster was charging that the South had only come to regard slavery as morally good when cotton plantations had become profitable, but he denounced Abolitionists, and pleaded for both sections to use sense if they wished to avoid war.

On March 7, the day Webster was to make one of his most memorable speeches, Sherman sent his card to Senator Corwin.

"Well," said the dark-faced Senator, "what do you want of me?" Sherman said that the gallery seats were all taken, and that he wished to sit on the floor of the Senate, where he had often seen persons "no better entitled" than himself. "Are you a foreign ambassador?" asked Corwin.

"No."

"Are you a governor of a State?"

"No."

"Are you a member of the other House?"

"Certainly not!"

"Have you ever had a vote of thanks by name?"

"No."

"Well, these are the only privileged members," said Corwin.

"You know well enough who I am," Sherman blurted out, "and if you chose you could take me in"—an outburst to which Corwin replied:

"Have you any impudence?"

"A reasonable amount if occasion calls for it."

"Do you think you could become so interested in my conversation as not to notice the doorkeeper?" asked the Senator, pointing to the functionary.

"There's no doubt of it, if you tell me one of your funny stories," said Sherman, and taking the lieutenant's arm, Corwin, by gestures, directed his face away from the quizzical doorman and talking as only Tom Corwin could talk, passed the portal.

"Now," said Tom, "you can take care of yourself."

Thanking the humorous old gentleman, Sherman brashly took a seat close behind Webster and near General Scott. But however much Webster's speech might set the nation seething, it left Sherman unmoved. "It was heavy in the extreme and I confess that I was disappointed and tired long before it was finished," he said later. At thirty years of age, Sherman was impatient with the logical oratory of a Webster. Intuition, the leap of sudden insight, was to be the way of Sherman's brain. As April closed, Clay's bill was still agitating the republic, but Sherman thought of it no more, at least for weeks.

His wedding was held in the Ewing home as the flowers of May bloomed over Washington. When he turned with Ellen on his arm to receive congratulations, it was the President of the United States, followed by the entire Cabinet, by Webster, by Benton, and by most of the capital's great men, who pressed forward. Only one face was absent —Henry Clay's. The lion of all social occasions, why didn't he come? At length here he was—Handsome Harry, so old, so feeble, walking slowly through the bright crowds to kiss the bride. Many brides, many babies, many women, he had kissed in his seventy-three years. He always did it well. To Ellen he gave a large bouquet and to Maria

Ewing he said, in his charming way, that his invitation had gone astray, but that he had come anyhow. That made the day supreme. The honeymoon trip was to Niagara Falls.

11

THE JONAH OF BANKING

LIFE danced for the bridegroom as the honeymoon continued among the many relatives in Ohio. With his father-in-law so close to the throne, he had learned that a bill adding four captains to the commissary department of the army was sure to pass Congress and that he was to have one of the posts. The added salary would keep the newly married pair in independence, at least.

But Washington was in turmoil when the bride and groom returned to the capital. On July 4 President Taylor, combating oppressive heat with ice water, iced milk, and a considerable number of cherries, had fallen ill, and by the ninth was dead. Out of courtesy for the incoming President, Fillmore, the Cabinet resigned. Sherman, attending the funeral as aide-de-camp of Adjutant General Roger Jones, wondered about the future. The Ewing family was determined to return to Lancaster, a far more pleasant place than Washington. The Salt-Boiler was to be appointed Senator from Ohio in the shoes of Tom Corwin, whom Fillmore wanted for his Secretary of the Treasury, and Corwin would take the large Pennsylvania Avenue house off the Ewings' hands.

The political shifting did not, however, affect the army bill, and on September 27 Sherman's commission arrived with orders moving him to the city of his choice, St. Louis. There on Choteau Avenue, not far from his beloved Mississippi, he leased a home. Soon Ellen was gone, returning to her mother's home to prepare for the baby that would arrive almost nine months to the day after her wedding. Sherman's married life had begun so soon to take on the character it would have ever afterward. Ellen would seem to be always going home on a visit.

In the absence of his bride, in the late winter months Sherman spent much time with Major Turner, the friend whom he had clothed in California, and who was now out of the army and a banking partner of James H. Lucas, the richest of St. Louis's property-owners. At the army post, Colonel Braxton Bragg and Major Van Vliet, old friends, were his intimates—the three of them, widely entertained by Southern families of the city and at various points down the river, heard new talk of how the slave States must link themselves with the Northwest against New England. A good proportion of the settlers in the Northwest had come from the South; agriculture was the common pursuit of the entire Mississippi Valley; geography had decreed that residents of the great center should unite against the industrial "sharpers" of the East. Not yet did the civilization that centered in St. Louis understand how the railroads creeping westward toward the muddy town of Chicago would, by the middle fifties, begin tying the Northwest with new bonds to the cities of New York, Philadelphia, and Boston.

Nor did the Southerners among whom Sherman moved perceive as yet how Clay's new bill, fixing a rigorous fugitive-slave law upon the country, would alienate fresh thousands in the Northwest. The law now allowed the agent of any slaveholder to take back into slavery any Negro whom he declared by affidavit to be runaway property, and a six months' term in jail and a thousand-dollar fine could be fastened upon any one who interfered with the recapture. In Ohio, a legislature was preparing to turn, in the coming year, from Thomas Ewing to that antislavery enemy of his, Bluff Ben Wade, when the time came to choose a new Senator. And Wade, breathing the resentment of Western woodchoppers against South Carolina slave barons who preached States' rights, was oiling his long squirrel rifle, which he would carry to Washington just in case the fire-eaters sneered at craven mudsills again.

To St. Louis, during Sherman's residence, came Old Solitude, working upon the lawsuit that would bring him $100,000, generally said to be the largest legal fee paid in America so far. A kinsman of Sherman's grandmother, Betsey Stoddard, had purchased a farm near St. Louis in the days when Spanish law ruled the wilderness and when he died in the War of 1812 had left his estate in confusion. In Dayton, Henry Stoddard, a cousin of Judge Charles Sherman, sought Ewing's aid in claiming the land, and the Salt-Boiler, at sixty-two years of age, sat himself down to learn the Spanish tongue so that he might read the ancient deeds. Winning the case, he took land in payment and interested Captain Sherman so heavily that the latter wrote his brother John in July, 1851, "I now own five quarter-sections, and prairie land 35 miles east of St. Louis—a tract of 20 acres woodland, seven miles from the city and am planning on getting more town lots." Over his own and Ewing's property he kept watch, making his reports in letters that began "My dear sir," and concluded "Affectionately your son, W. T. Sherman." The very closeness of family relationship was both a delight and a vexation. He appreciated the love with which Ewing welcomed Ellen to Lancaster for her confinement, yet after the birth of his baby Maria, on January 28, 1851, Cump felt constrained to apologize when in March he took the mother and child back to St. Louis. He understood the adoration that made Ellen want to return to Lancaster on frequent visits, and when she was gone, he tried to reason loneliness out of his mind. In the spring of 1852 Ellen was pregnant again, and to escape the heat of a St. Louis summer went to Lancaster, where she would remain well past the birth that autumn of her second child, Elizabeth.

Cattle-buying trips on the Missouri and Kansas plains filled Sherman with dissatisfaction for the commissary duties of the St. Louis post. On August 2 he was writing Ellen:

> I am getting tired of this dull, tame life and should a fair opportunity occur for another campaign on the frontier, I cannot promise to keep quiet. Commissaries are not fighting men.

He had smelled saddle leather again, had slept under the stars, had spent one night in a Shawnee Indian camp, and had ridden far in the open country, seeing much territory as he followed "my old rule never to return by the road I had come."

Relief came to him in his St. Louis office that September of 1852, when orders shifted him to New Orleans to end corruption in the commissary depot—a task that he accomplished speedily, if brusquely. New Orleans as a residence pleased him. As in Charleston, he was a favorite of society, General David E. Twiggs, the venerable Georgian, Richard Taylor and Colonel W. W. S. Bliss, respectively son and son-in-law of Zachary Taylor, seeing to it that he met the leaders of the aristocracy.

Yet Sherman was not happy. Some devil of unrest made him stir in his warm nest. He leased a house on Magazine Street and began furnishing it so that his wife and two infant daughters might join him when Christmas came, but he fidgeted at the monotony of army-post life. He wrote in November:

> Nothing but activity and continued interest contents me, and when these fail, an impulse moves me that reason, nor pleasure, nor any ordinary motive accounts for.

He could not understand himself. Perhaps he remembered, at these times, the one period in his life when he had been swallowed up in the bliss of absorbed interest, the days when he had sat painting pictures hour after hour, lost to the flight of the sun as it passed over Fort

Moultrie and sank behind the mists of South Carolina. His fingers, long and pointed, were those of an artist, his imagination was continually reconstructing the world as it ought to be. He was an artist without an art.

With so much time on his hands, he fretted. His mother had died in September. John was the one intimate link remaining with his own Shermans. An investment of fifteen hundred dollars' worth of stock in a Philadelphia soap concern proved worthless. He still owed between six and eight thousand dollars on his St. Louis real estate. Living costs were high in New Orleans and would soar when Ellen and the babies arrived.

Close behind his family, when it did come, appeared Major Turner, urging Sherman to leave the army. Lucas & Symonds, the St. Louis financiers who were Turner's partners, were to establish in San Francisco a branch called Lucas & Turner, and would pay Sherman forty-two hundred dollars a year and traveling expenses and give him a one-eighth interest in the branch if he would become its manager. Sherman restrained himself from leaping at the chance. Once before he had moved too impatiently and it had kept him out of Texas—and promotion. He did not want to rush to California again with such results. This time he would scout before he attacked. Obtaining a six months' leave of absence from the army, he broke up his home late in January, sent Ellen and the infants back to the Lancaster they had left six weeks before, and set sail for San Francisco.

The voyage, including a land trip across Nicaragua, was inauspicious. Bungling stewards registered him "Captain Sherman and Ladies" because he had been helpful to two women—one of them a blonde who sang sweetly in the ship's parlor. And although he finally established his freedom from connection with them, it did not make him proud, on reaching San Francisco, to learn that the blonde belle was a scarlet character of the town. Two shipwrecks met him on the last day of his journey, neither of them accompanied by any loss of life but each proving to him how cool and energetic he could be in times of confusion. Among the last to leave the first wreck, he managed "to get a can of crackers and some sardines out of the submerged pantry, a thing the rest of the passengers did not have." Even in peace he was a born commissary officer.

San Francisco was booming when Sherman came back to it after three years' absence. The dismal village of Yerba Buena, in whose future he had scorned to invest six years before, was now prosperous, with large brick and granite buildings, jutting wharves, busy ships, busier tradesmen and gamblers; raffles were never-ending; Oriental shawls, jewels, and Chinese gods were prizes. "This is a great country for rich people but death to a poor one," he wrote Ellen.

Nevertheless, with Major Turner, who had preceded him, at his elbow talking of the power of Lucas & Symonds, he felt secure. He remembered the quick money he had earned by the honest toil of surveying in 1849. Turner raised the offer to five thousand dollars' annual salary. The bank would be capitalized at three hundred thousand dollars. The job was a big one. So he accepted, and hurried home to gain Ellen's approval and to write Thomas Ewing on August 22, 1853:

> Thus far my case has been respectable and although in leaving California in 1850 I committed an error it was not vital, for by it I secured my wife and have established relations here of benefit to us all. . . . The removal to California of my entire family resolves itself into a separation from home. . . . I ask therefore your free and hearty consent to ease the shock of Ellen's leaving home.

To the Salt-Boiler, who was finding in grandchildren the delights that had faded as his own children had grown up, the news was a shock indeed. He busied himself with hasty plans for finding some counter-attraction for Cump in the Hocking Valley—one Hock had been dropped in the commercial rise of the region. But Cump was determined, and Ewing withdrew his plans. One memento he would keep—the elder child, nicknamed Minnie. Lizzie, the younger, less than a year old, would accompany her parents, carried by her nurse, Mary Lynch. On September 6, 1853, Sherman resigned from the army, discounting seventeen years of experience, and at the age of thirty-three embarked on a new career.

Another accident on the westward voyage. In transferring from land to ship at Nicaragua, the baby, awakening on her pillow, found herself carried by a dark-faced Indian, and shrieked lustily. Before she had become quiet in the arms of Mary Lynch, the nurse had taken fright at the roaring surf through which the Indians were carrying them and had begun screaming more loudly than had the baby. Lizzie went into convulsions, finally fainted, and, as Sherman later said, "for years showed symptoms that made us believe she had never entirely recovered from the effects of the scare."

In San Francisco Ellen was homesick and wrote her father that she feared the climate was bad for Cump's health, a warning that drew from Ewing a plea to Sherman to "come back if this is true, for your life and health are worth more than prosperity." Cump answered with a spirited defense of the California climate and of his opportunity; "I expect to clear $50,000 in six years. That amount of cash will enable me to live in ease in St. Louis or Cuba."

San Francisco brought Lucas & Turner success. Within a year the firm, under Sherman's management, had a new bank building and deposits of five hundred thousand dollars. But Ellen did not like the place. In June, 1854, she had borne another baby, William Ewing Sherman, and by September Cump was writing Ewing:

> I have given up hope that Ellen would become reconciled and therefore shall let her and all the family go home in the Spring to stay a long while. It's wrong for children to grow up without some knowledge of their father but it seems that such is my case. Of course I feel gratified to learn that Minnie is developing a fine disposition and character and would like to participate in its contemplation.

In December he was admitting to Ewing that the fogs of San Francisco were hurting him; "my bronchial tubes are bad." He was objecting to Ellen's plan for taking the children home. He feared they would catch malaria crossing the Isthmus of Panama. His objection would postpone her journey for a year and a half.

As a banker, Sherman was notable for firmness and foresight. His selection of a site for the bank building would prove faulty when the city drifted later in another direction, but at the time it was thought an excellent choice. Sherman's reputation for vision grew when, in the financial crash that fell upon the city in the winter of 1854-55, it was discovered that his bank had been prepared for the storm. Amid the prosperity that flooded the city at the time of his arrival, Sherman had within a few months noted a telltale sign. Real estate was declining. He began to contract loans. Furthermore he distrusted a financial "genius" of the town, a certain H. Meigs, and insisted, much to everybody's surprise, that the great man's loans must be guaranteed by other banks before he would continue them. When, in the crash, Meigs fled the city with bankrupt creditors in his train, Lucas & Turner's loss was, "compared with others, a trifle."

Sherman had prepared for a run on his bank while other institutions plunged blissfully onward making loans. He had been scrupulous, even to the extent of endangering a personal friendship when, asked by Captain Folsom, his intimate, to sign a roundrobin declaration of faith in an imperiled bank, Page & Bacon, he had refused. He would sign nothing until he had personal knowledge that the bank was solvent. A few days later Page & Bacon failed and terrific runs rocked all the banks in the city. So easily and readily did the Lucas & Turner depositors get their money that they soon lost their fear and replaced their funds.

With the passing of the crisis, Lucas & Turner emerged as one of the soundest of California banks, but there were no profits. Business lay in the doldrums—with the city crippled among its debts, worthless paper, and vanished dreams. In the chaos Sherman, as he wrote Ewing, had suffered personal losses because he had "thought more of acquitting my duties to my associates than of making anything for myself." His hopes of fifty thousand dollars in six years were gone, but "I have been so long identified with California that it would be foolish to change, so I look upon this as my home." Stubbornly he resisted hints from Turner and Lucas that he return to St. Louis and work for them there. He had made up his mind to stick to the last, and secured from the partners a loan of six thousand dollars with which to buy a lot and erect a house. Soon after the new home was opened on April 9, 1855, Ellen departed on her long-promised visit to Lancaster, leaving the children—Lizzie, now three, and Willy, ten months—in the care of Cump and Biddy, the capable nurse.

Before Ellen's return in November, Cump's annual income had been swelled by four thousand dollars and life had grown easier. But the incident that had occasioned the increase had revealed his essential hostility to the world in which he was moving. During the last week in May a Democratic committee, attracted by Sherman's conduct of the bank, had asked him to become their candidate for City Treasurer. The post would pay four thousand dollars and need not interfere with his banking job. Refusing on the ground that such an arrangement would be unethical, he added, "I am not eligible, because I have not graduated from the penitentiary." Hearing of this action, Lucas & Turner promptly added the amount of the treasurer's salary to their employee's yearly wage.

With politicians, and with a city whose finances gradually became so entangled in politics, Sherman grew disgusted. Loot and pillage were on every side, and in the following year—the summer of '56—an editor named Casey began printing articles that the banks accepted as a blackmailing effort. Representing his fellows, Sherman strode up the stairs of his bank building to the office that Casey occupied on the third floor. "If you repeat this," he said, "I'll throw you and your presses out of the window!" Casey promptly moved "to more friendly quarters," but continued to harass "the better element." Criminals seemed likely to rule the town openly. Leading citizens conferred with Governor J. N. Johnson. The State militia might be needed. Sherman was the man to head it. The commission of major general was offered him. He considered, and said that he would accept. But before he could take formal charge, the crash came.

Casey shot James King, a rival editor who, in defense of "society," had exposed his criminal past. The Vigilantes, who had brought order to the city in 1851, met in secret, the citizens of wealth and social standing prominent in their membership. Rumor had it that if King died Casey would be lynched. The Vigilantes did not trust the corrupt officers of the law. Newspapers took sides. Sherman was sworn in as major general. The governor arrived and secured a promise that the law would have its way, but when King died on May 20 the Vigilantes tightened their ranks and three days later took Casey from jail while Sherman and the governor watched from the roof of the International Hotel. Casey was hanged and the Vigilantes began exiling other "rowdies." The governor, who had shrunk from calling out the militia, since he had no guns or ammunition, now called his major general to Benicia, where on June 1 they asked the United States Army post commandant, General Wool, if he would supply munitions when Sherman called out the local National Guards. Sherman understood Wool to agree. Then the emissaries called on Commodore Farragut, the grim commandant at Mare Island, who agreed to place a warship off San Francisco for moral effect.

On June 4 Sherman summoned the National Guards to arms. Immediately the Vigilantes protested. Among them were many of his personal friends—dignified civic leaders. War must not come to the city streets, they pleaded. "It is for you to get out of the way," snapped the red-haired general. He sympathized with their wishes for a reclaimed city. As a financier and a citizen he was against their enemies—the rabble and the thugs—but the law was the law. The regular processes of government must be observed. No matter how good their intentions, their method was anarchical. Five generations of judges as ancestors and a boyhood spent under Thomas Ewing's tutelage had prepared Sherman to put principle above self-interest.

But in the midst of his preparations, Sherman was unhorsed. General Wool, after many evasions, took back his promise to furnish guns and ammunition. Governor Johnson withdrew outraged and Sherman resigned his commission, announcing "that I would thenceforward mind my own business and leave public affairs severely alone." Sitting in his bank, Sherman watched the Vigilantes work their will and noted how the world hailed them as reformers. He said later:

They controlled the press, they wrote their own history . . . but their success has given great stimulus to a dangerous principle, that would at any time justify the mob in seizing all the power of government. . . .

While Cump, who detested the pursuit of law, was following its principles along a lonely road, John, the lawyer, was playing politics. John had won his seat in Congress when the Northwest, in November, 1854, repudiated most of its Representatives, who at the last session had voted for the Kansas-Nebraska Bill of Senator Stephen A. Douglas of Illinois.

Crying expansion and manifest destiny, Douglas had forced the passage of his bill, which threw open Western territories to settlement and allowed them to decide for themselves whether or not they wanted slaves. This cast the North into turmoil, for it repealed the agreement made in 1820 that all States formed from Western lands would be free soil if located north of Missouri's southern boundary, and slave if located to its south. States' rights men acclaimed the move as a new victory in their old war against the Federal power. In the North resentment was so hot that old political fences were torn down and Whigs, Abolitionists, Free-Soilers, and many Democrats joined in demands that Southern "aggression" be curbed. The Northern clergy, hitherto lukewarm or evasive on the slavery question, swung into full cry against it. Thousands of Northerners who had no quarrel with slavery became anti-Southern on sectional grounds. In the slave States there was amazement at the spectacle of the whole North in agitation. Never had such unity of feeling been known, nor the common man been so inflamed and so rebellious against his leaders.

When the news of John's victory on an antislavery platform reached Cump, he wrote his brother:

Having lived a good deal in the South, I think I know practically more of slavery than you do . . . it is an old and historical fact that you must take as you find it. . . . Negroes free won't work tasks of course, and rice, sugar, and certain kinds of cotton cannot be produced except by forced negro labor. . . . The Nebraska bill was a mistake on the part of the South, a vital mistake that will do them more harm than all the violent abolitionists. . . . Let slavery extend along the shores of the Gulf of Mexico, but not in the high salubrious prairies of the West. . . . Slavery can never exist here or north of us, so the North now has the power and can exercise it in prudence and moderation. . . . Slavery being a fact is chargeable on the past; it cannot, by our system, be abolished except by force and consequent breaking up of our present government.

To Cump it was plain that if left alone the slavery issue would adjust itself. Economics and time were the proper rulers, not politicians. "Self-interest is the great motor," he wrote John in March, 1856; Kansans, Kentuckians, Missourians, were sure to see that slavery did not pay in their climate and would eventually abandon it. Lawyers would do well to keep their hands off, he said.

John, meanwhile, was touring Kansas with the Congressional committee sent to investigate the bloodshed and violence that had existed there ever since the organization of the Territory in May, 1854, when proslavery and Free-Soil forces had imported settlers to determine its future character. After three months' investigation, John returned to the capital convinced that the Free-Soilers had been right in refusing to accept a Territorial government set up by their proslavery rivals.

John was endorsing popular revolt while Cump was decrying mob rule. By August, Cump was telling his brother, "Unless people, both North and South, learn more moderation, we'll see sights in the way of civil war." In Lancaster, Thomas Ewing was agreeing with his boy. The old Whig had watched his party start to die as a new organization, the Republican party, arose. He refused to vote in the November elections, for the Republicans had nominated an Abolitionist, Colonel John C. Frémont—the same explorer whom Sherman had disliked in California. At the time of the Republican nominating convention Ewing had seen that the Illinois lawyer, Abraham Lincoln, had at one period received one hundred and ten votes for Vice-President before losing the nomination. Seven years earlier, Ewing, as Secretary of the Interior, had offered the post of Commissioner of the General Land Office to Lincoln, who had declined because he was in duty bound to support a friend for the appointment. The friend could not be named, and although Lincoln, on learning this, had sought the job, another Illinois Whig, Justin Butterfield, had been chosen, President Taylor and the whole Cabinet assisting Ewing in the decision.

When in November, 1856, the Democrats placed James Buchanan in the White House, the Salt-Boiler was more interested in another matter. A letter from California informed him that on October 12 Ellen had given birth to a fourth child, Thomas Ewing Sherman, and it was certain that she, her children, and her husband would soon come home to live.

Cump had advised his employers that California was deflated and the bank doomed to a profitless future. Respectable business men were daily surrendering to an "extremely easy bankruptcy law." Both State and city were repudiating debts. Foreign capital was being withdrawn. In February, 1857, Cump had written Ewing, "Ellen is down on the country, its morals and tendencies." And on March 22 he announced that sooner or later he would be transferred to the New York office of Lucas & Symonds:

> I may be forced to accept your kind offer of assistance, not in the way of money but to let my family have a home near yours till I can again feel able to provide them wherever I go. Ellen is so persistent in her dislike of this country that I have abandoned all hope of a change and think I had better make any sacrifice now to get away finally and make no calculations on ever returning. . . . I will have to have some house in Lancaster for it would be imposing too much on your kindness to turn loose in your house four children.

On May 1, 1857, the seventh anniversary of his wedding, Sherman closed the office and, with house safely rented, brought his family home. In bitter chagrin he borrowed $837.50 from his father-in-law. Two years later he repaid it with interest.

When in after years Sherman came to write his *Memoirs* he declared that at the opening of the firm's new offices at 100 Wall Street on July 7, 1857, "everything for a time went swimmingly." It was true that his bank's affiliations were with the cream of national financiers. Instead of salary he was to have an interest in both the New York and the St. Louis offices. But in his letters to Ellen at the time he sang a different song. Three weeks after the launching of the branch bank he wrote:

> Of all lives on earth a banker's is the worst, and no wonder they are specially debarred all chances of heaven.

Then he revealed to his wife a thing that had been preying on his mind, gnawing at his conscience all the time that his employers, and financiers generally, had been praising the skill with which he had extracted Lucas & Turner from the San Francisco crash without loss. He confessed to her that he was in debt to the firm, also that in California he had done a thing that obviously haunted his sleep.

What had happened was not as humiliating as Sherman, in his growing distress of mind—and suffering from asthma intensified by San Francisco's climate—made it appear. Soon after his removal to California, he had received money from old army friends, among them Braxton Bragg, with the request that he invest it for them. Their knowledge of his honesty and ability in business matters had given them the idea of asking him to obtain for them some of the rich profits of the West. Receiving these funds, totaling some hundred and thirty thousand dollars, as an individual and not as the representative of Lucas & Turner, he had placed portions of this money in apparently safe bonds. Other portions he had deposited in the bank, an act for which he had no specific authority, but which he unquestionably did in order to keep his friends' money earning interest. Furthermore, as he told them, this would protect their principal in case of his sudden death, since it made Lucas & Turner as much responsible as he himself was. Knowing the bank to be sound, he had thus safeguarded the trust fund, as he called it. When later on the City of San Francisco failed to meet its obligations, his friends suffered, for some of their money had been placed in city warrants, an investment recommended by all bankers at the time he had made it.

By all the rules of banking Sherman would have been justified and have been expected to say to his friends: "The fortunes of war have been against us. You asked me to speculate for you. I did the best I could, but could not foresee this panic." But Sherman's blood was not cold enough for a banker's veins. He could not shrug his shoulders. His father had taken over his underlings' debts. Sherman must repeat the point of honor. He assumed the responsibility for his friends' loss, even though it threatened to strip him of his last cent and cast him with his wife and four children upon the charity of his father-in-law. Not for months would he be able to admit his "folly" to Thomas Ewing. He wrote Ellen that the one unendurable loss in business was money "confided to me."

Facing this burden, Sherman saw that his expenses in New York were to be greater than his income. Yet he wrote John proposing that he himself, John, Hoyt, and Taylor each contribute fifty dollars a year to the support of their sister Elizabeth, whose husband was still dogged by poverty. Two days after he sent this letter, the financial depression became a panic in New York, with the great Ohio Life & Trust Company closing its doors. By October 6 his cousin James Hoyt was shaking him on his pillow in the early hours and brandishing a newspaper. Lucas & Turner had suspended too!

Hurrying to his office, he found telegrams instructing him to bring all assets to St. Louis at once. Before he took the train he wrote Ellen, "I am going to quit clean-handed, not a cent in my pocket. I know this is not modern banking, but better be honest." To John he wrote, "I am the Jonah of banking, wherever I go there is a break down." Would John buy his St. Louis and Illinois property? He described it: a lot worth $5,500; a twenty-acre tract costing $5 an acre in 1852, now worth $150 an acre, that he would let go at $100 an acre; four sections valued at $15 to $20 an acre which he would sell at $10; 40 acres bought at $20 an acre and worth much more but which he thought a bargain at $40.

In St. Louis he found that Lucas would liquidate without loss to any depositor—a glad piece of news, since it relieved him from loss as a partner. But there was no help, as he saw it, for his debt to army officers. "In the Spring I will be completely out of money, property and employment," he wrote John. "I ought to have had sense enough to keep out of such disreputable business. Banking and gambling are synonymous." From St. Louis, whose streets he walked, he wrote Thomas Ewing on November 17, "I see no chance for an income for my family and I don't like to have them despondent"; he saw no chance to recover ground lost in the last five years.

As he paced the sidewalks, almost distraught, one day he looked into the bearded, unkempt face of a wood-peddler. Where had he seen it before? On a horse vaulting over incredible barriers at West Point? Yes. The fellow had won honors in the Mexican War, risen to a captaincy, then had resigned in discouragement and in the hope that he could in industry earn a better living for his family. He had gone downhill rapidly, had drunk more whisky than was good for him, and was now dwelling on his wife's farm near St. Louis, squeezing out a dismal livelihood selling cordwood. A shabby and depressed little man he was, scarcely better off than his father-in-law's slaves. The two defeated men talked, then passed on, Sherman saying to himself:

"West Point and the Regular Army aren't good schools for farmers, bankers, merchants, and mechanics."

The two men slipped from each other's minds—William Tecumseh Sherman and Ulysses S. Grant.

12

DEAD COCK IN THE PIT

TACTFULLY Thomas Ewing began to discuss investments with Cump, asking his advice, trying to interest him in the several businesses that the old man carried on. Nor was this merely the scheme of a father-in-law to make a place for a jobless son. Sentiment was powerful in Old Solitude, but his son Tom said in later years, "Father always said Sherman was a fine business man."

Ewing was nearing his sixty-ninth birthday. His son Philemon, living next door, was capable and industrious in assisting with the law practice. Hugh and Tom, Jr., were off in Kansas, seeking adventure, wealth, and fame on their own account, the former organizing railways, the latter practicing law and politics, his warm heart afire with an antislavery zeal that his father could not share. Charles, the youngest Ewing son, was at the University of Virginia.

The old man needed Cump to handle his investments, his saltworks near Chauncey, his holdings in the rich natural resources of the Hocking Valley. Cump could make both himself and his father-in-law rich by seizing this opportunity. But the red-haired son-in-law was so wary of being patronized, so sensitive about independence, that he evaded Ewing's diplomatic, almost pathetic, proffers.

For the time being, Sherman felt in honor bound to stay with Lucas & Turner until the last accounts were squared, and as the dismal work went on, it became apparent that some one of the partners must return to San Francisco to liquidate some two hundred thousand dollars' worth of real estate and notes remaining there. Other members of the firm, their private fortunes still intact, were better situated to make the journey, but Sherman assumed it; "a self-imposed obligation," he later admitted it to have been. His debt of honor was ruling him.

Before he set off, he sent to Adjutant General Cooper of the United States Army a request "that in the event of an increase in the army, you consider my name for a commission above the grade of captain."

Then he went to Lancaster to the most unmerry Christmas of his life, so far. There he saw Thomas Ewing distributing gifts with that same grave tenderness which he remembered so well from his own childhood. The circle was complete—Ewing had fed, clothed, housed, and reared Judge Sherman's son, now he must do it again for that son's children.

Cump felt wincing memories of the other grandfather, Charles Sherman, dead among his debts. Did honor pay? Judge Sherman had thought so—and his children had been cast on his friends' doorsteps. William Tecumseh Sherman had believed in it, instead of evading debts as did reputedly honorable citizens in San Francisco.

Cump wrote John, "I am now adrift"; and on reaching San Francisco, where he camped in a lonely little office, minus clerical or janitorial help, he wrote Ellen, on January 28, 1858, his despair:

> . . . far away from you, far away from the children with hope almost gone of ever again being able to regain what little self-respect or composure I ever possessed. I wish I could, like most men, harden my conscience. . . . You know I worked as hard as anybody could. . . . What I failed to do, and my bad debts that now stare me in the face, must stand forever as a monument to my want of sense and sagacity.

Thoroughly whipped, he wrote Ewing on March 3 that he would take the job Old Solitude held open—the management of the despised saltworks:

> Were I alone in the world, or could I think that ultimately Ellen would become reconciled here, I would never leave California. . . . But I know it is idle to talk of Ellen living here for her lifetime. . . . Therefore I assure you of my willingness to undertake what you propose . . . so that I may feel I am not a burden on anybody. . . . All I need now say is that this Fall I will be adrift and will be happy to have the honest employment you suggest, provided you think I can earn a living for my family.

On April 2 he was writing Ewing that he was ready to take the salt post, which his father-in-law had offered to make more attractive by investing new capital in it:

> I never incurred a debt for myself, and hope never to know what it means, but Ellen's wants are artificial and though she professes great willingness to live in a log house, feed chickens and milk cows, I know better. She can't come down to that. She requires and must have certain comforts which to another would be superfluities and in whatever scheme I embark her wants and those of our children must be first considered. All I stipulate is that I don't want to live in Lancaster. You can understand what Ellen does not—that a man needs consciousness of position among his peers. In the army I know my place, and out here we are of the pioneers, and big chiefs—at Lancaster I can only be Cump Sherman.

What agitation was passing through Ellen's mind could only be guessed from Cump's words to Ewing:

> Of course Ellen is uneasy about me, but you must not let her think of coming out . . . she fears I will stay here. She don't appreciate the duties I owe my co-partners. It would be simply outrageous, under the circumstances, if I had not come.

Self-reproach and worry made him abject—possibly somewhat unbalanced. On March 21 he wrote one of his debtors a wretched letter, complaining that the California climate was hurting his health:

> I am sorely pressed for money. I appeal therefore to you to save me from disgrace at having lent money belonging to my brother officers and which you have. . . . And all this while my family is living on charity, and after I leave I must begin life without a cent and with no trade or occupation to fall back on. This punishment is more than I deserve for having lent money to my personal friends.

By April 15 he mustered up courage to confess his real trouble to Ewing:

> My situation is made peculiarly embarrassing by the fact that when times were seemingly prosperous, knowing not the danger, I undertook to invest for brother officers sums of money of moderate amounts, ranging in the aggregate to $130,000—all these are returned but about 15 or 20,000 which I think I see safe again though I must stand some of their loss.

In time Sherman found that this amount, with interest, would total thirteen thousand dollars, which he repaid, even though it stripped him of all his resources save a scant thousand dollars.

He wrote Ewing, in his letter of April 15, that the loss of his army commission, five years of his life, and all his property, and the experience of shipwreck at sea as well as at heart, all made his "show of sacrifice fully equal to that of any member of the firm." Consequently he would come home in September, in spite of Lucas's wish that he either represent the bank again in California or join it in St. Louis. He would accept whatever Ewing decided:

> I have been Captain so long that subordination will come a little hard, but I hope I can fill any post as well as my natural temper will admit. I must be either on the go or out doors. I prefer that to any mere sedentary work . . . if I extricate myself from this dilemma, I'll try and never again so complicate my duties and relations in life.

On June 2 he grimly revealed to John how the necessary step rankled, how wholly it was made for the sake of Ellen, and how much he preferred to stay in San Francisco. When Ellen wrote him that Minnie had been sent away to school, he replied:

> As long as we are vagabonds, I suppose we must give her up. Lizzie and Willy, will however cling to us in adversity and prosperity. If we live down Hocking Valley we must teach them ourselves since there are no schools.

By July 23 he had settled all matters possible of adjustment and was sailing home. From the ship he wrote Lucas:

> I conceive myself bound by every principle of honor or honesty to devote any portion of my remaining life to this California business and if in a year or two or three, or any time, business in San Francisco revives and your interest requires my service to return, I hereby agree to go without any other compensation than actual expenses. . . . Immediately on my arrival at Lancaster, I will account for every cent since my last account current.

To Major B. R. Alden of York, Pennsylvania—one of his army friends for whom he had been toiling—he wrote:

> I believe I have honestly watched your interests and though I would give a great deal had I never touched a dollar of any friend's money, still I did

so, and I must endure the mortification of having, in some instances, loaned it to the wrong person or on indifferent securities. . . . I go to Lancaster, Ohio, to start where I began twenty-two years ago.

His racing pen informed another army creditor, Major J. G. Barnard of New York, that his account would be finally settled in St. Louis:

But I have progressed far enough to know that in the settlements I have thus made, I have done better for you than for my own partners, and far better than I have for myself.

Finally, by August 8, he was free from all St. Louis connections, not only honorably discharged but urged by Lucas & Turner to remain with them. He wrote John:

I am done with banking. Ewing's plans are indefinite, doubtless to keep Ellen here. I do not want to live in Lancaster. . . . Ellen and Elizabeth [Reese] have declared war to the knife. Ellen thought Elizabeth reflected on her for bringing me away from California when she supposed me on the high road to wealth and fame. This was not the case. Also some foolish question about a lecturer named Nichols, involving the Catholic question. The quarrel has gone too far for reconciliation. I suppose it will spread to other members of the family. . . . What do you think of Kansas? My life here would be a struggle with family jars, so all round I am hedged. In San Francisco I would do anything, but I cannot live here.

While he waited in Lancaster, his nerves on edge, he wrote to Simon Bolivar Buckner, whom he had known at West Point, asking for news of work that might be done. Buckner, now a prominent lawyer of Louisville, replied that he had recommended him to George B. McClellan, who was vice president of the Illinois Central Railroad in Chicago. This hope soon faded. McClellan had nothing. All Sherman found to do was to send his creditors the driblets that his agents forwarded from the sale of his St. Louis land. On August 11 he sent to one man $343 in cash and three notes covering three years at $375 each. "I am well," he said in the accompanying letter, "but what I can do to maintain a family is yet in doubt."

On August 14 he wrote Dr. Bowie, the San Francisco physician who had ushered Tommy into the world:

He is hearty, strong and a rough customer, with a loud voice and a will to bring it into play. He goes everywhere and last evening I turned him loose naked with the other children into a fine stream of water that flows in the woods near us and he was the noisiest of the set. . . . Lizzie has entirely recovered of her deafness, but is otherwise delicate, and our eldest, Minnie, is growing out of all conscience.

The next day, however, in advising Major Barnard on bonds, he added: "I feel mistrust of everybody and everything," and to another army creditor, Colonel W. G. Freeman, he lamented a week later, "Matters have not improved with me in the least and I am on the point of going to the West to try my fortune, empty-handed."

In Leavenworth, Hugh, Tom, and their cousin Hampton Denman were practicing law and politics, as well as handling Old Solitude's extensive investments in real estate in and around the pioneer town. And soon Sherman was writing to a friend in St. Louis, "Mr. Ewing has set his mind on having me in Kansas, and I must and do respect his wishes, and shall conform to them as far as possible."

Through the hot dog days of August, he sat with his huge old father-in-law in the great brick mansion, children crawling around their feet, the fair fields and torn Kettle Hills drowsing in the distance. Inside his skull Sherman's thoughts went up and down, like animals that turn and turn endlessly in their cage, hunting among familiar bars for the opening that is not there. It was either Kansas or the saltworks down the Hocking Valley. And Kansas was farther away—farther from relatives, relatives whose very sympathy was a humiliation, relatives who witnessed, however tactfully, the spectacle of his botched career.

He was heartsick as he passed through St. Louis, where lay "all that we seek for, for ourselves and our children," as he wrote Ellen. When he went about inquiring what insurance agencies he might represent in Kansas, his friends "laughed at the idea of my living at Leavenworth"—a town of four thousand on the wild frontier. For a day he talked with an acquaintance, H. J. Patterson, about a real-estate partnership in St. Louis but, as he afterward wrote, "I was so reduced in finances that I could not afford to wait . . . without means or good profession I feared to undertake anything."

On September 1 he was in Leavenworth and he galloped on a borrowed horse to the fort two miles from town to explain his situation to Major Van Vliet, the quartermaster. This old friend promptly sent him on a ten-day job inspecting a military road near Fort Riley, and urged him to settle in the growing country; gold had been discovered near Pike's Peak and immigrants would soon be rolling past. The idea almost sickened Sherman—"California all over," he wrote Thomas Ewing.

Old Solitude, working hard to fix Sherman in the new land, deeded Ellen eight acres in Leavenworth and promised to give her eighty-four city lots if Cump would build a home upon it. Sherman resisted, explaining to Ewing that the lots were already in use as a slaughterhouse and that he could rent a good plastered house for less than he would be forced to pay in interest on the money spent in building. Curtly he wrote the old gentleman:

> Please consider it annulled so far as I am concerned. If, however, you desire to help us to that or any extent, please let the matter remain as now, till you learn I have concluded to stay here, when you can renew the proposition in such shape as you please.

If he should send for his family, he told Ewing:

> I shall insist on all, Minnie included. It is full time that she began to regard us as her parents. The propriety of this I know you will agree with perfectly, and therefore I need offer no argument.

Sagely, Ewing ignored the bridling tone in Sherman's letters and by early October he knew that everything was settled. Sherman had sent for his family. The trip to Fort Riley for Van Vliet had influenced Sherman strongly. Taking an army ambulance, a driver, and a string of mules, he had spent almost two weeks with officers on the road or in the fort. When the fifes blew and the drums rolled he knew what they were saying. When he talked with his own kind again he could forget that he did not wear the uniform. His letters to Ellen disclosed his nostalgia for the army, and admitted that he could never hope to know the "secret recesses" of civilians' souls as he knew those of soldiers. On his return to Leavenworth he wrote Ewing, "I made $50 and expenses and got the fever and ague thrown in for nothing."

On October 12 he wrote Ellen, giving her her "marching orders"; she was to come by way of St. Louis and collect two notes due them—one for $575, with $57.50 interest, the other for $550—"the wreck of my former estate," he told Ewing, ". . . we are almost absolutely dependent on that money." He explained that when Ellen had collected this, he would add $200 "cash in pocket" and that they would have a grand total of $1,382.50 on which to live for six months—safe enough, since the expenses in that time would be no more than $650. Out of the $732.50 remaining, he said that he would need $200 for his part of the expense of opening and equipping an office for himself, Hugh, and Tom, Jr.:

> So if we begin to earn money by January I will feel safe. If I were only brought up as a lawyer, I would not fear results, but I confess I will feel as an impostor if I should be left alone to counsel, advise and act in a capacity which I am not and which probably I never can become.
>
> As to office management, writing, outdoor work, making acquaintances and getting customers, I can do my full share, but in strictly professional

work I know my want of knowledge and feel more delicacy on that subject than a new adventurer should.

At the end of this long letter, which he wrote Ewing on October 13, Sherman reverted again to those two notes that Ellen must collect in St. Louis:

> Our whole plan rests upon them now. They are the only money in this world that I can call my own and I will not borrow—rather steal is my new doctrine. My bank experience has given me a greater abhorrence of a borrower than of an ordinary thief. Of course I know the wide distinction, but the result is too often the same.

Quietly the Salt-Boiler went ahead giving Ellen Kansas lands—an eighteen-acre tract a mile and a half from Leavenworth and two and a quarter acres in another tract. Sherman, learning of this, wrote Ewing, "Ellen is disposed to accept all you give her, and I hope you will retake any part should you need it." While he waited for Ellen's arrival, Cump wrote St. Louis insurance men asking for agencies—"I have determined to make this place my future home." He considered putting up a shanty to live in, but Tom Ewing, Jr., and his wife announced that they were soon to return to Ohio for the winter; the Shermans must take their house. Cump accepted, although he wrote his father-in-law, "It may be that in the spring I may see evidence enough to warrant me to recover from my California séance so far as to risk building on a choice spot."

Daily Sherman climbed a "crazy stairway" to the second floor of a rickety cottonwood building that stood between Delaware and Shawnee streets. Sherman & Ewing was the sign on the door. On the first floor was the land agency of Hampton B. Denman, ex-mayor of the town. Sherman and Hugh handled the real estate—Hugh being absent in Lancaster much of the autumn. Tom took care of the legal practice when not embroiled in his greater passion, politics. Tom had become one of the foremost Free-Staters in Kansas, and had gone far past his conservative father in antislavery sympathy. From the days in 1850 when he had sat in the Senate gallery at Washington hearing the great men of the nation debate the Compromise, Tom's zeal for the Free-Soil cause had grown. While studying law in Cincinnati he had watched Abolitionists sending armed emigrants to Kansas, and as soon as he had been admitted to the bar in the winter of 1856-57, Tom had married Ellen Cox, daughter of a Presbyterian clergyman in Lancaster, and had moved to Leavenworth. Hugh, the ready fighter of the family, was not in sympathy with Tom's politics. Hugh had come out of West Point a Democrat, and in 1858 had married Henrietta, daughter of George Washington Young, the largest slaveholder in Maryland and the namesake of a neighbor, the Father of his Country.

At thirty, Tom Ewing, Jr., was one of the leaders of the conservative faction among the Free-Staters; thanks to his skill in exposing ballot frauds of the proslavery and radical Free-Soil parties, he was now talked of for high judicial position. Tom's fame had come in the late days of 1857 and early weeks of January, 1858, when, acting on the advice of his father and various conservative Congressmen of the East, he had urged the voters of Kansas Territory to abide by an "ingenious and rascally" constitution—the Lecompton—which a proslavery legislature had fastened upon the people in defiance of the majority's wishes. While the radical faction of the Free-Staters, headed by a bold and clever politician, James H. Lane, urged that the party refuse to vote for Territorial officers under so obnoxious a constitution, Tom advised voters to go to the polls, elect their own men, then amend the constitution so that slavery would be outlawed. When Lane by trickery prevented a Free-Soil convention from adopting Tom's plan, Tom with others organized a rump convention, and spent a thousand dollars of his own money—including borrowed sums—to flood the Territory with propaganda exposing the fraud. In the subsequent election Tom stood beside the ballot box at Kickapoo, a Missouri River town, and, although menaced by pistols and spattered with rotten eggs, collected convincing evidence that the proslavery party was importing border ruffians from Missouri to stuff the boxes. Armed with his proof, Tom had gone to Washington and made such exposures as led Congress to kill the bill that asked for Kansas's admission as a State under the proslavery Lecompton Constitution. Violent though factional antipathies might be, Tom was sufficiently known as a lawyer to be hired by his adversary Lane to clear him from murder charges six months after their political break. "Your antlike industry saved me," said Lane.

Cump warned Tom not to take on debts for political purposes, and urged him to practice law rather than campaign for the attorney-generalship or the Supreme Court bench.

It was useless; Tom continued his work for the Free-Soil party, and because of his frequent absences another lawyer was added to the firm, Daniel McCook, an Ohioan who had graduated from the University of Alabama and come to Kansas to practice law. Sherman himself was admitted to the bar. He had asked Judge Lecompte what examination was necessary and had been answered, "None at all. I'll admit you on the grounds of general intelligence."

Armed with his certificate, Sherman began to acquire more confidence and to include legal opinions among his endless, fluent observations. He had reached what in 1840 he had regarded as the last choice of professions—the law. Tom Ewing and McCook, irritated no doubt by Sherman's sudden authoritativeness in their department, resolved to let him have his day in court. Managing to be absent one day when a certain client called, they forced Sherman to take the case and they were likewise gone when the case came to trial. Sherman, in panic, hunted for them, but was compelled to appear before the judge, who would not listen to his pleas that he was only the office counsel and that his trial partners were absent. The rival lawyers were ready, the judge was firm, and Sherman was lost. The case was one in which Sherman's client was being sued for illegal occupancy of land, and in picturing how the man kept proper rentals from the owners, opposing counsel denounced Sherman as a robber and a persecutor of the poor. Unused to this professional method of influencing juries, Sherman flew into a rage and, forgetting the case in hand, threatened loudly to thrash his critic. Naturally, the jury decided against him and he stamped back to his office swearing to have nothing more to do with the law. McCook, appearing innocently and smiling secretly, managed to save the client from damage, but Sherman ceased to advise his partners on legal matters. He devoted himself to real estate.

"He never mingled in our affairs," said the *Leavenworth Chronicle* in later years. It described him as nervous, muscular, with "a long, keen head, bluish-gray eyes that smouldered with fire, a sharp, well-cut mouth; complection fair, hair and beard sandy-red, straight, short and strong." He was full of "crotchets and prejudices" but "with gleams of saturnine humor and kindness around the mouth."

While he awaited Ellen's arrival, Cump ordered the last of his St. Louis properties sold to pay his final debt of honor on the San Francisco "trust fund." He would have some twelve hundred dollars for Major Barnard in New York—one of his heaviest creditors—as soon as Ellen arrived to sign the deed completing the land sale. But when Ellen arrived in mid-November she protested, and on December 8, Cump was forced to write Barnard, in deep humiliation:

> Mrs. Sherman obstinately refuses to sign the deed. She had previously objected to my deeding away all my St. Louis property to make up losses and interest in California for which I made myself responsible from an over-nice sense of right. I have already repaid such losses and interest to the extent of about $12,000 and had difficulty in getting Mrs. Sherman to sign the deeds and now that I am down to the last piece, she sees poverty too close and obstinately refuses to sign the deed. You must therefore indulge me a little longer.
>
> I have a wife and four children accustomed to ease and comfort, have

impaired health and to begin life anew, indeed having all prejudices of old professional ideas to contend with and whether I will ever again rise from present obscurity, an enigma. I would have tried some mercantile or mechanical business but was without capital, and have suffered enough by the false representations of others ever to give my note or borrow money for any purpose unless absolute necessity drive me to it. . . . Rest assured that I will send you the first $500 I can get. I owe no man and only have obligations similar to yours for about $1,000 in all.

To another creditor, Colonel A. C. Myers, he wrote on the same day a similar description of his plight, and concluded:

I have pitched in here as a lawyer at haphazard—have good partners and think if there be any business we can get it, but it is a pretty hard life.

Ellen was pregnant again; soon there would be five children dependent upon him—or, worse still, dependent upon Thomas Ewing. And in spite of his fiat concerning Minnie's removal to Leavenworth, the child had remained in Lancaster. Lack of good schools in Kansas had prompted Ellen to leave her there. In February she would be nine; undoubtedly she had grown to look upon her grandfather as her real father, and to think of that red-haired man who sometimes visited her home as a sort of romantic uncle.

Within two weeks after Ellen's arrival, Cump was making efforts to leave Leavenworth and secure work in St. Louis, where Minnie could join them. On December 8 he wrote Patterson, asking if their real-estate partnership could be discussed once more. He could move to St. Louis in the spring; "I have no money or capital and would have to begin empty-handed." Nothing resulting from this, he corresponded with St. Louis capitalists regarding a partnership in a wholesale grocery business, but that plan collapsed. On January 14 he was writing Tom Ewing, Jr., that Ellen was insisting that he rent a house, since Tom's family would soon be returning:

No house can hold two families in amity any length of time. . . . If I thought Ellen would be comfortable in the country I would prefer putting up a shanty in the Rudd tract [a Ewing farm outside the town] and scratch up a garden of potatoes but Church and the Doctor are obstacles in the way of that. I'll stave off action as long as possible.

Ellen was not apparently able at this time to mollify, as she usually could, the occasional gusts of temper that Cump showed toward her zeal for Catholicism. In the Ewing family there would live the story of how Cump at one time in his married life had made a remark that drew from his wife the reply:

"Why, Cump, why should you be surprised? You knew when you married me that I was a Catholic!"

"Of course I did," he retorted, "but I didn't know that you would get worse every year."

On that occasion Ellen had laughed and the skies had cleared. Her niece Eleanor, daughter of Phil Ewing, said of her:

> Always she had the gift of laughter which saved a situation. I remember hearing her tell that at one time when Uncle Cump secured a house and bought some of the furniture, she arrived to find three marble-topped tables all in a row. She said they reminded her of gravestones—and she laughed over them. Uncle Cump said of Aunt Ellen that whenever he left home he expected she would pull up stakes, take the children, and hike for Lancaster.

It was, however, with Cump's full consent that Ellen planned to return in March to Lancaster with the children. Medical care would be more satisfactory there when the time came for her child to be born. But in the winter months life was hard for both husband and wife. "Our business does not yet show signs of an income adequate to our necessities," Cump wrote his father-in-law on January 23. Concerning Old Solitude's continued proffers of help, Cump was still sensitive, declaring:

> I do not propose to touch a cent but leave all to Ellen, unless the cash part should be used in preparing a permanent home. On this subject I have thought much. If I can see a fair prospect for making a living here I shall not look elsewhere, but I am not content to stay here or anywhere unless I can be independent of assistance from any quarter. You can well understand that I am far from easy to receive assistance from you, and it is only in the start that I am willing to think of it.

Living in a borrowed house, working in a ramshackle office, oppressed by his own and his wife's dissatisfaction with Kansas, Sherman saw winter blow across the plains. Relief came from within his mind—in thoughts upon the nation as a whole, its problems and opportunities. It was like turning, heavily laden, to a religion. Upon the propagation of the majestic republic he dwelt fondly.

John Sherman fostered this quality in his brother, writing him through December his objections to the Union Pacific Railroad, which since 1853 had been considered as an object for eventual governmental subsidy. John thought it unwise to give land to private interests, since knowledge of the best route was yet too scanty and the Indians too hostile. Cump answered these objections on January 6, writing so long a letter that it became a short paper:

So large a number of workmen distributed along the line will introduce enough whisky to kill off all the Indians within 300 miles of the road.

In writing of the republic, Cump could be at ease, humorous, clear-headed. Few jests like this would appear in his personal letters of the time. For himself the present was dismal and the future hopeless—the destiny of the country was by contrast bright and clear. Writing of the railway's effect upon the land, Sherman sensed the harmony for which his life craved. "Politically it would unite the West, Center and East by the bonds of intercourse," he said in describing how the best of five possible railroad routes should link New York, St. Louis, and San Francisco. Such a road he pictured in detail—its cost, two hundred million dollars; its time of completion, ten years; the durability of iron rails and wooden cross-ties; the exact places where workmen might find coal and wood for fuel; the revenue to be expected from freight; the rates to be charged. The sale of public lands along the right of way would be insufficient for financing:

The General Government must build the road if at all. . . . It is a work of giants and Uncle Sam is the only giant I know who can grapple the subject.

In the paper Cump did not mention, as well he might, that in 1849 he had been the first to send exploring parties to search for an eastward route through the Sierra Nevada Mountains, and how in 1855 he had been vice president and a stockholder, to the extent of a few thousand dollars, in a small railroad, the Central Pacific, which was built twenty-two miles out of Folsom, California, as the beginning of the efforts at constructing a transcontinental line. Reprinted by John in the *National Intelligencer* of Washington on January 18, the paper brought Cump national notice, and, in later years, gave him the fame of a prophet among railroad men. Grenville M. Dodge, one of the chief builders of the Union Pacific Railroad, declared after the line's completion that Sherman's paper "stamped its author as a far-seeing statesman and an enlightened engineer . . . one of the most remarkable and instructive short papers to be found in the literature of trans-continental railway construction." The road would be finished in 1869, true to Sherman's vision of a ten-year job.

Perhaps worry, introspection, and humiliation had sharpened Sherman's senses abnormally. Henceforth there would be observers, again and again, to refer to him as almost clairvoyant. John, at this period, read a forecast from Cump regarding the national drift:

I think in the next ten years we will have plenty to do in the war line—Mormon war, civil broils and strife, contests growing out of slavery and other exciting topics.

Within a year the United States Army would be restoring order in Mormon Utah, and within two years "civil broils" would be indeed upon the land. But as to himself, Sherman was no seer. On April 9 he wrote to Ellen in Lancaster:

I am doomed to be a vagabond, and shall no longer struggle against my fate. . . . I look upon myself as a dead cock in the pit, not worthy of further notice, and will take my chances as they come.

13

SOLITUDE AND BANISHMENT

ELLEN returned to Lancaster and Cump fell to working clearing Ewing's land on Indian Creek, forty miles from town. He built cabins, directed workmen, cooked for himself.

When not at the farms he lived with Tom and Ellie Ewing in Leavenworth, where Ellie regarded him not only as a favorite brother but as an endlessly entertaining conversationalist. Her son Tom had from her, in later years, memories of this time:

She always spoke of how interesting he was. Once she had as guests several clergymen who were attending a Presbyterian meeting in town. He helped make their stay pleasant. They would hurry home from meeting to hear him talk. For example, one of them remarked that swearing was a wholly unnecessary and inexcusable vice.

He snapped out, "Were you ever at sea in a heavy gale, with spars creaking and sails flapping, and the crew cowardly and incompetent?"

"No."

"Did you ever drive a five-team ox-cart across the prairie?"

"No."

"Then you know nothing of the temptations to blasphemy—you are not competent to judge."

He and his wife were devotedly attached to each other in spite of frequent separation. He had grown up in affectionate relation not only to her but toward her sister, Sissie, with whom he was just as affectionate.

He flew from one of Ewing's properties to another, planting orchards, bargaining for cheap labor. No detail was too small for his attention, nor too large. He speculated heavily in corn, which he stored in new barns in the hope of selling it to covered wagons passing on the way to Pike's Peak. His accounts to Ewing were models of meticulous care, such sums as $3,244.92, for instance, being itemized so minutely as to include:

> 1 saddle and bridle, $5.00; shoeing 2 horses, $2.10; 2 candlesticks @ 10¢, 20¢; 1 doz. tin plates, 60¢; 1 curry comb, 25¢; 13 lbs. shot, 60¢; due Clements on 5000 bus. corn, $16.25.

The gold rush to the Rockies dwindled. The corn speculation did not turn out well. Some of the farm tenants quit. The law and real-estate office that Sherman had practically deserted to handle Ewing's farms paid no salary. As though to escape the life he lived, he began writing John more and more on political issues. All winter he had been dropping hints of leniency. The North had gained control of both Senate and the House, "and," he said, "all angry controversy ought to cease." He thought that the South, doomed now to minority and to the problem of handling three million slaves, was so weak "that it seems to me that the Northern representatives can afford to lay low and let events develop the solution of the dangerous political problem." He saw nothing in the Kansas quarrel that time could not solve. Let Congress admit it as a slave State:

> . . . her people will forthwith abolish it, and the South will never again attempt to coerce their Southern ideas upon any territory so illy adapted to slave labor. To taunt them with their want of success and weakness can do no good.

Educated Americans should stand on middle ground. On April 30 he told John that he would not vote in the coming election, which he foresaw as a Republican victory:

> My idea is that the Southern States should be more likened to a man having a deformity, like the fox who lost his tail and wanted all others to cut theirs off. . . . I would indulge them in their delusion with all the philosophy and complacency of a strong man.

They would never oppress the free States again. On May 1 he wrote Ewing that he preferred to see negroes kept politically subject to the whites wherever the two races approached numerical equality. He would be a Republican only if the party proved "moderate."

To carry his imagination further and further from its hopeless confines, there came letters from John, who was traveling abroad—letters describing the war between France and Italy. Cump sent him prophecies of results, the location of coming battles "near the Lake of Maggiore," criticisms of Napoleon III's strategy. He could see the French troops "glowing with a desire to battle." His blood grew hot. "I wish I were there to watch the operations and changes; but alas, I am in Kansas."

Perhaps it was thoughts of war that made him realize that the red gamecock was not dead, after all, in the pit of the frontier. On June 11 he determined to say farewell to Kansas, the law and real estate. His old friend Buell was now assistant adjutant general, and confidential adviser to Secretary of War Floyd and Sherman wrote him asking if there were any vacancies among army paymasters, "or anything in your line that I could obtain." Buell answered that there was none. Everything turned on politics. This was discouraging, for Thomas Ewing, who had been able to walk into the White House with a request during Whig régimes, was now a stranger to the Democratic President Buchanan. "However," said Buell, "I send you a paper which represents an opening that I have been disposed to think well of." Louisiana was planning a State military college and the vice president of the Board of Supervisors was General George Mason Graham, half-brother of the Colonel Mason who had been Sherman's commander and intimate in California. Graham was advertising for a superintendent.

Sherman speedily mailed an application, inclosing a recommendation from Buell, and gave himself over to the thought that in the gracious South he might find "solitude and banishment enough to hide from the misfortunes of the past." In that civilization his commercial failures would count for less than in the bustling North. Scarcely had he posted his application when from Lancaster came word that Cincinnati financiers were considering him as their representative in London. They had sent a man to England to investigate their needs and when he returned they would be ready to tell what was wanted. Obviously the Ewings were working hard for Sherman.

Sherman hurried to Lancaster to be on the ground if either or both of his chances materialized. Louisiana responded first. General Graham, remembering his dead half-brother's fondness for Sherman, began to campaign. His sister, a nun, remembered Ellen as one of her favorite pupils in the Georgetown convent. In open arguments and in anonymous eulogies inserted in Louisiana newspapers, Graham trumpeted Sherman's virtues. Sherman's letter of application helped his cause. It was opened at a meeting of the Board of Supervisors at a time when they were wading "through a mass of testimonials," as an observer described the scene, "flattering words of loving, partial friends, genealogies and such handsome nothings as only enthusiastic southerners can say of each other and of their ancestors for generations back when an office is in sight."

Sherman's statement was terse, realistic, and welcome in such an atmosphere:

Governor Wickcliffe, President, Board of Supervisors,
Sir:

Having been informed that you wish a superintendent and professor of engineering in the Military Academy of Louisiana, soon to be opened, I beg leave to offer myself for a position. I send no testimonials. . . . I will only say that I am a graduate of West Point and an ex-army officer; if you care to know further about me, I refer you to the officers of the army from General Scott down, and in your own State to Col. Braxton Bragg, Major G. T. Beauregard and Richard Taylor, Esq.

As the governor finished reading the letter, one of the Supervisors, a business man named Sam Henarie, spoke out: "By God, he's my man! He's a man of sense. I'm ready for the vote."

"But we have a number more of applications," protested the governor. "We must read them all."

"Well," snorted Henarie, "*you* can read them, but let me out of here. When you get through, call me and I'll come back and vote for Sherman."

The son and the brother of the late President Taylor, Dick and J. P. Taylor, urged the board to choose Sherman, the brother telling Graham:

"If you hunted the whole army from one end of it to another you could not have found a man in it more admirably suited for the position in every respect than Sherman."

On August 3 Graham notified Sherman that he had been elected. But the candidate made no immediate response. Ellen and all the Ewings were pressing him to wait until London could be heard from. The school would pay him but thirty-five hundred dollars a year, while the London post would certainly offer much more.

For almost two weeks he fidgeted, waiting, waiting, then he wrote Wickcliffe that he would accept. As his letter traveled South, Cincinnati bankers arrived in Lancaster with a proposition. New capital had joined the firm with the stipulation that Sherman be its London agent. It was too late, Sherman informed them. He had given his word to Louisiana, and as they departed amid the disappointment of the Ewings, Cump buckled to his new task. From his desk in Ewing's home flew letters asking army officers for information on military schools. George B. McClellan sent him French texts. He priced materials with the mastery of detail he had shown as a quartermaster.

This new position must be successfully held. Cump, looking ahead, began fortifying himself against danger. His brother John was being groomed by the Republicans for Speaker if they could organize the House of Representatives when it met in December. If elected John would be the first Speaker to be seated by a party wholly sectional. And no matter how loudly he and his colleagues might insist that they opposed only the spread of slavery beyond its present limits, the extremists of the South were believing that the Republicans planned eventually to attack slavery as it existed in the Southern States. Southern leaders pointed out that one of the Republican leaders, Abraham Lincoln, had told Illinois voters that the nation could not continue half-slave and half-free. Cump sent John a warning:

> As you are becoming a man of note and are a Republican, and as I go South among gentlemen who have always owned slaves and probably always will and must, and whose feelings may pervert every public expression of yours, putting me in a false position to them as my patrons, friends and associates, and you as my brother, I would like to see you take the highest ground consistent with your party creed.

Every day that Sherman spent in Lancaster preparing to move South, new groups of Southerners were converted to the idea of secession. The Democratic party had split North and South as a result of the Dred Scott decision of the United States Supreme Court. Jefferson Davis, Senator from Mississippi, was declaring that while ten years before Southern men had generally agreed slavery to be wrong, "truth and sound philosophy have progressed" until in 1859 "there is not probably an intelligent mind among our own citizens who doubts either the moral or the legal right of the institution of African slavery as it exists in our own country." Since 1850 Davis had been urging the South to build factories, to learn mechanical trades, and to free itself from commercial dependence upon the North. In its lack of industrial plants, the South had received only a fraction of the huge immigration from Europe, and while the North grew in wealth and population, the South was prevented by law from recruiting its own labor battalions abroad. Since 1808 the slave trade had been prohibited and although an illicit traffic in smuggled blacks had imported some twelve thousand chained Africans each year from 1856 to 1859, the supply was unimportant. A clamor for the raising of the Federal embargo on slave ships swept the South in 1857, conventions memorializing Congress and associations adopting resolutions. Such a change would increase Southern representation in Congress; it would lower the price of slaves so that small farmers could own them, thus solidifying the South; it would give the slave-power enough black men to colonize the Western Territories.

The campaign gained such momentum that in May, 1859, Sherman read that the flower of Southern statesmen, basing their representation on the electoral vote of each State, had met as delegates at a convention in Vicksburg and voted, two to one, that "all laws, State or Federal, prohibiting the African slave trade ought to be repealed." Everywhere in the North there could be found hitherto conservative men shaking their heads over this news. It was not the fire-eaters, but the sober representatives of the South, who now urged the restoration of the horrors that had shocked the civilized world. New groups of serious Northerners began to wonder if, since the South voted to legalize those floating hell-holes, the Abolitionists might not be right after all.

Then Sherman, one October morning, read that a lawless Abolitionist named John Brown had seized the government arsenal at Harpers Ferry, Virginia, hoping to arm slaves and lead them North to freedom. He had been captured. The South was seething. A revulsion against the Abolitionists swept the North. Republican leaders hastened to denounce the raid. The pendulum was swinging the other way. To Sherman, Virginia had been right in calling militia to attack John Brown, and the United States Army correct in protecting its arsenal. An attempt to fire slaves to insurrection would put women and children at the mercy of a race regarded as barbaric if not still animalistic.

Sherman believed that the new military school that he was to head had been conceived in Louisiana's determination to put itself in a position for self-defense. He could not believe that, as Abolitionists said, the school was part of a Southern preparation for aggressive war against the North. He knew that since 1854 Southern extremists had been urging their people to found military colleges and that several slave States, among them Alabama and Mississippi, had added military training to their State University courses. Smaller colleges were following the lead. Fire-eaters were demanding that Southern boys be sent no longer to such Abolitionist colleges as Harvard, Yale, and Princeton in the North.

But Sherman could not refuse the post on the supposition that extremists of both sections were right. He needed money, more money than ever, for on September 5 Ellen had borne him another baby—"Number Five," he described it to John—Eleanor Mary. He was forty—or would be in February.

So, late in October, he set off to learn his fourth profession, hoping that national events would not expel him from his school as they had from his bank. An unexpected piece of luck met him in St. Louis before he took the steamboat for New Orleans. It had to do with the house he had built in San Francisco with funds borrowed from Lucas. On the twenty-sixth Cump described the situation to Ewing:

When I finished, our profits did not enable me to repay. I put the title in Mr. Turner's name and considered it as Mr. Lucas' in lieu of the money advanced by him. An offer of purchase is now here, $6,150 and Mr. Lucas insists on my having it. I declined it peremptorily. Though I would prefer not to accept a gratuity, still they are so peremptory that I must take it or quarrel with them. I have therefore assented, and the deed will go out next steamer and money, less exchange, and commission, some $5,600, will return about January. I will consent that Major Turner send it to Ellen.

From Cairo on the twenty-ninth Cump wrote Ellen:

Should my health utterly fail me or abolition drive me and all moderate men from the South, then we can retreat down the Hocking and exist until time puts us away under ground.

In Louisiana Graham, Beauregard, the Taylors, and Bragg welcomed him, Bragg writing:

I heard something of your misfortunes and sympathized most deeply with you, but it is not too late for a man of your energy and ability to repair such disaster.

Bragg, now a wealthy planter, was an intimate friend of the new governor, Thomas O. Moore, and had pledged that executive to be Sherman's friend.

In the vast empty mansion among four hundred acres of pines, Sherman began to fashion a school. Sleeping on a cot, sharing quarters and meals with James, the carpenter, and fed by a black mammy, Sherman superintended the conversion of boards into tables, benches, desks, and blackboards. Too poor to buy a horse, he walked, when necessary, the three miles into Alexandria, the nearest town. His salary would not start until January 1. Lonely, he was tortured by his imaginary pictures of the Board of Supervisors, which had several politicians among its number, as coming to "attempt to extract from me promises I will not give"; his position might prove

inconsistent with decent independence—feeling runs so high where a nigger is concerned that, like religious questions, common sense is disregarded, and knowledge of the character of mankind in such cases leads me to point out a combination of events that may yet operate on our future.

When Ellen read these words, she had reason to look upon the slavery question as a religious one, for John Brown, having been hanged on December 2, was receiving a martyr's crown; church congregations were praying, belfry bells tolling, and clergymen, poets, and writers were likening him to Jesus. Southerners, stunned at the spectacle of such mourning for a "criminal," began in increasing numbers to feel that Northerners were a foreign people.

But the Supervisors said nothing to Sherman; Bragg, Graham, and Governor Moore were conservative, and moreover Sherman discovered that the motive behind the organization of the military school had been educational, not political. He learned that one group among the Supervisors had originally wanted to kill the military-training feature and that Graham had only succeeded in converting them by arguing "that Southern gentlemen would submit rather to the showy discipline of arms than to the less ostentatious government of a faculty." It was the same observation that the Supervisors would make in a report issued soon after the seminary had opened:

> . . . the greatest obstacle in the way of success of Southern schools is found in the inherent propensity of Southern youth to resist authority and control from any quarter with which they have no sympathy.

Bragg would write Sherman in February:

> The more you see of our society, especially our young men, the more you will be impressed with the importance of a change in our system of education if we expect the next generation to be anything more than a mere aggregation of loafers charged with the duty of squandering their fathers' legacies and disgracing their names.

Northern travelers, returning from the South, declared that the sons of slave-owners grew up in arrogance and conceit, "spoiled" by the presence of servile attendants upon whom they could, in the absence of parents, vent their childish passions.

But at the hour when Sherman, convinced that he was not being secretly used by secessionists, began to breathe easily, his brother John did the very thing Cump had cautioned him not to do—he appeared prominently in the robes of Abolition. Soon after the opening of Congress in December, John, without reading it, had endorsed for wide publication a pamphlet entitled *The Impending Crisis*, which a Southerner, Hinton R. Helper, had written to demonstrate how slavery brought economic and social degradation upon the "niggerless" white farmers of the South. Disapproved by Southern conservatives as unfair, and denounced by Southern extremists as a villainous attempt to alienate the ruling aristocracy from its poor-white supporters, the book started a terrific battle, which centered around John Sherman, the candidate for Speaker of the House. Representative Millson of Virginia led the assault upon him by declaring him "not only not fit to be Speaker, but not fit to live." Northern and Southern legislators carried knives and pistols in Washington's streets and halls, and the Helper scandal brought John's defeat by a margin of three votes when the Speakership was determined.

Frankly alarmed at the situation thus thrust upon him, Cump wrote to John, "I hoped you would be theoretical and not practical, for practical abolition is disunion, Civil War, and anarchy universal on this continent." But now that John was under fire, Cump said, "I hope you will conduct yourself manfully." As a boy he had raised no hand to protect his lawless brother from Mark Howe's whip, but now Cump told Ellen, "I do not intend to let any of them [the Southerners] reflect on John in my presence." He explained to her that he would leave the South and come north if the "insane politicians" organized for secession.

To Graham, Sherman explained that his brother's action in signing the commendation of Helper's book had been careless, the result of accepting other men's word that the work was not "incendiary," and "he is punished well." John, he knew, would do nothing aggressive against the South. He continued:

> I do think southern politicians are almost as much to blame as mere theoretical abolitionists. The constant threat of disunion, and their enlarging the term abolitionist has done them more real harm than the mere prayers, preachings and foolish speeches of distant preachers. . . . The true position of every gentleman, north and south, is to frown down even a mention of disunion.

Around Sherman rallied his friends, spreading the word far and wide that he was not in agreement with his brother. Bragg wrote him that if any one criticized him on John's account, he must

> keep silent, and refer the matter to your friends. I will answer any such insinuations and vouch for your soundness in any and all ways. I have known you too long and too well to permit a doubt to cross my mind as to the soundness of your views.

Only one Southerner, Dr. S. A. Smith, an aggressive politician on the Board of Supervisors, made—according to the records—inquiry of Sherman as to his views. Smith said to him on December 22 that it was important that all Southern educational institutions be in the hands of the friends of the South. Sherman replied that he was and had always been a strong advocate of the Union, and that "if disunion is meditated I will oppose it."

The following day Sherman wrote Tom Ewing, Jr., that his own views on slavery were more like Bragg's and other moderate Southerners than like Tom's:

I would not if I could abolish or modify slavery. I don't know that I would materially change the actual political relation of master and slave. Negroes in the great numbers that exist here must of necessity be slaves. Theoretical notions of humanity and religion cannot shake the commercial fact that their labor is of great value and cannot be dispensed with. Still of course I wish it had never existed, for it does make mischief. . . . The mere dread of revolt, sedition or external interference makes men ordinarily calm, almost mad. . . . I am willing to aid Louisiana in defending herself against her enemies so long as she remains a state in the general confederacy; but should she or any other state act disunion, I am out.

As he listened to Southerners talk of "peaceable secession" he shook his head. He wrote Tom Ewing, Jr.:

Disunion and Civil War are synonymous terms. The Mississippi, source and mouth, must be controlled by one government. . . . Therefore a peaceable disunion which men here think possible is absurd. It would be war eternal until one or the other were conquered—subject. In that event of course I would stand by Ohio.

It must have cooled Sherman's aching head, now and then, for him to look at the motto that he and the Supervisors had placed in marble over the main door: "By the Liberality of the General Government of the United States. The Union—*Esto Perpetua*." The school had been built and opened on funds chiefly Federal, a grant of lands having been given Louisiana some thirty years earlier for the purpose. An income of eighty-one hundred dollars a year had supplied the money for the structure. The State was now asked to appropriate sums for faculty houses and school equipment. In January the legislature would consider the matter.

While Sherman conferred with the Supervisors on this crucial question, there arrived word from Old Solitude that the London banking offer had been renewed. Beverly Tucker, United States consul at Liverpool, a Mr. Rupell, rich army contractor from Utah, William R. Roelofson, Cincinnati banker, and other capitalists had combined, and were insisting that Sherman handle their London branch bank. Ewing had suggested that Sherman be offered $3,750 in advance, a like sum at the end of two years, and payment of all office expenses. Ewing hoped Cump would take it; Northern teachers were distrusted in the South; Ellen would like London better than the backwoods of Louisiana, where epidemics of yellow fever raged.

As the seminary threw open its doors on January 2, with cadets enrolling, parents arriving in carriages, and Supervisors discussing the future, Sherman received another letter from Ewing; the offer was now seventy-five hundred dollars a year for two years—double his present income. Sherman debated, then wrote Ewing on the eighth:

> If I can hold off till the legislature shows its temper I will be in a better attitude to act. Here at $3,500 I could save little after bringing my family, but I would have good social position, maybe a good house and, taken all in all, a pleasant home, for such I should make it, designing to keep my children here summer and winter, always. Epidemics never originate here.

He felt responsibility to his employers, and explained to Ewing:

> The South are right in guarding against insidious enemies or against any enemies whatever, and I would aid her in so doing. All I would object to is the laying of plans designed to result in secession and Civil War . . . If I were to suspect that I were being used for such a deep laid plan I would rebel, but I see daily marks of confidence in me and reliance upon my executing practical designs, and if I were to say that I contemplated leaving, I would give great uneasiness to those who have built high hopes.

When Graham and Bragg learned of the London offer they flew to work to bind Sherman to the seminary; they lobbied among the legislators who were to assemble on the sixteenth, and urged them to pass the bills that would give the superintendent a house as well as the school a sufficient endowment. In the rush of attention showered upon him, Sherman let the London matter grow faint in his mind. Roelofson, he knew, would visit him with the formal proffer late in the month, but he did not feel like accepting. His mind centered on the house, which seemed assured. It would be the first home he had provided for all his children.

He wrote Tom Ewing, Jr.:

> I have no doubt one of our first troubles will be that Ellen's servants will all quit after we have gone into debt to get them here and then she will have to wait on herself or buy a nigger. What will you think of that—of our buying a nigger?
>
> But it is inevitable. Niggers won't work unless they are owned, and white servants are not to be found in this parish. . . . I suppose next fall we will bring some down from Ohio and after they leave and get married to some roving Texas trader or carpenter with a few hundred dollars in his pocket, we will be without servants and compelled to do without or buy.

As Sherman had found relief from his earlier woes in playing with his children, he now discovered it in the fifty-six boys who had enrolled. In youngsters he always found much that was humorous. The antics of Lizzie and Willy had amused him in California, and to Ellen he now wrote from Louisiana how his office was beset by ladies with children who part with tears and blessings, and I remark the fact that the dullest boys have the most affectionate mothers and the most vicious boys come recommended with all the virtues of saints. Of course I promise to be a father to them all.

After the first few weeks the cadets, wearying of the charm of the uniform, began to make trouble. Sherman wrote Tom Ewing, Jr., "The boys here are willful and govern their parents despotically."

The test came in late January, when one of the pampered young aristocrats taxed the superintendent with a "breach of propriety" in confiscating forbidden tobacco from a dormitory washstand. A gentleman's washstand was sacred! Fights broke out, a knife was drawn. Quickly Sherman expelled the cadet who had started the fight, the cadet who had drawn the knife, and the cadet who had been so sensitive about washstands. Thirty boys who had threatened to leave wilted after Sherman, turning sleuth, captured the cadet who had daubed the blackboards with hair grease, and forced him to hire a Negro to clean the premises. The superintendent was nobody to fool with.

One day Sherman discovered a marching line of boys convulsed with mirth. The cadet at the head of the line wore, unconsciously, a pig's tail attached to his coat tail. Sherman selected as the guilty man the boy who laughed loudest. He was correct. David French Boyd, the seminary's professor of ancient languages, a Virginian who admired Sherman without reservation, thought the superintendent "a born detective":

From the least clew he would infer what a cadet was doing. . . . He was well named Tecumseh. The wily old Indian was hardly superior to Sherman in reading the signs and divining the plans of foe or cadet. . . . Once I remember we were strolling in the woods and passed a group of cadets a little distance off. I had observed nothing unusual when he spoke up, "Those fellows seem a little flushed. They are up to something." I thought no more of it. The next day he called me into his office and said, "You remember those boys we passed yesterday in the woods? They were concocting a plan to rob the hen roosts of the neighbors. They have confessed it all to me."

By the middle of February the wave of insubordination had ebbed, with five cadets expelled or resigned. "Fifty-one still remain," Cump wrote Ellen, "not a recitation was missed, and I am fully supported. There can be but one master." Two days after he had passed his fortieth birthday he told his wife:

I have now crossed the line and suppose I must rest satisfied with the title of "The Old Man," the "cross old schoolmaster," but time won't wait and we must rush on in the race to eternity. . . .

But within a few days he found himself not so well supported as he had thought. Parents of expelled boys, and particularly the father of the young man whom Sherman had sent from class because he pinned pigs' tails to comrades' coat tails, had complained. Supervisor Smith, the politician, came inquiring into the conduct of the school. Smith had originally opposed military training, and as a legislator held in his hands the fate of the seminary appropriation bills. His investigation offended Sherman, who described it to Graham as "the first positive event that has shaken me and made me think seriously of Roelofson." Sherman said that if he remained in Louisiana he would always be dependent upon the whims and caprices of "boys and legislators." Either the legislature must provide funds for the school or he would accept the London offer. Graham wrote Governor Moore:

> . . . we are in imminent danger of losing our irreplaceable superintendent, the apprehension of which has kept me awake for more than half the night . . . we could not hope to get again exactly such another man . . . so clear, so quick and decided a mind—such practiced administrative and executive qualities—such experienced and varied knowledge of men, the world and its business, combined with such kindliness of heart and parental care and thoughtfulness.

Graham proposed that the State raise Sherman's salary to five thousand dollars a year. This was not Sherman's point, Graham knew:

> I have never known a more unsordid and unselfish gentleman, yet I think assurance of that amount, with a comfortable home for his family, will decide him immovable against Mr. Roelofson's offers. It will not be this amount of money which will influence him so much as the relief he will thereby experience from the apprehension, which is becoming somewhat morbid with him, that occurring political events and the position of his brother in the United States Congress may do or conspire to affect his position and impair his usefulness here.

If the legislature should fail to take action, Graham proposed that he, Dr. Smith, and the governor guarantee Sherman five thousand dollars a year from their pockets for the next five years. The governor was helpless, Graham was almost distraught, and Sherman was veering and changing his course as the contending winds buffeted him. Cump's letters to Lancaster betrayed his confusion. In one the London money tempted him, in the next he was "mistrustful of finance." Now he was satisfied that his berth was permanent, tomorrow he would be so angry at the dilatory legislators that he was ready to leave. Then he thought of how in New Orleans, seven years before, he had been approached by two as fine gentlemen as ever lived, with prospects more brilliant than those now offered me. I went and without any fault, negligence or want of ability, I was involved . . .

Even the arrival of Roelofson on February 11 with a note from Thomas Ewing did not conclude his indecision. Ewing had written:

My own opinion and all your friends' here is that you had better accept. Your present situation, the official annoyances in store for you, the personal and social comforts that it promises you and your family are not what we had hoped. Ellen will feel it at best but an honorable exile, cut off from social intercourse entirely with her friends, for the place seems inaccessible, your letters twelve to fourteen days in reaching us. Public office you may resign honorably. . . . You may choose a residence within fifty miles of London and enjoy good society in a civilized and orderly community. As to your family, you had better go without them and I will bring them to you in the course of the summer or autumn.

Sherman weakened, told Roelofson that if the Board of Supervisors would "willingly concur" he would accept, and took the financier to see Graham and five other board members at Alexandria. In flustered haste, the board passed resolutions of praise for Sherman and hoped he wouldn't resign. Graham begged for ten days in which to discover what the legislature would do. Roelofson departed with the observation that while the seminary was beautiful, it must be a "kind of exile."

After his harassing months in search of employment, Sherman grew confident when two sets of prominent people struggled for his services, so confident that he wrote to Ellen not only with humor but with a strange new note of authority. There need be no more occasion for her and the children to take refuge with her father:

Indeed if you hear that I have concluded to stay here, just make up your mind to live and die here, because I am going to take the bit in my mouth and resume my military character and control my own affairs.

Since I left New Orleans I have felt myself oppressed by circumstances I could not control, but I begin to feel footing and will get saucy. But if I go to England I shall expect a universal panic, the repudiation of the great national debt and a blow-up generally.

I suppose I was the Jonah that blew up San Francisco and it took only two months' residence in Wall Street to bust up New York and I think my arrival in London will be the signal of the downfall of that mighty empire.

Here I can't do much harm, if I can't do any good and here we have solitude and banishment enough to hide from the misfortunes of the past.

Therefore if Louisiana will endow this college properly and is fool enough to give me five thousand dollars, we will drive our tent pins, and pick out a magnolia under which to sleep the long sleep. But if she don't, then England must perish, for I predict financial misfortune to the land that receives me.

At Graham's insistence, Sherman went to the State capital, Baton Rouge, to lobby for the bill. The governor entertained him at dinner, Bragg and Dick Taylor introduced him everywhere.

In one day he wrote Ellen indicating that he wished to stay and to Tom that "the itch for change and adventure makes me strongly inclined to go. . . ." And to Graham he admitted that he was "confused." But to the legislators he said, "Whether I go or stay, the provisions made for the Seminary [in the bill] are essential to its success." When the ten days' grace had elapsed, the Seminary Bill was still unpassed, having been involved in a fight between wealthy planters and small farmers as to free scholarships. Bragg sought to hold Sherman by introducing another bill that would give the seminary superintendent an extra five hundred dollars if the school was made, as he proposed, a State arsenal.

On the day on which he must come to a decision, Sherman telegraphed Ellen, was answered, and promptly wrote Graham, "She is so strongly in favor of the London project" that he must choose it. "I confess I make this step in doubt and the strong preference of my family is all that turns the scale. . . ."

To Tom Ewing, Jr., Cump confessed Ellen's victory, but added that she

> will never be willing to live in England or indeed anywhere but in Lancaster. I only yield because I can see you and all determined, and Ellen's timidity about the bugbear of yellow fever would each year break us up and cost a fortune to travel to and from. England will be the same.

Therefore, he announced, he would go to England alone, remain two or three years, then return to find "some moderate employment" in Cincinnati.

But as the days passed, Sherman changed once more. He confided in Graham that he wished to remain and told him of his plan for accomplishing it. First he would put his resignation in the hands of the Board of Supervisors to be held for his signal of release, then he would go to Ohio to try and change Ellen's mind about yellow fever in Louisiana. Meanwhile he wanted the seminary to search for a new superintendent, since "I am fully conscious that I may fail." As he passed through Baton Rouge he was told that the Seminary Bill and Bragg's Arsenal Bill were sure to pass. He could be sure of four thousand dollars a year, a house, and a firmly established seminary, and the post could be his for as long as he liked. Against this, Roelofson's offer was, in its final analysis, seventy-five hundred dollars a year for two years, and one-tenth interest in the company.

Impatiently Sherman rode steamships and trains northward, making the last lap of his journey by night on a freight train in order to be in Lancaster at daylight on a Sunday morning. The first greetings over, he asked for Roelofson. He had sailed for Europe. Old Solitude was in Washington. On Tuesday Sherman hurried to Cincinnati to discuss the London matter with a banker, Gibson, one of the stockholders. The latter, ignorant of details, urged Sherman to await Roelofson's return before making a decision. Sherman refused. He demanded that Gibson pay him $3,750 in cash and secure the remainder of the $15,000, also that each partner individually guarantee him the full amount. Gibson was helpless in Roelofson's absence; plans could be completed when he arrived. "Therefore," as Sherman wrote Graham, "I notified him I would return to Louisiana."

Thomas Ewing, arriving in Lancaster, found his plan wrecked and Sherman preparing to return to the seminary, where his family must join him in the autumn. The Salt-Boiler calmly gave Sherman a fine saddle horse and his blessing. He sat on the hill, distilling logic in his mind as gravely as his hands had boiled salt among the Kanawha kettle fires so many years before. He had wanted the red-haired boy to be an army engineer. Failure! He had wanted the lieutenant to leave the army in 1844. Failure! He had tried to make the mature son-in-law his business manager. Failure! He had schemed to place him in affluent, cultured London. Cump had thrown away the offer in a huff.

Every employer had found Sherman as "transparently honest, faithful, reliable, correct and prompt" as Ewing had found him as a boy of nine—Anderson in Fort Moultrie, Mason and Smith in California, Lucas & Turner, the seminary board. . . . But would the fellow ever learn to serve himself as well as he served his masters?

14

WE DESERVE A MONARCH

MARCH lay on the dogwood blossoms as Sherman returned to the seminary and began preparing for the expansion that the legislature had at last authorized. Bragg's bill making the school a State arsenal had also passed and Sherman did not worry on being told, apologetically, that through an oversight the bill had neglected to give the superintendent his extra five hundred dollars in salary. Bragg and Graham assured him that this would be corrected when the lawmakers next assembled and that the back pay would be forthcoming.

In his determination to make the school successful, Sherman acted not only as superintendent and treasurer, but also as teacher of geography and American history and as substitute for most of the professors when they were absent. David F. Boyd, professor of ancient languages, saw him visiting the classrooms and sensing by "intuition" whether teachers of such unfamiliar subjects as Greek were doing their work well. Coming from the high-flown lecture of a professor one day, Sherman whispered to Boyd, "Every damned shot went clear over their heads." Boyd saw that he "soon clipped the wings of our grandiloquently soaring eagle and made him a plain barnyard fowl—a practical, useful instructor."

The worshipful Boyd thought Sherman "the prince of talkers," but conceded that the superintendent could not reason:

> That is, his mind leaped so quick from idea to idea that he seemed to take no account of the time over which it passed and if he was asked to explain how he came by his conclusions it confused him. This weakness, if weakness it can be called, was due to his genius. His mind went lightning-like to its conclusions and he had the utmost faith in his inspirations and convictions. Such minds have no patience with the slow, short steps by which the less gifted must plod along to their laboriously reached conclusions. . . .
>
> Once I remember he asked my opinion about something. I gave it and then began to give my reasons, when he stopped me with this remark, "I only wanted your opinion. I didn't ask for your reasons and remember, never give reasons for what you think or do until you must. Maybe after a while a better reason will pop into your head."

"A fine organizer and splendid executive officer," Boyd described him.

> He could organize and run successfully any enterprise—school included. . . . And if a cadet fell sick, the loving care and attention he gave him!

He was at the bedside several times a day and at night, watching him closely, consoling and encouraging him.

Although Sherman kept a contented face for the school to see, he was steadily losing weight. When Ellen saw him again in August she announced that he was "a mere skeleton," fifteen pounds under weight, and that the trouble lay in his excessive use of tobacco and in the bad food of the seminary. That Ellen was wrong in her diagnosis is to be argued from the fact that Cump throughout his life had astonishing immunity from indigestion and nicotine poisoning, despite his carelessness in eating and his almost incessant smoking of cigars. Asthma, which had annoyed him in San Francisco, lessened in the Louisiana pine country and he now resorted only occasionally to his home remedy, the burning of niter paper in his room. It is true that in November the seminary food was so bad that the cadets rioted in mess hall, denouncing worms in their rice and smashing crockery until Sherman burst into the room shouting, "Attention!" and quelled the disturbance with the expulsion of five boys; but the diet was obviously ample, if plain, in the springtime when the superintendent was losing weight so rapidly.

It was the state of the Union and its bearing upon his own future that was more probably the cause of Sherman's physical decline. Boyd observed how lean he was, how his red hair "when he was excited would stick straight out," how much he talked about the Union, and how he would always "stand by it."

Sherman watched the newspapers closely as the Democratic party assembled its delegates in Charleston on April 23 to nominate a presidential candidate. Heretofore the Northern and Southern delegates had always been able to compromise their differences, but now the sectional split had grown too wide. Slave-State delegates wanted a candidate and a platform committed to the principle that the Federal Government must protect slave-owners when they took their property into the Territories. The majority of Northern delegates, massing behind the candidacy of Stephen A. Douglas, insisted that settlers of Territories must be kept free to vote for or against slavery for themselves. It was Douglas's Northwesterners who held the power in the convention, a fact that William L. Yancey, Alabama disciple of Calhoun, recognized when he spoke of the Northwest as having "grown up from an infant in swaddling clothes into the free proportions of a giant people." He urged the new section not to rule slavery out of the Territories, since that would eventually bankrupt the South. In reproof he charged the Northern Democrats with holding "the common sentiment that slavery is wrong."

There were other items in the Southern bill of grievances; the protective tariff was a violation of States' rights, since it gave bounties to Northeastern manufacturers from the pockets of Southern agriculturalists; the North had flagrantly violated the mutual obligations of the States by allowing Abolition "nigger-stealers" to flourish. Some thirteen free States, it was charged, had passed laws hampering slave-owners in recovering fugitive blacks.

But keener than all other resentments was that of the air of moral superiority worn by the North. No matter how many laws were passed or ignored, no matter what compromises were made, the South knew that the Northern majority now believed slavery wrong. Conservative kindly Northerners might tell conservative kindly Southerners, "Yes, we know Abolitionists exaggerate the sins of slavery; we know *Uncle Tom's Cabin* was melodrama; we know many black slaves are better off than many free white workers in New England factories, and we will never see you robbed of your property." Yet the listener would know that the speaker, for the sake of manners, was refraining from adding, "But the institution *is* wrong."

Unwilling to see the Northwest triumph with Douglas in the convention, the delegates from seven cotton States withdrew, leaving the remainder of the members to adjourn until June 18, when the party would reassemble at Baltimore. As the politicians left Charleston, Alexander H. Stephens, the sage Georgian, observed that the seceding delegates meant to rule or ruin. He added:

> Envy, hate, jealousy, spite—these made war in heaven, which made devils of angels, and the same passions will make devils of men. . . . Mark me when I repeat that in less than twelve months we shall be in the midst of a bloody war. . . . The Union will certainly be disrupted.

On May 8, Cump Sherman wrote John, "I regard the Southern wing of the Democratic party at Charleston has made a vital mistake and is as dead as the Whig party." Conservative Southerners around him, like Graham, were preparing to support the presidential ticket nominated by the remnants of the Whigs at Baltimore in May—Bell of Tennessee and Everett of Massachusetts, a ticket weak and a platform conciliatory, the party renamed the Constitutional Union party.

At seventy-two Thomas Ewing was still too dynamic to become linked to such futility. He withdrew his support from the party that had counted him among its great men, and on his advice the Whigs of Ohio waited to see what the Republicans would do at their Chicago convention. The whole South waited too, wondering who the Black Republicans would nominate. Would it be Senator Seward of New York, who had talked of the "irrepressible conflict," or Abraham Lincoln, the Illinois politician who had said, "A house divided against itself cannot stand," or Senator Chase of Ohio, that antislavery renegade from the Democracy, or would it be a less decisive man like McLean of the United States Supreme Court or Judge Bates of Missouri?

Cump urged upon John the wisdom of nominating one of the last two; such men were conservative and would give the South no excuse to secede. He begged Tom Ewing, Jr.—now chief justice in Kansas—to be moderate. But his voice, crying in the distant pine wilderness of Louisiana, was as useless as he no doubt knew it to be. John and Tom joined in the rush to Lincoln. The Salt-Boiler noted how his plan for withholding party support from Bell helped to nominate Lincoln. The knowledge that blocs of voters were ready to support the Republican nominee if he be less colored than Seward with antislavery radicalism had led to the selection of the conservative Lincoln. But to the South, as to Sherman, Lincoln seemed as much an Abolitionist as Seward, and secession was talked with new fervor.

Ewing, who knew Lincoln to be "a reasonable, moderate man," began correcting Cump's impressions. The latter informed Tom Ewing, Jr., that after Lincoln's election, which now seemed sure,

> things may move on and the South become gradually reconciled. But you may rest assured that the tone of feeling is such that Civil War and anarchy are very possible.

The Democrats, reassembling at Baltimore in June, nominated Douglas, whereupon new blocs of Southern delegates withdrew, and falling back to reunite with the bolters of the Charleston convention, nominated their own ticket, Breckinridge of Kentucky and Lane of Oregon. The campaign was under way with four tickets in the field, vilification and hysteria predominant. To Sherman the spectacle was as offensive as the hard-cider campaign of 1840. He heard Southerners repeat the lies that politicians were spreading—Sumner, Lincoln, Frémont, were all baseborn—admittedly bastards—Hannibal Hamlin, the Republican vice-presidential candidate, was a mulatto!

"I only wonder that honorable men should seek office," Cump wrote Ellen. It disgusted him to hear rival parties rant about the legislation necessary to spread or to curb slavery. He wrote:

> All the congresses on earth can't make the negro anything else than what he is. He must be subject to the white man, or he must amalgamate or be destroyed. Mexico shows the result of general equality and amalgamation, and the Indians give a fair illustration of the fate of negroes if they are released from the control of the whites. . . .

The negro is made a hobby, but I know that northern men don't care any more about the rights and humanities of the negroes than the southerners.

It was to Governor Moore and a party of legislators, one night in the gubernatorial mansion, that Sherman declared himself most fully on slavery. After the ladies had left the dinner table, Moore asked Sherman for his views, and the latter, who loved to talk and who knew his increasing powers of conversation, held his listeners close for what may well have been more than an hour. Among the many ideas which he produced was that if he were a citizen of Louisiana he would work "to bring the legal condition of the slave more near the status of human beings under all Christian and civilized governments." He would never separate families on the auction block. Domestic slaves were better treated than any slaves on earth, but field hands were not so fortunate. He would repeal the statute that forbade any owner to teach a slave to read and write. Education would increase a slave's value. "By God, he's right," exclaimed a legislator, banging his fist among the wine glasses.

Sherman was angry with the North for denying slave-owners the right to take their blackamoors into the Territories, and angry with the South for making an issue of the point. Once, when away from the seminary, he wrote a letter that Boyd expurgated in two places before preserving it:

If any calamity should befall our country in this question, the future historian would have the pleasant task of chronicling the downfall of the Great Republic because one class of ——— would not permit theoretically another class of ——— to go where neither party had the most remote intention to go, for I take it no sensible man, except an army officer who could not help himself, ever went to Utah, New Mexico or Arizona or even proposes to do so. . . .

As he wrote this, the census of the nation was being taken and would show that although the Territorial legislature of New Mexico had thrown open that land to slavery ten years before, no slave was within its borders in 1860—and only twenty-nine could be found in Utah.

Sherman pointed out that Kansas and Nebraska of their own free will had excluded slavery. Why, he asked, was there so much commotion over a phantom issue? He told Boyd:

If we go to war for a mere theory, we deserve a monarch and that would be the final result, for you know perfectly well the South is no more a unit on that question than the North—Kentucky and Carolina having no sympathy.

Kentucky and other border States were, as Sherman saw, finding themselves at odds on the proposed restoration of the slave trade. If

Africans were imported, there would be a price decline in the slaves that the Border States bred and sold to the cotton plantations of the Gulf States.

When he heard Southerners talk of their new nation that might be formed with the Ohio River as its upper boundary, he grew impatient. It was idle, he said, to think that a Southern nation could survive. It would be based on slavery, the one institution that was certain to wreck it. Even if the North declined to fight for the preservation of the Union, the internal problem of slavery he thought certain to dissolve the proposed Southern republic. He pointed out to secessionists that their hoped-for nation would hold two geographic sections—the cotton States of the "deep South" and the tobacco and corn States of the border. In the former, slaves cultivated crops profitably, in the latter, very dubiously. Virginia, Tennessee, Kentucky, Missouri, Delaware, Maryland, and the hill sections of North Carolina, where slavery was less popular than in the Gulf States, would soon become the North of the new republic and the issue would be repeated on a smaller scale until "the same confusion and discord will arise, and a new dissolution till each State and maybe county will claim separate independence." He asked his neighbors, "If Louisiana joins this unhallowed movement to dismember our government, how long will it be till her parishes and people insult and deride her?"

He believed that geography had shaped the destiny of the United States, and that subdivisions would bring economic ruin upon the subdividers. His imagination speculated on the possibility of the North's allowing the South to set up its own government. This would be infamous, yet not necessarily fatal to the North and the Northwest provided they retained one thing—the Mississippi River. With that outlet secure, the United States could have "a strong compact Republic" by making its southern boundary the lower edge of Pennsylvania and Maryland and the Ohio River; it would hold the Mississippi, New Orleans, and the West to the Rocky Mountains. "Let California, Oregon and New Mexico slide into their original obscurity," he wrote John. But even this republic must fall if Louisiana, Mississippi, and Arkansas should secede. "Then," he said, "there must be war, fighting that will continue till one or the other party is subdued."

When school vacation time had come, he remained in Louisiana until July 31 arguing with his friends that

> even if Lincoln be elected he will not dare to do anything hostile to any section. Political majority has passed to the North and they are determined to have it. Let us hope they will not abuse it.

His friends, influential men of Louisiana, assured him that secession was highly problematical and that even if it came there would be no war. With this in mind he left for Lancaster to spend a few days with his family, then to travel to Washington to secure school supplies for the autumn term. Among these were muskets and ammunition for the cadets. In the office of Floyd, Secretary of War, he met Don Carlos Buell, who was still handling War Department business, as he was when he had directed Sherman to apply for the seminary post. Sherman said afterward:

> Major Buell took me into Floyd's room. I explained my business and I was agreeably surprised to meet with such easy success. Although the State of Louisiana had already drawn her full quota of arms, Floyd promptly promised to order my requisition to be filled.

If Sherman had any suspicion that Floyd was plotting to arm the South for rebellion—as was later charged by the North—he kept it to himself. His own position was that of a salaried and trusted servant of Louisiana who must fill his obligations.

When news of his success at the War Department reached Louisiana, the *Alexandria Constitutionalist* exulted, "That looks like getting the sons of Louisiana ready for any emergency of Civil War or servile insurrection that may arise." Braxton Bragg was working at the same time to have the War Department give the seminary the battery which he had commanded so famously during the Mexican War. Every schoolboy had thrilled to the printed tale of how he had decimated the enemy at General Zachary Taylor's command, "Give them a little more grape, Captain Bragg!"

Thomas Ewing, as a confidant of President Taylor, had received from the latter a somewhat different description of the incident:

> At the battle of Buena Vista Bragg was in full run with his battery and about to throw his guns into a ravine and follow them himself when he, Taylor, rode up to him, stopped him and ordered him instantly to put his guns in battery. Bragg remonstrated, saying they would all be captured but Taylor compelled him, and thus saved the day.

The seminary board, as if to assure conservative people that it was in no conspiracy to make war upon the Federal Government, voted, in Sherman's absence, to lessen the military features of the curriculum. Hereafter disciplinary measures were to be in the hands of a faculty committee—nonmilitary men—instead of in those of the superintendent. Parents had complained about the strictness of Sherman's régime. At news of this, Sherman resolved to find other work. He had feared that secession would sooner or later drive him from the State; now he had been offended by the board on administrative matters. He tried to get a position with an Ohio railroad, and when he failed he wrote John:

> . . . if Lincoln should be elected and you get a high seat in the synagogue, you must try and get me back where I rightfully belong into the army, the Inspector-General's department if a vacancy occurs.

The more he thought about the situation, the more often he wrote Boyd such sentiments as this: "Whoever is elected, forthwith will begin the war of secession." He thought of the coming storm—he felt temblors under his feet even while hunting hickory nuts in the autumn woods with his small sons, or while taking long buggy rides over the rolling Fairfield roads with Thomas Ewing, whom he observed to be "as active as he was forty years ago." One Sunday in late September he wrote Boyd:

> You can readily understand that I am sick of this war of prejudice. Here the prejudice is that the planters have nothing else to do but hang abolitionists and hold lynch courts. There, that all the people of Ohio are engaged in stealing and running off negroes. . . .
>
> The boys are back from church now and it requires more nerve to write in the midst of their noises than if a regimental band were in full career.

The sight of magnificent crops in the Northwest—the heaviest Thomas Ewing had ever observed—stirred Sherman's poetic imagination. He wrote Graham on August 12:

> May it not be providential? May it not be one of the facts stronger than blind prejudice to show the mutual dependence of one part of our magnificent country on the other. The Almighty in his wisdom has visited a vast district with drought but has showered abundance on another and he has made a natural avenue between.

He returned to Louisiana without his family. The house the seminary was building for him was under way, but the threat of war was near enough to make him doubt if Ellen and the children would ever see it. He was surer of his wisdom when, upon arriving in the South, he found disunion closer than ever. To his Northern friends he reported that Louisiana would not secede unless South Carolina started the rush, but that when such a thing happened, "the other Southern States will follow and soon general anarchy will prevail."

The more he thought of the national crisis, the less he blamed slavery; he wrote Graham that the cause lay in "a tendency to anarchy everywhere. I have seen it all over America and our only hope is Uncle Sam. Weak as that government is, it is the only approach to one." Vigilantes in California, border ruffians and Jayhawkers in Kansas, underground railways in Ohio! He told Graham that he would do his share by teaching boys good discipline:

> The law is or should be our king; we should obey it, not because it meets our approval but because it is the law and because obedience in some shape is necessary to every system of civilized government. For years this tendency to anarchy had gone on till now every state and county and town through the instrumentalities of juries, either regular or lynch, makes and enforces the local prejudices as the law of the land. This is the real trouble, it is not slavery, it is the democratic spirit which substitutes mere opinions for law.

When rumors came that citizens of Louisiana were secretly organizing in Vigilante committees to suppress what were whispered to be insurrections by the Negroes, Sherman planned to lead his armed cadets forth to suppress any and all illegal bodies. Whether he could force such work from his pupils was not the question. His own duty was to try it. The cadets in class spouted States' rights propaganda. They rioted over bad food and were quelled only with boldness. The whole nation seemed to Sherman to be careening into the abyss.

Then, on November 5, the day before the crucial presidential election, General Graham wrote the superintendent "that in case any others of the professors vote in the election tomorrow, you should also, lest cavillers say that you did not because there was no ticket here that suited you." It was fatherly advice from a disinterested friend, but Sherman leaped to the conclusion that the Supervisors were forcing him to vote for their candidate, Bell. This candidate was his own favorite, but to be *ordered* to vote for him was an insult. Sherman had never voted and would not now do so. He wrote Ellen: "If I am to hold my place by a political tenure, I prefer again to turn vagabond."

After the thunderclap of Lincoln's election, the South felt a wave of sobering moderation, with conservative men urging South Carolina to go slow with its plans for secession. But Sherman, knowing Charlestonians so well, saw that they must secede or "become the laughing-stock of the world, and that is what they dread . . . pride will drive her to secession." He told John that South Carolina would depart, the cotton States would follow her, then she would "drop far astern and the battles will be fought on the Mississippi River."

Through November and December swelled the howls for disunion and the prophecies of peril that the Black Republican President would soon bring to slave property. Men went mad over slavery. Cump wrote Ellen:

> I am sick of this everlasting subject. . . . I say "Damn the niggers!" I wish they were anywhere or could be kept at work.

On November 23 he wrote Ellen that if secession came

> I might have to go to California or some foreign country where I could earn the means of living for you and myself. I see no chance in Ohio for me. A man is never a prophet in his own land and it does seem that nature for some wise purpose, maybe to settle the wild lands, does ordain that man shall migrate, clear out from the place of his birth.

South Carolina called delegates to discuss secession. And while the citizens prepared for the fateful meeting on December 17, a vast flurry of conciliation swept the North. President Buchanan, General Scott, and Horace Greeley, the latter the highly influential editor of the *New York Tribune,* represented much Northern opinion when they agreed that while no State had any right to secede, the Federal Government had no authority to coerce a seceding State back into the Union. Conciliators proposed that Northern States repeal their local laws that interfered with the enforcement of the Fugitive Slave Law. Senator Jefferson Davis of Mississippi answered that it was too late for such concessions. Other peacemakers proposed that the nation go back to the old Missouri Compromise and extend to the Pacific the dividing line between slave States and free States. But in the confusion Lincoln, the President-elect, spoke from his Springfield home, where he sat waiting for the fourth of March and inauguration. He said that the people on election day had voted against any further extension of slavery. Votes for Lincoln and votes for Douglas too had been so cast. The tide of sentiment turned as he declared:

> Entertain no proposition for a compromise. . . . The instant you do, they have us under again, all our labor is lost. . . . The tug has to come and better now than later.

He prophesied that if the Missouri Compromise were restored, "then filibustering and extending slavery recommence. On that point hold firm as steel." Behind Lincoln, Northern opinion was slowly massing. It would waver, wander, ebb and flow, but in the end it would indeed hold firm as steel.

In the White House, as December passed, President Buchanan quaked and shifted. The United States Army forts in Charleston harbor, Moultrie and Sumter, needed supplies. But if they were provisioned, South Carolina would regard the act as "coercion" of a sovereign State. Buchanan sent Buell to Major Robert Anderson, the commandant of the forts, with verbal orders not to provoke the citizens. Cump Sherman wrote his brother, "Buchanan's refusal to reënforce Anderson was pusillanimous."

"Coercion" held no terrors for Sherman. His concept of government was that the Federal authorities had full power to prevent "absurd secession" and to reënforce its own forts without any intimidation from any State. Furthermore, he thought that the prompt and vigorous dispatch of supplies to Moultrie would make South Carolina pause in her headlong rush into secession. Indeed, the timid policy of the Administration did give South Carolinians confidence that their departure from the Union would not be opposed. All over the North Union men were groaning, "Oh, for one hour of Andy Jackson!"—the Jackson whose fearless stand in 1832 had aborted South Carolina's attempt at nullification of Federal power. But even with the Federal power shrunk to mere pretense, Sherman thought it better than State governments which were likely to disintegrate "at the call of any mob." To John he wrote on December 18:

> Though necessity presses me almost to extremity still I cannot bear the idea of being opposed to Uncle Sam. . . . The right of Secession is absurd, but the right of revolution always exists, but in my judgment there is not a shadow of justification. The United States seems melting away like a snowball in the sun. I feel needy, my family requires money and that a good deal, as much as I can possibly earn, but I fear I must cast myself loose again with nothing, as I look on Secession as a mere question of time. If possible get me something to do.

Right and left, now, Sherman scattered declarations of his faith:

> If Louisiana assumes a position of hostility toward the government, then this Seminary becomes an arsenal and a fort, and I quit. . . . I will do no act, breathe no word, think no thought hostile to the government of the United States. . . . You may assert that in no event will I forego my allegiance as long as a single state is true to the old Constitution.

Louisiana was to assemble delegates on January 8 to consider the crisis. All other Southern States but Texas had taken similar steps. Buchanan's Cabinet was breaking up. The evil day was close at hand.

"I wouldn't stay here if I could find employment elsewhere," Cump wrote John, and although his brother urged him to resign, there was no job to which the needy superintendent might turn.

It was painful for Sherman to look out of his office windows and see the new home rising on the campus. His family would never gather in it, he felt sure. On December 15 he wrote a description of it—a beautiful house "and all done but painting." He tried to explain matters to his daughter:

I know you would all like the house so much, but, dear little Minnie, man proposes and God disposes—what I have been planning so long and patiently and thought we were on the point of realizing, the dream and hope of my life, that we would all be together once more in a home of our own with peace and quiet and plenty around us. All, I fear, is about to vanish and again I fear I must be a wanderer, leaving you all to grow up at Lancaster without your Papa.

Men are blind and crazy, they think all the people of Ohio are trying to steal their slaves and incite them to rise up and kill their masters; I know this is a delusion—but when people believe a delusion they believe it harder than a real fact and these people in the South are going, for this delusion, to break up the government under which we live. You cannot understand this, but Mama will explain it to you. Our governor here has gone so far that he cannot change and in a month maybe you will be living under one government and I another. . . .

If this were only a plain college I could stay with propriety but it is an arsenal with guns and powder and balls and were I to stay here, I might have to fight for Louisiana and against Ohio. That would hardly do; you would not like it I know and yet I have been asked to do it. But I hope this will yet pass away and that our house and garden will yet see us all united here in Louisiana.

Your loving Papa.

Supervisors and legislators told Sherman many things—some, that Louisiana would not secede at all; others, that it would not secede for months; still others, that if it did there would be no war and that he could continue at the seminary without being asked to renounce his United States citizenship. Such promises were floating through his mind when December 24 arrived. He sat in his private room. The halls were empty of cadets, who had gone home for the holidays. Christmas Eve would be lonely so far from his own children. With him was his admiring Boyd. A man arrived with the mail, the newspapers days late, so slow was transportation into the pine woods.

Sherman opened a paper. South Carolina had seceded! It had left the Union by vote of its convention at Charleston on the twentieth. The expected calamity arrived, after all, as an incredible surprise.

Sherman began pacing the floor, tears falling, his tongue flinging despair—a tragic man walking up and down in his sadness, walking and walking until it became a sort of march that he was doing on the Louisiana floor, a march that might have been an omen, had the Virginian Boyd been able to read the future. Now and then Sherman stopped and addressed Boyd as if that mild professor of ancient languages were indeed the whole Southern people. Boyd always remembered that the superintendent talked as if broken-hearted.

> You, you the people of the South, believe there can be such a thing as peaceable secession. You don't know what you are doing. I know there can be no such thing. . . . If you will have it, the North must fight you for its own preservation. Yes, South Carolina has by this act precipitated war. . . . This country will be drenched in blood. God only knows how it will end. Perhaps the liberties of the whole country, of every section and every man will be destroyed, and yet you know that within the Union no man's liberty or property in all the South is endangered. . . .
>
> Oh, it is all folly, madness, a crime against civilization.

Boyd heard him say that if war came it would make him fight "against your people, whom I love best." He had more personal friends in South Carolina than in Ohio, he declared, weeping. Then he gave what Boyd would remember as a remarkable piece of detailed prophecy:

> You people speak so lightly of war. You don't know what you are talking about. War is a terrible thing. I know you are a brave, fighting people, but for every day of actual fighting, there are months of marching, exposure and suffering. More men die in war from sickness than are killed in battle. At best war is a frightful loss of life and property, and worse still is the demoralization of the people. . . .
>
> You mistake, too, the people of the North. They are a peaceable people, but an earnest people and will fight too, and they are not going to let this country be destroyed without a mighty effort to save it.
>
> Besides, where are your men and appliances of war to contend against them? The Northern people not only greatly outnumber the whites at the South, but they are a mechanical people with manufactures of every kind; while you are only agriculturists—a sparse population covering a large extent of territory, and in all history no nation of mere agriculturists ever made successful war against a nation of mechanics. . . .
>
> The North can make a steam-engine, locomotive or railway car; hardly a yard of cloth or a pair of shoes can you make. You are rushing into war with one of the most powerful, ingeniously mechanical and determined people on earth—right at your doors. You are bound to fail. Only in your spirit and determination are you prepared for war. In all else you are totally unprepared, with a bad cause to start with.
>
> At first you will make headway, but as your limited resources begin to fail, and shut out from the markets of Europe by blockade as you will be, your cause will begin to wane . . . if your people would but stop and think, they must see that in the end you will surely fail. . . .

Tears were bright on Sherman's red beard. It was Christmas Eve—the Union was falling . . . the Union of his foster father, of his father, and of four generations of judges behind that father . . . the Union of West Point. Another job—the fourth in four years—was crumbling under his feet.

He had been the Jonah of banking, now he was the Jonah of schoolteaching—he was the Jonah of everything.

15

EACH TO OUR OWN SHIP

AS the Christmas holidays danced across Louisiana, there flitted about the State one dark face that caught not even a fleeting reflection of the seasonal mirth. It might have been the face of John Calvin, so plainly did the scrawl of its scowling eyebrows write the word Duty on its forehead. It was the face of Braxton Bragg, a man whose high, clear-cut ideals of honor and pride had always fenced him off from easy friendship with other men, and whose fierce excitement made him now more unapproachable than ever. Bragg it was whom Governor Moore and the State Military Board had named to organize the commonwealth against the danger of war, and when his State commanded Bragg obeyed.

Few, however, as Bragg's friends might be and austere as his tense soul might become in this iron crisis, there was one man with whom he could be human—Sherman. And in the days after Christmas, the grim Mars relaxed long enough to write his friend a farewell letter. It was painful, he said, to realize that Sherman was going North; still, it was not surprising, and under the circumstances quite natural:

> You are acting on a conviction of duty to yourself and to your family and friends. A similar duty on my part may throw us into an apparent hostile attitude, but it is too terrible to contemplate and I will not discuss it.
>
> You see the course of events—South Carolina is gone, nothing can recall her. The Union is already dissolved. . . . The only question is; can we reconstruct any government without bloodshed? I do not think we can—a few old political hacks and barroom bullies are leading public opinion. . . . They can easily pull down a government, but when another is to be built who will confide in them? Yet no one seems to reflect that anything more is necessary than to secede.

Twenty-seven years later Sherman said: "I think I knew Bragg as well as any living man. His heart was never in the rebel cause." But Bragg was stern in whatever duty he undertook, and bravely faced the unpleasant task of informing Sherman that sooner or later quantities of the State's new muskets must be sent to the seminary arsenal for storage. This would place his friend in a delicate position, since to Sherman the purpose of the mobilization would seem treasonable, yet Bragg could not evade the situation. All he could do was to assure Sherman that the board would either hire a man to care for the arms or issue special orders to Sherman to receive them—an official move that would make the superintendent's action plainly that of a servant of the State and not that of a conspirator against the Federal Government. Bragg concluded:

> I shall continue to hope, though without reason, that Providence will yet avert the great evil. But should the worst come we shall still be personal friends.

At almost the same time that Bragg was writing to Sherman, the Virginian Colonel Robert E. Lee was writing to his son from a Texas fort, "Secession is nothing but revolution." The Constitution, thought Lee, had established a "perpetual Union" that might only be broken by revolution or by the consent of all the nation's people in convention assembled.

Another Southerner, Major Robert Anderson, was likewise declaring his position in Charleston Harbor. On the day that Bragg mailed his letter to Sherman, Anderson was dismantling Fort Moultrie and retreating to Fort Sumter, where he could resist better those South Carolina riflemen who were gathering near by in the sand hills. To him came Charlestonians saying that President Buchanan had promised them that no such moves would be made while negotiations between the State and the Federal Government were continuing in Washington. Anderson replied that he knew of no such agreement and that although his sympathies were entirely with the South, his sense of duty to his trust had made him retire to a fort in which he could defend, if necessary, Federal property. Three days later South Carolinians seized the United States arsenal and customhouse in Charleston and flew the Palmetto flag over all government property with the exception of the post office. The secessionists still wanted to be sure of receiving their mail.

For Buchanan to have permitted the South Carolinians to believe that he would neither enforce the Federal revenue laws nor hold public property was "utterly wrong" in Sherman's eyes. He told Ellen that he hoped Major Anderson would resist so that the people could be taught a lesson in obedience to authority:

> Our country has become so democratic that the mere popular opinion of any town or village rises above the law. Men have ceased to look to constitutions and law books for their guide, but have studied popular opinion in

bar rooms and village newspapers, and that was and is law. The old women and grannies of New England, reasoning from abstract principles, must defy the Constitution of the country. The people of the South, not relying on the Federal Government, must allow their people to favor filibustering expeditions against the solemn treaties of the land, and everywhere from California to Maine any man could do murder, robbery or arson if the people's prejudices lay in that direction.

As Sherman beheld Buchanan motionless while Alabama and Mississippi seized Federal forts he wrote Ellen, on January 8, that even if war came he would not serve under so spineless a government: "It merits dissolution." He told her that he felt no inclination to take part in the civil warfare which was imminent. "When the time comes for reorganization, then will come the time."

As he wrote, Louisiana's delegates were preparing to assemble on the 10th, many observers noting that the pro-Union element was in the majority. Sherman had no hope of their victory, for the political leaders had obviously willed otherwise. On the eve of the convention's first meeting, Louisiana's Senators, Judah P. Benjamin and John Slidell, telegraphed Governor Moore from Washington the sensational news that Federal gunboats were secretly bringing supplies to the forts at the Mississippi's mouth. In the resulting stampede Moore sent Bragg and 500 militiamen through the night of January 9 to seize Federal property. The Baton Rouge Arsenal was taken early on the morning of the 10th and the forts next day.

When the news reached the seminary, Sherman spurred to Alexandria to hand his resignation to Dr. Smith, who had now succeeded Graham in authority. Sherman's agreement had been to serve until Louisiana seceded, but here it was making war before it seceded. He bluntly told Smith that Bragg's action was "an act of war and a breach of common decency." Smith, talking rapidly to prevent Sherman's departure, asked him to hold his resignation until Governor Moore had disclosed the reasons for his action. Smith guessed that the governor had some reason not known to the public. Furthermore, he argued that Sherman could not abandon the seminary's money and management so quickly. If he would wait a few days, Smith would promise that he would be "in no wise compromised in any act of hostility to the general government." Reluctantly Sherman agreed, telling Graham in explanation:

If I had in view any occupation by which I could maintain my family I would not stay, but as I have no such employment in view, and as I cannot receive the compensation fixed by law for me as superintendent of the central arsenal and as I have laid by little or nothing, I have consented to wait awhile to allow the legislature to appropriate the five hundred dollars due for last year and for a little salary to accumulate to give me the means of retiring to Ohio and cast around for some means of support. . . . I feel no wish to take part in the civil strife that seems inevitable. I would prefer to hide myself, but necessity may force me to another course. Here in Louisiana you must sustain a large army and its commander will soon dispose of your governor and legislature and will keep them to the simple task of providing ways and means. Then Governor Moore will maybe see that it is not so simple a game to play. Our friend Bragg seems to be alert and most likely will be your king. You could not have a better. . . . Men have ceased to reason and war seems to be courted by those who understand not its cost and demoralizing results. Civilians are far more willing to start a war than military men, and so it appears now.

For eight days after Bragg's seizure of the arsenal, Sherman sat watching the wild horses of secession careen faster and faster toward the abyss. Mississippi, Florida, then Alabama, voted to break the old ties. Georgia was certain to follow when her convention met on January 19. Louisiana would now be sure to go when it voted on the twenty-fifth or twenty-sixth.

This insured war eventually if not immediately, for in Sherman's view there could be no peace between two confederacies one of which owned the source and the other the mouth of the Mississippi River. The laws of trade and commerce would force the two nations into war. How could it be otherwise with the agricultural South insisting upon free trade and the industrial North holding to its protective tariff? Importers at New Orleans, having no duty to pay, could send their commodities by boat to the upper border and undersell the Eastern merchants who shipped their merchandise by rail. To enforce custom duties along the whole length of the Ohio River would be a terrific task. Instead, the Northern confederacy would blockade the Southern ports. Would Europe permit that? No; there was no rhyme nor reason in Southern dreams of a peaceful future.

While Sherman waited dismally for Louisiana to secede, there came word from Thomas Ewing that if his boy would come home he could have charge of those saltworks in Chauncey—the post that since 1844 had threatened Sherman like some horrible Siberia to which his own failures must sooner or later condemn him. Fighting against this fate, Cump wrote to John on January 16 begging for help:

If I leave here I cannot come down to first principles, for however willing Ellen may be in theory, yet in particular she must have an array of servants, and other comforts that money alone can give.

Could John secure for him a place in the United States Treasury branch at St. Louis? In four years he could establish himself there . . . "otherwise I am doomed to the salt mills."

But suddenly Sherman's mind was made up to brave even Chauncey. News came that Governor Moore was sending to the seminary arsenal part of the United States arms that Bragg had seized at Baton Rouge. Before they could arrive Sherman felt he must be free. What was five hundred dollars to the mortification of receipting, as a Louisiana official, for property stolen from his own old United States Army? So on January 18 he wrote his resignation to the governor:

SIR:

As I occupy a quasi-military position under the laws of the State, I deem it proper to acquaint you that I accepted such a position when Louisiana was a State in the Union and when the motto of this Seminary was inserted in marble over the main door: "By the liberality of the general government of the United States. The Union—*esto perpetua*."

Recent events foreshadow a great change and it becomes all men to choose. If Louisiana withdraw from the Federal Union, I prefer to maintain my allegiance to the constitution as long as a fragment of it survives and my longer stay here would be wrong in every sense of the word.

In that event I beg you will send or appoint some authorized agent to take charge of the arms and munitions of war belonging to the State or advise me what disposition to make of them.

And furthermore as president of the Board of Supervisors, I beg you to take immediate steps to relieve me as superintendent the moment the State determines to secede, for on no earthly account will I do any act or think any thought hostile or in defiance to the old government of the United States.

The break had come! General Graham, almost distraught, turned toward religion, writing to Sherman:

For the share which designing, selfish politicians and editors have had in exciting the passions, alarming the fears, maddening the mind of the people on both sides, may God deal with them as they deserve. They have unchained winds which they will be powerless to control. I did what I could to make the people sensible of this before election but "Crucify him! Crucify him," was the Democratic cry and now we must all go over the cataract together, of which I have told them.

His resignation mailed, Cump wrote Ellen that he disliked to lose the five hundred dollars, but that it could not be prevented: "I must leave here with a clean record."

Bragg, who wrote the letter that Governor Moore signed accepting—regretfully and most flatteringly—Sherman's resignation, felt that there would be no war. On the day after Louisiana's convention voted secession, January 26, he told Sherman that

> a convention of Southern States will meet to organize a new confederacy. It will be in operation—a de facto government—before the 4th of March. We hope this course will lead to a peaceable solution of the matters. A separation is inevitable—nothing can prevent it now. Why should there be any strife over it? Wherever you go my fervent prayers attend you for success and happiness.

Sherman saw the future differently, as he pictured it to Graham: Lincoln would be inaugurated despite all Southern threats to the contrary, the government revenues would be collected, the Union would go ahead ignoring secession, and "the consequence is inevitable—war, and ugly war too. . . . But discussion is useless. The storm is on us and we must each to our own ship." He hoped that Graham would long survive to remember the time when "we started the Seminary in a vain belief that we were serving the cause of our common country."

As he waited for the supervisors and the governor to select his successor, there came to Sherman's door one day the guns Louisiana had seized at Baton Rouge—"stolen goods," Sherman called them. As they were counted out he saw with a pang that they were "in the old familiar boxes with the 'U.S.' simply scratched off." With that incident to symbolize the wreckage that was on the nation, Sherman wrote to Ellen:

> This rapid popular change almost makes me monarchist and raises the question whether the self interest of one man is not a safer criterion than the wild opinions of ignorant men.

On the very day that Cump wrote his resignation, John Sherman got to his feet in the House of Representatives to sound one of the few unstudied and emotional notes of his cold adult life. On January 18 John Sherman was again that schoolboy who feared no master, however large.

Earlier in the day Pendleton, one of his Ohio colleagues, had asked the North to be conciliatory toward the South. John roared that it was South Carolina who should conciliate; hadn't it fired on the flag and seized Federal property? And now the city of Vicksburg in Mississippi was compelling steamboats to dock and account for themselves. This touched the unwritten law—the law that

> the Mississippi River, gathering all the rivulets of the Northwest into one current, must be permitted to float our commerce, uninterrupted and untrammeled, to the sea, or thousands of men will float down upon its waters and make it free.

John went on:

> You and I see already rising in the West, where military feeling is rife, a spirit which will not brook much longer the insults already cast upon the flag of the country . . . if you have any misapprehension about the Northern people—if you suppose that because they are cold, because they are not fired by your hot blood, they will not perform their duty everywhere, you are very much mistaken. We are the equals of each other; we are of the same blood, the same parentage, the same character; your warm sun has quickened your blood, but our cold climate has steadied our intellects and braced our energies.

John discussed the army appropriation bill, which was before the House, and announced in ringing terms that he would vote for it in the expectation that the army would recover Federal property unlawfully taken. But if the South would only delay secession a little longer, he said, it would see that the incoming Lincoln Administration meant no harm to slavery as it existed in the States. "Try it in the name of God," he begged. Cump wrote Ellen, when he read the speech in the newspapers, that John was right in taking such bold ground, and that Anderson must be supported "if it costs ten thousand lives and every habitation in Charleston."

Sherman learned that Thomas Ewing, as a delegate to the Peace Convention held at Washington February 4, had worked to hold the Border States from seceding. This he knew to be wise, but there was a military clang in the command Cump sent John: "Key West and the Tortugas should be held at once. . . . Quick!" Then in his next letter the warrior's pulse had quieted and he said:

> I feel no inclination to take part in this civil strife because I have no confidence in the military dispositions that may be attempted unless I am high enough to have a word in the council.

So long as the army was ruled by politicians and their schemes and plots, he wanted to be free.

John must still work to get him that Treasury post in St. Louis, he said, provided the appointment could be made "without indelicacy." John must not represent him "as a Republican, but as an American, one who believes that in a few short years the inhabitants of the Mississippi will command this continent." He liked St. Louis, and moreover Major Turner, who was urging him to come there to rejoin him in business—the exact nature of which was as yet undetermined—said that Missouri would never secede.

There seemed good reason for the opinion Turner had given Sherman in February, 1861. The precipitate rush of the cotton States into secession, organizing the Confederate States of America at Montgomery, and electing Jefferson Davis President and Alexander H. Stephens Vice President on February 9, had built up a strong pro-Union sentiment in the slave States of the upper tier. Conservatives were in the majority among the delegates elected to consider secession in State conventions in Virginia, North Carolina, and Arkansas, and both Kentucky and Tennessee had voted to hold no convention at all. Every one of Missouri's delegates was pro-Union and the voters had rolled up a majority of eighty thousand against secession.

Except for the awful menace of war on the horizon, the daily life of the Northern and the Southern people went ahead as if nothing had happened. The United States mails continued to serve everywhere. Business went on between the two sections. The Southern Congress, anxious to woo the Northwest, voted to keep the Mississippi River open for free navigation. Here and there the most optimistic Confederates said they believed the Northwest would secede from the Union too, and join with the South. Southern politicians pointed out the fact that the Northwest was agricultural like the South, that it had been exploited by the Eastern manufacturers under the tariff laws as had the South. Wall Street was a greater enemy of the farmer and the West than the slave States could ever be.

There were strong, sensible arguments for such an alliance in 1861, but neither strong enough nor sensible enough. The Northwest was still fully aware that it had been the first child of the Federal Government. In spite of many confusions, many tangled motives, that had come with the years, it now felt something of what a man feels for the mother whom he has not seen since boyhood, but to whose distant home he turns instinctively when trouble comes. And Sherman, for all that he had said he loved the South and disliked Ohio, in February of '61 was a son of the Northwest coming home.

Boyd saw him bid the cadets farewell. The boys wept, the superintendent wept. Sherman finally managed to say that he couldn't make the speech he had intended; he "put his hand on his heart, saying, 'You are all here,' wheeled on his heel and was gone." With his accounts balanced, he had them receipted in New Orleans, where Beauregard thanked him for having cared so well for his two sons and a nephew at the seminary. The Creole was starting for Montgomery, where, it was announced, Jefferson Davis was waiting to make him commander of all Confederate armies. Sherman heard his friend Bragg rail against Davis for this assignment; his own rank in the old United States Army entitled him to this Confederate honor.

"You know," said Mrs. Bragg, over the teacups in the hotel where she, Braxton and Sherman spent their last hours together, "my husband is not a favorite with the new President."

Sherman answered, "I didn't know Bragg knew Mr. Lincoln."

"I didn't mean *your* President, but *our* President."

The time came for Sherman to go. His accounts were endorsed as final and full, his five-hundred-dollar arsenal salary was assured of payment, his record pronounced clean. He engaged passage up the Mississippi for the twenty-fifth. But before he departed he wrote a farewell letter to Boyd. In it he was writing sadly of their friendship's break when all at once his pen began to write a sort of vagabond's hymn to his country, a song strangely like those which Walt Whitman, the Quaker democrat, would sing—the theme of two men as different as day and night except for one common feeling of superiority over local pride, State loyalty, sectional confinement: the feeling that above all they were Americans. Sherman wrote:

> There is no pleasure or satisfaction in life when one's associate is devoid of feeling, sense or judgment. With these and a few companions I have never cared much whether my abode was in Wall St., San Francisco, in the Desert, in Kansas or Ohio.
>
> But the truth is I have socially been too much isolated from my children and now that they are at an age when for good or ill we should be together, I must try and allay that feeling of change and venture that has made me a wanderer. If possible I will settle down—fast and positive. Of a summer eve with my little Minnie and Willy and the rascal Tom I can live over again my Florida life, my ventures in California, and my short sojourn in the pine woods of Louisiana and I will teach them that there are kind, good people everywhere, that a great God made all the world, that He slighted no part, that to some He assigned the rock and fir, with clear babbling brooks but cold and bitter winters, to others the grassy plain and fertile soil, to others the rich alluvium and burning sun to ripen the orange and sugar cane, but everywhere He gave the same firmament, the same gentle moon and to inhabitants the same attributes for good and evil.
>
> What a beautiful task in theory, which may all explode the first moment of its realization, but still one to dream of—and I know you will believe me sincere when I hope that, in that little group, wherever it may be, you will some day drop in and try my hospitality. I assure you I know of no gentleman whom I would more gladly receive under my roof—because I feel you would appreciate what is good in fact, good in intention, and make allowances for poverty or mismanagement. If the present politicians break up our country, let us resolve to reëstablish it. . . .

With that he was gone north up the great river.

16

A CHIP ON THE WHIRLING TIDE

"A LADY'S thimble will hold all the blood that will be shed. The Yankee traders and mudsills will never fight."

For more than a year, Sherman had listened to Southerners repeating this sneer, and as he came north through the last days of February, he began to fear that it would prove true. From train and steamboat he saw the people of Indiana, Illinois, and Ohio blandly pursuing their daily tasks, seemingly confident that their statesmen would find a compromise, as in the past, for sectional trouble.

Chafing and brooding in Lancaster, Sherman read Lincoln's inaugural address of March 4. The new President denied that he would interfere with slavery, and he asserted that the Federal Government would hold its property and collect its duties. There need be no bloodshed. This sounded like firmness, but to Sherman there was nothing but disappointment in the President's failure to reënforce Sumter. Was he going to prove as pusillanimous as Buchanan? Sherman saw the future as dark for the nation as for himself. He wrote John, "I see nothing to do, but I still cannot remain thus, and am not willing to move my family down to the salt wells where they would grow up in rudeness and without fortune." Thomas Ewing was still trying to fix Cump in the post of manager of the family investments; Cump was still resisting.

Then all at once two letters came for Cump; John called him to Washington for a conference; Major Turner inquired if he would accept a job at two thousand dollars a year as president of a horse-car street railway in St. Louis. If so, Lucas would arrange it. Quickly Sherman answered Turner that he would accept if nothing came of a visit he must pay John.

The train that carried Cump eastward took him from the world of Thomas Ewing into that of John Sherman. Thus far in his life Cump had been reacting, one way or another, to the influence of his foster father; now it would be to his brother that he looked. At last John had a seat high in the synagogue. The Speakership of the House could have been his but for a more tempting post. Senator Salmon P. Chase had resigned to become Lincoln's Secretary of the Treasury, and the Ohio legislature had chosen John to fill his shoes. The bad boy of the Sherman family was now its brightest flower, successful in politics, successful in private business. As a friend of Chase, John was expected by Cump to have no trouble in securing the St. Louis Treasury post for him. But on his arrival Cump was told that the thing was impossible. That job was under the patronage of Frank Blair, Lincoln's trusted supporter in Missouri. All John could offer was a chief clerkship in the Government Loan Office. Brusquely Cump refused it as beneath him. Evidently he did not listen, in his anger, to John's reasons; at least John was forced to explain them carefully in a letter weeks afterward. John had been told by General Scott, and by other friends of Cump at the War Department, that if Cump took the clerkship he could use it as a stepping-stone for the quick recovery of his former rank in the army. This was as good as a promise with the head of the army, departmental bureaucrats, and Administration wheel horses interested in Cump's case, but Sherman was in no mood for reason. When his dignity was touched, his head grew too hot for rationality. The pressure of repeated failure was beginning to tell upon his nerves.

Nor was his anger all personal. It outraged him to see John and the rest of the national leaders paying no heed to the treason, the pro-Confederate talk, that was heard openly on the capital's streets. He was revolted by the spectacle of job-hunters weltering in the offices, lobbies, and sidewalks of the city, armies of desperate creatures, scrambling to get their noses in the public trough. Army friends of Sherman were sneering at the Rail-splitter in the White House. The democracy that had made Sherman almost a monarchist was enthroned. Noting how patronage was dispensed, Sherman thought the Administration little above a group of village politicians in dignity.

In his brittle state of mind, Cump decided to ask the President directly for reappointment to the army. John ushered him into Lincoln's room, which was full of visitors. At one end of a table, surrounded by men, he saw the President, a lanky, dark-faced man, coarse of feature and skin but with sad eyes. When the delegation cleared away, John stepped forward, shook Lincoln's hand, and dropped into a chair. He held out papers that he asked the President to sign, appointing some of his constituents to minor offices. Lincoln took the recommendations, saying that he would be glad to comply if the jobs had not been previously promised. John turned to Cump, saying:

"Mr. President, this is my brother, who is just up from Louisiana; he may give you some information you want."

"Ah," said Lincoln, "how are they getting along down there?"

"They think they are getting along swimmingly; they are preparing for war."

"Oh, well," drawled the slow, cool President, "I guess we'll manage to keep house."

And that was all Cump could ever remember of the interview. Feeling rebuffed, he said no more. John's memory of the occasion was that Cump definitely offered his service to the army and that it was not accepted. John understood Lincoln to say that he expected to handle the situation without help from soldiers and that the Union could be preserved by peaceful compromise. What undoubtedly happened was that Cump, angered at Lincoln's casualness of manner, had lapsed into the blind confusion that he habitually felt when slighted—the legacy of a proud orphan boy. John and Lincoln could procure appointments for selfish, swinish Republicans, politicians who had helped provoke the war, yet could get nothing for a patriot who had risked vagabondage rather than desert the Union. So Cump felt as John led him away. Years later Cump would recall the scene as he and John left the White House:

> I was sadly disappointed and I broke out on John damning the politicians generally, saying, "You have got things in a hell of a fix, and you may get out of them as best you can," adding that the country was sleeping on a volcano that might burst any minute, but that I was going to St. Louis to take care of my family and would have no more of it. John begged me to be patient, but I said I would not, that I had no time to waste, that I was off for St. Louis, and off I went.

To Boyd he wrote:

> I acted with energy, went to Washington, satisfied myself that Lincoln was organizing his administration on pure party principles, concluded that it was no place for me who profess to love and venerate my country and not a pure faction. . . .
>
> On the question of secession, however, I am ultra . . . that any part of a people may carry off a part of a common territory without consent or purchase I cannot understand. . . . Had the Southern States borne patiently for four years, they could have had a radical change in 1864 that might have lasted twenty years.

At the height of his anger at Lincoln, there came to Sherman a letter from Smith offering him high command in the Confederate army which Louisiana was recruiting. Smith was confident Sherman would oppose "the mad career of the Union Splitter and his fanatical crew."

> How delighted we all should be to hear that in the coming contest we might boast of the possession of your fine talents and high military qualities.

How freely we would furnish you with the men and means to do anything possible in the line of your profession.

There was no record of any answer to Smith's letter.

With his mind stirred by fury, Sherman could not or would not observe how many of Lincoln's appointments had been given to Democrats and Whigs in an effort to make the Administration representative of Northern loyalty to the Federal Government. Nor could Sherman understand the President's difficulty in consolidating Union men of radically different party allegiances into one new group. From Lancaster Cump wrote John that if Turner failed him in St. Louis he would try to get a clerkship in a store:

All the Ewings think you have slighted me—that your mere demand would have secured me anything—that the offer of a chief clerk in the loan department was beneath my deserts, certainly a shock to my pride and in general that I have been slighted. . . .

It certainly is humiliating to me who have filled high posts with honor, credit and success to be compelled to go begging for mere manual employment, but I will not throw the blame on you for I am well assured if I had selected anything definite you would have aided me. . . .

Now if there is anything in St. Louis open to your influence I do think you should demand it for me as a means of mere livelihood till I can recover from the loss I have sustained in relinquishing my place South. . . .

Mr. Ewing is in no condition financially to help me at all and unless I get employment of some kind in four months I will be desperate. I do think the administration is committing a fatal mistake in giving the cold shoulder to all national men as compared with mere politicians. It may by so doing demoralize the army and navy so that when the time comes for action they will incline against your party.

New England has succeeded in substituting her local ideas for those of Virginia and these may be as unpalatable to the Great Center on which must depend the future of this country.

Frustrated, wretched, Sherman took up his life in St. Louis, where Major Turner and Lucas had him quickly installed as president of the street railway. His salary was $40 a week, to which Ellen could add some $20 a week in interest received from her investments. They had sold the St. Louis lots given her by Thomas Ewing in 1851 and had loaned the resulting $10,000. Also they had placed at interest the $5,600 received from the sale of the San Francisco house. This $15,600 was Ellen's. Cump himself had sacrificed on the altar of honor everything but forty acres in Illinois valued at only $1,000 and producing no income. Against this income of $60 a week, Cump had expenses of more than $70, even with Lucas providing a house for them at 226 Locust

Street for a nominal rent of $50 a month. Ellen's insistence that the children attend Roman Catholic parochial schools increased the outgo. Minnie and Lizzie had enrolled with the Sisters, but Willy was placed by his father in a public school—probably after a dispute with Ellen, for however content Sherman might be with the Catholic faith as a religion for his children, he would be found at various times insisting that the boys be educated in nonreligious schools.

Life for Ellen was now one of never-ending strain. From love and from necessity, she had learned to handle her husband with something of the fond devotion of an older woman for an impulsive boy. Her ideal would always be that stately, poised father of hers. Often it seemed as though she were regarding herself as the grateful daughter of a god and the wife of a mere mortal.

Sherman's mental state did not prevent him from operating the car lines with efficiency. It was child's play for him to reduce costs 20 per cent without injuring service, and the very ease with which he filled his post gave him an unfortunate amount of time to spend in introspection. He found opportunity to fill hours with the writing of letters to John, storming against politicians in general and Frank Blair in particular. Blair he called Lincoln's viceroy in Missouri; he loathed the man as the politician who had prevented his appointment to the Treasury position. When John urged him to woo this patronage-dispenser, Cump retorted: "I would starve and see my family want, rather than ask Frank Blair or any of the Blairs whom I know to be a selfish and unscrupulous set of ———." As John read this around April 1, 1861, he chilled. What if Cump blurted out such sentiments publicly? Let the Blairs hear of this and all John's plans for his brother would be dead, for the Blairs were close to Lincoln's ear, and their capacity for revenge was famous among politicians.

They were indeed like an old Scotch clan, the Blairs. Frank's brother Montgomery, Lincoln's Postmaster-General, had once said, "When we go in for a fight we go in for a funeral," and since 1830 political battlefields had been strewn with the graves of their enemies. Francis Preston Blair, Sr., father of Frank and Montgomery, as editor of the *Globe* in Washington, had been spokesman and confidant of President Jackson, political midwife for President Van Buren, and altogether one of the most sagacious intellects in the Democratic party. He had helped form the Republican party in 1856, because he held Jackson's love of the Union and hatred for the Calhounites of South Carolina. For the Union Old Man Blair, as he was called, would wreck reputations, sacrifice friends, trick opponents, and play either lofty statecraft or low politics as the emergency might demand. Although a slaveholder, he opposed slavery as a menace to the Union, and favored gradual emancipation. His cadaverous face, his frail, stooping body, had been seen hovering around the first Republican convention, whose candidate Frémont he had hand-picked. Four years later he had appeared at Chicago with Montgomery controlling Maryland delegates, Frank controlling Missouri's, and his own influence strong through all the Border State delegations. Throwing his support to Lincoln, he had become the President's intimate, just as he had been when Jackson and Van Buren had sat in the White House. With Montgomery Postmaster-General, his friend Bates Attorney-General, and Gideon Welles, his old companion in Democratic ranks, Secretary of the Navy, Old Man Blair was said to hold three Cabinet votes in his vest pocket. Moreover his son-in-law, S. P. Lee, was an admiral, and Montgomery's brother-in-law, Gustavus V. Fox, was Assistant Secretary of the Navy. In 1861, when Blair was seventy-three, Lincoln said to his private secretary John Hay that while it was possible to fool the Blair sons, the father "ain't so easy tricked."

Since 1850 the old man had been helping Frank to erect a powerful pro-Union political machine in Missouri by combining the ancient Jackson elements throughout the State with the huge German population in St. Louis. In 1856 this antislavery, anti-South Carolina party had sent Frank to Congress, and again in 1860. Shrewdly Frank had converted a political marching society, the Wide-Awakes, into Home Guards, and drilled them quietly against the day of war that the Blairs felt to be inevitable. When Missouri's delegates had assembled in February, 1861, to consider secession, Blair had put on a front so bold and savage that not a single vote was given for the dissolution of the Union.

"Frank Blair is the family's hope and pride," Lincoln noted. Some day, Montgomery and the old man expected the younger of the sons to be President. Hated, feared, loved, young Frank was no man for Sherman to have antagonized in March, 1861. Had he done so, it is not unlikely that he would have spent the next four years of his life in obscurity. And that he did not do so was in large part due to the warnings he received from John. "I think you do injustice to the Blairs," wrote John, adding that four members of the Cabinet, Blair, Cameron (Secretary of War), Chase, and Bates,

> have a high appreciation of your merits and you will find they will readily and cheerfully accord to you anything in their power in a military way. Remember, you are known as a military man, not as a civilian. It can scarcely be expected that they will look to you to occupy either a political or business position.

If it was a political job that Cump must have, John said:

> . . . remember I can get it only through the Republican party and by coöperation with its recognized leaders. . . . You and I have our futures to make. . . . I know you can at once place yourself at the head of what must be the dominant influence in Missouri unless you allow yourself to be controlled by old resentments or prejudices. . . .

At nine o'clock on the night of April 6, three days after John had written this letter, a knock came at Sherman's door. He read a telegram:

> Will you accept the chief clerkship of the War Department? We will make you assistant Secretary of War when Congress meets.
>
> MONTGOMERY BLAIR.

What had happened was that the Postmaster-General had united with his factional foe, the Secretary of the Treasury, upon Cump as the man who would be, as Chase told John, "virtually Secretary of War." Considering that the incapacities of Simon Cameron in the War Department were already apparent to his colleagues, it was obvious that they had selected Sherman as the assistant who would take control in everything but name. Within nine months Cameron would indeed be gone from the Cabinet and President Lincoln be wondering whom to name as his successor. At this time Chase would be intrusted with much responsibility as to army matters in the West, and with Bates, the Blairs, and John Sherman championing his cause, Cump might well have been made Secretary of War—and Edwin M. Stanton never called to that post. But on Monday morning, the eighth, Sherman telegraphed Montgomery Blair, "I cannot accept," and forwarded a letter of explanation:

> I have quite a large family and when I resigned my place in Louisiana on account of secession, I had no time to lose; and therefore after my hasty visit to Washington, where I saw no chance of employment, I came to St. Louis, have accepted a place in this company, have rented a house and incurred other obligations, so that I am not at liberty to change. I thank you for the compliment contained in your offer and assure you that I wish the Administration all success in its almost impossible task of governing this distracted and anarchical people.

Blair read the telegram at a Cabinet meeting, whereupon some of the Secretaries shook their heads, saying that John Sherman's brother was obviously planning to go with the Confederacy if war came.

And war was evidently coming, for on the day that Sherman refused so promising a post in the War Department, Lincoln notified the Governor of South Carolina that the Federal Government would provision

Fort Sumter. Stiffened to his decision by the Blairs, but cautioned against it by almost all of his other advisers, Lincoln had taken steps to uphold Federal dignity.

Jefferson Davis and the Confederate Cabinet stood now at the crossroads. If they allowed the Federal Government to supply its forts and collect its Federal taxes, yet maintained their own independent State governments in calm isolation, they would place Lincoln in a quandary. How then could he combat peaceable secession? Any act of aggression would put upon him the onus of having begun violence and would cost him untold support in the North. If instead the South decided to repulse the food-bearing gunboats, it assumed the blame for opening hostilities, placed the Federal Government on the defensive, and dramatized it as the defender of national property and honor. Robert Toombs, Davis's Secretary of State, saw this truth very clearly and informed his President that to shoot at the national flag meant

> suicide, murder and will lose us every friend at the North. You will wantonly strike a hornet's nest which extends from mountain to ocean, and legions now quiet will swarm out and sting us to death. It is unnecessary; it puts us in the wrong; it is fatal.

But such political sagacity was wasted; hot heads would not wait, and in the small hours of April 12 Beauregard's militiamen burst a shell over Fort Sumter. The South had fired the first shot and, handing their adversaries the moral advantage, stood condemned in the eyes of most hitherto neutral Northerners as treasonable.

That night John wrote Cump that the suspense was over, war had come, troops were to be called. Now was Cump's chance to organize a regiment and be available for the promotions that were sure to follow:

> You are a favorite in the army and have great strength in political circles . . . those who look on merely as spectators in the storm will fail to discharge the highest duty of a citizen and suffer accordingly in public estimation.

Two days later, when Major Anderson drew Fort Sumter's quivering flag down its pole and started with his men toward the North, which blazed with war fervor, John was trying to fire his red-haired brother to action:

> We are on the eve of a terrible war. Every man will have to choose his position. You fortunately have the military education, prominence and character to play a high part in the tragedy. You can't avoid taking such a part. Neutrality and indifference are impossible. . . . You can choose your own place. . . . Can't you come to Ohio and at once raise a regiment? It will

be immediately in service. The administration intends to stand or fall by the Union, the entire Union and the enforcement of the laws.

But Cump refused—refused even when he read how militiamen from the North rushed to camp at Lincoln's call for 75,000 men to serve three months—regiments marching through New York singing a new song, "John Brown's Body," while cheers broke like white seafoam over their banners. The Sixth Massachusetts Regiment was being mobbed by secession sympathizers in Baltimore; four of its men were killed. . . . Virginia, Arkansas, Tennessee, and lastly, North Carolina, followed the cotton States out of the Union. . . . Maryland, Kentucky, and Missouri were trembling with indecision.

Daily Sherman moved through scenes in which the fate of the Mississippi Valley was being determined. If Missouri seceded, it was practically certain that Kentucky would follow. Then the great river would be in Confederate hands. The Ohio River counties of Indiana and the lower tier of Illinois counties would be likely to prove disloyal, too. Cump wrote John on April 18:

All the leaders of the State are Virginia, Kentucky and Southern men, the Governor, the Lieutenant-Governor and all the leading politicians. . . . It is manifest that Missouri will not identify Lincoln with Uncle Sam.

In Sherman's eyes, the desperate attempts of Frank Blair to hold the State to the Union were little more than the attempt of an antislavery faction to rule. He told John:

He is rabid, and would not stop till the whole country is convulsed and slavery abolished everywhere. . . . As to abolishing slavery in the South or turning loose 4,000,000 slaves, I would have no hand in it.

Blair, conspiring vigorously to overcome the neutrality that Missouri's governor, Jackson, had proclaimed, was raising regiments in spite of the State's decision against such an act. One night he called Sherman to his house and asked him to head a regiment. Sherman refused, saying that he had been adrift when in Washington, had offered himself and been declined. Since then he had spent seven hundred dollars for rent, five hundred dollars for furniture and the like, and was "in no condition to volunteer for three months with only a naked chance of permanency." Cump described the meeting to John:

He wants to make use of me. In Washington I was not a citizen of St. Louis and not entitled to be thought of for any office that would support me, but now I am good enough to be consulted. . . . I have taken my course . . . I will not be drawn into such a muddle. I will not identify myself with a Republican government. . . . Volunteers and militia never were and never will be fit for invasion and when tried will be defeated and dropt by Lincoln like a hot potato. . . . I cannot and will not mix myself in this present call. The first movements of the government will fail and the leaders will be cast aside. A second or third will rise and among them I may be, but at present I will not volunteer as a soldier or anything else.

He gave John to understand that when Congress put the regular army on a sound footing and offered him a suitable place he might accept.

No charge of indifference toward Cump could be now leveled against John. He soon sent his brother stirring word, "I have substantially tendered your service as General of Volunteers." Through his influence with the Administration and with Ohio officials, John had arranged for Cump to go to Ohio, raise a regiment, become its colonel, then receive the appointment as commander of all that State's troops. John was sure that Lincoln had no notion of limiting action to the three-month volunteers. The leaders in that force would be in line for permanent command of the three-year men whom the President would soon call. "Indeed," wrote John, "I know of no man in the United States who has such a position and I pray you not to surrender it, as a few days' indecision will amount to."

Still Cump held aloof. He argued that no Ohio official had invited him:

Ohio has always ignored me. When, last fall, I sought employment on a railroad I could not get it. . . . Now she expects me to break a contract for a permanent employment in exchange for a three months' service. It may be said that war disturbs all prior engagements. But war existed when I was in Washington. The South had rebelled . . . insulted our flag in a thousand ways. I resented it with a sacrifice and that sacrifice was not appreciated, so that the present excitement changes not my attitude at all. . . .

I don't suppose I will take part in the present movement. This is spasmodic and chiefly useful to show the South that when the time comes the North is as excitable as themselves, and that Lincoln can command. I hope 500,000 men will respond although only 75,000 are to be accepted. . . .

I know this affair is not to be for a day, but will last thirty years, and as plenty of men are at the command of the President for immediate service, no consideration of patriotism appeals to me now.

Was he sulking in his tent, nursing the wound Lincoln had given him, or was he a genius foreseeing with prophet's eyes the future course of the war? It was a question that in later years those who knew Sherman best could not answer conclusively. To the wife of Tom Ewing, Jr., he spoke like a strange prophet.

"Ellie, I'm praying for war, pestilence and famine."

"Why, Captain," said the gentle Ellie, "you mustn't say that!"

"I'm praying for war so that I can get back into the army; pestilence and famine naturally follow."

There was self-pity in his words to John:

> I have already been so tost about that I need rest and repose and think if I can once feel myself able to support my expensive family, independent of Government or of any party, I will feel more confidence in my position.

With chagrin John saw Governor Dennison of Ohio look elsewhere for a general, choosing George B. McClellan, president of the eastern division of the Ohio & Mississippi Railroad, with offices in Cincinnati. Within three months' time McClellan, at the head of midland volunteers, would win easy and conspicuous victories in western Virginia and as a result would be called to Washington to lead the armies of the republic.

Cump's feet carried him daily from his horse-car offices to the United States arsenal, a few blocks away, where, as in Kansas, drums and fifes spoke a language that he understood. There he saw Blair's favorite, Captain Nathaniel Lyon, whom Sherman had known at West Point—a red-bearded, nervous visionary like himself, a man with "stormy eyes." With Blair, Lyon had organized Home Guards, armed them with fifteen thousand muskets that Blair had obtained from Lincoln, and was plotting to unseat Lyon's superior, General W. S. Harney, chief of the United States Army Department of the West. Harney had allowed Governor Jackson to assemble the State militia, a pro-Confederate organization, and had promised that Federal troops would not interfere so long as the State remained neutral.

But Blair and Lyon knew that Jackson was in secret correspondence with Jefferson Davis and that the militia was receiving cannon and ammunition in boxes marked "Marble." Many of these munitions were from Baton Rouge—the same guns whose seizure by Bragg had caused Sherman to leave Louisiana, guns that seemed to be haunting Sherman's footsteps calling for revenge.

Curious it was that on the same day, May 8, that Lyon, Sherman's intimate, learned of the arrival of these guns at Missouri, Sherman should suddenly notify the Secretary of War that he was ready at last to take part in the conflict. His action might have had no prompting from the event; on May 3 a more persuasive thing had happened—President Lincoln had called for three-year volunteers. Sherman notified Secretary Cameron that he had been prepared all along to serve his country in the capacity for which he had been trained:

> I did not and will not volunteer for three months, because I cannot throw my family on the cold support of charity, but for the three years' call made

by the President, an officer could prepare his command and do good service. I will not volunteer, because rightfully or wrongfully, I feel myself unwilling to take a mere private's place and having for many years lived in California and Louisiana, the men are not well enough acquainted with me to elect me to my appropriate place. Should my services be needed, the record of the war department will enable you to determine the station in which I can render the best service.

He was now on record as willing to fight the long fight. When Old Solitude advised him to get a colonelcy, since the war might last three years, Sherman blurted out: "Three years? It will take a hundred!"

War came quickly to St. Louis. Governor Jackson assembled the militia on the western edge of town. Captain Lyon, disguising himself in a gown, bonnet, and shawl borrowed from Frank Blair's mother-in-law, rode through the camp. His red beard was hidden beneath a veil and in his lap was an egg basket. Just old Mrs. Alexander going to market! But in the basket were no eggs, only two loaded revolvers with which Lyon would shoot his way to liberty if trouble came.

Returning undetected to Blair, Lyon reported that the militia was preparing to seize the Government arsenal. Soon the regular troops and their more numerous allies, Blair's Home Guards—7,000 men in all—had surrounded and disarmed the few hundred militia. Blair had broken the back of secession in Missouri.

Sherman was on the streets with his son Willy and his young brother-in-law Charles Ewing, a budding lawyer, when the victorious Home Guards, many of them Germans, returned from their bloodless victory. "Damn the Dutch!" came from the street crowds. A drunken man fired a pistol, wounding a guardsman; the regiments whirled. Veterans of the old Prussian army fired a volley into the crowd, killing some twenty-eight men, women, and children. Bullets cut the leaves over Sherman's head. It was the first time he had ever heard a shot fired in anger. As the crowd stampeded, Charlie Ewing fell to the ground, covering Willy from danger, Cump beside him. Then Sherman, raising his head, noted that the militiamen were loading for another volley. He snatched Willy and popping over a gully, raced the boy home.

In that same crowd that watched the fracas was the stubby man whom Sherman had seen three years before peddling cordwood on those same streets. Ulysses S. Grant now wore a rumpled blue uniform and felt more optimistic about life. A year earlier he had left his farm near the city and had crept home to his father bankrupt and hopeless. The elder Grant had sent Ulysses to take charge of his leather and hardware store at Galena, Illinois, with instructions to keep his family on eight hundred dollars a year. There the humble ex-soldier was droning time away, solacing himself upon occasion with whisky, when one day the news came that Fort Sumter had been attacked. Because he had been a soldier, Grant was made chairman of a mass meeting but, consumed by bashfulness, was unable to state clearly the purpose of the meeting. No matter. Volunteers pressed forward and a clamor arose for Grant to be their captain.

When their eyes had been on peace and profits, the people of Galena had seen Grant only as a bankrupt little tanner's clerk with whisky on his breath, but when they looked through the red film of war, the people saw him as some one to whom they could intrust their boys in the awful and thrilling presence of Death. Governor Yates of Illinois shared this same confidence in the shy little man, and when Captain Grant had seen his Galena company enrolled among Lincoln's ninety-day men, the governor sent him as mustering officer to Belleville, near St. Louis. Grant and Sherman did not meet this time on the streets of the city to remind each other that the army was not a good training school for civil life. They passed on, Grant to gather recruits, then to offer his services vainly to Washington, and at last, when ignored by the War Department, to become colonel of the Twenty-first Illinois Volunteer Infantry.

Sherman, returning to his horse cars, was offered Harney's post and declined. Blair, having discovered General Harney attempting to conciliate both forces, had hurried to Washington and persuaded the Administration to remove the departmental commander. Conciliation was precisely what Blair did not want. Yet he was no mere self-seeker, as Sherman conceived him. When the Administration had telegraphed him the request that he, himself, take Harney's position, he had answered, "I have no military training and am totally unfit for the position. Captain Lyon is in every way qualified. Are you damn fools?" Blair had decided upon Lyon when Sherman refused the appointment. Soon Lyon's red head was lying in the blue grass; he was dead in Missouri's first battle.

Having put from him three appointments at the hands of the Blairs and his brother John, Cump sat in his horse-car office. One of the appointments might have made him Secretary of War, the second, general in chief of the United States armies, the third, a corpse. At his desk Sherman wrote on May 13 his last letter to Boyd, who would soon be in a Confederate uniform:

> Already Missouri is humbled. I have witnessed it; my personal friends here, many of them Southern, admit that Missouri's fate is sealed.

Major Turner had been one of the citizens who had helped Jackson and Harney negotiate for the State's neutrality, and as such had been opposed to Blair. Sherman gave Boyd prophecies:

> I have no doubt 100,000 disciplined men will be in Louisiana by Christmas next. The Mississippi River will be a grand theater of war. . . . It is horrible to contemplate but it cannot be avoided. . . . Were it not for the physical geography of the country it might be that people would consent to divide and separate in peace. But the Mississippi is too grand an element to be divided and all its extent must of necessity be under one government.

Sherman dwelt sadly on divided friendships; he could not yet realize it all:

> I know that I individually would not do any human being a wrong, take from him a cent or molest any of his rights or property, yet I admit fully the fact that Lincoln was bound to call on the country to rally and save our constitution and government.
>
> Had I responded to his call for volunteers I know that I would now be a Major-General. But my feelings prompted me to forbear and the consequence is my family and friends are almost cold to me and they feel and say that I have failed at the critical moment of my life. It may be I am but a chip on the whirling tide of time destined to be cast on the shore as a worthless weed.
>
> But I still think in the hurly-burly of strife, order and system must be generated and grow and strengthen till our people come out again a great and purified nation.

The next day Sherman was handed a telegram from his brother Charles in Washington, "telling me to come on at once, that I had been appointed colonel of the Thirteenth Regular Infantry and I was wanted at Washington immediately." From a trunk Sherman took the saddle, the sash, and the sword that he had laid away in 1853 and which he had saved all these years in his abiding nostalgia for the life of a soldier.

17

SICKENING CONFUSION

WHEN Major Turner learned of Sherman's decision, he boarded a train for Washington. For all his Virginia birth and recent endeavors to hold Missouri neutral, Turner would stand by the Union as against the Confederacy, and he carried to President Lincoln a plea that Sherman be made at least a brigadier general. Politically, this gave Sherman the backing of the Missouri moderates as well as that of the dominant Blair régime, and with Senator John Sherman and so many Cabinet members supporting the horse-car executive, Lincoln promised Turner that his candidate should have what was asked.

It was the office of quartermaster general that Cump's friends planned to secure for him. The Virginian, Joseph E. Johnston, universally recognized as one of the army's most capable executives, had resigned that post—with tears—to join the Confederacy.

Closing his affairs in St. Louis, sending his family to Lancaster, and traveling by train toward Washington, Cump tried to persuade himself that he wanted no office so elevated. Years later he would insist that he had desired nothing above a colonelcy. But when, on arriving at Pittsburgh, he received word that the Administration had set aside both the rival nominees for Johnston's post, himself and a Georgian, Colonel Montgomery C. Meigs, and had settled upon some newspaper man, Cump wrote John, "My God, is this possible?" Even when on reaching Washington he found that Meigs had been appointed after all, he regarded the incident as proving how unmilitary and wholly political were the plans of the Administration.

Tom Ewing, Jr., who was in Washington at the time, understood that Sherman had reported to Lincoln in person, with other officers, and all had been told to ask for whatever positions they wanted. Sherman had requested and received a colonelcy in one of the ten new regiments of regulars that Congress had authorized. Leaving the White House, Sherman met his old West Point friend, Irvin McDowell, who was resplendent in the new uniform of a brigadier general.

"Hello, Sherman," said McDowell. "What did you ask for?"

"A colonelcy."

"What?" exclaimed McDowell. "You should have asked for a brigadier general's rank. You're just as fit for it as I am."

"I know it," snapped Sherman.

From General Scott's hands, Sherman received his commission in the Thirteenth Regular Infantry. The new colonel asked for permission to recruit his regiment in St. Louis, but met with refusal. Scott attached him to his own staff and put him to inspecting the recruits who were pouring into Washington. This increased Sherman's depression. He wanted to be out of the bureau-ridden capital and back among the Westerners. All around him were politicians who were loud with baseless confidence, and army officers who were morose with anticipations of defeat. As a class, officers had only disgust for the turbulent Northwestern politicians who, under Lincoln, ruled the situation. The heads of army departments and bureaus in the War Department averaged seventy-four years of age, and had no sympathy with the young, lusty West.

The field officers who had remained loyal to the Union felt inferior to the Confederates who were organizing down across the Virginia fields at Richmond. For the past twenty years, Winfield Scott, the lionized general in chief, had been favoring Southerners in army organization. A pompous, high-minded aristocrat of the most self-conscious school, he had considered Southern gentlemen as the best of all possible officers. Unconsciously, he had poisoned the minds of Northern officers with the belief that they were martially and socially inferior. This prejudice was personal, not political, with Scott, who, although born in Virginia, had left it early to join the much-traveled army, and had grown up to be a nationally minded Whig of the Websterian school, strongly opposed to the cult of State-worship. He had opposed Virginia's secession most emphatically.

Not until 1861 did the North, which revered Scott's generalship in the wars with England in 1812 and with Mexico, perceive how pro-Southern his administration of the army had been. Then it was realized how many young Northern officers had resigned their commissions during the past twenty years to seek brighter futures in civil life: McClellan, Halleck, Hooker, Burnside, Sherman, Slocum, Rosecrans—Grant! Only then did it seem significant that Scott should have said two years before, when making his staff all Southern save one man, "If the Southern rascals have so much merit, how are we to deny them?"

Scott's staff was preponderantly slave-State in birth and sympathy; the war secretariat had been ruled by Jefferson Davis of Mississippi or John B. Floyd of Virginia for eight years prior to 1861; Southern politicians had controlled War Department patronage for at least the last twelve years. When four new regiments had been added to the army in 1855, eleven of sixteen field officers were Southerners, and in one of these organizations, the Second Cavalry, thirty-one of fifty commissioned men were slave-Staters. Floyd's assistants were, in the main, Southern-born. Since 1852 the United States Military Academy had been commanded by either Robert E. Lee or William J. Hardee, both Southerners, and the departure of these two men for Confederate posts in 1861 made loyal officers feel like schoolboys who were suddenly asked to match skill with their teachers.

It was dismaying to realize that the three army officers whom Scott had valued most highly had all taken high posts with the Confederacy—Joseph E. Johnston, Lee, and Albert Sidney Johnston. In attempting to make Lee chief of the Federal army, Scott had emphasized the man's ability, and there was consequent depression in the military ranks when Lee refused the appointment and followed Virginia out of the Union. Samuel Cooper, New Jersey-born, had resigned the adjutant general's office to take a similar post with the Confederate Army. Two Virginians, Lawson, head of the medical corps, and Abert, chief of the topographical bureau, followed him. Young Southerners had been actually directing the commissary and ordnance departments, which were nominally headed by Northerners aged respectively seventy-eight and seventy. Of the army's three brigadier generals, Wool, Harney, and Twiggs, only Wool was Northern-born, and he was now seventy-seven. Twiggs, commanding in Texas, had surrendered his whole force to the Confederate militia, and Harney, as Sherman had seen in Missouri, was at least gentle toward secession. All but one of the geographical divisions of the field force had been ruled by slave-State officers, and Albert Sidney Johnston, Scott's favorite among them, had abandoned Utah to go home to Texas and don a gray uniform.

As a cadet at West Point Sherman had first observed the national readiness to accept Southerners as having superior fitness to command in politics and government as well as in the army. In the quarter century that had elapsed since that time, Southerners had strengthened their hold upon the executive posts of the Government—a hold which Alexander H. Stephens had cited in his arguments against secession during the Georgia convention in November, 1860:

> We have had a majority of the Presidents . . . as well as control and management of those chosen from the North. We have had sixty years of Southern Presidents to their twenty-four. So of the Judges of the Supreme Court, we have had eighteen from the South, and but eleven from the North; although nearly four-fifths of the judicial business has arisen in the Free States, yet a majority of the Court has always been from the South. . . .
>
> In choosing the Presidents (*pro tem*) of the Senate, we have had twenty-four to their eleven. Speakers of the House, we have had twenty-three and they twelve. . . . Attorney-Generals, we have had fourteen while the North have had but five. Foreign ministers we have had eighty-six, and they but fifty-four . . . we have had the principal embassies so as to secure the world-markets for our cotton, tobacco and sugar on the best possible terms.
>
> We have had a vast majority of the higher officers of both army and navy while a larger proportion of the soldiers and sailors were drawn from the North. Equally so of Clerks, Auditors and Comptrollers filling the Executive Department, the records show for the last fifty years that of the 3,000 thus employed, we have had more than two-thirds of the same, while we have but one-third of the white population of the Republic.

Of the four ex-Presidents living at the hour of Secession, one, a Southerner, joined the dissenters, and the other three were lukewarm in their allegiance to the Federal cause. One Supreme Court judge resigned. Only three Congressmen and one Senator from the seceding States, clung to the Union.

Three hundred and eighty-seven officers resigned from the army or were dismissed for sympathy with the Confederacy. At the time this number seemed sensationally large, yet when viewed in the light of the Southern atmosphere that had surrounded the army for almost a generation, it is seen to be strikingly small—only 387 in a total of 1,108. It was not so much the number of these resignations that demoralized the army as it was the fact that they transferred to the enemy's camp the most promising officers who had been trained in actual battle. No officer of outstanding experience in combat could be found among the men who had clung to their posts. Scott, it was said, had favored Southern officers during the Mexican War and had given them the best battle training and promotions. Of the officers who now made up the Federal force the majority had seen no active campaigning except on the Western plains, where they had learned far more about whisky-drinking and poker-playing than about Indians. Military treatises had been neglected and many of the officers knew little more of warfare than did those civilians whom Lincoln was now appointing to command the volunteers. General Scott, with his seventy-five years, his three-hundred-pound body sodden with dropsy and only to be lifted from its chair by a curious arrangement of ropes and pulleys, was unable to take the field.

Surveying the military prospect, Sherman grew more and more depressed. And when he surveyed the volunteer spirit of the public, so wild, so chaotic, he was ready for despair. Tom Ewing, Jr., had come on from Kansas and was giving his support to a motley swarm of Jayhawkers from his State, a rough and ready crew who, without uniforms and armed with squirrel rifles and bowie knives, camped in a large room of the White House howling in the hope that some excited Southerner would attempt to carry out the Virginia boast that Lincoln would be ousted from his chair.

Sherman felt foolish to have joined so jumbled a crusade. He boiled inwardly at the continued talk of disloyalty on the streets of the capital. Murat Halstead, friend of the Ewings and of John, and editor of the *Cincinnati Commercial*, saw Colonel Sherman sit silently in John's room while a group of Congressmen discussed the war. But when one of the statesmen said that he had been talking to Lincoln about Kentucky, that the rebellion would soon be crushed, and that he himself had been greatly impressed by change in public sentiment around Washington, Sherman spoke sharply:

"The sentiment of the people of Washington is such that they would cut the throats of our wounded in the hospitals or on the sidewalk with table knives if our army should meet with disaster in this neighborhood." The gathering broke up.

It was with relief that Cump obtained leave from his inspection duties late in June and visited John, who was a volunteer officer without pay in the army assembling near Hagerstown, Maryland. John had stirred Ohio with speeches, raised a brigade that had been named for him, and had brought it to serve under General Robert Patterson, a retired army officer of sixty-nine, who was moving against Harpers Ferry, where the Virginia militia held the old United States arsenal. There the brothers saw Major George H. Thomas leading his men waist-deep through a river into his native Virginia. Cump knew that there had been whispers about Old Tom's loyalty. He had belonged to the Second Cavalry, which Twiggs had surrendered in Texas, a regiment from which the Confederacy had taken Robert E. Lee, Albert Sidney Johnston, William J. Hardee, Earl Van Dorn, E. Kirby Smith, John B. Hood, and Fitzhugh Lee—seven Southern generals from one Federal regiment. Thomas had been on leave in the North when the regiment had been surrendered, had met it at the New York wharf when its remnants arrived by boat, and had helped re-form it.

Not for months, perhaps years, would Thomas tell even his closest friends what it had cost him to turn his back on comrades and family. The former charged that his wife, Northern born, had swayed him. She denied this flatly and firmly, going so far as to declare that she had purposely refrained from discussing the issue with him. His Virginia friends and relatives, discovering that they could not sway him, asked him to change his name. He refused this request as calmly as the first.

Colonel Sherman gave Thomas's loyalty no question. On a tavern floor that night the two friends crawled about over a map selecting the points where the decisive battles of the war would come: Vicksburg, Nashville, Knoxville, Richmond, Chattanooga—two pairs of far-seeing eyes together on the tavern floor.

Cump and Tom talked of the stand their West Point classmates were taking. Henry Davies Wallen, Florida-born, would fight for the North, Robert P. Maclay of Pennsylvania, Bushrod R. Johnson of Ohio, William E. Steele of New York, had joined the South. Of the Class of 1840 fourteen were dead, and of the twenty-eight remaining fifteen would wear blue uniforms, eight the gray. Five of the Southern-born classmates would fight for the North, and three free-Staters would join the South.

In June, 1861, Northern orators and editors were scoring West Point as a "breeding-ground for traitors." Secretary Cameron, finding that 288 of the departing officers were graduates of the Academy, reported that without "this startling defection, the Rebellion never could have assumed formidable proportions." In view of this "extraordinary treachery," he said, there must be some "radical defect in the system of education itself." Graduates of the Academy were everywhere declared to be "bound, by more than ordinary obligations of honor" to remain loyal to the Government that had given them free education.

To inflame further the Northern masses against the Academy, came the news that of the 288 "traitors," nineteen were of Northern birth, and among them were General Cooper, Major John C. Pemberton of Pennsylvania, and Captain Josiah Gorgas, another Pennsylvanian now heading Confederate ordnance. Among the twenty-six Northern-born men who would reach the rank of brigadier general or better in the Confederate Army, twelve would be West-Pointers. Roughly one-fourth of the United States Navy's officers—259, in fact—left the service.

In that hysterical hour few words of praise were given those officers who, discounting their slave-State origin, remained at their posts. Among them were 162 graduates of West Point. Some of these were from the Border States, but many were sons of the eleven Confederate States. These eleven States were given as the birthplaces of 308 United States Army officers in the winter of 1860. Only 222 of this number resigned in 1861; 86 continued to wear blue uniforms. Eighty-one Virginia-born officers resigned, 47 would not; 18 Tennesseeans resigned, 7 refused. Eight of 32 North Carolina officers fought on the Northern side; 6 sons of South Carolina failed to join their 28 fellows who resigned.

Cool brains might have noted in July, 1861, how many more were the slave-State officers in Federal uniform than the free-State men in Confederate gray, but there were no cool voices in July, 1861. The coolest, Lincoln's, was declaring in the message to Congress on July 4:

> It is worthy of note that while in this, the Government's hour of trial, large numbers of those in the army and navy who have been favored with offices, have resigned and proved false to the hand which had pampered them, not one common soldier or common sailor is known to have deserted his flag. . . . This is the patriotic instinct of a plain people.

Lincoln's pointed comparison between enlisted men and commissioned officers seemed to the latter demagogical. Private soldiers wishing to join the South must desert and become liable to execution, while officers in resigning were immune. Furthermore, the rank and file were almost wholly Northerners and foreigners, chiefly the latter. Southerners had not cared to become privates. Officers thought Lincoln was craftily appealing to the democratic hatred of West Point in his effort to arouse the masses. It was to be a people's crusade, not a professional soldiers' war.

Cump returned to Washington with John, who had resigned his army commission and resumed his seat in the Senate. Two days after Congress convened, Cump received word that a daughter, Rachel, had been born on July 5. He now had a wife and six children to support in a nation that was apparently headed for ruin.

Day and night there beat in Sherman's ears the roar of democracy—editors, politicians, preachers, volunteers, howling "On to Richmond!" The sound was as terrible as sea storms off Cape Horn, as angry as northwest winds in Hockhocking winter nights—and almost as senseless. Exuberant boys made light of drilling in McDowell's camps, which rose on the Virginia side of the Potomac. They played games, hunted spring flowers by day and town chippies by night. At trivial noises they rushed from their tents in the darkness shouting, "The Rebels are on us!" Young officers, returning late from Washington saloons, sounded alarms just to see how the men would turn out. Between July 5 and July 16 Sherman drilled his brigade but six times. A variegated affair was his command—Wisconsin farmers in the gray uniforms of their militia organization; New York Guards, some of whom wore the antiquated regimentals of 1812 design, others of whom wore Scotch kilts. One regiment, the Sixty-ninth Zouaves, carried a great green flag that had been presented to them as reward for having refused to march in a civic parade recently given in New York for the Prince of Wales. Every man of the Sixty-ninth was Irish-born—every Irishman wore the scarlet breeches and the red fez of a Turk. They called themselves the Northern Shovelry by way of comparing their native industry with the reputed indolence of Southern chivalry.

In another brigade were their comrades the Fire Zouaves—the Eleventh New York Infantry, made up of Manhattan firemen. These boys vowed to hang Jeff Davis's scalp in the White House, they rubbed their clipped hair and mentioned that they had had their heads "filed" to serve as weapons. They announced that they were "sociable with paving stones," and from their temporary quarters in the Columbia Market Building they came to roll calls down ropes like monkeys in their baggy red trousers and short jackets. More wicked had grown their temper since the killing of their commander, Colonel E. Elmer Ellsworth, by an Alexandrian tavern-keeper. They grieved that they had not been brought South through Baltimore, where pro-Southern mobs still threatened to stone Union soldiers. "We'd have come through Baltimore like a dose of salts," they growled.

On July 16 came the order to move south against the enemy. Lincoln, reasoning that however green his militia might be, the Southern mob was equally so, decided to risk a battle, and sent 25,000 yelling Federals to attack the Confederate militiamen who, under General Beauregard, waited behind a yellow-banked creek called Bull Run.

But as high as confidence burned in the 25,000, just so low it flickered in their officers. Not one of the Federal leaders had ever handled a brigade in the manoeuvers that would now become necessary. Only one of their three division commanders, Heintzelman, had ever seen a battle. Tyler, the second of the trio, had been out of the army since 1834 and had now, in his sixtieth year, forgotten most of the little West Point had taught him. The third, David Hunter, also a West-Pointer, was a Virginian who had been merely a paymaster in the Mexican War. Of the nine men leading brigades, six had never smelled an enemy's powder and one, Schenck, had never attended the Academy nor worn a uniform —lately ambassador to Brazil, he had been appointed to a brigadier's rank by Lincoln for political purposes.

From McDowell, who had seen fighting in the Mexican War, down to the newest brigadier, the Union leaders numbered thirteen, of whom eight were still maidens as to battle. And Scott was treating McDowell like a schoolboy, a handicap indeed to so sensitive and courteous a field marshal.

Across Bull Run waited the pride of the old regular army—Beauregard, Mexican fighter and famous engineer; Longstreet, Cocke, Jones, Early, Evans, Jackson, Bee, J. E. B. Stuart, and E. Kirby Smith, all fire-chilled veterans of serious battles with Mexicans or Indians. Joe Johnston, still bearing Mexican scars, was close by at Harpers Ferry; Lee, Scott's lost ideal, was organizing troops in near-by Richmond.

Leading some 22,000 Southern soldiers were fifteen individuals, thirteen of them West-Pointers, twelve of them veterans of battles. And the superiority of the Confederate force lay in the fact that in such a battle as impended, victory would presumably go to those leaders who could exert the most authority over untrained men. Strategy would mean little in the cat fight to come. Everything would depend upon the amount of primitive action to be extracted from armed mobs.

Grimly Colonel Sherman started his brigade—three militia regiments and a battery of his old Third Artillery—down the dusty road. As he left he posted a letter to Ellen with a message to Willy that another sword had been sent him for his armory, "though truly I do not choose for him or Tommy the military profession. It is too full of blind chances to be worthy of a first rank among callings."

Sherman's first day of actual warfare brought him failure at the task of marching his men. No other officer was bettering his record; certainly none was learning as much as he. Sweeping down on a two-day march toward the town of Centerville, McDowell's divisions trod on each other's toes, jumbled their formations, and howled at each other and their officers. When thirsty, the men climbed fences and grouped around wells, cisterns, streams; when hungry, they kicked aside the haversacks that they had emptied earlier and took to knocking apples, chasing chickens, shooting pigs, and occasionally killing a cow, the men slicing off steaks as they passed. The blackberries hanging ripe on every hand lured men to break ranks while officers dashed about screaming useless threats. The Fire Zouaves, finding houses burning by the road, told their officers to go to hell and ran gleefully to extinguish the flames.

The Sixty-ninth Irishmen jeered when couriers kept arriving with orders such as "Colonel Sherman says you must keep in ranks," "Colonel Sherman says you must close up," "Colonel Sherman says you must not chase pigs and chickens." Rich brogues answered, "Tell Colonel Sherman we'll be havin' all the water, pigs, and chickens we want! Who are ye, anyway?" Catcalls and hoots followed the vanishing couriers.

Scotch Highlanders burred angrily at the same aides of Sherman. They were New York city boys, unused to walking and already weary under even the light marching outfits that Sherman had ordered. One of their captains had insisted on wearing his kilts, and his bare knees now drew regimental witticisms. Defiantly he answered the privates, "Highlanders wore kilts in India, surely the gnats and mosquitoes of Virginia won't be worse than the venomous insects of the East." A little later, with waving sword, he led a squad after a pig which ran across a field. Up and down the line regiments stopped to watch the chase, howling, "Go it, piggy!" "Catch him, Captain!" The pig went under a rail fence . . . the captain threw himself across the top rail to seize it . . . the regiments chorused, "Where's your pants?"

Dogged old sergeants who had been trained in the British army walked among the Highlanders, trying to teach the boys, at this late date, to keep step. They kept barking:

> Left!
> Left!
> Now-you-have-it,
> Damn-you, keep-it!
> Left!

The July sun parched the throats of the men, blood dampened the dust in their nostrils; many fell by the roadside, overcome with heat, and paid no heed to their officers, who bounded about waving pistols and cursing. Some of the men carried patent water-filters, porous bulbs with long rubber tubes. Marchers jeered as these fools stood over mudholes in the road sucking and sucking at the tubes until their eyeballs started from their heads. Only yellow water came for all their pains and they threw the contraptions away and strode on spitting and grimacing.

To Sherman's mind all this confusion prophesied disaster. The mischief that war loosed in the hearts of men appalled him. Here privates disobeyed orders, rambled at will, stole oats and corn for their horses, apples for themselves, even fired houses for sport. "No curse," said Sherman a few days later, "could be greater than invasion by a volunteer army." His own men seemed to him, he said, Goths or Vandals. Violence to enemy property horrified him in 1861.

On the eighteenth, as the Union force gathered at Centerville, McDowell ordered Tyler to make a feint at Manassas Junction, the Confederate railroad center and base of supplies, and so lure Beauregard to weaken his line elsewhere. "Do not bring on an engagement," warned McDowell, but the innocent Tyler became embroiled in a heavy artillery fracas at Blackburn's Ford on Bull Run and called on Sherman's brigade for support. It was Sherman's first sight of a man with battle blood on him, the first time he had heard cannon roaring at each other. Wounded men stumbled back past him as he rode up—"the sickening confusion as one approaches a fight from the rear," Sherman called it. Round shot tore spitefully through the trees; a cannon ball demolished a man with a splashing thud. For half an hour Sherman's brigade stood under fire, losing only four or five men, then the army fell back to Centerville to rest for two days while McDowell and his captains drew up the plan of the Battle of Bull Run.

Years later Sherman thought the plan excellent, but at the hour of its conception it was doomed by events beyond McDowell's knowledge. McDowell had entered upon the campaign with assurance from General Scott that Beauregard would be his sole opponent. Scott said that he would see to it that General Patterson's 9,000 militiamen, with Thomas's regulars, would keep Joe Johnston too busy at Harpers Ferry for any help to be rushed to Beauregard. But Patterson, almost seventy, could not understand the telegrams of Scott, aged seventy-five, and the two ancients quarreled by telegraph while Johnston, warned of Beauregard's danger, marched calmly away, arriving at Bull Run on the twentieth.

On the night of this date, Sherman looked at his sleeping men and wondered what they would do on the morrow. The Irishmen would fight on principle, but they hated their colonel. Sherman had forbidden them to bring more than one ambulance on the march and when one of their captains had been accidentally wounded during the trip, they had cursed because there was no spare ambulance in which to send him back to Washington. It seemed horrible to carry a wounded man on into a fight.

"Colonel Sherman exhibited the sourest malignity towards the 69th," wrote an Irish captain, Patrick Meagher. The Celts abused Sherman still more when on the evening of the twentieth he ordered them to bivouac in a low meadow, where in the heavy dew their beds seemed like a swamp. After confessing to their priests, they bedded down in the damp and lay coughing and moaning from leg cramps. Once a loose horse stumbled over a stack of muskets, lost its head, and stampeded among the little skeleton tents made by the guns, alarming the whole brigade. Drummers, stupid with sleep, beat the long roll, and 5,000 men scrambled for their arms, thinking that the jingling of the upset muskets was the sound of Confederate cavalry swords.

Moonlit peace in the heavens . . . maiden nervousness in the bivouacs . . . commanders on both sides conferring with lieutenants over tables on which candles shone. Beauregard knew he would be attacked next day, had known it indeed for three days, but he had been unable to throw up intrenchments. His soldiers regarded themselves as Southern gentlemen, chivalrous warriors, not ditch-diggers. Many of them had their Negro slaves with them—private soldiers with valets—and carpetbags and horsehair trunks in place of knapsacks.

Arriving early at the farmhouse where McDowell had ordered a council of war, Sherman wrote Ellen a letter while awaiting his superior's arrival. It might be his last letter. He tried to be humorous to hide his emotion. His chief danger, he said, was from being shot by his own awkward men . . . he would do the best he could . . . the volunteers were apt to stampede . . . his best love to all at home . . . his faith in Ellen was perfect and whatever happened on the morrow, the children were in a fair way to grow up in goodness and usefulness . . . good-by for the present.

Late that night Sherman left McDowell's table with the other brigadiers, each clear as to his coming duty. At 2:30 A.M. three divisions were to sweep far to the right and fall upon Beauregard's weak left flank. Meanwhile one division was to watch the main body of the enemy at Blackburn's Ford. At 2 A.M. the drums rolled. The moon was disappearing in the west and the men shivered in the cold winds that were blowing. Baggage wagons were as white as ghosts against the dark forests. Too nervous to cook breakfast, as the regulars did, the recruits were slow at forming in line. Tyler's division, which was to lead the way, was slowest of all. Having failed to march well by daylight, the men were now asked to march at night, and made a fiasco of the effort. The July sun came up warm, then hot. Into the blackberry patches went the men. This delay spoiled the plan of battle, for it not only brought Tyler to his position three hours behind schedule but it also so clogged the road that Hunter and Heintzelman, moving behind with their divisions, were correspondingly slow in reaching their goal, two miles further on.

In the fields north of Bull Run, Sherman and his brigade waited till noon for orders to attack. Sherman's duty was to fire a cannon now and then and threaten the enemy till Hunter and Heintzelman had crashed down upon the Confederates' left wing. Then he was to strike the retreating Southerners. By 9:30 the roar of cannon, off to his right, came to Sherman's ears. Rumors arrived. The "Rebels" were falling back!

Tardy as the attack had been, it had caught Beauregard unawares. He had gone early in the morning to his right wing at Blackburn's Ford, miles away, and had been preparing for resistance there; now he came racing to his left to meet the enemy's main blow. With him came Johnston, Jackson, Early, and Bee hurrying up their reënforcements, and as they came, the Union militiamen, flushed with success, struck them fiercely.

Sherman, listening to the uproar, fidgeted about the field where his men lay. He was wondering where to cross Bull Run when the time should come. The enemy answered his question most obligingly. Major Wheat of the Louisiana Tigers rode out of the woods close at hand and shouted dramatic disapproval of the Abolitionists. Sherman did not waste ammunition on the major, who was only showing off. Instead Sherman rode after the fellow as he disappeared. Where one horseman had forded the stream, thousands might follow. So it was that when the call came at noon, Sherman had a ford ready and was quickly over the stream, the bristle of his bayonets flashing encouragement to Hunter's men as they crowded the scattered Southerners through the woods.

18

NO MAN CAN SAVE THE COUNTRY

SHERMAN'S brigade stood in line. Among the distant trees Confederates could be seen fleeing. As Colonel Sherman rode along the front of his men, Private Todd of the Seventy-ninth Highlanders stepped out, piping, "General, give us a chance at 'em before they get away!" Todd's sergeant, a veteran of the British army, snatched the boy back, growling, "Shut up your damned head—you'll get plenty of chance before the day's over!"

At the moment, however, it did not seem so. Three brigades of Confederates had started running for Richmond, far away. Union militiamen up ahead broke ranks and hunted water, thinking the battle over. War was fun but it made a man most damnably dry. Commands mixed, organizations were lost just at the moment when McDowell sought to deliver his knock-out blow. The general, who was racing about the field in a carriage, could not keep in touch with brigade commanders in the woods. His staff organization was wretched, and besides, he had eaten tainted fruit from a tin can the night before, and now suffered from a bowel complaint that made horseback riding almost unbearable.

Before McDowell could bring order out of the chaos of victory, Beauregard had brought order out of the chaos of defeat. This was made possible by the superior authority and greater experience of the Southern brigadiers, who from Mexican days knew the tricks by which fugitives were rallied. Beauregard, with a cigar burning between his large black mustachios, had regimental flags carried forward—an excellent psychological device when men were going backward. Longstreet, roaring loudly, whacked recruits' buttocks with the flat of his sword. Joe Johnston rode among his men, calling on them to re-form. Thomas J. Jackson, his pioneer-preacher type of face set as against the Devil, held so steadily that some one—just who, was never certain—said something about either him or his men standing like a stone wall. By morning he was Stonewall Jackson to the army.

Even with the steadying of the Southern mob, McDowell might have won had he been able to throw his brigades, wave after wave, upon the flustered enemy, but with his officers as ineffective as they were, he could only send up one regiment at a time. Once he ordered two batteries, Ricketts' and Griffin's, to charge to the front line, and the battle soon centered around these guns, which stood on Henry Hill shooting canister into the rallying Confederates. The gunners, alone on the hilltop, kept looking back for infantry reënforcements.

"Here they come!" some one shouted, as a blue-clad regiment marched toward them from the woods on one flank. "No, they're Rebels!" shouted other cannoneers. The gunners paused, ready to decimate the newcomers with a blast. "No," shouted a major, "they're our supports!" and rode toward them. The blue regiment came on warily, staring ominously. Its flag, hanging limp at the staff in the lifeless heat, told nothing. Suddenly the regiment raised its muskets. "Stop!" cried Griffin, "we're Union men!"

A vast belch of smoke answered him and musket balls knocked down every man in both batteries. The regiment was the Thirty-third Virginia militia, still wearing its old-time uniforms of blue. It held Henry Hill while against it came the Fire Zouaves, who raced past the black, helpless cannon, with their piles of moaning men. When a Zouave had emptied his musket, he fell, as Colonel Ellsworth had taught him, upon his back and reloaded his gun, gripping it between his knees; then he bounced up and came on. When these strange acrobats had progressed two hundred yards beyond the battery, the Thirty-third Virginia gave them a volley and ran away. So did the Zouaves. Franklin's brigade next charged the hill, but enough Confederate fire was concentrated upon it to sweep the newcomers away. The battle now roared on a three-mile front, columns of yellow dust rising from all the roads and the bluish white smoke of burned powder hanging over the green trees.

All his life Sherman would remember this, his first battle—a wretched Negro caught between the lines . . . one of Sherman's officers, a foolhardy fellow, spurring out alone to saber retiring "Rebels" and falling dead . . . men crumpled "into every conceivable shape and mangled in a horrible way" . . . a piece of canister that scratched his knee . . . a spent ball that struck his collar . . . a bullet that hit his horse's leg—wounded horses were worse than wounded men. Sherman had prepared himself for the spectacle of slaughtered men, but he had not fortified himself against the butchery of animals. Later he admitted that it "did not make a particle of impression on" him to see dead and dying men, but that it had shaken him to see horses dashing about riderless, spraying blood from their nostrils or "lying on the ground hitched to guns, gnawing their sides in death."

Word came for Sherman to send in his regiments one by one to capture Henry Hill. First went the Second Wisconsin. In its militia uniform of gray it was badly shot up by both foe and friend. Next went the Seventy-ninth Highlanders with Colonel Cameron, brother of the War Secretary, riding ahead to die at the second volley. The Highlanders at length retreated from the plateau and sank sullenly behind the brow of the hill. Sherman turned and called to his Irish.

It was a mediaeval moment . . . long lines of men on scarlet knees in green grass . . . a strange green banner above them . . . bayonets glittering like spears above their bowed heads . . . Latin words rolling from the lips of Father O'Reilly, who commended every soul to God. The benediction done, the men put on their caps, and as they rose, Captain Meagher, standing in front, ran his eye up and down the line and then in fond challenge cried, "Come on, boys, you've got your chance at last!"

Ten little drummers fluttered their sticks. The regiment leaped forward shouting an Old World battle cry, "For Ireland and Fontenoy!" Bullets filled the air, writhing, hissing, and twisting like unseen serpents. As the Irish ran on they saw tragic and comic sights flash past—batteries whose gunners hid ludicrously behind open ammunition boxes that any spark might explode, pools of water with men drinking beside floating corpses of men and horses. The Sixty-ninth kept firing, closing gaps in the line, leaving men kicking and floundering in agony. Now and then they saw Colonel Sherman galloping among them, peering up the hill through the smoke, grinning and snarling. Over the hill they went . . . volleys stopped them . . . they swore at each other and charged again . . . fell back, charged once more, and at last dropped behind the brow of the hill leaving many scarlet-legged comrades in scarlet pools.

Their green flag was gone. Color-bearer Keefe had gone down kicking under a squad of "Rebels" and had been sent to the rear with two guards. Out of sight in the woods, he whipped from his breast a concealed pistol, shot both his guards, and wormed his way back to the Union lines, bursting from the thicket to race across the open with the green banner streaming and the Irish howling with joy.

For two hours more the battle went on, with Union regiments crowding so thickly up Henry Hill that the plateau seemed theirs at last. Then through the woods, at the Confederate flank, massed bayonets gleamed. Kirby Smith was coming up with the last of Johnston's reënforcements from Harpers Ferry. Napoleon had said, "After fighting six hours, a soldier will seize any pretext to quit if it can be done honorably, and the appearance of a reserve is almost always sufficient reason." If this was true of Napoleon's veterans, it was doubly true of McDowell's recruits, all of whom had been under fire—or, what was equally trying to a greenhorn, under the sound of cannon—since 9:30 A.M. It was then 3:30 P.M. and the Union boys began to drift from the field singly, in twos, in threes.

The handicap under which their officers had been laboring, inexperience in morale, now became apparent. Where the Southern officers had owned the training and confidence that rallied routed men, the Northern officers knew nothing of the art. They had no more control over their regiments in the retreat than they had had in the march from Washington. With the exception of some bad jams on the roads, the Yankee militia straggled away from the fight much as it had straggled into it.

Commissary wagons, driven by civilians, at the announcement of victory had driven in close to the firing-line, and when the soldiers drifted back, they whipped their horses in terror toward Washington. This started panic winging. Behind the wagons had gathered crowds of sightseers: Senators, Congressmen, lesser politicians, newspaper correspondents, departmental clerks, most of whom had brought their lunches as to a picnic. These with the exception of such hard-headed Westerners as Senator Wade of Ohio, Senator Chandler of Michigan, and Representative Washburn of Illinois, struck off for the capital at full speed. Wade and Washburn seized rifles and menaced the flying civilians and soldiers in an attempt to stop "this damned runaway," but the tide flowed around them. Representative John A. Logan of Illinois had jammed his plug hat down over his ears earlier in the day and taken pot shots at the enemy with a rifle. One of these civilians, a noted Illinois Abolitionist, had come up to Sherman during the battle and offered him field glasses.

"Who are you, sir?" asked Sherman tartly.

"My name is Lovejoy and I'm a member of Congress."

"What are you doing here? Get out of my lines, sir! Get out of my lines!"

Since the history of the battle would be written, in the main, by officers anxious to excuse themselves within reasonable limits from the responsibility for the rout, the blame for the Bull Run defeat would be placed upon the militiamen. And true it is that wagons upset, cannon broke down on the road, shameful panics developed at certain points where wreckage stalled the retreat, but the vast majority of the troops returned to Washington in better formation than the newspaper accounts of the time admitted. Not more than 13,000 of McDowell's 25,000 men had been in action, and most of these 13,000 simply walked back toward Washington, many returning to their bed grounds of the previous night. Organizations tramped toward the capital in sufficient order to repel easily all raids attempted by the Confederate cavalry. Beauregard had started to assail the retiring Yankees but his men had halted, insisting that a large Union force was advancing. This proved to be only a blue-clad brigade of Confederates coming from another part of the field, but the shock had been enough to settle all possibility of further advance.

With honors almost even as to dead and wounded, the two armed mobs had fought magnificently for novices—and had taken turns running away. The mob that fled last was the loser.

Occasionally a Confederate battery hurled shells among the disorganized Federals who milled about the field, sifting to the rear. This surprised a boy of the Seventy-first New York Volunteers; he noted an officer beside him in the walking retreat, and said, "Captain, why do the rebels keep shelling us when we're doing our best to leave them alone?" Said the captain, "They're trying to kill every mother's son of us, that's what they're trying to do!"

Many of the dispersed Federals wanted to stay and fight, but in the confusion could find no officers. Squads wandering about could be heard calling pathetically for McDowell to come and lead them back into the fray. McDowell, however, had done all that he could and had ordered retirement all along the line. Sherman put his men into a hollow square and marched them from the field, covering the general retreat. Lieutenant J. H. Cumming, a South Carolinian serving as McDowell's aide, had been sent by McDowell to order Sherman to retire, and as he came in sight he saw Sherman forming this square to meet Confederate cavalry who were coming over the hill in half-moon formation. Cumming said later:

> The square closed just before I reached it and I was left outside. There was but one thing to do, get off my horse and get in under the row of bayonets. I did this and, picking up a musket, put it against my knee, and knelt there.
>
> Sherman was on horseback in the center of the square and just as the cavalrymen swept up, he gave the word to fire. I never heard such a volley in my life. It knocked Confederates out of the saddle right and left. A few of them had such momentum that they came on anyway. One of these struck at me with his saber; it glanced off and broke my middle finger. Another one of them cut at a sixteen-year-old boy standing above me. The boy sunk his bayonet in the rider's side and as the horse swerved, the musket was torn from his hands and bobbed away, fast between the Confederate's ribs. The boy sobbed, "He took my gun!"

Slowly the hollow square left the field, falling to pieces as danger disappeared. Sherman brought off his command in fair order, "disorganized but not scared," and bivouacked it at their Centerville camp of the night before. In the night, however, they were ordered to Washington and mingled with broken regiments on crowded roads while a slow mizzling rain ushered in the dawn of what Sherman, in his old age, thought as gloomy a day as he had ever seen. Weary, glum, so dismal that he was almost wordless, he nevertheless worked with fierce nervous energy, posting guards over the Potomac, halting all traffic, and sending white-faced men to their various camps. Immediately the soldiers, seeing authority return, began to brace up. Over in Washington, the city might be in turmoil, shrieking that Beauregard would soon appear, but on the hills protecting the town Union regiments were re-forming, and would at least fight behind redoubts. There was no pursuit, for the South, like the North, had swallowed all the fighting that, for a time, it could digest. In the universal wail of chagrin and the clamor for revenge that shook the North in subsequent days, one voice was almost triumphant. It belonged to Thomas Ewing, who told listeners in Washington that his boy, Colonel Sherman, had been the last officer to leave the field, and had protected the retreat.

But in his own mind Sherman was still a Jonah. In war, as in banking, real estate, schoolteaching, he had acquitted himself well, yet had gone down in a general collapse. Expecting to be discharged with all the other leaders at the battle, he grew bitter and wild. "Nobody, no man can save the country," he wrote Ellen; newspapers dared not tell the truth, Lincoln and the rulers were thinking of political power, not of the country; democracy had failed, as he had predicted it would.

In this mood he ordered several men of the Seventy-ninth New York Highlanders from a barn where they gathered to hide from Tuesday's rain, following the battle. "Go down in the woods and build bush huts," he snapped. "I want to put my horses in here." The historian of the Seventy-ninth wrote later, "The milk of human kindness was rather deficient in him at that time."

Mutiny rose among the Irishmen, who insisted that their three months' term of service had expired. Sherman, informed by the War Department that the men were mistaken as to the date when their service had begun, ordered his battery men, better disciplined regulars, to prepare to shoot the mutineers down if they left camp. Angrily they remained, but one morning soon afterward an officer called to Sherman from a crowd, "Colonel, I'm going to New York today; what can I do for you?" After Sherman had said that he remembered signing no pass, the fellow answered, "I need no leave. My time is up and I'm going." Thrusting his hand ominously inside his coat, Sherman said that if the officer tried to leave, "I will shoot you like a dog."

The captain retired to brood. His chance for vengeance came that afternoon. Into camp rode President Lincoln and Secretary Seward in an open hack. Lincoln told Sherman, who rushed to meet them:

"We heard you had got over the big scare and we thought we would come over and see the boys." Wouldn't the colonel get into the hack and drive them to his command? Sitting beside Lincoln, Sherman abruptly asked him if he intended to speak to the men.

"I would like to," answered the President.

Sherman bluntly asked him to discourage all cheering, since "we had had enough of it before Bull Run to spoil any set of men." He asked for "no more hurrahing, no more humbug." Standing in his carriage, Lincoln talked to each regiment in turn, speaking of high duties and brighter days to come. When the men would have shouted he drawled: "Don't cheer, boys. I confess I rather like it myself, but Colonel Sherman here says it is not military and I guess we had better defer to his opinion."

At the end of each speech the President asked soldiers to appeal to him personally, as their commander in chief, if they were aggrieved. This brought from one Highlander a complaint:

"Mr. President, we don't think Colonel Sherman has treated us very well"—and the soldier proceeded to tell how they had been driven from the barn to make room for the colonel's horse.

"Well, boys," said Lincoln when the tale was done, "I have a great deal of respect for Colonel Sherman and if he turned you out of the barn I have no doubt it was for some good purpose. I presume he thought you would feel better if you went to work and tried to forget your troubles."

And after Lincoln had finished speaking to the Sixty-ninth New York, the angry captain spoke up:

"Mr. President, I have a cause for grievance. This morning I went to speak to Colonel Sherman and he threatened to shoot me." From his towering height, Lincoln looked down at the officer and repeated, "Threatened to shoot you?" Lincoln glanced at Sherman, who sat quietly on the front seat of the carriage. Then he bent his long frame angularly until his face was close to the complainant's. Loudly he whispered:

"Well, if I were you and he threatened to shoot, I wouldn't trust him, for I believe he would do it."

Near-by soldiers whooped with laughter, and as the carriage rolled down the hill, Sherman explained the incident to Lincoln, who said:

"Of course I didn't know anything about it, but I thought you knew your own business best." Both the President and the Secretary of State complimented Sherman on the order and cleanliness of his camp; the visit, they said, was "the first bright moment since the defeat."

Lincoln's observation of Sherman on this visit may well have been the deciding factor in his appointment of John Sherman's brother to a brigadier general's rank. Previously he had seen Colonel Sherman's name on a list of some five or six that had been handed him by Ohio's Congressmen and Senators as their recommendations for promotions to native sons. On August 3, Sherman was sitting with a group of officers in the lobby of the Arlington House when a lieutenant arrived with a list of newly appointed brigadier generals. "Heintzelman, Keyes, Franklin, Porter, Sherman," and so on—all veterans of Bull Run.

"By —— ——, it's all a lie," hooted Heintzelman. "Every mother's son of us will be cashiered!"

Nevertheless the promotions stood; Lincoln would blame no one for the defeat. There followed days of hectic toil for Sherman. Three of the seven regiments assigned him for training mutinied at the War Department's decision that they had volunteered for three years instead of three months, as they had understood. Sherman threw a hundred rioters into irons and manned his cannon to shoot down the rest. For three weeks he slept in his uniform. "I shall make a requisition for two nurses per soldier to nurse them in their helpless, pitiful condition," he wrote Ellen.

Of McClellan, whom Lincoln summoned from West Virginia as the man of the hour, Sherman had less hope than most men. He noted how the dapper little general, boots shining halfway up his thighs, enthroned himself in Washington instead of living with his men in their camps. Sherman wished to escape to the West. He told Ellen that the war would last so long that he could not hope to survive it. He saw poor old General Scott, still squabbling with poor old General Patterson about the escape of Joe Johnston from Harpers Ferry, gently laid on the shelf by Lincoln. Chaos and decay everywhere.

One day before Scott's departure Sherman, passing through his office, met General Robert Anderson, the hero of Fort Sumter. They talked of old days at Moultrie. They parted. Anderson was set thinking. He had a desperate mission. Sherman was the man to help him. So it was that within a day or two—on either the fourteenth or the fifteenth of August—a note from Anderson asked Sherman to meet him at Willard's Hotel. The colonel was introduced to politicians from Kentucky and Tennessee, among them a stern Senator from the latter State, Andrew Johnson, famous as the man who had defied secessionists. Johnson told Sherman what was afoot. Anderson was to lead the Union army that was to be raised and equipped in the Border States, but since his health was bad, he had asked for three young brigadiers to accompany him. Sherman he wanted most of all, then Burnside, Thomas, or Buell. Would Sherman go? Certainly.

McClellan, always regarding himself as undermanned, insisted that Sherman remain in Washington, the matter hanging fire until Lincoln discussed it with Anderson and Sherman at Willard's. First of all Anderson brought up the question of George H. Thomas, whose nomination as a brigadier general had not yet been acted upon by the President. As a late member of that Second Cavalry that had furnished so many leaders to the enemy, Thomas was naturally still under suspicion. But Sherman, mentioning talks he had had with Thomas in Maryland six weeks before, said that he *knew* him to be loyal. At this Lincoln capitulated and told Anderson he should have both his old Moultrie boys, Sherman and Thomas.

After this victory, Sherman pressed Lincoln to promise that in no event would he be asked to take any high command. He did not want responsibility so great. Surprised, Lincoln gave his promise, observing quaintly that his chief trouble was to find places for all the generals who wanted to command armies; one who shunned an army was a novelty. Fresh from this conference, Sherman met Thomas on the streets and announced:

"Tom, you're a brigadier general." Even accustomed as he was to Tom's stolidity, Cump was evidently surprised at his lack of elation. Was it possible that Thomas did not propose to stay with the Union? Could the gossip about his disloyalty be true, after all? "Where are you going?" Sherman asked.

"I'm going South," said Thomas, as imperturbable as ever.

"My God, Tom," blurted out Sherman, "you've put me in an awful position! I just made myself responsible for your loyalty!"

"Give yourself no trouble, Billy," said Thomas. "I'm going south at the head of my troops."

The blood flowed freely again in Sherman's arteries.

19

I AM TO BE SACRIFICED

FOR a few days, while he awaited the glad change to the Western front, Sherman brightened. He pored over military texts, learning for the first time the evolutions of the line—major tactics that West Point had never taught him. Meanwhile McClellan rode the streets of Washington, glittering with glory, snubbing Lincoln, and feeling already in his small bosom the prickings of Napoleonic pride.

But the mercury of Sherman's emotions fell when, on arriving in Cincinnati on September 1, he realized that the West was weltering in a confusion equal to that of the East. Flying, at Anderson's command, to beg recruits from the governors of Indiana and Illinois, he learned that all regiments were taken as fast as organized by Frémont, the new commander of the Department of Missouri. Hurrying to ask aid of Frémont, he found that man, whom he had understood so well in California, madder than McClellan with Bonaparte's dream. Frémont had surrounded himself with a military court so pompous that Sherman could not gain access to the throne room until he had raised a loud and angry series of shouts in the antechamber. Admitting him, Frémont was lofty and unable to promise help. Sherman, departing, noted among the hangers-on notorious swindlers from California. "Where the vultures are, there is a carcass close by," he said.

It was the carcass of Frémont's political ambition that he had scented with his prophetic nose. On August 31 Frémont had suddenly committed such folly as to all but turn the hardened stomach of his sponsor, Old Man Blair. He had proclaimed freedom for the slaves of all owners who might rebel against the Government. Of all harmful acts at this juncture, this was the worst, for it turned the Federal cause into an anti-slavery crusade just when it was most necessary that Kentucky and Missouri be convinced that the war had no object but the salvation of the Union. Immediately Lincoln annulled Frémont's proclamation, and the Blairs prepared to hold another funeral. Soon Frémont's dreams were mere memories. Lincoln replaced him with Halleck, who had come from California to reënter the army.

Returning to Louisville, Sherman tried to understand the complexities that were dividing families across Kentucky. The State, having voted at the August elections against secession, had seated two pro-Union legislators for every pro-Southerner, yet Governor Beriah Magoffin was conspiring with Confederates. Many motives, some patriotic, some social, some selfish, were entangled. The majority of citizens, schooled in the Henry Clay tradition of compromise, hoped to remain neutral and see Kentucky act as mediator in this as in former crises. Many slave-owners felt for the Confederacy the kinship of blood, class, and common property interests; others realized that if Kentucky seceded, Lincoln might make the fight a clean-cut issue between slave and free States. Then they would lose the slaves when the Federals overran the State.

Frank Blair's triumph in Missouri was a powerful argument against secession, and his methods had been adopted by the Union leader in the Kentucky legislature, the portly, piratically mustached Lovell H. Rousseau, who loved Bourbon whisky, blunt speech, and the Constitution. Rousseau, respecting his State's neutrality, was collecting recruits at Jerfersonville, Indiana, across the Ohio River from Louisville. Another Kentuckian, Lieutenant William Nelson, was enlisting Federals more openly at Camp Dick Robinson, in the blue-grass region. The Confederates were receiving volunteers at a camp barely over the line in Tennessee. Side by side on Kentucky roads went mounted men, young planters heading for the South and tall mountaineers riding toward Rousseau's Legion.

Kentucky's dream of neutrality had really ended before Sherman arrived. In a few days he learned that on September 3 a Confederate army had marched up from Tennessee and had begun fortifying the Mississippi River bluffs at Columbus. At their head rode General—lately the Episcopal Bishop—Leonidas Polk, a solemn thinker and a hearty eater. Polk eyed Paducah, where batteries might control both the Ohio and the Tennessee rivers. Before he could move, however, Union forces swept down from Cairo and seized the strategic town. Sherman learned that the man who had done this was Sam Grant—the same Ulysses S. who had taken the high hurdles at West Point. Grant had had no authority to make the move, but having made it, quickly sent a request to St. Louis headquarters asking for the necessary permission. When the sanction came, Grant calmly reported the job done. Lyon might be dead, but the West had found a man for his shoes.

The fat of Kentucky was now in the national fire. The legislature stripped Governor Magoffin of all power, and gave the State rule into the hands of five pro-Union commissioners. A second Confederate army under General Zollicoffer swept into Kentucky, through the Cumberland Gap. Rousseau, throwing off the mask of pretense, announced that he would bring his Legion from Indiana to Louisville, and when citizens begged him to desist on the ground that there would be bloodshed, he roared:

> Gentlemen, we have organized in defense of our common country and bloodshed is just the business we are drilling for. If anybody wishes to begin it when we arrive, I tell you before God, you shall have enough of it before you get through!

His advent into Kentucky was not, however, as dignified as he had planned it to be, for on the night of September 17 he was awakened in his Jeffersonville camp by Sherman, who had hurried across the river from Louisville with the news that a large Confederate army, under the awesome Albert Sidney Johnston, was invading the State and had sent an advance guard under General Simon Bolivar Buckner against Louisville. Even that minute Buckner was burning a bridge over the Rolling Fork of Salt Creek, a scant thirty miles from the city. Back in

Louisville, said Sherman, 1,800 Home Guards under the command of the fire marshal were entraining to meet Buckner. Quickly Rousseau brought his 1,200 half-trained men on the run.

Two years before, Sherman had been appealing to his friend Buckner to find employment for him, and now Buckner had joined the Confederacy, after long debates. Had he waited but a few days longer, he would have received an appointment as a brigadier general in the Federal army. Lincoln had mailed it.

At daybreak Sherman led his men from the trains to find the ruins of the bridge still smoking but no Buckner in sight. Quickly Sherman's eye caught the importance of a steep hill near by, and he sent Rousseau to hold it. It commanded the country for miles around—Muldraugh's Hill, upon which a boy named Abraham Lincoln had no doubt sat in his fifth and sixth years, looking at the wild and beautiful country below and tracing the Rolling Fork to where his father's cabin stood near at hand.

On Muldraugh's Hill Sherman inspected his men—a motlier crew than those he had commanded at Bull Run. None of the Home Guards wore regulation uniforms and Rousseau's Legion was in varying attire. One young man dressed in civilian clothes was summoned by Sherman and quizzed as a Confederate suspect. Quickly the fellow explained that he had been called out so rapidly that he had had no time to dress. Sherman excused him, but the young man muttered something to an officer as he departed and the general barked:

"What did he say?"

"Well," said the officer, "he said that a general with such a hat as you have on had no right to talk to him about a uniform."

Sherman clapped his hand to his head and held forth, to his amazement, a battered stovepipe hat. He had worn his proper uniform, but not his regulation hat. "Young man," he laughed, "you're right about the hat, but you ought to have your uniform."

Haste may have accounted for this lapse, but it is also true that Sherman was now entering upon that phase of his life when people would call him "queer." Absent-minded, Rousseau thought him as they stood at the railroad station near Muldraugh's Hill. Sherman, who was smoking incessantly, found that his cigar was no longer burning and asked a sergeant for a light. The soldier, who had just lit a fresh cigar, handed it to the general, who used it to kindle his own cheroot, then threw it into the dirt. Rousseau broke out laughing, but Sherman remained preoccupied. Three years later when Rousseau recalled the incident to him, Sherman said: "I was thinking of something else. It won't do to let tomorrow take care of itself. Your good merchant doesn't think of the ships that are in, but of those that are to come in. I was thinking of something else when I threw away that sergeant's cigar." Then he laughed and bent on Rousseau his sharp eyes with their myriad crow's-feet at their corners, and said, "Did I do that, really?"

On Muldraugh's Hill he was irritable, denouncing the Home Guards as "a paltry lot of fellows" because they objected to being sworn into the United States service for thirty days. A gruff old cock, the men called him, and when they learned that they must spend a month under him, they said, "He's a bitter pill to take." But Old Pills, Sherman's first army nickname, was changed when he took active steps to bring his men tents and blankets. Old Sugar-Coated, he became then.

There was, however, little sweetness in him in the autumn of 1861. The scarcity of recruits and their total unpreparedness for war sickened him. Some boys arrived with ancient flintlocks that government arsenals had converted into percussion-cap muskets—faulty weapons that kicked brutally when discharged. "One end guaranteed death, the other six months' sickness," said the volunteers. Some regiments came depressed and homesick, others buoyant with the intoxication of what orators had told them as they left home. Indiana towns had staged grand celebrations when the troops left, besashed marshals of the day bawling up and down the parade line, "Stand back and give the brave boys air!" Some banners bore the words "Victory or Death," and it was said canny veterans of the Mexican War had observed, "Make it 'Victory or Damned Badly Wounded,' and I'm your huckleberry!" Measles and other epidemics swept the camps, finding easy victims among farm boys who, reared in isolation, had not been exposed to contagious diseases as had city boys. Diarrhea came with strange food and water.

Learning that two men sleeping between two blankets could be warmer than one man rolled in a single blanket, the youths began to "mate up like spring geese." When officers sterilized the blankets with carbolic acid, the country boys gagged, declaring, "It smells worse than a woodpecker's nest"—the home of that bird being a repository for decaying refuse and thus a frontier byword for nausea.

On furlough in Louisville, the recruits lavished their money on hotel feather beds and in consequence caught cold when they returned to the harsh night air of their camps once more. Many youths went to Louisville without leave. Drunkenness was common, whisky in the city often retailing at twenty cents a gallon. Occasionally a homesick volunteer went back to Indiana, Ohio, or Illinois for a week. Characteristically, the enlisted men felt themselves superior to their officers, so firmly did they hold to the Western credo that a common man was the noblest work of God. Jake Smith, a wagon-driver for the Twenty-third Ohio

Infantry, sauntered into a Louisville hotel, sat down at a dining-table, and bawled, "I want a good dinner! I'm no damned common officer!"

Food was scant, faulty, and irregular. Vendors sold pies, cakes, and fruit to the men, who overate, grew sick, and wrote home wild statements that the Secesh were poisoning them. Few of the volunteers knew anything but the simplest rules of cooking and one private of the Seventy-second Indiana, recalling the scene later, said:

> If there is ever a time when a great big man feels his helplessness it is when he begins to cook for himself in the army. He wants to jam both fists into his eyes, howl like a booby and say, "I want to go home." Of course we always said on such occasions, "The smoke hurts my eyes."

When a man fell sick, his comrades usually cared for him, so meager were medical facilities, and they made pathetic hashes of the food they tried to prepare for the invalids. One private of the Twenty-third Ohio Infantry went insane upon receiving word that his sweetheart, back home, had married the other man. Strapped to a straw mattress, he fancied himself in hell with the devil hooking him with his horns. The boy would feel the straws beneath him and wail, "My God, ain't they sharp?"

Company cooks were not in the plan of army organization. Each man received his rations and could prepare them as he pleased; pork or bacon, ¾ lb.; fresh or salt beef, 1¼ lb.; flour, 1⅛ lb., or hardbread, ¾ lb. or corn meal 1¼ lb. To every hundred rations were added 10 lbs. of beans or rice, or as a substitute, 9¾ lbs. of desiccated potatoes; mixed vegetables, 6¼ lbs.; green coffee, 10 lbs.; sugar, 5 lbs.; vinegar, 4 qts.; and candles, 1 lb.

If a soldier wished to add to his larder from neighboring hencoops, he ran the risk of punishment as severe as if caught absenting himself without leave. The War Department was insisting that the army ingratiate itself by good conduct in the Border States. Sherman, by his own statements and those of his men, was particularly severe against foraging, forbidding even the theft of an apple from an orchard. "I was a poor innocent then," he said of himself years later, remembering those early scruples. So strict was he that he sentenced Private Sim Kingsley of the Thirty-eighth Indiana to be shot at sunrise for having killed a cow, but he relented in time to let the soldier off with a rasping reprimand. Sim's comrades thought Sherman mean.

Sergeant William Shaw, however, saw him melt one day. William shook in his boots while answering Sherman's questions about the care of telegraph lines; he thought the general sharp and sarcastic. Suddenly, he heard the dread voice change:

"I hear you're short of rations."

"Yes, sir."

"Wait a minute," said Sherman, and disappearing into the kitchen of his headquarters house near Muldraugh's Hill, he buttered two slices of bread and handed them, with an apple, to the sergeant. "There, this will put some fat on your ribs."

Brooding over the tragedy of a war that sent novices unprepared into battle, Sherman grew morose. He found himself unable to care for their health, forbidden to let them take the fresh food they needed or to sleep in comfort. Regulations demanded that the men keep out of vacant houses even when they had no tents to protect themselves from the cold rain. This exposure brought sickness, for the youths, after the fashion of the time, had been taught to sleep at home with bedroom windows closed against the poisonous night air. Few companies owned axes with which to chop firewood and since Sherman sternly ordered them to obey rules about keeping Kentucky fence rails sacred, the men suffered from lack of warming, drying fires. In its first month, the Thirty-third Indiana saw 511 of its 1,000 members taken away to crude hospitals in the rear. Sixty-two of the sick men died. Physicians were few, and in the main young and inexperienced. There were no sanitary supplies, no organized nurses.

The very music of the fifes in the morning was sad. General Jacob Dolson Cox described them:

> I shall never forget the peculiar plaintive sound of the fifes as they shrilled out the reveille. How was so melancholy a strain chosen for the waking tune of the soldiers' camps? The bugle reveille is quite different, it is even cheery and inspiring, but the regulation music for the fifes and drums is better fitted to waken longing for home and all the saddest emotions than to stir the host from sleep.

Private soldiers testified that bugle calls, which became commoner in the army, were beloved by the men. On fine nights when the boys had become used to hard beds under the stars, the good-night trumpets would say, "Go-to-sleep—go-to-sleep—go-to-sleep, soldier"—and slumber would come in the shadows of red campfires.

For all the misery that attended the initiation of Northwestern boys into war, there was comfort in the sociability that the volunteer officers, free from West Point brusqueness, so often gave their men. The soldiers liked the way Brigadier General Ebenezer Dumont, the Indiana politician, cleansed camps of sutlers who charged outrageous prices. These civilian merchants had quasi-military standing, but not in Dumont's eyes. Upon one occasion sentries brought him a quaking captive, who admitted that he had been selling things to the boys.

"What's your nationality?" demanded Dumont.

"I'm a Jew."

"Great God!" roared Dumont. "A sutler and a Jew! Here, Officer of the Guard, take him out and hang him!" As the officer, understanding well enough that he was only to expel the prisoner from camp, moved to lead him from the tent, Dumont suddenly pointed his finger at the frightened sutler and bellowed: "If it hadn't been for just such damned cusses as you, our Lord Jesus Christ would be alive and well until this day." At that, the sutler broke away and started running, while Dumont's staff writhed with laughter.

Worry over the lack of discipline, the lack of proper equipment, the necessity for his assuming responsibility for boys whom he understood and liked far better than the Easterners of Bull Run—all this wore Sherman's nerves closer and closer to collapse. Furthermore, he could get only insufficient recruits. New regiments, such few as came, went to Thomas, the new commander at Camp Dick Robinson. Tom needed them, for Zollicoffer was said to be approaching. But everybody seemed to be forgetting Sherman. Wounded feelings filled his brain with tumult, combining with his patriotic distress in a manner to produce something like hallucination. To Thomas Ewing he sent a letter so sensational as not to be preserved, but which Ellen described to John as one that gave her "great pain and anxiety."

With overwrought imagination, he began to make wild statements about the enemy's strength and to fail utterly to understand the extent of Union sympathy in Kentucky. At the moment that he was declaring the State to be predominantly secessionist, General Polk was writing Jefferson Davis, "Kentucky is fast melting away under the influence of the Lincoln Government." When Sherman was insisting again and again that armed enemies in the State outnumbered Federal soldiers by five to one, Confederate reports were showing that the opposing forces were practically equal, and when General A. S. Johnston was despairing at the apathy shown the Southern cause in the blue-grass section, Sherman was drawing extravagant pictures of recruits flooding Confederate camps and ignoring Union depots. At the end of September, when Sherman was expecting to be overwhelmed in a hostile State, an actual survey would have shown that approximately 10,000 Kentuckians had joined the Confederate armies, while fully 20,000 had put on Federal uniforms. The State consistently gave two votes and two enlistments to the North to every one to the South.

Had Sherman's mind been normal he could have informed himself with more accuracy as to the true state of Kentucky's sentiment, for at his hand on Muldraugh's Hill was the one man who in all likelihood knew more than any other about the question—Rousseau. In May Rousseau had given the Kentucky Senate sentiments that were a fair expression of the majority opinion in the State:

> I am for the old Constitution of Washington and his compeers; for the old flag and against all factions that would take them from me. It matters not who they are or whence they come, whether they come from England, France, Massachusetts or South Carolina. . . . The politicians are having their day. The people will yet have theirs.

On September 27 Sherman wrote, "I am to be sacrificed," and estimated that Buckner was menacing him with 15,000 men. Buckner was informing his War Department that he had only 4,500. And on October 4, when Sherman was protesting that Buckner could cut the railroad in his rear and gobble him up, he had 5,000 bluecoats in line with 3,000 more guarding the railway—and Buckner, lying low, could count barely 6,000 noses in his own camp.

With spy systems unorganized, fantastic rumors came to generals in both armies. In his mental agitation Sherman credited the Southerners with plans for a great move. Grant, at Cairo, coolly sifted these same rumors and announced that the Confederate leaders in Kentucky had "but little idea of risking anything upon a forward movement."

But with his sudden weakness for believing wild tales of the enemy's strength, there was flashing through Sherman's mind a brilliant comprehension of the need for censorship regarding his own force. Months, it seemed, before other generals grasped this necessity, it was clear to him. Murat Halstead, sending a reporter to interview Sherman at Muldraugh's Hill, learned Sherman's views on this point. Armed with a letter of introduction from Tom Ewing, Jr., the reporter approached Sherman, who was pacing up and down "at a little hot railroad station whose platform was washed by rain and sun, his sword scratching on the planks."

"Letter from Tom, eh?" said Sherman. He read it, took out his watch and said: "It's eleven o'clock; the next train for Louisville goes at half-past one. Take that train! Be sure you take it; don't let me see you around here after it's gone!"

"But, General! The people are anxious. I'm only after the truth."

"We don't want the truth told about things here—that's what we *don't* want! Truth, eh? No, sir! We don't want the enemy any better informed than he is. Make no mistake about that train!" For a time he paced the platform, then he broke out with, "See that house? They will feed you—say I sent you—but don't miss that train!"

On one other question his mind was functioning with startling clarity. He was elaborating the maps that he had begun to make upon his arrival. He rode the country for miles around, drawing details of the terrain. Far more than the majority of officers, North or South, he understood that war was to be won by those who best knew the ground. But over and above all military understanding played his instinct for the earth, for nature. Passion for order and unity, perhaps a subconscious craving for something settled, definite, and immutable, had led him as a boy to walk far on hunts, and as an adult to ride alone over hills and plains, finding some inner satisfaction in the shoulders of hills, the waistlines of river valleys. He loved the earth as a sailor loves the sea.

From whatever peace these map-making rides brought him, Sherman was torn on October 5 when General Anderson, declaring his health ruined "under the mental torture" of his command, resigned. By reason of his seniority, Sherman inherited the office "in direct violation," he said, "of Lincoln's promise to me." Of this promise Sherman reminded the War Department, and in time he received word that Brigadier General Buell would relieve him as soon as he arrived from California.

With no staff to assist him in the management of departmental routine, with Louisville citizens complaining about the petty offenses of soldiers, with Thomas demanding reënforcements, and with pressure from politicians reminding him that President Lincoln expected him to drive through the mountains and deliver eastern Tennessee, Sherman grew morbid. "Our arms are insufficient." . . . "They have not sent me a single officer from Washington, so engrossed are they with Missouri that they won't do us justice." . . . "We are moving heaven and earth to get arms, clothing and money necessary in Kentucky but McClellan and Frémont had made such heavy drafts that the supply is scant"—these were telegrams he sent to his subordinates. To President Lincoln he sent terse descriptions of the inadequacy of his force, the danger of defeat, the lack of all war material, and ended his telegram with the abrupt word, "Answer!"

To secure money with which to pay his recruits their wages, Sherman personally endorsed all drafts at Louisville banks—business details that, once so easy for him, now weighed him down. Runaway Negroes complicated his duties. Crisply he ordered his officers to return all fugitives upon "application of owner or owner's agent." "Sherman's policy of paying for all property taken for Federal use and of punishing depredations has produced a marked change in favor of the Union cause," commented the *Cincinnati Commercial* on October 17. "Sherman is the very man to fill the retiring hero's [Anderson's] place," wrote Sherman's friend, George D. Prentice, in his *Louisville Journal*. Such newspaper praise was, however, rare and due to grow rarer, for Sherman was nearing the warfare that he would wage with correspondents and which would cost him so heavily.

Henry Villard, the correspondent, saw the red-haired general appear nightly at nine o'clock in the office of a press association in Louisville. Through the telegraphic instruments there, the Government sent dispatches in cipher. At 3 A.M., when the office closed, Sherman would go to his hotel. He seemed never to sleep. Villard said:

> He lived at the Galt House on the ground floor, and he paced the corridor outside his rooms for hours, absorbed. The guests whispered about him and the gossip was that he was insane.

Much of the gossip was spread by newspaper correspondents. Some of them had thought him all but demented as they watched him in the office of the press association, where he smoked furiously, leaving from eight to ten cigar stumps on the floor each evening—Sherman's old soldiers, they were called. For hours he would be silent, pacing up and down the room, puffing white smoke, his head bent forward, his hands crossed behind his back, his eyes darting here and there but seeing nothing. At times he would throw himself far back in his chair, his thumbs in his vest, and launch into vivid, rapid speech, commenting on every item of news, every general, every seeming possibility of the war. Villard said:

> He spoke with unwise vehemence of his own connection with the military situation in Kentucky . . . he was simply appalled by the difficulties . . . and could not rid himself of the apprehension that he was due for defeat if the rebels attacked.

Villard estimated Sherman as having "intense patriotism and despair." So apprehensive had Sherman become by October 14 that he telegraphed to Lincoln, "I have reliable information from Bowling Green that Simon Buckner has over 20,000 men with cars sufficient to move them." Buckner's report on October 19 revealed this force to be 9,956.

Sherman saw no need, under these circumstances, for stopping to explain to the newspaper men his orders forbidding them to visit the camps. Filled as they were with the American doctrine of free speech and a free press, these journalists regarded the withholding of military secrets as an unwarrantable intrusion upon their rights. Patience and diplomacy might have enabled Sherman to convince them that the publication of such news would give aid and comfort to the enemy, but patience and diplomacy were far from Sherman's mind. When two journalists ignored his orders and visited camps at the front, Sherman expelled them beyond the picket lines, and when after he had refused a pass to a *Cincinnati Commercial* reporter he discovered the man disobeying him, Sherman clapped the fellow in prison.

Excoriating a reporter who had written that the general's manners were like those of a Pawnee Indian, Sherman was angered still further, a few days later, to read that the correspondent had apologized not to him, but to the Pawnee Indians. Correspondents passed the word to each other and their editors that Sherman was the enemy of the press. Through the profession there began to smolder a determination to "get" this red-haired martinet if opportunity should offer.

The opportunity was at hand. Since the thirteenth of the month Sherman had been feverishly anticipating a visit from Secretary of War Cameron, who had come West to investigate the muddle of inefficiency, corruption, and Napoleonic delusions that had characterized Frémont's régime in Missouri. Cameron would stop at Louisville, Sherman had been advised. It was Sherman's chance and he awaited it in excitement. On the seventeenth he was at Jeffersonville when the noon train brought the dignitary to the platform attended by Adjutant General Lorenzo Thomas and six or seven civilians. Now Sherman would get satisfaction. He approached all afire with pent-up speech.

Cameron dashed him by asking, first of all, when he could catch a boat for Cincinnati, as he must hurry back to Washington. Desperately, Sherman spoke up, begging the Secretary to come to Louisville, since there was business there "as important as any in Washington." The Secretary stared in amazement, asking if all was not well. No, said Sherman, it was as bad as bad could be. Cameron debated and consented only when he learned that he could make his Cincinnati connections safely if he left Louisville by railroad early in the morning. Rejoiced, Sherman hurried the party to his hotel rooms, ordered up food and liquor, and prepared to talk. But again his boyish eagerness must wait, for Cameron, who was ailing, stretched himself upon the bed and conversed with his traveling companions about other matters. Frémont's extravagance, which they had just beheld, occupied them long, but at length Cameron called, from his pillow, "Now, General Sherman, tell us your troubles."

Sherman objected to talking in the presence of so many strangers, but Cameron silenced him with "They are all friends, all members of my family, and you may speak your mind freely and without restraint." Thereupon Sherman locked the door and poured out his entire bill of grievances—recruits were being sent elsewhere . . . Buckner could take Louisville in a day's time if he chose . . . Kentuckians were not joining the Union colors . . . young Kentuckians were going South and older Kentuckians, the pro-Union element, would not fight against their relatives.

"You astonish me!" exclaimed Cameron. Kentucky's representatives in Washington had assured the Government that the State had plenty of men and lacked only ammunition and money. Sherman, driving hard at his theme, lectured the Secretary for having sent Kentucky only 12,000 muskets and those Belgian ones which Pennsylvania and Ohio had rejected. McClellan with 100,000 men was protecting less than a hundred miles of the front, Frémont had 60,000 for a like sector, while he, Sherman, was expected to protect three hundred miles with but 20,000 equally divided between himself and Thomas. For defense alone, said Sherman, we must have 60,000 men and "for offense, before we are done, 200,000." "Great God!" burst out Cameron, waving his hands above the pillow. "Where are they to come from?"

Concerning Sherman's use of the figure 200,000 there would be a dispute later on. Adjutant General Thomas understood that when asked what force would be necessary to expel the enemy from Kentucky, Sherman had "promptly replied 200,000 men." Five years later Major General Thomas J. Wood, who was in the room at the time, recalled that Sherman had specified that number of troops as necessary to clear the entire Mississippi Valley. Cameron obviously understood the statement as Lorenzo Thomas did, and in what could only be interpreted as anger, advised Sherman that he was overestimating the enemy, that he himself was tired of this defensive war, that the Government would furnish troops, and that Sherman must attack.

In his excitement Sherman thought the Secretary friendly, hearing him order Washington to send 10,000 troops and 6,200 muskets to Kentucky at once. When the official party had entrained, Sherman visited Old Tom's forces at Camp Dick Robinson and was seen by the men at the review to be grinning and chatting pleasantly.

But this optimism was fleeting, for Cameron had betrayed him into the hands of the newspaper men, who were awaiting the opportunity.

20

A LETTER TO LINCOLN

AMONG those civilians whom Sherman had asked Cameron to exclude from their conference was one man whom the general did not know or observe, Samuel Wilkerson, correspondent of the *New York Tribune.* Before leaving Louisville with the War Secretary, Wilkerson confided to Henry Villard that Cameron regarded Sherman as "unbalanced and that it would not do to leave him in command." And at Cameron's side during subsequent days, Wilkerson no doubt saw the telegrams and letters with which Sherman continued to demand protection for Kentucky. Sherman's letters were like fists banging on Cameron's desk, hoarse voices crying that the loss of the State would defeat the whole Union cause, and that it was wrong to expect miracles from untrained, unarmed soldiers.

Rival journalists believed that Wilkerson was writing the official report of Cameron's tour, a report that General Lorenzo Thomas would sign as his own, and when this document was published in the *Tribune* on October 30, Villard attributed to Wilkerson's hand those paragraphs which made "broad insinuations that Sherman's mind was upset." The report described Sherman's "gloomy . . . overestimate" of the enemy's force and recited how Cameron had "begged Sherman to assume the offensive."

Although Sherman boiled with anger at reading implications of his timorousness and lack of balance, he did nothing more violent than to write the War Department of his "dissatisfaction" at the publication of a private interview, and to repeat his request that he be relieved from the command. But he stood manfully to his guns, writing Cameron that even though his estimate of 200,000 troops "had been construed to my prejudice," he would repeat it. On November 6 he wrote:

> Do not conclude as before that I exaggerate the facts. They are as stated and the future looks as dark as possible. It would be better if some more sanguine mind were here, for I am forced to order according to my convictions.

On the previous day General Alexander McD. McCook, commanding the advanced force, had told Sherman that the powder supplied the soldiers was useless. "With our present force it would be simple madness" to move forward, Sherman wired Lorenzo Thomas.

In the midst of Cameron's requests that he attack the enemy, Sherman began to receive wires from McClellan suggesting that he retire from his advancd position and concentrate his troops near Louisville. McClellan asked how long Sherman could keep Buckner out of Louisville, and how many days McCook could hold out, retreating along the railroad, fighting mile by mile. It was this dispatch that Thomas Ewing, when he saw it, would insist betrayed McClellan's willingness to give up Kentucky. In army circles it was said that McClellan's confidential adviser, Colonel T. M. Key, had been sent to investigate Sherman and had reported that "Sherman was not sufficiently master of his judgment to warrant the intrusting to him of an important military command." Determined neither to advance for Cameron nor to retreat for McClellan, Sherman held his lines and demanded reënforcements. "Our forces are too small to do good, and too large to be sacrificed," he wired McClellan.

Sherman's enemies, the war correspondents, now began to interpret his actions as both irresponsible and disloyal. When he gave a pass to the wife of the Confederate officer Ingraham to allow her to go South from Louisville, newspapers repeated a paragraph, including the sentence: "His sympathy and kindness to such persons is entirely misplaced and unpatriotic." Sherman had not told them that the woman had asked for a pass on the ground that she was consumptive and needed Southern air, nor that before allowing her to depart he had told her, "Shut yourself up in a room and keep up a good fire and it will do you just as much good."

From November 5 to November 7 newspapers ridiculed Sherman's "motherly tendencies" in forbidding the exile of political prisoners. The United States Marshal in Louisville had been arresting Southern sympathizers with a view to deporting them to States further North, and Sherman had ended the practice. War could not stampede him into disregard for law; political prisoners should have civil trials. The incident provoked the *Chicago Tribune* into an attack upon Sherman for this "impolitic spirit of conciliation that has encouraged treason and spies." Reporters charged him with showing "contempt of the Kentucky ladies who were sending clothes to the boys." He had ordered the coddling of his men to be halted, and had declared female nurses a great nuisance. Between his anxiety to halt sickness among his men and his determination that they should become hardened to the long military life ahead of them, he was adrift. However, he met the Kentucky ladies in assemblage and spoke to them so gallantly that they were reported as having thought him charming.

But Louisville, as a whole, considered him erratic, if not a little "off."

One of the war correspondents in the city, Richardson by name, thought too many cigars responsible:

> When I first saw him in Missouri . . . his eye had a half-wild expression, probably the result of excessive smoking. . . . Sherman was never without a cigar. To the nervous-sanguine temperament, indicated by his blond hair, light eyes and fair complection, tobacco is peculiarly injurious. . . . He looks rather like an anxious man of business than an ideal soldier, suggesting the exchange and not the camp. Sometimes he works for twenty consecutive hours. He sleeps little; nor do the most powerful opiates relieve his terrible cerebral excitement. Indifferent to dress and to fare, he can live on hard bread and water and fancies any one else can do so.

The *Chicago Tribune's* reporter wrote in early December:

> I know not whether it is insanity or not, but the General . . . indulged in remarks that made his loyalty doubtful. He even spoke despondingly; said the rebels could never be whipped; talked of a thirty years' war.

As the press campaign against him progressed, Sherman talked of barring all correspondents from his department and elation came to the newspaper fraternity on November 9 when the War Department's General Orders 97 appeared announcing that Buell was to replace Sherman. The correspondent of the *Chicago Tribune* wrote, "Anderson was a gentleman of no mind. Sherman is possessed of neither mind nor manners. We are thankful now that we have a man who combines both." The *Cincinnati Commercial* congratulated the press on escaping from "the peevishness, prejudice and persecution" of the man who "is a perfect monomaniac on the subject of journalism":

> His favorite often proclaimed plan for the successful management of the war is the suppression of every newspaper in the country—a theory which he advocates the more strongly since the comments of the press on his requisition of only 200,000 men. The telegraph as a means of transmitting news is also an intolerable nuisance in his eyes. He considers the press alone responsible for all the defeats of the Federal arms, inclusive of Bull Run. How can such a narrow mind be capable of the successful management of such great and delicate interests as are entrusted to him by this state?

Waiting for Buell's arrival, Sherman fancied that the enemy was moving to crush both himself and Thomas. He sent Old Tom word to halt the slow, steady advance he was making toward Cumberland Gap; Zollicoffer was coming with overwhelming force! In reality, Zollicoffer at that moment was begging for reënforcements so that he might resist Thomas's larger army.

Old Tom, whose imagination never troubled him, retreated obediently, listening the while to Sherman's hysterical warnings that Albert

Sidney Johnston was marching from Bowling Green with 45,000 men to separate the two Federal armies and seize Louisville. Thomas discredited these rumors and said so, but Sherman was too agitated to heed his level-headed friend. Time would prove that Johnston, instead of marching with 45,000 men, was quiescent at Bowling Green begging his War Department for muskets, since a large number of his total force of 12,500 were unarmed. Anxiously Johnston asked Richmond to consider "the great superiority" of Sherman's army.

On November 11 Sherman wired Thomas not to give battle while retreating and "if outnumbered, you are not to sacrifice the lives of your command." In such sentences, creeping into his orders and letters and conversation at this crisis, Sherman was revealing one of the motives for what had been so paradoxical in his war life thus far. Crying for swift blows against the Confederacy, he had been slow to come to the front. A born executive and unselfishly dutiful, he had refused high command. Criticizing Lincoln for favoring civilian volunteers over professional soldiers, he had forced the President to promise that he himself—an army man—should be exempt from high authority.

Among the intellectual and emotional reasons for such contradictions was now visible a subconscious hatred of bloodshed. Sherman's mind was naturally tender, and shrank from the thought of sacrificial blood. And it would be nothing short of sacrifice to send untrained recruits into battle without proper arms. He would not take the moral responsibility for their slaughter. If the piteous butchery were to be made, some one else must give the word; he would obey orders, nothing more.

He was glad when Buell arrived on November 15. His friend was full of compliments for the progress in the training of the recruits. "Sherman," he said, "you should be a major general," but to McClellan Buell telegraphed that Sherman's apprehensions of attack were groundless, Sherman's fortifications were unnecessary, and although "Sherman still insists I need 200,000 men, I am content to try with a good many less." Buell halted Thomas's retirement, and injured Sherman's feelings additionally by opening in his presence each day letters from McClellan, all beginning "Dear Friend" and giving elaborate directions. Sherman had never received a letter from McClellan, only a few carping telegrams. Also, as he rode about the camps with Buell, Sherman saw arriving the regiments he had asked for—Northwestern regiments in such numbers that whereas the roll had shown 40,000 present on November 1, a month later it would hold 100,000 names.

It was these innocents who were on Sherman's mind as on November 21 he packed his baggage for the trip to St. Louis, where he had been ordered to join Halleck. That day he wrote John:

I cannot but look upon it as absolutely sacrificing them. I see no hope for them in their present raw and undisciplined condition, and some terrible disaster is inevitable. . . .

I suppose I have been morose and cross and could I now hide myself in some obscure corner I would do so, for my conviction is that our Government is destroyed and no human power can restore it.

At Benton Barracks he was soon seeing recruits as pathetic as those in Kentucky, brave, eager blunderers handling the faulty muskets that Frémont, with such loud self-congratulation, had imported from Europe. Some of the weapons refused to fire at all, others blew to bits at the first discharge, and the young soldiers from Chicago laughed, remembering how Methodist clergymen, mounting recruiting stands, had urged them to enlist on the ground that the fighting would be sanctified. Now the volunteers called their useless guns "damn sanctified rifles," and when a sentry passed, they yelled, "There goes another sanctified Methodist sharpshooter!" Boys of the Seventh Ohio remembered how a clergyman of Cleveland, the Rev. Mr. Beattie, had given a recruit a revolver, saying, "If you get in a tight spot, ask God's blessing if you have time, but be sure and not let your enemy get the start of you. You can say 'Amen' after you shoot."

Sherman's pity for the novice soldiers and his forebodings of "some terrible disaster" brought him difficulty shortly after his arrival in Missouri. Sent by Halleck to inspect troops at Sedalia, Sherman was seized by a nervous fear that the Union commander, General John Pope, had scattered his regiments so loosely that the Confederate Price might gobble them up. Pope, who knew that Price was not advancing, was astonished when Sherman began concentrating the forces. Pope wired Halleck such protests that the latter suddenly ordered Sherman back to St. Louis, specifying in his message that Mrs. Sherman was at headquarters. Ellen, from Cump's letters and newspaper descriptions of him, had sensed that her husband was in serious trouble. She had hurried to St. Louis and interviewed Halleck—probably demanding a furlough for Cump. She found Cump soon after he had returned from Sedalia. He was sitting alone and disconsolate in a great barn of a building.

"Ellen," he cried, "what are you doing here?"

"I've come to bring you home."

"I wouldn't think of going!"

Nevertheless, he went, Halleck urging him, telling him that a twenty-day rest would do him good. But on the following day, December 2, Old Brains sent McClellan his more candid opinion of Sherman's condition. He said that Sherman at Sedalia had thought there was danger of an attack and had commenced the movement of troops in a manner which I did not approve and countermanded. . . . I also received information from officers there, that General Sherman was completely stampeded, and was stampeding the army. I therefore ordered him to this place and yesterday gave him a leave of absence for 20 days to visit his family in Ohio. I am satisfied that General Sherman's physical and mental system is so completely broken by labor and care as to render him for the present entirely unfit for duty. Perhaps a few weeks' rest may restore him. I am satisfied that in his present condition it would be dangerous to give him a command here.

Shame now beat Sherman down. He could see that his brother officers viewed him askance; everybody thought he was mad. His wife was taking him home—he was like a boy whose mother has come to school to lead him away. Once more life had thrown him like a weed on his father-in-law's doorstep.

Ellen took Cump to the house she had rented near the Ewing mansion and, as they arrived, Sissie hurried in to welcome them. She stopped wide-eyed. Cumpy was so old, so wrinkled, his red beard streaking with gray, his eyes so queer as he stared from the window on the bleak December streets.

On December 11 Ellen wrote John that Cump had told a Lancaster friend, Hocking Hunter, "Sometimes I felt crazy in Kentucky; I couldn't get one word from Washington."

Fear added its force to the natural love and energy that were inherent in Ellen. She drew from her husband a confession which she believed gave the key to his condition. He told her that while he had been ruling in Kentucky some east Tennesseeans, hearing that he was coming over the mountains to rescue them, had set out to coöperate. While burning bridges to harass Confederates in their neighborhood, a few of them had been killed. Over this, Sherman had brooded, heaping morbidly fantastic reproaches upon his own head. Ellen wrote John:

I find that the keenest source of trouble to Cump is in the fact that he could not go to the relief of the East Tennesseeans at the time the bridges were burned. Can you not bring him to the belief that he is in no way responsible for that?

How much worse it would have been to have had his small force cut off at Cumberland Gap, than the death of the poor bridge burners! The fault lies in McClellan who refused to send out the smallest portion of his idle force on the Potomac. McClellan is called a stick. I say he is a mill stone. The army never would have done anything had not Mr. Stanton gone in.

Meanwhile the war correspondents in St. Louis turned in their cheeks the news of Sherman's demotion. Before his departure they had hounded him, anxious to give instructions in the proper respect due their profession. They had spread suspicion of his loyalty, pointing out his continued intimacy with Missouri families who were admittedly pro-Confederate. Sherman later confessed that "in spite of myself, they tortured from me words and acts of imprudence." He had stubbornly refused to break off friendships merely because of political disagreements.

On December 12 Cump and Ellen discovered how avid were the reporters to strike at an enemy. That day there arrived in Lancaster the *Cincinnati Commercial* of the 11th, and from its columns a paragraph leaped:

GENERAL WILLIAM T. SHERMAN INSANE

The painful intelligence reaches us, in such form that we are not at liberty to disclose it, that Gen. William T. Sherman, late commander of the Department of the Cumberland, is insane. It appears that he was at the time while commanding in Kentucky, stark mad. We learn that he at one time telegraphed to the War Department three times in one day for permission to evacuate Kentucky and retreat into Indiana. He also, on several occasions, frightened leading Union men of Louisville almost out of their wits by the most astounding representation of the overwhelming force of Buckner and the assertion that Louisville could not be defended. The retreat from Cumberland Gap was one of his mad freaks. When relieved of the command in Kentucky he was sent to Missouri and placed at the head of a brigade at Sedalia, when the shocking fact that he was a madman was developed by orders that his subordinates knew to be preposterous and refused to obey. He has of course been relieved altogether from command. The harsh criticisms that have been lavished on this gentleman, provoked by his strange conduct, will now give way to feelings of deepest sympathy for him in his great calamity. It seems providential that the country has not to mourn the loss of an army through the loss of mind of a general into whose hands was committed the vast responsibility of the command of Kentucky.

His enemies had him bayed now, like an exhausted stag. Ellen wrote John:

I will not dilate upon the peculiar nature of the pangs inflicted upon us both by this last. Nature will paint to your mind and heart what I felt when Tommy came in to us just now to say that a boy had told him that "Papa was crazy."

Cump wrote Ewing in Washington, that the most distressed feeling

of my life is that arising from a consciousness that you will be mortified beyond measure at the disgrace which has befallen me by the announcement in the *Cincinnati Commercial* that I am insane.

Ewing answered that John Sherman and he had decided Cump must bring suit for damages against "the scoundrels who have libeled you."

Then he proceeded to lecture "my dear son" sagely and gently upon the subject of free speech:

> You estimate the comparative power of the South higher than most men, and I think too high, but right or wrong, it does no good but evil to express the opinion until you can in some way control and change the matter.

Ewing asked Cump not to say things that would dishearten Union men:

> You have kindly feelings toward many engaged in the contest on the other side arising from old friendships. You ought not to give it voice.

Ewing said that he had seen in print criticisms of Cump's loyalty—"You are engaged in the war and can say nothing with propriety against its justice or policy."

Sherman sent Halleck a letter asking "if the steps I took at Sedalia were evidence of a want of mind." He defended himself:

> They may have been the result of an excess of caution on my part . . . but I set a much higher measure of danger on the acts of unfriendly inhabitants than most officers do because I have lived in Missouri and the South and know that in their individual characters they will do more acts of hostility than Northern farmers or people would bring themselves to perpetrate. In my judgment Price's army in the aggregate is less to be feared than when in scattered bands.

To Halleck he declared that the newspaper attack upon him had been written by a reporter

> whom I imprisoned in Louisville for visiting our camps after I had forbidden him leave to do so. . . . These newspapers have us in their power and can destroy us as they please, and this one can destroy my usefulness by depriving me of the confidence of officers and men.

On the day that they read the article, Philemon Ewing sat down with Cump and drafted a long and categorical denial of the newspaper charges. Then he hurried to Cincinnati to demand that Editor Halstead publish the refutation. Halstead explained the affair to Phil. He said that Henry Villard had come to him from Louisville saying that Sherman was crazy, but that no newspaper man at the front dared print it for fear Sherman would kill him. Yet the story *must* be published, else Sherman's insanity would wreck the army. Villard begged Halstead to bell the cat, and reluctantly, so the editor said, he had consented. He would now gladly publish Phil's answer, and on the thirteenth it appeared, branding "every material paragraph false" in the story of the eleventh.

But by the fifteenth the stricken family in Lancaster learned that other midland newspapers, including the *St. Louis Democrat*, had published the insanity article concurrently with or immediately after the *Commercial*. Ellen concluded that a plot had inspired these attacks, and she demanded that Halleck tell her what was behind it. Old Brains answered in smooth nothings:

> Tell the General I will make a Yankee trade with him. I will take all that is said against him if he will take all that is said against me. I am certain to make 50% profit by the exchange.

And to Philemon, who likewise bombarded him with letters, Halleck said that newspapers constantly did such blackguard tricks without injuring anybody. He explained his own part in the matter:

> When General Sherman came here his health was much broken by long and severe labor and his nervous system was somewhat shaken by continuous excitement and responsibility. Those who saw him here may have drawn wrong inference from his broken-down appearance and rather imprudent remarks, but no one who was personally acquainted with him thought that anything was the matter with him except a want of rest. I have no doubt that the quiet of home will enable him in a short time to resume his duties and silence all these scandalous and slanderous newspaper attacks.

On December 18 Halleck comforted Sherman with a letter saying that he had countermanded the latter's orders at Sedalia not because he thought them unwise but because, having later news than Sherman, he desired to postpone the movements Sherman had commenced. Since that time, he said, he had carried out the orders as Sherman had given them. However, Halleck continued, he would say in all frankness that many of Sherman's remarks about the probability of the Confederates' taking St. Louis had "led to unfair comment."

Sherman stood staring out of the windows—winter leaves and rain on the cold streets of the village. All he could get from his superiors was words, words, words. He let thoughts of suicide dart back and forth through his mind. Ellen, watching him, wrote John:

> I cannot persuade Cump to go to Washington. He is feeling terribly about this matter. If there were no kind of insanity in your family and if his feelings were not already in a marked state, I would feel less concern about him, but as it is, I cannot bear to have him go back to St. Louis haunted by the specter and reading the effects of it in any apparent insubordination of officers or men.
>
> It will induce and fasten upon him that melancholy insanity to which your family is subject but which is far removed from what they have represented. I think Cump ought to take a leave of absence until Spring. He

can spend his time usefully and avoid the bad effects of idleness on his mind by attending to Father's affairs at Chauncey.

But Cump was readier to face the suspicions and shrinkings of his fellow officers than those saltworks which had been waiting for him so long, like purgatory. When his leave was up he returned to St. Louis, noting as he did so how his friend Editor Prentice was printing ridiculous laudations of him in the *Louisville Journal* of the nineteenth:

> His [Sherman's] mind is probably unsurpassed in power and comprehensiveness by that of any military man of our country. . . . In his dauntless heroism he is the equal of Richard the Lion-heart. His deportment at the battle of Bull Run, as we have heard it described by eye-witnesses, was worthy of the greatest hero of any age. He has been deemed insane only by those who could not comprehend him . . . his intellect, we are happy to learn, is as calm and firm as it ever was.

Sherman took up his new assignment—the drilling of recruits at Benton Barracks—in dejection. He wrote John on January 4 that he did not feel qualified to rise to a major general's rank and responsibility:

> I am so sensible now of my disgrace from having exaggerated the force of our enemy in Kentucky that I do think I should have committed suicide were it not for my children. I do not think I can again be entrusted with a command. . . .
>
> I believe myself better qualified for a disbursing department. Suppose you see McClellan and ask him if I could not serve the Government better in such a capacity than the one I now hold. I do not feel confident at all in volunteers. Their want of organization, the necessity to flatter them, etc., is such that I cannot prosper with them. . . .
>
> Affectionately,
>
> W. T. SHERMAN.

Experience with and anecdotes of the recruits brought him occasional amusement, as for instance the story of an Iowa major, W. W. Belknap, in collecting men at Keokuk. Riding out of the rural town with his volunteers, he turned back at the sound of a woman's screaming. A mother was hauling her son from the ranks and protesting:

"Major, he can't go; he shan't go! He's not old enough; he's not eighteen and he must stay here."

"Madam," said Belknap, "he must go. He is seventeen; he has sworn it and the law says that the oath taken by the recruit shall be conclusive."

Still the mother held her son by the collar while the grinning crowd gathered. Belknap talked rapidly, saying, as he later recalled his words, that if her boy were killed he would be embalmed in the hearts of his countrymen; "if he was wounded he would perhaps receive a pension in twenty, forty or fifty months—or years." At last the woman relented, wept, blessed her son, and called after him:

"Darby, be a good boy and stay by the major and you'll never be hurted." On the way to St. Louis, Belknap made Darby his orderly and in after years would remember him as "the biggest forager and the greatest thief I ever knew."

When training regiments at Paducah, a few weeks later, Sherman was sardonic. He asked officers of the newly arrived Fifty-third Ohio:

"How long do you expect to remain in service?"

"We've enlisted for three years and expect to serve our time."

"Well," he barked, "you've got some sense. Most of you fellows come down here intending to go home and run for Congress in about three weeks."

They asked, "Where shall we camp?"

"Oh, anywhere, it's all as flat as a pancake and wet as a sponge."

To John Sherman and the Ewings, Cump's descent to the rôle of a mere drillmaster behind the scenes loomed as a tragedy. Ellen was sure that Halleck did not mean to restore Cump to a post of importance. Halleck wrote favorably, but with what Ellen described as "true lawyer-like ambiguity." Finally on January 10 Ellen decided to do what so many war-torn women were doing when everything else failed, she would lay her troubles in the bosom about which men sang half jocularly but which women understood to be what it was—the bosom of Abraham.

She wrote a letter which began: "Mr. Lincoln, Dear Sir":—She asked him for "some intervention in my husband's favor and in vindication of his slandered name." She recited how in Kentucky "he was almost ignored by the military authorities in Washington," how with but 30,000 recruits he had been expected "to protect an extent of territory larger than that which General McClellan held his choice and immense army to protect," and asked how with no muskets "to give the East Tennesseeans could he have sent a force through Cumberland Gap?" She described how his demands for a sufficient army had been ridiculed by Adjutant General Thomas's report:

> Being of a nervous temperament, he shrank from the responsibility of his position which secured him no adequate means of protecting those under him. His request to be relieved was very coolly complied with and much more readily than any request for men or arms had been.

Ellen reminded Lincoln that Buell, who had been reënforced immediately after taking command, had moved forward but seven miles, yet had not been ridiculed. She said that army conspirators, using newspapers as tools, had timed their attack well, and although contradictions had been published, "who gives credence to them?" No official contradiction had appeared.

As the minister of God to dispense justice to us and as one who has the heart to sympathize as well as the power to act, I beseech you by some mark of confidence to relieve my husband from the suspicions now resting upon him. He is now occupying a subordinate position in General Halleck's department which seems an endorsement of the slander. I do not reproach Gen. Halleck, for Gen. Sherman's enemies may have shaken the confidence of the men in him by the suspicions that he is insane and thus rendered it impolitic to appoint him to a command there.

His mind is harassed by these cruel attacks. . . . Newspaper slanders are generally insignificant, but this, you will perceive, is of a peculiar nature and one which no man can bear with stoicism, particularly one who is so sensitive and nervous.

Will you not defend him from the enemies who have combined against him, by removing him to the army of the East? If I were sure there would be no forward movement of the Missouri troops down the Mississippi I would ask you to telegraph him to come to Washington when you could dispose of him in your wisdom. . . . Adg. Gen. Thomas has shown himself more than an enemy of my husband. He had it in his power and he seized the occasion to present him in an unfavorable light to you. As malice cannot prevail where justice rules, I look for a speedy relief from the sorrow that has afflicted me in this trial of my husband.

ELLEN SHERMAN.

Then she enclosed the newspaper accounts of Cump's "insanity" and sent her plea to the White House.

In November it had been assumed by the Pennsylvania politician Alexander K. McClure that Lincoln credited the stories of Sherman's insanity current in Washington. And when he had heard that Sherman had been removed, McClure had rushed into the War Department, asking Thomas A. Scott, the Assistant Secretary, what it meant. "Sherman's gone in the head," said Scott. "And upon inquiry," McClure wrote later, "I found that Scott simply voiced the general belief of those who should have been better informed on the subject."

Years afterward Lincoln's secretaries, Nicolay and Hay, defended the President from the charge that he had removed Sherman for "suspected insanity." In proof they offered a paper that Lincoln had endorsed. It was a letter from James Guthrie, the pro-Union railroad president of Louisville, asking Lincoln to send Sherman "back to Kentucky to serve under Buell." Guthrie had said that this would please "most if not all the Union men of the state and most of the officers in the field, I am told." The one way to adjust the conflict in the two generals' rank would be to promote Buell and allow Sherman to serve as his second in command. On November 27 Lincoln had written across Guthrie's letter, "If General McClellan thinks it proper to make Buell a major general, enabling Sherman to return to Kentucky, it would rather please me." But McClellan, who did few things to please the President, and who was moreover anxious for his favorite, Buell, to win honors in the West, let the proposal die.

There are no records to show that Lincoln responded to Ellen Sherman's plea. There were, however, "forward movements down the Mississippi" afoot at the moment, movements in which Halleck would find use for Sherman. While these secret plans progressed, Ellen continued to inform John that Cump's brother officers were trying to "annihilate him" and "kick him into obscurity."

PART TWO: THE SUMMIT

21

UNCONDITIONAL SURRENDER GRANT

GENERAL HALLECK sat in his headquarters in St. Louis, rubbing his elbows in that curious way that was habitual with him, and fixing his bulging eyes on maps. He was now finding good use for all those French military texts over which he had pored in his cabin while Sherman and the other boy lieutenants caught sea birds with fishhooks. Also, he was finding good use for all his political experience in California Territorial affairs.

Great opportunity was before him. So far, he was only ruler over the Department of Missouri. What he wanted was the supreme command in the West. The obstacle to this was Buell, commanding the rival Department of the Cumberland. The prize would unquestionably go to whichever of the two generals won the first smashing victory. As McClellan's entry, Buell held the inside track. And if he should make any kind of a showing in a drive through Cumberland Gap to relieve the pro-Union population of East Tennessee, he would delight Lincoln, who was in special anxiety for that region.

Halleck had no particular friend at court, and moreover he had antagonized Northern Abolitionists by the thoroughness with which he had undone Frémont's antislavery work in Missouri. One opportunity to make powerful friends presented itself. On his desk were letters from Senator John Sherman and Thomas Ewing asking that General Sherman be given fair treatment. Senator Sherman carried weight with Lincoln, and the President's regard for Thomas Ewing had been lately dramatized. Lincoln had asked and taken Ewing's advice in solving the international problem created by the navy's seizure of two Confederate commissioners, Mason and Slidell, on a European-bound ship flying the British flag. Halleck knew, furthermore, that Secretary Chase, whom Lincoln had delegated to give special attention to Western matters, was closely allied with John Sherman and had shown official interest in General Sherman's transfer to Kentucky the previous September.

Even if such thoughts were not determining Halleck's action in January, 1862, they were assuredly in his mind, for his history was one of shrewdness and cautious schemings to be on the winning side. The lawyer general began all at once to pay attention to Sherman, to make him his confidant and to ask his advice on the inner strategy of the coming spring campaign. "I have the fullest confidence in him," Halleck wrote the Ewings, and on February 8 he had grown so enthusiastic that he telegraphed McClellan that Sherman and not Buell ought to command the forthcoming campaign from Kentucky into Tennessee. The suggestion that McClellan demote his pet in favor of a man who had been sent home as unsound two months earlier was naturally doomed to failure. Learning this, Halleck promptly began to make Sherman one of the main cogs in his own organization.

One night in the Planter's Hotel Halleck and Sherman bent over a map. It was obvious that Albert Sidney Johnston was not the superman that the old army had believed. Here was proof. Johnston had fortified the Mississippi against Union attack, yet until late January had neglected to protect those other rivers, the Cumberland and the Tennessee, on which Northern armies might steam straight into the heart of the Confederacy. Within the past few days Johnston had made hasty efforts to guard those streams, erecting Fort Henry and Fort Donelson, but it was too late to expect them to check Halleck's advance, once it started southward. Furthermore, Johnston had divided his army, stationing approximately 14,000 men at the new forts and as many more at Bowling Green to watch Buell.

Discussing these things, Halleck drew a line on the map from the Mississippi eastward. This was the Confederate line of defense. "Now where," he asked, "is the proper place to break it?" Sherman answered, "In the center"—an A B C of military education. Halleck drew a perpendicular line. It coincided with the Tennessee River. "That's the true line of operation," he said, and within a month was hewing at it. To command the advance guard, he chose Grant, since at the Battle of Belmont in November that dusty, slouching little man had filled his recruits with the faith that they could whip many times their weight in "Rebels."

On February 6 word came back to Halleck that Grant had captured Fort Henry, and on the thirteenth that he had invested Donelson. To keep Grant supplied was now of first importance and before night of the thirteenth Halleck placed Sherman in charge of the District of Cairo, with headquarters at Paducah, Kentucky, the key to the Cumberland and Tennessee rivers. Sherman went to his task with new heart. Energetically he sent men, food, and cheering messages to Grant. At last things were beginning to move.

Move, indeed! Sherman had barely settled into his new post when dispatches announced that Grant had taken Donelson too—captured it with between 12,000 and 15,000 prisoners—the first decisive victory of the war! Militarists opened their eyes, for Grant had violated an orthodox rule by besieging a fort that held as many as or more men than he commanded. Textbooks said never to attack fortifications unless possessed of a five to one advantage.

The Northern populace bothered not over such details—all they knew was that Grant had told the defending general, Buckner, that he would accept nothing but unconditional surrender. The two words sent a paroxysm of joy through the Union States. No longer did U. S. Grant mean merely Uncle Sam Grant to a few old army acquaintances. Now it meant Unconditional Surrender Grant to millions. At last the North had a hero! "He has knocked the rebellion in the head," ran a current phrase.

The victory had enabled Halleck to defeat Buell in their race for honors; "Give me the command of the West," he had telegraphed the War Department when it congratulated him on Donelson's capture. But Old Brains had now a new rival, Grant, and as though to deflate the hero, Halleck began reporting to Washington that General C. F. Smith, the second in command, had been the mainspring of the attack, and that he should be made a major general. True it was that Smith, with his white mustachios waving, had ridden so resolutely into the Confederate fire that his regiments had been inspired to crushing charges, but he had been plainly secondary to Grant in responsibility for the triumph.

Halleck began to find fault with Grant for failure to make out reports. The latter had admittedly too little of the bookkeeper in him for a perfect major general. Also Grant, hurrying to Nashville, which had been thrown open to Buell as the result of Donelson's fall, was for some days out of touch with Halleck. The latter, not waiting to discover that Grant's visit was for wise military purposes, assumed that the new idol was absent on a drunken spree, and sent word of this to Washington. Old Brains had tattled on Sherman in December, and on Grant in February.

Restricted to his tent without a command, Grant puzzled over his fate during the following weeks as Halleck prepared to strike the Confederates in their new base at Corinth in upper Mississippi. General Smith's thrilling mustachios now led the field forces. Finally Grant asked to be relieved and might have vanished from the war had not

Lincoln, discerning in him the real victor at Donelson, awarded him a major general's stars.

In the period of his misery Grant took consolation in the discovery of a new friend, Sherman. In his shy, silent way, Grant had appreciated deeply the speed with which Sherman at Paducah had kept him supplied. Many years later, Grant wrote in words that were, for him, sentimental:

> At the time he was my senior in rank and there was no authority of law to assign a junior to command a senior of the same grade. But every boat that came up with supplies or reënforcements brought a note of encouragement from Sherman, asking me to call upon him for any assistance he could render and saying that if he could be of service at the front I might send for him and he would waive rank.

Keeping himself clear of the Halleck-Grant difficulties, Sherman busied himself with strategy. His mind was functioning clearly; intense apprehension had turned into acute penetration. Ceasing to brood over himself as a wronged man and a Jonah, he studied the enemy. Suspecting that Bishop Polk would abandon Columbus, on the Mississippi, Sherman urged Halleck to attack before the heavy cannon could be carted away. But Halleck was too cautious and the guns were gone when on March 2 the Union flotilla seized the town.

Slowly Halleck prepared to strike Corinth, which bestrode the Memphis & Charleston Railroad—East-West artery of secession. The South was nearing panic; committees of citizens were begging President Davis to demote Johnston. Another Confederate army had been defeated in Arkansas at the Battle of Pea Ridge. An ironclad *Monitor* had suddenly halted another ironclad *Merrimac's* expectations of wrecking the Union fleet on the Atlantic. Confederate victory must come in the West, and to reënforce Johnston there arrived Beauregard, Bragg, John C. Breckinridge, Pillow, Floyd, Polk, Cheatham, Hardee, Cleburne, Hindman—the flower of the South, excepting three Virginians who still watched McClellan in the East: Lee, Jackson, and J. E. Johnston.

While the Federals concentrated, Sherman saw steamers arrive with the Donelson prisoners. Buckner was aboard. Sherman found him sitting on the floor of his cabin, surrounded by his officers and in great vexation. Colonel William B. Hazen of the Forty-first Ohio had, as a former friend of Buckner's, accompanied Sherman, and he observed that "the meeting was destitute of any element of cordiality—a few cold words only passing between Sherman and Buckner." He heard the Southerner upbraid the Northerner for "opposing peaceable secession" and the Federal answer that "the Southern people had no right to seize the public property."

On March 10 Halleck set his huge force steaming south on transports. The following day he was announced as commander of all Federal armies between the Rockies and the Alleghenies. Buell was now one of his underlings. Old Brains had won, and it was his new favorite, Sherman, who led the advance guard. With orders to precede the army far up the Tennessee, land, march inland, and break the Memphis & Charleston Railroad, Sherman steamed rapidly. At one point he saw a wharf beside some aged warehouses at the foot of yellow cliffs—Pittsburgh Landing, where travelers went ashore for the twenty-mile trip overland to Corinth. Quickly Sherman sent a courier back to Smith, commanding the main flotilla, with the news that here concentration would be easiest. By the time he had returned from his railroad raid—a failure due to unfordable streams—he was met by orders to disembark at the spot he had chosen.

Up sticky saffron bluffs he led his regiments. On the heights peach orchards spread over rough country, their blossoms beginning to show like a faint pink rain. On the right was Snake Creek, fed by Owl Creek, on the left was Lick Creek—all of them swollen by spring storms and making the high ground a natural citadel. If an enemy attacked, he must come marching down between the streams as a Lilliputian would stride down the ribs of an open fan toward the Landing in the handle. Pushing forward two miles from the river, Sherman pitched his camp on a knoll hard by a log church—Shiloh Meeting-house, where but lately gaunt clergymen had called upon half-literate farmers to defend the South and slavery as God's special creations.

No superior officer ordered Sherman to intrench. Brigadier General James Birdseye McPherson, chief engineer of the army, thought when he arrived that breastworks were unnecessary. General Smith, whose illness, due to an infected leg, kept him on board a transport, told Grant when the latter was given the active command, "By God, I want nothing better than to have the Rebels come out and attack us! We can whip them to hell. Our men suppose we have come here to fight, and if we begin to spade, it will make them think we fear the enemy." Grant and Sherman agreed that digging was bad psychology. From their West Point training, the officers still believed that the ideal soldier stood up to the enemy's fire like the British at Waterloo. "Fight man fashion," was the slogan. Charles Francis Adams said later on:

> I cannot tell how often I heard that agreeable aphorism set forth in war days. The old fogy, West Point, regular army theory that fieldworks made the men cowardly.

Newspaper correspondents, at some time around April 1, asking Sherman what prospects there might be of Confederate attacks, were told, "We are in great danger." And when they asked him why he didn't urge his views on Grant, he said with a shrug of his shoulders, "Oh, they'd call me crazy again." Most of the time, however, he expected no attack. "Beauregard is not such a fool as to leave his base of operation and attack us in ours," he told his officers. Perhaps this was only his gesture of showing army men that he did not overestimate the enemy—his recent failing.

Grant, arriving for inspection on March 17, learned from Sherman that the enemy in Corinth numbered no more than 20,000. In reality 40,000 were there. Grant, confident that no attack would come from them, returned to his headquarters at Savannah, some nine miles down the river.

It seemed safe by the sleepy church among the peach blossoms. Soon there were 33,000 men on or near the yellow bluffs. The Army of the Tennessee—henceforth to be Grant's or Sherman's—was forming. Seven miles north down the river camped Lew Wallace's division, 7,000 strong, while a little farther back Buell rested with 20,000 more—the Army of the Ohio. Thus in the region there were 60,000 Federals, young, strong assurance of victory running through them. From the hills by the Shiloh Meeting-house, the boys could see Southern cavalrymen now and then. Sherman knew of one private who wrote a letter—"I gazed from a lofty eminence, my darling sweetheart, and looked upon the Rebels with vigor and contempt."

Through the Southern ranks at Corinth ran the same naïve confidence—"One Southerner can whip three Yankees." Sometimes it was "ten Yankees." Their generals were planning the very thing that Grant, McPherson, and, perhaps, Sherman were sure they would not dare—a surprise attack upon Grant before Buell could arrive. In after years there would be interminable quarrels as to whether the plan was made by Albert Sidney Johnston or by Beauregard. The former was known to be eager to redeem his loss of Kentucky and Tennessee. Beauregard, sick with throat trouble, was anxious for a victory that would show the Richmond authorities how wrong they had been to remove him from the Eastern command so soon after his "victory" at Bull Run.

At noon on Thursday, April 3, Johnston set 40,000 men walking toward Pittsburgh Landing. "You can march to a decided victory over your mercenary enemies," he told them. "The eyes and hopes of eight millions of people rest upon you." With Johnston, Beauregard, and Bragg at their head, the Confederates overshadowed their opponents in prestige. Except for the confidence that the Federals had in Grant, the conqueror of Donelson, the situation was almost identical with that at Bull Run. Of the twenty-six officers, from Johnston down, who commanded units of brigade size or larger, ten were West Point graduates and eleven had seen fighting in the Mexican War. Of a similar number that ranged from Grant to the lowest brigade officer in the Federal army, only four were West Point graduates and only one, McPherson, had come directly from the regular military force. No more than seven were veterans of Mexican War battles. Sherman was the only one of six division commanders to have had regular army experience.

From his position by Shiloh Meeting-house, Sherman looked across to the organization on his left, the division of Brigadier General Benjamin M. Prentiss—a Virginia-born, Missouri-reared man who had learned ropemaking in Illinois, fought in the Mexican War, and been a commission merchant in 1860. Beyond Prentiss in the line, Sherman saw Brigadier General Stephen A. Hurlbut, who had left his native city of Charleston, South Carolina, at the age of thirty to practice law in Illinois. Behind Sherman was the division of Major General John A. McClernand, an Illinois lawyer and Congressman who had fought Chief Black Hawk in 1832. Near the Landing was the division of Brigadier General W. H. L. Wallace, an Ohio lawyer who had had some experience fighting Mexicans.

But the scarcity of battle-trained officers was not to prove as serious a handicap in the West as in the East. Western farmers were in no event as dependent upon leadership as were the clerks and factory hands of the seaboard States. The industrial and social regimentation that had been working for generations in the Northeast had been largely absent from the Northwest, where a farmer's only master was Nature, and where individuals boasted that they were "as good as the next man." The Western excess of independence might make discipline more difficult than in the East, but it meant superior initiative and self-reliance in fights.

Fresh from log schoolhouses, Western boys in their teens treated officers as though they were teachers, stealing clothing, books, and liquor from them with prankish delight. When the uniformed schoolmaster grew too strict with discipline, it was common for the martial pupils to threaten him with defeat at the next election of officers three years hence. Many officers, having been politicians and office-holders before the war, feared to punish insubordinates lest they offend constituents back home. Major Garber of the Thirty-third Indiana Infantry found himself embarrassed after imprisoning privates who had stolen clapboards from a barn to be used as beds. For days the major heard nothing but derisive yells of "Cla-aa-aapboard!" wherever he went. Eventually he freed the prisoners and publicly apologized to the regiment.

Recruits did not object to such disciplinary sentences as parading with a knapsack full of stones, but they were often unruly when a man was tied up by the thumbs. They understood and approved the reason for drumming deserters out of camp with one side of their heads shaved. Such spectacles made men roar with laughter. Some of the culprits faced such punishment with shameless glee, rejoicing to be out of service. Alonzo L. Brown of the Fourth Minnesota Infantry saw one culprit who after expulsion "thumbed his nose at the edge of camp, kicked up his heels and waved good-by." Regiments howled with merriment to see offenders mounted backwards on a mule and paraded with their crimes chalked on a board that hung from their necks. Soldiers were eager to be in the details of guards who marched on such occasions with fixed bayonets pointing at the mule's posterior. It was likewise enjoyable to see other culprits embracing a tree with hands tied together.

Boys of the Seventy-second Indiana Infantry, in Buell's army, saw their colonel, John T. Wilder, give terrible punishment to a private who had deserted and attempted to shoot an officer. The prisoner was seated on a stool with the regiment looking on, his head shaved "slick as an onion," and held fast while Colonel Wilder took an iron from a fire and pressed it against the man's right cheek. "There was a sizz and a jet of steam, the iron was withdrawn and there was a great D showing fiery red." The regimental musicians struck up the "Rogue's March," while the deserter, stripped to the waist, a blanket on his shoulder, a canteen and one day's rations at his belt, was marched along in front of the soldiers and sent beyond the lines.

When soldiers died of disease in the early days of the war, regiments and even brigades and divisions massed in open squares to hear sermons and hymns. To signal a warrior's death there would be salutes by battalions—"the heaviest volleys we heard during the war," said boys of the Seventy-second Indiana. Soon, however, the novelty of death wore off, and military funerals were abandoned.

Influenza, bronchial ailments, and pneumonia ravaged the camps. "In the night we could hear the chorus of 'graveyard coughing,'" said veterans of the Seventy-second, in recalling their Shiloh days. The indigestible messes made by awkward cooks out of the rice, flour, grease, salt, and water that were employed to make flapjacks added to the digestive horrors of already weakened men. The craving for sugar led to the gobbling of it in quantities, and the men believed this to be one of the causes for the almost universal blight of dysentery. Strange water and perhaps excitement spread the ailment.

Wanly the boys tried to laugh at diarrhea, nicknaming it the Tennessee quickstep. The surgeons, as superior as only young surgeons can be, treated the depressing complaint with jocosity more often than with medicine. When the hospitals, crude affairs at best, refused to receive sufferers, boys of the Fourth Minnesota complained to their officers, receiving the answer, "Try red-hot pokers; that's a sure cure!"

In both armies, Northern and Southern, sanitation was bad, logs serving as latrines. Few officers knew enough to teach their men how to dig small ditches around their tents; water ran in during rains to dampen sleeping figures.

Through the young days of April these two great mobs of innocents ripe for slaughter drew together—two herds of apprentice killers, pathetically eager to learn their trade in what Sherman, then and later, frankly reminded his men was "horrid war."

Probably 80 per cent of each army had never heard a gun fired in hatred. The average soldier was no more than twenty-two years of age, and in all likelihood younger. Three of the five Union divisions were, in Grant's language,

> . . . entirely raw and many of them had only received their arms on the way from their States to the field. Many had arrived but a day or two before and were hardly able to load their muskets according to the manual. Their officers were equally ignorant of their duties.

Of these greenhorn divisions, Sherman's was as raw as any.

In the Southern mob that came blundering across the fields, chaos was so universal as to drive methodical Braxton Bragg almost to frenzy. It angered him, Puritan that he was, to see how airily the cavaliers took the job of soldiering. "A very large proportion of the rank and file had never performed a day's labor," he said, and one of his brother officers admitted that he had never seen a military drill nor heard a lecture nor read a line on the subject.

Uniforms in each force were as weird as any Sherman had seen at Bull Run. "One Irishman and three yards of flannel make a Zouave," ran the saying in the West. Several Confederate regiments were in Union blue. Here and there a Northerner clanked about in a steel vest for which he had given seven dollars and a half to some oil-tongued salesman in St. Louis or Louisville on the guarantee that it would stop bullets; "if it don't, bring it back and we'll give you another." Many Confederates wore odd hats, some, little girls' hats of straw—anything, everything.

Weapons were of comic assortment. Hundreds, perhaps thousands, of Confederates carried shotguns because muskets were lacking. Others sneered at the guns that had been issued and fondly patted the bowie knives in their belts. Most of the Federals still carried flintlocks remodeled into percussion-cap weapons. A few shouldered the cumbersome foreign muskets that they had not yet found opportunity to lose.

On Thursday night rain fell in torrents, turning the yellow roads to mire and making the Southern privates fearful that their powder was damp. To see if their guns would work, they discharged them into the air, blazing away in spite of the pleadings of their officers that quiet was necessary to a surprise attack. The rain dribbled down the necks of officers as they squabbled about the right of way. Orders were misunderstood and repeated in comic jumbles. Bishop Polk's men stalled and held up the whole advance, the bishop growing irate when accused of inefficiency. So ridiculous were the delays that by Saturday night the Confederates had progressed only eighteen miles—one of the slowest military marches on record. In that time the Southern boys had whooped, cheered, and shot at deer that broke cover at their approach; they had eaten up their five days' provisions in two days' time and thrown their haversacks away.

Disgusted with the conduct of the men, on Saturday night Beauregard wanted to give up the whole enterprise, arguing that by no amount of negligence could the Federals have missed discovering the approach of 40,000 men of whom so many were yelling and shooting. "We will find the enemy intrenched to the eyes," he said, all the leaders but Johnston agreeing.

Johnston had sent his underlings through the regiments to learn their temper, and when the report came back to him that if the army retreated now it would melt away, the disappointed boys leaving for their homes, he made up his mind to attack Grant at all costs. Neither he nor the South could afford another retreat such as he had made from Bowling Green. "I would fight them if they were a million," he announced, and ordered the attack for dawn.

The night was starry, with 33,000 Northern boys snoring in their tents and 40,000 Southern boys drowsing fitfully on their muskets a mile or two away—two virgin armies ready for their maiden embrace.

22

SHILOH, BLOODY SHILOH!

THE dawn came up on Sunday, April 6, to shine red on the peach blossoms that were flowering in Tennessee. Among the fluttering petals, buglers in blue uniforms stood up and their horns wailed "The-devil-is-loose, the-devil-is-loose." The routine reveille snarled through the tents and the Army of the Tennessee awakened to remember that they were soldiers face to face with another day of camp life. There had been a little scare on Friday evening when some gray cavalry had galloped up with a few cannon to annoy the outposts, but that meant nothing more than bluff. Sherman had pursued the enemy for five miles with his brigade, only to find no respectable force menacing him. On Saturday afternoon Colonel Jesse J. Appler of the Fifty-third Ohio, holding the most advanced position, had sent Sherman word that a large force of the foe was approaching, and the red-haired commander, bulging with confidence, had answered, "Take your damned regiment back to Ohio. There is no enemy nearer than Corinth." That afternoon he had wired Grant, "I do not apprehend anything like an attack upon our position."

Ever since his arrival at Pittsburgh Landing, Sherman had been listening to wild-eyed pickets rushing in with tales of massed armies "out there," and always he had found on investigation merely a few squads of Southern cavalrymen scampering away. He had had enough of these camp rumors in Kentucky and would not make the same mistake again. In Sherman's tent, his new aide-de-camp, Lieutenant John T. Taylor, asked why he didn't march out to fight the "Rebs" over in Corinth. Sherman replied, "Never mind, young man, you'll have all the fighting you want before this war is over."

Now the Confederates, looking at the red dawn, exclaimed, "The sun of Austerlitz!"—so filled were they with Napoleonic mottoes. No bugles blew; the whole Southern army stepped quietly into battle array. "Tonight we will water our horses in the Tennessee," said Johnston, his large mustachios flaring. At half-past five the brigades, spread wide, came marching through the dew, straight down the ribs of the giant fan, aiming at the Landing in the handle. Men in the ranks carried their muskets at right-shoulder shift; the skirmishers ahead bore their guns like quail-hunters.

Johnston's battle scheme was to strike the Union right, then let the whole Southern line, as it came up, roll down the length of the Union front—a method that would begin with Sherman, proceed to Prentiss, then engage Hurlbut and W. H. L. Wallace on the left.

"What a beautiful morning this is!" said boys of the Eighty-first Ohio as they washed their faces in front of their tents, stuffed their shirt tails inside their trousers, and stretched themselves. The birds and insects sang with that especial loudness which they seemed to possess on Sundays. Breakfast was cooking. Shots popped among the trees, far away. "Those pickets again," everybody said. The Eighty-first, well to the rear—they were in W. H. L. Wallace's division—did not know that the shooting came from skirmishers whom Prentiss had sent out to reconnoiter. Prentiss, the volunteer officer, was warier than his neighbor Sherman, the trained soldier.

In Sherman's lines, so much nearer the sound of this first clash between the opposing skirmishers, there was deadly calm. One man, that timorous leader, Colonel Appler of the Fifty-third Ohio, took alarm and had his drums sound the long roll. He had cried "Wolf" so often that his men, grumbling, took their own time about falling into formation. Suddenly a private of the Twenty-fifth Missouri, one of Prentiss's outposts, stumbled out of the thicket, holding a wound and calling, "Get into line, the Rebels are coming!" Appler sent a courier to Sherman, who sent back word, "You must be badly scared over there." Neighboring regiments, accustomed to Appler's chronic uneasiness, went on with their breakfasts.

An officer of the Fifty-third who had gone into the bushes half dressed came scrambling back howling, "Colonel, the Rebels are crossing the field!" Appler hurried two companies out to see and one of their captains rushed back with the news, "The Rebels are out there thicker than fleas on a dog's back!" At that moment the quail-hunting skirmishers of the Confederate advance stalked into view within musket shot of Appler's right flank. "Look, Colonel!" an officer shouted. A Union skirmisher dashed in yelling, "Get ready, the Johnnies are here thicker than Spanish needles in a fence corner!"

"This is no place for us," wailed Appler, and ordering battalions right to meet the Southern threat, shook in his shoes. His men, who had never held a battalion drill, were confused and milled about pathetically. Cooks left their camp kettles and ran. The sick, one third of the regiment, were carried to the rear. Sherman, one orderly behind him, rode up and trained his glasses on a part of the field that was as yet clear. The quail-hunters raised their rifles. "Sherman will be shot!" cried the Fifty-third. "General, look to your right!"

The general looked, threw up his hand, snapping, "My God, we're attacked!" As he said it the Confederates fired and his orderly fell dead, the first mortality at Shiloh. "Colonel Appler, hold your position! I'll support you!" shouted Sherman, and he spurred away for reënforcements. Appler received the encouraging news, walked over to a tree, and lay down behind it, his face like ashes. His men, forming in a wavering line, began to shoot at the Confederates, whose main line, guns flashing in the sun, came out of the woods. "Retreat! Save yourselves!" bawled Appler, and jumping up from the shelter of the tree, he bounded away to the rear and so out of the Civil War. The Fifty-third wavered. Some boys followed their colonel; the rest began to shoot at the enemy.

An incessant humming was going on among the tree tops. The boys said it sounded like a swarm of bees. Then the leaden swarm drew lower and lower until men began to fall down under its stings. It was all new and puzzling. When a man fell wounded his friends dropped their guns and helped him to the rear, staring at the blood with horror and curiosity. There were no stretchers, no hospital attendants at hand, no first-aid kits. Men bled to death because no comrade knew how to stanch the flow with a twisted handkerchief. One boy of the Fifty-third was hit a glancing blow in the shin and sat down, rubbing the place and squalling loudly. It hurt, bad!

Private A. C. Voris of the Seventeenth Illinois, which stood close by, left his regiment and came over to help the leaderless Fifty-third. He had served at Fort Donelson and was therefore a veteran among these apprentice killers. Walking calmly among them, Voris taught the trembling youngsters how to use their guns. He would aim, fire, reload, and talk. "I've met the elephant before and the way to do is to keep cool and aim low." His rifle would go "Crack!" then his voice would resume: "It's just like shooting squirrels, only these squirrels have guns, that's all." The Fifty-third began to do better. Soon Voris, seeing his own regiment moving off, called "Good-by!" and left, but the Ohio boys never forgot him, even if a little later they all ran away. After their flight they re-formed, promoted Captain Jones to the colonelcy, and marched back into the fight in scattered units.

Recruits like those of the Fifty-third were scampering away from all parts of the field before nine o'clock, and soon a number, estimated by Grant to be 8,000, were hiding under the bluffs by the river screeching in terror. Grant, who had hurried down from Savannah at the first sound of guns, wasted no time trying to re-form the fugitives. "Excluding these troops who fled, panic-stricken before they had fired a shot, there was not a time," he said, "when during the day we had more than 25,000 men in line." This 25,000, however, learned the business of battle quickly. Considering their lack of training it would not have been surprising if they had all run; so said British military critics when they studied the battle years later. The average Federal stood his ground, shooting at enemies sometimes not more than thirty feet away. When the Confederates derisively shouted "Bull Run!" the Union boys gave them back "Donelson!" in a jeering bellow.

To join them came a thin trickle of soldiers who, after fleeing, regained self-command on the river bank. Surgeon Horace Wardner, Twelfth Illinois, was working among the wounded on the wharf when he heard a large splash and looked up to see a demoralized horseman trying to swim the river on horseback. Some fifty yards from shore the animal wheeled, unseating its rider, and headed back. Frantically the cavalryman caught the passing tail and was towed to land. The ducking had cooled his blood and, gathering up weapons, he mounted and rode toward the battle.

So stoutly did Sherman hold the Union right that Johnston failed in his scheme for rolling up the Federal line like a sheet of paper. With his face and red beard black with powder, Sherman dashed up and down the field, re-forming regiments as fast as they crumbled, plugging leaks in the human dike, drawing back his force, step by step, and succeeding, somehow, in keeping the stormy tide of Southerners from breaking through. Confederate batteries were shelling his force heavily and volleys of musket balls and buckshot swept the ground. One buckshot penetrated his palm, but without taking his eyes off the enemy he wrapped a handkerchief about it and thrust his hand into his breast. Another ball tore his shoulder strap, scratching the skin. Captain William Reuben Rowley, aide-de-camp to Grant, arriving to ask how the battle was going, found Sherman standing with his uninjured hand resting on a tree, his eyes watching his skirmishers.

"Tell Grant," he said, "if he has any men to spare I can use them; if not, I will do the best I can. We are holding them pretty well just now—pretty well—but it's as hot as hell."

Four horses had died between Sherman's knees. At the death of the first, Lieutenant Taylor dismounted and handed his reins to the general. Swinging into the saddle, Sherman said, "Well, my boy, didn't I promise you all the fighting you could do?" Albert D. Richardson, collecting descriptions of Sherman from his men after the battle, said that at this point in the encounter:

> All around him were excited orderlies and officers, but though his face was besmeared with powder and blood, battle seemed to have cooled his usually hot nerves.

Other soldiers said that during the battle Sherman hadn't waved his arms when he talked, nor talked so much, as in the past. His lips were shut tight, his eyelids narrowed to a slit. He let his cigars go out more often than in peace times. He didn't puff smoke as furiously as in camp. John Day of Battery A in the Chicago Light Artillery saw Sherman halt his spurring progress over the field by the guns, again and again. Brass missionaries, the cannoneers called their pieces, having vowed to "convert the Rebels or send 'em to Kingdom Come." Day remembered that during the fight "Sherman had trouble keeping his cigar lit and he used up all his matches and most of the men's."

Thomas Kilby Smith, officer of the Fifty-fourth Ohio, and a family friend of the Ewings, watched Sherman with worshipful eyes and wrote home, "Sherman's cheek never blanched." For the second time in his life, Sherman had found something to make him forget himself, completely, utterly. He had caught that sharp rapture of absorption as a youth painting pictures on canvas in South Carolina. Now he had found it again—the strange joy of profound selflessness. Here in the storm and thunder of Shiloh, the artist found his art. His nerves, so close to the thin skin, congealed into ice. Sometimes when he held his horse motionless for a period, studying the enemy, the dead and wounded piled high before him. He did not notice them, yet they were the same boys for whose safety he had worried himself in Louisville to the brink of lunacy.

Soldiers around him thought he saw and foresaw everything. When his right wing fell back, he grinned, saying, "I was looking for that," and loosed a battery that halted the charging Confederates in stricken postures. When his chief of staff, Major Dan Sanger, pointed out Southern cavalry charging the battery, Sherman produced two companies of infantry that had been held for this emergency. They shot riders from saddles while Sherman went on with his cannonade.

For all its absorption, his mind—perhaps his subconscious mind—was photographing hideous pictures, sharp negatives, and storing them away. Later on they would become vivid positives:

> . . . our wounded mingled with rebels, charred and blackened by the burning tents and grass, crawling about begging for some one to end their misery . . . the bones of living men crushed beneath the cannon wheels coming left about . . . 10,000 men lying in a field not more than a mile by half a mile.

The field of which he spoke was a cocklebur meadow in the front. Across it Beauregard had sent his Irish-born dare-devil General Patrick R. Cleburne, to lose one third of the brigade in the fury of Sherman's fire. Probably all that saved the life of Cleburne was an accident; his horse stumbled at the start of the charge, sinking the general in the mud and separating him from his command. When the day was done, many observers said that a man could have walked all over the cocklebur meadow using bodies for stepping-stones.

Novitiates though the Northern boys might be at the profession of war, most of them were trained squirrel-shooters who, once they had mastered the complexities of the newfangled muskets, did lavish execution at point-blank range. After the first flurry, nothing could terrify them, not even the Rebel yell that had first been heard at Fort Donelson. This incoherent battle cry was distinguished by a peculiar shrillness from the deeper shouts of the Federals.

By ten o'clock the Northerners had steadied enough to begin countercharges, the Twentieth Illinois, for instance, fighting back and forth through its camps a half-dozen times. At this hour Grant, making the rounds, had ridden quietly up to Sherman, upon whom the full fury of Southern determination continued to fall. Grant said that he had anticipated Sherman's need of cartridges, and that he was satisfied the enemy could be held. He said that he was needed more elsewhere and galloped away. It was their first meeting under fire, and in the smoke they gauged each other. Later Grant said, "In thus moving along the line, I never deemed it important to stay long with Sherman."

It was at this hour of 10 A.M. that the battle settled into what most of those participants who survived the war would describe as the fiercest they ever saw. Regiments mixed, blue and gray, in the hit-trip-smother. Men carried away confused memories—awful sheets of flame . . . the endless zip-zip of musket balls, canister . . . the shudder of grapeshot . . . dirt, gravel, twigs, pieces of bark, flying in their faces . . . splinters like knives ripping open bodies . . . men tearing paper cartridges, ramming them down musket barrels, capping the guns, firing, and as likely as not forgetting to remove the ramrods, not missing them, in fact, until they saw them quivering like arrows in the throats of enemies fifty feet away. Sense and hearing were stunned by the crash of exploding powder and the death shrieks of boys. Fountains of warm wet blood sprayed on the faces and hands of the living, brains spattered on coat sleeves. Men moved convulsively, wondering whether this moment—now—would be their last. When the Fifty-fifth Illinois retreated into a blind ravine, Confederates slaughtered them from the gully edge. "It was like shooting into a flock of sheep," said Major Whitfield of the Ninth Mississippi, and years later he was still saying, "I never saw such cruel work during the war."

Prentiss, who had been forced slowly backward, finally anchored his regiments in a sunken road and by a concentrated fire was achieving a carnage hitherto unimagined by any one of the youths involved. The

Hornet's Nest, the Southerners called this sector as they worked in it for six hours, trampling their own dead and wounded. Federals noted how the charging lines would wave like standing grain when a volley cut through them. Others said the lines when hit wobbled like a loose rope shaken at one end. At times the graycoats simply bent their heads as to a sleet storm. For beginners the Southerners were as brave as the Federals, and vice versa—farm boys all, learning a new trade.

A young private of the Fourteenth Illinois came up to Lieutenant Colonel Cam, fumbling at his entrails, which were trying to escape through a great slit in his abdomen, made by a passing shell. The slippery intestines kept working through his fingers. "Oh, Colonel, what shall I do?" he pleaded. Cam laid him gently behind a tree, whipped tears off his own cheeks, then walked back into the killing. Johnson, an officer of the same regiment, spurred his horse after an elderly Confederate officer, shot him through the body, reached out and seized his victim by the hair. To his horror the whole scalp came off as the Southerner slipped dead from the saddle. A roar of laughter arose above the battle clash, and Johnson saw that he held a wig.

Private Robert Oliver of the Fifty-fifth Illinois saw Private James Goodwin walk off the field resembling Mephistopheles in a play: "He looked like he had been dipped in a barrel of blood." Goodwin carried seven bullet holes in his skin. The Union Sergeant Lacey saw George F. Farwell, a company bugler, sitting against a tree reading a letter. Lacey shook him and found that he was dead, his sightless eyes still fast upon his wife's handwriting. Colonel (afterwards General) Joseph Wheeler of the Southern force said, "The Yankee bullets were so thick I imagined if I held up a bushel basket it would fill in a minute." A boy of the Fifty-third Ohio, joining another outfit, was wounded and sent to the rear, but was soon back saying, "Captain, give me a gun, this damned fight ain't got any rear." Units were surrounded at times without knowing it and were rescued only by the equality of their enemy's ignorance.

Lieutenant James H. Wilson of Grant's staff caught a youth starting for the rear, shook him, and called him a coward. The soldier protested indignantly. "I've only lost confidence in my colonel," he said. Private Sam Durkee of Waterhouse's Battery, close to Sherman often during the day, felt a blow on the seat of his trousers as he bent over his cannon, and looking around, he saw the heels of his lieutenant's horse flirting past. Durkee yelled above the cannonade, "Why did you let your horse kick me?" "I didn't," screamed the officer. Sam felt his posterior with his hand and found blood. "Oh, I'm wounded!" he screeched. Ed Russell, thumbing the vent of a cannon near by, went down with a solid shot through his abdomen, lived twenty minutes, and shook hands with every man in the battery before he died. Men with lung wounds lay heaving, every breath hissing through holes in their chests.

The most ghastly killing of all took place when Albert Sidney Johnston assailed the Peach Orchard, a knob left of the Union center. Hurlbut, defending it, placed his men on their stomachs in a double row to shoot Johnston's men like rabbits "a-settin'." Before such a blast the Confederate boys at length withered and refused to try again. Johnston rode along the front. In one hand he carried a small tin cup that he had picked up in the sack of a Union camp and forgotten to drop. He touched bayonets with it, crying, "Men, they are stubborn; we must use the bayonet!" The Southern boys admitted that Johnston was magnificent and that his horse Fire-eater was beautiful, but they did not want to go into that sheet-flame death again. Suddenly Johnston swung his horse toward the foe and shouted, "Come, I will lead you!" Boys felt hot blood in their veins once more and, rushing past him, took the Peach Orchard, although they left comrades in rows behind them.

Fire-eater was hit four times. Johnston's clothes were pierced, one ball ripping the sole of his boot. He flapped the sole, laughing— "They didn't trip me that time!" Then he reeled. Searching hands could at first find no wound, but at length came upon a boot full of blood. Johnston was dead at two-thirty in the afternoon. A tourniquet might have saved him from the thigh wound that drained his life.

The capture of the Peach Orchard was not decisive. Hurlbut fell back to another strong position, and his men fired so rapidly as to shave down saplings and thickets as if with gardeners' shears. Between the lines thirsty men from both forces drank side by side. Wounded soldiers died while drinking, staining the water red. The Bloody Pool, it was called long afterwards.

In the retirement from the orchard, two wounded gunners tried to move their cannon with one horse. Mud stalled them. They decided to give up. Just then a stray bullet obligingly struck the horse at the base of the tail and with an astonished snort and lurch the animal took the gun off to safety.

Battered slowly, steadily backward, Grant did not lose confidence. At 3 P.M. he calmly began to assemble cannon on high ground near the Landing, parking the guns wheel to wheel and collecting enough ammunition for a final burst of flame, which at close quarters was expected to destroy any possible number of assailants.

At 4 P.M. the crisis of the battle came. In nine hours of fighting the Confederates had captured 23 cannon, and pushed the Union line back a mile or more. At the beginning Sherman had prevented them from turning the Union flank, yet they had seized three out of five Northern division camps, shooting some Federals in night clothes among the tent ropes. Some of the attackers who reached the camps so suddenly owed their success to their blue uniforms, Union batteries having let them advance unmolested. These rows of tents had helped save the Northern battle line from complete breakage, for the Confederates halted to loot the camps. It had been almost twelve hours since many of them had eaten, and they forgot the battle in their hunger for the half-cooked breakfasts standing on Union fires. They rifled haversacks, drank whisky, and read the letters of Federal privates that fluttered on tent floors.

The Confederates had been at fault, too, in attacking in long lines on so rough and broken a front. The battle had promptly split up into many individual struggles, with coöperation between generals impossible. Bragg, smashing fiercely at Prentiss, finally surrounded him, but could find no brother Confederate to push in through the open spaces on right and left to divide the Union line into three sections. By the time Prentiss had surrendered to save the lives of his remaining 2,000 men, Grant had patched up a solid front line again, Sherman and McClernand had fallen back into a more solid array, and the Federals waited for the next assault.

It never came. Beauregard, succeeding to the Confederate command on Johnston's death, saw that his men had had enough. Many had left their posts to go over and stare at the Union prisoners. Organization was broken, officers were separated from men, losses had been frightful. Furthermore, a dull, heavy, and monotonous pum-pum had begun to sound from the river. Two Union gunboats, escorting Buell's army in its advance up the stream, had begun to throw shells into the Confederate lines.

Shortly after six o'clock that morning, Grant had sent word for Buell's advance guard, under General "Bull" Nelson of Kentucky, to make haste. A steamer with rush orders had gone on to tell Buell at Savannah to bring up his whole force. To his men Buell seemed negligent as he listened to the distant guns. Boys of the Fifty-first Indiana Volunteers said he was "seemingly unconcerned—a condition of mind and heart almost universally attributed to him by the men of his command." Their regimental historian described the scene:

> Colonel Streight stormed around at a great rate and Captain Will Searce became so impatient that he cried like a child and railed out against Buell, characterizing him as a rebel. Looking up he saw Buell not forty feet away.

He had certainly heard the remark but took no notice. We paced up and down the bank like caged animals.

Although there was no convincing proof of the not uncommon charge that Buell's loyalty was doubtful, the man had too much of his friend McClellan's jealousies and prima donna's outlook ever to fit into the Western way of war. Twenty-two years after Shiloh, Sherman wrote James B. Fry, one of Buell's officers:

> General Grant believes, and we all do, that you [Buell's army] were derelict in coming by the short line . . . so deliberately and slowly as to show a purpose, while Sidney Johnston moved around by the longer line and made his concentration and attack on us before you arrived, and long after you should have been there to help us on the *first day*.

Buell arrived at the Landing in mid-afternoon, in advance of his men, and concluded from the sight of 8,000 fugitives at the wharf that the Army of the Tennessee had been defeated. He later insisted that Grant, whom he soon met, gave him a similar impression. But Sherman, who conversed with Grant at almost the same time, declared that the latter had talked quite differently, saying that at Donelson he had noticed that there came a time "when either side was ready to give way if the other showed a bold front." He had decided to be the bold one, and had won. Now, he said, the enemy had shot its bolt and with Buell's force available by morning, victory was sure.

Near dusk, Sherman, meeting Buell and Fry, told them that the Army of the Tennessee had 18,000 men in line, that Lew Wallace's 6,000 "had just come in and that I had orders from General Grant in person to attack at daylight the next morning." He was glad Buell had come, but thought victory certain even without him. Buell regarded this as a poor way to welcome him, "the savior of the day."

The battle dwindled as twilight spread. Grant and Sherman had narrow escapes at almost the same moment. A shell, missing Grant, tore the whole head, except for a strip of chin, from a captain beside him, ripped a cantle from a saddle behind him, and bowled on to clip both legs from one of Nelson's men as he came up from the river bank.

Sherman was swinging into his saddle when his horse pranced sufficiently to tangle around his neck the reins held by Major Hammond. As he bowed while Hammond raised the reins, a cannon ball cut the straps two inches below the major's hand and tore the crown and back rim of Sherman's hat.

Up from the Landing poured Nelson's men, stepping over piles of wounded on the wharf. The 8,000 fugitives had already trampled these bloody victims, sailors had dragged heavy cables across them, and they were now so caked with mud and dried blood that they were as black as Negroes.

The fresh legions cursed the cowards at the Landing. They thought them as terrorized as sheep who have been visited by killer dogs. In answer to these taunts, the deserters answered, "*You'll* catch it; *you'll* see. They'll cut you to pieces!" Nelson wanted to fire upon them. Colonel Jacob Ammen, the Virginia-born leader of a Union brigade, found his way blocked by a clergyman who exhorted the refugees, "Rally for God and country! Oh, rally round the flag! Oh, rally!" Always a pious Episcopalian, Ammen forgot himself this once and burst out, "Shut-up, you God-damned old fool! Get out of the way!"

The first of Nelson's men to reach the top were Rousseau's brigade—the Kentuckians who had originally disliked Sherman at Muldraugh's Hill. Now when they saw him with his hat in tatters, black powder on his red beard, his hand bandaged, they put their hats on their bayonets and cheered for Old Sherman. He pretended not to notice, but he remembered it always. It was the first really good word he had had since the beginning of the war.

While the Union officers rearranged their battered forces, Bragg had been moaning, "My God! My God!" because Beauregard would not order the one final charge that, Bragg was sure, would bring complete victory. But several days later he admitted to his wife that "our force was disorganized, demoralized and exhausted and hungry." Some of his men he described as

> too lazy to hunt the enemy's camps for provisions. They were mostly out of ammunition and though millions of cartridges were around them, not one officer in ten supplied his men. . . . Our failure is entirely due to a want of discipline and a want of officers. Universal suffrage, furloughs and whisky have ruined us.

It was just such a letter as Sherman would have written had he been in Bragg's shoes.

That night Bragg and Beauregard slept in Sherman's vacated tent. Near by, the captive Prentiss slept among Confederates he had known before the war. He twitted his hosts about the defeat awaiting them on the morrow. "Do you hear that?" he would say, awakening them in the night, when the boom of United States Navy cannon came from the river. Colonel Nathan Bedford Forrest, lately a slave-trader, now an unmilitary but surpassingly warlike cavalry leader in the Southern army, walked through the bivouacs of his men confiding to brother officers, "If the enemy attack us in the morning they will whip us like hell."

Grant was riding through the Union camps with substantially the same message, hunting out his commanders in the chaos to tell them that he was going to attack at daylight. To General Rusling, he said quietly, "Whichever side takes the initiative in the morning will make the other retire, and Beauregard will be mighty smart if he attacks before I do."

Across the torn field, men slept with the roar of the gunboats and the screams of the wounded ripping the air. Hospitals had broken down. Surgeons, swamped with work, did what they could, slicing and sawing in desperate haste. Flies had been blackening wounds all day. A mixture of whisky and chloroform was the only antiseptic, and when it was poured on mangled flesh it brought out maggots "on a canter," as the sufferers grimly said. Rain fell, bringing misery to the tentless warriors and relief to the burning lips of the sufferers.

When the lightning flashed the wet and weary Confederates saw sickening sights all around them—naked, bloating flesh, ghastly white faces—and they heard the moaning refrains, "Water! Water!" in the storm. A. H. Mecklin, a Bible student who had joined a Mississippi regiment, thought he heard wild hogs in the bushes. "Through the dark I heard the sound of hogs quarreling over their carnival feast." He admitted, however, that the sound was "not unmistakable."

As the night grew gray with morning, Lieutenant William George Stevenson, of Beauregard's staff, rode the field searching for his chief. Stevenson had seen a cannon ball take off the head of an earlier mount and was sick of everything. His new horse balked at a little ravine. He said afterward:

> He hesitated and I glanced down to detect the cause. The rain had washed leaves out of the narrow channel down the gully some six inches wide, leaving the hard clay exposed. Down this pathway ran a band of blood nearly an inch thick, filling the channel. Striking my rowels into the horse to escape the horrible sight, he plunged his foot into the stream of blood and threw the already thickening mass in ropy folds up on the dead leaves on the bank.

Through both battered and bleeding armies ran the folk saying, "Nobody ever wins who starts a battle on a Sunday."

Monday saw sharp, bitter fighting but victory for the North was certain. General Lew Wallace with 5,000 men arrived and took their places in the line. Wallace had started early on Sunday morning to march the five miles to Shiloh Meeting-house, but had wandered around the country all day within sound of the battle without being able to find it. Whether the mistake was his or that of Grant's aides was a matter of dispute for years to come. Beauregard, calling the roll at dawn, found only half of his original 40,000 men at hand—and these were disorganized. Nevertheless the Confederates fought stoutly for eight hours more.

At 3 P.M. on Monday Grant, gathering up fragments of regiments, led them in one last charge that broke Confederate resistance, and Shiloh was won. That evening the cold, drizzling rain resumed, gradually turning to sleet and hail that bruised the butchered Southern boys who lay in the young spring grass or who had been piled like bags of grain into open wagons for the jolting trip to Corinth. Against orders, Confederate privates crowded into the tent of General Breckinridge and stood there packed and wretched while the water ran in under the tent flap. In defeat they had lost their awe of great men.

The hail pelted Union wounded too, as they lay shrieking on the field of victory; it knocked from the trees the last few peach blossoms that the bullets had spared.

23

AS SMART AS TOWN FOLKS

ON Tuesday morning Sherman awakened in the tent he had occupied on Sunday night. It was riddled with bullets, dead men lay close to it swelling in the April heat. Two of his horses had been killed at the picket rope at the start of the battle. The general was afoot. Even his colored cook, Bustamente, had fled. The only food he had eaten in two days had been brought him at night by a Negro boy who served his aide-de-camp, Major Sanger. Now through the air so putrid with decomposing bodies, the servant appeared with a large cheese that he said he had found at a sutler's camp. Sitting on a log with his aides, Sherman ate it. Months later the sutler filed suit against Sherman for payment.

On the field all around them Union soldiers were burying the dead. Some boys shrank from touching the mangled corpses, others grew sick at the odors of putrefaction, but they quickly hardened to their trade, casually discussing trivialities with each other while they shoveled the dead men under. One elderly German recruit was caught trampling ten Confederate corpses into a hole large enough for no more than six, and growling as he did so, "Dot's too good for secesh. To de tefil mit ye!" An officer leaped, kicked the man's posterior, and sent him to the rear.

Sunday's fighting—the largest battle up to that hour on the North American continent—would remain to the end of the war as probably its bloodiest one-day strife in proportion to the number of men engaged. Of the 25,000 Federals exposed to the enemy's fire, 280 in every 1,000 were killed or wounded; and, reconciling the many conflicting claims as to Confederate losses, it was estimated that 225 in every 1,000 Southerners had been hit. Almost every survivor in both armies would go the rest of his days saying that he had never seen such bloodletting as at Shiloh. Grant thought it the worst he had ever seen. Sherman would tell veterans of the Eastern army, thirty years later, "So help me God, you boys never had a fiercer fight than we had there." George W. Cable, the New Orleans author, wrote, "The South never smiled after Shiloh."

Among the many wild rumors published throughout the North concerning the slaughter was one that Sherman had been killed. For a few hours at least, it was flying around Lancaster, unconfirmed but none the less agonizing. An old Irish woman who helped Ellen with the housework was thinking of those five fatherless children—two of them red-haired—when she told townsfolk, "Ellen Sherman need only to set her children on the rail fence and the woodpeckers will feed them."

The rumor reached Virginia, where in the camp of the Louisiana Tigers along the Rappahannock, ex-Professor Boyd, now a Confederate soldier, heard it with a start. The bulletin, issued at the end of the first day's fighting, had announced General Sherman's death as part of the great Confederate victory. While his comrades cheered, Boyd went off alone to weep.

It was almost as a soul redeemed that Sherman now rode his camps. Praise was heaped upon him by his brother-officers. Rousseau told listeners in later years, "Sherman gave us our first lessons in the field in the face of the enemy." Nelson would soon be saying, "During eight hours the fate of the army depended on the life of one man; if General Sherman had fallen, the army would have been captured or destroyed." Halleck, arriving on April 11 to take command of both Grant's and Buell's armies, commended Sherman to the Secretary of War:

> It is the unanimous opinion here that Brig. Gen. W. T. Sherman saved the fortune of the day on the 6th instance, and contributed largely to the glorious victory on the 7th. He was in the thickest of the fight on both days. . . . I respectfully request that he be made a major-general of volunteers.

Stanton announced the promotion on May 1. In Washington, Tom Ewing, Jr., doing legal work for the Union Pacific Railroad, had joined with Ohio's two Senators, John Sherman and Ben Wade, to secure Cump this honor. Tom wrote his father on May 2:

> Tell Ellen that the General's name was confirmed immediately on Wade's motion and unanimously without a reference; no other name but Grant's and Hitchcock's was ever confirmed without reference save Sherman's.

In his official report Grant praised Sherman's "great judgment and skill" and added later, "To his individual efforts, I am indebted for the success of that battle." Cump wrote Ellen:

> I have worked hard to keep down, but somehow I am forced into prominence and might as well submit. . . . The scenes on this field would have cured anybody of war. Mangled bodies, dead, dying in every conceivable shape, without heads, legs; and horses!

He wished that the war would end, but "I never expect it, or to survive it." After having lavished such anger on the newspapers, he saw no irony in his own request to Ellen to cut out of the papers and preserve all paragraphs mentioning him at Shiloh. Franc B. Wilkie, the war correspondent, visiting Sherman in the flush of his fame after the battle, described him:

> Built narrow and almost effeminate, voluble and smiling, eyes light gray and flashing incessantly in every direction, if he walked, talked or laughed, [he] walked, talked or laughed all over. He perspired thought at every pore. . . . I found Sherman pleasant and affable to his inferiors and engaging his equals with a mood that shifted like a barometer in a tropic sea.

This bright mood, however, soon met an eclipse. Into camp a few hours after the battle had come a slender correspondent of twenty-three years, Whitelaw Reid, reporter for the *Cincinnati Gazette* and author of the widely copied articles signed Agate. Wilkie noted that Reid habitually held an expression like that of a man who had recently escaped "from an imminent and frightful danger," although he could not agree with Sherman's declaration that Reid "would run like a scared wolf."

Reid had been at Cairo when first reports of the battle had begun to arrive, and had gathered that the Federals were being badly whipped. Arriving at Pittsburgh Landing on Sunday night, he had begun sending out accounts of how great had been the "surprise" of Grant's army, how pitiful had been the slaughter of Sherman's and Prentiss's men in their tents, without a chance for their lives. To add to the public's revulsion of feeling from the Tuesday morning elation of victory, there wound north steamers loaded with wounded men. The horrors of war came home to the Northwest, particularly to Ohio, which was smarting under the shame of having had several of its regiments run away at the outset of the fighting. Governor Tod of Ohio announced that the men were not cowards, but had been surprised as the result of the "criminal negligence" of their generals. Public opinion demanded a scapegoat and Grant was named by Ohio editors and politicians. In Congress, Harlan of Iowa declared that Grant had blundered at Belmont, had lost at Donelson until saved by C. F. Smith, had been surprised at Shiloh and saved by Buell. "With such a record those who continue General Grant in an active command will in my opinion carry on their skirts the blood of thousands of their slaughtered countrymen." Lieutenant Governor Stanton of Ohio visited the camps, talked to Sherman, then rushed to publish in a Bellefontaine newspaper on April 12 a resounding defense of the Ohio "cowards" and a blast against "the blundering stupidity and negligence of the general in command." He declared that there existed "a general feeling among the most intelligent men that Grant and Prentiss ought to be courtmartialed or shot."

Although he himself had not been named by Stanton, Sherman seized a pen and dashed into the lists to defend Grant. He wrote Stanton that the charges against Grant and Prentiss were false in every particular and that Stanton knew it. He said he was not surprised at the lies published by newspaper men, "It is their trade." But men in official life should not descend "to this dirty work."

> As to the enemy being in their very camps before the officers were aware of their approach, it is the most wicked falsehood that was ever attempted to be thrust upon a people sad and heartsore at the terrible but necessary casualties of war. That the cowards who deserted their comrades in that hour of danger should, in their desperate strait to cover up their infamy, invent such a story was to be expected. . . .
>
> It is simply ridiculous to talk about a surprise. To be sure very many were astonished and surprised not so much at the enemy's coming, but at the manner of his coming and these sought safety at the river and could not be prevailed to recover from their surprise till the enemy had been driven away by their comrades after two days of fighting. . . .
>
> If you have no respect for the honor and reputation of the generals who lead the armies of your country, you should have some regard for the welfare and honor of the country itself. Our whole force, if imbued with your notions, would be driven across the Ohio in less than a month and even you would be disturbed in your quiet study where you now in perfect safety write libels.

When Charles Eliot Norton, the Boston editor, read Sherman's words, he said, "How his wrath swells and grows; he writes as well as he fights!"

In Lancaster, the Salt-Boiler wrote a twenty-four-page pamphlet defending Cump and Grant and sent copies to friends for broadcasting. In it he riddled Stanton's evidence as if he were conducting a case before the Supreme Court. He quoted the Duke of Wellington, who, when asked if he had not been surprised at Waterloo, said, "No, but I am now." Ewing quoted what many witnesses on the battlefield had said about Sherman. One, General Boyle, had remarked, "If Bonaparte had commanded at Shiloh, he would have made Sherman a Field Marshal on the field of battle."

The dispute persisted in the newspapers for weeks as politicians tried to whitewash the soldiers who had fled. Cump explained to Ellen that the purpose of war was to obtain results through slaughter and to Ewing he wrote:

> If the newspapers are to be our government, I confess I would prefer Bragg, Beauregard or anybody as my ruler, and I will persist in my determination never to be a leader responsible to such a power. . . . I am not in search of glory or fame, for I know I can take what position I choose among my peers.

The question of the "surprise" at Shiloh was to remain as a topic for quarrels in years to come, the most convincing statement regarding it coming from Prentiss, who said, "We were not surprised, but we were not prepared."

In the new organization of Halleck's army, McClernand commanded the reserve, Pope the left, Buell the center, and George H. Thomas the right. Sherman, in spite of all Halleck had said of him, was subordinate to Old Tom, a situation that he was as willing to accept as Thomas had been content to serve under him in Kentucky. It was Grant who had cause for complaint. Halleck, massing the army for the advance against Corinth, relegated Grant to the empty post of second in command. Halleck's reasons for this were never made clear. Sherman, who still admired Halleck, obviously attributed the affair to damage done Grant by the newspaper attacks. He showered upon Ellen descriptions of Grant's bravery, sobriety, goodness; "Grant is as kind as a child," he said.

One day Sherman heard Halleck casually mention that Grant was leaving the army in the morning. When Sherman asked the reason, Halleck said he didn't know; Grant had simply asked for a thirty-day furlough. Quickly Sherman rode to Grant's tent, outside of which aides were packing up. Grant was seated on a campstool, sorting letters. Sherman pressed questions hot upon him.

"Sherman," said Grant, "you know that I'm in the way here. I have stood it as long as I can and can endure it no longer."

"Where are you going?"

"St. Louis."

"Have you any business there?"

"Not a bit in the world."

Then Sherman began to talk. He begged Grant to stay. He said that he had once allowed himself to be overwhelmed by the mere assertion of newspapers that he was crazy. But he had remained in the army, and now behold! the battle at Shiloh had given him new life. "Now I am in high feather," he said. He told Grant that if he left the war would progress and he would be forgotten; if he remained fortune might turn and lift him to his true place. At the end of a long session Grant had been won. He thanked Sherman and promised to stay around for a while anyway. At all events he wouldn't leave without first talking to Sherman. On June 5 Sherman, while on a scouting expedition, received a note from Grant assuring him that he would stay with the army, and in glad reply Sherman sent congratulations: "For you could not be quiet at home for a week when the armies were moving."

The two men were being drawn together. Sherman was feeling for Grant that powerful fervor which a man feels for the person whom he has befriended in effective fashion. Grant's taciturnity attracted Sherman. In years to come, when both of them were aging, Sherman would pathetically wish that he had been able all his life to hold his tongue as had Grant—an ability which, he said, "came from Grant's will-power and nothing else." Grant's laconic habit was dramatized for Sherman by the fulminations, blathering pronunciamentos, orations, and addresses of so many other generals, North and South. To the camps came a copy of the *New Orleans Picayune* containing a poem with which the Confederate General Jeff Thompson had sought to embolden his men:

I'll suffer hardships, toil and pain,
For the good times sure to come;
I'll battle long that I may gain
My freedom and my home.

I will return though foes may stand
Disputing every rod.
My own dear home, my native land,
I'll win you yet, by God!

All over the North orators were thundering prophecies of how peace was now close at hand. The West had won it. Sherman was writing Ellen his conviction that there would still be many battles—the next one would be worse than Shiloh and he expected to be killed in it or soon thereafter:

> This gives me little trouble, but I do feel for the thousands that think another battle will end the war. . . .
>
> I hope the war won't come to an end until those who caused the war, the politicians and editors, are made to feel it.

Then, without any apparent realization of inconsistency, he began to pull political wires with the Ohio administration that he had been so lately assailing. A friend had come to camp, Captain Philip Sheridan, who had returned from army service on Western plains to get into the fighting. So far, he was only serving as Halleck's quartermaster-general, and Sherman, remembering their boyhood days around the Catholic Church at Somerset, wrote Ohio's governor asking that the captain be given a regiment. There was nothing forthcoming, and on May 25 the State of Michigan claimed the dark little officer as Colonel of its Second Cavalry and started him on his battle life.

In the business of army organization, which was now the order of the day, with Halleck moving his 100,000 slowly toward Corinth, Sherman was at home. Old Brains's progress was so cautious—advancing from one elaborate breastwork to another at a rate of twenty miles in twenty-five days—so leisurely, that Sherman had a chance to teach his division the minutiae of militarism. To his boys, who were scarcely older than the seminary pupils, he became a painstaking instructor, talking, writing, explaining tirelessly. He placed sentries with his own hand—a detail too small for other division commanders. He ignored Confederate sharpshooters who aimed at him as he galloped along the picket lines. He taught his men how to fell trees for breastworks, how to clear away underbrush behind as well as in advance of a trench—"not to retreat on, but to afford means of drawing assistance." His injunction was, "Let every ax and spade be busy." It had taken costly lessons to teach the Western generals the value of intrenchments, and with Shiloh's slaughter on their minds they now dug excessively.

The snail-like progress of the advance gave Sherman time to lead his men on swift lateral movements during which he could drill into them the art of marching. "By keeping a steady pace," he said in one lengthy paper on marches issued to his men on June 17, "a weak or sick soldier will experience far less fatigue than if he rests for a while and then follows behind." Officers must keep their plodding men grouped, let them halt often to "breathe."

When his regiments encamped, Sherman showed them how and where sinks should be dug. He improved sanitation. He explained to cannoneers how to cut hay for their horses the moment a march paused. He worked to end the malingering of officers and men who indulged laziness, spring fever, and nostalgia by remaining in tents and hospitals. In General Orders he wrote,

> If the men are unable to bear arms they will form on the left of the company unarmed. If not in the hospital, but suffering from diarrhea, they can be hauled to the drill-ground by the colonel's order and there must be silent and observe the movements of the division.

Colonel Kilby Smith, who made a presentation speech when a group of officers gave Sherman a sword in honor of Shiloh, wrote home that the general would allow no furloughs, however sick an applicant might be.

Sherman set a stern example. Stricken by malaria while building bridges in swamp land, he scorned shelter and lay by the roadside directing the work. The following two days he was unable to leave the ambulance, but kept it at the scene of activity so that he could hear the men working and send them orders. He was ashamed of illness and thirty years later wrote that this "was the only time I ever did such a thing in the whole war."

How to train his hungry boys to forage for their brigades without pillaging civilians was Sherman's most serious problem. Both he and Grant continued to pour out orders and warnings on the subject. Later Sherman would say that at this time he had "personally beaten and kicked men out of yards for merely going inside." He was nevertheless drifting by the process of logic toward a slightly different view. On June 7 he relaxed somewhat the principle of giving farmers receipts for foodstuffs commandeered; his new orders read: "Brigade quartermasters must give receipts with promise to pay at the pleasure of the United States on proof of loyalty at the time." He was beginning to understand that in ways other than mere fighting, the army ought to try and wean noncombatants from allegiance to Jefferson Davis's government.

Still, he insisted to his men that foraging was "a delicate right" and carefully he wrote out for his foragers lists of articles which they might and might not appropriate. They could condemn hay, fodder and firewood, but no fence rails unless all other wood was unavailable. They must never touch personal belongings, never enter houses. To steal a hen was "as much stealing as though committed in our own country." He lectured his officers and men with such injunctions as, "Our mission is to maintain, not to violate, all laws human and divine." And on July 7 he posted orders reading:

> Stealing, robbery and pillage have become so common in this army that it is a disgrace to any civilized people. This demoralizing and disgraceful practice of pillage must cease, else the country will rise on us and justly shoot us down like dogs and wild beasts.

Urged by home orators to go forth and destroy the enemy, many of the Western boys innocently interpreted "the enemy" to mean all Southerners armed or unarmed. Sherman, repressing them, thought that they had "as much idea of war as children." Grant meanwhile was telling his aide, Lieutenant James H. Wilson, "The common soldiers are as smart as town folks."

There was truth in both viewpoints. The boys of the old Northwest might be still contemptuous of discipline, nevertheless they were working out their salvation in their own way. As became pioneers, they could do many things with their hands, and a rough and hardy frontier optimism was helping them. Instead of allowing the obstinacy of army mules to frazzle their nerves, they paid the beasts mock compliments: "A mule is so patient he'll wait three days for a chance to kick a soldier."

They knew the tricks of subsisting in the forest; they took torches into thickets at night and knocked dazzled robins, doves, and wild turkeys from limbs; they "shined" frogs that were "so big they bleated like lambs." The Indiana troops were said to be "great ramblers," eating "not only the blackberries but nibbling the thorns off the bushes." Coffee was consumed in enormous quantities, the Government issuing it roasted in the whole berry to prevent adulteration. Soldiers placed quart pails on flat stones and crushed the berries with musket butts while companions fed grains into the primitive mills. At daybreak the camps were musical with this clangor. Canteens, made of tin and covered with a woolen cloth, held three pints of water. When thrown into a fire an old one came unsoldered, and furnished a soldier with two dishes, one of which served as a washbasin, the other, when mounted on a split stick, as a skillet. Half a canteen, stabbed full of holes, was a perfect grater for corn fritters.

With pay only fourteen dollars a month—an additional allowance of fifty-two dollars being made annually for clothing—the boys found it thrifty and exciting to steal from the sutlers. Mouths of cannon were excellent hiding-places for loot when officers appeared with outraged sutlers to search tents.

Many privates supplied themselves with rubber ponchos to supplement the regular equipment of a light woolen blanket. Sporting gentry among the men chalked squares and numerals on the rubber surfaces for the playing of the gambling games, chuck-a-luck and Honest John. From the North came stockings knit by women who massed patriotically to do what they could. Many a girl tucked into the toe such romantic messages as:

Brave sentry on your lonely beat,
May these blue stockings warm your feet;
And when from wars and camp you part
May some fair knitter warm your heart.

The men sang "Hail Columbia," "The Girl I Left Behind Me," "Jay Bird," "Mary's Dream," "Do-da Day," and "Roll On, Silver Moon." They loved a chorus:

Weeping sad and lonely,
Hopes and fears how vain,
Praying when this cruel war is over,
Praying we may meet again.

For the first year and a half of war the boys slept in Sibley tents, huge affairs in which from twenty to twenty-two lay spoon fashion, with their feet to the small sheet-iron stove in the center. When one sleeper wished to shift position, he would shout "Spoon!" and the complete circle of drowsing men would turn over, hunting new depressions for hip bones. Soldiers protested when the War Department, late in 1862, abandoned the wigwam Sibleys for small service tents that came in two pieces, each some four by six feet in size. Every soldier carried half a tent, and at night must find another man with a companion piece, button the two flaps together, mount them on a ridgepole, pin down the sides and ends, and then share with his mate a space six feet by seven. To give up the sociability of the Sibleys for the cramped irritations of the service tents angered the men.

General Rosecrans, appointed to replace the unsuccessful Buell at Nashville in the fall of '62, rode out to inspect the new tents the day after their installation. On the white canvas, which stood in endless rows, he saw charcoal letters, also signs before the tent-flaps—Pups . . . Dog-hole No. 1 . . . Pups for Sale . . . Rat-Terriers . . . Bull Pups Here . . . Sons of Bitches Within. It was raining and the men were all inside their tents as the general started to ride down the line. Suddenly he saw the red face of a soldier who was on his hands and knees peering out at him. The soldier barked "Bow-wow!" and quickly the inverted V of every tent filled with faces yowling, barking, baying at the general. Rosecrans, his great red nose gleaming genially, roared with laughter as he passed down the line.

In time the soldiers became reconciled to pup tents, noting how much more easily they were transported than the huge Sibleys had been. New quarters enforced greater comradeship between pairs of soldiers. Once when a shell was seen to hurtle neatly through a raised tent flap, soldiers rushed up to find that it had buried itself in the earth without injuring the occupants, one of whom was heard saying, "There, you damn fool, you see what you get by leaving the door open!" To secure floors for these tents was a difficult matter, since rules forbade the theft of boards. One squad of soldiers stealing a barn door were carrying it home when a provost marshal loomed ahead. Quickly one of the men stretched himself on the door and groaned dismally under a blanket while his companions, with anxious faces, hurried past the sympathetic guard.

Chaplains worried because young men in war became irreligious. Drinking was common. Many officers kept barrels of beer in their tents. Before one tent stood a sign, "New Grocery. Wilson & Ellsworth. Fresh Beer 3c a Glass. Give us a Call." Wilson and Ellsworth were respectively captain and first lieutenant.

Despite all this irregularity, Halleck's 100,000 men were becoming soldiers. For Old Brains Sherman had personal gratitude and personal respect. He attributed to Halleck, in the main, the major general's stars that reached him on the twenty-ninth. The promotion, coming so soon after his misfortune in Kentucky, comforted Sherman far more than he pretended when he wrote to Ellen, "I know not why it gives me far less emotion than my old commission as 1st Lieutenant of Artillery." He said that he knew he had merited that initial promotion, and doubted if he was worthy of the later one.

He was seen by Captain Bouton to grow expansive, although not vain, as he put on the insignia of his new rank and received congratulations in his tent. His staff, taking advantage of his mood, asked him to tell them about Bull Run, one of the few subjects upon which he had been studiously silent. Graphically he described the fight, saying, "I could have taken any brigade nowadays and whipped either army."

He was proud of his division when it repulsed a Confederate counterattack on May 29 while Grant and Thomas looked on. Sherman then stormed the enemy's line and stood peering into Beauregard's main works outside Corinth. Next day his division was among the first to sweep into the town, which had been evacuated during the night.

So great was Sherman's feeling of personal indebtedness to Halleck that he did not join in criticism of Old Brains's slow march upon Corinth nor of the commander's decision to halt after the capture of the city and scatter his immense army about strategic points in the West. Years later Sherman would agree that this scattering program had been "a fatal mistake," since if Halleck had kept his 100,000 men—in reality 120,000, due to reënforcements—concentrated and had marched them against Beauregard at Tupelo, Mississippi, he could have given the Confederacy a crushing defeat. Beauregard at the time had only 60,000 effective soldiers, and discouragement was preying upon them. But at the time Sherman was so whole-heartedly in sympathy with Halleck that he grew desperate when on July 11 President Lincoln summoned Old Brains to Washington to become general in chief of all Federal armies.

McClellan had been a failure during the summer campaign in Virginia, and had been relieved. Lincoln, turning to the West for a fighting general, chose Pope to organize a new, more aggressive unit of the Eastern forces. Next he summoned Halleck to sit in the War Department and organize victory. To Sherman Halleck declared that he did not want to accept; he agreed with Sherman that there was too much politics at Washington. But in the end he accepted obediently enough, news of which brought Sherman "heartfelt pain."

To make Sherman particularly emotional was his discovery that Halleck, in preparing to depart, had arranged with Grant, next in rank, to place Sherman in one of the most important and pleasant posts in the western field—the command at Memphis. On July 16 he sent Halleck protests against his departure:

> You took command in the Valley of the Mississippi at a period of deep gloom when I felt that our poor country was doomed to a Mexican anarchy, but at once rose order, system, firmness and success in which there has not been a pause . . . all I have done has been based on the absolute confidence in your knowledge of national law and your comprehensive knowledge of things gathered, God only knows how. . . . The man who at the end of this war holds the military control of the Valley of the Mississippi will be *the* man.
>
> You should not be removed. I fear the consequences. . . . Instead of that calm, sure, steady progress which has dismayed the enemy, I now fear alarms, hesitations and doubt. You cannot be replaced here and it is too great a risk to trust a new man from the East.

Crossing Sherman's letter in transit came Halleck's farewell. It was marked Confidential:

> The change does not please me, but I must obey orders. Good-by and may God bless you. I am more than satisfied with everything you have done. You have always had my respect, and recently you have won my highest admiration. I deeply regret to part with you.

Halleck went East and Grant, who was only commander of a military district embracing western Kentucky and Tennessee, sat uncomfortably in the vacated chair. Officially there was no successor to Halleck as the director of the Department of the Mississippi, nor would there be any successor for three months and more. Buell with the Army of the Ohio was independent, and from Washington was moved toward Chattanooga. Sherman saw again arising the same confusion and lack of unity that had existed before Halleck's ascendancy in the West.

Sherman did not expect Grant to develop the necessary qualities for the high command. Grant was the man for battles, but he had obviously never heard of the military maxims, organizational principles, and campaign rules which came so profoundly from Halleck's tongue. A month after Old Brains had gone, Cump wrote John, "The loss of Halleck is almost fatal. We have no one to replace him."

24

WE CAN MAKE WAR TERRIBLE

ON a Sunday morning late in July, 1862, General Sherman sat with his staff among the starched and crinolined parishioners in the leading Episcopal church of Memphis, Tennessee. While the preacher prayed, the Southerners peeped from under their eyebrows at the Union leader who had come to control the city. Their own soldiers had departed soon after the fall of Corinth, and for a time General Grant had come to rule them, but with the departure of General Halleck to the East, Grant had gone back to Corinth to command the Army of the Tennessee and this red-haired Sherman had arrived.

Many parishioners in the Episcopal congregation knew him from days when, living in St. Louis and New Orleans, he had been a part of the social life that had played up and down the Mississippi. They watched his bowed head as the preacher spoke a ritualistic prayer of the service. The preacher asked God for many things, but after the fashion of Southern Episcopalians since secession, omitted the standard request that divine protection be given the President of the United States. Sherman's head came up. He remembered the prayer from the days when he had listened to it every Sunday in the chapel at West Point. He knew what the clergyman had omitted. He rose to his feet abruptly, and repeated the missing words in a strong, clear voice. Then he sat down. "Next day," as his admiring Captain Bouton described it, "he ordered the ceremony observed or the church closed."

The incident was a signal that Sherman had come to regard himself as more educator than warrior. Shiloh's bloodletting had drained the phantoms from his mind, the weeks spent in inching toward Corinth had allowed him to develop as an efficient instructor of soldiers; now he began to teach Southerners that war was terrible and peace beautiful, that rebellion meant ruin, while obedience to law meant, in the end, prosperity. His philosophy of war was beginning to take form. War could do something even more important than restore the authority of the Constitution; it could chasten a willful democracy—teach it obedience and humility.

His first task in this purpose which animated him was to show Memphis that the Federal army brought punishment for "Rebels" and blessings for the loyal. Soon after his entrance on July 21, he had reorganized the city police, routed the thugs who had preyed on the householders ever since the Confederate army had fled, started the idle steamboats carrying trade northward, encouraged stores, theatres, schools, and churches to reopen, and put Mayor Park and the city government to functioning again. His concept of obedience to law had never included interference with private morals and he took no action to close the "parlor houses" that had made the river port celebrated for sin. A general, he thought, had more important duties than acting as nursemaid for his men. One of the soldiers, O. L. Jackson, described Memphis as "one of the first places of female prostitution in the country . . . virtue was scarcely known within the limits of the city proper and many a soldier contracted diseases there." Sherman took no notice of the frequency with which his men sought those Negro girls who, accustomed to the carnal visits of Southern males before the war, now were willing or even eager to give themselves to white men from the friendly North. Clustering on the fringe of many Federal encampments, these slave women, in the words of one Union cavalryman, "felt loving toward us because they thought we were bringing them freedom, and they wouldn't charge us a cent." To halt the smuggling of liquor into the city, Sherman reopened the shuttered saloons and licensed them. "I traverse the city day and night," he wrote after several weeks, "and assert that Memphis is and has been as orderly a city as Saint Louis, Cincinnati or New York."

While Sherman demonstrated to civilians the advantages of Federal rule, Congress and the President came to his aid in showing Southerners the disadvantages of clinging to the Confederate Government. On July 17, four days prior to Sherman's arrival in Memphis, a Confiscation

Bill had been passed, allowing enemy noncombatants sixty days' grace in which to recant; after that their property was liable to seizure. Although the law was in John Sherman's words "more useful as a declaration of policy than as an act to be enforced," it made a sweeping change in the Federal attitude toward runaway slaves.

On August 6, 1861, Congress had turned into law an idea advanced by a Federal general from Massachusetts, Benjamin F. Butler who, in Virginia, had seized as "contraband of war" Negroes who labored on Confederate military works. But the army as a whole, East and West, had held to the course of noninterference between master and slave. Led by Halleck, the Western forces had repulsed runaway slaves. Here and there Abolitionist privates encouraged blacks to leave their masters, and companies of soldiers sometimes shielded fugitives from owners who came to camp for them, but the vast majority of escaping slaves were handed back to claimants or driven beyond the lines.

"Have nothing to do with the Negro," Sherman had ordered while at Paducah, ". . . it is deceiving the poor fellow to allow him to start and have him forcibly driven away afterward."

Now in July, 1862, Congress declared that any slaves captured or escaping from any person "in armed rebellion or abetting it" should be retained by the army and should be "forever free of their servitude"; moreover, any slave escaping into a Free State should be free unless his master could take oath that he had never given aid or comfort to "the present rebellion."

In Memphis Sherman welcomed this sweeping change. He was as anti-Abolitionist as ever, yet he saw slavery as a weapon against those who would nullify Federal law. Indeed, long before the War Department had interpreted the new statute for army commanders, Sherman had made his own interpretations and begun enforcing them. On August 8 he officially informed Memphis that "in the absence of instructions from his superior officers" he had decided what he would do. Runaway slaves, of whom some 1,300 were loafing about the city, could go home to their masters or stay; no "force or undue persuasion" would be put upon them to make them decide. But if they remained they must work for the Federals, receiving, in lieu of salary, food, clothing and "one pound of chewing tobacco a month." Later on more equitable wages would be agreed upon and paid. When the United States courts were reëstablished, said Sherman:

> Loyal masters will recover their slaves and the wages they have earned during their temporary use by the military authorities; but it is understood that all masters who are in open hostility to the Constitution of their country will

lose their slaves, the title to which only exists by force of the very Constitution they seek to destroy.

In September, Sherman would learn that still more distinguished support had come to his policy. Lincoln's Emancipation Proclamation would free the slaves of people in rebellion and promise to seek compensation for those loyal citizens in the rebellious States. Ironically, logically, Sherman impressed his rule upon slaveholders. When one asked how he might round up his runaways, Sherman snapped:

"I know of only one way—through the United States marshal."

On the street, the Southerner asked for the marshal and was told that he had left town. "When did he go?"

"When Sumter was fired on." Back to Sherman he raced asking if there were no other recourse.

"No," said Sherman. "The law provided a remedy for you slaveholders in cases like this; but you were dissatisfied and smashed the machine. If you don't like your work, you had better set it running again."

By the end of August's first week Grant had received instructions as to the new policy and relayed them to Sherman with particular reference to real estate. Sherman, informing Memphis that he was trustee for the United States until questions of rightful ownership could be settled by proper courts, seized all vacant buildings and set up his quartermasters as a huge renting company. Writing out for them thirteen sample problems that might arise, he attached lengthy solutions and soon was collecting twelve hundred dollars monthly in rentals which he credited to the Government. The training which had seemed so futile in Kansas now bore fruit. Under his management, the rental department was operated meticulously, efficiently and became a powerful factor in the revival of business that came to Memphis.

Grant in Corinth read revealing sentences from Sherman's letters of August 17 and October 4:

> Your orders about property and mine about niggers make them [the Southerners] feel that they can be hurt and they are about as sensitive about their property as Yankees. . . . We cannot change the hearts of the people of the South but we can make war so terrible that they will realize the fact that however brave and gallant and devoted to their country, still they are mortal and should exhaust all peaceful remedies before they fly to war. This is all I hope for and even this will take time and vast numbers.

If he could agree with the Government's policies in condemning real estate and slave property, he was not so fortunate in his attempt to stop trade with the enemy interior. Upon entering Memphis, the greatest cotton mart north of New Orleans, he found traders buying cotton on Federal permits—the Government having permitted the trade in order to encourage loyal planters in the Border States as well as the textile-mill owners of New England. Into Memphis came farmers demanding gold for their bales. Gold, Sherman knew, found its way to the Confederate authorities, who bought arms and ammunition with it in the West Indies. So he forbade the traffic. When the Northern speculators who thronged the city found the farmers willing to accept salt, Sherman forbade that exchange too. "Salt is as contraband as powder," he said, knowing how the farmers used it to cure ham and bacon for Bragg's soldiers to live on all winter long.

For a few days, Sherman's embargo held. Once he relaxed it when some forty farmers convinced him that they would exchange their cotton for shoes and medicine needed by their suffering families. "Their plain, simple story impressed me," he told Grant. But he mixed wisdom with sentiment, insisting that the farmers, in return for this favor, help him suppress the guerrillas who roamed their regions.

When news came that the Government would not sanction his rulings and that he must allow open trading, Sherman made a cunning attempt to keep within the letter of the law and yet enforce his principle. He required buyers to pay cash which would be held in escrow by quartermasters until the end of the armed rebellion; or if they chose they could sign notes redeemable at that far-off time. Explaining this plan to Secretary of the Treasury Chase, who controlled the cotton traffic, Sherman wrote, "Under these rules cotton is being obtained about as fast as by any other process, and yet the enemy receives no 'aid or comfort.' "

But his statesmanlike device was not acceptable, and through Halleck the Government ordered him to abandon it and allow the transfer of gold. With a growl to Grant that he did not see how Halleck could countenance such a thing, Sherman obeyed. However, he snarled:

> Commerce must follow the flag, but in truth commerce supplies our enemy with the means to destroy the flag and the Government whose emblem it is.

He was careful not to heckle the Washington authorities, as he had when he had been stationed in Kentucky. Now that he had command of his nerves, the tact and diplomacy he had shown as a young officer began to return to him. He made no such error as did Grant concerning the Jewish speculators who were so numerous in the cotton markets. Where Sherman limited his strictures to personal letters, Grant on December 17 expelled Jews from his department--a move that Lincoln revoked on January 4.

Sherman reported to Halleck that his work in organizing Union

Clubs and fostering antisecession sentiment was "really a substantial beginning of the conversion of the people to our cause." Yet to his brother John he was writing such sentences as:

> It is about time the North understood . . . that the entire South, man, woman and child is against us, armed and determined. It will call for a million men for several years to put them down. . . .
>
> My opinion is that there never can be peace and we must fight it out. The war is, which race, that of the North or South, shall rule America. . . .
>
> The greatest danger North is division and anarchy, but I hope the pressure from the South will keep all united until our armies begin to have some discipline and see how important it is to success.

How far he was prepared to go to root out rebellion he made plain to John on August 13:

> I would be willing to revolutionize the Government so as to amend that article of the Constitution which forbids the forfeiture of land to the heirs. My full belief is that we must colonize the country *de novo*, beginning with Kentucky and Tennessee, and should remove four millions of our people at once south of the Ohio River, taking the farms and plantations of the Rebels. I deplore the war as much as ever, but if the thing has to be done, let the means be adequate. Don't expect to overrun such a country or subdue such a people in two or five years. It is the task of a century.

That Sherman should tell Halleck that the Memphis people were showing signs of conversion and tell John that the Southerners were irreconcilable, did not mean that he had sacrificed his old ideals of honor; it meant merely that he had learned the responsibility of public place. Thomas Ewing had advised him not to speak officially or publicly in a way to discourage Union men. He would obey.

While he wrote privately to Grant and John Sherman regarding the wisdom of making war terrible and of employing depopulation, he was doing acts of kindness for acquaintances in the Confederate Army. Through subterranean channels he let General Pillow know that the latter's concern over starving slaves was unjustified; the slaves were not wandering in Memphis, they were on the Pillow plantation. And learning that his old West Point friend Earl Van Dorn was suffering for the comforts of life in his headquarters at Holly Springs, Mississippi, he connived at smuggling through the lines cigars, liquor, boots, and gloves for the Confederate's personal use. When the poor of Memphis suffered in the winter's cold, Sherman organized a charity drive, established a bureau of relief, donated a thousand dollars from his rental collections, and called upon his troops to give money, food, "or anything needed by poor or sick families. Generosity and benevolence to the poor and distressed are characteristic of good soldiers."

When Judge John T. Swayne, the police magistrate whom Sherman had restored to office, stubbornly attempted to pass upon cases touching ownership of slaves, Sherman labored patiently to teach him to keep within his province—criminal cases:

> For God's sake, don't let this accursed question of slavery blind your mind to the thousand and one duties and interests that concern you. . . . In my seeming leaning toward men of your character I have risked my reputation and ability for good.

Abolitionists in the North were attacking him for his failure to set free all Negroes in his district.

He drew a sharp line between acts of personal kindness and stern duty. When Tennessee bankers sought to protect their funds by professing friendship with both Federal and Confederate forces, he wrote Andrew Johnson, the loyal governor of the State:

> All men must now choose which king. This by-play is more dangerous than open, bold rebellion. A large amount of the success of our enemies has resulted from their boldness. They have no hair-splitting. We, too, must imitate and surpass their game and compel all men and corporations to espouse the cause.

He himself split no hairs in enforcing the ancient *lex talonis*, the law of retaliation, in his attempts to suppress the guerrillas whom he recognized as the most anarchical creation of the war. The looseness with which the Confederacy employed Partisan Rangers had made the status of these irregularly enlisted bands very vague, some generals recognizing them as legitimate soldiers, others excommunicating them as outlaws. The persistence of these guerrillas in firing upon nonmilitary steamboats plying the Mississippi caused him to terrify Memphis on September 27 when he issued Special Orders No. 254:

> Whereas many families of known rebels and of Confederates in arms against us have been permitted to reside in peace and comfort in Memphis, and whereas the Confederate authorities either sanction or permit the firing on unarmed boats carrying passengers and goods for the use and benefit of the inhabitants of Memphis, it is ordered that for every boat fired on, ten families must be expelled from Memphis.

A few days later when guerrillas near the town of Randolph poured lead into two steamboats, Sherman burned the village and informed the countryside that a repetition of the outrage would cause him to fill boats with captive guerrillas and use them as targets for Union cannon. "God himself has obliterated whole races from the face of the earth for sins less heinous . . ." he roared. With universal wails the people of Memphis begged him to recall the order. He replied that he would suspend it for fifteen days so that they might beg the Confederate armies to suppress guerrillas, although he felt sure no such disavowal would be forthcoming. Sternly he lectured the Memphis lady, Miss P. A. Fraser, who had sent him an appeal. He wrote her:

> Would to God ladies better acted their mission on earth . . . that instead of inflaming the minds of their husbands and brothers to lift their hands against the Government of their birth, and stain them with blood [they] had prayed them to forbear, to exhaust all the remedies afforded them by our glorious Constitution and thereby avoid "horrid war," the last remedy on earth.
>
> . . . when the time comes to settle the account, we will see which is more cruel—for your partisans to . . . shoot down the passengers and engineers with the curses of hell on their tongues, or for us to say the families of such men engaged in such hellish deeds shall not live in peace where the flag of the United States floats.

Having made the incident serve his disciplinary purposes, he refrained from exiling Memphis families under his decree. He made a determined effort to help the citizens when their officials voted to debase currency and issue the so-called shinplasters in denominations as low as ten cents. Sardonically he asked why they did not imitate Mexico, "where soap is money." He asked them if, as the South had boasted, "Cotton is King," why they did not put up cotton in "parcels of 5, 10, 25 and 50 cents." He said that if it was the last thing he did, he wished to spare the people from the folly of the shinplasters.

While he paced the streets of Memphis he saw from afar a change come over the spirit of war. On August 2 Grant had been ordered by the Administration to live henceforth off the enemy's country, and in the subsequent sixty days Sherman beheld a striking object lesson in the wisdom of this course.

He knew that Bragg, replacing Beauregard on June 27 as commander of the Confederate army at Tupelo, Mississippi, had accomplished marvels in rescuing the secessionists of the Mississippi Valley from the despair into which Albert Sidney Johnston's régime had cast them. Rasping, scolding, drilling night and day, Braxton had revivified not only the army but the civilians. Even the Confederate politicians of Kentucky promised their State to Bragg if he would march there.

In September he took them at their word, and came North with an army keyed to the daring manoeuvers required in a campaign which skirted the immobile garrisons left by Halleck and recalled from East

Tennessee the Federal army of Buell. In the contagion of his high resolve, he was joined by another Confederate army under Kirby Smith, and as he thrust even to the gates of Louisville, Smith menaced Cincinnati. Panic agitated the Northwest. Indiana rushed half-trained recruits to Buell in Louisville; farmers drilled in Cincinnati.

But Bragg found how baseless were the promises of Kentucky politicians. He had carried in his wagons some 15,000 muskets for the citizens who were to rise and join him. They did not appear. Kentucky was as pro-Federal as ever. At this discovery Bragg abandoned the moves which had so far wrung the compliments "very skillful and bold" from Sherman. Veering away from Louisville, Bragg avoided battle. But the weather was hot and dry and on October 8 some of his privates took to fighting with Buell's skirmishers for some water holes near Perryville and, before any one quite knew it, a battle had been fought. Although Bragg held minor advantages at the day's end, he withdrew into Tennessee, and as he retired he cast off the scruples which had led him to protect civilians' property. Living off the country he moved far more rapidly than his pursuer Buell who still fed his men from a huge slow wagon train.

As Sherman thought over this campaign, he saw that his old friend Braxton had shown how marches must henceforth be marched.

Rapt in war plans, Sherman was regarded by the Ewings as excessively conscientious when he neglected to assist his youngest brother-in-law, Charles. Some months earlier the youth had secured, without help from Cump, appointment as captain of the Thirteenth Regulars, and was now fretting at the obscure task of guarding prisoners in Illinois. Tom, Jr., wrote home that one word from Cump would rescue the boy, and when Old Solitude also grew restive, Sherman took action, sending pleas to Halleck. Soon Charley was at the front where he would later serve on Cump's staff as lieutenant-colonel and inspector-general, these promotions coming, however, more from zeal and courage than from favoritism. To the Ewings, Cump explained why he had been so slow to want Charley brought down to the battle-zone:

> . . . the chances of war are so uncertain that I almost dread to have him exposed to them. I don't want him to become enamored of military fame, but to devote his time to the profession of the law. I feel that all the sacrifices we are now making enhance the dignity of the Profession of Law rather than the influence of the Military class, which is too costly to endure long.

In September Charles was writing from Memphis that the officers and men worshiped Cump "particularly since Shiloh," and that his staff loved him for the many thoughtful things he did for them. Lieutenant Kilby Smith was writing his mother: "Sherman never utters a word to bring the blush to the cheek of a maiden. . . . He rarely smiles yet has cheering amiability. The men love him."

Ellen, visiting Memphis in the late autumn, wrote her father that the war was changing Cump. His red beard was grizzled. "He looks more wrinkled than most men of 60."

25

THE VULTURES ARE LOOSE

THE autumnal haze of 1862 was on the Mississippi Valley. Sherman stood watching the great river writhe past in dark, constrictor coils. Since he had first seen the Mississippi River, twenty years before, it had been a majestic satisfaction to him—the symbol of geographic unity. It was the trunk of the American tree, with limbs and branches reaching to the Alleghenies, the Canadian border, the Rocky Mountains. "The spinal column of America," he called it, "the seat of coming empire."

No matter where his nomadic feet had carried him, they had kept turning back to the Mississippi. He could have understood the Romans who prayed to Father Tiber. He did understand the Indians who had reverenced the Father of Waters. In hours when the Union, the Constitution, became phantoms—words, nebular guessings—the Mississippi River was still a fact. Men might say that it was half-Federal, half-Confederate, but it still rolled on—the physical refutation of sectionalism. He wondered why men should not see that this was true.

Sherman understood that whoever won the river won the war. Let either Richmond or Washington fall, and the war would continue. But let Federal steamers roll from St. Louis to New Orleans and the Confederacy, cut in two, must wither and die. Already the Union forces held it as far south as the mouth of the Arkansas River, a hundred miles below Memphis; also it held New Orleans at the river's end, but between the two extremes stretched more than two hundred miles still ruled by Confederate cannon.

The key to this stretch of enemy river was Vicksburg, from whose high bluffs the strongest of massed batteries frowned on waters that cut a giant hair-pin curve in the lowlands—Vicksburg, the golden apple

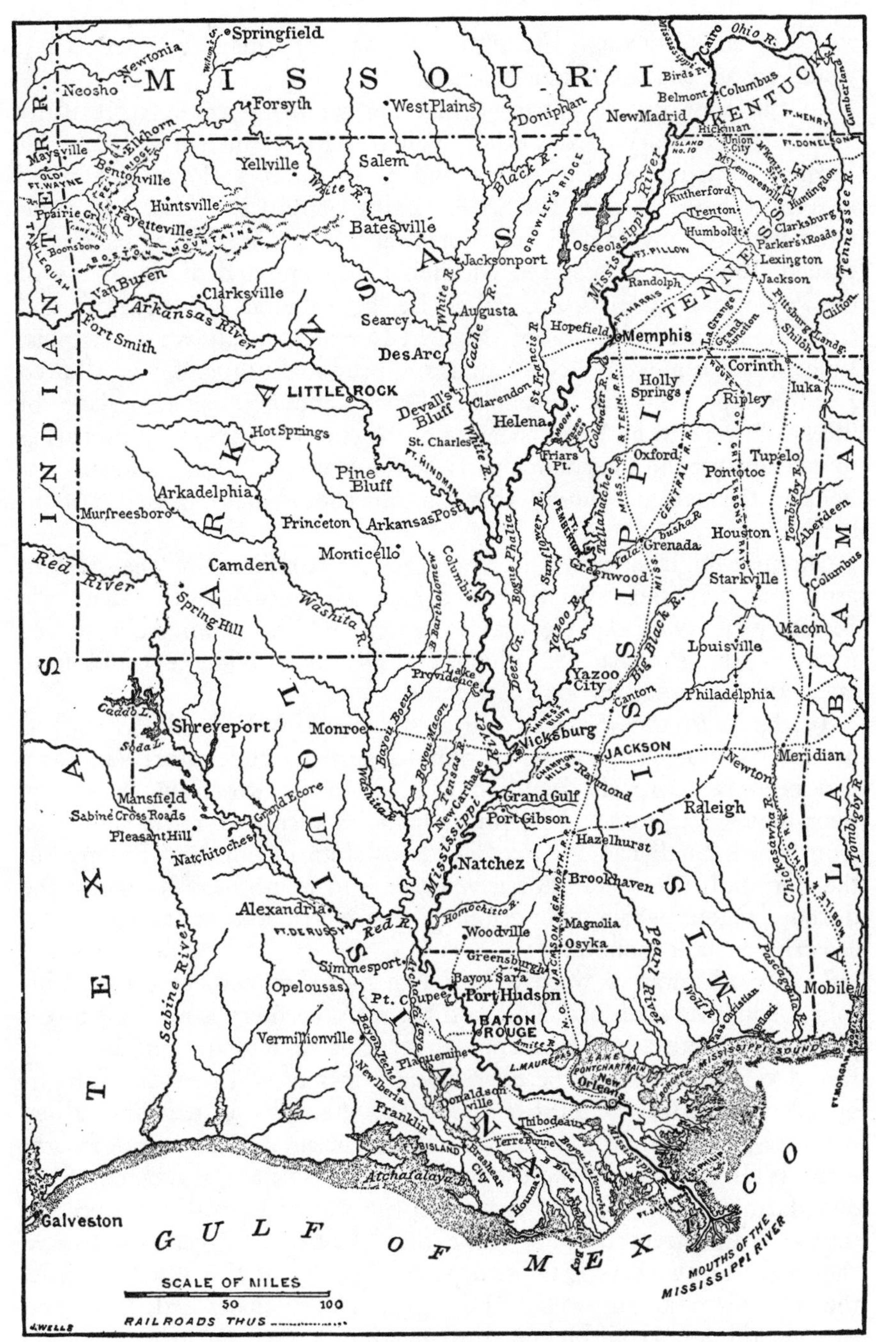

SECTION OF THE MISSISSIPPI VALLEY

(From *Battles and Leaders of the Civil War*; vol. 3)

that now shone through the autumnal haze. Sherman saw that its fall would rescue the war from stalemate.

In the East it was apparent that neither army could successfully invade the territory of the other. Where McClellan had failed in his Virginia campaign of the spring and early summer, Pope had failed in August, beaten back at the Second Battle of Bull Run. Lee had countered with the invasion of the North, and in the free-State panic that ensued, Lincoln had restored McClellan to command of the Army of the Potomac. McClellan had halted Lee at Antietam in September, and from the bloody indecision of the field Lee had withdrawn to Virginia. Lincoln had removed McClellan again, presumably for having allowed Lee to escape scot-free. Lincoln had issued announcement that slaves of "Rebels" were to be freed. Masses of Northern voters were preparing to vote against the President's party at the State and Congressional elections in the autumn—angry that Lincoln should have turned "Abolitionist."

Sherman in later years declared that the condition of the Eastern army was desperate with four men issuing orders—the President, the Secretary of War, the General in Chief and the commander of the Army of the Potomac. "Nothing but Divine Providence could have saved this nation at this crisis," he said.

In the West the war was also at stalemate. A Federal victory had been won on October 4 when a Confederate army under Earl Van Dorn had been murderously repulsed at Corinth by Rosecrans—a victory sharp enough to decide Lincoln to name Rosecrans for the command from which Buell had been removed for sloth in pursuing Bragg. But the Corinth battle was not decisive enough to weigh heavily against the discouragement which was gripping the Northwest as tax rates and conscription talk mounted.

Democratic orators were telling Northwestern audiences that Lincoln's Administration had delivered them to the mercies of Wall Street plutocrats. With the Mississippi River closed, midland produce was forced to find markets in the East. Cheap water freight was cut off, high-priced railroad freight must be used. And the railroad magnates, allied with Eastern capitalists of other lines of business, had raised freight rates. Wall Street was using the war to fatten itself at the expense of the poor farmer, and Wall Street wanted the war continued at its present status. Wall Street did not want the Mississippi River opened. So chorused the Democratic politicians, asking why, if this were not true, the Administration allowed Vicksburg to remain unattacked. Here and there wild orators could be heard demanding that the Northwest secede and form its own Confederacy. Then it could make peace with the

Southern Confederacy and have cheap water freight to the sea. Secret societies grew in the Northwest, plotting revolt.

General Grant, sitting at his headquarters in upper Mississippi, listened to Sherman's pleas that Vicksburg be taken. Grant's hands were tied. He had inherited an army that Halleck had scattered so widely that now only 35,000 could be assembled for a campaign. He would need more to take Vicksburg and must wait until they came from the North. But volunteering had almost ceased, and the North was not yet reconciled to the universal conscription that the South had already adopted.

To Grant strange rumors came sifting down from the North. One of his generals, John A. McClernand—the same division commander who had fought so well at Sherman's side during the Battle of Shiloh—had turned on his commander, fed the newspapers with criticism of Grant's generalship at Shiloh, and gone North on leave of absence, saying, "I'm tired of furnishing brains for the Army of the Tennessee." Political ambition was fermenting mightily inside McClernand. As a Democratic Congressman from Illinois—representing Lincoln's home district—he had leaped to support the Union in 1861 and, partly as reward for this and partly because he had been a convenient peg upon which to hang honors that would please wavering Democrats, the Republican President had made him a brigadier general.

To Lincoln in September, 1862, McClernand had taken a secret plan. If he could be commissioned to raise a separate army for the capture of Vicksburg and the opening of the Mississippi, he would preach a great crusade through the Northwest, bring thousands of hesitating citizens into uniform, and save the section from secession. On October 20 Lincoln, who had been friendly with him in prewar days, wrote out a paper marked Private and Confidential and gave it to the ambitious man. McClernand, he said, could, if he chose, show the paper to governors in the Northwest. It authorized him to organize recruits then enrolled but unmobilized in Iowa, Illinois, and Indiana, to enlist new regiments, and to forward them South

> to the end that when a sufficient force, not required by the operations of General Grant's command, shall be raised, an expedition may be organized under General McClernand's command against Vicksburg and to clear the Mississippi River and open navigation to New Orleans.

Vicksburg had now become a golden apple to McClernand as well as to Sherman. From its seizure, however, Sherman wished no personal gain. McClernand was dreaming of the political honors—the United States Senatorship, perhaps the Presidency—that would come to the conqueror of the Gibraltar of the West. Western newspapers exulted at the patriotic fervor that McClernand kindled with his recruiting drive. Soon the new apostle of Westernism had 60,000 soldiers drilling or departing southward. He became known as the President's favorite. Frank Blair, in Missouri, strengthened this popular belief when he asked Lincoln to attach him to McClernand's force.

Grant was worried. Regular-army men about him said that the President was trying to win the war with citizen soldiers like McClernand instead of with West-Pointers. Sherman, who apparently took no notice of the McClernand movement, sent Grant a plan of campaign: March the army straight south along the railroad tracks that ran from Memphis to Vicksburg; batter back the Confederate army under General John C. Pemberton, which now protected those railroads; and in the meantime send a second force in transports down the Mississippi to demonstrate against the city's water front. Between the two forces Vicksburg could be pinched off.

Grant liked the plan. On October 26, less than a week after McClernand had made his noisy entrance into the Northwest, Grant began telegraphing Halleck of his readiness to take Vicksburg with his own force provided "small reënforcements" were sent him. Halleck was silent. Two weeks later Grant telegraphed that if the reënforcements did not "come on rapidly, I will attack as I am." Halleck replied that twelve regiments would soon be in Memphis, the depot for the Vicksburg expedition. This puzzled Grant, who asked if he was to lie still while the expedition was fitted out, and if Sherman was to remain under his command. Halleck answered, "You have command of all men sent to your department and have permission to fight the army as you please." This was probably more than a declaration to Grant that McClernand's recruits were not reserved for a special force, as McClernand understood; it was in all likelihood a signal to Grant to make haste. Halleck did not approve of McClernand; few West-Pointers did.

Meanwhile there was arriving at the flotilla base at Cairo, Illinois, Admiral David D. Porter, a man who had risen to his post without the help of the United States Naval Academy, and who had told Secretary of the Navy Welles that he preferred to coöperate with McClernand, since he dreaded association with West Point generals as being "too self-sufficient, pedantic and supercilious." To Porter Lincoln said that McClernand was "a better general than either" Grant or Sherman, "a natural-born general" who had been the real victor at Shiloh. At least in later years Porter would so quote the President.

Grant was making haste. First he ordered Sherman to bring two divisions overland and merge them with the main army. Sherman, having built scientific fortifications around Memphis, felt it secure with four regiments as defenders, and brought three divisions. But when he arrived Grant had changed his mind. On the night of December 8 Sherman learned that Grant now planned a surprise attack on Vicksburg. Sherman was to hasten back to Memphis, collect 40,000 men—many of them the recruits McClernand was pouring into the city—load them on steamers that Admiral Porter had already started southward from Cairo, then float down the Mississippi to the mouth of the Yazoo, eight miles above Vicksburg. Turning into the Yazoo, Sherman was to storm the bluffs rising above the river and fight his way to the high plateau in the city's rear. With 40,000 he should be able to master the 6,000 Confederates who garrisoned the citadel. Grant said that he would prevent Pemberton from detaching any of his 25,000 for the reënforcement of the garrison. From his new base of supplies at Holly Springs, Mississippi, Grant planned to march south down the railroads, hammering Pemberton while Sherman took the city.

Immediately Sherman returned to Memphis and began what he later described as "preparations hasty in the extreme." Grant in after years admitted that he had organized so hurried an attack to forestall McClernand:

> I feared that delay might bring McClernand who was his [Sherman's] senior. . . . I doubted McClernand's fitness; and I had good reason to believe that in forestalling him I was by no means giving offense to those whose authority to command was above both him and me.

Who those higher-ups might be, Grant never explained. In all likelihood he was not candid with Sherman in describing his new move as a "surprise attack." Grant was too good a militarist not to know how impossible it was for a flotilla bearing 40,000 men to steam down the river for days without its progress being described in many telegrams to Vicksburg and Pemberton.

In reality the only principal in the whole drama who could be surprised was McClernand, who was happily recruiting in the fields of war, politics, and marriage. At fifty-one years of age, he celebrated his approaching conquest of Vicksburg by marrying a lady whom Ellen Sherman later described in some scorn as his sister-in-law. On December 12 McClernand asked the War Department to send him to the front. He had his men transported to Memphis. He was ready. Silence hung on the wires. Knowing well the wiles of politicians and suspecting the cunning of Halleck, on the seventeenth McClernand telegraphed both Stanton and Lincoln, "I believe I am to be superseded." Stanton replied soothingly that McClernand was to command the expedition under the supervision of the departmental commander. This was not exactly what Lincoln had authorized in his private instructions—"a sufficient force, not required by the operation of General Grant's command." But McClernand's situation was worse than even Stanton's telegram had indicated. On December 18 Halleck telegraphed Grant:

> It is the wish of the President that General McClernand's corps shall constitute a part of the river expedition and that he shall have the immediate command under your directions.

But Halleck did not send this word to McClernand until the twenty-second, and even so, did not send with it necessary orders directing the impatient man to quit his official recruiting station at Springfield, Illinois. It took McClernand another twenty-four hours to secure this.

At last on December 23 he entrained with his bride, the bridal party, and an accompanying rain of old shoes. On the twenty-sixth they steamed south from Cairo, and soon docked at Memphis, where the ladies thought to see the bridegroom take command of his legions. His men were gone! The whole expedition was gone! It had sailed off without him! Sherman had started with it on the nineteenth!

McClernand could never prove a conspiracy against him. Grant, he discovered, had tried to telegraph him on the eighteenth the information just received from Halleck, but Confederate cavalrymen had cut the wires and the message had not come through. However, such a telegram would have come too late to be of any use, with Sherman stealing out of Memphis on the nineteenth. McClernand believed that the guilt lay primarily in Washington. No Confederate cavalrymen had snipped wires between the capital and Springfield. The responsibility for his disappointment, he told Stanton, lay either with Halleck "or a strange occurrence of accidents." Sadly he left Memphis on December 30 and steamed after Sherman, his bride and her party still accompanying him.

Sherman had departed in such eagerness as to forget to take along necessary portions of pontoon bridges—a rare, almost unique instance in the career of a military leader whose memory and foresight were remarkable. His desire for secrecy on the trip had been unusually keen, even for him. He had commanded that his officers should seize "any unauthorized passenger and conscript him" into the military service for the unexpired term of the regiment that captured him. Not only had he excluded newspaper correspondents but he had also threatened to shoot Colonel A. H. Markland, regional superintendent for the United States Army mails, when that official had insisted upon joining the expedition. At length Sherman had relented and carried Markland with him as his guest on the *Forest Queen.* Markland's trustworthiness was soon apparent and Sherman made him a friend for life.

Picking up General Frederick Steele's division at Helena, Arkansas, on the twentieth, Sherman turned into the Yazoo on the twenty-sixth, landed his men on swampy ground, and made preparations in a steady rainstorm. Admiral Porter declared that the rainfall had so swollen the Yazoo current that "the vessels had to be fastened to the trees." He heard the "wind howl like a legion of devils, though which side it was howling for, I have no idea."

On the twenty-ninth Sherman sent his men to the bluffs. Each division commander had been given maps and carefully written, detailed orders, but the attack was a prompt failure and Sherman drew off, counting 208 killed, 1,005 wounded, and 563 captured and missing. On the bluffs, the Confederates admitted only 63 dead, 134 wounded, and 10 missing. Sherman was fuming with anger at one of his division commanders, General George W. Morgan, for having moved so awkwardly as to miss a chance at carrying the bluffs. Morgan had failed to lead his men in person. Up spoke General Frank Blair, who after having tried so earnestly to get Sherman into uniform now found himself serving under the admired soldier. Blair urged Sherman to name Morgan as officially responsible for the repulse. But Sherman refused and in his report took the blame. He wrote:

> I know General Morgan's enthusiasm and devotion to the cause, and will not question these, and assume to myself the consequences of failure rather than throw it off on any generous and brave man or set of men.

The rains persisted. Sherman glanced at trees and saw that the high-water mark of previous floods was ten feet above his head. It was time to leave. His first independent command had been a failure. He searched in imagination for a chance to redeem himself. He thought of Arkansas Post, a Confederate fort in the Arkansas River. The mouth of the Arkansas was only a hundred and twenty-five miles northward. The fort held but 5,000 men, yet it might prove dangerous if neglected; it could be used as a Confederate base against subsequent assailants of Vicksburg. Drenched and disheveled, he entered Porter's cabin. After long silence he said:

"I've lost 1,700 men and those infernal reporters will publish all over the country their ridiculous stories about Sherman being whipped."

"Pshaw," said Porter, "that's nothing; simply an episode in the war! You'll lose 17,000 before the war is over and think nothing of it. We'll have Vicksburg yet, before we die. Steward! Bring some punch. . . ."

"That's good sense, Porter, but what shall we do now? I must take my boys somewhere and wipe this out." Porter said that he would go anywhere with him. "Then," said Sherman, "let's go and thrash out Arkansas Post."

On the morning of January 2, 1863, Sherman was passing in a rowboat from transport to transport, inspecting his men, when a long hail came from the deck of the *Black Hawk*, Porter's flagship. The admiral was shouting from the bridge: "McClernand is at the mouth of the Yazoo waiting to take command of your army!" Earlier in the morning, a colonel dressed in glittering new regimentals had arrived at Porter's cabin saying that McClernand "wants you to call and see him as soon as possible." Whatever thoughts Porter had originally held about McClernand's superiority over West-Pointers now disappeared. He said that it was McClernand's place to make the first call. The colonel departed in heat.

Angry though Sherman was at being superseded, he told Porter that he would have to call on McClernand, "for he ranks me." And a little later he was looking at McClernand on the latter's ship, the *Tigress*. He saw a swarthy, black-bearded man of slight figure and transparent egotism. Wilkie, the war correspondent, thought McClernand "fussy, irritable and nervous—something fidgety about him—lacking the composure of Grant and the cynical indifference of Sherman." Frankly Sherman explained his situation and added that he supposed the obvious influx of Confederates into Vicksburg meant that Grant had driven Pemberton back.

Then McClernand, no doubt with great pleasure, told him that Grant was not coming at all. On December 20 Confederate cavalrymen had captured and destroyed Grant's base of supplies, Holly Springs. The Union commander, Colonel Murphy, from either cowardice or treachery, had failed to defend it. Grant, conceiving it impossible to conduct a campaign without a base of supplies, had withdrawn into Tennessee, helpless to recall Sherman, who had steamed on to certain defeat. Pemberton, warned plentifully of the flotilla's descent upon Vicksburg, had sent to the city enough men to make Sherman's repulse an easy one.

Such events gave McClernand fresh hope. He did not blame Sherman for the hurried use of his recruits. To Washington, he praised Sherman for having "probably done all in the present case any one could have done." He said that Grant's failure to coöperate had been the cause of defeat.

Quickly McClernand issued orders that in effect declared his independence of Grant, renaming the expedition the Army of the Mississippi and dividing it into two corps, the first to be commanded by General Morgan, the second by Sherman—a bitter pill for Sherman to swallow, since he felt that Morgan had been to blame for the Chickasaw defeat. Moreover, Morgan had been a Democratic politician of Ohio—a McClernand man. But Sherman swallowed the dose manfully. "His promise of support was generous," said McClernand, and on January 4 Cump worked to compose the differences between McClernand and Porter. "My God, Porter," he said, after separating the quarreling rivals, "you'll ruin yourself if you talk that way to McClernand; he is very intimate with the President and has powerful influence." Porter, who had grown angry at what he said was an insult given Sherman by the new leader, replied, "I don't care who or what he is, he shall not be rude to you in my cabin."

Outwardly Sherman was conciliatory, cool, and self-possessed as he helped adjust differences so that army and navy worked in harmony in the storming of Arkansas Post on January 11 without serious loss. In the moonlit night preceding the attack Sherman crawled to a stump close to the enemy's lines and lay there till morning listening to voices, and during the attack he sent his staff to safety while he pressed forward alone under fire. In the surrendered fort he noted among the prisoners "a good deal of feeling" against Garland, the Confederate colonel who had flown the white flag. He took the Confederate under his wing, borrowed a battered coffeepot and some scraps of hardtack from a soldier, cooked the captive a meal, and slept with Garland the night after the fight in a hospital room whose straw pallets stunk of blood and corruption. Making peace among Confederates as well as among Federals, Sherman seemed pacific, yet he was writing Ellen so wildly about injustices and Lincoln's "insults" and "the dead set to ruin me for McClernand's personal glory" that she feared his mental condition of a year previous had returned. He was discussing "sliding out" and returning to St. Louis.

And by January 28, soon after discovering that Northern newspapers were hinting at his "insanity" in sending men to be butchered without chance for victory at Chickasaw, he was writing Ellen:

> Indeed I wish I had been killed long since. Better that than struggle with the curses and maledictions of every woman that has a son or brother to die in any army with which I chance to be associated. . . . Seeing so clearly into the future I do think I ought to get away.

On January 8, at the receipt of Cump's first letters describing the Chickasaw defeat, Ellen had written John:

God help us but I fear the effect on Cump. Do not desert him for if he goes down in an hour of adversity it brings woe upon his family. Burn this letter as soon as read.

And Thomas Ewing was writing his son Hugh, who after distinguishing himself at Antietam had been promoted to a brigadier general's rank and sent to join Sherman's division:

General Sherman was badly used by the President in placing that wooden-headed McClernand over him. He talks of resigning but this will not do—it would be a terrible mortification to his family and friends and a triumph to his enemies. See him and tell him how strongly we all feel on the subject.

Perturbed though he was, Sherman had not entirely lost his sense of humor. On January 24 he wrote McClernand that a Mrs. Groves near whose home he was encamped was complaining about "the burning of rails, the noise, tumult and confusion of the mass of men." He said "the poor woman is distracted and cannot rest . . . Either the army must move or she."

Grant, mortified at his own failure, the arrival of McClernand to command his friend, and the seeming folly of an invasion of Arkansas, sent McClernand orders to hold his army in the Mississippi at Milliken's Bend above Vicksburg. To Halleck Grant sent word that the Arkansas Post raid was "a wild goose-chase," but when a letter arrived from Sherman stating the strategic purpose of the move and that he, not McClernand, was its author, Grant promptly reversed himself and began wiring Halleck descriptions of the affair as having been "very important." McClernand was, unwittingly, welding the bonds of friendship between Grant and Sherman.

Both Sherman and Porter were busy now writing Grant urgent pleas that he come and take command of the expedition, but although Halleck on the twelfth had sent authority to relieve McClernand and give the command to the next in rank, Grant withheld the blow. On the sixteenth McClernand wrote Lincoln:

How can you expect success when men controlling the military destinies of the country are more chagrined at the success of your volunteer officers than the very enemy beaten by the latter in battle? . . . Do not let me be clandestinely destroyed, or, what is worse, dishonored without a hearing. . . . It should be made an independent command as both you and the Secretary of War, as I believe, originally intended.

On the seventeenth Grant arrived, listened to Sherman and Porter, then on the twentieth solved the difficulty by assuming the chief command himself, and moving to Young's Point, opposite the Yazoo's mouth. While Sherman idled there, supervising the pick-and-shovel work that his men were doing before the heights of Vicksburg, a family matter troubled him. The ancient feud between Ellen and his sister Elizabeth had broken out again, centering now about the Sherman house, which the brothers and sisters had agreed should be kept for the use of any one of them needing it. Elizabeth had rented it to a Protestant clergyman and had somehow quarreled with Ellen over the old religious issue. The women would spat until April, when Cump asked John to see Elizabeth and tell her to write him no more, since between herself and Ellen "my choice is soon made."

Another and greater vexation was the revival of his war with the newspapers. During his youth in the South Sherman had acquired the sectional belief that ladies and gentlemen were never discussed in print—a lady's name could be published but twice in her life, once when she married and once when she died. In Memphis Sherman had lectured an editor for eulogizing him:

> Personalities in a newspaper are wrong and criminal. I don't desire my biography to be written till I am dead. It is enough for the world to know that I live and am a soldier.

In general, Western war correspondents had grown bolder with personalities since the departure of Halleck, who had curbed them severely. Wilkie, the reporter, said, "Whisky flowed for correspondents with the coming of Grant." It was on tap at most brigade headquarters. Correspondents served as staff officers, demanded and received horses, saddles, official and private papers. Major General Henry W. Slocum said:

> The result was a daily revelation of secrets . . . the promoting of discord among officers and of jealousies between the different commands. Month by month they became more independent and more defiant of military authority.

The man who stopped their major abuses, said Slocum, was Sherman, who belled the cat in the spring of 1863. And the cat he selected had claws, for it was the star war reporter of the *New York Herald,* chief journalistic supporter of Lincoln's Administration. This was Thomas W. Knox, a large-headed, ponderous, sardonic, and overbearing New Englander. As a friend of Frank Blair's, Knox had defied Sherman's prohibition of correspondents on the Vicksburg expedition in December and had accompanied Blair on the steamer *Continental.* After the Chickasaw battle, Knox had posted a letter to the *Herald,* but Colonel Markland, watching the mails, had refused to send it. Angry at Sherman for this censorship, Knox had traveled to Cairo and sent out a description of the battle, charging the commanding general with bungling the attack, denying hospital facilities to the wounded, and behaving in ways that were "unaccountable." Knox's brother correspondents, similarly censored by Sherman, joined in filling their papers with accounts of Sherman's failure. These reports of the slaughter were especially horrible to the North since they came so hard upon the depressing news of twelve thousand men lost at Fredericksburg, Virginia, on December 13 by the Federal Burnside who had replaced McClellan. Sherman arrested Knox on January 31.

"Of course, General Sherman," drawled the supercilious reporter, "I have no feeling against you personally, but you are regarded as the enemy of our set and we must in self-defense write you down."

The answer drove Sherman almost mad. "The insolence of these fellows is insupportable," he wrote Grant. He court-martialed Knox as a spy. Knox blamed Blair, who after a period of suspicion on Sherman's part, cleared himself. So emphatically did Blair defend himself against the charge of having invented Knox's falsehoods that Sherman lost the last of his old-time distrust of Lincoln's viceroy, and began with him a friendship warm and strong. To Blair he sent a formal statement:

> I am glad that your letter enables me to put the fellow where he really belongs, as a spy and infamous dog. . . .
>
> Without further declaration I declare that if I am forced to look to the *New York Herald* as my law and master my military career is at an end.

Also he sent Blair a personal message, explaining his attitude toward his men. It had hurt him to be accused of sacrificing lives carelessly:

> I may be and am too reckless of public opinion, but I am not of my officers and men. I would not have them think or feel that I am reckless of their safety and honor or that I neglect to take every possible precaution against danger or fail to study every means to attain success. . . .

On the night before the court-martial of Knox, Sherman wrote Porter:

> The spirit of anarchy seems deep at work at the North, more alarming than the batteries that shell us from the opposite shore. . . . Reporters print their limited and tainted observations as the history of events they neither see nor comprehend. . . . We cannot prosper in military operations if we submit to it, and as some one must begin the attack, I must assume the ungracious task.

This held an echo of the letter he had written a few months earlier to his staff officer, Colonel W. H. H. Taylor:

> See the number of leaders already made the butt of all the arrows of the envious and disappointed. . . . Success is demanded and yet the means to

attain success are withheld. Military men are chained to a rock whilst the vultures are turned loose.

To Ellen he stormed:

I will never again command an army in America if we must carry along paid spies. I will banish myself to some foreign country first. I shall notify Mr. Lincoln of this if he attempts to interfere with the sentence of any court ordered by me. If he wants an army he must conform to the well-established rules of military nations and not attempt to keep up the open rules of peace.

The court-martial voted that Knox should be banished from the department, a verdict that suited Sherman but which he had small faith that Lincoln would sustain in the face of powerful appeals made by the *Herald* and by politicians whom it and other newspapers could control. While he awaited the President's decision, his aide Major Sanger returned from a St. Louis trip with a copy of the *Republican* that charged him with having again gone insane. Seizing a lead pencil, Sherman scrawled off a voluminous open letter to a half-dozen St. Louis friends—among them Lucas, Turner, and Patterson:

I assure you I am the same sane person who in San Francisco fought mob violence, the same who in the beginning of the war begged the leaders to pause and make due preparations before they dashed into it. . . .

I believe thus far no one has attacked my honesty or sense of truth or personal courage but I suppose in all else that goes to make up personal character I am in public estimation robbed and stripped. . . . I had thought of retiring and seeking another profession. . . .

Among all the infamous charges none has given me more pain than the assertion that my troops were disaffected, mutinous and personally opposed to me. This is false, false as hell. My own division will follow me anywhere. . . .

If you see a chance for me to make a living I would be much obliged for an early notice, and though I left the position of President of the Railroad too suddenly, you know it was because I thought I was called by my superior government. Next time I will think more of my own interest and less of the demands of a public that is so ready to believe all that is infamous of one who has ever been in the advance and unable to hear of the work of his traducers till months after they have effected their base purposes.

From Lancaster came such volleys of caution and pleadings that Cump retreated from his thoughts of resigning and told Ellen that he would abandon his warfare against newspaper "spies." But he still believed that a free press would eventually defeat the Union cause unless the people have resources enough to learn by the slow and sad progress of time what they might so much easier learn from books or the example of our enemy. . . .

I feel also that our government instead of governing the country is led first by one class of newspapers, then another, and that we are mere shuttlecocks flying between.

In Washington Thomas Ewing was telling Orville H. Browning, the Senator from Illinois, that

it is impossible for any human creature to tell how the war will come out. The Administration is very weak and the government may be utterly overthrown.

A movement was on foot among the Moderates and anti-Abolitionists, led by Old Man Blair, to force the antislavery leaders, Seward and Chase, from the Cabinet, with Thomas Ewing scheduled for Secretary of the Treasury. The plan failed but the Salt-Boiler still ranked high in the opinions of the Northern conservatives.

Late in March, Sherman learned that on the twentieth of the month Knox had been notified by Lincoln that his sentence would be revoked if Grant would concur. McClernand and General John M. Thayer, presiding officer at the trial, had advised Lincoln that Knox's offense was technical rather than "wilfully wrong." The interposition of two civilian officers, but lately frontier politicians, offended Sherman, but he waited silently while Knox took his case to Grant. He strained in anxiety. Would Grant weaken? Grant knew that Lincoln was his friend, and that the President was anxious to mollify the *Herald*.

One day Sherman opened a letter from Knox; it contained Grant's decision. Grant reminded the reporter that he had violated Sherman's order, attempted to blast his reputation, and made insinuations against his sanity:

General Sherman is one of the ablest soldiers and purest men in this country. . . . Whilst I would conform to the slightest wish of the President where it is formed upon a fair representation of both sides of any question, my respect for General Sherman is such that in this case I must decline, unless General Sherman first gives his consent to your remaining.

Grant had bound Sherman to him with new hoops of steel. Sherman speedily notified Knox that his plea was useless:

Come with a sword or musket in your hand, prepared to share with us our fate in sunshine and storm, in prosperity and adversity, in plenty and scarcity, and I will welcome you as a brother and associate; but come as you now do, expecting me to ally the reputation and honor of my country and my fellow-soldiers with you as the representative of the press which you yourself say makes so slight a difference between truth and falsehood and my answer is Never!

Having carried his point, Sherman, as he had promised Ellen, made no further efforts to bar the press generally, but, said General Slocum:

> . . . from that date to the end of the war, there was less vilification of the officers, fewer attempts to destroy the confidence, not only of the country, but of the army in our military leaders.

The affair had alienated Sherman still further from Lincoln. He told Grant that the President "must rule the *Herald* or the *Herald* will rule him; he can take his choice." And writing to Murat Halstead, he classed Lincoln with Buchanan in weakness, and compared them both unfavorably with Andrew Jackson:

> All I propose to say is that Mr. Lincoln and the press may, in the exercise of their glorious prerogative, tear our country and armies to tatters, but they shall not insult me with impunity in my own camp.

26

I TREMBLE FOR THE RESULT

AS springtime came up the river, Grant grew embarrassed. He was no nearer success than when he had arrived at Young's Point, and begun watching Vicksburg on its heights down the river. One thing was clear—nothing could come of attacks from the river front. Vicksburg could only be taken from the rear, that plateau which stretched to the east of the city. It could not be reached by sailing up the Yazoo and ascending the bluffs on its north. Sherman's defeat in December proved the defenses there to be impregnable. There was no chance to penetrate further among the bayous and reach the plateau by landing east of these bluffs. Sherman and Porter had tried in mid-March to find a route through the jungles and had been turned back.

There was another way of reaching the manoeuvering ground behind Vicksburg: Go down the river, below the city, land, march northeast, and then swing in upon the defenses. Lincoln, who had been interested since young manhood in canals and waterways, had urged Grant to dig a large ditch through the big bend made by the river in Vicksburg's front, and to run his transports through it, out of range of the massed batteries on the heights. All spring Grant held his engineers at work on various canals, and his soldiers spading. It kept them busy and Lincoln satisfied; but Grant had no hope of its success. Water levels were not right for the plan and furthermore, no canal that could be dug would place transports beyond the reach of Vicksburg's cannon.

One last desperate resort lurked in the back of Grant's mind: Abandon all ruses, devices, schemes—run the batteries! Sherman, when he learned that Grant was considering this bold move, begged him to forget it—the gunboats and transports "wouldn't live a minute," they were "mere egg-shells."

Grant waited, debating and silently smoking cigars. The weather grew hotter. Perched on knolls and levees above the rising river, soldiers of the Army of the Tennessee said that in the evening the air was "a saturated solution of gnats" which "came out of the leaves like smoke" to swarm on a man's neck "like a band of hot iron." Soldiers burned cotton to drive them off, and often sat coughing and choking all night long. But there were compensations. Honeysuckle and roses were blooming. Strawberries were ripe. Green figs hung exotically on trees. A new game, baseball, could be played where ground was solid. Alligators could be shot. "These Minié balls are good," soldiers said, as the new ammunition in practice shots penetrated alligators' hides. The invention of a French captain, and named for him, the Minié bullets were conical, with a hollow base that concentrated loose powder and gave the missile greater range and force than had been possible when balls were spherical and fitted so loosely that powder seeped past them.

Northwestern boys marveled at Spanish moss hanging gray from trees. In the moonlight it waved in ghostly gestures. On picket duty, in deep forests, sentinels shivered at the mournful wailings of the chuck-will's-widow, larger cousin of their own doleful whippoorwill. Home from his March explorations among the farms that dotted the jungles of the Yazoo, Cump wrote Ellen:

> The trees are now in full leaf, the black and blue-birds sing sweetly and the mocking bird is frantic with joy. The rose and violet, the beds of verbena and mignonette, planted by fair hands now in exile from their homes occupied by rude barbarians, bloom as fair as though grim war had not torn with violent hands all the vestiges of what a few short months ago were the homes of people as good as ourselves. You may well pray that a good God in his mercy will spare the home of your youth from the tread of an hostile army.

To planters of the Yazoo Sherman restored farming implements carried off by his soldiers, and wrote his division commander, Steele:

War at best is barbarism, but to involve all—children, women, old and helpless—is more than can be justified. Our men will become absolutely lawless unless they can be checked. . . . I always feel that the stores necessary for a family should be spared and I think it injures our men to allow them to plunder indiscriminately.

Sherman began urging Grant to pull up stakes, transport the whole army to Memphis, then march it down the railroads to Vicksburg's rear—the plan he had suggested in the previous autumn. Grant knew that from a military view this was the correct campaign, the easiest, the most promising. But his own haste in sending Sherman to Chickasaw Bayou in December had in the public view committed the army to a river attack. If the whole force were now to retire to Memphis and start over again by a different route, the North would ring with cries of defeat. The Northwest, which was growing more impatient daily, might even revolt. The Administration feared to allow the retirement that Sherman urged upon Grant. On March 20 Halleck telegraphed Grant:

The eyes and hopes of the whole country are now directed at your army. In my opinion the opening of the Mississippi River will be to us of more advantage than the capture of forty Richmonds.

In the West it was said that the Easterners wouldn't fight. By that was meant that the Army of the Potomac would die but that it had not the will to victory. It was awed by Lee. Lincoln was turning to a new leader, Joseph Hooker, still as handsome as when Sherman had known him in California.

In the North public feeling was strong against Grant. McClernand's friends were creating clamor for his appointment to head the expedition. The Republican editor of the *Chicago Tribune*, Joseph Medill, was writing Schuyler Colfax, the Indiana Speaker of the House of Representatives in Washington:

Army deaths, taxation, the continued closure of the Mississippi, exorbitant charges of transportation companies for carrying the farmers' products eastward—all combine to produce the existing state of despondency and desperation. . . . Sometimes I think nothing is left but "to fight for a boundary."

Rumor had it that Lincoln was saying, "I think Grant has hardly a friend left except myself." In all probability, this remark—if made—was not intended to be taken literally, for as the pressure tightened upon Grant, friends rose. Frank Blair, who had entered the war as a McClernand man, was now whole-heartedly a believer in Grant. This undoubtedly meant that his brother, the Postmaster-General, and his father were similarly minded. Charles A. Dana, whom Stanton had sent to

Grant's headquarters to observe and report, was writing Ulysses's praises. William P. Mellen, the United States Treasury supervisor for the Mississippi Valley, was writing his chieftain, Chase, such ardent defenses of Grant that the Secretary used them to keep Lincoln convinced of Grant's ability. Cump Sherman was telling Ellen, "Grant is as honest as old Zack Taylor," and he was stimulating John to defend the commander in Washington.

Considering the political power that these friends at headquarters gave Grant, it is unlikely that his position was as much endangered as most historians would later indicate it to have been. But at the time his friends were in dread that Lincoln would supplant him with McClernand. Sherman even worked out a plan for tying McClernand's hands. On the night of April 8, after a discussion at headquarters, Sherman wrote Grant a letter urging him to call upon all his corps commanders for detailed opinions as to the best plan for capturing Vicksburg. He said, "Unless this be done, there are men who will, in any result falling below the popular standard, claim that *their* advice was unheeded." He would, herewith, begin it by stating his own plan. Then he repeated his long-held idea—the retirement to Memphis and descent upon Vicksburg by land.

But Grant pocketed Sherman's letter, refusing to use the weapon. He had made up his own mind. He was done with jockeying strategy. He would move by the simplest route of all—he would run the batteries. The simplest and most direct ways, he thought, were almost always the best. The gunboats would go first, after them would come barges and transports, carrying enough supplies and men to hold the river near Grand Gulf, fifty-five miles south of Vicksburg. Then the army could march from Young's Point down the west bank of the river to the new concentration point and find enough provisions on the barges to feed it while it captured Grand Gulf. That accomplished, Grant expected to float two hundred miles on down the river to meet General Banks and Admiral Farragut at Port Hudson. When that fort fell, they could all come back together and attack Vicksburg from the southeast.

Sherman was writing Ellen, "Grant trembles at the approaching thunders of popular criticism and must risk anything," but he added, "and it is my duty to back him." He did not resent Grant's assignment of McClernand as the corps commander to lead the invasion down the west bank. McClernand was the senior corps commander and had, moreover, surprised every one by approving Grant's plan—the only lieutenant to welcome it. The others seemed to share Sherman's distrust of the scheme, yet all would support their leader. "I have no faith in the whole plan," Cump told Ellen, yet he worked day and night to make it succeed.

On the night of April 16 Grant boarded an anchored ship, with his wife and children about him, and gave the word. Admiral Porter, in his ironclad *Benton,* led six gunboats, three transports, and a small fleet of barges down toward the hairpin that twisted in front of Vicksburg's bluffs. Confederates saw moving forms on the dull silver face of the river, set houses afire on both banks, and poured shells upon the flotilla that came downstream like a parade through a city mad with celebration. For an hour there was thunder, flame and thunder—flash and jar of batteries and gunboat cannon answering each other, Porter's cannoneers stripped to the waist . . . the splash of shells . . . the splintering thud of balls ripping transports' sides . . . shrill, defiant yells of blue-coats crouching behind cotton bales on decks . . . the sky exultant with flames shining on clouds of powder smoke . . . thunder, flame and thunder.

Out in the stream, barely below the southernmost Vicksburg battery, Sherman was standing in a yawl watching the fleet go by, his blood dancing to the artillery step that Shiloh had taught it—his heart tuned to the big guns. Earlier in the day he had worked his way, with soldiers and rowboats, along the Louisiana shore to this spot, where he would be ready to pick up survivors if, as he expected, many ships were destroyed. As the black form of the *Benton* came past the last of the vicious waterspouts, Sherman pulled to her, boarded, and shook hands with Porter. Then he visited each ship in turn as she emerged from the gauntlet run.

He was not, however, elated. He returned to headquarters and wrote Ellen, "I tremble for the result. I look upon the whole thing as one of the most hazardous and desperate moves of this or any other war." How was Grant to supply his army when every pound of food and munitions must be shipped past seven miles of hostile cannon or carted along thirty-seven miles of almost impassable road? Grant had turned back from his December campaign because his supplies had been burned at Holly Springs; now in May, he was committed to a far more dangerous campaign with no supply-base.

What Sherman could not see was that Grant had, in those silent months before Vicksburg, evolved a new psychology for the Federal armies. At Donelson the seed of the new idea had started to grow when he had noted that if two fighters were exhausted the first to revive would be the victor. Lying at the foot of Vicksburg's cliffs, Grant had come to the irrevocable belief that, in the end, triumph would come to that army which never counted its dead, never licked its wounds, never gave its adversary breathing space, never remembered the past nor shrank from the future—the army which dismissed old rules and which ignored rebuffs—the army which held implicit faith in a simple and eternal offensive.

Grant had a concrete plan for making an easy landing at Grand Gulf. He sent General B. H. Grierson on a cavalry raid up and down the interior, and he told Sherman that he wanted an elaborate feint made on May 1, along the Yazoo toward Haines' Bluff. He would not order Sherman to make this move, for, as he said, Northern newspapers would interpret it as another of "Sherman's defeats." Captain Wm. L. B. Jenney, Sherman's chief engineer, saw the reception of Grant's note:

> Sherman remarked, "Does General Grant think I care for what the newspapers say!"; jumped into a boat at once and rowed to Porter's flagship, where Sherman and Porter then arranged a jolly lark. . . . Sherman spread his command over the decks of the transports with orders that every man should . . . look as numerous as possible. Porter ordered every boat to get up steam, and even took a blacksmith shop in tow, which he left behind a point near to and concealed from Haines's Bluff with orders to fire up every forge and make all the smoke possible. The gunboats and transports whistled and puffed and made all the noise they could. They showed themselves to the garrison . . . and then drifted back and landed the men, who were marched through the woods . . . until they were seen by the enemy . . . taken on board to go through the same farce again.

By such devices Sherman made his ten regiments seem so enormous that the Confederate commander on Haines' Bluff telegraphed Pemberton, "The demonstration at Grand Gulf must be only a feint. Here is the real attack. The enemy are in front of me in force such as have never been seen before at Vicksburg. Send me reënforcements."

Pemberton halted large detachments that were hurrying to repulse Grant, and countermarched them furiously to meet Sherman. Shuttled back and forth so hysterically, the Southern infantrymen fell to the ground, panting like animals. Citizens brought up carriages and helped the weaker to Haines' Bluff in time to see Sherman steam blandly away. Grant had sent him a message: "All right; join me below Vicksburg." Thanks to Sherman and Grierson—principally the former—Pemberton had been prevented from interposing but a scant and easily whipped 4,000 men to Grant's landing party of 10,000 at Grand Gulf. But Sherman, returning to Young's Point, disembarking his men and marching them south toward the ferry, was still pessimistic. He heard that Banks could not meet Grant down at Port Hudson on scheduled time—not before May 25 at the earliest. This had decided Grant to attack Vicksburg alone, moving direct from Grand Gulf. Sherman saw that his friend was going to lead an army of 43,000 with no base of supplies into a region where some 60,000 enemies, all told, awaited him with superior arms and a friendly civilian population on ground that was familiar to them and strange to the invaders.

In Washington the Administration was more frightened than Sherman to hear of Grant's decision. Halleck and the Staff said Grant was violating all military tradition. Less than a week before, the Army of the Potomac under Hooker had been cruelly tricked and defeated by Lee at Chancellorsville, and now lay in discouragement close to Washington. Lee was threatening to invade Pennsylvania. If Grant should lose the Western army, the Federal cause was as good as lost. Hastily the Administration sent Grant word to halt his drive, to play safe and to wait till Banks could join him. The message came too late. Grant's very daring had placed him beyond the reach of the telegraph and when the order finally came to him he was smashing to victory and paid it no heed.

One week after leaving the Yazoo Sherman was eighteen miles east of Grand Gulf—a prodigious march—following Grant along a dirt road that led to the rear of Vicksburg. Sherman trembled more than ever for the result. Grant had no wagon train and only such ammunition as his men could carry on their backs and in a few nondescript farm wagons and buggies picked up along the way; he was driving to disaster. Sherman sent a courier begging Grant to "stop all troops till your army is partially supplied with wagons . . . this road will be jammed, as sure as life." Back came Grant's amazing words:

> I do not calculate upon the possibility of supplying the army with full rations from Grand Gulf. I know it will be impossible without constructing additional roads. What I do expect is to get up what rations of hard bread, coffee and salt we can, and make the country furnish the balance.

As he prodded his men to overtake Grant, Sherman's eyes began to open, the old military world of West Point to spin around beneath him—then disappear. This was a new kind of war—and Grant was making his own rules as he went along. Here was an army caring not a whipstitch for a base of supplies. From field, barn, smokehouse, and cellar they were extracting epicurean meals. When they squatted on their haunches at noon, they fried ham, bacon, pork chops, beefsteak; when they lay in their tentless bivouacs in the twilight they broiled spring chicken, duck, turkey, guinea hens; and at breakfast they ate the eggs of all kinds of poultry. They filled canteens at black molasses barrels in cellars. They rolled blankets around bottles of wine and whisky lifted from baronial sideboards. They seized plantation gristmills and within a few minutes ground enough cornmeal to supply themselves with cornbread for days. What was a base of supplies to them? They were not professional soldiers. They were Western pioneers—a new generation of pioneers loose in a new country with rifles and axes. Had their fathers or grandfathers given a damn about a base of supplies when they had crossed the Ohio long ago to enter the wilderness?

Twenty-four hours after sending Grant that message of protest concerning the dangers of moving without a supply line, Sherman's education was complete. While his men built a new bridge over the Big Black River, he lay down in a Negro's cabin to snatch a few moments of sleep. It was midnight, axes and hammers rang, pine torches flared. An aide wakened him, saying that Grant had just ridden up. In a second Sherman was out of the door, his red head shining in the flare of the flambeaux. Twenty-five years later Sherman recalled the scene in detail:

> I rushed out bareheaded and taking him by the hand said, "General Grant, I want to congratulate you on the success of your plan. And it's your plan, too, by heaven, and nobody else's. For nobody else believed in it."

It was as near to hero-worship as Sherman would come in a lifetime that held no heroes.

27

THIS FELLOW McCLERNAND

AS the Army of the Tennessee drove forward, wedging itself between Vicksburg and Jackson, the State capital, forty-five miles due east, Sherman began to reap the benefits of the long hours he had spent in teaching his men the art of marching. The stragglers at Bull Run had shamed him and ever since that fiasco he had trained men by example, order, and lecture, to keep together on the march. In the past when moving at the double-quick he had at times walked with the troops so that "no man could complain." When in the saddle, it was his habit to ride in the fields beside the men instead of in the road among them; it irritated them to be crowded this way and that by the iron shoes of a horse. The soldiers knew well why he did this and it pleased them. They called him Uncle Billy and Old Billy, shouting gay questions at him.

Sometimes he answered, sometimes he merely grinned. The faster he forced them to walk, the oftener he awarded them short breathing-spells.

From the first he had been teaching them that it was no use to beg rides in wagons. Always disdaining personal luggage, he despised wagon trains as little more than so many continuous temptations to man's weaker nature. Now as he forged on in Grant's flying column he notified his corps that only two ambulances would follow each brigade. None could ride except the desperately sick or the wounded. "Men found in ambulances, on mules, or horses without a written ticket of a surgeon must be dismounted and sent to their ranks," he ordered. Straggling now was "as much a crime as rebellion and will justify extreme and summary punishment. Our corps . . . must be compact and strong."

Various militarists had spoken of the heart or the stomach or the artillery of an army as its index of strength. Sherman, realist that he was, understood it to be the legs.

> Thirst and fatigue are to be expected, but the safety and success of all will make all good soldiers bear cheerfully the deprivation of rest and water.

This was his order while his men swung down the Mississippi road in that long, rolling stride they had learned on plowed ground back home in Ohio, Iowa, Illinois, and Missouri.

The swiftness with which Sherman's corps covered the miles was one of the chief factors in the success with which Grant inserted himself between Pemberton and the rescuing army that Joseph E. Johnston, newly arrived, was assembling at Jackson. When Grant, on the night of the twelfth, learned that McPherson's Seventeenth Corps had routed Pemberton at Raymond, a vital crossroads only fifteen miles from Jackson, he ordered McPherson on into the capital and sent Sherman hurrying after him. Although the rain fell in torrents, often covering the road with a foot of water, Sherman's men came with incredible speed. Marching out of Dillon's plantation, twenty-two miles from Jackson, early in the morning of one day, they were fighting in the outskirts of Jackson at 10 A.M. of the next. They had covered the last stretch of fourteen miles while McPherson's men were traversing ten miles on a parallel road. And in the Civil War fourteen miles, according to General Lew Wallace, was "the average day's march for a division of infantry under the most favorable circumstances."

For a day, after scattering Johnston's weak defensive army, Sherman's Fifteenth Corps remained in Jackson, obeying its commander's order "to destroy everything public not needed by us." Then they were out on one of the most prodigious marches of the war.

Grant had learned from a spy that Joe Johnston was planning a shrewd countermove. The wily Confederate had ordered Pemberton to halt Grant's advance by striking the Union communications. He expected Grant, when nipped in the rear, to turn, and in that moment Johnston expected to circle rapidly to the north and join Pemberton in front of Vicksburg. Grant outgeneraled Johnston badly by ignoring the threat entirely and by calmly throwing enough brigades to the north to keep Johnston from his run around the end. Then he hurled his main blue-clad force straight west at Vicksburg while poor Pemberton was thrashing around in the Union rear with 18,000 men hunting those communications which were nowhere to be found. After performing like a fever patient striking at phantoms, Pemberton recovered in time to meet Grant's thrust at Vicksburg and receive an overwhelming defeat. Except for tardiness on McClernand's part, Grant felt sure he could have separated Pemberton from Vicksburg at this battle—the Battle of Champion's Hill. As it was, the Confederates, dazed and disheartened, fell back to the Big Black River and intrenched.

Sherman, summoned from Jackson to help with this direct drive at Vicksburg, had come on the double-quick. His men had left on the morning of the sixteenth and by noon of the seventeenth were at Bridgeport on the Big Black, twenty-seven miles away—"an almost unequaled march," as Grant informed President Lincoln.

It was during this flying advance that Sherman met the irony of war face to face in the road. Drinking with his soldiers at a roadside well, he saw a book on the ground, asked a soldier to hand it up to him in his saddle, opened it, and read *The Constitution of the United States.* He turned to the flyleaf and saw two words written there—Jefferson Davis. Negroes told him that the plantation was indeed that of the Confederate President.

The eager legs of the Fifteenth Corps enabled its commander to reach the Big Black in time to help in a second rout of the Confederates. Restlessly Sherman worked his way to the river's very edge, where, from the shelter of a corncrib, he observed the enemy's position on the opposite bank. With his own hands he pointed the guns that shelled the defenders out of their trenches, and that night he sat with Grant beside a rapidly built pontoon bridge while his strong-thighed boys crossed in the flare of pitch-pine torches.

Next day, while the Confederates tumbled into the strong trenches around Vicksburg's edge, Sherman and Grant made a sentimental journey to the Walnut Hills, which the Fifteenth Corps, as the right wing, was passing. Ostensibly Grant was making the side-trip to select a roadway up which salt, coffee, and hardtack could be brought from

Yazoo River steamers to the army. His men had sickened of endless chicken and lamb chops and craved wheat foods. In all probability Grant was riding, as was Sherman, to look at the now empty forts of Chickasaw, where their first Vicksburg campaign had ended so disastrously. The companions spurred their horses far ahead of the marching columns, up among the most advanced skirmishers. On the heights they drew rein and sat in silence looking down at the muddy Yazoo—a brown ribbon tangled in the trees. They stared at that narrow and hopeless shelf of swamp land where Sherman's men had lain groaning. Grant saw for himself how impossible it had been to expect victory at such a point.

The comrades had come at last to the rendezvous that they had set for the past Christmas. Sherman had kept it then, Grant had not. But Grant had kept it in the end. It was his habit to finish his war plans sooner or later—the war habit of inevitability. He was here now, after six months. Here they both were. Abruptly Sherman broke the silence:

"Until this moment I never thought your expedition a success; I never could see the end clearly till now. But this is a campaign; this is a success if we never take the town."

While they sat on the heights, their men streaming past behind them, General Pemberton was riding through a fleeing horde into Vicksburg and lamenting to a companion, "Just thirty years ago I began my military career by receiving an appointment to a cadetship at the United States Military Academy—and today—the same date, my career is ended in disaster and disgrace." Wretched man! He had been no more confused than his superiors, Jefferson Davis and Joseph E. Johnston. Throughout the campaign Davis had been commanding him to protect the citadel at all costs, while Johnston had been ordering him to forget the city, march out, join other Confederate forces, and crush Grant; then Vicksburg could be reclaimed even if the Yankees had seized it. Attempting to reconcile the two policies, Pemberton had tried to meet Grant in the field and at the same time protect the town. In the face of Grant's incredible manoeuvers he had been helpless. Furthermore, the Army of the Tennessee had outfought his men unmistakably. The Westerners seemed invincible. At home they had learned to walk far, shoot straight, care for themselves, and fight with willingness. Now they were fighting for many causes, among them love of the Union, cheaper freight rates for their wheat, and plain, ordinary fun.

The Army of the Tennessee was ready when, on the nineteenth, Grant sent his men against the looming bastions of Vicksburg. Hadn't they tackled Donelson with a force smaller than that of the fortified enemy? Now they could certainly storm Vicksburg, even if they were but 45,000 men in the open against 35,000 behind parapets, trenches, hills, thickets, fallen timber dotted with sharpened spikes and with pitfalls covered with dry cane.

They were a little giddy with pride. In the twenty days that had passed since they had crossed the Mississippi, they had claimed two hundred and fifty miles of the river, fought and won five separate battles, not to speak of endless skirmishes, captured a State capital, marched a hundred and eighty miles, made 6,000 enemies throw down their muskets, killed and wounded as many more, seized 27 heavy guns, 61 lighter pieces—and fed themselves.

At two o'clock in the afternoon, three signal guns boomed and the Yankees ran forward through the little ravines, open spaces, and brakes toward the Confederate works, which on the instant turned into a cloud of smoke perpetually shattered by bursts of flame. Captain J. J. Kellogg, Company B, One Hundred and Thirteenth Illinois, saw "the very sticks and chips, scattered over the ground, jumping under the hot shower of Rebel bullets." Surprised, riddled, and half-stunned, the regiments tumbled into the ditches at the foot of the parapets and except for sporadic and futile attempts to scale the steep embankments did nothing all afternoon but shoot off the hats—or heads—of such Confederates as attempted to rise and aim at them. By lying low they could escape the enemy fire, which, cutting through the cane, broke off the stalks one by one until, as Kellogg said, "they lopped gently upon us" as if in a delicate gesture of protection.

To the left of the One Hundred and Thirteenth Illinois, the Thirteenth regulars lost 77 of their 250 men, among them their captain. Every officer was wounded and Captain Charles Ewing took command, carrying the flag after three color-bearers had been shot down. A bullet chipped the staff in his hand, carrying away part of a finger. "He saved the colors," Cump wrote Ellen. "The heads of columns," he told her, "have been swept away as chaff thrown from the hand on a windy day." When night came, the Union men raced back to their own lines, remaining only in some advanced rifle pits that they had wrested from the enemy. As Captain Kellogg reached safety he "stopped and took one long breath—bigger than a pound of wool."

On ridges that were often parallel and ranging from fifty to four hundred yards apart, the two armies now faced each other, the Confederates on a seven-mile semicircle, the Federals on a line that from the river on the north to the river on the south would soon be twelve miles of intrenchments. Sherman held the right, McPherson the center, and McClernand the left.

For two days the Northerners threw up breastworks and fired at the red flashes in the opposite parapets' loopholes. Then Grant ordered another attack. It would come at 10 A.M. on the twenty-second. For this assault Sherman scouted the ground carefully, and although the place looked almost impregnable, he supported Grant's view that it would be wise to try it. Joe Johnston might raise an army large enough to interfere with a siege. Moreover the Union men would never willingly settle down to a long, dull investiture unless convinced that Vicksburg could not be taken by storm.

During the night of the twenty-first Sherman asked his brigadiers how they wished to cross the deep ditch that lay at the foot of the breastworks. Hugh Ewing, whose brigade—calling itself the Forlorn Hope—was to lead the Fifteenth Corps, suggested that the men cut cane stalks and fill the ditches with bundles of them. Sherman, judging that a wooden bridge would be better, sent his officers out to find lumber. One house was all that could be found—and Grant was sleeping in it. Hugh Ewing, however, decided to awaken the chieftain and tell him the situation. Grant arose, dressed himself, and stood in the night watching while the house came down and supplied lumber for the bridge.

Next morning Union cannon, flanked by the captured Confederate guns, shelled the Vicksburg defenses for more than an hour while the blue regiments, with fixed bayonets, stripped down to their lightest attire and tried to compose themselves. Every commander's watch had been set by Grant's and at ten, when the cannonade ceased, the whole line sprang into action and ran across the gullies, fallen trees, and open spaces again. Captain Kellogg saw Grant, Sherman, and the latter's brigadier, Giles A. Smith, peering through field glasses from behind trees as he started with his company. A minute later Kellogg envied them as he sprang into bounding action, running rapidly, as he admitted, not so much in any anxiety to be where the enemy was as to escape having his posterior transfixed by the gleaming bayonets of his own men. As he ran he saw a brother captain, wounded in the wrist, racing for the rear while an unhurt private, attempting to assist him, pursued, snatching at his superior's coat tails. The two vanished from the fight while onlookers laughed.

Most of the charging men piled into the ditch, tried to clamber on the slick parapets, and fell back in the face of the fire that had already laid many of their comrades on the field behind. Hugh Ewing, whose bridge was too short for the ditch, lay with his shattered band close against the parapet. He produced a new flag, saying, "I want this planted on the top." A captain took it up and was killed; his younger brother planted it successfully and rolled back to safety. All day Hugh's men kept it flying, risking their necks to pick off all Southerners who approached it. When night brought orders to retire, a private crawled up, snatched the banner, and slid away untouched by the pelting bullets.

The attack had been a failure from beginning to end. Here and there some outer works were captured, but to no important purpose. Upon these most advanced Federals the defenders had rolled twelve-pounder shells with fuses sputtering. Scattering shrapnel, they were murderous. The best defense was to reach up with bayonets while the infernal things teetered on the crest and push them back into the Confederate trenches.

From the mutilated regiments in the ditch soon rose cries of "Ammunition!" Cartridges were needed to keep down Confederate heads. Volunteers raced through the open field to fill boxes and hats with the cartridges of dead and wounded men. One of these dare-devils was linked with Sherman in poems, stories, orations, for years after the war. Orion P. Howe, aged twelve, had marched away from his home at Waukegan, Illinois, with a brother of fourteen, to serve among the drummer boys of the Fifty-fifth Illinois Infantry. With their father, who led the regimental band, they had escaped injury. By some oversight, Orion accompanied the regiment in its charge on the twenty-second and lay with the men in the ditch. When ammunition ran low, Orion flitted about the field harvesting cartridges and running with his little blouse full to the riflemen. Flattered by the regiment's praise, he announced that he would return to the rear and order up new supplies from the ordnance wagon. As he departed, his colonel, Oscar Malmborg, enjoined him to be sure and ask for cartridges caliber .54, since the ordnance held varying sizes of musket balls. Only caliber .54 would fit the regiment's weapons, the colonel warned him. The regiment's historian wrote:

> We could see him nearly all the way . . . he ran through what seemed a hailstorm of canister and musket-balls, each throwing up its little puff of dust when it struck the dry hillside. Suddenly he dropped and hearts sank, but he had only tripped. Often he stumbled, sometimes he fell prostrate, but was quickly up again and he finally disappeared from us, limping over the summit and the 55th saw him no more for several months.

Sherman's eye caught Orion just as the boy vanished from the Fifty-fifth's vision. Standing on the ridge brow watching his whole line, Sherman turned as

> this young lad came up to me wounded and bleeding with a good healthy boy's cry, "General Sherman, send some cartridges to Colonel Malmborg; the men are all out."
>
> "What is the matter, my boy?"

"They shot me in the leg, sir, but I can't go to the hospital. Send the cartridges right away."

Even where we stood the shot and shell fell thick and fast and I told him to go to the rear at once, I would attend to the cartridges, and off he limped. Just before he disappeared he turned and called as loud as he could, "Caliber .54."

In the confusion, the ammunition never reached the Fifty-fifth, and as Colonel Malmborg gallantly admitted, it would have done no good had it come, for in his excitement he had made a mistake in directing little Orion to bring caliber .54. The regiment's rifles used caliber .58 instead. But Orion was a hero just the same, and on August 8 Sherman wrote Secretary Stanton a recommendation that the lad, who was too young for West Point, be sent to the Naval Academy and educated to become a midshipman. "I'll warrant the boy has in him the elements of a man and I commend him to the Government as one worthy of the fostering care of some one of its National institutions." Official red tape withheld the boy's appointment for more than a year, during which time the brigade commander Giles A. Smith made him his orderly and saw him wounded at Dallas on May 28, 1864. Then Orion journeyed to Annapolis. But after so stirring a boyhood, schoolbooks failed to interest him, and he was dropped in his second year, becoming in succession a sailor, a Texas cowboy, an Indian fighter, and finally disappearing from sight, in the language of the Fifty-fifth's historian, as having "settled quietly somewhere in Illinois."

Orion's exploit—the most widely sung and celebrated of the hour—had no such military effect as did that of a nineteen-year-old Welsh immigrant, Joseph E. Griffith, who as a member of the Twenty-second Iowa Infantry was in the front of McClernand's attack. Leading eleven comrades, Griffith had climbed into an artillery emplacement of the enemy, to be stunned by the rifle volley that was poured into their group. Arising unwounded, he saw all of his comrades dead or helpless, and fifteen Confederates staring at him, their muskets empty. He had in his hand a repeating rifle that he had picked up on the field where some Federal officer had dropped it, and aiming it at the enemy he ordered, "Lie down!" They obeyed. Then, backing out over the parapet on his stomach in a groove made by a Union cannon ball, he forced his captives to follow him into the Federal lines, losing only one of them in the storm of lead that swept the open spaces through which he herded his little band.

This exploit and a few similar feats by his men flooded McClernand with pride. Three of his regiments placed their flags in outer trenches of the enemy. To his unpracticed and overambitious eyes, such achievements seemed to signal the rise of his star. He began sending Grant notes asking for a general assault all along the line so that his men could complete their victory and take the city. "We have part possession of two forts and the Stars and Stripes are waving over them. A vigorous push ought to be made all along the line," he said in the first of the notes. Grant read it and handed it to Sherman, saying, "I don't believe a word of it." But Sherman argued that it was official and could not be ignored; he offered to renew the attack instantly. Grant said that he would ride over and examine the claims. If he sent no word by three o'clock—it was then noon—Sherman could attack.

McClernand sent more notes, and Grant, thinking that the "reiterated statements might possibly be true," allowed the assault to be resumed from end to end of the line—an attack that, as Grant afterward reported, "resulted in the increase of our mortality list fully 50 per cent without advancing or giving us other advantages." When Grant described this action to Halleck on May 24, Stanton, through Dana, authorized McClernand's removal. But still Grant hesitated, although he admitted that "looking after his corps gives me more labor and infinitely more uneasiness than all the remainder of my department." Jealousy was making McClernand do foolish things. For instance he once told Colonel Wilson, who came from Grant with a minor order, "I'll be God-damned if I do it. I'm tired of being dictated to. I won't stand it any longer and you can go back and tell General Grant." However, he tempered his remarks when Wilson threatened to jerk him out of his saddle and beat him out of his boots. When Wilson reported the incident Grant said, "I'll get rid of him the first chance I get."

But he did not, even though the chance was at hand. McClernand, noting how, with the arrival of fresh divisions, siege guns, and supplies, Grant was certain to capture Vicksburg, wrote a hasty glorification of himself and sent it on May 30 to the *Missouri Democrat* in St. Louis. Under the guise of congratulating his troops on their bravery during the assault, he magnified his own generalship, insinuated that Sherman and McPherson had neglected to support him, and that Grant, by failing to reënforce him, had lost a probable victory.

With the paper stealthily on its way to St. Louis, McClernand entered Grant's headquarters on June 4 and demanded that he be given official relief from the "slanders" that other officers were spreading about him and his responsibility for the slaughter of the Twenty-second. Grant evaded a direct answer and said that he would reply in writing. But for nine days Grant failed to write the answer. It was not a time when Grant was at his best. On June 6 his chief aide, General Rawlins, sent him a letter:

> The great solicitude I feel for the safety of this army leads me to mention what I hoped never again to do—the subject of your drinking. . . . I have heard that Dr. McMillan, at General Sherman's a few days ago, induced you, notwithstanding your pledge to me, to take a glass of wine, and today when I found a box of wine in front of your tent and proposed to move it, which I did, I was told you had forbid its being taken away, for you intended to keep it until you entered Vicksburg . . . and tonight when you should, because of the condition of your health if nothing else, have been in bed, I find you where the wine bottle has just been emptied, in company with those who drink and urge you to do likewise, and the lack of your usual promptness of decision and clearness in expressing yourself in writing tended to confirm my suspicions.

Rawlins was stalking the camps with many forces, many fires, making his eyes so bright and his face so livid behind his black beard—tuberculosis, hate of liquor, zeal for the Union, concern for Grant. He reminded men of a profane Crusader and of a mother hen. On June 13 a copy of the *Missouri Democrat* of the tenth came to Grant's headquarters, bearing McClernand's paper of self-congratulation. It struck like a bombshell. Grant asked McClernand if it were really from his pen, and was told that it was; but, said McClernand, he thought his adjutant had sent a copy to Grant before it was mailed. The seriousness for McClernand now lay in the fact that he had committed a technical error. Since 1862 the War Department had ruled that it was insubordinate for any officer to publish any official paper or report without permission from his superiors. McClernand, labeling his paper "General Orders 72," had made himself liable for dismissal.

But Grant sat for four days more without action. Then on the morning of the seventeenth Sherman stamped into headquarters, holding the offensive newspaper. He was so shaken with wrath that for a time he could not speak. At length he broke out in a tirade against "this fellow McClernand" and demanded that he be cashiered. He had just seen the *Democrat*, and to a man like himself who never threw off on others, McClernand's attempt to accuse both Sherman and McPherson of neglect was plain cowardice.

The next day Grant signed an order relieving McClernand from duty and sending him home to Illinois. When Colonel Wilson handed him the summons, McClernand read it, then said, "I am relieved. By God, sir, we are both relieved." From Cairo, on the way home, he telegraphed his friend Lincoln, "I have been relieved for an omission of my adjutant. Hear me." In time there came to him at Springfield the sad, sweet words of Lincoln's answer. The President said he knew Grant had sent in an explanation, but he hadn't asked to see it, "because it is a case, as appears to me, in which I could do nothing without doing harm." Lincoln wrote as an Oriental sage might write of a friend already dead:

> I doubt whether your present position is more painful to you than to myself. Grateful for the patriotic stand so early taken by you in this life-and-death struggle for the nation, I have done whatever has appeared practicable to advance you and the public interest together. . . . General Grant and yourself have been conspicuous in our most important successes and for me to interfere and thus magnify a breach between you could not but be of evil effect. . . . Force me to force you back upon General Grant would be forcing him to resign. I cannot give you a new command, because we have no forces except such as already have commanders . . . he who has the right needs not to fear.
>
> Your friend as ever,
>
> A. LINCOLN.

Everything had happened for the best. The Confederacy was cut in two and, as Sherman had foreseen, was doomed. Tens of thousands of Northwestern Democrats had been committed to blue uniforms for three years, and within a few months, the majority of them, together with their families at home, would be found viewing Lincoln with new enthusiasm.

McClernand had helped knock the golden apple, anyway. He had been the means of uniting Grant and Sherman in stronger bonds of a friendship that would prove most advantageous to the Federal cause. He would go the rest of his life blaming them and Halleck, not Lincoln, for his injury. Perhaps John A., out of his deep knowledge of politics as it was played on the prairie, believed that a President of the United States must do anything to save the sacred Union—anything!

28

MANY SOLDIERS

IT was the twenty-fifth of May, three days after the assault on Vicksburg. Federal dead between the lines were "swelling to the stature of giants" and were making the air so unbearable that Confederates had sent out the request that they be buried. Under a white flag soldiers threw dirt on late comrades, while in their midst Sherman and a Confederate officer sat on a log. The Southerner, Captain S. H. Lockett, had come out to gather information, but had become so fascinated by Sherman's conversation that he had forgotten his mission. "Intentionally or not," said Lockett afterward, "his civility prevented me from seeing many other points on our front that I, as chief engineer, was very anxious to examine."

To all appearance, Sherman was callous toward death. In reality, his days and nights were full of resentment against the Administration for what he believed was its indifference towards boys' lives. When reënforcements had been sent to the front during the past winter, the regiments had averaged 900 men, now they had been reduced by disease and bullets—principally the former—to around 300 per regiment, and were thinner than veteran organizations that had seen eighteen months more of service. Sherman knew that if the War Department had used most of these recruits as replacements in older regiments, many youths now dead would be alive. Politics, however, demanded that volunteers be gathered in new regiments so that officers could be appointed by State governors, or elected by the men. Jobs must be made for deserving patriots. Sherman refused to admit that President Lincoln was forced to employ many political devices to keep the war spirit alive in faint-hearted sections of the North. He wrote to Grant on June 2:

> All who deal with troops in fact instead of theory know that the knowledge of the little details of camp life is absolutely necessary to keep men alive. New regiments, for want of this knowledge, have measles, mumps, diarrhea and the whole catalogue of infantile diseases whereas the same number of men, distributed among the older regiments would learn from the sergeants and corporals and privates the art of taking care of themselves which would actually save their lives and preserve their health against the host of diseases which invariably attack new regiments. Also recruits, distributed among the older companies catch up, from close and intimate contact, a knowledge of drill, the care and use of arms and all the instructions which otherwise would take months to impart.

When newspapers announced the passage of a new Conscription Law, Sherman pronounced it "the best act of our Government," but his approval disappeared as he read that the 300,000 drafted men were to be divided into two groups—100,000 sent as replacements to veteran regiments, 200,000 to be formed into fresh regiments with new officers. To Sherman this proved Lincoln unintelligent, and he sent Grant a plea to start work against so reckless a scheme:

> I do not believe that Mr. Lincoln or any man would at this critical period of our history repeat the fatal mistakes of last year. . . . The economy, too, should recommend the course of distributing all recruits as privates

to the old regiments, but these reasons appear to me to be so plain that it is ridiculous for me to point them out to you or even to suggest them to an intelligent civilian.

I am assured that the President does actually desire to support and sustain the army and that he desires to know the wishes and opinions of officers who serve in the woods instead of in the "salon." If so, you would be listened to.

His sense of outrage grew as he read that the President was intending to consolidate veteran regiments whose membership had fallen below 300. Such an order would drive from the service scores of battle-trained and competent officers, and supplant them with "political colonels" of greenhorn regiments. Sherman begged Grant to persuade Lincoln to abandon this idea and to use all recruits as replacements:

If adopted it would be more important than the conquest of Vicksburg and Richmond together as it would be a victory of common sense over the popular fallacies that have ruled and almost ruined our country.

To Ellen he railed against the consolidation scheme:

If the worst enemy of the United States were to devise a plan to break down our army, a better one could not be attempted. . . . It may be that the whole war will be turned over to the negroes, and I begin to believe that they will do as well as Lincoln and his advisers.

The public's attitude toward Grant strengthened Sherman's contempt for democracy. On June 2 he wrote Ellen:

Grant is now deservedly the hero . . . belabored with praise by those who a month ago accused him of all the sins in the calendar, and who next will turn against him if so blows the popular breeze.

Vox populi, vox humbug.

The siege was progressing toward inexorable triumph. Little things happened to please Sherman—for instance, the arrival, one day, of ex-Professor Boyd as a prisoner of war. Sherman entertained him at his headquarters and introduced him to Admiral Porter as "Mr. Boyd; he thinks he is a Confederate captain, but in reality he's my old professor of foreign languages." He saw to it that Boyd was given his desired transfer home.

The spectacle of Vicksburg's bombardment delighted Sherman's artistic eye. On clear nights he saw pickets sitting on their rifle-pit embankments, staring at the grandest pyrotechnics they had ever beheld—thin red trails of light, sparkling like comets' tails, soaring into the sky to halt, then curve downward to vanish among the housetops of the dark city. After a pause, a jarring concussion would come on the wind. From land and river Union siege guns and navy mortars were throwing shells with burning fuses. All around on the horizon crazy lights were swinging like witch torches, gyrating in half-circles and ellipses—signalmen handling lanterns. Through the darkness a squad of bluecoats would drop over the trench tops and steal out into the bullet-torn thickets between the lines to dig rifle pits nearer the enemy. Many soldiers elected to dig rather than to occupy the dangerous shooting-posts.

Six to twelve marksmen manned a rifle pit—half of them shooting at Confederate heads while the other half read newspapers or novels, or slept. Snores mingled with the explosions of cartridges. When shells hurtled past their ears the men would try to put words to the deadly music. The missiles said, "Where-is-he—where-is-he—where-is-he," or "I'se a-coming—I'se a-coming." Solid shot would either bury itself in the ground or skip along the surface. A ball rolling with apparent sloth was still dangerous. A bluecoat put out his leg to stop one; it crushed his foot. Mortality from artillery fire was, however, light. It was the noise of cannon and bursting shells that bothered. Privates of the Twelfth Wisconsin said that their Negro cooks lay so flat during a bombardment that soldiers mistook them for rubber blankets and carried them to camp over their shoulders at the day's end. During the night batteries were rolled forward to new emplacements. One morning the guns of the Union General Ransom displayed iron trapdoors over embrasures in the parapets. Confederate sharpshooters trained their rifles on the mysterious affairs. Suddenly the mantelets flew down, the cannon belched fire, and the Confederates poured bullets in. But the mantelets had closed in time. A blue-clad gunner leaped on his cannon, howled, "Too late!" and ducked.

Between the ever-nearing lines, blackberries ripened. Opponents declared truces so that they might pick the fruit. It was the best cure for diarrhea. During one impromptu truce a Union lieutenant saw one of his privates, an Irishman, suddenly throw a spade into the enemy trench. He explained, "One of thim grayback divils hit me with a clod." Once in the midst of tiresome pot-shooting, a private of the Eleventh Wisconsin announced, "I'm goin' out to shake hands with them Rebs." He went. A Johnnie came out to meet him. Squads, then hundreds, followed from each trench. Everybody shook hands. Opponents discussed the weather, good shots, narrow misses, their own diseases, and the errors of their generals. They traded coffee for tobacco, swapped knives, compared their sweethearts' tintypes. One Confederate was overheard by the Wisconsin boys to lament, "I want to see my ma." He sat apart on a log. Suddenly a Union officer appeared, scolded both forces severely, and ordered them all back to their respective rifle pits. Bullets began to hunt victims once more.

By the end of June opposing rifle pits were so close together that dirt from their garrisons' spades met in the air. Conversation was almost constant. Captain Kellogg once heard a voice calling from the Confederate trench,

"Is any of the boys of the Sixth Missouri there?"

"Lots of 'em," came the answer.

"Is Tom Jones there?"

"Here I am; is that you, Jim?"

"Yes, and say, Tom, can you meet me between the lines? I've got a roll of greenbacks and I want to send 'em to the old folks in Missouri." Both forces held their fire while the brothers met between the lines.

By common consent it was regarded as bad form to shoot at a picket who was stationed in an exposed position. Captain Frederick E. Prime, Grant's chief engineer, thought the enemy so conservative of its own lives as to make the defense "far from vigorous":

> This indifference to our approach became at times almost ludicrous. . . . On one occasion our pickets, in being posted, became intermixed with the enemy's and after some discussion, the opposing picket officers arranged their picket lines by mutual compromise, these lines in places not more than 10 yards apart . . . the advantage of this arrangement, novel in the art of war, was entirely on our side.

When a sharpshooter was narrowly missed by an enemy marksman he would leap up, thumb his nose, and shout, "Shoot again!" No opponent could recharge a muzzle-loading weapon in less than thirty seconds. The infiltration of repeating rifles, although few in number, stopped this game. A squirrel-shooter of the Fifty-fifth Illinois secured a five-shot Colt rifle with which, after planting a ball near an enemy's head, he could drill the fellow through as he bobbed up and twiddled his fingers.

The siege was on the whole monotonous. Newspaper correspondents, in the dearth of excitement, made much of the shambles resulting from the explosion of Union mines under Confederate defenses. In reality these were idle affairs. The largest of them, upon which weeks were spent in tunneling, blew up only six Confederate privates and one Negro, the latter being lofted unhurt into the Union lines. General John A. Logan maintained the petted and delighted fellow in camp for months, more as a souvenir than as a servant. Two attacks following mine explosions cost Grant only some thirty in killed and wounded.

With reënforcements swelling his army to a total of 75,000, Grant erected elaborate defenses in his rear. East of the Big Black were only 20,000 Confederate troops, yet they must be watched, for they were commanded by the only Southern general for whom Grant would ever admit to hold fear. When the war was done, Grant declared that he had never valued Robert E. Lee so highly as Joseph E. Johnston.

With as few as 20,000 men, Johnston might make trouble, for he was known to be a past master at strategy, a highly cerebral, experienced, and courageous leader. Wounded while opposing McClellan near Richmond in May, 1862, Johnston had been removed from the supreme Southern military command and supplanted by Lee. A feud had grown up between him and Jefferson Davis owing to a dispute over the technical position of his name in the seniority list of officers. Furthermore, the wives of the two men had quarreled. Davis had sent Johnston West in the summer of 1863 when the general was still weak from wounds and from dysentery. The two men had quarreled again over details of the Vicksburg campaign, in which Johnston had not appeared to advantage. Officers in both opposing armies talked of Johnston's scholarship, how he knew astronomy, French, and Greek. They regarded him as "refined and remote." His staff thought him "rather cold" and held him in great awe, yet he liked a "social drink" and shared with his aides a single table fork that boasted but one prong. Habitually he rode his horse through camp at a gallop, explaining that his father had taught him to ride so always. A. J. L. Freemantle, the British war correspondent, saw him as "below middle height, spare, well set-up, wearing a greyish beard." Johnston told the Englishman that he had been wounded in battle ten times—most of his scars had been received in the Mexican War.

According to his lieutenant and admirer, General Joseph Wheeler, Johnston told but one humorous story—that of the chaplain who when asking a profane muleteer, "Do you know who died to save sinners?" was answered, "Damn your conundrums, I'm stuck in the mud!"

With so many men at hand, Grant decided that it would be better to send a force out to the Big Black to watch Johnston. Looking over his generals, Grant selected Sherman as the best match for Johnstonian strategy. Sherman, he knew, wished to remain in front of Vicksburg and to be assigned to rule the city when it should fall. Considering Sherman's success in governing Memphis, such a step would have been logical, but Grant needed protection from Johnston. "I never suggest anything to myself, personal," Cump wrote Ellen in describing his disappointing assignment to the backwoods. To John he wrote, "With Grant, I am a second self . . . personal and official friends."

On June 20 he marched east with seven divisions and soon was intrenched and watching the awesome Confederate who had graduated from West Point the year Sherman was nine. Desultory skirmishing was all that occurred. Johnston manoeuvered up and down, helplessly peering toward Vicksburg, where Pemberton starved. Soldiers in the city were eating rats. Sherman found his task easy. One day—according to camp rumor—a captive lieutenant was brought to his tent, a soulful youth with long hair. As he sat by the general, he fell to admiring magnolia trees.

"How beautifully those leaves wave—be-ee-utiful!" Sherman snorted and gave his stool a hitch. "Be-ee-ee-utiful!" continued the poet.

"Well, damn it, can't you let 'em wave?" roared Sherman. Onlookers reported that "the exquisite subsided."

In Vicksburg, about this time, General Pemberton was reading a paper labeled "Appeal for Help" that had been mysteriously thrown into his headquarters. His eye ran down it, catching sentences:

> We as an army have as much confidence in you as a commanding general as we perhaps ought to have. . . . We give you great credit for the stern patriotism you have evinced in the defense of Vicksburg. . . . Everybody admits that we have all covered ourselves with glory, but alas, alas, general, a crisis has arrived in the midst of our siege. . . .
>
> Men don't want to starve, and don't intend to, but they call upon you for justice. . . .
>
> If you can't feed us, you had better surrender us, horrible as the idea is, than suffer this noble army to disgrace themselves by desertion. I tell you plainly men are not going to lie here and perish, if they do love their country dearly. . . . This army is ripe for mutiny, unless it can be fed.
>
> Just think of one small biscuit and one or two mouthfuls of bacon per day. General, please direct your inquiries in the proper channel and see if I have not stated stubborn facts which had better be heeded before we are disgraced.
>
> From—
>
> Many Soldiers.

Pemberton knew that the end was at hand. In places, Federal intrenchments were within five yards of his own line. In a minute's time, a torrent of Union bayonets could surge over the parapets and stab weakened defenders to death.

Surrender came on July 4, Grant paroling the 31,600 wasted Confederates in the knowledge that the great majority, sick of the war, would go home never to shoulder arms again. As the disarmed Johnnies came out, Grant observed that "not a cheer went up, not a remark was made that would cause pain." Confederates declared they heard one cheer—and that it was for *them*, not their downfall. The Twelfth Wisconsin boys wrote:

It was good to see them eat . . . we could never remember anything that gave us greater pleasure than the eagerness of the rebels to get a drink of coffee. . . . It was a moonlight night and many of us did not sleep at all, talking with the prisoners.

Pemberton was haughty and approached insolence; Grant was courteous. He counted 172 cannon, 60,000 muskets—most of them superior to his own—and huge stocks of ammunition. Up North men were declaring that they had always had faith in Grant, the Northwest was happy because the Wall Street railroaders were now due to get their come-uppance—the cheap water freights could soon be resumed.

Grant had become a hero to the North, but not nearly so great a hero as American children in future generations would be taught. Public attention had been largely diverted from the immeasurable significance of his victory by military affairs in the East. In June Lee's army had come North on a terrifying invasion. The cities of Washington, Baltimore, Philadelphia, Harrisburg, trembled. General George Gordon Meade, the new leader of the Army of the Potomac, found himself, by good fortune, on advantageous ground just as Lee bumped against him. There were three days of fighting around Gettysburg, Pennsylvania, then on the Fourth of July the North heard that Lee had drawn off his shattered brigades and was retiring to Virginia.

With cruel fear lifted from their souls, the Union populace cheered far louder for Gettysburg than for Vicksburg, and while it was regarded as providential that two Federal victories should thus coincide on the republic's birthday, it was felt that God had shown His hand more clearly in protecting His chosen people from invasion than in conquering an enemy city away off down in Mississippi.

Halleck was sending Grant congratulations:

Give my kindest regards to my old friends among your officers. I sincerely wish I was with you again in the West. I am utterly sick of this political hell.

Sherman was lonely, too, far out in the interior, twenty miles from the scenes of victory—lonely and happy, as he wrote Grant:

I can hardly contain myself. Surely I will not punish any soldier for being "unco happy" this most glorious anniversary of the birth of a nation. . . .

Did I not know the honesty, modesty and purity of your nature, I would be tempted to follow the example of my standard enemies of the press in indulging in wanton flattery; but as a man and soldier and ardent friend of yours I warn you against the incense of flattery that will fill our land from one extreme to the other. Be natural and be yourself and this glittering flattery will be as the passing breeze of the sea on a warm summer day. To me the delicacy with which you have treated a brave but deluded enemy is more eloquent than the most gorgeous oratory of an Everett.

This is a day of jubilee, a day of rejoicing to the faithful, and I would like to hear the shouts of my old and patient troops, but I must be a Gradgrind—I must have facts, knocks and must go on. Already are my orders out to give one big huzza and sling the knapsacks for new fields.

For the first time since the beginning of the war, Cump now wrote Ellen as if he expected to come home alive. On July 5 he wrote her:

I shall go on through heat and dust till the Mississippi is clear, till the large armies of the enemy in this quarter seek a more secure base, and then I will renew hopes of getting a quiet home where we can grow up among our children and prepare them for the dangers which may environ their later life.

He told Ellen that Grant's victory gave him his "first gleam of daylight in this war." He could now see that the Confederacy was doomed. The Mississippi would soon be cleared; Port Hudson must fall; then the whole valley would be certain to come, little by little, into Federal control. Also Grant's triumph was in itself a sort of spiritual declaration of freedom for the army. The Administration had meddled in his affairs far less than in those of the Eastern army. In fact, Grant had ignored a sudden demand from Halleck that he give up his daring manoeuvers in mid-May and return to Grand Gulf until reënforcements came. Grant, receiving the order in battle, dropped it and spurred ahead after an infantry charge. It was about this independence of Grant's that Cump wrote Ellen on July 5:

Thank God we are free from Washington and that we have in Grant not a "great man" or "hero" but a good, plain, sensible kind-hearted fellow. . . . Thank God, no President was near to thwart our plans.

Could Sherman have seen what Lincoln was writing Grant, a little later, he might have begun to see the President in a different light. Lincoln was thanking Grant

for the almost inestimable service you have done the country. . . . When you got below Port Gibson, Grand Gulf and vicinity, I thought you would go down the river and join General Banks, and when you turned northward, east of the Big Black, I feared it was a mistake. I wish now to make the personal acknowledgment that you were right and I was wrong.

After General Banks captured the doomed Port Hudson on July 8, Lincoln announced to the nation, "The Father of Waters goes again unvexed to the sea." Sherman felt a thrill of pride when Admiral Porter wrote him regarding Port Hudson, which had defied Banks for weeks, "The Army of the Tennessee would not have stopped to dig a ditch before such a place."

29

THEY CRY ALOUD FOR MERCY

DURING the new campaign, which was to drive General Johnston far into the interior, Sherman saw additional signs that led him to believe that the war should be ended. He noted how the Federal privates had become filled with a confidence and skill that doomed their enemies. The Vicksburg campaign had hardened even the newer regiments into a veteran poise.

On July 6 as he began his march toward the enemy in Jackson, Sherman heard a cheer arise while he passed down a column. He looked to see who had shouted; his own men were not so effusive. He saw that the noise had come from a new regiment—the Seventy-ninth Highlanders. When he had last seen them, they had been boys and had cursed him in their camps after Bull Run. The Highlanders had been sent West down the Ohio River in a side-wheel steamer "so light of draught that it could sail on a heavy dew" and they had rioted for a night or two among the saloons and "parlor houses" of Louisville before entraining for the Vicksburg front. They had arrived to find their first commander, Sherman, a general. They marveled at the swiftness with which his Westerners covered ground with a fast, swinging walk, a short rest, another drive, and so onward, day and night.

The march to Jackson was demonstrating the power of Sherman's marchers. The heat was awful, the dust ankle-deep, the creeks dry, the ponds foul with dead animals that the retreating Confederates had led into the water, then shot. Food was mainly "horse-corn" roasted in the husk over fence-rail fires, and although the half-ripe ears physicked men seriously, they marched on. Thunderstorms revived them; they unrolled rubber ponchos and let water trickle into their mouths as they walked. When the rain came at night they thanked the lightning for showing them mudholes and stalled artillery caissons. Said Leander Stillwell, private of the Sixty-first Illinois:

> The dirt road would soon be worked into a loblolly of sticky, yellow mud. Thereupon we would take off our shoes and socks, tie them to the barrel of our muskets, poise the piece on the hammer on either shoulder, stock uppermost, and roll up our breeches. Splashing, the men would swing along, singing "John Brown's Body" or whatever else came handy.

Sherman noted, "Rain cheered men on the march and depressed them in camp."

On his march to Jackson, Sherman taught his men to camp without tents. He refused to let his officers pitch the tents that their orderlies carried on horses. It was effeminate, he said, for commissioned men to sleep inside when privates were resting, dead-tired, in corn furrows with stalks for mattresses. One night he weakened, however, when a storm broke and sought refuge in a tent that, against orders, Major William L. Jenney, his chief engineer, had erected. He called in his staff and spent the night "talking and smoking, with an occasional drink." Jenney noted that he habitually awakened earlier than any other man in the army, and that he grew sarcastic at hearing officers shouting from their blankets for orderlies to bring them wash water and eye-openers. "Do they think they're in the Fifth Avenue Hotel?" he growled. Jenney saw him, on entering the town of Clinton, look around for a headquarters house and then, on discovering that regimental commanders had seized the best homes, select for himself the meanest log cabin in the town.

As cunning as an Indian tracker, Sherman read Johnston's mind in the dust. "There will be no fight this side of Jackson," he told Jenney. "Joe Johnston has marched all day in the broiling sun, passing two places where it would have been most advantageous to have made a stand had he desired to do so." Then he ordered his men to abandon the marching formation that kept them ready for instant action. Instead, they could hurry forward, loose and free, to rendezvous at Jackson. The speed with which this more informal method carried the men brought them to the city of Jackson before the Confederates could erect powerful earthworks. Nevertheless Sherman refused to attack. He had seen the costliness of frontal attacks at Chickasaw and at Vicksburg. As he settled down to a week's bombardment of the enemy lines, his men passed along the word that Uncle Billy wished to spare the lives of his soldiers.

Sherman had come to know his men during the Vicksburg campaign. He now regarded the corps—the Fifteenth—as his own; and in its own undemonstrative way, the corps admired him. As time went on, it would reflect his personality, his carelessness of attire. It was a farm-boy organization. Of the fifty regimental organizations included or represented in its ranks, thirteen were from Illinois, twelve from Missouri, eleven from Iowa, and ten from Ohio. It was the model that he held up to the other corps, Ord's Thirteenth and Parke's Ninth, as on July 17 the whole army rushed into Jackson, from which Joe Johnston, seeing no chance for further resistance, had withdrawn.

"One day's work by the Fifteenth Corps in Jackson in May prevented Johnston from handling his troops in the Vicksburg campaign," Sherman told the army. It took the hint and spread the flames that had been burning among Johnston's abandoned stores when they entered the town. Factories, railroad shops, and warehouses were added to the fire. Homes were not deliberately burned, but raiding parties sent out to destroy railroads in the country around Jackson carried the work of devastation to such lengths that Sherman said that for thirty miles on all sides of the city the land "was terrible to contemplate." However. he added,

> It is the scourge of war to which ambitious men have appealed rather than [to] the judgment of the learned and pure tribunals which our forefathers have provided for the supposed wrongs and injuries.

To Grant he wrote at the end of the first day's occupancy:

> We have made fine progress today in the work of destruction. The enemy burned the greater part of Jackson and we have done some in that line; the place is ruined.

In the flames of Jackson four months of destruction came to a pause, four months in which the attitude of Grant and Sherman toward enemy property had undergone revolution. The change had not been primarily of their making. Halleck was the real author. As lately as March both Grant and Sherman had been subsisting their armies only in part on the farms around them, and they had been insisting that their foragers differentiate between loyal and disloyal planters in the seizure of grain, horses, and Negroes. Receipts must still be given for produce that was commandeered. But with the beginning of April Halleck had sent an unofficial but nevertheless emphatic letter to Grant giving the cue for future conduct.

> The character of the war has changed very much with the last year. There is now no possible hope of reconciliation with the rebels. The Union party in the South is virtually destroyed. There can be no peace but that which is forced by the sword. We must conquer the rebels or be conquered by them. The North must conquer the slave oligarchy or become slaves themselves, the manufacturers mere "hewers of wood and drawers of water" to the Southern aristocrats.

He told Grant to begin taking slaves into the lines. "Every slave withdrawn from the enemy is equivalent to a white man put hors de combat." He wrote General Hurlbut in Memphis that since the enemy in West Virginia had adopted the policy of driving off all live stock, be it friend's or foe's,

> we must live upon the enemy's country as much as possible and destroy his supplies. This is cruel warfare, but the enemy has brought it upon himself by his own conduct.

During the Vicksburg campaign both Grant and Sherman had tried to temper the War Department's new policy to the shorn civilians; Grant had ordered, "Cripple the rebellion in every way without insulting women and children," and Sherman, commanding his men to "use freely" all corn and meats, had added, "Protect houses and families as much as possible." He had driven loafing soldiers from Southern homes and had tried to save heirloom portraits in mansions that had been deserted. He still had keen liking for paintings. In his eyes it was still anarchy to burn houses. To appropriate food, to destroy mills and warehouses, was business—the business of war.

Under the necessity of feeding his men in the recent campaign, when there were no supplies arriving from the rear, Sherman had abandoned many of the rules he had observed in less strenuous periods. He had stopped demanding that his foragers give receipts for produce. How could such formalities be observed when men must march twenty miles a day fighting Pemberton, and feed themselves? No longer did he call chicken-stealing a crime. How could men obey his orders as to the free use of meats without disobeying his other orders about holding houses inviolate? The meat was in smokehouses, and the Fifteenth Corps could construe a smokehouse as something other than a residence. But when meat was in a cellar, what then? Nothing to do but call the cellar a smokehouse.

In Jackson Sherman found Southerners pressing around him with submissiveness. "The inhabitants are subjugated. They cry aloud for mercy," he wrote Grant.

Always when an army of either force swallowed an enemy region, a certain number of citizens could be relied upon to lick the conqueror's boots, but here in Jackson Sherman saw signs of something more serious. Men whom he knew as "very intelligent and influential" came to him to discuss, with sad dignity, ways and means of bringing themselves and their State back into the Union.

This was the moment for which Sherman had been waiting since the beginning of the war. If Confederates would only admit themselves wrong in rebelling, he would show them how kind the Federal power could be. In Memphis he had, for policy's sake, pretended to see signs of such a change, but in private he had admitted such hopes groundless. Now he was convinced that this talk of conversion was sincere.

A dinner given him and his staff by the chief justice of Mississippi on his second night in town had seemed symbolic. The State official had welcomed him with what he told Porter had been "a beautiful supper." Wine had flowed; laughter, songs, and toasts had rung among the paling stars. Witty Frank Blair had been toastmaster. So gay had been the party that when Major Jenney, hunting a missing brigadier next day, sought Blair's aid, the latter struck off for the banquet hall. Blair remembered the brigadier in a certain chair. Then he remembered hearing some one say that the brigadier had gone home early. Blair and Jenney looked under the table. There slept the brigadier and beside him snored two other generals whom no one had missed.

While his officers recovered from the banquet wine, Sherman busied himself on errands of mercy. Beginning with the dispatch of food and medicines to the hospitals and asylums, he obtained from Grant permission to feed eight hundred helpless women and children from army stores. Sherman's heart was touched, but his brain was equally sensitive to another appeal—the opportunity to wean these crushed civilians away from the Confederacy. It was not enough that a few thoughtful inhabitants were disgusted with Jefferson Davis's régime. The commoners must be influenced. "I delay here," he wrote Grant, "to encourage the people to rebel against a Government which they now feel is unable to protect or support them." Not only did he proceed to feed the destitute; he also began to reëquip the looted farmers with horses and mules. Turning the army's bag of live stock—not needed for transport—into a stockade, he summoned owners to reclaim their property. No proof of loyalty did he ask. Simple ownership was all any one need establish. He told his officers:

> Provisions are issued as a pure charity to prevent suffering just as we would to Indians on the frontier or to shipwrecked people . . . and the fewer conditions the purer the charity.

But if he made no conditions, he missed no opportunities to impress upon the sufferers their debt of hate to secession leaders. After arranging with the Confederate cavalryman, General W. H. Jackson, to establish Hinds County as a neutral zone so that farmers might raise crops unmolested by either army, he admonished the people to use their surcease in thinking upon the errors of rebellion.

By the first of August, Sherman saw Grant adopt his plan of feeding the helpless and expand it to include the whole Army of the Tennessee in Mississippi. "It should be our policy now to make as favorable an impression upon the people of the State as possible," said Grant. Sherman pointed out the significance of this act to a committee of penitents:

> I do not think that any nation ever undertook to feed, supply and provide for the future of the inhabitants of an insurgent district. We have done so here and in other instances in this war.

If the committee could find anywhere in history other instances, he would be glad to learn of them. Modestly he refrained from mentioning that one of these "other instances in this war" had been his own work among the destitute in Memphis. It obviously gratified him in August to see his men carry bread and beans into homes from which they had taken hams and molasses in May.

But the spirit of license unleashed during the Vicksburg campaign would not down. After he had marched his men from Jackson back to their camps on the Big Black, Sherman wrote Grant:

> The amount of plundering and stealing done by our army makes me ashamed of it. I would quit the service if I could because I fear we are drifting to the worst sort of vandalism. I have endeavored to repress this class of crime, but you know how difficult it is to fix the guilt among the great mass of the army.

He restored his policy of giving receipts for food and in one case went to the extreme of ordering his men to pay cash for provisions. In sending a cavalry detachment on a pacific trip to a distant station he gave the colonel several thousand dollars in currency; it was to be spent for food taken from "Union people and the poorest farmers, without being too critical as to politics."

All around him were increasing signs of submissiveness. To all Federal generals in the Mississippi Valley there came such floods of letters and so many delegations asking peace and return to the Union that both he and Grant believed Mississippi, Louisiana, Tennessee, and the major part of Arkansas to be subjugated.

He was happy. Ellen arrived in mid-August with Minnie, Lizzie, Willy, and Tommy. His commission as brigadier general in the regular army arrived. Grant had recommended both himself and McPherson for the promotion, praising their "purity and disinterestedness." Grant had cited Sherman's feats, his "unequalled march" from Jackson, his "great merits as a soldier," which "entitle him to more credit than it usually falls to the lot of one man to earn." Sherman replied saying that he valued the commission far less than the fact that it would associate his name with "yours and McPherson's"; all he wanted to do would be "to serve near you and under you till the dawn of that peace for which we are contending." From John came the glad news that Northern newspapers, even "your old enemy the *Cincinnati Gazette*," were now "especially laudatory." He needed defenders no more. Hugh Ewing was writing his father: "The army is confident Cump can defeat anybody. His praise is on every tongue."

Sherman was secure for the first time in his life—secure and independent. Even if the war should end, he would hold his rank. He was back in the regular army. He would never be rich on a brigadier general's salary, but his wife and children need never go running home to Lancaster again.

He took immense pride in the energy and brightness with which his son Willy, now nine, rode beside him around the camps. Charles Ewing, stationed with the Thirteenth Regulars immediately behind Cump's tent, saw to it that Willy learned the manual of arms. The regiment made the boy a sergeant.

In the round of picnics, parties, and calls Ellen saw that most social of the Federals in the West, General James Birdseye McPherson, a man so attractive of person and manner as to be a favorite of even the Yankee-hating belles of Vicksburg, where he now commanded. As ruler of the captured city, McPherson's popularity with secession women would in time set certain brother officers to whispering about his loyalty, but Sherman would quiet the rumors and in brotherly fashion warn his friend to be more circumspect.

"The best scholar in his class at West Point, the highest moral character of the whole student corps," was General W. B. Hazen's description of McPherson. "The very man to handle volunteers," he was called by Logan, who was ever slow to praise a West-Pointer:

> . . . his disposition made easy the troubles of the march when organizations clashed . . . a gentle, sweet man, six feet in height, graceful, captivating, polished of manner, soft of temper, totally unconscious of fear, full of natural sweetness.

Sherman said:

> If he lives, he'll outdistance Grant and myself, a noble, gallant gentleman and the best hope for a great soldier . . . in my mind's eye.

A half-orphan, born in an Ohio log-cabin, chief support of a widowed mother and a grandmother, honor man at the United States Military

Academy, a young engineer in California, skillful enough to attract the notice of Halleck, McPherson had been called to St. Louis when Old Brains had taken command. He had been chief engineer of the army at Donelson and Shiloh and had been a major general of volunteers at thirty-three. Grant rated him as highly as he did Sherman, and admired him, but did not feel for him the intimacy that he felt for his red-haired lieutenant.

"When the time comes that to be a soldier, a man has to forget or overlook the claims of humanity," said McPherson, "I do not want to be a soldier." He was religiously inclined; officers spoke of him as "a practising Christian." However, Colonel Markland, who knew him intimately at Vicksburg, was sure he was not Puritanical. "A troubadour under the windows of fair ladies of that war-stricken city," Markland called him, remembering how McPherson, with himself and two other generals, had sung on the midnight streets.

Ellen did not see those two outstanding volunteer officers, Logan and Blair. Logan was at home in Illinois building Republican fences among his late Democratic constituents, and Blair was in Washington scheming with his shrewd old father and his Postmaster-General brother—possibly the President also—to make himself Speaker of the House of Representatives. This youngest of the Blairs had never resigned his seat in Congress and now in the autumn of '63 Lincoln was advising his family to let Frank

> help organize a House which will really support the Government. If elected Speaker let him serve, if not, let him retake his commission and return to the army. For the country this will heal a dangerous schism.

Frank was obviously rising in military skill, said Lincoln: "his appointment to the command of a corps by one so competent to judge as General Sherman proves this." Wilkie, the war correspondent, described Frank:

> . . . tall, well-formed with a sandy complexion, light-gray eyes, heavy moustache, clean-shaved face, a fine forehead covered with a mass of reddish hair, distingué in style and bearing, handsome and commanding, slow and deliberate in speech, doing everything well from leading a charge to uncorking a bottle.

Ellen heard Cump and his brother officers talk of the Confederates—of Earl Van Dorn, who after riding through Union fire for two years, had been assassinated in May, 1863, by a civilian, Dr. Peters, who insisted that Van Dorn had betrayed one of his female relatives. Ellen heard talk of Bragg's readiness to quarrel with his companions, and of how his staff could never decide which was worse, his health or his temper. She heard tales of General Nathan Bedford Forrest, the Confederate horseman, whose temper was as vicious as Bragg's and who had indeed once told Bragg that he would slap his face if he weren't too damned a scoundrel to be touched. A Tennessee cabin boy, reared in the backwoods, Forrest had never learned to spell with accuracy, nor to acquire the traits of a Southern gentleman. Having amassed a fortune selling slaves as well as real estate in Memphis, he was disliked by the West-Pointers and the aristocrats. He refused to learn the manual of arms, he tore limbs from trees and whipped troopers whom he thought liars or cowards. Once when a Tennessee regiment ignored his rallying cries, he peppered their posteriors with a shotgun. When a lieutenant, resenting Forrest's ungovernable temper, tried to shoot him, Forrest disemboweled him with a pocketknife. As the dying man begged forgiveness, Forrest wept. He often wept from excitement in battle. He disliked liquor, tobacco, and smutty stories, and was fond of arranging religious revivals for his men. He could count eight brothers and half-brothers in gray uniforms. Eccentric, original, full of aggressive genius, he would in time earn from Sherman the compliment—"that devil Forrest."

Ellen did not find Cump wasting much anxiety on his opponents in the late summer of 1863. He expected the war to end shortly. By all that was rational, the Confederacy should surrender. It could now quit with honor. It had defended the Mississippi and lost. "The war has been virtually and properly settled. It was a certainty," Sherman said.

Something hinting at serenity—as near as he had ever come to it—came into his nature. He tried to persuade Grant to reinstate poor General Lew Wallace, who had been pining in Indiana ever since his failure at Shiloh. When Grant refused his suit, Sherman advised Wallace:

> . . . avoid all controversies, bear patiently temporary reverses, get into current events as quick as possible and hold your horses for the last home stretch.

Wallace felt a surge of admiration for the man "who practised what he preached."

Sherman counseled another fallen leader, Buell, not to write his proposed history of the early war, but to accept any rank in order to be back in active service:

> . . . it looks childish, foolish, yes, criminal—for sensible men to be away at the rear, sitting in security, torturing their brains and writing on reams

of foolscap to fill a gap future historians will dispose of by a very short and maybe an unimportant chapter or even paragraph. . . . Like in a race the end is all that is remembered by the great world.

He was pleased when a soldier asked one day if he might name his newborn baby W. Tecumseh Sherman. A letter from the North had just announced the event.

"How long have you been in the service?" asked Sherman.

"Two years, General."

"Have you ever had a furlough?"

"No, sir, I've been with the regiment every day."

"Been two years in the service, never had a furlough, and your wife has a bouncing boy? Why, really, I don't understand this," said Sherman with mock gravity.

The soldier's face reddened while staff officers exchanged winks. "General, my wife visited me three weeks when we were in Memphis," said the man sheepishly. The officers roared with laughter and the petitioner left with the desired permission and Sherman's promise that when the boy was ten he would receive something worth while from the general. Keeping track of the child, in time Sherman learned that he had died before his tenth birthday.

Handling the routine affairs of his corps with ease, Sherman found time to help in what would be the first use of the railroads as traveling post offices. Postmaster-General Montgomery Blair, introducing into the postal department money orders and free delivery in cities, had decided to experiment with the sorting of mail on fast trains. In the army to which his brother was attached he found generals willing to attempt the new scheme. Colonel Markland described it:

> General Grant first made it a distinctive feature of army service. . . . To the Army of the Tennessee is due the credit for demonstrating that mails could be accurately distributed in transit under the most adverse circumstances, and to that Army as much as to any other agency is due the credit of originating the mail service in the United States.

Markland noted the efficiency with which Sherman saw to it that letters from home reached even the most scattered of his commands. This, according to several observers, was one significant cause for the exceptional morale in the Fifteenth Corps.

Not so obliging was Sherman when another Administration experiment was commenced—the enlistment of Negro soldiers. Propaganda for the arming and training of blacks had been strong ever since Lincoln's issuance of the Emancipation Proclamation. Certain Federal generals approved the step as one that would strengthen the army; Abolitionists insisted that the Negro should have the right to fight the civilization that had enslaved him; shrewd manufacturers covertly pushed the plan in the hope that it would keep the Government from drafting white laborers. More Southern than Northern on this question, Sherman wrote Ellen:

> I would prefer to have this a white man's war and provide for the negroes after the time has passed, but we are in revolution and I must not pretend to judge. With my opinions of negroes and my experience, yea, prejudice, I cannot trust them yet.

In May, 1863, the Confederate Congress made the Abolitionists more determined on the issue. It passed a law condemning to death any white Federal officer captured while commanding black troops. The law would rarely, if ever, be officially enforced, since the Federals threatened reprisals.

Although the organization of black regiments went on near his corps, sometimes reaching into his territorial domain, Sherman kept aloof. He would give no helping hand to a project so obviously doomed to failure. He flew into rage when planters complained to McPherson that Sherman had sent Negro soldiers to plunder and kill them. This was, he answered, "the very reverse of my practice. On the contrary I have done more than most persons to restrain the violence and passion of the Negro." He knew these same planters as friends of guerrillas and for them to talk of depredations stirred him to irony:

> By breaking up the only earthly power that could restrain the negroes, by openly rebelling against the Government of the United States, they prepared the way for those very acts against which they now appeal to us to shield them. . . . All we are bound to do in the name of humanity is to invite them into our lines for personal safety and to leave their property to revert to a state of nature for the use of alligators and negroes.

His one employment of Negroes for military purposes he described to McPherson as "a kind of picket" on the outskirts of his corps, a comic band, which he allowed to use a few mills for grinding their corn:

> . . . under the command of a venerable George Washington who, mounted on a sprained horse, with his hat plumed with an ostrich feather, his full belly girt with a stout belt from which hangs a terrible cleaver, and followed by a trusty orderly on foot, [it] makes an army on your flank that ought to give you every assurance of safety from that exposed quarter. Should, however, the secesh be rash enough to gobble up that picket, I still think we could survive the loss.

He did not share the excited Southern planters' fears regarding the runaway slaves who roamed the country. Such wanderers were, he said:

> . . . a poor, ignorant class of human beings that appeal to all for a full measure of forbearance. . . . If they mistake their just relation to the Government or the people, we will soon impress on them the truth.

To his subordinates who came in contact with the field hands who capered so frantically, he gave the order, "Impress upon the Negroes that to deserve freedom, they must respect the rights of humanity."

Toward the world Sherman felt genial as the summer of '63 waned. He even grew a little smug, for once in his life, as he wrote John:

> Though full of corruption and base materials our country is a majestic one, full of natural wealth and good people. Our progress has been as rapid as any philosopher could ask . . . we have had as much success as could be hoped for.

30

BLOWS THICK AND FAST

IN the heat of Mississippi dog days Sherman began to realize that he had been a fool to believe that both North and South had understood the significance of Vicksburg's fall. Instead of recognizing the hopelessness of further warfare, the Confederacy was electing to revive it. It had called up conscripts between the ages of eighteen and forty-five.

Sherman believed that the Federal Government was blundering almost as badly. The Administration had evidently learned nothing from Grant's stupendous victory. Not yet could it see that the road to success lay in the direction of allowing Grant freedom of action. He wanted to keep the Army of the Tennessee compact and aggressive, to drive on Mobile and to wipe the Gulf Coast clean of enemies. If the war was to go on, he knew that the Western army must be forever on the offensive—a hammer always ringing. Against this psychology was Halleck's scholarly fondness for defensive warfare, and Halleck was at Stanton's and Lincoln's ear. The orthodox traditions of military art still could curb the heterodox, independent Westerners. So Grant saw his army scattered, on the ancient formula, about the Mississippi Valley as garrisons for captive towns.

There it lay as September began. Grant, departing for inspection of forces in New Orleans, asked Sherman to substitute for him as commander. But Sherman, still dodging major responsibility, refused, although he agreed to do the work and issue the routine orders in Grant's name.

Newspapers arrived with descriptions of how Rosecrans was leading the Army of the Cumberland against Chattanooga, and how he had occupied it on September 9. With Vicksburg, this gave the Federals the two most important points in the West. General Burnside, with the Army of the Ohio, seized Knoxville. Now the rich coal fields of the South were in Union hands, also the niter beds that supplied the Confederacy with two thirds of its gunpowder. But Rosecrans was failing to wait in Chattanooga and consolidate his triumph. Lunging on into the hills of northern Georgia, he felt Bragg's resistance stiffen on September 12.

That same day, Sherman on the Big Black saw by the newspapers that the war was definitely to be resumed—"a great and terrific battle is predicted between Bragg and Rosecrans." In the absence of Grant there was nothing that the Army of the Tennessee could do. It was ironic that the army should be lying idle. If the Administration had let Grant have his way, the army could now have been raiding Mobile, and the Confederacy could not have concentrated against Rosecrans. As matters stood, this concentration was a large one. Gray-clad divisions had rushed up from lower Mississippi and a crack corps from Lee's Virginia force under Longstreet had come over the mountains to join Bragg.

Five days after discovering the new and tragic turn of affairs, Sherman sat down to answer a letter that Halleck had sent him in late August, asking for his views on reconstruction in Louisiana, Mississippi, and Alabama. Halleck had said that President Lincoln needed the

> opinions of cool and discreet [men]. . . . I think he is disposed to receive the advice of our generals who have been in these States and know much more of their condition than gassy politicians in Congress.

General Banks had contributed, Grant had not; would Sherman oblige? If so, Halleck would treat it as personal and not make it public.

The problem facing Lincoln was baffling. Had the seceded States "committed suicide" and lost their original status, or had they merely succumbed to the insurrection of certain citizens? Abolitionist statesmen and violent leaders, known as Radicals, held to the theory that by the act of secession the States had reduced themselves to the position of mere Territories and that action must be taken before they, in penitence, could be restored to their former rights. Against this view liberal statesmen argued that the States need do nothing but renounce secession, reëlect loyal officers, and then automatically resume their places in the Union. Lincoln, although leaning toward the liberals, was feeling his way slowly through a maze of unprecedented legal entanglements.

The Sherman who sat down on September 17 to write out his views was a man angry from the fresh discovery that all his recent work in feeding and converting Southerners had been useless. Labeling his letter Private and Confidential, he scrawled twenty-seven hundred words, an essay, a survey, a declaration of faith, a course of future action—and in more paragraphs than one a prose poem. Into it he poured his artistic conception of America as it ought to be, and his realistic analysis of it as it actually existed. Above all, he saw the nation as a dream of symmetry and proportion—a creation of majestic, unsentimental brotherhood.

> The valley of the Mississippi is America, and, although railroads have changed the economy of intercommunication, yet the water-channels still mark the lines of fertile land, and afford cheap carriage to the heavy products of it.
>
> The inhabitants of the country on the Monongahela, the Illinois, the Minnesota, the Yellowstone, and Osage, are as directly concerned in the security of the Lower Mississippi as are those who dwell on its very banks in Louisiana; and now that the nation has recovered its possession, this generation of men will make a fearful mistake if they again commit its charge to a people liable to misuse their position, and assert, as was recently done, that, because they dwelt on the banks of this mighty stream, they had a right to control its navigation.
>
> I would deem it very unwise at this time, or for years to come, to revive the State governments of Louisiana, etc., or to institute in this quarter any civil government in which the local people have much to say. They had a government so mild and paternal that they gradually forgot they had any at all, save what they themselves controlled; they asserted an absolute right to seize public moneys, forts, arms, and even to shut up the natural avenues of travel and commerce. They chose *war*—they ignored and denied all the obligations of the solemn contract of government and appeal to force. . . . I know them well.

For Lincoln's eye he sketched the four classes into which the South was divided. First, there were the large planters, some still "bitter as gall," others conservative:

> I know we can manage this class, but only by action. . . . If our country were like Europe, crowded with people, I would say it would be easier to replace this class than to reconstruct it . . . but, as this is not the case, it is better to allow the planters . . . to hire any species of labor and to adapt themselves to the new order of things.

Second, there were the small farmers, storekeepers, and laborers, three fourths of the Southern population. They had no real interest in the war and "would slink home if they could." Sherman was again leaning toward monarchy when he thought of them:

> These are the real *tiers état* of the South and are hardly worth a thought; for they swerve to and fro according to events which they do not comprehend or attempt to shape. When the time for reconstruction comes . . . they will want the old political system . . . to amuse them and make them believe they are the real sovereigns; but in all things, they will follow blindly the lead of the planters. The Southern politicians, who understand this class, use them as the French do their masses—seemingly consult their prejudices, while they make their orders and enforce them. We should do the same.

Third, there were the Union men of the South:

> Afraid of shadows, they submit tamely to squads of dragoons and permit them without a murmur to burn their cotton . . . and when we reach them they are full of complaints if our men take a few fence rails. . . . I account them as nothing in this great game of war.

Fourth, he listed:

> The young bloods . . . who never did work and never will. War suits them, and the rascals are brave, fine riders, bold to rashness and dangerous in every sense. They care not a sou for niggers, land or anything . . . they don't bother their brains about the past, present or future . . . the best cavalry . . . the most dangerous set of men this war has turned loose upon the world . . . when the resources of their country are exhausted, we must employ them.

For such a people, he said, "a civil government now . . . would be simply ridiculous." The interests of the United States "demand the continuance of the simple military rule after *all* the organized armies of the South are dispersed, conquered and subjugated." The only real issue, he wrote, was, "Can we whip the South?"

> Another great and important natural truth is still in contest, and can only be solved by war. Numerical majorities by vote have been our great arbiter. Heretofore, all men have cheerfully submitted to it in questions left open, but numerical majorities are not necessarily physical majorities. The South, though numerically inferior, contend they can whip the Northern superiority of numbers, and therefore by natural law contend that they are not bound to submit. This issue is the only real one. . . . War alone can decide it.
>
> I would banish all minor questions, assert the broad doctrine that a nation has the right, and also the physical power to penetrate to every part of our national domain, and that we will do it—that we will do it in our own time and in our own way; that it makes no difference whether it be one year or

two, or ten or twenty; that we will remove and destroy every obstacle, if need be, take every life, every acre of land . . . that we will not cease till the end is attained. . . .

I would not coax them or even meet them half way but make them so sick of war that generations would pass away before they would again appeal to it. . . .

The people of this country have forfeited all right to a voice in the councils of the nation. They know it and feel it and in after-years they will be better citizens from the dear-bought experience. . . . Let them learn now, and learn it well, that good citizens must obey as well as command. Obedience to law, absolute—yea, even abject—is the lesson that this war, under Providence, will teach the free and enlightened American citizen. As a nation, we shall be the better for it.

When the letter was finished, Sherman sent it to Rawlins asking him to read it before forwarding it to Halleck. With it went a note:

I know that in Washington I am incomprehensible, because at the outset of the war I would not go it blind and rush headlong into a war unprepared and with an utter ignorance of its extent and purpose. I was then construed *unsound;* and now that I insist upon war pure and simple, with no admixture of civil compromises, I am supposed vindictive . . . indeed, I know and you know that the end would be reached quicker by such a course than by any seeming yielding on our part. . . .

The South has done her worst, and now is the time for us to pile on blows thick and fast.

When Sherman learned from Halleck that President Lincoln wished to publish the twenty-seven-hundred-word treatise, he wrote, "I think it won't bear publication. . . . If I covet any public reputation it is as a silent actor. I dislike to see my name in print." The paper remained unpublished until Sherman himself gave it out twelve years later. In writing it, Sherman had introduced himself to Lincoln as an independent thinker; also he had clarified his own ideas of duty. Heretofore his bark had been much worse than his bite in dealing with the civilian populace of the South. Now that they had elected to continue the wasteful struggle, he was preparing to make his bite a death grip.

As he mailed his letter, the war entered a new phase. Bragg, catching Rosecrans's army scattered, routed it on September 19 and 20 at Chickamauga Creek, killing, wounding, or capturing 16,000 out of 60,000. Only the stalwart defense of George H. Thomas's wing prevented the loss of the entire force. In Chattanooga the demoralized remnants gathered to endure Bragg's siege.

Hysteria ran through the North. Telegraph wires sang with fear. Grant was fast in a New Orleans bed, his leg and side swollen from an injury received in the fall of his saddle horse. His explanation, years later, was that the animal had taken fright at a street car. General William B. Franklin told Samuel L. Clemens that he "*saw* Grant tumble from his horse drunk." Reading Halleck's wire ordering troops east from Memphis to threaten Bragg, Grant now ordered Sherman to lead the movement. "He had superior fitness for an independent command," he said later.

Haste now on the Big Black, drums rolling, muleteers cursing, wagons loading, the roads to Vicksburg black with marching men, Ellen and the children packing up for the return trip to Ohio. Vicksburg's wharves were smoking with transport engines. The *Atlantic* was the last to leave for Memphis. On it rode Sherman and his family. Sherman noticed that Willy was carrying a small double-barreled shotgun in the confidence that he was a soldier embarked on high adventure. The boy gloried in his sergeant's uniform. While Sherman was showing the family his old camps as the steamboat passed Young's Point, he looked twice at Willy; the small face was pale. Ellen rushed the child to bed. Surgeons summoned from regiments below deck diagnosed the illness as typhoid fever, and said that it might prove fatal.

The river was low and the steamer's progress was tortuous. Sherman haunted the bedside, denouncing himself for having brought his family to Mississippi. Willy, more than any other child, "took an interest in my special profession," said the father; he was "that child on whose future I based all the ambition I ever had."

Twenty-four hours after he had been carried ashore at Memphis, Willy died among helpless physicians—the best of the city. Helpless too, and overwhelmed, Sherman watched the small life disappear. "His loss is more to me than words can express," he telegraphed Halleck, "but I would not let it divert my mind from the duty I owe my country." Sherman moved through a nightmare, securing railroad cars to transport his men to Corinth; hunting a metallic casket for Willy's body; attending to the details of thousands of men who must be fed. For two days the torture was acute, then on the fourth of October, the Thirteenth Regulars escorted their mascot's body to the steamer *Gray Eagle* and Cump waved good-by to Ellen and the remaining children. That night he wrote his thanks to the Thirteenth Regiment:

> The child that bore my name and in whose future I reposed more confidence than I did in my own plan of life, now floats a mere corpse, seeking a grave in a different land, with a weeping mother, brother and sisters clustered about him. For myself I seek no sympathy. . . .
>
> But Willy was or thought he was, a sergeant of the Thirteenth . . . he had the enthusiasm, the pure love of triumph, honor and love of country,

> which should animate all soldiers. God only knows why he should die this young.

He wanted the Thirteenth to know that they could call upon him and his family in future years and find "that we will share with them our last blanket, our last crust." Early the following morning he was writing Ellen:

> Sleeping, waking, everywhere I see poor little Willy. His face and form are as deeply imprinted on my memory as were deep-seated the hopes I had in his future. Why, oh, why should that child be taken from us, leaving us full of trembling and reproaches? . . . I will go on to the end but feel the chief stay to my faltering heart is now gone. . . . I will try and make poor Willy's memory the cure for the defects which have sullied my character . . . all that is captious, eccentric and wrong.

When he passed the hotel room where Willy had died, he saw the children of new guests playing there, and it seemed sacrilege. While he loaded his staff, clerks, and a battalion of the Thirteenth on a special train for Corinth, he was seeing Willy stumbling over the sand hills of San Francisco, drumming on the dinner table at Leavenworth, running to embrace his father on the banks of the Big Black—"and last, moaning in death." He wrote Ellen, "Why was I not killed at Vicksburg and left Willy to grow up to care for you?"

Then he entrained for Corinth, passing the Fourth Division of marching men. His Thirteenth guards, on top of the fleeting cars, waved good-by to the troops. In the rear car Sherman tried to find forgetfulness in sleep. Noon came as the train passed Colliersville. Major Jenney, sitting near Sherman, opened a package that a German had given him in Memphis. It was a cake. Jenney started to cut it. The engine shrieked. The train stopped. Jenney put down the cake and looked out. Soldiers were running toward the head of the train, cocking their rifles. "The road is cut ahead by Chalmers's cavalry," came the word. Jenney heard Sherman order the train backed to Colliersville, where the brick station had been previously turned into a blockhouse and surrounded by shallow trenches. A telegrapher hurried orders to the Fourth Division to come on at the double-quick. Across a ridge, four hundred yards away, Confederates were pouring, infantry and cavalry. Just before enemy horsemen cut the wires, Brigadier General John M. Corse, commanding the division, answered, "I am coming."

For four hours Sherman with 600 men kept 8,000 attackers at bay. He knew from the enemy's mode of assault that "there was not a military man along." All were militiamen, and although they used eight cannon and Sherman none, the guns, as Sherman noted, "were handled as bad as possible. . . . It was a big scramble for plunder and bunglingly managed throughout." Twice the charging Confederates reached the rear end of the train, looting it and attempting to set it afire. They kindled the blaze with the extra shirts of Colonel Audenreid, Sherman's aide-de-camp, and stole Sherman's second-best uniform. They led off five horses, among them Sherman's favorite Dolly. But the fire of the regulars from the hill above the tracks drove the looters away before the train could be destroyed. One marksman aimed at a Southerner who emerged from the rear car hobbling on one foot and attempting to force the other into a captured boot. The bullet knocked the pillager flat and, in the language of a spectator, "before he was done kicking the soldier that shot him had the boots on."

Each time the resurging Confederates clustered about the train, some Federal would note a body lying on top of a car. "There's a Rebel!" he would say, and take aim. "That's not a Rebel," the Thirteenth would chorus. "That's Tom Smith. He's dead-drunk and couldn't get off." But in the cross fire that swept the train, it was obvious soon enough that Tom must be dead. Late in the afternoon when Corse and his panting rescuers drove off the attackers, the Thirteenth sent men to the train top to bring off Tom Smith's body. When they began dragging him, Tom sat up, rubbed his eyes, and asked where he was. No bullet had touched him. All he could ever remember about the fight at Colliersville was that it had sobered him up.

Major Jenney stood on the chipped platform of the rear car. The enemy had stolen his cake. Suddenly he saw a Union soldier pass, eating something. Jenney saw that it had frosting on it. He heard the soldier calling to nobody in particular,

"Who had the cake?"

"I did," said Jenney.

"Well," mumbled the man with his mouth full, "I got this out of a dead Rebel's hand under the fence there. It's real good. He had his mouth full, but I let him keep that."

31

VISIBLE INTERPOSITION OF GOD

THERE was a chill in the October days and a chilled fury in Sherman's blood. The war was to go on; Willy was dead; and the army was back under the thumb of Washington again. The way to make Bragg abandon the campaign against Chattanooga was to loose the Army of the Tennessee in devastation around Meridian, Selma, and Mobile. That would bring him down out of the mountains soon enough.

Here was Sherman inching along the railroad, at Halleck's orders, repairing the line, making ready to ship supplies into Chattanooga, where Rosecrans's men were starving—scraping in the mud around horse troughs for grains of corn that had fallen. It was a slow way of relieving such distress. Loyalty and gratitude kept Sherman from criticizing Halleck, yet he was disagreeing on policy. He disapproved Halleck's plan for garrisoning so many captured towns, since it kept troops exposed to capture and death—made them stationary targets for continual raids. He saw that it was wasteful to guard so many outlying railroads—another of Halleck's practices. Sherman wrote Hurlbut, whom he had left commanding the troops at Memphis, to abandon the railroad south of the city: "I don't want to hear of the loss of any public stores or small detachments of men trying to save that railroad. It is not worth the life of one soldier." He also urged the abandonment of Corinth, that depot for which Halleck had labored so mountainously in 1862. Send the garrison into the field to destroy other Southern strongholds! If the enemy occupied Corinth, it would be easy to expel them when necessary! Keep the Union forces moving, devastating, piling on blows "thick and fast."

Personally, Sherman enjoyed the open country and disliked garrison life. He had liked the hardships of the Vicksburg campaign immeasurably better than the soft months in Memphis. He noted that soldiers were healthier on the march than in camp; it was disease, not battle, that was still Death's great friend. War was won by wasting everything but the blood of your men!

Often in his past life as a civilian Sherman had lamented the fate that had made him a "vagabond." The word had played through his conversation and correspondence. Had that bugbear been a secret attraction all along? How much of his admiration for wild, fast, devastating marches was the result of war logic and how much was purely instinctive yearning—a poetic yearning for open roads? There was personal joy as well as military astuteness obvious in his comment during these railroad-mending days:

> I never saw such greedy rascals after chicken and fresh meat. I don't think I will draw anything for them but salt. I don't know but it would be a good plan to march my army back and forth from Florence and Stevenson to make a belt of devastation between the enemy and our country.

An arid swath across upper Mississippi and lower Tennessee would keep Confederate raiders from menacing Kentucky.

Under Halleck, however, he could not follow so logical a plan. Nor was there time for it. Stanton had summoned Grant to Kentucky, making him commander over all Western armies. Sherman must become head of the Army of the Tennessee. Rosecrans was relieved from the leadership of the Army of the Cumberland. Thomas was in his place. Thomas was telegraphing Grant in Louisville, "We'll hold the town till we starve"—a remark that the admiring Union populace would soon convert into "We'll fight till hell freezes over and then we'll fight on the ice." By October 9 Grant was in Chattanooga and putting into effect the plans that Rosecrans and Thomas had drawn up for the importation of food. Soon the "cracker line" was open and the danger of starvation was passed.

On October 24 Sherman received notification of his promotion. He wrote Secretary Chase, whose advice he wanted on details of border trade:

> By the vicissitude of war, I am again forced into the command of a department. I almost shrink from a command that involves me with civil matters which I do not understand. Politics or the means to influence a civil people are mysteries I do not comprehend, but am forced to act.

Having admitted this, he promptly issued an order that called for nothing less than the conscription of Southern civilians into the Union army. Hurlbut had written him that the departure of so many troops had left Memphis dangerously weak, and that he wished to form militia companies from the many Northern civilians in the city. Sherman had already impressed idle citizens into service as teamsters during his slow march toward Chattanooga. Why not extend Hurlbut the same privileges? It was new to war, but this was a new kind of war. So, on October 28 he issued general orders that declared the district insurrectionary and one in which

> every citizen is liable to be called for military service. . . . Every commanding officer of a fixed military post may impress any citizen whatever and may compel his services in any of the old organized regiments.

A Southern civilian taken in this way could expect no more compensation than if in other days he had been called out by a United States marshal to serve on a posse comitatus.

Dryly Sherman observed to Grant that this extension of the war power was "somewhat novel," but he justified it on the ground that "in times of insurrection the army is vested with all the executive powers of the nation. In case of riot any sheriff can summon the bystanders." By the end of the year Sherman would learn that Hurlbut had used the order to form 2,700 men in line at Memphis alone.

Before Sherman had time to develop this bold policy all over his department more important matters interrupted. On October 27 Grant wrote him to "drop all work, hurry eastward with all possible dispatch toward Bridgeport," the concentration point on the Tennessee River below Chattanooga. Grant meant to fight. Sherman assembled his enormous wagon trains—he had started with so many of them because it might be necessary to provision Chattanooga in this manner, and he could not now abandon them to the enemy. In Corinth he had done everything possible to lighten them, even allowing his men to appropriate sutler's supplies that had been secreted among army boxes. "You have stolen transportation belonging to these men while they have had to make a forced march," he had roared. "You are served right!"

Rain fell; mud was abysmal. There were delays while bridges were built, and while steamboats were brought up to act as ferries. River banks were slippery and mules were stubborn. Sherman grew nervously ill. "I feel as if I had a 30-pound shot in my stomach," he wrote Porter. "It is not villainous saltpeter that makes one's life so hard but grub and mules." He would not take time to provision a detachment left to mend the railroad leading to Nashville. All he could do was to say, "The quicker you build the railroad, the quicker you'll get something to eat." So slow was his progress that it required thirteen days to march the last stretch of his journey to Bridgeport—an airline distance of one hundred and fifteen miles. It was like escaping from a treadmill when, spurring ahead of his columns, he caught a supply ship at Bridgeport and rushed into Chattanooga to confer with Grant.

Patiently Grant had been awaiting him. Through the smoke of his cigars he had studied the Army of the Cumberland, which occupied the city, and had decided that it was too demoralized by defeat and trench life to attack Bragg on the mountains before them. It would take fresh troops, acting as bellwethers, to lead the way. He looked at the two corps that had been sent West from the Army of the Potomac. Under General Hooker, they lay along the river, just outside the ring of mountains. They were not accustomed to victory. Grant did not propose to rely upon them. He could only wait until his own Army of the Tennessee arrived under Sherman.

Grant noted how rival pickets regarded each other with something more than the traditional absence of the killing instinct. They paid each other long social calls, stationing lookouts to announce the approach of officers. When one appeared, the visiting delegation departed saying, "Good night. Get a good rest, for we'll give you hell tomorrow." But the morrow brought little in the way of hell, only desultory long-distance shelling. So absurd was the situation that Grant, riding the picket lines, saw Confederate outposts a few feet from him on the opposite side of a creek come to attention and salute him as politely as if he had been one of their own generals. And once while conversing with a private who was filling a canteen at the stream, he discovered that the fellow was not one of his own men but a member of Longstreet's corps, which wore blue uniforms. The general and the private parted in amity. On the heights Bragg's men, polishing their cannon, grew lazy, thinking their position impregnable.

A few days after receiving his illuminating view of the general apathy, Grant learned that Bragg had detached Longstreet's corps and sent it to besiege Burnside in Knoxville. Now was the time to strike, for Bragg's lines were weaker by 18,000 men. Also President Lincoln, still sensitive about East Tennessee, was urging that Grant help Burnside. It was with joy that Grant saw the red beard of his friend Sherman appear at headquarters on November 14. Immediately Grant, Thomas, and other officers rode out with Sherman to view the field of the coming battle.

Sherman stared at a granite amphitheater stretching from the northeast to the southwest. He stood on the stage, a plain that stretched away to the mountains three to four miles distant. Behind him lay the city and behind that, the river. On the northeast Missionary Ridge rose near the river and stretched across to the southwest, where it sank into bottomlands traversed by Chattanooga Creek. Then the rocky formation rose again, climbing up to become Lookout Mountain, a craggy pile, noble enough to inspire the war correspondent Benjamin F. Taylor to the tribute, "An everlasting thunderstorm that will never pass over." Every foot of the semicircle seemed to be covered with the white tents or black cannon of the Confederates. Trenches had been strung along the front of Missionary Ridge, and halfway down its steep slope; also a line of rifle pits lay at its bottom. Sherman spoke up:

"General Grant, you're besieged!"

"It's too true," answered Grant.

A finger pointed out Bragg's headquarters on the crest of the ridge.

"Tom, have you seen Bragg or had any communication with him?" asked Sherman.

"Damn him!" growled Thomas. "I'll be even with him yet."

"What's the matter?"

Thomas explained how a harmless message had come down from the North for a Confederate officer and how:

> I put a slip of paper around it with a note asking Bragg to forward it to its address. The same parcel was returned with a flag of truce with Bragg's endorsement, "Respectfully returned to General Thomas. General Bragg declines to have any intercourse or dealings with a man who has betrayed his State."

Thomas related the tale "with many threats of what he would do when the time came."

When Thomas's idolaters, in later years, pictured him as having been unshakable in his poise, Sherman would scoff, "He was not so imperturbable as the world supposes."

Grant outlined to his generals the plan of battle. Perhaps he was more explicit in explaining it to Sherman than to Thomas, with whom his relations were not cordial. Perhaps Sherman's quickness of mind let him grasp the scheme more clearly than could the slower-witted Thomas. Later their views of the plan would be found to differ. Sherman understood that he was to bring up his Army of the Tennessee, sneak them past Lookout Mountain, cross the river, pass behind the city, then recross the stream at night and in the following morning fight his way up on to the northern end of the ridge. That would make Bragg's position untenable, for Sherman could roll along the crest, or dip down behind the mountain to seize Bragg's railroad communications at Chickamauga depot. Meanwhile Hooker with his Eastern corps would demonstrate against Lookout Mountain and with Bragg assailed on left and right, Thomas would move against his center. As a manuscript for a drama, the plan was sensible, but Grant's stage directions were poor. Both Thomas and Hooker were uncertain just what was expected of them and their staff officers were angry, declaring that Grant intended using the resident armies as mere supernumeraries, while Sherman was to have the star rôle.

Sherman studied the terrain through his spyglass for a time, then with a quick gesture telescoped his glass and told the Cumberland chief engineer, General William Farrar (Baldy) Smith, "I can do it!" He was off through the November moonlight in a rowboat and, taking his turn at the oars "spelling" each of his four rowers, he reached Bridgeport in the morning.

The route by which Sherman led his troops inward from Bridgeport carried the Fifteenth Corps past Hooker's Easterners. Two sections of the North were face to face—one spick and span in paper collars, polished buttons, well-brushed coats, knapsacks topped with neatly rolled blankets, French fatigue caps on their heads, faces shaven or neatly whiskered; the other ragged, muddy, many shoeless, all shaggy of hair and beard, rakish slouch hats on their heads, few wearing knapsacks, the average man carrying his belongings in a blanket roll swung over one shoulder. The East was more pleasing to the eye, the West was more comfortable.

Sherman's men called Hooker's dudes and brass-mounted soldiers. They jeered, "What elegant corpses they'll make in those good clothes." The Easterners answered, "Tramps!" Chaplain John J. Hight of the Fifty-eighth Indiana thought the Easterners far better disciplined:

> They make better guards and indeed are superior on any kind of detached duty that requires style. But the Western men are better fighters. I have often been pained by hearing our men make contemptible reproaches at the Eastern troops. They are better bred and do not retort to the same extent. This bellowing of one body of soldiers at another is all wrong.

Passing Hooker's Twelfth Corps, one of Sherman's privates, an Irishman, left the ranks to stare at a five-pointed star that the Easterners wore on their caps, tents, and wagons. All the stars he had ever seen had been on generals' shoulders. "Are you all major generals?" he asked. They explained that the star was a corps badge, a feature of both Federal and Confederate armies in the East. "What's your badge?" they asked him—a little loftily no doubt. The Irishman promptly patted his leather ammunition pouch at his belt and replied, "Badge, is it? There, be Jasus—forty rounds in the cartridge box and twenty in the pocket." When John A. Logan succeeded Blair a little later as head of the Fifteenth Corps, he heard the story and adopted as the corps' badge an engraving of the box with "40 rounds" upon it.

Work as hard as he might, Sherman could not bring up his men in time to attack at the date set by Grant—November 21. Grant postponed it twenty-four hours and advised Sherman, "Time is of great importance to us." But still Sherman was late. Mud was deep. Dana, writing Stanton of all he saw, said:

A lamentable blunder has been committed in moving Sherman's forces from Bridgeport with enormous trains they brought from West Tennessee following in usual order in the rear of each division instead of moving all the troops and artillery first. Grant says the blunder is his; that he should have given Sherman explicit orders to leave the wagons behind; but I know no one was so much astonished as Grant on learning that they had not been left, even without orders.

Shamed and mortified by his failure, Sherman was sending couriers with apologies. Blair had reported to him that his men were all up from the march, and on the strength of this Sherman had promised to meet Grant's first appointed hour for the attack. Blair had been wrong; his men were detained by a road that was nothing but "a ditch full of big rocks," as Sherman reported. Dana said:

But the fault of marching with trains Sherman attaches to himself. Grant's orders that he should get all troops here before Friday night [Nov. 20] having been positive and it was his own duty to see that nothing hindered his arrival.

Sherman would not throw off on Blair.

It was the night of the twenty-third before Sherman, stealthily circling along the hills, came to the river. There he learned that his secrecy had been in vain. Grant had begun the attack during the day. Warned by the telegraph that the enemy had commenced assaulting Knoxville and that Lincoln was "in an agony of suspense," Grant had been much impressed by a Confederate deserter who told him that Bragg was leaving the ridge. Throwing Thomas's men forward, Grant had seen the heights blaze with cannon fire. The deserter had lied. The demonstration, aside from warning Bragg of approaching battle, had accomplished nothing except the seizure of Orchard Knob, a bald foothill in front of the ridge. During the storming of this dome, Thomas had revealed a curious detachment of mind. From his observation post he had seen several of his men shot down on the hill, and as they lay kicking he had said to an aide, "Kellogg, what a beautiful spot that knoll will make for the burial of our dead." Later on he helped make Orchard Knob a National Cemetery.

The moods of the generals were becoming somewhat fantastic. Perhaps it was stage fright that was responsible. In previous battles both Federal and Confederate commanders had worked in broken, wooded country which shut from sight everything but the action of a few brigades close at hand. Now in the theatrical openness of Chattanooga's plain, a general could see everything and became self-conscious, if not confused.

Furthermore, there was an almost total eclipse of the moon on the night of the twenty-third. Major James A. Connolly, inspector general of a division in the Army of the Cumberland, noted how the soldiers gabbled about this lunar event:

> It was considered a bad omen among the ancients on the eve of battle; we concluded also that it was ominous of defeat, but not for us; we concluded that it meant Bragg because he was perched on the mountain top, nearest the moon.

During that night there were several different views of the morrow's plan. Sherman was sure Grant expected him to hammer Bragg's right flank until enough Confederates moved there to underman their center; then Thomas would strike the middle. Hooker understood that he was to demonstrate against Lookout and only to attack seriously if Confederate weakness developed. It was vague what Thomas thought.

While his men ate supper around campfires on the evening of the twenty-third, Sherman inspected 116 crude boats in the willows. They had been prepared for him by his one-time law partner, Dan McCook, now colonel of the Fifty-second Ohio. At midnight Sherman sent thirty scouts across the river in a boat and by two o'clock knew that the enemy pickets had been surprised and the way cleared. He called the advance guard, armed with rifle and spade. As they stepped into the boats he walked among them asking them to move quietly. Captain S. H. M. Byers of the Fifth Iowa recognized him with a start:

> Few of us had ever before heard the voice of our beloved commander . . . his attention to every detail of the dangerous adventure waked confidence in every one. He was with us, sharing the danger.

By daylight 1,000 men were over and intrenched; a pontoon bridge went down with celerity and the main body crossed. Sherman pushed forward through a drizzling rain to find that the maps given him were wrong. The ridge was not continuous. Instead of sweeping along a level crest, he found that he must climb a series of fortified hills and batter his way up valleys choked with canister. He took the first hill, intrenched, and waited for orders. Sounds of battle were coming from his right—evidently from Lookout Mountain, seven miles or more across the plain and hidden now in fog. Toward sundown winds tore the fog away and Hooker's men were seen like pigmies racing here and there, almost to the summit. Hooker, refusing to be a minor actor in the great drama, had promptly sent his troops straight for the peak, and it was apparent that he would soon have Lookout cleared. Major Connolly described the scene:

Oh, such a cheer as then went up in the valley! Manly cheeks were wet with tears of joy, our bands played "Hail to the Chief," and 50 brazen throated cannon, in the very wantonness of joy, thundered out from the fortifications of Chattanooga, a salute to the old flag. . . . Lookout was ours, never again to be used as a perch by rebel vultures.

When night fell, Hooker's campfires sprinkled the black mountainside as thickly as stars dotted the heavens. A gigantic hunter's moon, full to the brim, emerged from the east as if from theatre wings on to a stage. At midnight one of Grant's staff officers arrived with orders for Sherman to attack at dawn; Thomas would go forward "early in the day."

As the sun of the twenty-fifth flamed, Sherman crowded his men up hills, arroyos, and wooded gullies under a plunging fire. At the other end of the vast stage Hooker was being sent by Grant down off his mountain to ford Chattanooga Creek and start flailing Bragg's left flank.

Grant and Thomas stood together on a knoll in the center of the amphitheater. From among rocks Confederate riflemen and cannoneers shot Sherman's troops to pieces, capturing eight stands of color and some 500 prisoners. This was to be expected. Sherman understood his rôle to be that of Chickasaw Bayou again—to pound the enemy until the latter concentrated at a single point and thus exposed himself to the main thrust, which in this case would be Thomas's. Officers of the Army of the Cumberland were of the opinion that Grant meant Sherman's attack to be the main one. Everything was vague. Sherman decided to throw Hugh Ewing's division forward on the extreme left.

"I guess, Ewing, if you're ready you might as well go ahead," he said, between puffs of his cigar. "Keep up formation till you get to the foot of the hill."

"And shall we keep it after that?" asked Hugh.

"Oh, you may go up the hill if you like—if you can." And pushing Hugh by the arm as he talked, Sherman nervously propelled him away. "I say, Ewing, don't call for help until you actually need it."

Hugh needed no pushing and, as at Vicksburg, charged fiercely, taking and holding a point well up the hill. Meanwhile Sherman was asking Grant for news, the signal flags wigwagging briskly. At noon, his abrupt signal, "Where is Thomas?" brought Grant's answer that the Cumberlanders were beginning to move. This was an error. Thomas was standing motionless. He was understood by Grant's staff officers, grouped close in the rear, to be waiting, according to Grant's orders, for the two flanks to be turned before hurling his Cumberland men at the rifle pits at Missionary's base. Grant's staff buzzed; something must be done—Sherman was checked and Hooker was fussing with a bridge job at Chattanooga Creek. Wilson, watching his chieftain, Grant, noted that he seemed discouraged. With his brother aides, Wilson decided that Grant ought to make Thomas attack; it was the one hope of victory. General Rawlins, ranking staff officer, stepped up to Grant and told him what the boys thought. Grant walked over to Thomas and said, in a conversational tone, "Don't you think it's about time to advance against the rifle pits?" Thomas made no reply and continued to stare through his field glasses.

Noon passed, and Sherman continued his hopeless battering at invincible rocks. Finally at 3 P.M. he rested his bleeding soldiers and caught a signal from Grant, "Attack again." "I thought 'the old man' was daft," said Sherman later, "and sent a staff officer to inquire if there was a mistake." Grant replied that there was none; keep pounding! Major Jenney, the staff officer in question, remembered Sherman's words as, "Go signal Grant. The orders were that I should get as many as possible in front of me and God knows there are enough. They've been reënforcing all day."

About this matter of Southern reënforcements mystery would always hang. Regarding it, witnesses either made honest mistakes or were touched by the moon. Grant, Rawlins, Sherman, Hazen, and General O. O. Howard (who had arrived from the East and been sent with his division to support Sherman) all declared emphatically that they saw column after column of Bragg's troops pouring eastward from the center along the crest to meet Sherman's attack. Hazen, who stood with Grant and Rawlins on Orchard Knob in easy view of the ridge top, was very specific in his statement. Yet General E. P. Alexander, the Confederate, said that no such regiments had been sent, and Wilson, studying the reports, concluded that Alexander was correct. The most sensible explanation seemed to be that the eclipse of the moon had made everybody a little crazy.

The last message of Sherman, however, may have helped jog the center into action. At least soon after its arrival Rawlins walked up to Grant in his mother-hen manner and urged him to make Thomas move. Wilson noted that Grant, "with unusual fire, ordered Thomas to command the attack." The grave Virginian came to life and sent word to his troops down on Orchard Knob to be ready to take the rifle pits at the ridge base when six cannon should be fired in rapid succession. Thomas's aides understood that the move was to relieve the pressure on Sherman.

What was really intended was never clear. Grant recalled that he had considerable difficulty in getting the order to attack through

Thomas to the division commanders. Grant also said that he had ordered the troops to take the rifle pits, then to re-form "preparatory to carrying the ridge." The Cumberlanders understood that they were merely to carry that line of rifle pits.

When the orders, such as they were, came to the Cumberland troops, they jumped up and down with excitement. The battle had so far been a failure, the short November day was nearly done. Thomas's soldiers had Chickamauga on the brain and burned for revenge. For a day and a half they had lain off stage seeing and hearing the action of their rivals, the Army of the Tennessee and the Easterners. Grant's implication that they were not first-rate combat material had fermented inside them. Also, Sherman's ragged marchers in passing had dropped contemptuous remarks. "We were crazy to charge," said boys of the Sixth Indiana, who lay waiting for those six signal guns. Hazen noted that in his brigade "all servants, cooks, clerks, found guns in some way" and crowded into line, avid for a chance at the Johnnies.

At 3:40 the cannon began booming, and, at "Five!" the men began to run forward like the wind. They howled back epithets, huzzas, incoherent defiances, at the rifles and cannon that blazed from the bottom to the top of the ridge. Lead sang past them as they jumped fallen trees. Over their heads curved Union shells to splash fire against the mountain. Confederates, withdrawing from the rifle pits, backed up the slope, shooting as they went. Many of them seemed dumfounded, fascinated as at a mammoth review. Into the pits leaped the Federals. Officers began urging them to convert the shelter holes into trenches facing in the opposite direction. But the men paid no heed. They were sucking great chunks of air into exhausted lungs, while their muscles twitched as if under some dervish intoxication and their eyes rolled hungrily upward to the summit, six hundred feet away.

All at once they began to howl and to run again, breaking out of the pits to scramble up the steep slope, their bodies bursting through entanglements, heaving up rocky faces, their eyes fixed on the heights. Officers stood bawling at them to come back, waving swords, cursing them, finally joining in the race. Soon the leading Federals were running neck and neck with the slowest Confederates, and came tumbling with them into the second line of Southern defense, out of which other graycoats tore like rabbits. Unionists were too winded, and secessionists too astonished to do much fighting. Both sides simply raced and bellowed.

Back in the rear, Grant said sharply to Thomas, "Who ordered those men up the ridge?" Thomas didn't know. "Granger," persisted Grant, turning to the next Cumberlander of rank, "did you order them up?"

"No," said Granger, "when those fellows get started all hell can't stop them." Grant said something about somebody catching it if the attack failed. The common soldiers were taking the battle into their own hands. Later Hooker, who hated Grant, declared that the latter had been disappointed at the unexpected development, spoiling as it did his plans for Sherman's glory. Hooker insisted that Grant had said, at the day's end, "Damn the battle! I had nothing to do with it."

One of Thomas's division commanders in the charge, Phil Sheridan, had tried to recall his men when they surged out of the rifle pits, but he had wound up by joining them. One drink he would take before starting up the mountain. He whipped out his silver whisky flask, threw back his head. Far up on the crest a Confederate officer was looking down at him. "Here's to you!" shouted Sheridan, and drank deep. The Confederate answered with a wave of his hand and a volley from six cannon. Brushing dirt out of his eyes, Sheridan growled, "That's damned ungenerous; I'll take those guns for that!" Up he spurred, jamming his flask into his pocket wrathfully.

Sixty battle flags were climbing the mountain, the soldiers now traveling in wavering wild-goose formations behind the banners. Upon them rolled rocks and shells whose fuses had been touched with matches. The air whimpered with musket balls which gray gunners had tossed by the hatful into cannon and discharged point-blank down the cliff. The angle was not favorable to execution, but the Federals were paying no attention to the enemy, anyway. They seemed to have forgotten the foe; they began to race with each other as they neared the summit. Now and then a man fired perfunctorily upward, but they were more absorbed in the obstacle race before them—bowlders, entanglements, precipices, thickets, fallen trees. Captain Briant of the Sixth Indiana was in the lead when one of his privates, Tom Jackson, passed him. Snatching Tom by the coat tail, Briant jerked him back and forged ahead, but just at the finish Tom rushed by to win. Before his eyes the Johnnies were scampering; only one Confederate captain remained to defend the crest. Dropping his gun, Tom stalked the officer, his hands low and extended. Suddenly the captain, brave enough in the face of hot lead or cold steel, saw those bare hands, lowered the point of his sword, and ran off after his men.

Briant's Hoosiers, pulling themselves on to the crest, saw Tom Jackson looking down the rear face and calling, "My God, come and see 'em run!" His comrades said, "It was the sight of our lives—men tumbling over each other in reckless confusion, hats off, some without guns, running wildly." Everywhere the defenders were fleeing; a squad here and there lingered to battle on for a few minutes before tearing off down the back slope.

The Confederate flight was as sudden and inexplicable as had been the Federal assault. "We ran because we could see too much," said Southerners after the battle. "When we saw the number of lines coming up against us, we got demoralized." Poor Bragg, striding among the men as they began to break, shouted, "Here's your commander!" and was answered, "Here's your mule!" He raved that night in the valley behind the ridge, calling the flight shameful; the Yankees, he said, had arrived exhausted "and the slightest effort would have destroyed them. . . . The position ought to have been held by a line of skirmishers against any assaulting column."

No one could explain the turn of the battle. "In a superstitious age," said General Cox, "the victory would have been attributed to supernatural influences." Dana wired Stanton:

> The storming of the ridge by our troops was one of the greatest miracles in military history. No man who climbs the ascent by any of the roads that wind along its front can believe that 18,000 men were moved up its broken and crumbling face unless it was his fortune to witness the deed. It seems as awful as a visible interposition of God.

Eyes lifting from the valley saw the victors capering on the crest, officers embracing privates, orderlies hugging colonels. Above them danced what was apparently a flock of blackbirds. The men were throwing their haversacks into the twilight air. On to the ridge top the generals were now coming. Thomas J. Wood shouted at the soldiers, "You'll all be court-martialed!"—and then he laughed. Sheridan, his horse shot out from under him, came up on his short legs to rush at one of the cannon that had offended him and straddle it, quarreling with General Hazen as to its ownership. General Howard stopped on the slope to ask a dying soldier where he was hurt.

"Almost up, sir!"

"I mean what part of your body?"

"Oh, I was almost up and but for that"—pointing to his wound—"I'd have reached the top."

Between deep, puffing breaths, the color-bearer of the Thirty-eighth Indiana was telling late-comers on the heights, "A fellow of the Twenty-second Indiana was up here first, but he wouldn't have been if I hadn't had on my overcoat." Captain D. F. Bremmer of Company E, Nineteenth Illinois, was counting fourteen bullet holes in his overcoat, but none in his skin. Almost 5,500 Federals and 3,500 Confederates had been killed or wounded in the two days' fighting, most of them in the dramatics of the twenty-fifth.

The November twilight was fading. Chaplain Nixon D. Stewart of the Fifty-second Ohio stood among the dancing men, looking past them at the hunter's moon that now came climbing the mountain too—a full white moon.

"There is no blood in it," he said. "The earth has drunk it up."

32

PREPARE THEM FOR MY COMING

UP one of the roads that wound to the crest of Missionary Ridge went General Grant, halting to talk to wounded men. "We're even with them now for Chickamauga," one bleeding private told him. "All we needed was a leader." Quite generally the common soldiers attributed to their commander the miraculous victory. Not for months or years to come could they realize that the triumph had been their own, and that the chief generals, both North and South, had been singularly inept in the fighting.

Yet there was a sort of cosmic justice in the manner in which soldiers, civilians, newspapers, and statesmen awarded the credit to Grant. Out of his own skill, determination, and originality he had won the far more crucial triumph of Vicksburg, and had received no commensurate appreciation. Now when the focus of dramatic attention was upon him, he would receive hosannas immeasurable for what the common soldiers had, on mob inspiration, accomplished.

As the news of the victory spread across the North, Grant's fame echoed to the stars. Clergymen who in the spring had clamored for his recall as "a slothful drunkard" now thumped their pulpits with elation as they lauded him. Politicians who in April had denounced Lincoln for not removing so inert a general, now berated the President for not having made Grant general in chief long ago. The Democrats were sure they would nominate him for President in the coming June. Congress started striking off medals in his honor. The magnitude of Vicksburg became at last apparent. "Thank Heaven," ran a current phrase, " 'the coming man,' for whom we have so long been waiting, seems really to have come." Babies were named for him; his photographs were kissed by exultant women. Old ladies wept at the mention of his name. All small boys, it seemed, wanted to play that they were General Grant.

Sherman, unable to see much of the battle of Missionary Ridge—not knowing indeed until late on the night of the twenty-fifth that the Ridge had been stormed—got the impression that everything had gone as he had understood Grant to have planned it, and that the whole affair was a perfect example of his friend's genius for coördination and timing. From what he could see in his isolated valley off to the left, this had seemed to be the case, and so strong was his initial impression that it became permanently fixed in his mind.

At daylight on November 26 Sherman hurried his men forward to find their enemies gone. They pushed down the opposite slope and found that Bragg had set fire to supplies at Chickamauga station. Bluecoats snatched scorched beans from the flames, knocked in heads of molasses barrels and scooped the thick liquid into their hats. As the barrels emptied, men leaned farther and farther inside, giving comrades opportunity to kick their feet from under them. When hands drew them out, they stood dripping while laughing soldiers "sopped" on them, scraping off mouthfuls on crooked forefingers. One private, by mistake, was tipped into a barrel half full of soft soap and before his comrades could notice their error, they were "sopping" him vigorously, then tumbling away, spitting and coughing and "howling with indignation."

All day the Federals pushed forward through the débris of Confederate retreat—Sherman, Sheridan, and Hooker crowding onward and sending back such bags of captives and munitions that Grant soon counted 6,100 prisoners, 40 cannon, 7,000 muskets, and almost numberless wagons. But before his tabulation was complete a message arrived:

> Well done. Many thanks. Remember Burnside.
>
> A. LINCOLN.

Immediately Grant started General Gordon Granger with his corps for Knoxville, eighty-five miles away. Then Grant wondered if Granger were not too slow. After all, there was no man who could streak across country—minus wagons—like Sherman. The Fifteenth Corps's iron legs behind Sherman's red head could save Burnside without question. Sherman read his new orders on the thirtieth. He disapproved. Here was Lincoln crowding him to enter East Tennessee exactly as in 1861. Sherman believed the President's motive to be sentimental and political rather than military. Sherman agreed with Lincoln that control of the East Tennessee railroad was important, since it was the shortest and swiftest line between Lee's army in Virginia and Bragg's in upper Georgia, but he was not prepared to accept Lincoln's statement that if Knoxville were held, the Confederacy would perish "like an animal with a thorn in its vitals."

He knew that East Tennesseeans were wringing Lincoln's heart with tales of how Confederates butchered them for their loyalty to the Union, but to him it was plain that the larger humanity required that Burnside's 15,000 men should be out wrecking Confederate armies and cornfields instead of garrisoning the threatened region. Better sacrifice a handful of citizens than let the whole war run on to slaughter millions across the larger field. While he pushed his men rapidly toward Knoxville, Sherman sent Grant a message of protest:

> Recollect that East Tennessee is my horror. That any military man should send a force into East Tennessee puzzles me. Burnside is there and must be relieved, but when relieved I want to get out and he should come out too. I think, of course, its railroad should be absolutely destroyed, its provisions eaten up or carried away and all troops brought out. Cumberland Gap should be held simply as an outpost of Kentucky.

He began the march in keen sympathy for his men, who had been walking and fighting for seven consecutive days on two days' rations. They had no tents, only a few had blankets. Many were shoeless and ice was forming an inch thick each night in puddles on muddy roads. One cold rain in the mountains would annihilate his soldiers, for they must embark upon a winter campaign in the attire to which they had stripped themselves when attacking Missionary Ridge. Later he said:

> But twelve thousand of our fellow-soldiers were beleaguered in the mountain town of Knoxville . . . needed relief, and must have it in three days. This was enough—and it had to be done.

Having been told that Burnside had but three days' food, Sherman drove fiercely through the rocky country, many of his men limping in moccasins made of cowhide rudely laced with thongs and worn with the warm hair next the flesh. On December 3, the scheduled date for relief, he pushed cavalry through to Knoxville. They arrived in the city to find the place comfortable, with large pens of cattle, and with a bloody victory recently won. Longstreet's Confederates had tried to storm the Federal bastions, had been wrecked, and now lay in distant hills licking their wounds. When he learned of this victory, Sherman halted his Fifteenth Corps some fifteen miles from Knoxville and let them rest while he rode on into the city, to observe that Burnside's men were fatter and better clothed than his own, and that Burnside's dinner table was epicurean.

Grant now proposed that Sherman pursue Longstreet over the Blue Ridge Mountains into South Carolina, but Sherman declined. "A stern chase is a long one," he said, pointing out that his men had marched five hundred miles. Yet a few days later Sherman was writing General Jefferson C. Davis, who had supported him at Missionary Ridge with a division of Cumberlanders, "My troops are in excellent heart, ready for Atlanta or anywhere." The distance to South Carolina was approximately the distance to Atlanta. It was apparent that Sherman was resisting every move that might shift him from the Mississippi Valley into the Eastern sphere. He had begun to think of wrecking Atlanta, the transportation hub of the Confederacy, now that the Mississippi River was in Federal hands.

Word came to march back to Bridgeport and go into winter quarters along the Tennessee River. Grant was giving Sherman leave to go home for a few weeks. Ellen was still broken-hearted over Willy's death; Thomas and Maria Ewing were both ill. As Sherman departed, consigning his army into Logan's hands, he said, "There is no better body of soldiers in America."

The soldiers wintered in new uniforms, good houses, and much revelry. They made friends with families up and down the river, danced "The Alabama Flat-rock" with mountain women, or when no women were present waltzed gander fashion, tying handkerchiefs on half the men to designate them as women. They talked much of "fair yellow girls" in this or that locality. They revenged themselves on belles who refused sociability by writing home long descriptions of how ugly Southern women really were, after all.

Foraging was easy and not often dangerous. Dan McCook's men, gathering food, asked a Negro boy what he would do when he was free. "I'se gwine sleep in de sunshine," he answered, "wrapped up in pancakes, and yaller gals will pour 'lasses ober me." Foragers of the Tenth Illinois, while foraging, captured Confederate cavalrymen in the Sequatchie Valley near Chattanooga, locked them in an old stable and heard them wail, "You're not going to keep us in this damned hole all night, are you?" "Your Saviour was born in a stable," called the Federal Captain Wiseman as he rode past, "and it's a damned pity if you can't stay in it for a single night."

With Grant Sherman spent two days in the former's headquarters at Nashville. He learned that he must bring up 20,000 veterans from the Mississippi River garrisons for the spring campaign. Just where the campaign would lead, Grant couldn't say; it might lead into Georgia, it might go into East Tennessee—at least it would be eastward. Sherman grew apprehensive that in the absence of so many trained troops guerrillas would menace Mississippi River ports. Already they were firing on steamers again. He must make a trip down the river and put such fear into the citizens that they would remain quiescent after the Federal garrisons had been weakened. To Logan he wrote:

> To secure the safety of the navigation of the Mississippi River I would slay millions. On that point I am not only insane, but mad. Fortunately the great West is with me there. I think I see one or two quick blows that will astonish the natives of the South and will convince them that, though to stand behind a big cottonwood and shoot at a passing boat is good sport and safe, it may still reach and kill their friends and families hundreds of miles off. For every bullet shot at a steamboat, I would shoot a thousand 30-pounder Parrotts into even helpless towns on Red, Ouachita, Yazoo or wherever a boat can float or soldier march.
>
> Well, I think in all January and part of February I can do something in this line.

Before leaving Nashville, Sherman had a heart-to-heart talk with Grant about the sneers that Hooker and certain officers of the Army of the Cumberland were making about his failure to storm the northern end of Missionary Ridge. They were saying that he had never shown sufficient resolution in attacking enemy lines. Hadn't he failed at Chickasaw Bayou too? Hooker was writing Chase that Sherman's "four repulses" at Missionary Ridge could

> only be considered in the light of a disaster. . . . Sherman is an active, energetic officer, but in my judgment is as infirm as Burnside. He will never be successful. Please remember what I tell you.

But on the whole Sherman's two days in Nashville were entertaining. He was "rather disgusted" to hear Andrew Johnson, the military governor, rant and storm against the enemy, but he had sport going with Grant, Granger, and General Grenville Dodge to restaurants and theatres, unrecognized in their rough clothing by the townsfolk or soldiers. At his suggestion the four men attended a performance of *Hamlet*, where Sherman found such loud fault with the acting that Dodge warned him the audience, mainly soldiers, would recognize them and start an ovation. But Sherman persisted, "so indignant at the butchery of the play that he could not keep still," and finally Grant led the party away from its front-row balcony seats before the drama was done.

Granger entertained Sherman at his mother-in-law's home and Dodge heard the old lady upbraid the guest of honor for the stealing done by his soldiers on the march to and from Knoxville. "She pecked and pounded away until finally Sherman turned upon her." As a matter of record he had burned no mills on this march and had attempted to discriminate between loyal and disloyal farmers, but he made no such defense to the lady. Instead, Dodge heard him say:

> Madam, my soldiers have to subsist themselves even if the whole country must be ruined to maintain them. There are two armies here; one is in rebellion against the Union, the other is fighting for the Union . . . if either must starve to death, I propose it shall not be the army that is loyal. There is nothing too good for the soldiers who wear the blue.
>
> War is cruelty. There is no use trying to reform it, the crueler it is, the sooner it will be over.

Dodge observed, "The response put a cold douche on the dinner and no efforts of any of us could relieve the strain. The lady said no more, for it was a great rebuke."

On Christmas Day Sherman arrived in Lancaster for the first holidays he had spent there in twenty years. Ellen and the children were living in the mansion on the hill, caring for the old couple. Thomas Ewing grew better, perhaps from the satisfaction of seeing Cump hailed as a hero by the people for miles around. Photographers, autograph-hunters, reporters, neighbors, curious hand-shakers, crowded around Cump for seven days, driving him to gruff repulses or into hiding himself. Meeting the soldier whom Sissie Ewing had recently married, Sherman realized that Old Solitude now had three sons and two sons-in-law wearing uniforms. Theresa had found romance in 1862 when Major Clemens F. Steele had come to Lancaster on recruiting duty. West Virginian, drummer-boy in the Mexican War, a "forty-niner" in California, traveler in South America, one of the first to enlist in 1861, Steele was attractive to the girl. And when he had won a colonelcy and wounds in the Federal assault upon South Carolina's Fort Wagner in the summer of '63, he came home to marry her. Invalided from service, he faced the task Cump had evaded—the management of those saltworks down at Chauncey.

Reading newspapers and talking to the Salt-Boiler, Cump began to catch up on political events in the North. He found that on December 8 Lincoln had acted in direct opposition to the advice he had sent from the Big Black in September. The President had offered amnesty and pardon to all Confederates below the rank of brigadier general and exclusive of certain other classes of leaders. All the penitents need do would be to take the oath of allegiance to the Federal Government. Lincoln had also suggested that whenever a rebellious State sent one tenth of its recognized voters to the polls, under Federal practice, and reëstablished a State government, their work should be recognized, and Congress should be asked to decide upon the qualifications of Senators and Representatives to take seats at the Capitol. Cump described the plan to John:

> Unwise . . . it but protracts the war by seeming to court peace. It, to them, looks like weakness. I tell them that as they cool off, we warm to the work.

Likewise he opposed the Northern system of paying bounties to men who would enlist and thus keep conscription from being enforced in certain localities. To see thieves, vagabonds, riffraff, receive four hundred dollars and more for enlisting angered him. Within a few months the system would be a national scandal, with bounty-jumpers deserting their companies to sell themselves in other States under other names. Sherman was delighted to hear praise thundering around Grant's name, but it distressed him to hear such insistent demands that Grant be sent to take charge of the Army of the Potomac—demands like that of Senator Doolittle of Wisconsin:

> Grant has won seventeen battles, he has captured 100,000 prisoners, he has taken 500 pieces of artillery. . . . He has organized victory from the beginning and I want him in a position where he can organize final victory and bring it to our armies and put an end to this rebellion.

As the old year died, Sherman wrote Grant a letter warning him of danger:

> I hardly realized till I got here the intense interest felt for us. The army is on all lips, and were you to come to Ohio, you would hardly be allowed to eat a meal, from the intense curiosity to see you and hear you.
>
> . . . you occupy a position of more power than Halleck or the President. There are similar instances in European history, but none in ours. For the sake of future generations risk nothing. Let *us* risk and when you strike let it be as at Vicksburg and Chattanooga.
>
> Your reputation as a general is now far above that of any man living, and partisans will maneuver for your influence; but if you can escape them, as you have hitherto done, you will be more powerful for good than it is possible to measure. . . . Preserve a plain military character and let others maneuver as they will. You will beat them not only in fame, but in doing good in the closing scenes of this war, when somebody must heal and mend up the breaches made by war.

In 1861 Sherman had thought of himself as one of the men to help build up the reunited nation. Now he had been carried too far into the fire to hold any such position. He thought of himself as the destroyer of illegality and rebelliousness, the scourge of the lawless, the punitive force—the performer of work that some one must do before the gentle tasks of healing could begin. Grant had shown the healing touch by his treatment of surrendering Confederates at Vicksburg. He was the ideal man to keep in that character, so natural to him. Sherman thought of both Grant and McPherson as leaders who must keep themselves unsullied for benign tasks at the war's end. As for himself, he would do the harsher, more terrible tasks of devastation, which must fall on somebody's shoulders.

Soon he would be writing General Edward R. S. Canby to hold Southern civilians accountable for guerrilla outrages, "for if they fire on boats with women and children in, we can fire and burn houses with women and children." He wrote this when he was fresh from Lancaster, where he had wept with Ellen over Willy's death. When New Year's Day had flown, he hurried South, taking Minnie with him as far as Cincinnati, where she would attend a convent school. They parted at the door, she turning into the cool sanctuary, he plunging back into the world of death and wounds.

At Memphis, in his inspection tour of his department, he found the citizens asking to give him a banquet. The socially and politically elect wanted to honor him. Among them were prominent secessionists who had admired his pacific and sound rule of their city. He made a speech and was told on all hands that it had been good. He appealed to the aristocrats at the banquet table with the plea that

> . . . according to the rules of honor as prescribed at the best clubs of Paris, London, New Orleans and Charleston, the South was wrong. They had willingly gone into an election and because that election did not result as they wanted, they refused to abide by the result and appealed to war.

Instead of striking at guerrillas, as he had intended, Sherman organized a blow at the city of Meridian, lying a hundred and fifty miles east of Vicksburg. As a railroad center and arsenal, Meridian was particularly useful to Confederate bands that carried war toward the Mississippi River. To destroy it would cripple guerrillas far more seriously than to pursue their bands. Furthermore, Sherman saw a chance to ruin Meridian and defeat the Confederate cavalry raider General Forrest at one stroke. He planned to lead the infantry himself from Vicksburg and to have Grant's chief of cavalry General W. Sooy Smith ride down from Memphis with 7,000 horsemen, overwhelming Forrest's 4,000 on the way. He and Smith would unite at Meridian and defeat the Confederate army, which on the demotion of Bragg after Chattanooga was commanded by Lieutenant General (Bishop) Polk.

Muzzling the press, Sherman made his march with swift secrecy while Polk was enjoying his habitual war sermons against "the barbarous hordes of fanatics and Puritans and German infidels" who were trying to "crush our altars." Spies came to the huge old cleric warrior as he sat in his tent making life arduous for his cooks. On January 23 they said that Sherman was coming. But the bishop brushed the thought aside with, "He'd gain nothing by it." It was not until February 3 that Polk awakened to the fact that Sherman's army in two columns was across the Big Black. Even then the bishop was confused, thinking Sherman bound for Mobile. Sherman, pretending such a course, saw the Confederates scatter their forces, sending some toward Mobile, some to Meridian. Almost without the firing of a shot, Sherman's infantry rolled into Meridian on February 14 to find immense quantities of Confederate food, arms, and clothing that the befuddled bishop had not removed. "This is worth fifty millions to the Government," Sherman said, and put his destroyers to work. The supplies, the arsenal, two large hotels, and gristmills were burned and the railroads for twenty-five miles in all directions were destroyed.

Through the smoke Sherman watched for Sooy Smith, but the cavalryman never came, and on the twentieth Sherman started the return march to Vicksburg. He wrote Ellen that he was really glad there had been no battle: "It would have been terrible to have been encumbered with hundreds of wounded. . . . As it was I scared the bishop out of his senses." He wrote Halleck that he had ruined "a full hundred miles of railroad . . . and [made] a swath of desolation fifty miles broad across the State of Mississippi which the present generation will not forget." Southerners insisted that Sherman's raid had been a failure, since within twenty-six working days the railroads were again in operation. But in their denunciation of his ravages they revealed the extent of the wreckage he had made. One of Polk's subordinates, General Stephen D. Lee, charged Sherman with "taking back 300 more wagons than he started with" and with "burning 10,000 bales of cotton and 2,000,000 bushels of corn and carrying off 8,000 slaves, many mounted on stolen mules." Lee estimated the damage at five million dollars, of which "three fourths was private property." Lee named the devastation the Sherman Torch and asked in later years, "Was this the warfare of the civilization of the nineteenth century?" For years to come Lee and his fellow-critics in the South could not or would not admit that Sherman had been anything but wantonly vindictive in this his first spectacular punitive campaign. They remained blind to the fact that he had been working to paralyze the Confederacy so that the Mississippi might remain peaceful during his forthcoming campaign.

Sherman did not count the Negroes who followed him into Vicksburg—a singing, praying, exulting mob. "We bring in," he reported, "some 500 prisoners, a good many refugees and about ten miles of Negroes." It was the largest bag of slaves yet made by a Federal army on so brief a raid, and the spectacle set the soldiers talking excitedly. Men of the Twelfth Wisconsin saw Negresses carry two children for two hundred and fifty miles and drag others who clung to their skirts. The privates remembered the Southern claim that slaves were happy in bondage. They asked, "Why then are so many of them glad to walk three hundred miles to escape?" Many Western boys felt compassion for sobbing and weary pickaninnies and wished to carry them, but the speed at which Sherman moved his columns prevented such kindnesses. One man in every six was barefoot as the legions returned to Vicksburg; many men were in their underdrawers. Bill Scott of the Twelfth Wisconsin slit the remnants of his frayed trousers into ribbons and walked into town with the lilting step of a ballet girl—skirt aflutter.

While the word of his fearsome raid went up and down the Mississippi Valley, Sherman sent messages to his subordinates to heighten Southern fear of the Federal army. To Major R. M. Sawyer in Alabama he sent a paper to be read to the civilians "so as to prepare them for my coming." He wished Sawyer to make his position clear to the people:

> In Europe whence we derive our principles of war, wars are between kings or rulers through hired armies, and not between people. These remain as it were neutral and sell their produce to whatever army is in possession. . . . Therefore the general rule was and is that war is confined to the armies engaged and should not visit the houses of families or private interests.

However, he pointed out, insurrectionary wars had different rules. The English had dispossessed Irish rebels and populated the North of Ireland with Scottish immigrants. The United States had an unquestioned right to do this, but in view of the peculiar situation out of which the war had arisen, Sherman would not advise it. "I believe this war is the result of false political doctrines for which we all as a people are responsible." For this reason he would

> bear in patience that political nonsense of slave rights, States' rights, freedom of conscience, freedom of the press and such other trash as have deluded the Southern people into war, anarchy, bloodshed and the foulest crimes that have disgraced any time or any people. . . .

If they want eternal war, well and good, we accept the issue. . . . Three years ago by a little reflection and patience they could have had a hundred years of peace and prosperity, but they preferred war; very well.

Last year they could have saved their slaves, but now it is too late. All the powers of earth cannot restore them their slaves any more than their dead grandfathers. A people who will persevere in war beyond a certain limit ought to know the consequence. Many, many people with less pertinacity have been wiped out of national existence.

Solemnly he warned the South that if they persisted three years more, they might reasonably expect the confiscation of their homes and lands. He laid down the policy of sparing "dwellings used by women, children and non-combatants" so long as no correspondence was held with armed enemies. He would take vacant houses, provisions, forage, wagons, and live stock, since "it is clearly our duty and right to take them, otherwise they might be used against us"; this he said was a well-established principle of war. His last words in the long warning were:

To those who submit to rightful law and authority, all gentleness and forbearance; but to the petulant and persistent secessionists, why, death is mercy and the quicker he or she is disposed of the better.

Satan and the rebellious saints of Heaven were allowed a continuous existence in hell merely to swell their just punishment. To such as would rebel against a Government so mild and just as ours was in peace, a punishment equal would not be unjust.

Cump sent a copy of his war fiat to John asking that it be published for all Americans to read—"its publication would do no harm except to turn the Richmond Press against me as the prince of barbarians."

He had been many kinds of a prophet in the past. Now he felt the duties of the Archangel Michael upon him. For years he had pleaded with the South to see the light. They had refused; they had resumed warfare after Vicksburg had proved their cause doomed. In this, as he saw it, they had sinned and merited stern punishment. Over and over he had warned them what he considered justice to be.

Let them now prepare for his coming! With the springtime he would be ready.

33

THE MAN ON HORSEBACK

SOOY SMITH'S failure to keep the rendezvous at Meridian strengthened Sherman's belief that as an instrument for achieving major results in war cavalry had been much overrated. Late in leaving Memphis, Smith had been early in returning—driven back by Forrest, whose numbers had been ridiculously inferior. While waiting in Meridian to hear from his horse chief Sherman had said, "It will be a novel thing in war if infantry has to await the motions of cavalry." Distrust of cavalry had been occasionally apparent in Sherman's correspondence during the past year; henceforth it would increase and be voiced more candidly. Soon the horse wing of the Federal armies would be complaining that Sherman was prejudiced against it.

By temperament Sherman was opposed to the psychology that developed in men when they adopted the traditions and traits of professional horse soldiers. They were romantic, he was practical; they were reckless, he was efficient; they were dramatic, he was realistic. They viewed war as a series of isolated jousts, he regarded war as work, battles as but incidents. Cavalrymen as a class, North and South, clung to the European standards—brilliant, thundering charges, spectacular hurricanes of steel. Sherman knew that all this was nonsense in a country as wooded and broken as the South. The plains of France permitted manoeuvers impossible in the wilds of Tennessee. Sherman told his subordinates:

> Infantry can always whip cavalry and in a wooded or mountainous country can actually thwart it and even at times capture it. . . . I have not seen in this war a cavalry command of 1,000 that was not afraid of the sight of a dozen infantry bayonets, for the reason that the cavalry to be effective have to have a road or smooth fields, whereas the infantryman steps into the bushes and is safe, or can block a road in five minutes and laugh at the man on horseback.

Sherman perceived that the cavalry's chief usefulness lay not in fighting, but in collecting information about the enemy, and in tearing up his railroads. But it went against the grain with the riders to do such unthrilling drudgery. Sherman asked them to become section hands on horseback; they wanted to keep the rôle of *beau sabreur*. They found satisfaction in waving sabers—although in private they admitted that the blades were rarely stained with blood. Throughout the war surgeons' reports showed significantly few wounds from swords. Some cavalrymen admitted that in a skirmish a man was more apt to slash off the ears of his own horse than the head of an enemy.

Back of the cavalryman's mental attitude was the Old World tradition that a gentleman went to war in the saddle, a peasant on shoe leather. This idea had thrived in the Southern States, where the military and social ideals of Europe had stronger hold than in the North. Aristocratic planters, especially in Virginia and South Carolina, called themselves cavaliers. Enthusiasm for Sir Walter Scott's novels had helped prepare the sectional mind to regard horsemen as chivalric knights, fitted by their eminence to command rightfully the plodding foot soldiers who did the digging, tramping, and wrecking required by war. It was Ivanhoe whom many a Southern mind visioned when newspapers trumpeted the cavalry exploits of J. E. B. Stuart, Forrest, Joseph Wheeler, Wade Hampton, and W. H. F. Lee. "The best blood of the South rode in the cavalry," was a common saying. War correspondents fostered the public belief that cavalry was romantic and effective. Readers demanded such stories, and reporters found it far easier to write about melodramatic, hell-to-split cavalry action than to analyze the tedious and complex movements of infantry.

It was a spectacular equestrian feat of the Confederate Jeb Stuart that created the first great popular enthusiasm for cavalry, North and South. In June, 1862, he rode his dragoons completely around McClellan's huge army, and while the raid was of no military importance other than to make McClellan feel foolish, it fired the Southern populace with the dream that their native genius for horsemanship would win the war. The *Richmond Examiner* of October 19, 1864, looked back upon those early days and said:

> The idea was that Southern men, being accustomed from childhood to the saddle and to arms and having good Virginia horses under them, must necessarily ride over everything the Yankees could get up in the shape of horsemen.

News of Stuart's ride set the populace North and South to demanding more and more cavalry. The two governments were forced to enlist more horse regiments than they had planned. And in the expansion the Confederates fared better than did the Federals, for the latter found that their horse recruits were chiefly town boys, mechanics, shoe clerks, hatters. Laborers and bookkeepers, especially of Eastern cities, felt a keen desire to mount horses and become gentlemen. Union farm boys as a class shunned the cavalry, unless they happened to come from Kentucky or Missouri, where riding was more fashionable. Sons of self-sufficient pioneers of the Northwest did not seem to suspect that a man could acquire social prestige by simply climbing on a horse. From experience they knew the drudgery of feeding, watering, and currying a mount. They preferred to walk through the war with only themselves to do for. So they sat on cantonment fences laughing at the city boys floundering on the practice ground. Don Piatt, the Cincinnati editor, observed, "The only cavalrymen killed were from falls. Brush against one and he would fall off."

The ignorance and recklessness of Federal dragoons in wearing out their mounts kept Sherman angry; especially did it rouse him when he discovered that his cavalry could not revenge Sooy Smith's defeat because of a scarcity of horseflesh. Smith had started for Meridian with 7,000 horses, had picked up 4,000 more on the trip, yet within a few weeks after his return to Memphis his men had reduced the number to 2,400. "They will bankrupt the Government," growled Sherman. Quartermaster-General Meigs complained, "No government can keep 120 regiments of cavalry mounted while such a system is tolerated. They have killed off ten times as many horses for us as for the Rebels." He and Sherman agreed that 30,000 horses had perished in the Western armies during the winter of 1863-64.

The greatest fault Sherman detected in cavalry was its refusal to destroy railroads. This art consisted in burning the wooden ties, heating rails red-hot in the flame, then twisting the iron around trees until nothing but a rolling mill could restore it to usefulness. Rails that were merely bent could be quickly straightened and relaid. But the twisting process was toilsome. Usually a squad of young horsemen were far from the sight of superior officers when they met a duty of this kind. It was easy to slight the task. Moreover cavalrymen, in their aristocratic delusions, thought iron-twisting better suited to those yokels, the infantrymen. "The cavalry has not the industry to damage a railroad seriously," Sherman would conclude late in 1864. "Usually it can be repaired faster than they can damage it."

He agreed with that judicious observer, the Union General Jacob D. Cox, that the cavalry's fondness for brilliant raids was "never worth the candle." Cox declared that from the date of Jeb Stuart's exploit in 1862 "every cavalry commander burned to distinguish himself by some such excursion and chafed at the comparatively obscure but useful work of learning the detailed positions and movements of an opposing army, and patrol work." In these raids, he said, "men and horses were used up wholesale without doing any permanent damage to the enemy." Sherman once wrote angrily to officers who wished him to halt a large infantry movement because Southern horsemen were in his rear: "I can't turn back for a cavalry raid. It is designed for clamor and nothing more." He had seen a foray by the Union Colonel B. H. Grierson create helpful diversion during the Vicksburg campaign, but almost all other expeditions of the kind had been disasters. In April, 1863, Colonel A. D. Streight had been captured with most of his 2,600 riders while raiding in northern Alabama, and General John H. Morgan, the Confederate, had fared similarly in Indiana and Ohio a few weeks later.

Too much "love of the éclat of a bold raid" was said by Lee's aide, Long, to have been responsible for Jeb Stuart's tragic absence from the Confederate Army at Gettysburg. Stuart had not returned from an independent and melodramatic ride when Lee, feeling his way across unfamiliar ground toward an unknown enemy, had been drawn unwillingly into battle. When the gaudy horseman returned, Lee met him with a rare outburst of anger, being seen by Major McClellan, Stuart's adjutant, to raise his arm and exclaim, "General Stuart, where have you been? I have not heard from you for days, and you the eyes and ears of my army!"

"I have brought you a hundred and fifty wagons and their mule teams," explained Stuart.

"Yes, General," replied Lee, "but they are an impediment to me now." Then he controlled himself, and "spoke to Stuart in great tenderness."

General Hooker was believed by many Northern critics to have suffered seriously at Chancellorsville because General Stoneman's cavalry was away on a fruitless raid when needed on the battlefield. In the East it was said that Hooker was the author of that popular epigram, "Who ever saw a dead cavalryman?" In the West this was credited to Sherman. It was certain that Sherman did say, "I do wish to inspire all cavalry with my conviction that caution and prudence should be but a small element in their characters."

Even when, in late '64, the Federal cavalry were brought up to an efficiency that began to win them victory in their brushes with Southern horsemen, Sherman was still unable to share the valuation put upon this military arm by distant newspaper readers. As to General Wheeler, whom he would later oppose, Sherman held essentially the views of Grant—"Wheeler is easily whipped if boldly attacked by half his numbers." In 1865 Sherman said of the dragoons of Wheeler and Wade Hampton, "My marching columns of infantry don't pay the cavalry any attention, but walk right through it." His occasional statements in

1863-64 as to the superiority of Confederate horsemen when matched against Northern dragoons were found upon examination to apply almost invariably to Forrest's "critter company"—an organization of mounted infantry. Forrest, as a volunteer officer and unorthodox militarist, paid scant heed to cavalry standards or traditions. He merely supplied horses to his riflemen so that, farmers as they were, they could ride to work. Their work usually consisted of infantry action performed while their horses remained tied to trees in the rear.

While studying the enemy centaurs in the Mississippi Valley, Sherman came to the conclusion that on the whole they helped him more than they harmed him. They irritated him by gobbling up his pickets, but they made Southern civilians sick of the Confederacy. Operating in highly independent units, clattering far and wide, a large proportion of them gravitated toward lawlessness. Sherman often phrased his opinion of them in letters and orders such as this:

> I don't want those rebel bands captured. They are doing us excellent service. They are disgusting the minds of Southern people with Confederate pretension and government. I want the people to feel that their rebel authorities care but little for them.

The Confederate General D. H. Hill of North Carolina was in many respects as nervously alert and as penetrating as Sherman, and his views on cavalry were almost identical with the Federal's. Near the end of the war he concluded:

> My experience with the cavalry in this war has not been favorable and I make no secret of my opinion. . . . What we need is efficient cavalry, not immense bands of plunderers scattered over the country. Nine-tenths of the so-called cavalry never see and cannot be induced to see an armed Yankee.

Although the valor of the average Southern horseman was not open to this suspicion, there developed unlimited proof that the cavalry plundered its farmer friends. Zebulon B. Vance, the Confederate officer who became Governor of North Carolina in 1862, wrote his Secretary of War at Richmond on December 1, 1863:

> If God Almighty had yet in store another plague for the Egyptians worse than all others, I am sure it must have been a regiment or so of half-armed, half-disciplined Confederate cavalry.

The same Secretary of War read among the sheafs of similar complaints one made on January 27, 1864, by Sergeant L. G. Sleeper of the Forty-fourth Mississippi Infantry:

> The cavalry in Southern Mississippi is a most perfect nuisance, a terror to the people and a disgrace to all civilized warfare. All men who are conscripted join this cavalry and consider themselves out of service.

By the late months of 1864 there were many realists in the South who understood that the mediaeval ideals of chivalry had betrayed Confederate cavalry. Economy had contributed to the Southern plan for having each cavalryman supply his own mounts, but back of all else lay the chivalric idea of a knight bestriding his own horse and riding off to the wars—a gesture at once antiquated and romantic. Major E. H. Ewing, Inspector of Field Transportation in the Western Confederate army, reported to Richmond on September 1, 1864:

> The policy adopted at the beginning of the war by the Government of making cavalrymen mount themselves is, in my opinion, the most extravagant to the Government, and has done more to demoralize the troops of this branch of the service than any other cause. When a soldier is dismounted . . . he is entitled to a furlough of thirty days to go home and remount himself. This makes every cavalry soldier, or at least all that desire to be, mere horse traders, selling their animals whenever they desire to go home. Many even go further than this; they steal every animal whether public or private, when it can be done with any show of success in retaining him for a few days, until they can sell or swap him. Some stations through which the army has passed have in this way been entirely swept of animals, thereby taking from the people their only means of support. . . .
>
> I respectfully suggest that all private animals now ridden by cavalrymen be taken possession of by the Government and paid for . . . and when a soldier is dismounted, if it can be shown that it was through no carelessness of his, let him be remounted by the Government. . . . This mode of mounting troops will, in my opinion, be beneficial to the service and do away with much of the odium now attached to the cavalry arm.

In 1863 General Hooker had begun to reform the Federal cavalry, but it was not until the spring of 1864 that substantial progress was made. Grant and Sherman began such changes in organization and discipline that the mounted force was soon able to win more skirmishes than they lost. The basis for improvement had been laid somewhat earlier with the supply of repeating rifles to Federal horsemen—weapons that the South had failed to secure. General Lee had disapproved of magazine guns because he feared their holders would waste ammunition; then too, in the latter part of the war, the Confederacy had been unable to import or manufacture them.

The *Richmond Examiner* among its many criticisms of Confederate horsemen declared that the Federal superiority in cavalry during the last months of the conflict was due to the fact that "the Yankees are a practical and acute race of people." They had studied organization and armament "well assured that in the long-run chivalry and ostrich feathers would be no match for movements in armed mass with weapons of terrible power and range." The editor lamented that "our chivalrous cavaliers" were eventually overcome by "squadrons of factory-hands and preachers, half-barbarous Dutch and Irish clod-hoppers."

Much of these later developments was apparently plain to Sherman in the early months of 1864. His disgust with his own cavalry could have occupied his pen for days. But a trip to New Orleans intervened. Grant was ordering him to lend 10,000 soldiers for thirty days to General Banks, who was preparing to sail from New Orleans and clear the Red River Valley. Grant also suggested that Sherman command the whole expedition, but Sherman declined, not wishing to offend Banks. However, he would confer with Banks, and took a steamer south. At Natchez he halted to rescue ex-Professor Boyd, who was again a prisoner. On the steamer and in New Orleans hotels the Confederate was his guest. Cump described their association to Ellen:

> I never saw a man evince more gratitude. He clung to me till I came away. . . . Boyd tells me that the motto over the door of the Seminary is chiseled out. You remember it . . . "By the liberality of the General Government of the United States, the Union—*Esto Perpetua*." The fools!

Two days and nights of Banks's régime were enough for Sherman. Banks was postponing his military expedition in order to take part in the inauguration of the pro-Union State government, which President Lincoln with the help of Federal bayonets had set up in Louisiana. The Administration had not heeded Sherman's advice sent from the Big Black. With the war entering its last and fiercest phase, Banks was talking reconstruction, not destruction, and was worrying over how his cannon would work when discharged by electricity in the novel celebration of Governor Hahn's inauguration. In disgust Sherman sailed north the day before the festivities. He was writing Ellen his joy at serving under Grant in the coming spring campaign—"if we can't whip Joe Johnston, we will know the reason why." But a few hours—perhaps a few minutes—after he wrote this, Sherman saw Captain Adam Badeau, Grant's aide, clamber over the ship's rail with a letter. Grant had been made a lieutenant general—the first since Scott, the second since Washington—and had been ordered to the capital. He said in his letter that he would "accept no appointment which will require me to make that city my headquarters." But what he had started out to say was to thank Sherman and McPherson "as *the* men to whom above all others I feel indebted for whatever I have had of success." The news frightened Sherman. "Grant would not stand the intrigues of the politicians a week," he thought. He dashed off an answer:

> You do yourself injustice and us too much honor . . . at Donelson also you illustrated your whole character. I was not near and General McPherson in too subordinate a capacity to influence you. Until you won Donelson, I confess I was almost cowed by the terrible array of anarchical elements. . . . I believe you are as brave, patriotic and just as the great prototype Washington; as unselfish, kind-hearted and honest as a man should be; but the chief characteristic is the simple faith in success you have always manifested, which I can liken to nothing else than the faith a Christian has in a Savior.
>
> This faith gave you victory at Shiloh and Vicksburg. Also when you have completed your last preparations, you go into battle without hesitation, as at Chattanooga—no doubts, no reserves; and I tell you it was this that made us act with confidence. I knew wherever I was that you thought of me, and if I got in a tight place you would come if alive.
>
> My only points of doubt were in your knowledge of grand strategy and of books of science and history, but I confess your common-sense seems to have supplied all these.

Never to his brother John had Cump written in such brotherly emotion.

Self-interest did not cross Sherman's mind. It was almost certain that if Grant went East, Sherman would inherit the command in the West. He had long since ceased to doubt his own ability for high command; he was now prepared to take the responsibility for the lives of veteran soldiers. Nevertheless he wrote to Grant:

> You are now Washington's legitimate successor. . . .
>
> For God's sake and your country's sake, come out of Washington! . . . Come West; take to yourself the whole Mississippi Valley. Let us make it dead-sure, and I tell you the Atlantic slope and Pacific shores will follow its destiny as sure as the limbs of a tree live or die with the main trunk. . . . Here lies the seat of the coming empire; and from the West when our task is done, we will make short work of Charleston and Richmond and the impoverished coast of the Atlantic. . . .
>
> I foretold to General Halleck, before he left Corinth, the inevitable result and I now exhort you to come out West. . . .

Two days later he wrote Ellen asking her to hunt up this prophecy he had made Halleck in June, 1862, and added:

> I feel that whilst my mind naturally slights the events actually transpiring in my presence, it sees as clear as any one's the results to be evolved by time.

Eight months earlier he had told her, "I am somewhat blind to what occurs near me, but have a clear perception of things and events remote."

He had written her after the Meridian raid that its success had been due to the thoroughness with which he had silenced newspaper correspondents, the plan he had urged from the first. "Am I not right?" he had asked her. "And does not the world see it?" His artist's mind had pictured life as a thing of rounded justice and balanced diversities, with the people of all sections compensated equally under "the same gentle moon." He had gone to war so that the United States might go on to its destiny as symmetrical as a tree. Now he had come to feel that time was itself something that could be sensed as a whole—something rounded, logical, predictable, comprehendable.

In this faith in his own prescience there was no touch of mysticism. He saw his ability as nothing more than the insight and foresight of a logical mind. "I usually prefer to make my estimates of the enemy upon general reasoning than from the words of spies and deserters," he once wrote Thomas. In June and July, 1863, he had written his subordinates to be chary in crediting scouts and spies: "I prefer to be governed by what I think the enemy should attempt."

Like all men who feel themselves to be prophets, Sherman could not remember the times when his forecasts had been wrong; he could only see those instances when his imagination had been true. And the latter cases had been so many and so conspicuous as to give him confidence. With assurance he wrote in the sand, in March, 1864, for his friend Grant to read. A week later, he knew that his warning had been sent too late.

Lincoln, assuring himself that Grant had no political ambitions such as had complicated McClellan's generalship, had named Grant to command all the armies, superior to Halleck, almost superior to the President himself, since Lincoln was prepared to let him have freedom of action. Grant, visiting the White House for conference, soon saw that it would be impossible to direct the war from Tennessee. The Army of the Potomac was so low in morale that he must command it in person.

On the seventeenth Sherman learned the truth. Grant, returning to Nashville, summoned him, and told him that he must become responsible for all the armies between the Alleghenies and the Mississippi. For a few days Sherman kept close to his friend, laughing at the bashfulness with which Grant received the adulatory delegations from the North. They had no chance for a last conference, so many were the visitors, and Grant suggested that Sherman accompany him to Cincinnati on his eastward trip. They could talk on the cars. But the railroad train rattled so loudly that they fell silent.

In Cincinnati Ellen was awaiting Cump, and there was more delay. At length, however, when Ellen and Mrs. Grant were occupied in discussions of domestic affairs, the warrior husbands secreted themselves in a room at the Burnet House and bent their beards above their maps. To Sherman it was still marvelous that Grant should decide "to go East, a stranger almost among strange troops . . . a more daring thing was never done by man on earth." But at any rate he and his friend had the war in their own hands. Each believing that "in war a town is a military weakness," they did not need to reassure each other that from now on there would be no more scattering of troops to hold citadels. Grant, with the simplicity of genius, said that there were but two objectives: one, Lee's army in Virginia, the other, mobilized at Dalton, thirty miles south of Chattanooga, under Joseph E. Johnston, who was now restored to command. The Confederacy would have its best leaders against them. Every effort must now be bent toward endless, relentless fighting, summer, winter, all the time—the kind of warfare both Grant and Sherman had preached, "blows thick and fast." It would be hideous carnage, but the most merciful in the end if it could halt these years of wastage. A quarter of a century after he and Grant had sat there, Sherman stood in the Burnet House pointing at the room and saying:

"Yonder began the campaign . . . we finally settled on a plan. He was to go for Lee and I was to go for Joe Johnston. That was his plan. No routes prescribed. . . . It was the beginning of the end as Grant and I foresaw right here. . . ."

34

THE BEAUTY OF TIME

TO the great assignment of organizing the Western armies in Nashville Sherman turned with one executive principle in mind—harmonious action without rigid discipline. His kind of war was to be that of a business in which every man would be asked to become selfless. To follow such a course meant sacrificing somebody's feelings in almost every situation that arose. McPherson was the first to be hurt.

When Sherman and McPherson had been together in Vicksburg, earlier in the year, the latter had confessed that he was engaged to marry Mary Hoffman of Baltimore, and that he wished to have the ceremony performed before the spring campaign began. Sherman, agreeing to help arrange it, had posted a letter before meeting Grant in Nashville, urging McPherson "to steal a furlough and run to Baltimore *incog.*, but be back to take part in the next move."

The next move had come too quickly, however, and summoning McPherson, Sherman said, "Mac, it wrings my heart but you can't go now." There was immediate need of McPherson's singular talent for making peace between West-Pointers and volunteers. In Sherman's absence Logan, as commander of the Army of the Tennessee, had taken offense at Thomas's refusal to let the Tennessee army have equal rights with the Cumberlanders on the Chattanooga-Nashville railroad, which was under Thomas's command. Logan rushed to Sherman, when the latter arrived from Cincinnati, and told his story, adding that Thomas was acting in bad grace toward a brother army that had marched five hundred miles to rescue him at Missionary Ridge. Such a rift at the start of the campaign was perilous, and Sherman quickly gave all departmental commanders equal authority on the railroad. He smoothed Thomas with the statement that he knew "the slights were unintentional on your part." Then he placed McPherson in command of the Army of the Tennessee.

Disturbing rumors were afloat, whisperings that Thomas was dissatisfied at not being given Sherman's place, ruling the three armies—those of the Tennessee, the Cumberland and the Ohio. When Lieutenant Colonel Willard Warner, a devoted inspector general, asked Sherman if there was any truth in the rumors, Sherman snorted:

> Not a bit of it. It don't make any difference which of us commands the army. I would obey Tom's order tomorrow as readily and cheerfully as he does mine today. But I think I can give the army a little more impetus than Tom can.

Hurlbut, his friend at Memphis, was writing complaints at not being given the supreme command, under Sherman, on the Mississippi River. That post had been given to Major General Henry W. Slocum, one of the Easterners sent to Chattanooga but moved to Vicksburg because hatred between himself and Hooker made it unwise to let them serve near each other. Sherman sent an appeal to Hurlbut:

> Surely in times like these patriotism should influence us all to do anything and everything to make union and harmony prevail everywhere. So help me God, I will cheerfully subside and, if required, will take command of a company post if ordered or even suggested by those who, from success, merit or even chance, have the lawful control.

Hugh Ewing was fuming in Louisville because Cump had not called him to a post in the new organization. At the end of the Missionary Ridge-Knoxville campaign, Hugh had asked to be transferred for the winter to some city where he and his wife might enjoy the social environment to which they were both adapted. Cump had obliged him, yet in the spring would not restore him to the command that he had led so spiritedly at Vicksburg and Missionary Ridge. Cump said that to do this would mean the displacement of some officer who had endured irksome camp duty through the winter. Hugh was left to command at Louisville, and to console himself with the promise sent by his father on January 31, "I intend that you shall own, when you leave the service, a Major-General's commission."

Sherman found political ambitions of various volunteer generals opposing his radical new plan for re-forming the cavalry. Upon his announcement that cavalry and infantry would be no longer brigaded together, he was resisted by Brigadier General Alvin P. Hovey, who said that he had brought down from Indiana five regiments of foot and five of horse, and they must be kept under him. As a former judge of Indiana's Supreme Court and United States District Attorney, Hovey had been one of the War Democrats commissioned by Lincoln, and was supposed to have the President's interest. Sherman, refusing to abandon his reorganization plans, finally persuaded Hovey from his irate intention of resigning. But the Hoosier nursed wrath.

General Hazen, the Cumberland officer who was later transferred to the Army of the Tennessee, noted that in these days of organization "jealousies, dislike and dissensions were developing in the Army of the Cumberland while they were nearly unknown in the Army of the Tennessee." Sherman, he observed, had built morale in the latter army by making promotions strictly on merit. Hazen also declared that "as to discipline, instruction and administration the Army of the Cumberland was so far the superior as scarcely to admit of comparison." In Sherman's army there had been "a singular omission in these particulars."

Shanks, the war correspondent, doubted "if there was ever a division, brigade, or even regimental drill in the Army of the Tennessee after Sherman took command in 1863." He saw discipline slacken in the Army of the Cumberland as in the months that followed Sherman's advent as ruler of all Western armies it began to feel his method of supervision.

When in August Hazen was appointed to command the second division in Sherman's hand-trained corps, the Fifteenth, he was torn between admiration for its fighting qualities and despair over its intense democracy. Vainly he tried to teach the men that they must cut their hair—locks that hung as low as on the shoulders of frontier Leather-stockings. He issued commands for the men to abandon "their vicious and almost mutinous habit, if rations were late, of calling 'Hard-tack' . . . to general officers who rode near them, or making catcalls and other disrespectful demonstrations." He heard the boys bellow, "Sow-belly!" behind the back of Brigadier General Peter J. Osterhaus, whom they suspected, as a German immigrant officer, of attempting to Prussianize them. Once when men of the Seventeenth Corps thought Frank Blair driving them like sheep on an unnecessary march, they bleated "Blaa-aa-ir" at his back. Yet all these men refrained from shouting disrespectfully at Sherman. They called to him freely as he rode along the lines, addressing him as "Uncle Billy," yet their intimacy was friendly.

In the Army of the Cumberland marched two regiments, the Thirty-first Indiana and the Ninth Ohio, whose officers issued commands in "undefiled high Dutch" and who followed German manuals and drills very different from those of the regiments around them. Their very bugle calls were strange, although their musicians were admitted to be the best in all the armies.

The springtime of 1864 found Sherman and Thomas far apart in militarism. Cump had drifted ever away from the West Point teachings that Tom religiously observed. Thomas drilled soldiers diligently and repeatedly warned his officers that an army's fate might depend upon the proper fastening of a buckle.

Sherman had brought to the mobilization an army holding far fewer West-Pointers than had Thomas. None of the officers who commanded corps and divisions in the Army of the Tennessee had ever attended the Academy. In Thomas's force similar units were commanded by ten West-Pointers and seven men from civil life. The third army, that of the Ohio, was divided equally between the regulars and volunteers.

With the new leader of the Army of the Ohio, Major General John M. Schofield, Sherman was satisfied, and when newspapers revealed that friends of Buell were working to place him in Schofield's position, Sherman stormed, "The damned newspaper mongrels seem determined to sow dissension wherever their influence is felt."

Toward two generals in the Army of the Cumberland Sherman was particularly drawn, one, Jefferson C. Davis, the other, Oliver O. Howard. The former was a shaggy-bearded Hoosier who, as the son of Kentucky Indian-fighters, had run away from home at sixteen to fight Mexicans and to enjoy it so thoroughly that he refused a West Point nomination in order to remain on the frontier. Continuing in the army, he had earned a commission and had aimed the first gun that answered Charlestonians from Fort Sumter. He had fought in all the Cumberlanders' battles, was reputedly the most talented swearer in the whole

Federal force, believed in slavery, and was half admired, half feared as the killer of the bullying General William Nelson at Louisville in September, 1862. Nelson had insulted him, and in the midst of a dispute studded with God-damn-you-sirs had been shot by Davis's pistol.

Contrasted with so satanic a figure was Puritanic Howard, who, as a New England Abolitionist at West Point, had fought with his fists sons of slaveholders and prayed to God to aid him. As a devotee of Bible classes, Howard had been called goody-goody, and cadets had shunned him until a certain Virginia student, nicknamed Beauty in respect to his lack of chin, befriended him, taking him "to see the girls." The Southern boy's name was J. E. B. Stuart.

When Hardee had been made commander at West Point, he had named young Howard instructor in mathematics and Sunday-school classes. At thirty-one Howard was a brigadier general, and had lost a right arm in the fight of the Army of the Potomac at Fair Oaks—a calm, God-fearing patient who said to General Philip Kearny, when he visited him in the hospital, "Now we can buy our gloves together"—a reference to Kearny's loss of a left arm in Mexico. "Don't worry," Kearny had answered, "the ladies won't think any the less of you." Meade, after Gettysburg, had said of Howard, "He always votes to fight," and at the end of the Knoxville march Sherman had reported that Howard should be praised "as one who mingles so gracefully and perfectly the polished Christian gentleman and the prompt, zealous and gallant soldier."

Carl Schurz, the German-American general from St. Louis, had seen Sherman, Howard and Davis together on this Knoxville campaign. Howard had entered a house where Sherman, Davis and Schurz were warming themselves.

"Glad to see you, Howard," said Sherman. "Sit down by the fire. Damned cold this morning."

"Yes, General," answered Howard, "it is *quite* cold this morning."

At this prim reproof, Sherman had winked at Davis, who promptly launched into a tale that had no other purpose than to give his gift for profanity full play. Schurz reported:

> Howard made feeble efforts to turn the conversation, but Davis, encouraged by repeated winks and sympathetic remarks from Sherman, grew worse and finally Howard, with distress all over his face, left, whereupon Sherman and Davis made the house ring with laughter.

When Schurz protested, Sherman said, "Well, that Christian-soldier business is all right in its place, but he needn't put on airs when we are among ourselves."

There was one thing in Sherman's generalship Howard disapproved—the total disregard for Sunday. Howard shared McClellan's belief that "one day's rest in seven is necessary to men and animals. More than this, the observance of the holy day of the Lord God of mercy and battles is our sacred duty." Whenever possible, Howard spent the Sabbath carrying fruit to hospitals and singing hymns with soldiers.

With Schofield, Sherman got on smoothly without any particular intimacy. The new man was a New-Yorker, graduating from West Point with McPherson and Sheridan, a scholarly fellow, leaving his post as teacher of natural philosophy at the Academy to become professor of physics at Washington University in St. Louis. He had entered the war under Lyon, had risen to head the Department of Missouri, and had become so entangled in the fratricidal politics of the region that Lincoln had sent him to Knoxville to replace Burnside. At his first review of the Army of the Ohio, the men had stared at him, a plump blond of thirty-three whose beard was flowing and whose undershirts were red. "It's all right, boys," a private had drawled. "I like the way the Old Man chaws his tobacco."

Through his immense army that mobilized from Nashville to Chattanooga, Sherman spread the word that no promotions should be asked for until the end of the coming campaign. When Halleck wrote that Lincoln wished to make him a major general in the regular army, he answered:

> I wish you to say to the President that I would prefer he should not nominate me or any one. . . . I now have all the rank necessary to command and believe all here concede me that ability, yet accidents may happen and I don't care about increasing the distance of my fall. The moment another appears on the arena better than me, I will cheerfully subside . . . I know my weak points. . . . I will try and hold my tongue and pen and give my undivided thoughts and attention to the military duties devolving on me.

It was a Herculean task to have 100,000 men ready by April 25, when he expected Grant to sound the general advance. He could not count on those 10,000 men loaned to Banks. The Red River campaign he summarized as "one damned blunder from beginning to end," and the 10,000 were still needed to protect the Mississippi. Thousands of furloughed soldiers must be hurried back into the ranks. Northwestern governors were refusing to send cavalry recruits because Sherman had no horses for them. Sherman persuaded Stanton to send them forward anyway—"a horse needs twenty pounds [of food] daily, a man but two."

Acting as his own chief quartermaster, Sherman telegraphed his aides over the Northwest to buy, buy, buy, quibbling not on price. Food, grain, hay, saddles, uniforms: all the endless equipment for three armies and 35,000 horses must be ready. He wrote Meigs, "Commissaries are too apt to think their work done when the vouchers of purchase are in due form, and the price in Chicago or the moon is cheap." General Rusling heard him storming at a quartermaster, "I'm going to move on Joe Johnston the day Grant telegraphs me he is going to hit Bobby Lee; and if you don't have my army supplied, and keep it supplied, we'll eat your mules up, sir—eat your mules up!" Rusling saw Nashville become "one vast storehouse—warehouses covering city blocks, one a quarter of a mile long—stables by the ten and twenty acres, repair shops by the fieldful." Preparing for the day when, deep in Georgia, he must provision his huge force by railroad, Sherman drilled repair gangs in the art of mending tracks and mending bridges. In the final analysis his success would depend more upon transport than upon fighting, and he made his supreme preparations accordingly.

Sherman's mind was driving at a new speed; he wrote letters all day and sometimes all night. Such recreation as he took was in his old love, the theatre. Scorning a private box, he sat, according to Shanks, in the pit of the New Nashville Theatre "surrounded by his boys in blue, laughing and applauding 'the points' with as much gusto as any in the audience."

On his first day in office, March 24, Sherman began reorganizing the single line of railroad that was to supply him in his campaign against the enemy. His initial order, forbidding the road to private interests or persons, brought a roar of protest from East Tennessee, which had been supplied from Nashville. Citizens protested so fervently to Lincoln that he wrote Sherman saying, "anything you can do consistently . . . for those suffering people I shall be glad of." Sherman replied that either the East Tennesseeans or the army

> must quit and the army don't intend to unless Joe Johnston makes us. . . .
>
> We have paid back to Tennessee ten to one of provisions taken in war. . . . I will not change my order, and I beg of you to be satisfied that the clamor is partly humbug and for effect; and to test it, I advise you to tell the bearers of the appeal to hurry to Kentucky and make up a caravan of cattle and wagons and come over the mountains by Cumberland Gap and Somerset to relieve their suffering friends on foot as they used to do before the railroad was built.

He was angry when, a little later, the War Department ordered him to allow a certain Philadelphia Quaker passage into East Tennessee with food for his coreligionists. To Dana, who was now Assistant Secretary of War, he wrote testily concerning people "who cannot grasp the great problem," and although he allowed the Quaker to make the trip, he refused passage to the supplies. He explained his philosophy of war to Dana:

> In peace there is a beautiful harmony in all the departments of life—they all fit together like a Chinese puzzle, but in war all is ajar. Nothing fits, and it is the struggle between the stronger and weaker, and the latter, however much it may appeal to the better feelings of our nature, must kick the beam. To make war we must and will harden our hearts. Therefore when preachers clamor and sanitaries wail, don't join in, but know that war, like the thunderbolt, follows its laws and turns not aside even if the beautiful, the virtuous and charitable stand in its path.
>
> When the day and hour comes, I'll strike Joe Johnston, be the result what it may; but in the time allotted to me for preparation I must and will be selfish in making those preparations which I know to be necessary.

On April 24 he wrote Halleck, "Stability is what we lack in our government. . . ." To Christian Commissioners who demanded that he send Bibles and religious tracts over the railroad, he snapped, "Rations and ammunition are much better." To keep freight conductors from secretly selling rides to civilians, he urged Meigs to make the offense punishable by death. He railed against the red tape of railroad tradition. Only 60 cars a day were traveling from Nashville to Chattanooga. This must be increased to 130, and to accomplish it, Sherman proposed doubling the track and running trains on an endless circuit. He wrote Meigs, ". . . these railroad men are so accustomed to time-tables that I believe they would run on a single track if a double one lay side by side."

Defeated in this scheme, Sherman ruthlessly seized all freight cars arriving from the North and persuaded James Guthrie, president of the Louisville & Nashville road, to do the same with all cars arriving at Louisville. Guthrie obeyed and together they soon had the daily average of cars on the road at 130, then 145, and finally 193, with railroad men staring at Sherman in horrified admiration. He watched his quartermasters closely, and wrote Chase:

> I want an army to be far above the contaminating influence of trade and gain . . . the soldier is lost if he dream of a cent.

He found time to prophesy disaster for the Administration's plan of colonizing ex-slaves along the Mississippi River under the protection of Negro soldiers. On April 12 he wrote General Lorenzo Thomas, director of the project:

All Southerners, old and young, rich and poor, educated and ignorant, unite in this, that they will kill as vipers the whites who attempt to free their slaves, and also "the ungrateful slaves" who attempt to change their character from slave to free.

On the very day that he sent this warning, Forrest's horsemen were massacring white and Negro soldiers in Fort Pillow, which protected a trading-post some fifty miles from Memphis, and which Sherman had ordered abandoned before he left Vicksburg. Hurlbut, presumably at the insistence of Lorenzo Thomas, had reoccupied it with 557 soldiers, half black, half white Tennesseeans. During and after an assault Confederates had slaughtered 350 of these, many dying while trying to surrender. Forrest later declared that he had tried to halt the horror but his report to superiors declared, in his subliterate spelling: "We busted the fort at ninerclock and scatered the niggers. The men is a cillanem in the woods."

The affair shook the North; pulpit and press denounced Forrest, Congress launched an investigation, and Stanton ordered Sherman to send officers to collect affidavits from survivors. Sherman, reading these reports, joined in the universal Northern belief that Forrest had passed beyond the pale. He should be killed. But, sympathizing with Hurlbut, who was removed from office for "timidity" in not having driven Forrest from the territory, Sherman wrote Grant that the fault was primarily the Administration's in garrisoning such posts with Negro troops. However, he wasted no time in horror or hate. "You know how I like to be on time," he wrote McPherson, prodding him forward to be ready for the great day, which Grant had now postponed to May 5. To Colonel C. B. Comstock of Grant's staff he wrote:

> I believe in fighting in a double sense, first to gain physical results and next to inspire respect on which to build up our nation's power. . . . We saw the beauty of time in the battle of Chattanooga and there is no reason why the same harmony of action should not pervade a continent.

As he began stripping his armies for action he wrote that he wanted no tents at all for marching troops and only the common A tents for encampments:

> My entire headquarters transportation is one wagon for myself, aides, officers, clerks and orderlies. I think this is as low down as we can get until we get flat broke and thenceforward things will begin to mend. Soldiering as we have been doing in the past two years with such trains and impediments is a farce and nothing but absolute poverty will cure it. I will be glad to hear Uncle Sam say "we cannot afford this or that . . . you must

gather your own grub and wagons, and bivouac and fight not for pay but for self-existence."

General Hickenlooper, of the Army of the Tennessee, noted that Sherman intended to have "no councils of war"—no chiefs of staff: "Adjutant Generals were to him simply clerks and scribes . . . his official papers he carried in a side-pocket and finally filed them away in an empty candle-box." At last Sherman was ridding himself of wagon trains; he had said that the delay of waiting on such impediments on a country road fatigued men more than marching. Soldiers were told to carry on the coming campaign "five days' bacon, twenty days' bread and thirty days' salt, sugar and coffee, nothing else but arms and ammunition." In this way, he estimated, each corps could bear on its back enough to eliminate three hundred wagons. One supply wagon and one or two ambulances were all that a regiment would have.

In the midst of his desperate hurry, there appeared before him one day a woman in a surgeon's uniform, and with a commission and orders assigning her to that rank. Sherman later described how she

> complained that my men had guyed her, and asked me to issue an order to stop them. I said, "Well, if you want them to stop, why don't you take off those clothes?"
>
> "What's the matter with these clothes? Aren't they strictly physiological?"
>
> "Yes, but damned unfeminine!"

In telling this incident, Sherman would add, "Would you believe me, that damn fellow Stanton had sent that woman out just to bother me." The woman soon disappeared from camp, riding toward the enemy, who she insisted wouldn't harm her. Quickly she found herself in Libby Prison, not to be exchanged till August, when she came North declaring that her guards had shot at her through the floor of her cell. She would in time become famous as an advocate of male attire for women—Dr. Mary Walker.

As April died, Sherman moved to Chattanooga. His warehouses were full. Thomas moved his Cumberlanders to Ringgold, eighteen miles south of the city; Schofield brought his Ohio army from Knoxville to a parallel point; McPherson drew up at the right end of the barrier at Lee & Gordon's Mills.

The men waited, tense, strong, healthy, eager. They said that even the mules, who had grown fat and dull, caught the excitement, and brayed, "Jo-HOOK-er; HOOK-er, HOOK-er." Men of the Thirty-third Massachusetts were angered when in the midst of their straining impatience "the rebel widow Haynes" complained that vandals had stolen her drawers and chemise. Officers paraded men past her so that she might pick out the guilty. Then she remembered that the thieves had not the number 33 on their caps, but 88. The regiment broke ranks in disgust. Sherman sat at Ringgold reading census reports of every county in Georgia, a State that, as he wrote Grant, "has a million of inhabitants. If they can live, we should not starve." He was selecting the places where forage would be best. Grant said of him, "He bones all the time while he is awake, as much on horseback as in camp or in his quarters."

On May 6 Halleck telegraphed that Grant was moving on Lee. Sherman gave the word; 254 cannon began to rumble, the barrier went up on 98,000 men, most of them between eighteen and twenty-five. They marched through wild flowers and fruit trees in bloom. Bees hummed. As the One Hundred and Fiftieth New York marched past the battlefield of Chickamauga, Private Charles E. Benton saw trees dead from bullet wounds, human skeletons working their way out of shallow graves. He saw "hands sticking up, skin dried to bones and weathered to the color of granite—fingers curved as if beckoning—one, with index finger pointing upward." Thrushes sang, humming birds tossed among blossoms. It was May.

35

TERRIBLE DOOR OF DEATH

THE blue tidal wave rolled up to the first Confederate intrenchments. The Fifty-second Ohio now skirmished ahead of the advance. Around its ears bullets slit the air. Then the Johnnies—a mere picket guard—scurried to the rear. From them there floated back a jeering cry,

"Bring on your God-damned nigger wool!"

For months Southern generals, editors, politicians, and clergymen had been telling the people that Sherman would come with hordes of armed and savage Negroes. Captain Conyngham, serving as an artillery officer and war correspondent in the Federal force, read in a Southern newspaper:

> Neither life nor virtue is sacred from these northern barbarians; the old and infirm perish by their bloody hands, while lovely women—our wives and daughters—are reserved for a fate even worse than death. Strike, men of the south and exterminate such polluted wretches, such living demons!

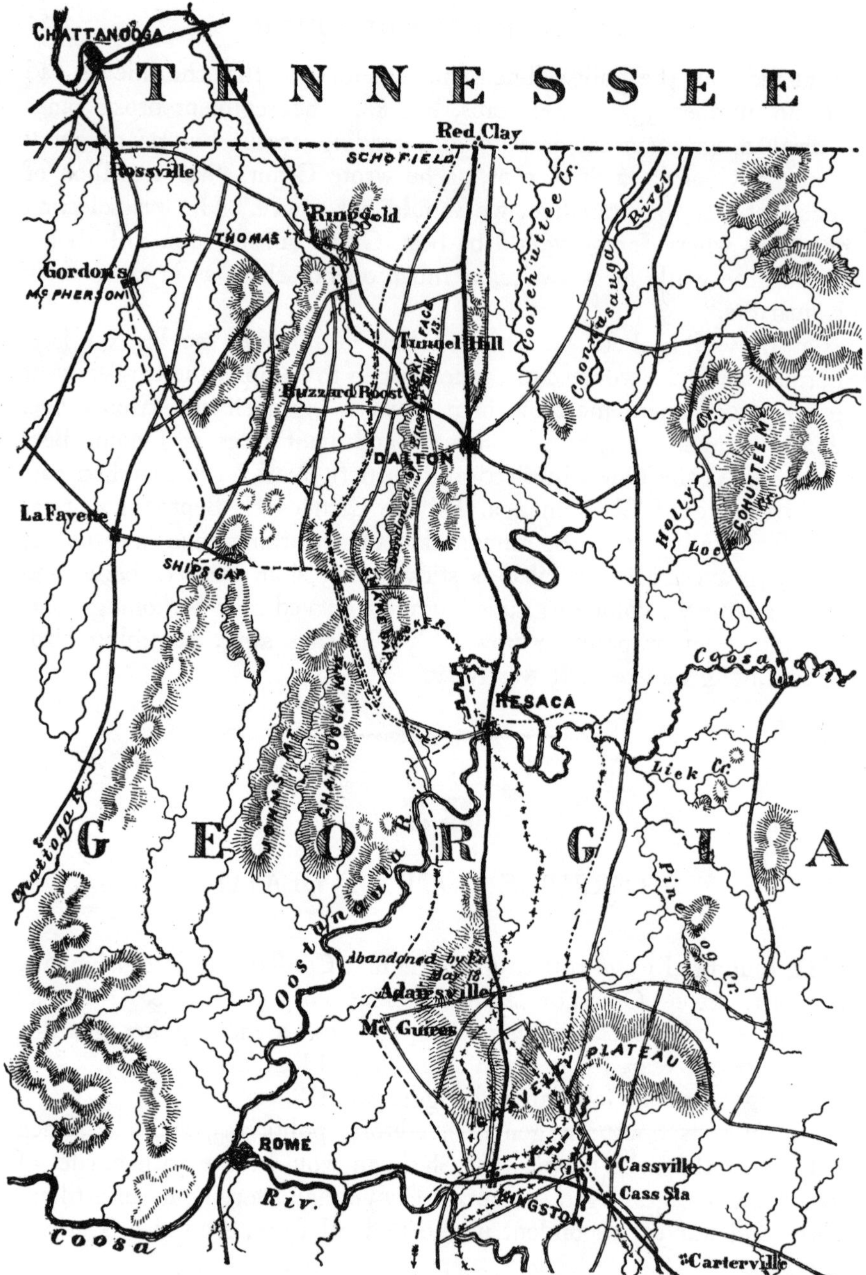

THE ATLANTA CAMPAIGN, SECTION ONE

Simplified version of map drawn in 1865 by Sherman's chief engineer, Brigadier General O. M. Poe for the Bowman-Irwin military biography, *Sherman and His Campaigns.* Dotted lines indicate routes of Sherman's armies; blackest of lines indicates railroad; lighter parallel lines, wagon roads.

It would be months before the South realized that Sherman was making only a white man's war.

From a hill Sherman stared at the Confederate defenses in the mountain range that separated him from their headquarters at Dalton, Georgia. Cannon crowned ridges. The narrow pass through which Sherman must strike, if he drove head on, was flooded—Buzzard Roost. Sherman had no idea of storming through so stout a gate. He would flank it. He poised his center and left it at the threshold, while his right, the swift-legged Army of the Tennessee, stole on cat's feet around the enemy's left, skirting the mountain range to fall on the railroad town of Resaca, eighteen miles back of Dalton.

Psychologically, this plan made the best use of the Union generals—slow, unconquerable Thomas in the center as a bulwark against counterattack; McPherson and Schofield, younger, more aggressive men, on the flanks with smaller, fleeter armies marching in swiftly traveled arcs, feinting, swerving, feinting again, then suddenly striking like hammers into Johnston's ribs. If McPherson should seize the railroad in Johnston's rear, the latter would be driven into the less hilly country to the east, where Sherman felt certain he would destroy half the Confederate army and capture all its cannon.

Waiting with the Cumberlanders, Sherman seemed to observers to have "electric alertness." Late in the afternoon of May 9 came the first word from McPherson. He was within five miles of Resaca. Success was imminent.

"I've got Joe Johnston dead!" roared Sherman, beating the supper table till the dishes rattled. "Now we'll ride and tell Tom."

But in the night couriers arrived with different news—McPherson had failed to take the railroad; he had found intrenchments too strong; his cavalry had not arrived. Disappointed, Sherman threw secrecy to the winds and pushed Thomas and Schofield toward Resaca, but Johnston was first on the field, abandoning Dalton and clinging to his precious railroad. "I regret beyond measure you did not break up the railroad," Sherman wrote McPherson, "but I suppose it was impossible." When next they met he said, "Well, Mac, you missed the opportunity of your life." But in reports to Washington Sherman protected his friend, declaring that he had acted on orders.

The campaign had failed, at its beginning, to end itself. Nevertheless it had shown Johnston that Sherman was an artful flanker, just as it had shown Sherman that his adversary was one of the leading defensive artists in military history. It had also shown men of the Cumberland and Ohio armies that their new commander would conserve their lives. Within ten days, Cump wrote Ellen:

> The officers and soldiers realize that by bringing up McPherson's army with secrecy and dispatch . . . I saved them the terrible door of death that Johnston had prepared for them in the Buzzard Roost.

In the march to support McPherson, on the morning of May 14, a Cumberland private passed a red-bearded officer sleeping against a tree. "Is that a general?" he asked an orderly who stood near by. And when he was told that it was, he growled, "A pretty way we're commanded when our generals are lying drunk beside the road!" "Stop, my man!" shouted Sherman, leaping to his feet. "I'm not drunk! While you were sleeping last night, I was planning for you, sir; now I was taking a nap." "Uncle Billy sleeps with one eye and one ear open," was the word that passed through the army.

In dry weather Sherman camped under trees, in wet weather he used empty houses. Deep in the night marching men saw his red head, inclining toward baldness, passing to and fro in the firelight; his beard was sunk in his neck, his arms locked. Now and then he spoke to a guard; around him lay his staff under blankets. Soldiers thought him so full of marching that he had to keep it up all night. They wondered if he would always expect them to march all night, too.

Sherman had become, indeed, a friend of night. In it he found himself the complete artist, letting his imagination roam across space and time unhampered by the distractions of the daytime. On the walls of darkness he could picture what was happening far off, and what impended. Night hours, he said, were his favorites, because then his ears could tell him what the enemy was doing. Sleeping but four hours a night, he usually added three more in daytime cat naps, sitting against trees or boxes. Asthma, chronic since San Francisco days, made his bed fitful. When his cannon had established their range he told Howard to open fire: "The moon gives light enough, and night is better than day for artillery." Cannoneers were then free from enemy sharpshooters. "Moonlight nights are the very thing for marching," he would say, eager to spare his men from the Southern sun.

As the Federal armies battered fiercely at Resaca, Confederate leaders realized that this crisis was like no other in the Western war. Hardee, quicker than others to perceive the danger, had put his affairs in shape before Sherman had left Nashville. He had married, in Dalton, the belle to whom he had been engaged. General John B. Hood sensed the danger when Sherman approached Rocky Face. On the night of May 11, while riding the lines with Bishop Polk, who had just arrived at Resaca with 18,000 men, Hood asked for baptism. Up to that moment, he had thought little of the hereafter; he had not considered it when surgeons sawed off his wounded arm at Gettysburg, his maimed leg at Chickamauga, but he thought of it when Johnston began retiring before Sherman. A six-foot Kentuckian riding strapped to his saddle, always hungry for conflict, Hood owned a spirit that belied the sad, hound-dog expression in his blue eyes and in his drooping blond-bearded lips.

At midnight the bishop came to Hood's headquarters, lit tallow candles, blessed water in a tin bucket, and lifted his hands. Hood began scrambling with his crutches. Polk told him to remain seated. Hood fought his way to an erect position. He had met everything standing, and at thirty-two was too old to change. The fat bishop inducted a new lamb into the Protestant Episcopal fold while vandal cannon muttered blasphemies on the horizon.

A wave of religious conversion went through the staffs of Johnston and Hood. All spring, evangelists had been holding revivals among soldiers who stood bareheaded in the light of bonfires, or knelt while hymns rose in the dark forests. Southern soldiers as a class held chaplains in greater respect than did Northwesterners, who in general were as reserved toward the spokesmen of Jehovah as toward the representatives of Mars. Sons of frontiersmen were apt to be skeptical toward any experts who assumed to speak with the authority of old conventions. Much of this was Jeffersonian deism, transplanted French republicanism, free thought. Part of it was sturdy self-reliance, and part of it was sheer bumptiousness and backwoods irreverence. During the past winter, when hundreds of dollars were offered as bait to recruits, one bystander in the Northwest had grown weary of listening to a clergyman appealing to men to enlist for the Lord's sake. "What bounty is He offering?" he called, interrupting the exhorter.

General Schofield thought this spirit of independence partly responsible for Sherman's policy of continually flanking, rather than assaulting, Joe Johnston. He described the Western privates:

> . . . intelligent soldiers . . . they felt strongly against attacking entrenchments . . . felt no necessity of fighting on unequal terms . . . veterans, they were very loath to attack unless they saw a chance for success . . . they fought much like they worked farms or sawmills, demanding a fair prospect that it would pay. Commanding such an army, the general must maneuver to fight the enemy on fairly even terms.

Technical officers who criticized Sherman's indifference to drills and military tradition unanimously praised the business efficiency of his campaigns. In Nashville he seemed to have prepared for every detail of forthcoming action. Field telegraphers had been trained to bring their light wagons close to the front, and to string wires and insulators to trees so that a general might have a clicking instrument at his elbow when under fire. Sherman was delighted with the operators, observing how when they were separated from their instruments they could "by cutting the wire . . . receive a message with their tongues from a distant station." Topographical engineers reflected Sherman's passion for their art; they pressed ahead of the advance, accompanying the scouts and charting, mapping the terrain in detail—their drawings being rushed back to "dark wagons," which multigraphed them in a stream of rapid editions.

The speed of Sherman's pontoniers depressed the enemy, so quickly did the experts stretch canvas over the boatlike frames, transfer them from wagons to water, string them together with guy ropes, plank them with boards, and offer them to waiting legions. The Thirty-third Indiana saw a Confederate prisoner watch this process, then drawl, "Boys, anybody who could make a bridge out of them damned dog-tents could beat us!" And, as Johnston retired from Resaca on the sixteenth to a new line five miles south, he found that it did small good to burn bridges ahead of Sherman. The latter had come with a great stock of bridges, prepared in Nashville on a standard pattern with duplicate parts, and his engineers, working with what General Cox thought

> efficiency and speed beyond praise, renewed bridges as if by magic, and perhaps nothing produced more moral effect upon the enemy than hearing the whistles of locomotives in the rear of our armies within a few hours after they had received reports that the railroads had been broken.

J. P. Austin of the Ninth Kentucky Cavalry in the Confederate army said:

> Sherman's immense bridge across the Chattahoochee was done so quickly that he was ever afterward regarded by our boys as the champion bridge builder of the world.

Sherman was creating such an atmosphere of invincibility that a few weeks later Confederate soldiers scoffed at the news that Forrest had ruined a tunnel in the Yankees' rear. "Sherman carries a duplicate tunnel," sighed the cynics. His artistic skill in flanking awed Southerners. One of them, surrendering to the One Hundred and Third Illinois, drawled, "Sherman'll never go to hell; he will flank the devil and make heaven in spite of the guards." Stretcher-bearer Benton heard a prisoner say, "You-uns swings around on your ends like a gate."

Nor did it add to Confederate assurance when word seeped through the army that Joe Johnston had got religion on May 17 at Adairsville, where the gray legions had intrenched most formally after leaving Resaca. Mrs. Johnston had written Bishop Polk asking him to baptize her husband, who had at last consented to such a step. Having snatched Hood from the burning, the bishop officiated over Johnston.

Two days later the Confederate leader, as if in response to a new power, gave official notice that the retreat, which had covered twenty-seven miles in ten days, was ended. On May 19 he told his men, "You will now turn and march to meet his advancing columns. . . . I lead you to battle. We may confidently trust that the Almighty Father will still reward the patriots' toil." But on second thought Johnston decided that it would be unwise to test divine favor in open ground, and instead ordered a ten-mile retreat to a line between Kingston and Cassville, where he laid a trap. Deftly he poised his men like steel jaws around two roads down which he expected to see Sherman come in full cry. But Sherman, scorning the orthodox method of pursuing with massed columns, approached with wings spread wide—so wide that Schofield's cannon suddenly began to enfilade the trappers' right flank. The steel jaws shut softly on open air, the stirring battle orders were torn up, and Johnston retired once more.

In the absorption of this deadly game, Sherman was self-possessed. Men who had remarked how his facial muscles twitched while preparing for the campaign, now observed that the habit was gone. General Cox would carry in his memory one instance that showed "how completely Sherman's nerves were unaffected" during the campaign. A courier dashed up with word that Schofield had been injured beneath a falling horse. Sherman sprang from his bed beside a log and rode to Schofield's column where, sitting on a fallen tree, he drew a map for the next movement, sketching "in firm delicate lines and neat touches, even to the fine lettering of houses and roads."

The imagination that had once made Sherman overestimate the enemy was now so harnessed that it pictured Johnston's force as less than it was. Success as a fighter as well as a strategist was sweet—a little too sweet, perhaps, since it led him to blurt out tactless comparisons in writing to Stanton on May 23 from Kingston:

> If General Grant can sustain the confidence, the esprit, the pluck of his army and impress the Virginians with the knowledge that the Yankees can and will fight them fair and square, he will do more good than to capture Richmond or any strategic advantage. This moral result must precede all mere advantage of strategic movements and this is what Grant is doing.
>
> Out here the enemy knows we can and will fight like the devil; therefore he maneuvers for advantage of ground.

This dispatch was read by Dana to Grant, Meade, and other Union officers soon after the fighting around Spotsylvania, Virginia, where the soldiers of the Army of the Potomac had fought so desperately that their death roll made the whole North shudder. Colonel Theodore Lyman, aide to General Meade, saw his leader's eyes

> stand out about one inch as he said, in a voice like cutting an iron bar with a handsaw, "Sir, I consider that despatch an insult to the army I command and to me personally. The Army of the Potomac does not require General Grant's inspiration or anybody's else inspiration to make it fight!" He did not get over it all day, and, at dinner, spoke of the western army as "an armed rabble."

After the war it was Sherman's belief that the superiority of the Western forces over their opponents was in large part due to the moral effect of having won the first great clash, Shiloh, while the Eastern army had the disadvantage of defeats suffered at the start of the war.

Perhaps it was the success of his first trial as an independent campaigner that made Sherman seem gentle in Kingston. Howard saw an example of it on a Sunday morning. Sherman sat near the window of a cottage, absorbed in the chess tournament he was playing with the Confederacy. "Now what is Joe Johnston's game?" he would habitually ask his subordinates, although he sought the answer not so much from them as from his own mind. This morning, a bell in the town jangled erratically, on and on, until Sherman sent the guard to have it stopped. Tracing the sound to a church, the sergeant found the Rev. E. P. Smith, a Christian Commission worker, in difficulty. The preacher had discovered an empty meeting-house and in preparing it for service had climbed to the ceiling to repair a broken bell-rope. In his descent he had split the seat in his trousers and in confusion had retained so tight a hold upon the rope that the bell had jangled crazily. The sergeant told him to come on and explain things to the general.

"But I can't go in this plight," protested the cleric. "Take me where I can fix up."

"Them's not the orders," said the sergeant. "Fall in!" To Sherman the good man said that he had only been ringing for Sunday service.

"Sunday? Sunday?" said Sherman in bewilderment—then, "Didn't know it was Sunday; let him go!"

Staff officers noted that while in Kingston the general was kind to one of the few noncombatants who was authorized to follow his army—Mother Bickerdyke. This Illinois widow had accompanied the Western army ever since Fort Donelson's fall, toiling in hospitals, ladling water out to men on march, rushing home delicacies to their camps.

By preference she worked with Sherman's army, and women who labored with her said:

> She had a great admiration for several of our great generals, but most of all for Sherman. She loved him . . . and considered herself a part of his force.

Between herself and Sherman there played some unintimate but powerful understanding; both were forceful and each was an instinctive forager. Between campaigns, Mrs. Bickerdyke went North to demand that civilians support her work "as with a big spoon." She kept housewives knitting, wrapping bandages, preserving fruit for invalid soldiers. With sweet bravado she took checks from strange bankers and a dozen eggs from a Negro's cabin. From Illinois farmers she had begged in 1862 a drove of cows and a thousand hens for use near a Memphis hospital. Worn out by the awful heat of the Jackson campaign in July, 1863, she had been sent home by Sherman to recuperate, but she had rejoined the army at the Battle of Missionary Ridge and had assembled barrels of food and bandages in Nashville for the spring campaign of '64.

It had been these barrels which troubled her when she learned that Sherman, leaving Nashville for Chattanooga, had commanded that nothing but military articles could travel on the railroad. But she had outwitted him. His train of ambulances had not yet departed, and although he had ordered that no barrels of supplies be carried to the front in these mule-drawn conveyances, she quietly emptied the contents of her barrels into bags, shifted them into the ambulances, saw them off, then, deliberately defying the general's orders against noncombatant railroad passengers, bullied her way on the next train to Chattanooga. There she brushed past aides who said Sherman was busy.

"Good morning, General," she said. "May I come in?"

"I should think you had *got* in," growled Sherman, pretending to be busy with papers on his desk. "What's up now?"

"Why, General, we can't stand this last order of yours. You'll have to change it as sure as you live. . . . After a man is unable to carry a gun and drops out of line, you don't trouble yourself about him, but turn him over to the hospitals. . . . We must have supplies."

"Well," said Sherman, turning back to his work, "I'm busy today."

"No," commanded the gray-eyed woman, "fix this thing as it ought to be fixed. Have some sense about it."

At this he laughed, and there was an exchange of badinage from which she suddenly brought him up standing with, "Well, I can't stand fooling here all day . . . write an order for two cars a day." The general obeyed.

From Chattanooga Mother Bickerdyke had followed the army with a traveling laundry that cleansed dressings, and often enough sick or wounded men. Once she was heard to say that when hot water was scarce she had not emptied the tub after bathing a wounded major general, but had put fifteen private soldiers through it too. At Kingston army surgeons complained to Sherman that she was cluttering up the hospital with relief articles not on the military list. But the general only threw up his hands, saying: "She outranks me. I can't do a thing in the world."

A letter from home may have softened Sherman somewhat during his Kingston stay. There he received word that his seventh child, Charles Celestine, had been born, but that he was so frail that he might not live. Over this loss, however, he could not brood as he had when Willy sickened. He now had a hundred thousand sons of other fathers in his sole charge.

As May ended, Sherman counted his losses at 9,000, a surprisingly small number considering the terrain, which he thought to be "as difficult as was ever fought over by civilized armies." Reënforcements had filled the gaps in both forces. Johnston had lost 8,500, but had 60,000 in line and was gathering new strength as he retired.

Care of the wounded was probably as efficient in Sherman's army as in any other force of the time. Ambulances were two-horse spring wagons with canvas tops and with benches seating eight or more patients on either side. On the floor or in swinging stretchers three prostrate men could be carried. During slow, jolting trips to the hospitals, green flies "blew" wounds or worked around bandages. Often when a man had lain for hours on the field before receiving aid, these eggs had hatched by the time surgeons cut bandages away. Nurses were convalescent soldiers, or volunteer workers, male and female.

The Seventieth Indiana cherished a motherly soul, Mrs. John L. Ketcham, who wrote home moving accounts of her work with the wounded of that regiment. One, a boy whose leg was shot off above the knee, she said,

> . . . lay white and still; he might bleed to death at any moment. I read hymns, placing myself so that the sound of my voice might surely reach him, and he not see the distressed sympathy in my face. In reading "O Mother Dear, Jerusalem," when I would come to that line, "O God, if I were there," it thrilled me so I could hardly bear it.
>
> When I read, "On Jordan's stormy banks I stand," I thought I heard a sound, but he was so weak I did not like to ask if he spoke, when a nurse

sitting on the floor by the fire, with head all shaven from erysipelas and face all discolored with iodine said, "He said, read it again."

There was an old green-house on our ground. About all that was left was a rose geranium blooming alone. I daily plucked some of those leaves and took them to him. They looked green and fresh and their fragrance is rare.

The nurse told her each day that the boy kept the leaves in his fingers all night long. "I came in one morning; he was not there. The nurse said, 'He held onto them greens to the last, and told me I was to give his respects to you.' "

But it was not wounds that gave Sherman's soldiers most worry, although General Howard, listening to "the woods moan and groan with the voices of sufferers," thought so. The men soon learned that the chances of being struck by enemy lead were, after all, slight in proportion to the number of troops engaged. They were told by their officers that five hundred or six hundred bullets were fired for every man killed.

What tortured the soldiers most were the many kinds of vermin, which were grouped under the epithet "graybacks." Unable to change clothing or bathe since leaving Chattanooga, privates of the Seventieth Indiana observed:

The men's bodies are alive with creeping things of every description . . . the poor private drags his tormented carcass in utter hopelessness to the end of the campaign. Every man from the Colonel down is broken out horribly and cannot get a moment's rest for the intolerable itching.

Into the diaries of privates in the One Hundred and Third Illinois went descriptions of men scratching the skin from their bodies:

Chigres are big, and red as blood. They will crawl through any cloth and bite worse than fleas, and poison the flesh very badly. Many of the boys anoint their bodies with bacon rines which chigres can't go. Salt water bathing would cure them but salt is too scarce to use on human flesh.

As the heat of Georgia in mid-June broke upon the army, privates saw maggots hatching "in everything from the wounds of men even to the sugar in the mess boxes. The only way to get any good of beef was to kill it in the night and cook it and eat it in the morning." They cursed when advances forced them to tarry where the retreating Confederates had camped. Excrement, decaying food, and refuse produced horrible smells.

36

BIG INDIAN WAR

AS Johnston fell back, nearer and ever nearer to Atlanta, which Jefferson Davis had pronounced vital to the life of the Confederacy, there arose a Southern demand that he either fight Sherman or resign in favor of some one who would. Civilians protested that a battle would stop Sherman for good and all. Hood was insisting that his superior ought to turn and fight. The private soldiers, although still rapt in admiration of Johnston's brilliant skill in retirements, were beginning to say, "General Sherman never makes but one speech, 'Now, boys, let's get ready to go!' and we get ready on both sides."

Johnston's wisdom was not apparent to many observers in the South. By nature silent, contemptuous of civilian and political advice, he made no verbal defense. Sagacious and cunning, he did not propose to inform Sherman of his plans. By retiring slowly, he might some day catch Sherman in an awkward position and ruin him. Also, through Johnston's gray head was running statesmanlike strategy. If he could keep Sherman from winning a victory before early November, he could aid the Northern peace party, as he after admitted, "to carry the presidential election, which would have brought the war to an immediate close."

Up North, Lincoln and the most astute political experts were agreeing. By mid-June Grant's remorseless attacks upon Lee's intrenchments had cost 65,000 Union casualties, and the whole North was in mourning. Inside the Republican party, a small but powerful group of Radicals were denouncing Lincoln as infirm, slow, weak, and although they had been unable to prevent his renomination at the national convention on June 7, they still hoped to make him withdraw in favor of some candidate who would have a chance of election. They said that he was still under the thumb of the Border State Moderates, like the Blairs. They pointed to his choice of a Tennessee Democrat, Andrew Johnson, for the vice-presidential nominee as proof of his faltering hesitancy to crush the South.

Joseph E. Johnston's great difficulty lay in finding ground on which to halt Sherman's flanking movements. When he made a stand at Allatoona Pass, eighteen miles below Kingston, Sherman side-stepped nimbly, threaded his way to the southwest, and in three days' skirmishing around New Hope Church menaced the railroad. There was no guesswork behind this feat—nothing but memory.

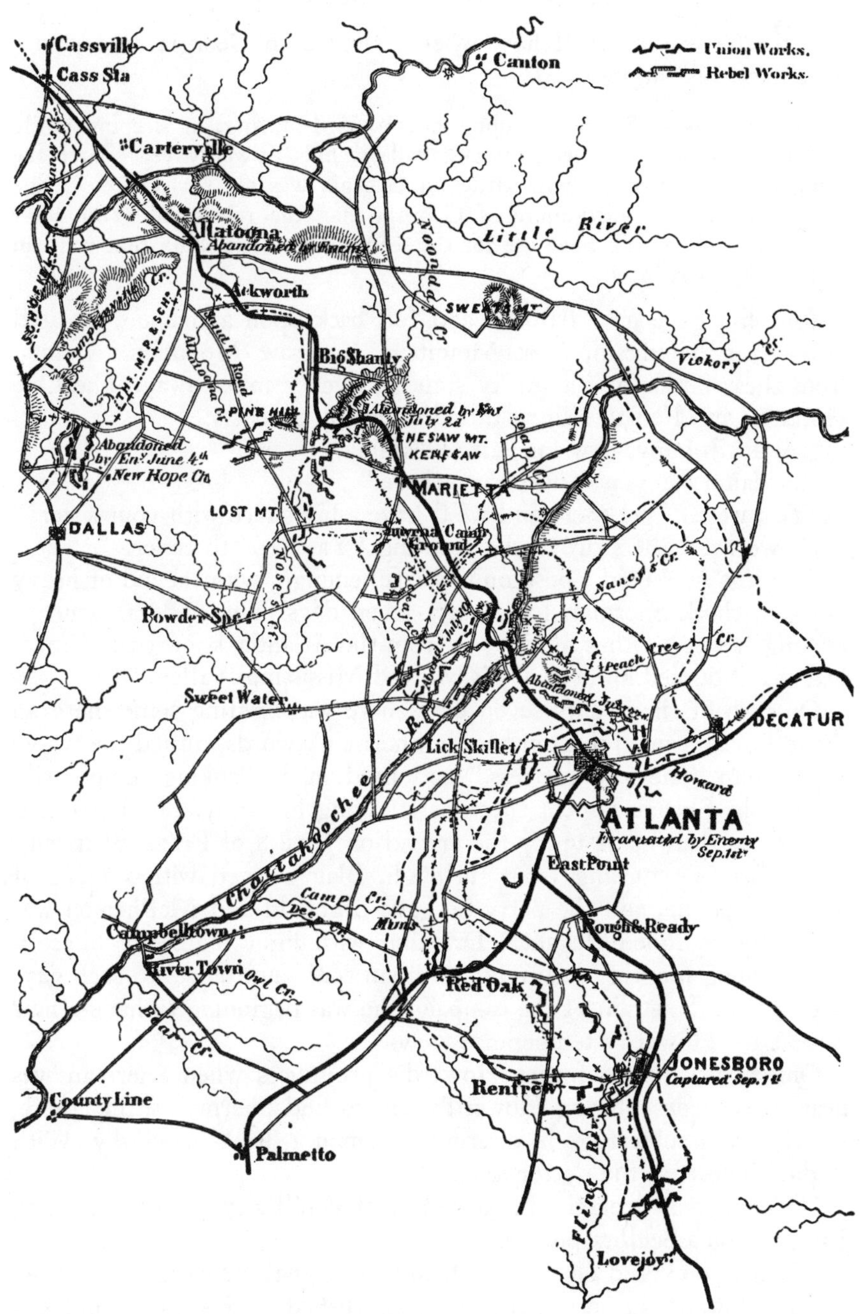

THE ATLANTA CAMPAIGN, SECTION TWO

Simplified version of map drawn in 1865 by Sherman's chief engineer, Brigadier General O. M. Poe for the Bowman-Irwin military biography, *Sherman and His Campaigns.* Dotted lines indicate routes of Sherman's armies; blackest of lines indicates railroads; lighter parallel lines, wagon roads.

Later he would recall how when stationed in Georgia as a young lieutenant, his comrades

> spent their leisure Sundays reading novels, card-playing, or sleeping while I rode or walked, exploring creeks, valleys, hills. Twenty years later the thing that helped me to win battles in Georgia was my perfect knowledge of the country. I knew more of Georgia than the rebels did. You don't know how soon you'll have use for the seemingly useless thing that you can pick up by mere habit.

Johnston gave up Allatoona and fell back upon a chain of isolated hills—Pine Mountain, Lost Mountain, Kenesaw Mountain. Atlanta, from these peaks, was a smoky smudge twenty miles away. The One Hundred and Fourth Illinois called to enemy outposts:

"Hello, Johnny, how far is it to Atlanta?"

"So damn far you'll never get there."

"Yes, we *will* get there and we'll have a big dance with your sister!" A shower of bullets drove the taunting "Yankees" to cover.

Johnston now held a position powerful enough, with the aid of heavy rains, to check Sherman for twenty-seven days. The Federal general, looking at wet weather blowing in from the Atlantic, knew that the war had at last carried him out of his beloved Mississippi Valley.

On each of the twenty-seven days there was fighting somewhere on the ten-mile front. Johnston had, in Sherman's words, turned the whole region into "one vast fortress," and mud made flanking temporarily impossible. Sherman spent the time studying his army. His losses had been more than made up by the arrival on June 8 of Frank Blair with two divisions returning from furlough. Blair arrived with wagons of iced champagne, and the party he gave Schofield and McPherson was reputedly "damned elegant." Drinking with light regularity himself, and scorning morality lecturers, Sherman could not object to such gayeties, yet in the strain of the campaign he was beginning to have a new respect for Howard's temperance views.

Officers learned to forget Howard's prejudices when Sherman was near. A surgeon entering Howard's tent to find Sherman sitting there, resorted to a subterfuge in offering Sherman a drink of whisky. With studied innocence the doctor said:

"General, you look tired and weary. If you'll step over to my tent, I'll give you a Seidlitz powder."

"Thank you," said Sherman, catching the signal, "I will."

But Howard, always literal-minded, rushed to his valise and extracted a powder, saying, "There is no need for you to go over there, if that is what you want."

Sherman surrendered, and took the dose.

Liquor was reputedly ruining one of his chief hopes in these early days of June, bogging the steps of his Brigadier General S. D. Sturgis, whom he had ordered to leave Memphis on June 1 with 8,000 horsemen, to destroy Forrest's 3,500 cavalrymen. Both Sherman and Johnston had been holding Forrest much in their thoughts, Sherman scheming to end his riding days, Johnston begging authorities in Richmond to send the cavalryman up from Mississippi to cut Sherman's communications between Dalton and Chattanooga. Sturgis met Forrest at the Battle of Brice's Cross-Roads on June 10, lost 2,240 men, 16 cannon, and his reputation. Although a court-martial would fail to prove that whisky had been responsible for Sturgis's defeat, evidence was introduced to show that the general had embraced many bottles and at least one woman before the expedition had left Memphis. Sherman, who had written Stanton as the first news reached him, that if Sturgis were proved drunk, "he shall have no mercy at my hands," softened as the weeks went by, and he finally excused the cavalryman in his report to the War Department:

> I know what misfortunes may befall us all. He was dealing with a foe unencumbered with trains. I consider a train of wagons reduces a command just half, for it cannot move without covering its trains.

Years later when it became apparent that much of the evidence against Sturgis was questionable, Sherman noted how after the tragedy the officer's morals were unchallenged.

Southern newspapers were revealing that Sherman had been correct in predicting that Negro troops would wreak vengeance for the massacre at Fort Pillow. Sturgis, on his own responsibility, had included some 1,200 black soldiers in his expedition and on June 14 the *Atlanta Appeal* charged that they had called themselves the Avengers of Fort Pillow:

> In one instance the grandmother, daughter and granddaughter were each, in the same room, held by drunken brutes, and subjected to outrages. . . . A young wife, enceinte, taken to a negro encampment and tied to stakes driven in the ground, was made to minister to the hell-born passions of a dozen fiends.

Admitting that this description savored too strongly of stock propaganda put out in all wars, and conceding that the story of the woman staked out had been told of Cossacks, Prussians, Turks, and French, there was unquestionably enough brutality shown on the Sturgis raid to justify Sherman's objections to the whole scheme of exposing childlike Negroes to war's temptations.

The Sturgis fiasco, following so hard upon the Sooy Smith rout and the Fort Pillow "outrage," prompted Sherman to write Stanton on June 15:

> Forrest is the very devil. I have two officers at Memphis who will fight all the time, A. J. Smith and Mower. I will order them to make up a force and go out and follow Forrest to the death if it cost 10,000 lives and break the Treasury. There will never be peace in Tennessee till Forrest is dead.

Smith was steaming into Memphis that moment with the two divisions Sherman had loaned Banks—strong-legged marchers of the Army of the Tennessee. They could do the job. Sherman had finally set infantry to pursuing cavalry! He ordered McPherson to have Smith or Mower start out

> and to pursue Forrest on foot, devastating the land over which he has passed or may pass, and make him and the people of Tennessee or Mississippi realize that though a bold, daring and successful leader, he will bring ruin and misery on any country where he may pause or tarry. If we do not punish Forrest and the people now, the whole effect of our past conquests will be lost.

He sent word to Memphis that "if Mower will whip Forrest I will pledge him my influence for a Major General and will ask the President as a personal favor to hold a vacancy for him."

Soon the telegraph announced that Smith and Mower, marching out of Memphis on July 1 with 14,000 men, had tricked Forrest into leaving a strong defensive position and attacking them with only 12,000. Their victory was overwhelming and, said the telegraph, Forrest had been wounded and had died of lockjaw. Sherman answered, ". . . tell General Mower I am pledged to him for his promotion and if Old Abe don't make good my promise then General Mower may have my place." Although Forrest recovered from his wound, Lincoln gave Mower his promotion.

Upon a calmer examination of the Fort Pillow evidence after the war, Sherman wrote Forrest's friends that he was satisfied the Confederate had done what he could to halt excesses, and that the slaughter of Negro troops was not, properly speaking, a "massacre" so much as the rather unnecessary killing of blacks due primarily to their panic.

Forrest's defeat added to the woes of Joe Johnston, who must have more troops from somewhere. Bragg, acting as Davis's adviser, declared that Johnston already had every available man,

> and he has retained several commands deemed absolutely necessary elsewhere, after receiving orders to move them. No doubt he is outnumbered by the

enemy, as we are everywhere, but the disparity is much less than it has ever been.

All that remained for Johnston to do was to strengthen his defense to the uttermost and conserve lives as carefully as did his adversary. Technical eyes found the Confederate fortifications more pleasing than the Northern, but attacking parties found each equally unconquerable. Johnston's engineering corps superintended his intrenchments, employing Negroes and Georgia militiamen as laborers. Union breastworks were in general laid out and thrown up by the infantrymen themselves, although as time went on Sherman organized wage-earning Negroes to do the heavy work whenever possible. Instinctively the Western skirmishers dug pits whenever they advanced, burrowing into the ground with fingers, bayonets, and halves of canteens. When secondary ranks rushed up, spades were handed from man to man, each digger employing the implement for one minute before an officer, calling time, signaled its passage to the next worker. Trenches soon stood where rifle pits had marked the advance; parapets of dirt, four to six feet high, rose; ditches were dug on the outside; trees and bushes were cut for a hundred yards in advance of the breastworks; brush was piled as entanglements for an onrushing enemy; axmen chopped trees behind the lines so that they fell in front of parapets and with their tops pointing toward the enemy. Soldiers bored holes in logs and set sharpened stakes therein—chevaux-de-frise, West-Pointers called these wicked contraptions, sheep racks, the Westerners said, as they laid them where they would harm assailants most. Axmen stood on parapet tops amid raining shells and cut down trees with such exactitude that trunks fell along the crest to serve as head logs under which riflemen could thrust their muskets. Smaller trunks were notched to fit under these head logs and to form skids down which the heavy timbers could roll harmlessly if knocked backward by a solid shot. Leafy branches were placed over the trenches to shut off the sun's rays.

Warfare in the woods fitted the handicraft traditions of the Western farmers, a fact that Johnston recognized when he reported to Richmond that the enemy was well adapted to the kind of fighting required. Cump described to John the whole campaign as "a big Indian war." Colonel C. J. Dilworth oriented his Eighty-fifth Illinois privates to their environment by calling out as they entered thickets seeking Confederate sharpshooters, "Well, we will turkey-hunt this morning." Frank Blair's men once crawled on their bellies, Indian fashion, toward an apple orchard midway between the lines and, lying on their backs, knocked off apples with clods and sticks while Confederates raked the grove with Minié balls that helped bring down the fruit.

Sherman's soldiers were sons and grandsons of pioneers who had adopted Indian tactics in winning the Western forests. The Shawnee name of their general symbolized the Indian quality of the fighting.

In Johnston's army, Major General Samuel G. French, a New Jersey Quaker who after graduation from West Point had married and settled in the South, wrote in his diary:

> It does seem strange that we cannot have one quiet Sabbath. Sherman has no regard for the Fourth Commandment. I wish a Bible society would send him a prayer book instead of shipping them all to a more remote heathen, but it would be the same in either class. The one is uncivilized by nature—the other, I fear, becoming so from habit. Perhaps "Tecumseh," has something to do with it. There is much in a name.

Sherman was seen in battle to discuss coming movements with private soldiers who stood near by. Colonel O. L. Jackson thought the general at such times spoke to common soldiers as if they were members of his staff. Logan insisted that almost any private of the Fifteenth Corps was capable of commanding it—a tribute identical with Napoleon's declaration that every man in some regiments carried a marshal's baton in his knapsack. Yet few of the Western privates aspired to be generals or to remain in the army after the war. The year before, in Memphis, Sherman had explained to the Russian military observer, Lessoffski, that the expert artillerymen who drilled for them were not professional soldiers, only "mechanics, clerks, and laborers a few months before." The elegant Russian had asked what such men would do after the war. "I told him," said Sherman, "they would go back to their homes." The Slav shook his head in disbelief.

Regarding themselves as essentially riflemen called from home to extinguish an insurrection, the Western soldiers kept surveying the battles and campaigns in their entirety. They took eager interest in what was happening at the other end of their lines. Men of the Seventieth Indiana described the intensity with which they listened to the cannonading far on the flanks, hearing the lulls,

> then the hurrahing, sometimes the shrill, boyish rebel yell, sometimes the loud, full-voiced, deep-toned, far-sounding chorus of Northern men; then again the roar of cannon, the rattle of musketry and the awful suspense to the listeners. If, as the noise grew feebler, we caught the welcome cheer, answering shouts ran along. . . . But if the far-off rebel yell told of our comrades' repulse, the silence could be felt.

As June wore on, the army's respect for Sherman increased. The railroad was repaired with such rapidity that the United States mails arrived twice and sometimes three times a week as the army edged toward Kenesaw Mountain. A soldier of the Seventy-third Indiana wrote in his diary on June 14:

> Our profoundest admiration goes to the way Sherman keeps up his railroad and our rations. On the 11th the High Tower Bridge was completed and an engine crossed immediately . . . crying in its loudest whistle, "How-do-you-doo-oo-General-Sherman!"

The cheers of 50,000 men answered. Up to then the Indiana writer had always thought engines screamed, "Make-way for-Li-i-i-iberty."

It was this same day, June 14, that Sherman, riding up among his advanced forces, came out on a hill to select a point where he might push in between Kenesaw and Pine mountains. Eight hundred yards away on the slope of Pine, he noted a group of Confederates studying him through their glasses. "How saucy they are," he said. "Howard, make 'em take cover. Have one of your batteries fire three volleys into 'em." Then he rode off.

By chance, Howard gave the order to the man who was probably the best artilleryist in either of the opposing forces—Captain Hubert Dilger, famous as Leatherbreeches. Dilger had been an artillery expert in the Prussian army in 1861 when his uncle, a New York merchant, had written him that this was the time to visit America. On leave of absence, Dilger joined the Army of the Potomac, fought diligently and happily, then came West with Hooker. Like other Easterners, he discovered that Sherman placed his cannon much nearer the front than did the orthodox technicians of the Army of the Potomac. Dilger, adopting the principle, pushed his guns, Battery I, First Ohio, so far up among the riflemen that both General Stanley and General Granger were quoted as having said they would order bayonets for his cannon. Recognized as a genius, Dilger was allowed to place his guns wherever he wished, and to rove about as a free lance. Clad in immaculate doeskin trousers, a white shirt with rolled sleeves, and shining top boots, the handsome Prussian was the darling of the Army of the Cumberland. Although he spoke many languages, he preferred to command his gunners with carefully rehearsed claps of his hand. Standing close to the breech, often sighting himself, he worked the cannon with deadly precision.

Soldiers of John Sherman's Brigade described how Dilger had received the order from Howard to drive the saucy Confederates from Pine Mountain. They saw him sight his guns, heard him say, "Shust teeckle them fellows," then clap his hands. Shells burst near the party of Johnnies on Pine Mountain. Three central figures separated, two running for cover, one lingering to depart with more dignity. The two who ran were Joe Johnston and Hardee, the one who made off so slowly was Bishop Polk, whom Sherman, after a conversation with Johnston in later years, described as having refused to run because of his dignity and corpulency and also because he did not wish "to appear too much hurried or cautious in the presence of his men." At any rate the bishop stopped in the open to have another look at the enemy and gave Leatherbreeches time enough to catch him through the stomach with a cannon ball on the second volley. Down went the old man and back through the exploding shells came Johnston and Hardee to kneel above him.

"I would rather anything than this," said Johnston.

"My dear, dear friend," moaned Hardee, the tears falling.

Years later there would be Southerners to spread the legend that Sherman had sighted the gun that killed the bishop, when as a matter of fact the Federal commander had ridden away before the shots were fired and did not know until evening that there had been any results from the discharge. Toward sundown, signal-corps men, who had for some days been reading the Confederate wigwag flags, translated messages betraying the bishop's death. Hardened to killing, Sherman telegraphed Stanton twenty-four hours later, "We killed Bishop Polk yesterday and made good progress today."

The death of Polk brought spiritual rather than military misfortune to Johnston. The good old man had been a buffer between the hostile temperaments of Johnston and Hood, and when he was gone, hot heads began to knock together. Hood, acting in sympathy with President Davis and Bragg, fumed because Johnston would not give battle. He writhed as during the day after the bishop's fall Johnston gave up Pine Mountain, and two days later withdrew from Lost Mountain. The lines converged on and around impregnable Kenesaw.

On June 13 Sherman wrote, "We cannot risk the heavy losses of an assault at this distance from our base." On the sixteenth he telegraphed Halleck:

> I am now inclined to feign on both flanks and assault the center. It may cost us dear but in results would surpass any attempt to pass around.

He had many reasons for considering this sudden reversal of policy. His temperament said, "Flank Kenesaw"; his logic said, "Attack it." Johnston's lines were thin in the center, strong on the flanks—a natural reaction from Sherman's style of offensive. A swift thrust at the Confederate middle might break through and if it did, there would be a rout with fleeing Confederates butchered as they crossed the deep

Chattahoochee River in Kenesaw's rear. Also, Sherman feared the arrival of Georgia militia would soon enable Johnston to send veteran divisions to relieve Lee in Virginia. To Halleck and Grant Sherman sent messages of cheer almost daily—"Grant may rest easy that Joe Johnston will not trouble him, if I can help it by labor or thought."

Jealousy of Grant was the curious reason given by Don Piatt for Sherman's decision to attack Kenesaw. Piatt, who disliked Sherman, said after the war that Logan had told him of a dramatic interview in McPherson's tent on the night of June 26. Sherman was reading a newspaper filled with accounts of how, early in the month, Grant, abandoning his bloody frontal assaults on Lee, had dropped below the James River and suddenly appeared on Lee's flank, attacking from the south—his Vicksburg technique again. Logan said that Sherman had looked up from the newspaper to say

> that the whole attention of the country was fixed on the Army of the Potomac and that his army was entirely forgotten. Now it would fight. Tomorrow he would order the assault. McPherson quietly said that there was no necessity for the step since Johnston could be outflanked and that the assault would be too dear.

But Sherman had answered that "it was necessary to show that his men could fight as well as Grant's." Some color of truth was given Logan's tale by telegrams Sherman had sent Grant a week earlier:

> You may go on with the full assurance that I will continue to press Johnston as fast as I can overcome the natural obstacles and inspire motion into a large, ponderous and slow, by habit, army. Of course it cannot keep up with my thoughts and wishes, but no impulse can be given it that I will not guide.
>
> My chief source of trouble is with the Army of the Cumberland which is dreadfully slow. A fresh furrow in a plowed field will stop the whole column and all begin to entrench. I have again and again tried to impress on Thomas that we must assail and not defend; we are on the offensive and yet it seems that the whole Army of the Cumberland is so habituated to be on the defensive that from its commander down to its lowest private I cannot get it out of their heads.

He told Grant that Thomas had ignored the order about limiting tents for the sake of mobility and that he maintained a "headquarters camp on the style of Halleck at Corinth." Conyngham described Thomas's camp as "a most gorgeous display of tents of all kinds, every officer and servant had one . . . Sherman would frequently rein up and ask, 'Whose quarters are these?' " Orderlies would reply, "General Thomas's, General." "Oh, yes," Sherman would say in irony, "Thomastown—Thomasville, very pretty place, appears to be growing rapidly."

On June 18 Sherman had written Grant that Thomas had "cost me two splendid opportunities which never recur in war." Once, in the late-May fighting around Dallas, Thomas had delayed four hours in preparing for an advance, and again on June 15 when a gap had appeared in Johnston's line:

> I ordered Thomas to move at daylight, and when I got to the point at 9:30 I found Stanley and Wood quarreling which should not lead. I'm afraid I swore and said what I should not, but I got them started and instead of reaching the Atlanta road back of Marietta, which is Johnston's center, we only got to a creek to the south of it by night, and now a heavy rain stops us and gives time to fortify a new line.

During the weeks before Kenesaw, Sherman saw that his men were rapidly settling into the frame of mind of besiegers, as at Vicksburg. Boys of the Twelfth Wisconsin watched the artillery duels, and told each other that Sherman had said he would take Kenesaw or fill it full of old iron. They sat on parapet tops like crows on fence rails watching rival batteries exchange missiles. Once a jocular Confederate deviated his gun's muzzle and sent a shot directly at the spectators. Homeric laughter rose from Confederate trenches when the entire row of Northerners presented their posteriors as they tumbled backward into their trench.

At night the Wisconsin men stood with other regiments on their parapets watching for the "fire-sheet lightning" that told of a Confederate cannon's discharge. Then they would "duck while the shell swooped over," popping up again like prairie dogs to repeat the performance. When the shells passed, an Irish private shuddered as at a banshee's flight. "By the power of mud, byes," he would groan, "lay low, lay low! . . . Oh, hear the murtherin' thing a-screamin'!"

All at once Sherman's mind was made up. The attack was ordered for June 27. Back in Nashville he had heard that officers had sneered at him as "not a fighting general." At that time he had answered, "Fighting is the least part of a general's work, the battle will fight itself." Every frontal attack in his past had been made at the command of his superiors, and all had been failures. Now he would launch one on his own responsibility.

37

WITH BOOTS ON

EARLY in the morning of June 27 Federal cannon began bursting shells on Kenesaw, and for an hour iron rang on rock and tore at green wood. Sherman was giving McPherson directions as to how the ascent should be made on the front of the Army of the Tennessee.

"About halfway up the mountain," he said, "you will find a plateau where there is a peach orchard; it will be a good place to stop and let your men get breath for the assault." Sherman remembered how when he had ridden up the mountain in 1843 he had conversed with a farmer on this plateau, and how the farmer had said the spot was chosen for an orchard because it was on the northern slope of the mountain where peach buds would not develop prematurely in the springtime and fall victim to early frosts.

The soldiers viewed the attack with distrust. They thought Uncle Billy might be wrong for once in expecting them to storm those heights. Something ominous lurked behind the exhortations that officers poured into their ears. Colonel Dan McCook, who was to lead the way, stood before his ranks reciting Horatius's speech: "Then how can man die better than facing fearful odds . . ." The men listened attentively, for he was one of the Fighting McCooks, with two brothers already dead in uniform and his father, Daniel, Sr., killed while commanding militia against Morgan's raiders in Ohio. Four other brothers of Dan were at the front, also five first cousins, whose father John had died in an army surgeon's uniform. Altogether the Tribe of Dan and the Tribe of John had sent fourteen McCooks to war. One would be a major general, three would be brigadiers, three colonels, one a captain, three lieutenants, and the only one to miss shoulder straps would be Old Dan's youngest, Charles, who at seventeen had been killed at Bull Run.

Rivaling Dan McCook in battle preparations was Brigadier General Charles G. Harker, a West-Pointer who read the Bible in his tent each night and who in 1862 had delighted his men by wooing and winning a Tennessee belle while camped upon the estate of her relative, General Pillow's brother.

With the officers exhorting and the cannon roaring, Sherman waited for the attack as a dancer waits for the music to which he will try a new step. For seven weeks he had led Johnston in a dance that they both knew by heart, a dance of poised, balanced rhythms. Even the private soldiers recognized this quality in the campaign. A Confederate deserter described how the Johnnies at their coffee each morning would listen to the jackasses of Federal wagon trains braying in the dawn, and would say, "It's time to git up and git; there are Sherman's trumpeters!" There had been a steady tempo to the skirmishes, a clocklike regularity to the digging, shooting, flanking, retreating—two armies in the hands of two artists. Now Sherman proposed to break the rhythm and to see if Johnston could step to a new measure.

The cannon sputtered into silence and Kenesaw stood quiet with summer. Then McCook and Harker went up the slope, and 25,000 Confederate rifles and 50 cannon wrapped the mountain in smoke. In less than an hour Sherman knew that the new step had tripped him. Harker and McCook were dying, 2,500 others had been killed and wounded, while the enemy held their trenches with a loss of only 808. The Army of the Tennessee had suffered far less than the Cumberlanders, thanks to the loose, Indian formation of their advance. Thomas's men had gone into battle in formal columns, like British grenadiers. For a time Sherman hoped that a second trial would carry the blue wave over the earthworks before which the men lay, close to rocks and stumps, shooting at slouch hats. "One or two more such assaults would use up this army," said Thomas when Sherman asked his opinion. And that night when Sherman, in calling off the attack, told Tom, "Our loss is small compared with some of the East," Thomas replied, "I think it decidedly better than butting against breastworks twelve feet thick."

The dancers returned to the old routine, Sherman pushing Schofield forward on the flank—a movement that had begun even while the attack was in progress. To Halleck Sherman sent a letter of self-defense:

> The attack I made was no mistake; I had to do it. The enemy and our own army and officers had settled down into the conviction that the assault of lines formed no part of my game, and the moment the enemy was found behind anything like a parapet, why, everybody would deploy, throwing up counter-works, and take it easy, leaving it to "the old man" to turn the position. . . . Even as it was, Johnston has been much more cautious and gives ground more freely.

In later years military experts disagreed among themselves as to the wisdom of the attack, but all admitted that Sherman had not risked enough men to place his army in danger.

Sherman looked at himself in something like amazement. He, who had been so fearful of assuming responsibility for men's lives, was now sending thousands to death. Two days after the slaughter he wrote Ellen:

> It is enough to make the whole world start at the awful amount of death and destruction that now stalks abroad. . . . I begin to regard the death and mangling of a couple of thousand men as a small affair, a kind of morning dash—and it may be well that we become hardened. . . . The worst of the war is not yet begun.

Down from its trenches, part way up the mountain, Sherman drew McPherson's army, putting into its place the dismounted cavalrymen of Brigadier General Kenner Garrard. McPherson was sent to help Schofield flank Johnston, and at dawn of July 3 Sherman saw his skirmishers capering on the heights of Kenesaw. Furiously he pushed Thomas around the mountain on Marietta, the city nestling in its rear. He arrived in the city before Garrard, and the Seventy-second Indiana infantrymen heard him "swearing horribly" and asking, "Where's Gar'd? Where's Gar'd, where'n hell's Gar'd?" Garrard, arriving, explained that it took time to get men down, mount and provision them:

> But Sherman got madder and madder and finally yelled, "Get out of here quick!" Garrard said, "What shall I do?" "Don't make a damned bit of difference so you get out of here and go for the rebels."

Sherman was sure that "no general such as he [Johnston] would invite battle with the Chattahoochee behind him." But Johnston amazed him by dropping into superb fortifications that his engineers had prepared in front of the river, as though he expected the Federals to try to redeem their Kenesaw failure. The Confederate privates had been attempting to provoke their adversaries into attacking on the Fourth of July. The Seventy-second Indiana, marching to Marietta, had seen nailed to a tree a board on which was sketched a white man embracing a Negress. Under it was written, "Billy Sherman hugging a nigger wench. Come on and we'll give a warm reception on the 4th."

Intrenching opposite Johnston, Sherman scattered troops up and down the river hunting fords by which he might flank again. As a blind he sent the bulk of his cavalry one way to attract Johnston's horsemen, then seized crossings in the opposite direction. Johnston attributed the discovery of these fords to the fraternization between pickets. These outposts declared truces and bathed in the river, exchanging anecdotes and scrubbing each other's backs. Federal engineers, disguising themselves as innocent pickets, mingled with the bathers and in gabbling with the Confederates learned much topography.

Up and down the river Sherman kept raiding parties demolishing war property, railroads, provisions, mills. To reach the town of Roswell, some twenty miles north on the river, a division of the Army of the Tennessee marched thirty-one miles in a day. There Garrard had burned a cotton mill over which waved the French flag, but which had spun Confederate uniforms. When the Gallic owner protested, Sherman wrote Garrard, "Should you, under the impulse of natural anger, natural at contemplating such perfidy, hang the wretch, I approve the act beforehand." And to Halleck Sherman wrote, "Such nonsense cannot deceive me. I take it a neutral is no better than one of our own citizens." Years later, according to General Dodge, a court of claims awarded damages to the French mill-owner and censured Sherman.

Far and wide swept Sherman's men. He brought his old Kentucky associate, Rousseau, down from Nashville with cavalry to raid Alabama's railroads and crops. Both Rome and Marietta were partially burned, and as the troops swept down toward the Chattahoochee, they saw smoke rising from buildings along its banks. "Charley," said one soldier to another, "I believe Sherman has set the river on fire." During the sack of Roswell, a squad of Federals halted in a cemetery when one of their number called, "I smell meat!" Following his nose, the men knocked a hole in a burial vault and were extracting ham, bacon, and molasses when, as the Seventy-second Indianans told it, "An old woman pounced on the men, shouting, 'I allus heerd you-uns robbed the cradle and the grave but I never expected to see it.' "

Howell Cobb, the Georgia statesman and leader of militia, wrote his wife on August 3 concerning the Federal invaders, "I have heard of no cruelty or outrages to white women, but cases are reported of them outraging women in the presence of their mistresses." Understanding as he did the uses to which warring nations put the propaganda of horror, Cump wrote Ellen:

> Though not conscious of danger at this moment, I know the country swarms with thousands who would shoot me and thank their God they had slain a monster, and yet I have been more kindly disposed to the people of the South than any general of the whole army.

On the morning of July 5 Major James A. Connolly, adjutant of a division in the Fourteenth Corps, emerged on a bluff overlooking the Chattahoochee and saw such a sight as made him write his wife, back in Illinois:

> Mine eyes have beheld the promised land. The "domes and minarets and spires" of Atlanta are glittering in the sunlight before us and only 8 miles distant. . . . Generals Sherman and Thomas (who are always with the extreme front when a sudden movement is taking place) were with us

on the hilltop, and the two veterans for a moment gazed at the glittering prize in silence. I watched the two noble soldiers—Sherman stepping nervously about, his eyes sparkling and his face aglow—casting a single glance at Atlanta, another at the River, and a dozen at the surrounding valley to see where he could best cross the River, how he best could flank them.

In the night of July 9, Johnston, finding Sherman's men across the river and endangering his retreat, withdrew to the other bank and entered trenches along a new line of defense, Peach Tree Creek. Up to the river now dashed the whole Federal army, wild for a bath—their first chance for a thorough cleansing in two months. While pontoniers laid bridges, thousands of naked men basked on the banks, playing cards and boiling their clothes in odd containers. Sherman, naked too, was seen squatting in the Chattahoochee discussing the temperature of the water with a teamster who admired him from dry land.

Arraying his armies on the east bank, Sherman approached Johnston in a stupendous wheeling movement, with Thomas's heavy force acting as the hub, Schofield's in the middle, and McPherson's swinging fifty miles on the outer rim to change from the right wing to the left. It was one of the manoeuvers that Sherman had in mind when, long after the war, he spoke of the Army of the Tennessee as

> never checked, always victorious, so rapid in motion, so eager to strike, it deserved the name of "the whip-lash." It swung from one flank to the other as danger called, night and day, in sunshine and storm.

The majesty of this approach impressed Sherman's adversaries, one of whom, as a prisoner of the One Hundred and Fifth Illinois, said, "Sherman ought to get on a high hill and command, 'Attention! Kingdoms by right wheel!' "

Inside the Confederate ranks Sherman's great opponent, Joe Johnston, had come to the end of his dance. At Decatur, McPherson had cut the railroad running to the northeast. The Federals were ranged within five miles of Atlanta. Calls for Johnston's retirement were beating like a sea around Jefferson Davis in Richmond. Southern politicians and editors were in panic lest Atlanta be surrendered without a blow. Throughout the campaign, Johnston had been enigmatic if not cryptic with Davis, never giving him a satisfactory answer as to when he intended to fight Sherman. Now Johnston was still imperturbably laconic. He received Davis's emissary, Bragg, with politeness but would say nothing about future plans. His lieutenant, Hood, had written bitterly to Bragg saying that Johnston's refusal to give battle many miles north had been "a great misfortune to our country" and that Johnston had "lost 20,000 men without having fought a decisive battle."

Finally, on July 16, Davis made one last demand for a statement and received from Johnston the cool reply:

> My plan of operations must depend upon that of the enemy. It is mainly to watch for an opportunity to fight to advantage.

With that the camel's back broke, and Davis sent word that since

> you have failed to arrest the advance of the enemy to the vicinity of Atlanta, far in the interior of Georgia, and express no confidence that you can defeat or repel him, you are hereby relieved. . . .

Back came Johnston's answer, asserting that Sherman's army was much stronger in comparison with his own than was Grant's in comparison with Lee's:

> Yet the enemy has been compelled to advance much more slowly to the vicinity of Atlanta than to that of Richmond and Petersburg, and has penetrated much deeper into Virginia than into Georgia. Confident language by a military commander is not usually regarded as evidence of competency.

With this thrust at Davis, who had been much more closely identified with Lee's campaign than with any other, Johnston surrendered his office to Hood, explaining with cold courtesy that he had planned to fight Sherman at Peach Tree Creek. Then he joined his wife at Macon, Georgia, and awaited developments.

His comparisons between himself and Lee had been approximately correct. Allotting to both generals all available soldiers within their beck and call, Johnston had controlled some 60,000 and Lee some 90,000. Against them Sherman had assembled 100,000 and Grant, 120,000. Odds had been five to three against Johnston and four to three against Lee. Grant had progressed eighty-five miles in a month, while it had taken Sherman six weeks to travel an equal distance.

Although careless commentators, South and North, would in time ascribe to Grant the opprobrious title "Butcher," implying or confidently asserting that his battle methods were characteristically more costly than those of any other general in either force, an examination of statistics would tell a different story. In his average battle, across four years of war, Grant would lose one hundred and thirteen, killed and wounded, in every one thousand men. Lee's comparable loss, exclusive of the Wilderness battles in 1864 (on which he kept no figures) was one hundred and forty-nine. Hood, while opposing Sherman, lost one hundred and fifty-four in every one thousand, while Sherman's methods sacrificed only sixty-two by contrast. Johnston, in his average battle with Sherman throughout 1864-65, lost eighty as against Sherman's ninety.

Sherman's average across his entire career was only sixty-three in each one thousand.

When news came on July nineteenth that Hood was now facing him, Sherman found himself in the unexampled position of having at his elbow three men who had known Hood intimately at West Point. McPherson, Schofield, and Howard agreed that Hood, for all his lack of limbs, would attack; in school he had been rash, erratic, headstrong, precipitate, and not intellectual. Through the Federal ranks went the story that a Kentucky colonel had come up to tell Sherman how in a poker game, "I seed Hood bet $2,500 with nary a pair in his hand." Thomas, who had served with Hood in the United States Army in Texas, agreed that he would strike quickly.

Bracing for a fight, Sherman warned his generals to be on the alert. He hoped for a battle because his force as it stood was not strong enough to besiege Hood in Atlanta. If only he could have beaten Hood into the city, he could have avoided fighting. But it was too late now for regrets.

In his trenches, Hood thought he saw Sherman blunder in the wheeling movement—a gap was visible between Thomas and Schofield, and into this opening, on the morning of the twentieth, the Confederates came.

Private Henry E. Cist, Company I, Twenty-third Indiana, stood on his trench looking at blackberries just beyond the skirmishers. He had been awaiting battle for three days, and was tired of it. He wanted those blackberries, and as the quiet of noon descended he stole out to them. He rambled nearer the forest, picking and eating. Suddenly a flash of light dazzled his eyes. He blinked. It was the sun striking on gun barrels of gray-coated men pouring out of the forest—six lines of them, muskets at right-shoulder shift. Cist screamed murder, Rebels, help, get ready, and bounded homeward through the briers, berry stains on his open lips. His comrades dropped their noonday meals, cannon boomed, musket volleys crashed—and the fight was on.

Hooker's corps was beaten backward by the rush. A perilous hole opened on his flank, and toward it the Southerners charged, heads down, "yelling like demons." But into the breach, like a mountain, moved Pap Thomas, who seemed to live for these moments of defensive crisis. From his guns came a barring torrent of canister and Hooker, who seemed to live for moments of offensive drama, ordered a counterattack. Thomas, standing on the banks of Peach Tree Creek, was being observed by an officer of the Seventieth Indiana:

> He is always working at his short, thick whiskers. When satisfied he smooths them down, when troubled, he works them all out of shape . . . and it was at that moment, when our right and left, fighting in the woods, seemed ready to give way, he had his whiskers all out of shape. . . . But when he saw the rebels running, with us after them, he took off his hat and slung it on the ground and shouted, "Hurrah! Look at the Third Division! They're driving them!" His whiskers were soon in good shape again.

After this bloody repulse, Hood was expected by Sherman to evacuate Atlanta, since his main line was now crowded back to less than a mile and a half from the city. But Hood, unsatisfied, decided that Sherman was moving "in reckless fashion" to enfold the city on three sides, and that McPherson's army at Decatur was "in the air." Through the night of the twenty-first, Hood sent four divisions on a stealthy march of fifteen miles to strike the Army of the Tennessee.

At ten o'clock on the morning of the twenty-second, Sherman sat under a tree by his headquarters house, near the center of the line. With him was McPherson, who had ridden over for instructions. Sherman drew a map of the operations he wanted to make as soon as McPherson should be done with the ruination of the railroad at Decatur. McPherson was in good spirits, having just seen his artillery prepare to shell factories in Atlanta. A week earlier he had wondered to Schofield when he might get off to get married. His plump friend had replied, "After the capture of Atlanta, I guess." Now romance seemed near as the walls of the city prepared to come tumbling down.

Sherman and McPherson talked. Occasionally a solid shot cut through the trees above them with a tick-tick-ticking sound. Suddenly a louder note came in the firing—a new roar from the left, where McPherson's men were moving. The two generals leaped to their feet and figured by Sherman's compass exactly where the fighting must be. McPherson swung into the saddle and spurred away, calling back to Sherman something about sending him word when the cause of the firing was discovered. Sherman noted how handsome and manly he was—"He had on his boots outside his pantaloons, gauntlets on his hands, had on his major general's uniform."

Sherman in his dusty, rumpled flannel uniform turned back to the headquarters house. In a few minutes one of McPherson's aides flung off a foaming horse and cried to Sherman that the general was either killed or wounded. McPherson had sent his aides away with orders as he galloped toward the fight, and had disappeared down the forest road almost alone. Shots had been heard and his horse had raced back, bleeding and with saddle empty. Sherman told the officer to run his horse to the Army of the Tennessee and give the command to Logan.

Tell Logan to fight on! Then Sherman sent couriers to order Thomas to pour into Atlanta—Hood was out of it.

The battle rose like an approaching thunderstorm on the left. Rifle bullets began to strike around the house. Hoofs thudded as messengers came and went. Up rolled an ambulance and into Sherman's room came officers carrying McPherson. Somebody ripped a door off its hinges and laid it across two chairs for the body to rest upon. Sherman bent forward while surgeons examined the wound. No use. McPherson had died a few minutes after receiving a rifle ball near his heart. Sherman noted that "he was dressed just as he left me, with gauntlets and boots on."

Beside the corpse Sherman paced the floor, shouting orders at the staff officers who plunged in and out of the open door with reports. Bullets pattered on the roofs and walls, shells crashed in the forest, the roar of battle was an unending crescendo. Sherman's feet marched up and down the room; his voice barked, barked, against the storm; his eyes turned constantly back to the white face of his friend; tears ran down his red beard and off on to the dusty floor.

Couriers came shouting that the Army of the Tennessee was surrounded—lost. Sherman said that it couldn't be. He would send no help. It had never been whipped and could win now as always. Furthermore, he wanted both Thomas and Schofield free to push into Atlanta. He sent couriers to demand aggressive action from Tom.

Across in the woods, the Army of the Tennessee was at the greatest crisis in its career. Hood's attack had caught it moving and unprepared. It had lost many cannon. But, fire-chilled veterans that they were, the men fought from tree to tree until hasty intrenchments were erected, then from scanty parapets of branches and dirt they killed their assailants in shoals. Confederates drove at them from three sides, and sometimes from four. When attacked strongly in the rear, the Tennessee Army men merely rolled to the other side of their parapets and shot away their assailants. Then they rolled back and fired at the front once more. Seven distinct assaults the Fifteenth Corps beat off during the afternoon.

Across one trench top the Fifteenth Iowa and the Forty-fifth Alabama fought hand to hand, clubbing, stabbing, shooting, throttling. Flags were snatched away, the snatchers were shot, the flags retrieved. Once the opposing colonels, Confederate Lampley in a white slouch hat, and Federal William W. Belknap, a large man in a monstrous red beard, were face to face. Belknap, lately a Democratic politician of Iowa, knew how to encourage his men. Reaching over he snatched Lampley by the shoulders and threw him kicking into the Union lines. When Lampley died a few days later, his captors believed shame more responsible than wounds.

Capable of fighting a battle without officers—so it was thought by many observers—the Fifteenth Corps had taken fiery satisfaction in the sight of their commander, Logan, spurring among them with the shout, "Don't disgrace the Fifteenth Corps! Will you hold this line with me?" The men looked up, their faces black from biting cartridges, to see Logan's raven hair shining in the hot sun and his eyes blazing—those eyes so black that no pupil was visible. His black hat was swinging over the black sheen of his stallion's hide. "We will!" bellowed the soldiers, then they fell to chanting, "Black Jack! Black Jack! Black Jack!" Later when he roared to them the news of McPherson's death and asked that it be avenged, they charged savagely, swinging musket butts like axes and howling, "McPherson and revenge!"

It might have been the knowledge of acute danger to this corps—his own—that prompted Sherman to give up his resolution to spare it the humiliation of being "rescued." To headquarters came one of the corps's division commanders, General Charles R. Woods, to say that his men, on the extreme right and close to Sherman, had now been cut off from Logan and the main body. They were about to go under. Sherman sent Woods back with orders to attack, then he hurried Schofield with twenty cannon to a hill overlooking the position.

Although in his official report Sherman gave Schofield credit for the movement, it was his own hands that trained the first gun for Woods's relief. As he sighted down the barrel, a bullet glanced past his cheek. "Ha!" he exclaimed, "close shaving—we'll pay back that compliment. Fire! Very good, very good; that kicked up the dust and some of their heels, too."

Rallying, Woods charged and recaptured most of the cannon lost to Hood at the first onset. The Confederates retired a little, and fell to bombarding the lines with shell and Minié balls. Sherman stepped behind a tree. Near by, a soldier crouched in the shelter of a mass of earth and tree roots, and whenever a shell burst close at hand, the fellow wailed, "O Lord, Lord, if I once get home . . . Oh, I'll be killed!" Captain Conyngham saw Sherman grin and, stooping, pick up stones that he threw against the barricade of tree roots. At each handful the private howled afresh. "That's hard firing, my man," called Sherman. "Hard?" moaned the soldier. "It's fearful. I think thirty shells have struck this tree while I was here." "It's all over now, come out," said Sherman, stepping forth as the musket fire subsided. Conyngham saw that "as the trembling man came out and saw who it was, he ran away."

Riding back to headquarters that night, when Hood had retired into Atlanta, defeated, Sherman said to Willard Warner, "I expected something to happen to Grant and me; either the Rebels or the newspapers would kill us both, and I looked to McPherson as the man to follow us and finish the war."

It was Warner who telegraphed the tragic news to Mary Hoffman, who awaited McPherson and marriage in Baltimore. Thoughtfully he addressed the message to Mary's mother, but the old lady on receiving it said, "Mary, I haven't my glasses, won't you read it?" Mary fell in a faint. Warner knew that Sherman wrote the girl a kindly letter explaining why he had not let her fiancé come to Baltimore in December for the wedding. "He seemed to regret not having let him go," said Warner. "He talked about it with tears."

To Lorenzo Thomas, Sherman wrote on July 24 of McPherson as "a man, who had he survived, was qualified to heal the national strife which had been raised by ambitious and designing men." For years to come, Sherman would wonder exactly how McPherson had met his death. He could find no eyewitnesses. Then, on the fourteenth anniversary of the fatal day, there came to him a letter from a veteran, A. C. Thompson, who as a member of the Fourth Ohio had been McPherson's orderly. He had been alone with the general when Hood's skirmishers had broken through on to the forest road down which they were galloping:

> Just as I saw the rebels upon us, they yelled out, "Halt, halt, you damned sons of bitches." The General checked his horse and raised his hat as if to salute them, then with a quick turn to the right, he tried to get away. I saw them raise their guns to shoot. I slid down on my saddle and as I bent over I saw the leaves fly from under the General.
>
> My head struck a tree and knocked and stunned me I suppose for about three minutes. When I got over my stun I got up and started to help him up; he was lying on his right side with his right hand under his breast; his left hand was on his left leg and I called him, asking if he was hurt and he said, "Oh, orderly, I am."
>
> Then I went to pick him up and there was a big rebel caught hold of my revolver belt and jerked and dragged me away from him, called me a Yankee son of a bitch and told me to go to the rear or they would shoot me.
>
> At this the General turned over on his face trembling—I think he was dead.

38

CHANGE FRONT ON WASHINGTON

IT was ten o'clock on the night of July 22. The three corps commanders of the Army of the Tennessee met in the woods where the wounded were screaming. They expected that Sherman would send fresh troops from the Army of the Cumberland to relieve the battered Tennesseeans. Logan, as the commanding officer, sent Dodge to ask Sherman for help. "He seemed surprised to see me," said Dodge, "but was cordial. I stated my errand."

"Dodge," barked Sherman, "you whipped them today, didn't you?"

"Yes, sir."

"Can you do it again tomorrow?"

Dodge stiffened, the pride of corps spurting once more in his arteries. "Yes, sir," he said, turned and went back to his troops. Sherman later said that "the Army of the Tennessee had fought the great battle without aid and, all alone, could whip Hood's whole army." He seemed as proud of that army as if every man in it had been his son.

Thomas had been unable to penetrate Atlanta while Logan resisted Hood. Moving up to the intrenchments, Thomas thought them too well manned to risk an attack, and Sherman hid his disappointment even when, in later days, it was apparent that a bold assault could have brushed aside the comparatively few defenders. Located so deep in the enemy's country, Sherman wanted complete harmony among his officers, and was prepared to make sacrifices to obtain it. On the twenty-third his diplomacy met a rigorous test when Thomas came to headquarters asking,

"What are you going to do about the Army of the Tennessee?"

"Well," said Sherman, "there is Logan in command. I don't know that it exactly suits me, but it will make him terribly mad not to give him the situation permanently. What do you think about it?"

"That is what I came to see you about," Thomas answered. "I don't think it is going to do to keep Logan there. He is brave enough and a good officer but if he had an army I am afraid he would edge over on both sides and annoy Schofield and me. Even as a corps commander he is given to edging out beyond his jurisdiction. You cannot do better than put Howard in command of that army."

Sherman argued that to import Howard "would make a rumpus among these volunteers." Coming from the East, Howard would arouse the jealousy of the Western men, "who put a good deal of store upon their achievements and natural talents." Wouldn't such a step dampen their enthusiasm?

"If you give it to Logan," said solemn Thomas, "I should feel like asking to be relieved." In Old Tom's memory still rankled the thought of how Logan had complained about him to Sherman in Nashville.

"Why, Thomas," exclaimed Sherman, "you would not do that?"

"No," said Thomas slowly, "I would not, but I feel that army commanders should be on friendly terms and Logan and I cannot. Let the President decide it."

Sherman snapped, "No, it is my duty and I'll perform it."

They talked on. Hooker, as the senior corps commander, expected to succeed McPherson, but Cump and Tom agreed he was impossible. Sherman's heart prompted him to name Logan, whose battle conduct entitled him to command the army that was already his in spirit. But Sherman's reason argued that Logan as an officer from civil life might fail in the purely technical manoeuvers that must come within the next few days. Telegrams from Grant had arrived warning Sherman that Lee might send reënforcements to Hood. This possibility made it necessary to throw the Army of the Tennessee to Atlanta's rear for the destruction of the railroad that ran to the southeast. With this road ruined, Lee's men would be delayed. To move an army from its trenches ten miles through the night in battle array and fit it into a new sector of the line was one of the most difficult feats in generalship, and Sherman wondered if Logan could manage it. Furthermore Sherman resented the freedom with which "political generals" like Logan and Blair left the army in quiet times to campaign among Northern voters. He liked Tom's candidate, Howard, who was serene where Logan was fiery. Howard would be better for a campaign; Logan would be better in battle. And Sherman cared not who won the battles so long as the Federals won the campaigns.

"Well, Thomas," said Sherman at last, "we cannot get along here without you. We must continue together in harmony to produce results. . . . If you are decided in the matter, I will telegraph to Washington and suggest Howard."

He issued Howard's assignment without comment. That he felt badly about Logan was apparent in the tributes he gave him in messages to the War Department, but he made no explanations, no apologies. When the affair later became a political issue between regulars and volunteers, Sherman refused to throw off on Thomas; he said that the whole responsibility had been his own. Only when the issue had died did he admit that Thomas's complaint had been the deciding factor.

Sherman's selflessness was apparent in the prompt approval he gave the War Department's plans to take from him the southern Mississippi portions of his department and award them to General Canby. As late as July 24 he had been proud of his command over the Mississippi River, and had written Slocum:

> Though far away here in Georgia thundering away at Atlanta, my thoughts revert to Mississippi and that great valley which appears to me the spinal column of America.

When the change was announced, he informed Halleck:

> As long as we can pull together, it makes little difference who commands, and I perfectly accord to General Canby the control of matters on the great river.

In contrast to his own attitude, Sherman found Hooker raging because he had not been given the post assigned Howard. Sherman made no effort to hold the prima donna in line, and when Hooker left for the North to take an inactive department, Sherman calmly moved the man's worst enemy, Slocum, into his place. Hard on Hooker's heels went General John M. Palmer, the Cumberland corps commander who took offense because he had been asked, during the heat of battle, to take temporary orders from Schofield, whose commission made him technically Palmer's junior. "I had not thought of relative rank," Sherman told Palmer, begging him not to resign as he threatened to do. As a Republican politician of Illinois and a reputed friend of Lincoln's, Palmer felt that the West-Pointers were discriminating against him, and insisted upon departing. To the last Sherman urged him to trump up some dignified excuse rather than brand himself a petty quibbler.

With the campaign settling into a siege of Atlanta, Sherman wired Halleck:

> After we have taken Atlanta I will name officers for promotion. In the meantime I request that the President will not give increased rank to any officer who has gone on leave from sickness or cause other than wounds in battle.

General Cox, thinking over this matter, later concluded that Sherman was attempting to forestall the list of promotions that the War Department announced on the day following his request. On that list were two new major generals: Hovey, who had departed from the army at Kenesaw still fuming because his infantry and cavalry were brigaded separately, and Osterhaus, who had been absent for a time on sick leave. It outraged Sherman to see around him worthy officers ignored "because they had no politicians to speak for them." He believed politics had dictated the advancement of Hovey and Osterhaus, and he telegraphed the War Department:

> . . . it is an act of injustice to officers who stand by their posts in the day of danger to neglect them and advance such as Hovey and Osterhaus, who left us in the midst of bullets to go to the rear in search of personal advancement. If the rear be the post of honor, then we had all better change front on Washington.

By the next afternoon Lincoln answered, saying that both Sherman and Grant had earlier recommended the two men for promotion. As to Hovey, "we knew he had reason to feel disappointed and mortified, and we felt it was not best to crush one who had certainly been a good soldier." Lincoln said that he had long before promised to promote Osterhaus: "The word was given on what we thought was high merit and somewhat on his nationality."

Sherman hastened to apologize to Lincoln, and to beg that he be not regarded as faultfinding, "for I assert that I have been well sustained in every respect during my entire service. I did not suppose my dispatches would go outside the War Department. I did not suppose you were troubled with such things." His own recommendation of Hovey and Osterhaus had been given after Vicksburg's fighting and if they had been acted on at that time, all would have been well, but coming at the present time, he said, the promotions had made all his officers believe that advancement "results from importunity and not from actual service."

Since early in June, Sherman had been at odds with the Administration over its policy of enlisting Negro soldiers from among the refugees. From the start of the campaign Sherman had hired fugitive slaves at ten dollars monthly to do heavy manual labor, and when recruiting agents wooed these hands away with the offer of fourteen dollars a month, Sherman had, on June 3, ordered the agents arrested. Adjutant General Lorenzo Thomas, still organizing Negro troops in the West, complained to Stanton that since Sherman commanded the regions where the chief supply of recruits was to be found, his order virtually crippled the whole enlistment plan.

It astounded Lorenzo Thomas, and Abolitionists who believed the formation of Negro regiments an act of justice to the bondsmen, when Sherman attacked the whole scheme on the ground that it was an act of injustice. He wrote Lorenzo Thomas that it was wrong to take Negro men away from their women:

> The first step in the liberation of the negro from bondage will be to get him and his family to a place of safety, then to provide him the means of providing for his family. . . . If you divert too large a proportion of the able-bodied into the ranks, you will leave too large a proportion of black paupers on our hands. . . .
>
> For God's sake, let the negro question develop itself slowly and naturally, and not by premature cultivation make it a weak element in our policy. I think I understand the negro as well as anybody . . . he, like all other of the genus homo, must pass through a probationary state before he is qualified for utter and complete freedom.

Sherman had warned Southerners in 1860 that their institution of slavery was weak in its separation of families. In 1864 he saw the Federal Government making the same mistake. Before the war he had begged Northerners and Southerners to let time solve their quarrels; now he must revive his request. Impatient in regard to personal matters, he could feel the need of long, cool years and slowly whirling ages in questions that touched anything like the basic nature of mankind.

He saw nothing but error in Congress's law, passed July 4, authorizing Northern governors to send agents into the South to recruit Negroes "who shall be credited to the State which may procure the enlistment." Instrumental in the lobby which pushed this bill were New England manufacturers anxious to have their white mill hands exempted from conscription in a time when war inflation brought factories swollen profits. If Negroes could be lured into uniform by the new army wage of sixteen dollars monthly and the Federal bounty of a hundred dollars, then the draft need not touch so many white laborers.

Although he had been informed by Halleck on this phase of the matter, Sherman astutely avoided the temptation to denounce the bill on so political a score. His objections were military, as he wrote Old Brains on July 14:

> Before regulations are made for the States to send recruiting officers into the rebel States, I must express my opinion that it is the height of folly. I cannot permit it here and I will not have a set of fellows hanging around on any such pretenses. We have no means to transport and feed them. The Sanitary and Christian Commissions are enough to eradicate all traces of Christianity out of our minds much less a set of unscrupulous State agents in search of recruits.

Almost as he wrote, letters arrived from a swarm of the hated tribe who, clustering in Nashville, asked him where they might begin to enlist Negroes. On July 30 he answered, naming eight cities, all deep in Confederate territory and far from any Federal force—cities such as Selma, Montgomery, Savannah. It was his ironic way of telling them to go to hell. His reply, addressed to John Spooner, agent for Massachusetts, continued:

My opinions are usually very positive and there is no reason why you should not know them. Though entertaining profound reverence for our Congress I do doubt their wisdom in the passage of this law, first, because civilian agents about an army are a nuisance; second, the duty of citizens to fight for their country is too sacred a one to be peddled off by buying the refuse of other States; third, it is unjust to the soldiers and volunteers who are fighting, to place them on a par with the class of recruits you are after; fourth, the negro is in a transition state and is not the equal of the white man; fifth, he is liberated by act of war, and the armies in the field are entitled to all his assistance in labor and fighting in addition to the proper quota of the states; sixth, this bidding and bartering for recruits, white and black, has delayed the reënforcement of our armies at the time when such reënforcements would have enabled us to make our successes permanent; seventh, the law has delayed the universal draft which I firmly believe will become necessary to overcome the widespread resistance, for under the providence of God it will separate the sheep from the goats and demonstrate what citizens will fight and what will only talk.

Stoutly Sherman protested that he was the friend of the Negro; that he had escorted to Federal lines more Negroes than had any other general, but that he preferred the blacks kept as servants and laborers or if as soldiers on probation in local garrisons.

But I would not draw on the poor race for too large a proportion of its active athletic young men, for some must remain to seek new homes and provide for the old and young, feeble and helpless.

Not even a direct plea from Lincoln could swerve Sherman. The President, writing on the eighteenth, reminded his general that the act "being a law, must be treated as such by all of us. . . . May I ask, therefore, that you will give your hearty coöperation?" Standing to his guns, Sherman wrote Halleck that he did not wish to be "construed as unfriendly to Mr. Lincoln" but that "it is not fair to our men to count negroes as equals. Cannot we at this day drop our theories and be reasonable men?" He had seen recruiting agents in the past take Negroes back to Nashville, "where, so far as my experience goes, they disappear." He pointed out that while Lorenzo Thomas had thousands of Negro soldiers on the Mississippi, "I cannot draw away a white soldier. . . . All count the Negroes out." Then he continued:

We want the best young white men of the land, and they should be inspired with the pride of freemen to fight for their country. If Mr. Lincoln or Stanton could walk through the camps and hear the soldiers talk they would hear new ideas. I have had the question put to me often: "Is not a negro as good as a white man to stop a bullet?"

Yes; and a sand-bag is better; but can a negro do our skirmishing and picket duty? . . .

Can they improvise roads, bridges, sorties, flank movements, etc., like the white man? I say no.

Time would prove the soundness of Sherman's objections, for while a total of 180,000 Negroes would be enlisted by the Federals during the war, no more than half actually bore arms, and except in a few instances were not effective in aggressive action. In only one item of war were they exceptional; they had little of the white man's dislike of the bayonet. With only a few generations separating them from the jungle they still felt familiarity with cold steel.

By early August the letter to Spooner had found its way into the newspapers North and South, with the result that Sherman found himself assailed by Abolitionists and praised by Confederates. The *Richmond Enquirer* said on August 24:

> We wonder if any spectacle can be more degrading than to see Massachusetts, whose machinations for supremacy in the Union have culminated in the present conflict, sneaking in the rear of the Yankee army to pick up negroes enough to keep her citizens out of the fight. She has received an appropriate rebuke from Sherman.

Although Sherman protested to Lincoln that he meant no interference, his failure to coöperate was given by the adjutant general's investigators as one of the chief reasons for the virtual collapse of the Negro-recruiting scheme in and around his armies. They reported months later that 237 agents had obtained only 400 black recruits, of whom one fourth were physically unfit. Many of the remainder deserted, and almost all of the hundred-dollar bounties were stolen from the ignorant volunteers by the agents.

That Sherman escaped reprimand was, in all probability, due to two reasons: first, Lincoln was slow to let political questions interfere with a general who would fight; second, he was relying upon Sherman to save him at the November elections. As the summer waned, Lincoln saw political retirement approaching. Nothing but a military victory of sensational scope could alter the obvious intention of the voters to make a change in their ruler. Horace Greeley, capable of swinging hundreds of thousands of votes through his *New York Tribune*, was manoeuvering for peace and declaring that nine tenths of the people North and South were utterly sick of war—"our bleeding, bankrupt, almost dying country . . . shudders at the prospect of fresh conscriptions and new rivers of blood." Grant's mortality lists kept the North in mourning. The Democratic *New York World* asked, "Who shall revive the withered hopes that bloomed at the opening of Grant's campaign?"

Many patriots were losing heart, declaring that neither side could win, and that European monarchies would soon seize the exhausted republic. Abolitionists and liberals, accusing Lincoln of weakness in antislavery matters and of tyranny in his restraints of civil liberty, had put a ticket in the presidential race, headed by the disgruntled John C. Frémont. Secretary Chase was resigning the Treasury portfolio; paper money had fallen to thirty cents on the dollar. Radical Republicans were denouncing Lincoln's reconstruction plans in Louisiana and Arkansas as merely a czar's ruse to fatten his factional power. Still more Republican politicians were preparing to ask Lincoln to resign in favor of some nominee who had a chance of election. Rosecrans in St. Louis thought the antiwar secret society, the Sons of Liberty, strong enough in Union States to send the Northwest into revolt. Holt, judge advocate general of the Army, numbered the Sons at half a million, with their principal strength in Ohio, Illinois, Indiana, Kentucky, and Missouri. Guerrillas were ravaging Kentucky, aided and abetted by aristocratic blue-grass families who saw in the general weakness of the Federal garrisons the hope of eventual victory for the Confederacy in the West.

There was no hope that Grant could conquer Lee in time to change the drift of sentiment before election day in November. Sherman was the one man in a position to produce a triumph spectacular enough to save Lincoln. If he should ruin Hood's army, or capture Atlanta, the North would be dramatically surprised, for his campaign had received relatively less public notice than Grant's. War correspondents had been hampered and all but driven off by Sherman. Grant had never discouraged them. Furthermore, on July 7 Sherman had asked Halleck to give out no news from his army: "Absolute silence in military matters is the only safe rule. Let our public learn patience and common sense."

But if a victory were to be won in Georgia, it were well for Lincoln that it were won quickly, for on September 5 the new conscription was to go into effect—an event that would solidify new thousands against the President, who was apparently sending herds of unwilling youths to fruitless slaughter. And Sherman, upon whom Lincoln must rely, was not only indifferent to the election, but was also disgusted with democracy.

Before starting the campaign, Sherman had sought to fortify Kentucky against the guerrillas who would arise as soon as his back was turned. He had urged Governor Bramlette to organize in each county a band of loyal riders who, acting under the sheriff, could arrest every suspicious citizen. When Bramlette had refused so antidemocratic a step, Sherman had done nothing. But when in early June rumors of depredations reached him, he sent back orders for the military in Kentucky to hunt guerrillas like wild beasts, and

> to arrest all males and females who have encouraged or harbored guerrillas or robbers, and you may cause them to be collected in Louisville, and when you have enough, say 300 or 400, I will cause them to be sent down the Mississippi through their guerrilla gauntlet, and by a sailing ship, send them to a land where they may take their negroes and make a colony with laws and a future of their own. If they won't live in peace in such a garden as Kentucky, why, we will kindly send them to another, if not a better land, and surely this would be a kindness and God's blessing to Kentucky.

To James Guthrie, his Louisville friend, Sherman wrote that the trouble-makers must be exiled for some years

> . . . and take time to study and reflect on the great theory of self-government which began with Old Adam and has made precious little progress since. . . .
>
> Joe Johnston would never sanction such dogs as call themselves guerrillas in Kentucky, nor would Lee or Bragg or any other man who thinks he is fighting to establish a new and independent government better suited to their interests and honor.

General Burbridge, Sherman's chief lieutenant in Kentucky, read his chief's words:

> The fact is in our country personal liberty has been so well secured that public safety is lost sight of . . . and we are thrown back a hundred years in civilization, law and everything else, and will go right straight to anarchy and the devil if somebody don't arrest our downward progress. We, the military must do it. . . .

Suspecting that Lincoln would not sustain him in a move so radical as the deportation of enemy civilians, on June 21 Sherman had asked Stanton to sanction the scheme. He asked that he be allowed to select a foreign home for the malcontents:

> Honduras, British or French Guiana or San Domingo would be the best countries but they might object to receive such a mass of restless democrats. Madagascar or Southern California would do.

He argued eloquently with Stanton:

> Our civil powers at the South are ridiculously impotent, and it is as a ship sailing through the sea—our armies traverse the land and the waves of

disaffection, sedition and crime close in behind, and our track disappears. But one thing is certain, there is a class of people, men, women and children who must be killed or banished before we can hope for peace and order, even as far south as Tennessee.

Although the Administration would not permit him to try his exile scheme, he saw Lincoln on July 5 place Kentucky under the military law that in Nashville Sherman had foreseen to be necessary.

As his army lay around Atlanta, Sherman began to feel that even it, upon which he pinned his faith to restore law and order in the land, was after all but part and parcel of a tragic and vicious circle of factors that were wrecking the future of harmonious, intelligent government. He voiced his doubts to the Southern divine, Bishop Henry C. Lay, who was passing through his lines:

This war ought to be arrested. It is intensifying the greatest fault and danger in our social system. It daily increases the influence of the masses, already too great for safety. The man of intelligence and education is depressed in value far below the man of mere physical strength. These common soldiers will feel their value and seek to control affairs hereafter to the prejudice of the intelligent classes.

That Sherman knew how the Administration's future awaited upon his campaign, was not to be doubted. John had written him on July 24, "We all feel that upon Grant and you . . . the fate of the country depends"; but Cump would make no condescension to politicians. He grew angry when John, on August 2, sent him a request that he oblige Schuyler Colfax, Speaker of the House, who wished nine Indiana regiments furloughed home to vote at the State election in October. Sherman refused, and added, "Congress cannot be worsted. . . . Had I a vote I would not give it to one of you."

His every thought was now centered upon concentrating all Federal force upon the enemy and, as he wrote Grant, "Any sign of let-up on our part is sure to be falsely construed. . . . We must manifest the character of dogged courage and perseverance of our race." And on August 14 he wrote to James Guthrie:

War is the remedy our enemies have chosen . . . and I say let us give them all they want; not a word of argument, not a sign of let-up, no cave in till we are whipped or they are. . . . The only principle in this war is, which party can whip. It is as simple as a schoolboy's fight and when one or the other party gives in, we will be the better friends.

He told Guthrie that "those side-issues of niggers, State rights, conciliation, outrages, cruelty, barbarity, subjugation, etc., are all idle and nonsensical." He reminded Guthrie that Confederates had "first burned bridges on your railroad," and had commandeered slaves in Kentucky to do military work

> when I would not let our men burn fence rails for fire or gather fruit or vegetables though hungry. . . . We at that time were restrained, tied by a deep-seated reverence for law and property. The rebels first introduced terror as a part of their system. . . . Buell had to move at a snail's pace with his vast wagon trains . . . Bragg moved rapidly, living on the country. No military mind could endure this long, and we were forced in self-defense to imitate their example.

To Leslie Coombs, his friend in Frankfort, Kentucky, who protested at the devastating turn taken by the war, he wrote on August 11:

> and did they not begin to burn the houses of Union men in Kentucky and carry off the slaves of Union men in Kentucky, when I, poor innocent, would not let a soldier take a green apple, or a fence rail to make a cup of coffee?
>
> Why! we have not yet caught up with our friends of the South in this respect for private rights. . . . I pledge my honor when the South ceases its strife, sends its members to Congress and appeals to the courts for its remedy and not to "horrid war," I will be the open advocate of mercy and a restoration to home, and peace, and happiness of all who have lost them by my acts.

In practically every section where there was bold Federal action in the summer of 1864, there was a Westerner in command: Grant in Virginia; Sheridan in the Shenandoah Valley; Sherman in Georgia; Admiral Farragut, born in East Tennessee, volleying and cursing at the forts of Mobile Bay; and assisting Farragut on land Canby, Kentucky-born and scion of the teachings of Henry Clay.

The West was in the saddle: Lincoln of Illinois in the White House; Stanton of Ohio in the War Office; even Halleck, as chief of staff, had lived from his thirtieth to his forty-seventh year west of the Alleghenies and longed now to be back in the Mississippi Valley. Under the gentle Lincoln had arisen informal, rugged, aggressive Westerners to supplant the more technical and suave Easterners who had ruled at the beginning of the war. Grant had cleared the Army of the Potomac of the cliques and professional cabals that had flourished under McClellan. The devious political manipulations of Secretary Cameron had been supplanted by the blunt, crude, offensively-mannered methods of Stanton. Dishonest manufacturers feared Stanton, whose notorious rudenesses were a blend of fierce incorruptibility in departmental matters and bad health—health ruined by tireless work, night and day.

And in all this list of Westerners who believed in war to the finish, there was not one man who had asked in 1860 that the South should be stripped of its slaves.

39

GLORIOUS LAUGHTER

KNOWING that the new Confederate leader, Hood, would be aching for a chance to redeem his reputation as an attacker—the bold attacker who would show Joe Johnston the error of defensive warfare—in late July Sherman proposed to tempt his adversary. "Act with confidence . . . act offensively to show him that you dare him to the encounter," he wrote Logan as on the twenty-seventh the Army of the Tennessee swung to the right, and with its wagon wheels muffled in hay marched around the city aiming at a new position southwest of Atlanta. With Schofield stretching his Army of the Ohio on the north and northeast, Thomas on the west, this would give Hood but one avenue for bringing in supplies—the railroad to the south. On the twenty-eighth, as the Fifteenth Corps swept past the new trenches that Hood had erected in the neighborhood of Ezra Church and the Lickskillet Road, the Confederates accepted the dare. Out they came, yelling and shooting. Two miles away, Sherman heard the thunder. "Logan is feeling them, and I guess he has found them," he said. Presently one of Howard's staff officers galloped up to say that Logan was fighting off a heavy attack. "Good—that's fine—just what I wanted, just what I wanted," said Sherman, while Major Connolly stood close by, staring at him in admiration. "Tell Howard to invite them to attack, it will save us trouble, save us trouble, they'll only beat their own brains out, beat their own brains out." Connolly heard him "talk on gayly; he understood his own strategy was working."

"Hold 'em! Hold 'em!" Logan was howling, and his Fifteenth Corps, crouching behind a rail fence, beat off five attacks, and were holding their ground at nightfall. They had repulsed the Johnnies twelve times in a week. When Sherman arrived to compliment them, they showed him the field carpeted with dead and wounded enemies and lied proudly about it all, saying, "It was easy." The Fifty-fifth Illinois counted graycoats "in windrows, sometimes two or three deep." Howard, who had tactfully remained in the rear so that Logan might have all possible honor, said, "I never saw fighting like this before."

A prisoner confessed to men of the Fifty-fifth Illinois, "Our generals told us that the Fifteenth Corps had bragged long enough that they had never been whipped, and today we'd drive you to the river or hell before supper." From a Union rifle pit at the day's end a voice called, "Well, Johnny, how many of you are left?" "Oh, about enough for another killing," came the answer.

Desertions were increasing in the Confederate Army. Jefferson Davis advised Hood to avoid frontal attacks. Here and there privates shouted, "Give us Johnston!" That master of his art had been justified. He had known better than to expose his men so openly to the sharpshooters of the Northwest.

Sherman's men said that Uncle Billy had atoned for his Kenesaw mistake. In three pitched battles before Atlanta he had let the enemy make the attacks. Sherman wrote Halleck:

> We have good corporals and sergeants and some good lieutenants and captains, and those are far more important than good generals. They all seem to have implicit confidence in me. They think I know where every road and by-path is in Georgia, and one soldier swore that I was born on Kenesaw Mountain.

It was not purely chance that gave Sherman the nickname of Uncle Billy. The fatherly Thomas was well called Pap, and Brigadier General Alpheus S. Williams of the Twentieth Corps was paternal enough at fifty-four to be universally known as Pop. Marse Robert and Marse Joe were fitting nicknames for Lee and Johnston among Southern privates, who were, on the whole, more respectful of their generals. Sherman's attitude of distant friendliness and unsentimentality made him seem like an uncle who watches over nephews zealously yet without paternalism. Had he been more dramatic he might have won such names as Hooker and Logan did—Fighting Joe and Black Jack. But Sherman was too practical and too scornful of heroics to become an idol.

The one Western general to become an idol was Logan. The men cheered and leaned forward to touch his stallion when he galloped past. He loved it; his hat seemed always to be off, his walrus mustachios streaming in the wind.

It was the correspondent of the *Washington National Tribune* who after the war gave the nation the romantic tale of Logan and the "Rebel" baby. As he advanced after the Battle of Ezra Church, surgeons told Logan of a neighboring accouchement. They wanted Logan to christen the baby. Excited at the thought of life entering so confidently into a world of death, Logan agreed to act as godfather. He found a cabin with its roof half shot away, and an interior looted by both armies. On the bed lay a white-faced girl whose husband, she said, had died in Lee's army. Beside her sat her mother, a crone who was smoking tobacco given her by the surgeons. Among the covers was a microscopic scarlet face—a girl baby.

"This looks damn rough," said Logan, and sent officers to bring poles and fix the roof, set them to sweeping out the place and building a fire. He asked his staff to empty their haversacks in a clean spot in a corner. When the last colonel was down off the roof, the old crone brought a gourdful of spring water, Logan took the infant in his arms, and the chaplain prepared to officiate. Shells crashed in the woods not far away. "What are you goin' to give her for a name?" quavered Grandma. "I want it to be right pert, now." The chaplain began to speak holy words. He came to the naming of the baby. "Shell-Anna," said Logan, and as he departed, he gave the grandmother a gold coin for the child, adding, "Put it in a safe place or some damned bummer will steal it in spite of everything."

War correspondents had no such hero tales of Sherman. They still disliked him, although he was now too successful to be hounded. One of them described him:

> . . . no symptoms of heavy cares—his nose high, thin and planted with a curve as vehement as the curl of a Malay cutlass—tall, slender, his quick movements denoted good muscle added to absolute leanness, not thinness.

General Rusling thought Sherman

> too busy to eat much. He ate hardtack, sweet potatoes, bacon, black coffee off a rough table, sitting on a cracker box, wearing a gray flannel shirt, a faded old blue blouse and trousers that he had worn since long before Chattanooga. He talked and smoked cigars incessantly, giving orders, dictating telegrams, bright and chipper.

He had seen to it that men fought off scurvy by eating turnip tops, dandelion greens, sassafras root, and pine-leaf tea. A country boy himself, he had learned the pioneer trick of subsisting in the wilderness. He noted that men sickened of the patent compounds with which the War Department sought to vary rations—desiccated vegetables, concentrated milk, meat biscuit, and curious extracts. It amused him to hear the soldiers jeer at "desecrated vegetables and consecrated milk." Often a strip of raw pork sprinkled with brown sugar and eaten on hardtack was the fare in isolated rifle pits. Around campfires men toasted hardtack, or pounded it into flour and mixed it with boiled rice to make griddle cakes to be eaten with molasses filched from plantations. Cracker crumbs fried in pork fat and seasoned were called hell-fire stew.

But the favorite food to be found in the commissariat was baked beans—beans prepared as by a ritual, thrown into an iron pot, covered with fat pork, sunk in a pit of coals, and kept baking all night. Sentries threw chunks on the fire, bayonets lifted out the kettle at dawn, and in the sunrise the beans and pork were found melted together—a rhapsodic memory for the years. Around the fiery pit soldiers lay, shadows flickering on their blankets, their minds gloating upon the millions of beans that had been eaten and the millions more waiting in warehouse caverns back in Nashville.

One hundred days after the start of the campaign, Cump wrote Ellen that his greatest triumph was not that of battle or strategy, but in so handling his supplies that not one of his men had missed a meal.

Vigilantly Sherman protected his slender railroad from the passengers who would have kept it from its primary task—the bringing of food. "A single messenger's bulk and weight in bread and meat would feed 100 men a day or one man 100 days," he said in denying the Governor of Minnesota the right to send extra commissioners to care for the wounded. There were already too many commissioners on the ground, one from each State, county, and congressional district in addition to the agents of the Sanitary and Christian commissions. Sherman denied powerful editors transportation for huge bundles of newspapers. He was, however, becoming more philosophic, temporarily at least, about the press. He wrote Thomas forbidding them to suppress "mischievous and treasonable newspapers" in Nashville:

> I have no objection whatever, but in human nature there is so much of the mule left that prohibition of a newspaper increases its circulation . . . it would be like damning a few of the tributaries of the Kanawha to stop the flood of the Mississippi.
>
> . . . the proper remedy is in punishing the men who publish malicious and false articles. . . . Thus, put in public stocks any venders of obscene or libelous sheets and give a good horse-whipping to any editor who would dare advise our soldiers to avoid their honorable contracts of enlistment.

Demanding cold logic and unsentimental reasoning from all others, in the campaign Sherman allowed himself to stray from his ideal when he thought of Federal prisoners starving in Southern prison pens. Before commencing his shift of forces to the southwest of Atlanta, he had sent two large groups of cavalry against the sole Confederate railroad entering the city. General Stoneman, commanding one of these forces, had begged Sherman to allow him to ride on to Macon and Andersonville, where some 30,000 prisoners were suffering. Evidently without stopping to question how so many weakened men, if rescued, could be brought back across a hundred and thirty miles of hostile territory, Sherman bade Stoneman God-speed. When both groups of horsemen were defeated—Stoneman and many of his men captured—Sherman made explanation to Halleck, writing on August 7:

> Nothing but natural and intense desire to accomplish an end so inviting to one's feelings would have drawn me to commit a military mistake at such a crisis, as that of dividing and risking my cavalry so necessary to the success of my campaign.

To the Sanitary Commission he wrote later, "I don't think I ever set my heart so strongly on any one thing as I did in attempting to rescue those prisoners."

With the return of the vanquished horsemen, Sherman thought of sending infantry against the railroad, but he decided that this would stretch his lines too thin; he gave it up, sent to Chattanooga for large siege guns, and began to bombard the city. In late June he had said that he had no thought of attacking Atlanta; his objective was the Confederate Army, and now in August, when it became necessary to focus his attention upon a citadel, he wrote Halleck, "I am too impatient for a siege," but "whether we get inside Atlanta or not, it will be a used-up community by the time we are done with it."

Scouts and his own reason told him that the city was depopulated. "Most of the people are gone," he wrote Ellen on August 2; "it is now simply a big fort."

By August 10 he was writing Howard, "Let us destroy Atlanta and make it a desolation." He informed his generals that since Atlanta was a fortified town "whose inhabitants have, of course, got out," they must shell not only the Confederate lines, which were close to the suburbs, but the railroad depots, arsenals, and ammunition and provision warehouses in the city proper. Soon his infantrymen in their trenches lay under a canopy of hurtling iron. The ground shook night and day from the roar of 223 cannon.

The Twelfth Wisconsin was troubled by a gun in their rear that was deficient enough to drop its shells into Federal rather than Confederate trenches. "She slobbers at the mouth—take 'er away!" they shouted through cupped hands to the gunners. They rejoiced when the huge siege guns arrived from Chattanooga. Soon the largest of the new cannon began a monotonous dispatch of a shell at five-minute intervals. "There goes the Atlanta Express," said the men as it boomed.

Federal trenches were topped by sandbags, and at danger points signs read, "Keep down here! Don't stand on the works." At night both armies burned cotton balls, soaked in turpentine, between the lines to aid their sharpshooters in picking off soldiers who wormed through the open spaces stringing telegraph wire, ankle-high, between stumps. Other workers dug little pits, two feet deep, and covered them with twigs. Attacking was made difficult. Often in the evening brass bands played while Northerners and Southerners sang the same song. The campaign became everything that Sherman detested, immobile, tedious. He fidgeted because health and morale declined in trench and camp. He and his men craved the open country, the swinging march. "The enemy hold us by an inferior force," he told Schofield; "we are more besieged than they." His orders became irritable—"I don't hear those guns." . . . "Move up the pickets." . . . "Move up the guns."

A duel of nerves was being fought between himself and Hood—two impatient men. Hood weakened first. He sent Wheeler with almost all the cavalry to threaten Sherman's long railroad. Sherman's nerve held. The threat, he announced, was only a wild-goose chase. He had enough guards in blockhouses and repair gangs in cities along the way to keep the road mended no matter how often Wheeler dashed in to break it. His prediction came true. Wheeler, unable to do serious harm, galloped on into East Tennessee, where he could affect Sherman not at all. General Cox observed that Wheeler had yielded "to the common temptation of cavalry to make too much of the distance they may go behind the hostile lines."

Sherman recognized that Hood had made a capital blunder. Minus his horse scouts, the Confederate was now like a blind man. Quickly Sherman sent his own cavalry to break Hood's one remaining railway. He knew from past records that his horsemen would do railroad tracks as little damage as Wheeler's were doing, but Sherman pinned his faith on the general whom he selected to lead the cavalry raid—Brigadier General Hugh Judson Kilpatrick.

Kilpatrick was a headlong youth of twenty-nine whom Grant had sent Sherman from the Army of the Potomac in April—a bristling little man with a long red nose and longer and redder side-burns. At West Point, Little Kil had gone outside the curriculum to practice amateur acting, political oratory, and fisticuffs with Southern cadets who advocated secession. He had married on the day of his graduation in June, 1861, had ridden away to become the first regular-army officer to be wounded, also the first of the younger West-Pointers to command either a brigade or a division. A precipitate Celt he was, fearing no present and no future and believing that, if spared, he would some day become governor of his native New Jersey, and later on President of the United States. Much given to fictitious descriptions of his feats, his accounts of battles were as boastful and unreliable as were those of his ex-classmate and present rival, Joe Wheeler. Legends about him ran through the army. Men said he neither drank whisky nor gambled—but women! Don Juan of the cavalry! Not all of the romance attributed to him could have been true, however, for he carried with him much of the time Billy, a nephew of fourteen, whose lessons Little Kil heard in his tent. A few months after the Atlanta campaign, Union soldiers were laughing about the two Negro wenches who cooked for Kil, and the *Macon Telegraph* charged that he seated them at his dinner table—most likely an invention.

Sherman favored Kilpatrick over Garrard because the latter would, in Sherman's language, retreat "if he can see a horseman in the distance with a spyglass." Sherman admitted that Kilpatrick's treatment of his own horses entitled him to the name Kil-Cavalry, but when selecting him in November, 1864, to head a raid involving fighting, Sherman said, "I know that Kilpatrick is a hell of a damned fool, but I want just that sort of a man to command my cavalry on this expedition."

In August, 1864, however, Sherman imagined that Kilpatrick would work and toil as well as fight. In sending him to destroy the Confederate railroad, Sherman wrote Kil's superior, Schofield:

> Tell Kilpatrick he cannot tear up too much track nor twist too much iron. It may save this army the necessity of making a long, hazardous flank march.

His orders to Kil were "not to fight but to work."

In a few days Kilpatrick was back from his raid, boasting that he had disabled the road for ten days at least; but next morning Sherman saw supply trains calmly puffing into Atlanta over the "demolished" tracks. Inquiry revealed that Kil had spent most of his time fighting and charging. Sadly Sherman dismounted his cavalry and put it into the trenches to free infantry for the dangerous march that must now be made. As Sherman slipped all but Slocum's corps from the west to the southeast, he was courting danger. Joe Johnston, hearing of it some days later in his retirement, said, "It is Sherman's one mistake of the whole summer." But Sherman, beginning the movement on the night of August 25, relied upon Hood's lack of cavalry scouts to keep the secret. Thomas thought the whole affair "extra-hazardous," since it obliged the army to cut loose from its base of supplies—the depot near the Chattahoochee—and to march with only ten days' rations. But as they rode with the men, Cump showed Tom privates gathering and husking roasting ears—he had timed his march to the ripening of the corn.

To Hood came spies saying that Sherman was marching with scant supplies. Not stopping to think of the roasting ears, Hood leaped to the conclusion that Sherman had abandoned the siege . . . Wheeler had cut the Federal line . . . Sherman was starving . . . retreating! Hood telegraphed Richmond of the "great victory" and planned a civic celebration in Atlanta. Trainloads of ladies, fluttering with joy, arrived from Macon, singing songs of triumph and dreaming of a victory ball.

On to the railroad over which the happy ladies had traveled came the Federals, with Sherman saying to Thomas, "I have Atlanta as certainly as if it were in my hand."

It was the thirtieth before Hood awakened to the fact that Sherman was attacking, not retreating. Quickly he sent Hardee with two corps to Jonesboro, some twenty miles south of the city, to protect the railroad. Then, while these troops clashed with the Fifteenth Corps outside the town, Hood learned that Schofield was on the tracks at Rough and Ready, halfway between Jonesboro and Atlanta. Quickly Hood brought half of Hardee's men back to Atlanta; he was attempting Pemberton's method at Vicksburg—to defend a city and fight an open battle at the same time. Paying no attention to Atlanta, other than to assure himself that Slocum was still watching it from the trenches on its north, Sherman brought Schofield and Thomas down the railroad—twisting iron—toward Jonesboro, and sent Howard to cut the tracks south of the town. On September 1, Hardee was in Sherman's net. The Fourteenth Corps, in Thomas's army, which the profane Jefferson C. Davis, supplanting Palmer, had turned into a most aggressive unit, assailed Hardee so fiercely that Sherman cried, "They're rolling 'em up like a sheet of paper!"

Sherman kept watching the left of the line, where Stanley's Fourth Corps—one of Thomas's—was expected. If it kept its appointment no earthly power could prevent the capture of Hardee's force. Sherman sent courier after courier to cry Stanley on. Finally he sent Thomas himself, and said later that it was "the only time during the campaign I can recall seeing General Thomas urge his horse into a gallop."

Meanwhile Davis's men almost annihilated a much smaller organization known as Govan's Arkansans, and, breaking through, fell upon the flank of an equally famous Confederate brigade, Granbury's Texans. Next day the surviving Arkansans—a pitiful handful—sent a bandaged delegation to ask if the Texans had "lost confidence" in them. Granbury's remnants said, "No."

In the race between Stanley and night, Stanley lost, finding himself tangled in dense forests, and in the darkness Hardee slipped out of the bottle neck and circled south to intrench again at Lovejoy's Station, seven miles lower on the railroad. Stanley had cost Sherman a chance to establish himself as a notable leader in battle and in private Sherman was inclined to blame his lack of "dash and energy" for the enemy's escape. But in public Sherman blamed the impassable forests and said nothing against Stanley.

With such long stretches of the railroad in Union hands, it was certain that Hood must sooner or later evacuate the city. Sherman consoled himself for Hardee's escape by thinking of how his strategy had fooled Hood. The *Macon Telegraph* of November 23 reported how Sherman, talking with a Southern lady, had said:

> I played Hood a real Yankee trick that time, didn't I? You can beat us fighting, madam, but we can out-maneuver you; your generals do not work half enough; we work days and nights and spare no labor nor pains to carry out our plans.

During the night of this Thursday, September 1, that ended the fighting at Jonesboro, citizens in the North sat by their lamps reading the platform that the Democrats had adopted at their Chicago convention earlier in the week and which declared that the war must be ended "in the name of humanity, liberty, and public welfare." McClellan was the candidate, with bright prospects of victory.

That same Thursday night Lincoln sat in the White House, outside whose windows the darkness was black indeed. The draft would go into effect on Monday! In the President's desk was a memorandum, penned a week before:

> This morning, as for some days past, it seems exceedingly probable that this administration will not be reëlected.
>
> Then it will be my duty to so coöperate with the President-elect as to save the Union between the election and the inauguration; as he will have secured his election on such ground that he cannot save it afterward.

In that same darkness Sherman paced beside a campfire upon which, now and then, he absent-mindedly tossed a Georgia pine knot. He strained his ears for sounds from Atlanta twenty-six miles away. Eleven o'clock; all quiet. Sherman sent couriers to order Slocum on the north of the city to feel Hood's defenses. Midnight; muttering thunder on the north wind—cannon?—and faint shudders that might be rifle volleys? Sherman pointed his nose into the wind like a hound. He walked to a farmhouse in which lights had burned earlier in the evening. Knocks brought a sleepy farmer into the yard. Had he lived there long? Yes. Had he ever heard those noises before? Yes, that was the way it sounded when there was fighting up at Atlanta.

The low rumblings died, but Sherman, returning to his campfire, stood listening, listening—alone in the night time, when he was freest, most alive. He was painting imaginary pictures on the vast black canvas above—pictures of Hood attacking Slocum . . . pictures of Hood blowing up his magazines and leaving the city . . . pictures of Hood falling upon the flank of Sherman's own army. If he could be sure what the thunder meant, he would know what to do. If Hood was evacuating, Sherman should rouse his army and strike forward to cut off the retreat.

Four in the morning—another muttering on the horizon. Sherman sent an aide to warn Schofield to be on the alert against attack. The sounds died. Sherman paced. The sky grew gray against the pine forests to the east. Officers stirred in their blankets. Sherman heard bugles blow. The great army awakened. Fires winked in the twilight of dawn. Coffee scented the air. With daylight, Sherman pressed forward, ordering a mass attack upon Hardee. "We want to destroy our enemy," he said.

Too late. Hardee had gone. At 8 A.M. Schofield sent word that *he* had heard those noises last night and thought Hood was destroying his stores. At 10 A.M. Schofield reported that a Negro, just in from Atlanta, said Hood was evacuating the city in great confusion. But at 8 P.M. Sherman was still wondering if the rumor was true. He had sent couriers to find out, but they had not yet returned. He knew how ready soldiers were to believe what they were anxious to hear. Perhaps the bulk of Hood's army was south of him. Nothing was certain. He now moved cautiously, indeed, he ordered his generals to avoid battle: "I do not wish to waste lives by an assault." At 9:30 that night came a courier from Schofield, stating that while everything was still indefinite, all reports indicated Hood's retirement during the night. At 11:20 Sherman wrote Schofield: "Nothing positive from Atlanta, and that bothers me."

Between midnight and 6 A.M. a courier arrived with Slocum's word of victory. Slocum, hearing the noises Thursday at midnight, had crowded forward at daybreak to find the Confederate trenches empty. Federals had broken into town to see the last of Hood's men departing at the other end of the city. Slocum had telegraphed Stanton: "General Sherman has taken Atlanta." The wire was in Lincoln's hands soon after 10 P.M. Friday, September 2. On Saturday the North was rocking with joy. The President set Sunday aside as a day of thanks to the Supreme Being for the victories of Farragut in Mobile Bay and Sherman at Atlanta.

At 5:30 P.M. on Sunday Halleck was handed the first word from Sherman:

> So Atlanta is ours and fairly won. I shall not push farther on this raid, but in a day or two will move to Atlanta and give my men some rest. Since May 5th we have been in one constant battle or skirmish. . . .

Sherman had filed the message with the nearest telegraph operator at 6 A.M. on Saturday. From his bivouac he had sent the news to Thomas, who hurried over to see Slocum's note. Tom could scarcely believe his eyes. He studied it in delight, snapped his fingers, whistled, and tried, in his elephantine way, to caper. Sherman said, "He almost danced."

In the woods couriers ran with Sherman's announcement of victory. Sherman listened to the "wild hallooing and glorious laughter" of his men. They were thinking of how they had cut from the Confederacy Kentucky, Tennessee, Arkansas, Texas, Louisiana, Mississippi, Alabama —now Georgia and Florida were theirs for the marching. The Confederacy had been reduced to Virginia and the Carolinas.

Up North, boys rode horses down dirt roads between tall walls of plumed and whispering corn. They waved newspapers and shouted to gray-bearded farmers who were cutting weeds in rail-fence corners:

"Sherman's taken Atlanta! Atlanta's fallen!"

The men in fence corners threw down their scythes and waved their hats. On porches women listened to the shouting neighbor boys, then threw their aprons over their heads and ran into the house sobbing in joy.

Sherman's old enemies, the *Cincinnati Commercial* and the *New York Herald*, led the chorus of acclaim that rose. The *Herald* said his blows were "cyclopean." Soon Northern newspapers were reprinting the *Richmond Examiner's* condemnation of President Davis for his removal of Johnston from the command:

> The result is disaster at Atlanta in the very nick of time when a victory alone could save the party of Lincoln from irretrievable ruin. . . . It will obscure the prospect of peace, late so bright. It will also diffuse gloom over the South.

Secretary of State Seward was saying, "Sherman and Farragut have knocked the bottom out of the Chicago platform."

In the Army of the Potomac sat a twenty-nine-year-old officer, Charles Francis Adams, Jr., listening to the artillery salutes that Grant was firing in honor of Sherman. Scion of a patrician and intellectual family of New England, son of the American ambassador to Great Britain, grandson of one President of the United States and great-grandson of another, young Charles Francis, Jr., felt the cold blood of the Adamses grow hot in his veins. He wrote his mother:

> How superbly Sherman—Sherman "the unlucky"—has handled that army. It almost brings tears to my eyes to read of the boldness, the caution, the skill, the judgment, the profound military experience and knowledge of that movement, all resulting in its brilliant success and condensed in that one immortal line, "So Atlanta is ours and fairly won."
>
> Why should not Sherman rank only second to Gustavus, Frederick and Napoleon? . . . Unquestionably it is THE campaign of this war, not more brilliant or so complete as Vicksburg but reviewed as a whole, with its unheard-of lines of supply and unceasing opposition, it rolls along like a sonorous epic. The enemy swarms on his flank and rear like mosquitoes, they do not turn him back a day. They stand across his path, he rolls around them and forces them back. At last he brings them to bay and all observers shout, "A deadlock!"
>
> Lo, his cannon thunder in their rear and astonished and demoralized, outgeneraled and outfought, they save themselves in confessed defeat. It is superb. . . .
>
> I only look at the campaign in an artist's point of view as a poem.

40

WAR IS WAR

TO Sherman, as he took up his headquarters in Atlanta, came "the applause and thanks of the nation" as voiced by the President. Grant wrote:

> You have accomplished the most gigantic undertaking given to any general in this war, and with a skill and ability that will be acknowledged in history as unsurpassed if not unequaled.

Halleck called the campaign "the most brilliant of the war."

Reading the newspapers, which rang with hosannas for him, Sherman found that in late August the Democrats had talked of him as the dark horse upon whom their national nominating convention might unite if the leading candidate McClellan were not able to win the prize. Border State leaders were urging Sherman as the proper nominee, an anti-Abolitionist and a successful general. Two of Sherman's Kentucky friends, Leslie Coombs and James Guthrie, were convention leaders, and Guthrie, while the favorite son of his State in the early balloting, did not expect the presidential nomination. He was scheduled for the vice-presidential place.

But by the time the delegates assembled in Chicago on August 26 newspapers had printed Sherman's letter to Spooner, the Massachusetts recruiting agent, and the Sherman boom was dead. In that letter, which castigated Negro-recruiting, Sherman had spoken of slaves as unalterably free and of slavery as dead. It was to this declaration, so unpalatable to Border State delegates, that Mack, political expert of the *Cincinnati Commercial,* referred when he telegraphed his paper from Chicago on August 26:

> General Sherman had some friends here but they have all forsaken him since the publication of his letter in favor of universal emancipation.

In Atlanta, Sherman read news of his candidacy with disgust. He wrote Halleck:

> Some fool seems to have used my name. If forced to choose between the penitentiary and the White House for four years . . . I would say the penitentiary, thank you. If any committee would approach me for political preferment I doubt if I could have patience or prudence enough to preserve a decent restraint on myself and would insult the nation in my reply. . . . We as soldiers best fulfill our parts by minding our own business and I will try to do that.

None of Sherman's officers knew which of the rival candidates, Lincoln or McClellan, he favored. He would not talk politics. His silence set gossips to imagining that he was secretly working for McClellan, and soon Northern newspapers were declaring that he had pledged ninety-nine out of every hundred soldier votes to the Democratic candidate. "Pure fabrication," Sherman pronounced these rumors, when next he wrote Halleck; he was not a voter and would support neither candidate.

> I hate to express a political opinion because it is tested not by reason or general principles but by some dirty political platform. . . . Show this to the President, except this conclusion; Damn the mischievous newspapers.

But scarcely had Sherman seen his name escape the "contaminations" of the Democratic politicians before it was besooted by Republicans. At Chicago, on August 29, the Democrats had nominated McClellan for President and, eliminating Guthrie, had named for Vice President George H. Pendleton of Ohio—a move to conciliate the strong peace faction in the Northwest. And although it was obvious to astute observers that since Atlanta's fall the Democratic ticket had no real chance for success, the campaign began with such a flourish that on September 6 the Republican *New York Herald* called upon both Lincoln and Frémont to withdraw so that the two factions of the Republican party might unite on Grant for President and Sherman for Vice President: "That is the only way they can preserve the republic." And even after Vermont and Maine gave the Union party the majority in early September, the *Herald* kept declaring that the President was such "a failure in manners and administration, in manliness and management" that he should give way to one of "the men who have really proved themselves great—Grant, Sherman, Farragut."

Sherman scorned this movement, which speedily dwindled. The more he heard of politics, the closer he drew to Halleck, who he knew shared his antipathy. He wrote Old Brains on September 4:

> I owe you all I now enjoy of fame, for I had allowed myself in 1861 to sink into a perfect slough of despond, and do believe I would have run away and hid from dangers and complications that surrounded us.

He turned to Halleck in concern over the draft, which was to go into effect September 5, and which Republican leaders were begging Lincoln to postpone until after election. Unless he did so, they said, the voters would elect McClellan. On the fourth Sherman was sending Halleck a plea:

> Tomorrow is the day for the draft and I feel more interested in it than any event that ever transpired. Some of those old regiments that we had at Shiloh and Corinth have been with me ever since and some of them have lost 70% in battle. . . . They feel discouraged whereas if we could have a steady influx of recruits, the living would soon forget the dead.

To his dismay the draft was postponed for a few days on technical grounds, and newspapers published an address of the Secretary of State declaring that it would never be enforced—an utterance that provoked Halleck to write Sherman on September 16, ". . . these infernal old humbugs cannot tell the truth when it is to their interest to do so. You are right in avoiding them." On the following day Sherman telegraphed Stanton that if Lincoln modified the draft "to the extent of one man or wavers in its execution, he is gone. Even the army would vote against him." Stanton, recognizing the value of Sherman's telegram, relayed it over the Northwest as proof to politicians that conscription must be enforced.

Sherman's telegram gave Lincoln an opening of which he made quick use. For two years and more he had been worried over Indiana. That State had elected a Democratic legislature in 1862 and had taken a troublesome stand against the war. Only the Herculean toil and courage of its governor, Oliver P. Morton, had kept it among the vigorously pro-war States. Now in early September, 1864, its Sons of Liberty, its peace partisans, and its natural Democratic strength made it likely to vote Democratic in spite of the drift toward Lincoln. It would hold its State elections in October and if lost to the Administration might start an unlikely but possible stampede to McClellan. At any rate, if lost it would carry to defeat the dogged Morton. In August Speaker Colfax had been rebuffed when he had asked Sherman to let his Indiana regiments go home to vote. With twenty-nine regiments of Hoosiers in Sherman's army alone, a furlough to Indiana troops might well determine the State's issue. After Sherman had curtly refused to coöperate, Stanton had ordered home six prominent Hoosier officers—among them Colonel Benjamin Harrison, grandson of President William Henry Harrison. Sherman had seen them go North almost simultaneously with Logan and Blair, to stump Indiana and neighboring States. But the six were not, in Lincoln's mind, enough. And on September 19 he sent Sherman a gentle but insistent message:

> The State election of Indiana occurs on the 11th of October, and the loss of it, to the friends of the government, would go far toward losing the whole Union cause. The bad effect upon the November election, and especially the giving the State government to those who will oppose the war in every possible way, are too much to risk, if it can be possibly avoided.
>
> The draft proceeds, notwithstanding its strong tendency to lose us the State. Indiana is the only State voting in October whose soldiers cannot vote in the field. Anything you can safely do to let her soldiers, or any part of them, go home and vote at the State election will be greatly in point. They need not remain for the Presidential election, but may return to you at once.
>
> This is in no sense an order, but is merely intended to impress you with the importance, to the army itself, of your doing all you safely can, yourself being the judge of what you can safely do.
>
> Yours truly,
>
> A. LINCOLN.

Sherman had declared the draft more important than any other thing. Lincoln was showing him that he agreed. The Administration was putting conscription above its own interests in Indiana; would he coöperate in defeating the Hoosier Democrats who opposed the draft? It was a letter that caught Sherman as neatly as had Lincoln's concerning Hovey and Osterhaus, and placed him in a dilemma.

Whatever Sherman had in mind as to the solution of his problem was never revealed, for Hood came to his rescue. The Confederate began such impressive military moves before the Indiana election time that it was transparently unwise to detach troops from the army at Atlanta. Some Hoosier regiments from stations in the Tennessee and

Kentucky portions of Sherman's department did, however, slip across the line to vote.

Also it is unlikely that Lincoln would have pressed the matter further, for on September 19, the very day that he wrote Sherman, General Sheridan won over the Confederate Early a dramatic victory, including a spectacular bit of histrionics in the way of a twenty-mile ride to Winchester. With the Shenandoah Valley conquered, it was plain to the North that Lincoln's generals were now certain to win the war. Democratic orators who called the war a failure lost their audiences to laughter when hecklers shouted, "Sherman and Sheridan!"

To add to the Democratic rout, Lincoln persuaded Frémont to withdraw from the race, and thus brought back into Republican ranks Abolitionists and Radicals. This removal of a third ticket was accomplished by the sacrifice of Postmaster-General Blair, whose head was the price demanded by the Frémonters. Resigning, Blair stumped the Border States manfully for Lincoln and held his following in line.

To the very eve of the election Cump held aloof. On the day Indiana voted he sent John a letter denying that he was for McClellan and adding:

> . . . if government must be inflicted I suppose Lincoln is the best choice, but I am not a voter . . . not a citizen of any State unless it be Louisiana. No man should vote now unless he has a musket on his shoulder.

To his generals he said that soldiers should be the only voters.

He appreciated the arrival of his commission as major general in the regular army, but he was not content with what he had accomplished. He had, after all, failed in his primary purpose, the ruin of the Confederate Army. He had taken Atlanta and kept his opponents from reënforcing Lee, but Hood still faced him with 40,000 men. On June 30 he had written Ellen that he had "no idea of besieging Atlanta." Now that he had besieged and taken it, his words were chickens come home to roost. He must pretend, to his army at least, that the city and not the Confederate Army had been the great objective of the campaign. His troops were in no condition to resume the offensive. They had fought and marched for a hundred and twelve consecutive days, and their ranks were thin. Many men were going home, their three-year enlistment term over.

So on September 8 Sherman congratulated his troops officially and proclaimed the capture of Atlanta as having "completed the grand task which has been assigned us by our Government." And so skillfully did he spread this doctrine that soon the whole army, forgetting that they had failed to bag the army that they had set out to bag, hailed as conclusive the capture of a city that had been but an incident in Sherman's original aims.

For days prior to Atlanta's fall Sherman had considered what to do with it. To hold it along Hood's abandoned works would require a garrison of 30,000 men. Tentatively he decided to shrink the city to one fourth its area, depopulate it, and refortify it with short trenches that 7,000 soldiers could man. But he did not want to garrison it permanently with any soldiers. He had seen Halleck's folly in anchoring 10,000 men in Vicksburg and 10,000 more in Memphis, and to Old Brains he now wrote:

> Atlanta is a fortified town, was stubbornly defended, and fairly captured. As captors we have a right to it. The residence here of a poor population would compel us sooner or later to feed them or see them starve under our eyes. . . . If the people raise a howl against my barbarity and cruelty, I will answer that war is war and not popularity-seeking.

The howl was forthcoming when Sherman, arriving in the city, notified Mayor James M. Calhoun that citizens must prepare to evacuate their homes; those who wished to go north would be transported free; those who chose to go south would be hauled in Federal wagons to Rough and Ready, a station halfway to Hood's lines. When Calhoun and two aldermen protested that the people could not find shelter in the region south of the city, which was already overcrowded by refugees from upper Georgia, on September 12 Sherman answered that he granted the truth of all that they said, but he would not revoke his orders,

> . . . because they are not designed to meet the humanities of the case, but to prepare for the future struggles in which millions of good people outside of Atlanta have a deep interest.

Reading Sherman's letter, the citizens were sampling the general's letter-writing art at its best. Phrases and sentences rose powerfully from its text—

> . . . sooner or later want will compel the inhabitants to go. Why not go now . . . instead of waiting till the plunging shot of contending armies will renew the scenes of the past month? . . .
>
> You cannot qualify war in harsher terms than I will. War is cruelty and you cannot refine it. . . . I know I had no hand in making this war, and I know I will make more sacrifices today than any of you to secure peace. But you cannot have peace and division of our country. If the United States submits to a division it will not stop but will go on until we reap the fate of Mexico, which is eternal war. . . .
>
> Once admit the Union . . . I and this army become at once your pro-

tectors and supporters, shielding you from danger, let it come from what quarter it may. . . . You might as well appeal against the thunder-storm as against these terrible hardships of war. . . .

You deprecate its horrors, but did not feel them when you sent car loads of soldiers and ammunition, and molded shells and shot, to carry war into Kentucky and Tennessee, to desolate the hundreds and thousands of good people who only asked to live in peace at their old homes, and under the Government of their inheritance. . . .

I want peace, and believe it can only be reached through union and war. . . .

But, my dear sirs, when peace does come, you may call on me for any thing. Then will I share with you the last cracker, and watch with you to shield your homes and families against danger from every quarter. . . .

Now you must go . . . until the mad passions of men cool down, and allow the Union and peace once more to settle over your old homes at Atlanta. . . .

To effect the transfer of citizens, Sherman asked Hood for a truce, and on the ninth the Confederate accepted in a letter denouncing the deportation as "unprecedented" and one that "transcends in studied and ingenious cruelty all acts ever before brought to my attention in the dark history of war." Hood protested against the act "in the name of God and humanity."

On the following day Sherman made answer in words that would be printed and reprinted across the North and in England—a letter that students of Sherman's life in later years would agree was the most eloquent and vivid ever to come from his inexhaustible pen. Hood's eye met striking phrases and sentences as it passed over the pages:

It is not unprecedented; for General Johnston himself very wisely and properly removed the families all the way from Dalton down. . . . You yourself burned dwelling-houses along your parapet, and I have seen today fifty houses that you rendered uninhabitable because they stood in the way of your forts and men. You defended Atlanta on a line so close to town that every cannon-shot and many musket-shots from our line of investment, that overshot their mark, went into the habitations of women and children. General Hardee did the same at Jonesboro and General Johnston did the same, last summer, at Jackson, Mississippi. . . .

I say that it is kindness to these families of Atlanta to remove them now, at once, from scenes that women and children should not be exposed to, and the "brave people" should scorn to commit their wives and children to the rude barbarians who thus, as you say, violate the laws of war, as illustrated in the pages of its dark history.

In the name of common sense, I ask you not to appeal to a just God in such a sacrilegious manner. You who, in the midst of peace and prosperity, have plunged a nation into war—dark and cruel war—who dared and badgered us to battle, insulted our flag, seized our arsenals and forts . . . falsified the vote of Louisiana; turned loose your privateers to plunder unarmed ships; expelled Union families by the thousands, burned their houses, and declared, by an act of your Congress, the confiscation of all debts due Northern men for goods had and received!

Talk thus to the marines, but not to me, who have seen these things, and who will this day make as much sacrifice for the peace and honor of the South as the best-born Southerner among you!

If we must be enemies, let us be men and fight it out as we propose to do, and not deal in such hypocritical appeals to God and humanity. God will judge us in due time, and he will pronounce whether it be more humane to fight with a town full of women and the families of a brave people at our back, or to remove them in time to places of safety among their own friends and people.

Hood replied on the twelfth in a letter much longer than Sherman's. He denied that Johnston had depopulated villages—he had only "extended friendly aid to his unfortunate fellow-citizens who desired to flee from your fraternal embraces." He charged Sherman with violating the rules of war in not notifying Atlanta that he intended to shell it. He said that Sherman had fired into the city

for weeks . . . far and above and miles beyond my line of defense. . . . I have too good an opinion of the skill of your artillerists to credit the insinuation that they, for several weeks, unintentionally fired too high for my modest field-works.

That Hood was discussing the long-range bombardment by the siege guns while Sherman was discussing the position of Confederate works near houses in the outskirts of the town, was apparent in this exchange. Point by point Hood disputed Sherman's statements regarding the origin of the war, but as he wrote it became apparent that he could not make the arguments for the South that an abler representative could have put forth. Hood's West Point record of intellectual dullness came to the mind of officers who read his statement that Negro slaves and Indians were "with a unanimity unexampled in the history of the world, warring against your attempt to become their masters." The truth was that slaves were practically unanimous in welcoming the "Lincoln soldiers," and only a handful of Indians in the Southwest had joined the Confederate Army, and then only as a sort of adventure. Hood's declaration that not one family of Union sympathizers had been expelled from the South was a confession of rank ignorance, since both opposing forces had practiced the offense in almost numberless instances in the Border States. The debate lost its zest for Sherman when he read Hood's concluding paragraph:

> You came into our country with your army avowedly for the purpose of subjugating free white men, women and children and not only intend to rule over them, but you make negroes your allies and desire to place over us an inferior race which we have raised from barbarism to its present position. . . . You say, "Let us fight it out like men." To this my reply is . . . we will fight you to the death. Better die a thousand deaths than submit to live under you or your Government and your negro allies.

Sherman terminated the correspondence with a short note, pointing out the obvious truth that he had no Negro allies, never had used any, knew of none south of Chattanooga and even those had been introduced by another general. As to the bombardment of Atlanta, Sherman did not cite the fact, so plain in his orders of early August, that he had believed the inhabitants gone from the city. All he would say was:

> I was not bound by the laws of war to give notice of the shelling of Atlanta, a "fortified town" with magazines, arsenals, foundries and public stores. You were bound to take notice. See the books.

By "the books" Sherman perhaps referred to Article 19 of the *Instructions for the Government of Armies of the United States,* issued by the War Department on April 24, 1863:

> Commanders whenever admissible, inform the enemy of their intention to bombard a place, so that the non-combatants and especially the women and children, may be removed before the bombardment commences. But it is no infraction of the common law of war to omit thus to inform the enemy. Surprise may be a necessity.

A half-century later, the British war lawyer, J. M. Spaight, would decide that "Sherman's view as expressed in his quotation [to Hood] cannot be reconciled with the principle laid down in this article."

Hood's continuance of verbal assaults upon Sherman lost much significance when it became known that he was also berating Joe Johnston, Hardee, and other fellow Confederates for a wide variety of alleged faults. However, Spaight, studying the situation from the vantage point of time, concluded that Hood had triumphed over Sherman in a debate concerning the exchange of prisoners. When Hood suggested trading captives, Sherman agreed on condition that since the Confederates could and would place their reclaimed men immediately in the ranks, they should give him only those soldiers who belonged to his army and who were physically fit to take their places in the ranks. "I am not willing," he said, "to take equivalents belonging to other armies than my own or who belong to regiments whose times are out and who have been discharged." For the weakened invalids sent him from Andersonville, he would trade Hood noncombatants whom he had captured in Confederate railroad and munition shops of Atlanta. He had seized some thousand of these workers because "by your laws all men eligible for service are *ipso facto* soldiers . . . simply detailed soldiers," who had been as useful in factories as in the field.

Spaight decided that no rules of war justified Sherman in stipulating conditions regarding the fighting ability of prisoners, nor was he justified by precedent in "capturing even the males of fighting age in a country in which universal service is compulsory." Precedent obliged him to leave the "peaceable civil population free from the liability of capture." Sherman, in Spaight's view, "undoubtedly deviated from the accepted usage of war in this instance. An invader had no war right such as he claimed."

Yet Hood was in error, said Spaight, when he accused Sherman of inhumanity in refusing to exchange prisoners on such terms. War rules gave a commander complete justification for using his own judgment as to whether exchange was advisable. If eventual victory would be hastened by nonexchange, the larger humanity might well be served by leaving prisoners to suffer in prison pens.

By early October Sherman knew that the Administration had sanctioned his original adventures in military law. A letter from Halleck written September 28 brought the news—a long letter from which Sherman's racing eye caught high lights:

> The course you have pursued in removing rebel families from Atlanta, and in the exchange of prisoners, is fully approved by the War Department. Not only are you justified by the laws and usages of war in removing these people, but I think it was your duty to your own army to do so. . . .
>
> The safety of our armies, and a proper regard for the lives of our soldiers, require that we apply to our inexorable foes the severe rules of war. We certainly are not required to treat the so-called non-combatant rebels better than they themselves treat each other . . . they strip their own families of provisions leaving them as our army advances, to be fed by us. . . . We have fed this class of people long enough. . . .
>
> I would destroy every mill and factory within reach which I did not want for my own use. This the rebels have done. . . .
>
> I have endeavored to impress these views upon our commanders for the last two years. You are almost the only one who has properly applied them.
>
> I do not approve of . . . burning private houses. . . . That is barbarous. . . . But I approve of taking or destroying whatever may serve as supplies to us or to the enemy's army.

That Hood's charge of inhumanity had stung Sherman was apparent to the Southern bishop, Henry C. Lay, who was entertained at headquarters in Atlanta in mid-September. The bishop heard Sherman say:

> To be sure, I have made war vindictively; war is war, and you can make nothing else of it; but Hood knows as well as any one I am not brutal or inhuman.

The Atlanta campaign with its wordy aftermath had dramatized Sherman to the North as a great war leader, to Europe as a strategic genius of the first rank, and to the South as its chief anathema. Henceforth European war colleges would study his campaigns, remarking in admiration the skill with which he, driving into an enemy's country, had lost no more—and probably fewer—men than his opponents, who had fought on the defensive. To have invaded such wild country, to have fought so endlessly and to have lost no more than the 31,687 that he reported as his killed, wounded, and missing, awakened European militarists to the Americans' skill at war. Haughty professionals of the Old World would talk less, after this, of the American war as merely the scramble of two armed mobs. Johnston too was now marked abroad for generalship of high order. How many men the Confederates had lost was uncertain. Sherman estimated the number at 34,979, while the highest estimate by other students put the figure at 40,000 for each side.

Wide republication of the Sherman-Hood correspondence clarified the war's aims in countless Northern minds, the *Cincinnati Commercial* declaring that Sherman's letter was "a model of condensed history." In the Army of the Potomac, Charles Francis Adams, Jr., was writing his brother Henry, in London:

> What do you think of Sherman's letter to Hood? What a "buster" that man is. He really seems to be the most earnest and straightforward of the whole war. In him and in him alone we seem to get the glimpse of real genius. Here is the most scathing exposition of rebel nonsense of old standing which has yet enlightened the world.

It was this same scathing quality of his letters that drew to Sherman the full flood of Southern hatred. To the bitterness of military defeat he had now added the gall of rebuke. His tongue, as much as his sword, had made him the obvious symbol of all that the South felt to be "overbearing" in the North, and he was to become thereafter the convenient target for the denunciations that eased the pangs of chagrin, outrage, and despair—the same process by which the North, in similar pain, had focused its passions on Jefferson Davis.

Southerners who had known Sherman before the war wondered if this "ogre" could really be he. In Baltimore, Mrs. Annie Gilman Bower thought of the days when, with her famous clergyman father, Samuel Gilman, and her equally famous authoress mother, she had welcomed young Lieutenant Sherman to their Charleston home. She read sentences in a letter General Sherman had sent her on June 30 from Marietta:

Your welcome letter of June 18th came to me amid the sound of battle, and as you say little did I dream when I knew you, playing as a schoolgirl on Sullivan's Island beach, that I should control a vast army pointing, like the swarm of Alaric, toward the plains of the South.

Why, oh, why, is this? If I know my own heart, it beats as warmly as ever toward those kind and generous families that greeted us with such warm hospitality in days long past . . . and today . . . were any and all our cherished circle . . . to come to me as of old, the stern feelings of duty would melt as snow before a genial sun, and I believe I would strip my own children that they might be sheltered.

And yet they call me barbarian, vandal, a monster. . . . All I pretend to say, on earth as in heaven, man must submit to some arbiter. . . . I would not subjugate the South . . . but I would make every citizen of the land obey the common law, submit to the same that we do—no more, no less—our equals and not our superiors. . . . God only knows how reluctantly we accepted the issue, but once the issue joined, like in other ages, the Northern races, though slow to anger, once aroused are more terrible than the more inflammable of the South. Even yet my heart bleeds when I see the carnage of battle . . . but the very moment the men of the South say that instead of appealing to war they should have appealed to reason, to our Congress, to our courts, to religion, and to the experience of history, then will I say, peace, peace. . . . Whether I shall live to see this period is problematical, but you may, and may tell your mother and sisters that I never forgot one kind look or greeting, or ever wished to efface its remembrance, but putting on the armor of war I did it that our common country should not perish in infamy and disgrace. . . .

I hope when the clouds of anger and passion are dispersed, and truth emerges bright and clear, you and all who knew me in early years will not blush that we were once close friends. . . .

41

I CAN MAKE GEORGIA HOWL

SHERMAN walked the streets of Atlanta, happy that at last he could rule captured territory without being compelled to receive cotton-buyers and traders in and around his army. The old political interference seemed over. One trader for each of the three armies was all he would tolerate. The others—an army of carpetbaggers—had been checked by the Administration when Grant had advised that Sherman be allowed to handle affairs in his own way.

One day Sherman saw a sign over a door proclaiming the opening of an Indiana relief agency. He said to Henry Hitchcock, his new military secretary:

> I haven't any *Indiana* army down here, but a United States army. I am not going to have any man coming here to make distinctions among my men. . . . I won't have one man nursed because he is from Indiana and his next neighbor left to long and pine for what he couldn't get because he was from Ohio.

And with that he closed the Indiana depot, and stubbornly refused to weaken when Stanton, under political pressure from several governors, urged him to abandon his stand against State agencies. Sectionalism had no place in an army warring against disunion.

To the citizens of Atlanta Sherman was personally kind, if the reports in the *Macon Telegraph* and the declarations of Hood's officers, who received the deported citizens, were accurate. By September 25 Sherman was given an official list of 446 families, totaling 1,651 individuals, including slaves, who had gone south. The *Macon Telegraph* of September 13 had estimated that half of Atlanta's permanent population of 13,000 had fled before his approach. For the needy who remained in the city Sherman arranged theatrical benefits which, running for seventeen nights, raised eight thousand dollars. A Federal regiment—the First Georgia—was recruited from among Confederate deserters, most of whom claimed to be pro-Union men who had been conscripted into the enemy's service. On September 22 Zebulon B. Vance, the thirty-four-year-old Governor of North Carolina, wrote a friend that "the army in Georgia is utterly demoralized. . . . They are deserting by hundreds." He thought "the utter demoralization of the people" had arrived:

What does this show, my dear sir?

It shows what I have always believed, that the great popular heart is not now and never has been in this war.

It was a revolution of the Politicians, not the People, and was fought at first by the natural enthusiasm of our young men and has been kept going by State and sectional pride assisted by that bitterness of feeling produced by the cruelties and brutalities of the enemy. . . .

Saturday night may yet come to all of our troubles and be followed by the blessed hours of rest. God grant it.

As one who had found bitter fault with President Davis all along, Vance might have been suspected of excessive depression. But Howell Cobb, head of Georgia's militia and a believer in war to the end, had written his wife on August 19 that Georgians were "depressed, disappointed and too many of them disloyal. A little hanging would do immense good." And to Sherman in Atlanta came a certain Colonel Joshua Hill of Madison, Georgia, to sit talking all night about peace. As a former friend of John Sherman's in the Federal Congress, Hill was candid with Cump. He had seen the desolation from Resaca to Atlanta—a desolation that, incidentally, the *Indianapolis Journal* described thus:

So startling is the utter silence that even when a wild bird carols a note you look around surprised that amid such loneliness any living thing should be happy.

When Hill said that "further resistance was madness," Sherman urged him to see Georgia's governor, Joseph E. Brown, and invite him to come to Atlanta and address the citizens on peace. Sherman authorized Hill to offer Brown a proposal—if Brown would withdraw Georgia's troops from the army, Sherman would keep his men thereafter on main roads and would buy produce instead of appropriating it. Soon Hill returned to report that Brown had refused the offer on the theory that "the people were too feverish." But Sherman persisted. Another Georgian who had known John in Congress—a Mr. Foster—joined Hill in attempting to bring Sherman into conference with Vice President Stephens of the Confederacy, who was now advising friends that peace was not far away. Sherman telegraphed word of this prospect to Lincoln and in answer received strong encouragement. But Robert Toombs, that leader who had begged Davis not to fire on Sumter, warned Stephens that it would be "wrong, very, very wrong" to confer with Sherman, and the plan collapsed. To Hill Sherman said, "There is nothing left for me to do but to proceed."

A few months later Sherman would discuss his feelings at this time:

I contended at first, when we took Vicksburg, by all the rules of civilized warfare, they should have surrendered, and allowed us to restore Federal power in the land. But they did not. I claim also when we took Atlanta, that they were bound by every rule of civilized warfare to surrender their cause. It was then hopeless, and it was clear to me as daylight that they were bound to surrender and return to civil life. But they continued the war, and then I had a right, under the rules of civilized warfare, to commence a system that would make them feel the power of the Government, and cause them to succumb to our national authority. . . .

I lived among them . . . but at the same time, if their minds are not balanced so as to reason aright, we have the right to apply the rod. . . .

The question then arose in my mind, how to apply the power thus entrusted by my Government so as to produce the result—the end of war—which was all we desired; for war is only justifiable among civilized nations to produce peace.

Where to apply the rod became now a matter of friendly dispute between himself and Grant. It was to James H. Wilson, now a major general and the officer sent to him by Grant to re-form Western cavalry, that Sherman at this time gave his frankest estimate of Grant's character:

Wilson, I'm a damned sight smarter man than Grant; I know more about organization, supply and administration and about everything else than he does; but I'll tell you where he beats me and where he beats the world. He don't care a damn for what the enemy does out of his sight but it scares me like hell. I'm more nervous than he is. I am much more likely to change my orders or to countermarch my command than he is. He uses such information as he has according to his best judgment; he issues his orders and does his level best to carry them out without much reference to what is going on about him. . . .

At almost the same time Grant was telling Bishop Henry C. Lay, the Southern clergyman who was passing through his lines, that Sherman was "a most superior general—a good, kind man, too." The bishop, who had visited Sherman in Atlanta, replied, "Very unrelenting, however, in his character in walking the path marked out for himself." "Yes," said Grant, "that is his character." In the succeeding weeks Grant and the bishop were to find their estimate of Sherman far truer than Sherman would find his evaluation of Grant, for through late September, October, and early November it would be Grant who would become the apprehensive one who changed his orders, and Sherman the man who refused to be scared.

At their last meeting in Cincinnati, the preceding January, Grant had hoped that once Johnston was defeated, Sherman would hold a line running from Chattanooga to Atlanta to Mobile—a fact which Grant admitted to Halleck on October 4, saying, "When this campaign was commenced, nothing else was in contemplation . . ."

But after Farragut's fleet had won at Mobile Bay, dooming the Confederate forts to surrender, Grant suggested that Sherman march from Atlanta to Augusta, Georgia, a distance of a hundred and seventy-five miles. This would be an arduous campaign, with Hood defending every step, and it would only be possible if, as Grant proposed, Farragut and Canby sailed from Mobile and steaming up the Savannah River to Augusta, seized the city and held it as a base for Sherman's army. When this idea was abandoned, owing to the need for Canby in Missouri to repel raiders, Grant suggested that he might send down divisions from the Army of the Potomac to seize Wilmington, North Carolina, and hold it as a terminus for Sherman's march. Sherman, however, began to argue that his true objective was Savannah:

> The possession of the Savannah River is more than fatal to the possibility of Southern independence. They may stand the fall of Richmond, but not of all Georgia. . . . If you can whip Lee and I can march to the Atlantic, I think Uncle Abe will give us twenty days' leave of absence to see the young folks.

While Sherman and Grant debated, President Jefferson Davis intruded most dramatically. Across Georgia came the stout-hearted Executive, rousing his people with bold speeches. To audience after audience he announced that Hood was soon to move against Sherman's rear, and that the latter would quickly be seen fleeing northward "through slaughter," harried and hounded like Napoleon from Moscow until the Confederate banners waved "on the banks of the beautiful Ohio." Reading Davis's words in Southern newspapers, Sherman was amazed to find that the man had "lost all sense and reason," and that he should have revealed "the full key to future designs." Delighted with the information, Sherman was nevertheless irritated by the boast that he would be forced to retreat. All his adult life he had nursed a curious antipathy toward returning from a trip by the route upon which he had come. Now Davis made him doubly resolved and unrelenting in his decision to walk the path to Savannah he had laid out for himself.

Davis's announcement affected Grant differently. Immediately Sherman's superior dismissed all talk of an eastward campaign and began urging the protection of the rear. Sherman, having sent Thomas with a portion of the army to Tennessee, argued that this force, plus reserves collected in the Northwest, could protect Chattanooga and Nashville. On October 1 Sherman telegraphed Grant that if Hood dared move against the railroad, "I shall attack him," but that if Hood circled out through Alabama on a swing toward Tennessee, it would be better to let Thomas receive him, "and for me to destroy Atlanta and march across Georgia to Savannah or Charleston, breaking roads and doing irreparable damage. We cannot remain on the defensive." He said he would watch Hood closely, for the fellow was "eccentric and I cannot guess his movements as I could those of Johnston, who was a sensible man and only did sensible things."

As he wrote this telegram, Sherman learned that Hood was marching through the country parallel to the tracks. Sherman marched along the railroad, watching closely. He had strong guards in blockhouses and a division under General Corse at Rome. On October 4 signal officers, who dotted the mountain peaks, sent Sherman word that Hood was swinging in on Allatoona Pass, the chief supply depot of the region. In its warehouses were a million rations of hardtack and on either side of a deep railroad cut were two forts manned by 941 soldiers, of whom 200 were raw recruits. Behind the forts in mountain valleys were 9,000 Union cattle. It was a tense moment for Sherman. The loss of a million rations would not be ruinous—he had cared nothing for the loss of a train now and then, saying, "It is a button from my coat"—but the moral effect of Allatoona's loss would strengthen Grant's argument that he should forget the seaward march and devote himself wholly to Hood.

From mountain peaks wigwag flags sent messages across the heads of the marching enemy. Sherman summoned Corse to entrain with a brigade for Allatoona. Then at 2 P.M. on the fourth he signaled Allatoona, "Sherman is moving in force. Hold out." At 6 P.M. he signaled, "General Sherman says hold fast. We are coming." Luckily the next day dawned clear, and Sherman, riding to the signal station on Kenesaw, saw Allatoona across fourteen miles of autumnal forests that were so beautiful he longed to be able to paint them. A cotton ball of smoke hung over the distant fort. Fighting had begun.

"Find out if Corse is there," he snapped. A signal officer waved a dark flag on a pole against the bright background of the sky. (The army since the late fifties had used this system of communication, which a surgeon, Albert J. Myer, had developed in 1856 from a system of signs made with spears by hostile Indians in New Mexico.) From a shanty on Kenesaw's crest, another officer trained a telescope on Allatoona. For two and a half hours he caught nothing but glimpses of the answer as waved by a signal man from a stump in the beleaguered fort. Billows of smoke interrupted the message. Finally the officer left the telescope.

"General, I can't make anything from what I have here, C-S-H-E-H-E."

"I understand it! Corse is there all right. He'll hold out. I know the man!"

Corse was a comfort to Sherman—a slender little fellow of twenty-eight, whom no one expected to live long but whose chief ailment was evidently nothing but hypochondria. He had quit West Point at the end of his second year, emigrated to Iowa, taken up law, abandoned it for politics, then, in the words of Wilkie, the war correspondent, had "joined the army in 1861 to relieve the pain of political defeat." Bad luck had restricted him to inactive commands, and he had sought relief in religious revivals which he conducted noisily in camp. Then he had gone home on sick leave, his comrades expecting never to see him again. But he had been back for the spring campaign of 1862 and, although dismal from lack of fighting, had managed to remain until assignment to Sherman's Fifteenth Corps in the winter of 1862 had brought him the activity he craved. He had shown speed in relieving Sherman from danger at Colliersville, and had fought ferociously at Missionary Ridge, where Sherman had reported him badly wounded. The Union officer M. L. Jamison reported, however, that when Corse had been borne, "boisterous and blasphemous," from that field, Surgeon Henry R. Payne had "removed his clothes tenderly to find a little blue spot where a spent ball had struck him—nothing more."

To rescue Corse now, Sherman ordered Cox to march rapidly and to "burn every house and barn . . . so that I can see where he is all the time." Through the whole day Sherman paced the mountain top, watching the powder smoke on Allatoona and the clapboard smoke in the valley—"vast panorama," he thought it—"a beautiful day." He chafed at Cox's slow progress, he worried when at 4:15 Allatoona signaled, "General Corse is wounded. Where is General Sherman?" "Near you," he answered. ". . . Hold on—General Sherman says he is working hard for you."

The fighting on the hill was as severe as any ever to be experienced by men in Sherman's command. It had begun at eight o'clock with a bombardment from three quarters, the garrison lying behind low, inadequate breastworks. In a lull there had come to Corse a demand for surrender "to avoid a needless effusion of blood." The demand had been signed by General Samuel G. French, who as a Quaker cadet had seen how Sam Grant could harbor the loud gong of a watch in his bosom while calmly solving problems in mathematics at a West Point blackboard. Corse had answered that he was "prepared for the 'needless effusion of blood' whenever it is agreeable to you."

Promising his half-starved troops their fill of those warehouse rations, French launched a determined attack upon the forts, and when his men were repulsed shelled it frenziedly. Four attacks and a murderous sleet of lead had been withstood by four o'clock, when another pause came in the battle. French was preparing for another attack. Corse lay unconscious from a face wound; a third of his men were bleeding. Colonel Rowett, Corse's second in command, and himself badly wounded, ordered his men to hold their fire; ammunition was running low. The words "Cease firing" beat into Corse's dazed brain and he came to his feet swearing and defiant. By fitting bayonets on muskets whose barrels had burst from overheating, and giving them to the sick and the wounded who were propped against the earthworks, Corse presented a show of false strength to the onslaught. Stuffing his cannon with hatfuls of Minié balls wrapped in torn blankets, and giving the lanyards to wounded gunners to hold, the unconquerable little general prepared to die fighting. The sun was rolling low in the west and both sides prepared for the final effort.

At length the Confederates came on, trampling their slaughtered or screeching comrades. Corse waited until they were close at hand, then cried, "Fire!" The wounded cannoneers yanked hard at their lanyards. It was as though by merely pulling strings they had jerked scores of opponents inside out. In the flame that wrapped the hill, Confederates charred or fled. "The needless effusion of blood" was over; 706 of the 1,944 defenders had been killed or wounded and 799 of the 3,197 attackers had fallen.

As night fell Sherman knew that Allatoona was safe. Next morning, back on Kenesaw, he signaled, "How is Corse?" The answer came, "I am short a cheekbone and one ear but am able to whip all hell yet." Sherman's gratitude swelled. "Your head is worth more than a dozen of any I have to spare," he signaled Corse, and for days insisted that the hero remain quiet and obtain rest. When the two men met a little later, Corse's bandage was removed, revealing strangely little scar on the cheekbone and no apparent damage to the ear. Sherman said, "Corse, they came damn near missing you, didn't they?" He had seen many brave men, in the heat of battle, imagine themselves to be wounded more seriously or less seriously than was the actual case. There was no question as to Corse's courage.

Instead of allowing the battle to be interpreted in Washington as an example of Hood's strength and as such, a reason for abandoning all thought of a seaward march, Sherman seized the opportunity to offer it as proof that just such a movement was the wisest thing. He telegraphed Grant on October 9:

It will be a physical impossibility to protect the roads, now that Hood, Forrest and Wheeler and the whole batch of devils are turned loose without home or habitation.

To station the army along the road would, he said, cost the lives of 1,000 men a month, with nothing gained. Artfully he appealed to Grant's long-established conviction that troops should be mobile and aggressive rather than defensive and garrisoned. He wrote on the ninth:

Until we can repopulate Georgia, it is useless to occupy it, but the utter destruction of its roads, houses and people will cripple their military resources. . . . I can make the march and make Georgia howl!

Grant protested that it was now impossible for him to prepare a seacoast base for Sherman. This, said Sherman, was quite all right; he would strike into Georgia without a base. Grant insisted that Thomas was likely to be defeated if left with scant forces to oppose Hood. Sherman answered that Thomas's force was "ample." On October 11 Sherman wired Grant that he would "infinitely prefer" to wreck the railroad and country between Chattanooga and Atlanta, "including the latter city," then march east "smashing things to the sea." He said he hoped Hood would trail him:

. . . instead of being on the defensive, I would be on the offensive. . . . The difference in war is full twenty-five per cent. I can make Savannah, Charleston or the mouth of the Chattahoochee. . . . Answer quick as I know we will not have the telegraph long.

Evidently prior to the arrival of this telegram Grant had written Lincoln a statement of reasons for disapproving Sherman's plan. At least he sent such a wire on October 11. Then at 1 P.M. on the twelfth Grant veered completely, wiring Sherman, "On reflection, I think better of your proposition. It would be better to go south than to be forced to come north." He advised Sherman to "clean the country" of railroads, live stock, and Negroes, arming and organizing the latter.

On the morning of the thirteenth Grant found himself in a predicament. His telegram to Lincoln had been a persuasive one, and the President had agreed with it. Stanton wired Grant:

The President feels much solicitude in respect to General Sherman's proposed movement and hopes that it will be maturely considered. The objections stated in your telegram of last night impressed him with much force, and a misstep by General Sherman might be fatal to his army.

Grant's task was now to undo what he had done, and he wired the President:

> Sherman's proposition is the best that can be adopted. . . . Such an army as Sherman has, and with such a commander, is hard to corner or capture.

Pressure upon Lincoln was heavy. Halleck was dubious about Sherman's plan, and Rawlins, Grant's imperious adviser, slipped away secretly from camp to warn Lincoln of the folly into which Sherman and Grant were straying. But within three hours after reading Grant's plea for Sherman, Stanton telegraphed Sherman official approval—"Whatever results, you have the confidence and support of the Government." Halleck wired him that "the authorities are willing" for him to march to Savannah, where a fleet would be waiting with supplies.

All seemed settled. Hood, after vainly attempting to frighten a garrison at Resaca into surrendering on the ground that he would take no prisoners if forced to storm the works, veered off south. Beyond the destruction of some twenty miles of track, which was quickly repaired, he had harmed nothing. Reporters noted that Sherman, who had edged up as far as Gaylesville, held Hood in "the most inexpressible contempt," and that he was heard to say, "Damn him, if he will go to the Ohio River, I'll give him rations. . . . Let him go north, my business is down South." According to Sherman's calculations it would take Hood weeks to collect sufficient shoes to prepare his men for another campaign.

At this point, Forrest raided to the Tennessee River and captured two gunboats and five transports, a feat whose brilliance staggered the Administration in Washington, yet which left Sherman unmoved. Grant proceeded to reverse himself, telegraphing Sherman, "If you see a chance of destroying Hood's army, attend to that first, and make your other move secondary." On November 2 Sherman replied that, with his wagon trains he could never overhaul the more lightly equipped Hood—"If I turn back the whole effect of my campaign will be lost." Grant, studying Thomas's forces, and noting that Sherman was to send 14,000 men from the Army of the Tennessee in Missouri—A. J. Smith's long-absent division—to Nashville, capitulated once more and on November 2 wired Sherman to "go as you propose."

By the next day Sherman was confident that, in his absence, Thomas would see action. Beauregard, assuming the general supervision over Confederate armies in the West, was issuing proclamations to which Sherman referred in a long optimistic telegram to Halleck on November 3:

> He purposes and promises his men to invade Middle Tennessee, for the purpose of making me let go Georgia . . . I detached the Fourth Corps (General Stanley's) 15,000 strong . . . and subsequently the Twenty-third

Corps (Schofield's), 10,000, which is now on the cars moving to Nashville. This gives Thomas two full corps, and about 5,000 cavalry, and all the new troops recently sent to Tennessee, and the railroad guards with which to encounter Beauregard should he advance farther. Besides which, Thomas will have the active coöperation of the gun-boats . . . and the two divisions of Smith and Mower, en route from Missouri. I therefore feel no uneasiness as to Tennessee, and have ordered Thomas to assume the offensive in the direction of Selma, Ala. . . .

I would advise the accumulations of all troops up the Tennessee . . . subject to Thomas' orders, and that General Canby leave the Mississippi to be watched by gunboats and local garrisons, and push, with about 15,000 men, for the Alabama River and Selma. These coöperating movements would completely bewilder Beauregard, and he would burst with French despair.

Thomas, who had been heretofore dubious as to the force left him, felt confident in early November. Rawlins, collecting recruits in Missouri, telegraphed that A. J. Smith's men would start for Nashville on the tenth. This would give him another aggressive lieutenant to add to Schofield and Wilson, the last of whom Sherman was to leave behind with the bulk of the cavalry.

From Kingston Sherman ordered all stores and invalided men to be rushed from Atlanta to Chattanooga, and as the trains roared past headquarters on November 6, he sat down to write Grant a farewell letter, a sort of summary of his reasons for the long and stubborn fight that he had won against his friend:

I propose to act in such a manner against the material resources of the South as utterly to negative Davis' boasted threat. . . . If we can march a well-appointed army right through his territory, it is a demonstration to the world, foreign and domestic, that we have a power which Davis cannot resist. This may not be war but rather statesmanship, nevertheless it is overwhelming to my mind that there are thousands of people abroad and in the South who reason thus: If the North can march an army right through the South, it is proof positive that the North can prevail. . . .

Now Mr. Lincoln's election, which is assured, coupled with the conclusion thus reached, makes a complete, logical whole. Even without a battle, the result operating upon the minds of sensible men would produce fruits more compensating for the expense, trouble and risk.

In his letter he revealed that it was his old passion for unification that had determined him to march to Savannah instead of to any other point. The easiest march would be to the Gulf burning cotton; also it would be the way his sentiment would impel him, for on the route he could set free 40,000 prisoners at Andersonville. The march that would allow him to destroy his "own enemy," Hood's army, would be by way of the Chattahoochee River to Montgomery, Alabama, and thence to the Gulf. But the march that would help Grant and coördinate the major campaigns of the war would be one to the sea, then up the coast to help the Army of the Potomac finish Lee at Richmond.

Any one of the three, he admitted, might be chosen, once he had penetrated into the heart of Georgia. Something might prevent him from reaching Savannah. All he could tell Grant was, "I will not attempt to send couriers back, but trust to the Richmond papers to keep you well advised." He would start as soon as the election was over. The news of Lincoln's triumph would dismay the South, and at that precise moment Sherman would add to their consternation by bursting upon Georgia with devastation. Outside his headquarters, as he wrote, his army was being paid. The Administration, anxious for the soldier vote, was seeing to it that the paymasters arrived at the moment when they would do most good.

On November 8, as Union voters went to the polls, Sherman maintained indifference to the election. He was working at business details. He had studied the last United States Census statistics regarding those Georgia counties through which he proposed to pass. "No military expedition was ever based on sounder or surer data," he wrote Ellen. He knew what he would destroy. To General Tyler in Louisville he wrote, "The world will lose sight of me shortly and you will hear more stories than when I went to Meridian."

While his soldiers cast the votes that would be mailed to their home States to be counted in the general results, Sherman issued orders for the new campaign. The march would be long and difficult, it would lead into hostile territory, but no one need know its destination. His men could rest assured, however, that "all chances of war have been considered and provided for, as far as human sagacity can."

In confidence he indicated to Howard his destination. Showing Howard a map of North Carolina he put his finger on Goldsboro, close to the Virginia line, and near enough Lee to be a serious menace if occupied. "I hope to get there," he said.

On the ninth, when it was certain that Lincoln had been elected, Sherman gave his men more details of the march. There would be two wings: the right, composed of the Fifteenth and the Seventeenth Corps under Howard; the left, made up of the Fourteenth and the Twentieth under Slocum. Men would travel lightly, one wagon and one ambulance to a regiment, and they would "forage liberally," since the wagons would carry only ten days' provisions. Each brigade would have foraging parties to gather food "under the command of one or more discreet officers." The army would march in four parallel columns, at a pace of fifteen miles a day. On the tenth Sherman gave the order to march and sent Corse in Rome word to begin burning all property that might be useful to the enemy. Next day he wired his engineering chief, Captain Poe, in Atlanta, to start knocking down factories.

Sherman, who had once described himself as too red-haired to be patient, had in the final analysis persevered longer than the stolid Grant in their friendly tussle over the campaign, but now that success was at hand, Sherman was excited. He knew that with so many skeptical superiors in Washington, an order might come at any moment countermanding his march. He would not be free so long as the telegraph was open.

No final telegrams did Sherman send to Washington. Let sleeping dogs lie! One he sent to Thomas at midnight on the eleventh; if the enemy attacked Nashville "you will whip him out of his boots. . . . You may act on the certainty that I sally from Atlanta on the 16th instant with about 60,000 men." Again at 8 A.M. he wired Thomas asking for a message at Allatoona that night. A half-hour later he was reading an answer; Thomas did not fear the enemy under Hood:

> and if he attempts to follow you, I will follow him as far as possible. I believe I shall have enough to ruin him. . . . I am now convinced that your success will fully equal your expectations.

They were the West Point cadets again, the young comrades in Florida, the friends of Kentucky days and in the march after Shiloh—Old Tom, slow, but as always, the rock.

Major Connolly arrived in the town of Cartersville shortly after 3 P.M. to see Sherman sitting on the hotel porch sending his last message to the North. It was to Thomas and read: "Dispatch received. All right." Connolly saw telegraphers, after they had sent the telegram, break the wires at Sherman's command. At last the army was beyond recall. A weight lifted from Sherman's soul. For the first time in his life he was utterly on his own resources. Now he was free from the affectionate sponsorship of either the Salt-Boiler, Ellen, John, Turner, Graham, Halleck, or Grant.

Through the late afternoon he spurred his horse—a rapid walker—beside his marching legions. Along the railroad track gangs of pioneers waited to start the work of destruction the moment the last train from Atlanta had passed. Night fell. Trains streamed by—the flash of a headlight gleaming on shining rails . . . a spray of sparks . . . a deafening roar . . . the white glove of an engineer leaning from his cab to wave good-by to the army . . . a whistle wailing farewell. On the horizon back to the west hung a faint glow where Rome burned.

Walls of blackness ahead and overhead, and on them Sherman painting murals of a size he had never attempted before—the first pictures his wartime imagination had ever painted without dark colors . . . gigantic pictures of himself sweeping a thousand miles to draw up at Grant's side for Lee's surrender . . . pictures of the South penitent among its empty fields and charred barns . . . pictures of the whole nation quiet under the law. . . .

Out of the darkness around him, from many roads converging on Atlanta, rose the voices of his men, chanting to the tempo of their route step:

Mine eyes have seen the glory of the coming of the Lord;
He is trampling out the vintage where the grapes of wrath are stored. . .

42

THE ANGEL OF THE LORD

"THE true way to be popular with troops is not to be free and familiar with them, but to make them believe you know more than they do," Sherman had confided to the Arkansas bishop, Henry C. Lay, at Kingston on November 11. "My men believe I know everything; they are much mistaken but it gives them confidence in me." Three days later a private soldier, staring at new orders that had been posted, said, "Old Sherman's got the big head now. He has captured Atlanta and he thinks he can go wherever he pleases; and he has started out." With almost limitless faith in their commander, four corps read the bulletin and saw that the campaign would officially begin in the morning. The cavalry was to feign at Macon to the south, the left wing at Augusta to the north, then everybody was to swing in upon Milledgeville, Georgia's capital, in seven days.

Through the night privates discarded extra clothing and helped load wagons. Guards on sidewalks forced officers and men to walk in the middle of the street; Sherman wanted no arson to delay departure. At sun-up slugs of liquor were rationed, and three corps began to move; the last—the Twentieth—was to wait for Sherman's leave-taking twenty-four hours later. Before sundown on the fifteenth Sherman rode into the city, which his aide-de-camp, Major George W. Nichols, viewed with sad eyes—"Beautiful roses bloom in the gardens of fine houses, but a terrible stillness and solitude cover all, depressing the hearts of even those who were glad to destroy the city." Only the industrial district had been demolished on orders—depots, warehouses, and factories in ruins awaited the torch. Sherman had commanded that no fire be lit until he was present. But through the residence district many empty houses had yielded clapboards to soldiers who had built huts for themselves in camps outside the city. Other abandoned homes, here and there, had disappeared entirely as men took them, a board at a time, for firewood.

In the evening of the fifteenth Captain Poe and his engineers fired the downtown débris, and as the flames reached shells in the wreckage of the arsenal, explosions rattled window sashes over the deserted town. Once fire spread to dwellings nearest the industrial inferno, so that approximately 37 per cent of the city's area was in ashes when at 7 A.M. Sherman departed. That the flames did not progress further was due to the work of soldiers, toiling through the night under Poe and Sherman. A part of the spoliation later charged to Federals was admitted by General W. P. Howard, who examined the city on December 7 for Governor Brown, to have been done by civilian robbers and deserters who swarmed into the town after Sherman's departure. Citizens flocked back to their homes so quickly that by December 9 the Southern Express was accepting packages for Atlanta, and within three weeks from the disappearance of the Union army, the post office was open, newspapers were publishing, and rebuilding had begun. The burning of the city sent hate and terror across the South, and in the violence of the epithets applied to Sherman by Confederate editors was visible the secret despair that he was spreading. The *Macon Telegraph* on December 5 was calling him Judas Iscariot for having betrayed the South that had nurtured him and given him position. The editor wrote of him as if he were some supernatural power—"the spirit of a thousand fiends centered in one." Readers felt fear when they repeated the *Telegraph's* words:

> It would seem as if in him all the attributes of man were merged in the enormities of the demon, as if Heaven intended in him to manifest depths of depravity yet untouched by a fallen race. . . . Unsated still in his demoniac vengeance he sweeps over the country like a simoom of destruction.

That such criticism for the destruction of Atlanta was unwarranted was the statement of the British war lawyer J. M. Spaight in after years. "A commander," said he, "has an undoubted right to destroy such places if he cannot hold them and if they would otherwise be used by the enemy." In Spaight's view Atlanta had been unquestionably "specialized for war."

Sherman, leaving the city by the Decatur road, halted on a hill and looked back at the smoke rising to the sky. The artist in him wished for canvas upon which to paint the stupendous scene—the "extremely beautiful day" . . . the sun glancing on 55,000 gun barrels all slanted west over shoulders of men whose faces pointed east . . . on the horizon white-topped wagons following the legions, 2,500 light trucks, and 600 ambulances drawn by mules and horses.

Never before in the lifetime of America had so many covered wagons followed an eastward trail. White-tops had always flowed inland from the Atlantic shore; now the West was sending them back, and as before riflemen walked alongside looking for food and enemies. In the counter-migration were 62,000 men, 55,000 of them afoot, 5,000 on cavalry horses, 1,800 riding artillery horses or the caissons of sixty-five cannon—Western farm boys marching back into the parent East to teach the old colonies how to respect the Federal Government. As it happened, they were moving against the original colonies of the Southeast. Many of them would have marched as readily against New England, believing that Massachusetts had been as guilty as South Carolina in putting States' rights above Federal welfare. Again and again Southerners heard

> soldiers from the Northwest damn the negro as the cause of the war and say that they would rather put a bullet through an Abolitionist than a Confederate soldier.

A lean, strong army it was—predominantly ruddy of face and blue of eye. Yellow-haired Germans and dark-haired, blue-eyed Irish, Scotch, and English were the bulk of the force. A reddish blur of skin and whiskers flowed past Sherman as the troops swung by his horse. Even brunet beards had been burned red by three years' exposure to the Southern sun.

It was an army of 218 regiments—or fragments of regiments—184 of them from the West, and of these 155 from the old Northwest Territory. Ohio led with 52 regiments; Illinois had 50; Indiana, 27; Wisconsin, 13; Michigan, 10; Minnesota, 3. Iowa, settled by sons of the Northwest Territory, had 15; Missouri, 10; Kentucky, 4. From the East had come 33 regiments; New York, 16; Pennsylvania, 10; New Jersey, 3; Massachusetts and Connecticut, 2 each. One company of white Alabama Unionists rode in the cavalry. Of all these regiments, in Sherman's opinion, Wisconsin's were the best. He said:

Wisconsin kept her regiments filled with recruits, whereas other States generally filled their quotas by new regiments, and the result was we estimated a Wisconsin regiment equal to an ordinary brigade—five hundred new men added to an old and experienced regiment were more valuable than a thousand in the form of a new regiment.

Conscripts and volunteers under the high-bounty system were inferior in character and ability to the volunteers of 1861-62. Each regiment now held veterans who were still too young to vote in spite of three years' service. Each man in the Army of the Tennessee was the survivor of four who had assembled at Cairo in 1861. In the Eighty-fifth Illinois it was said:

Thirty men now formed an average company. Many of the original files of four were now a single man. Colonels were often less than thirty years of age, captains and lieutenants much younger. The army gloried in its youthful strength.

The twenty-one officers who commanded divisions, corps, and armies averaged forty years of age; at the Battle of Bull Run men in similar posts had averaged forty-six. When Sherman had joined the army in 1861, he had served among commanders who stood ten West-Pointers to three volunteers. Now his own army had for its chief officers twelve volunteers and nine West Point graduates. Did he recall how in January, 1862, he had written John, "I do not feel confident at all in volunteers. I cannot prosper with them"? Privates noted that Sherman's pets, if he had any, were Mower, Giles A. Smith, and Corse, the first of whom had been a merchant before the war, the second a carpenter, and the third a man who had left West Point in failure after one year.

As the army streamed past Sherman on his Decatur Hill, privates called, "Uncle Billy, I guess Grant is waiting for us at Richmond." The superb confidence of his men sent a wave of questioning through his mind. If he should be leading those men to defeat, all the objections of Grant, Lincoln, and Thomas would come to light and the newspapers would howl him down as a lunatic. If Thomas should fail to check Hood in Tennessee, Sherman would be to blame. Exactly three weeks before starting his campaign he had written Ellen:

In revolutions men fall and rise. Long before this war is over, much as you hear me praised now, you may hear me cursed and insulted. . . . Read history, read Coriolanus and you will see the true measure of popular applause. Grant, Sheridan and I are now the popular favorites, but neither of us will survive this war. Some other must rise greater than either of us, and he has not yet manifested himself. . . .

From his hill Sherman looked back at the copse where McPherson had died. There might have been the great man! A stab of pain. Sherman turned his horse's head to the east, flicked a spur, and rode through the field beside his singing men. In a little while he had himself in hand, and was busy showing soldiers how to twist iron. He did not fancy a special hook-and-lever contraption that Captain Poe had invented in Atlanta for the quick twisting of red-hot rails, a method producing what the men called Lincoln gimlets. Sherman felt better about the work when men lifted the rails and wrapped their glowing middles about trees, adorning the countryside with symbols of destruction. Sometimes soldiers bent rails into the letters U and S and placed them on hillsides to serve, in the language of the Fifty-fifth Illinois, "as mute reminders of the majesty of the Union cause."

On the second day Georgia began to "howl." Soldiers began to feast, white citizens to protest, and Negroes to discover how false were the stories their masters had told them of Sherman's fondness for tossing black men into fires. Noting how the "Lincoln soldiers" laughed, the shrinking Negroes rushed to them shouting, "De day ob Jubilo hab come!" and "Massa Lincum done remember us!" Pickaninnies began to turn somersaults in the dust. Sherman saw the blacks turn "simply frantic with joy"; he watched a slave girl seize a regimental flag, embrace it, and scream that she was "jumping to the feet of Jesus." At every crossroads there emerged throngs of dancing, capering, singing Negroes. Boys of the Thirty-third Massachusetts were embraced by shuffling field hands, by spruce house servants, by bandannaed mammies, and by giggling "yaller gals" whose arms brought sheepish desire to white faces. The New England boys saw blacks hanging to Sherman's stirrups, pressing their faces against his horse, and hailing him as the Angel of the Lord. Major Hitchcock saw a Negress holding a baby whose mulatto skin betrayed the white blood of its father and pointing at Sherman with the cry, "Dar's de man dat rules de world!"

For miles on either side of marching columns, Negroes pointed by day to the cloud of dust that rose over the pine trees, and at night they watched the pillar of fire that stood above the myriad campfires of the army. Preachers with rolling eyes said that Jehovah had sent that same sign to lead the Hebrew children to the Promised Land. Panting runners came to distant shanties to say that a red-bearded Moses had come to the black man, sure enough.

Northern newspapers would soon hand round the prediction that Sherman would bring out of Georgia "two able-bodied Negroes for every white soldier in his ranks." But Sherman had set his face against such a possibility. On November 8 he had forbidden his army to encumber itself with refugees—"At some future time we will be enabled to provide for the poor whites and blacks who seek to escape from bondage." And on the ninth he had stipulated that only able-bodied blacks who could serve as workers should be taken with the columns. He steadfastly ignored Grant's suggestion that he "clean the country of Negroes" and arm them. He had Negro preachers brought to him so that he might explain to the race his reasons for denying them escape: this was not the proper hour for deliverance; he had barely enough food for his army; he could not take care of them if they came along; freedom did not mean escape from toil; it meant that those who had been slaves could now work for themselves—some day, at the proper hour, they would be delivered—they must not harm their masters. "We don't want that," he kept saying.

As many as 25,000 blacks joined his columns at one time or another, yet three fourths of them turned back after a few days, overcome by weariness and homesickness. Sherman saw that his plan for using the Negro preachers was working. An exodus of Negroes might mean starvation for both white soldiers and black admirers. Tabulation of the slaves who did follow the army to the sea revealed their number as only 6,800. Of these 3,000 had been accumulated by the Army of the Tennessee and 3,800 by Slocum's wing. It was significant that the Twentieth Corps, in which were concentrated the Eastern regiments, collected practically as many blacks as did the whole Army of the Tennessee. Abolition sentiment was still stronger in Easterners than in Westerners.

Brigadier General John W. Fuller of the Seventeenth Corps saw excited Negroes line rail fences like blackbirds or minstrels as the column passed. He heard a private shout, "Boys, this is a review and there's the reviewing officer!" An aged Negro was receiving salutes with amazement and delight. To cap his wonder, there came to him a black boy on a mule to announce that another army, just as big, was marching on a neighboring road. "Dar's millions of 'em, millions!" cried the old man, standing on the fence and lifting his arms. Then, in a lower tone, he asked the soldiers, "Is dare anybody lef' up Norf?" A few days later Fuller saw him, no hat on his white wool, no shoes on his dusty feet, trying to force his wobbling legs to keep pace with the young soldier strides. When an officer asked, "Uncle, how far are you going?" the patriarch gaped in serene wonder at so strange a question. "Why," he said, "I'se jined!" Major Nichols put the question to an aged Negress walking among the cattle herds at the army's rear. She looked up with beseeching trust to say, "I'se gwine whar you gwine." A black boy, Jess, attached himself to General Hazen and delighted the staff by always protesting, when warned against pillage, that he "would sooner go to hell uphill on his knees backwards."

Negroes walked beside soldiers, proudly carrying the warriors' muskets and cooking-utensils. They sang on the march and around campfires at night; they danced and talked African jungle tongues to make the Federals laugh. They cooked rare dishes. Many Negro girls gave love gladly to white soldiers in the shadows. Conyngham thought miscegenation common. He noted how the most sensuous of the Negresses

> led luxurious lives, stowed away in baggage wagons . . . and fêted at the servants' mess at night. It would be vexatious to the Grand Turk or Brigham Young if they could only see how many of the dark houris were in the employment of officers' servants and teamsters. I have seen officers themselves very attentive to the wants of pretty octoroon girls, and provide them with horses to ride.

The correspondent of the *New York Herald* saw General Williams's black servant Tom riding like a Sultan with sixteen dark females accompanying him in harem formation. The reporter declared:

> . . . a heavy stench arose from the moving mass of the free people so heavy that the soldiers remarked that bloodhounds were no great shakes after all; the veriest idiot of a dog could not miss such a trail as that.

Conyngham saw ancient mules bearing hampers stuffed with children, "a black head with large staring eyes peeping out of a sack on one side and a ham or turkey balancing it on the other." He laughed at groups of Negresses herding little bands of pickaninnies with switches as though they were black lambs. An officer of the Seventieth Indiana wrote his wife:

> It was very touching to see the vast numbers of colored women following after us with babies in their arms, and little ones like our Anna clinging to their tattered skirts. One poor creature, while nobody was looking, hid two boys, five years old, in a wagon, intending, I suppose, that they should see the land of freedom if she couldn't. Babies tumbled from the backs of mules to which they had been told to cling, and were drowned in the swamps, while mothers stood by the roadside crying for their lost children and doubting whether to continue longer with the advancing army.

Between feeling sorrow for the tragic Negroes and laughing at the comic ones, the Federal soldiers found the first week of the march most entertaining. The Confederates gave the army no trouble. Clouds of foragers and cavalry moving on the fringe of the army prevented the enemy from discovering either its size or its destination. Confusion dominated Sherman's enemies. Although Northern newspapers had, on November 9 and 10, "given Sherman's program exactly and his strength," as Grant angrily observed, the Southern leaders persisted in believing that the invading force was from 30,000 to 35,000 in number. On the theory that all Northern descriptions were mere "Yankee blow," they refused to credit the *New York Times's* revelations on November 11 that Sherman was marching on Savannah with between 40,000 and 70,000 men, and that he would destroy Atlanta, touch Macon and reach Milledgeville in seven days.

Beauregard, who had been sent West to help Hood, moved in a fog of misinformation. For a few days he thought that Sherman could be frightened into returning to Tennessee, and to accomplish this he sent Hood marching toward Thomas. Then he struck off for Georgia, imagining that he could assemble there a force sufficient to protect the State if Sherman chose to ignore Hood. He fancied that Sherman's force of only 36,000 men could be repulsed by 17,000 Georgia militiamen, 7,000 of Wheeler's horse, and 5,000 regular infantry summoned from seacoast garrisons. Soon the optimistic Creole discovered that Sherman's army was almost twice as large as he had imagined, that Wheeler had but 3,000 riders, and that the sum total of Confederate infantry and subsidiary cavalry was but a scant 13,000, divided almost equally between Augusta and Macon.

There was magnificent courage, pure propaganda, and empty bombast all mixed in the outburst of prophecy and prediction that came from the Southern press even after November 16, when Northern newspapers printed most convincingly the fact that Sherman's army numbered 60,000. Southern leaders sent Georgia reassurances that the invader could be repulsed. In Richmond a clergyman phrased it, "God has put a hook in Sherman's nose and is leading him to destruction." On November 30 the *Macon Telegraph* voiced the general view that Sherman was in reality fleeing from Hood:

> Sooner or later his crimes will find their Nemesis. . . . The desolator of our homes, the destroyer of our property, the Attila of the west, seeks sanctuary. His shrine is the sea.

Other gazettes declared that Sherman's mules were dropping dead, that he was making desperate efforts to reach the Gulf of Mexico, and prayed that "a gulf of perdition be upon him." On November 23, when newspapers agreed that he was stalled and "in a woeful state," Sherman's columns, fat, healthy, and equipped with more stout mules than were needed, marched into Milledgeville. Completely mystifying the enemy as to his condition as well as to direction, he had brought his two columns along with coglike precision even when their extreme flanks were fifty or sixty miles apart.

He looked eastward from Georgia's capital. As he had planned, the flustered enemy had divided their forces in response to his feints. The way to Savannah lay open—no river or intrenchments to bar the way, the whole path rich in harvested cereals that President Davis had persuaded Georgians to raise instead of cotton. The sweet-potato crop was ripe and waiting to be dug. A surfeit of food was exposed and defenseless.

"Pierce the shell of the Confederacy and it's all hollow inside," said Sherman to his military secretary.

43

THE BESOM OF DESTRUCTION

TWENTY years after his march into Georgia's farm lands, Sherman described the changes war had worked in his attitude toward Southern noncombatants:

> I know that in the beginning, I, too, had the old West Point notion that pillage was a capital crime, and punished it by shooting, but the Rebels wanted us to detach a division here, a brigade there, to protect their families and property while they were fighting. . . . This was a one-sided game of war, and many of us . . . kind-hearted, fair, just and manly . . . ceased to quarrel with our own men about such minor things, and went in to subdue the enemy, leaving minor depredations to be charged up to the account of the rebels who had forced us into the war, and who deserved all they got and *more.*

From Atlanta, Sherman's 62,000 men came into the fat fields of Georgia like a glacier that levels the terrain, like the Goths migrating into Italy, like locusts devouring a land. They marched with the remorselessness of winter descending upon harvest fields. They saw that it was not for speed that they had been ordered to travel lightly. Instead of the scheduled fifteen miles a day they were making ten—half the rate at which Sherman had trained them to march. They understood that the reduction had been made to enable them to waste the resources of the regions through which they walked. The campaign would be a protracted Hallowe'en.

FROM ATLANTA TO THE SEA

Prepared by

Brvt. Brig. Gen. O. M. Poe.

Chief Engineer.

Engraved for "Sherman and His Campaigns."

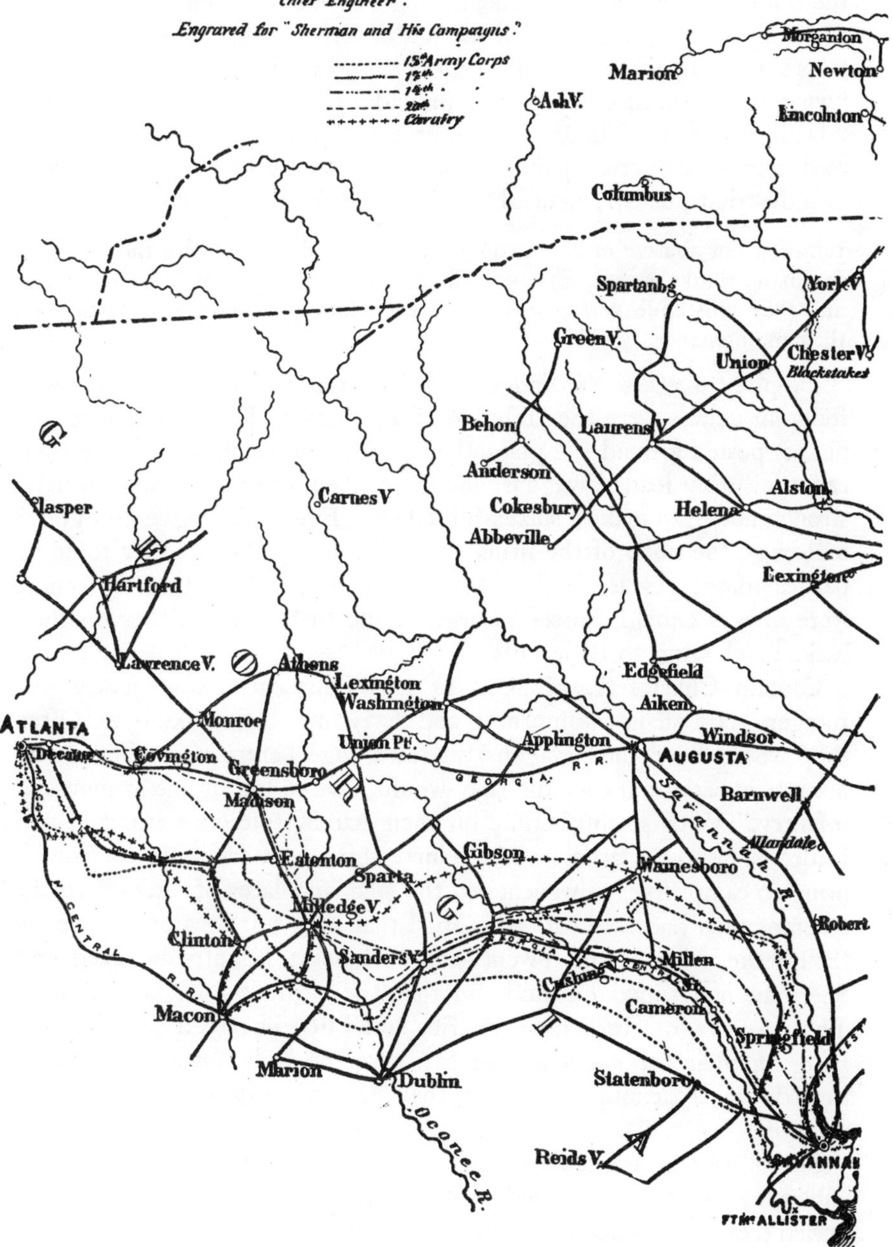

No fighting, no flanking; just foraging and twisting iron. Each morning, details of from twenty to thirty men—later extended in some commands to fifty—marched away from brigades. Their officers knew the route the column would take during their absence, and exactly where to rejoin it at sundown. Until night the foragers were at liberty to go where they liked. Sherman's orders authorized them to appropriate "whatever is needed by the command" but forbade them to enter "dwellings of inhabitants or commit any trespass" and enjoined them to discriminate "between the rich who are usually hostile, and the poor or industrious, usually neutral or friendly." Also, they must

> refrain from abusive or threatening language and may, where the officer in command thinks proper, give written certificates of the facts, but no receipts; and they will endeavor to leave with each family a reasonable portion for their maintenance.

Despite the occasional danger of being attacked by enemy horsemen, foraging details were the ambition of all soldiers. Few were killed, for pickets posted around the plantations kept good watch while their comrades leisurely loaded wagons, and if attacked, the parties were usually strong enough to make a successful defense. Even if beleaguered in farm buildings, the noise of the firing would be sure to bring other foraging parties to the rescue. And in the final event, if forced to flee, there were always enough horses to bring home the soldiers either on their backs or clinging to their tails.

Captain Charles A. Hopkins of the Thirteenth New Jersey saw foragers start off in the morning and "stay out all day like boys. Often they would have their wagons full of forage before noon, but would not return because if they did they would have to fall in line as mounted infantry." With so much time on their hands, soldiers unearthed and loaded unnecessary articles. The Thirty-third Massachusetts saw squads bring to camp "Negro wenches in the silks and laces of ladies." In the columns men had so much extra food that they left tons of it to rot in their wake. Men of the Twenty-sixth Missouri Infantry believed that Sherman had timed his raid "so that the corn was all in the crib." They saw wagons backed up to cribs and filled in record time by men lying on their backs kicking the ears into the beds. Often wagons returned rapidly enough to claim their original places in the moving columns.

Slaves usually assisted foragers in seeking out the spots where valuables or hams were buried. Captain Hopkins thought the idea of buried treasure touched boyish memories and helped men become expert poking into lawns and gardens with ramrods. An officer of the Seventieth Indiana noted

> that the times were propitious for the "poor white" to show the arrogant planter that "one man is as good as another" and for the revengeful who had cherished a grudge to get even with his neighbor.

Many soldiers observed that it was human nature for a family that had lost all its grain and live stock to seek company for its misery by explaining just where the neighbors had hidden their produce.

Sometimes brigades found difficulty in recognizing the foragers when at sundown the details came home. Through the late afternoon the columns marched between rows of wagons groaning with food and guarded by rows of men who seemed on their way to a fancy-dress ball. Here would stand an Indiana boy dressed in strange attire looted from an ancestral Georgian chest—Revolutionary regimentals, an ancient white wig, a three-cornered hat, and a sword. There would smirk a bronzed Illinois farmer decked out in the bell-crowned beaver, white trousers, and swallowtail coat of an 1830 dandy. Yonder would prance a bearded lady, an Ohio private wearing a low-necked evening gown, a pearl necklace around his throat, and by way of dramatic contrast howling humorous obscenities at the passing regiments. William Sharpe of the Seventieth Indiana saw the foragers arrive with "anything that had wheels, drawn by anything that could pull." Goats, cows, horses, mules, jackasses, drew wagons, chaises, buggies, sulkies, coaches, that were loaded with "every imaginable thing under the sun a lot of fool soldiers could take it in their heads to bring away." On top of one load of food, preserves, vegetables, baby carriages, and musical instruments Sharpe saw

> a man in an antique two-story stovepipe hat, a Revolutionary shad-belly coat, black velvet knee-breeches, legs hideously bare, who pressed to his lips a six-foot stagecoach horn and blew it as if his name was Gabriel and Judgment Day was just at hand.

From the wagons were dumped bushels of sweet potatoes. Colonel Charles D. Kerr saw one specimen three feet long, and heard men say, "The yams are so large you can sit on one end while the other roasts in the fire."

Foragers were fond of thrusting bayonets through beehives, then running at top speed toward their friends, bellowing with laughter as files of men broke ranks in fits of hysterical slapping while horses lunged and kicked. The Seventieth Indiana foragers were filling their canteens at a sorghum hogshead in a mansion one day when a

> buxom housemaid, black as night, rushed in at the command of her mistress, crying, "G'way from heah! Dese our 'lasses," at the same time striking one of the foragers on the head with an oak paddle. . . . Recovering himself he called out, "Let's baptize her, boys," and they immersed her in the syrup and let her run.

As they emerged from the cabin, the foragers of another brigade appeared with a large ox wagon.. The Seventieth awarded to them the prize supply of molasses, aided the newcomers in loading the hogshead, and then waited until it had been consumed next day before innocently mentioning that it had been used as bathwater for a Negress.

Southerners, who felt the natural emotions of despoiled householders and defeated partisans, suffered additionally from the fact that the Westerners treated the march as a huge joke. Soldiers laughed as they dragged forth heirlooms of the sacred Southern past. They bellowed when, during their stop at Georgia's capital, they found that stacks of Confederate banknotes made good kindling for coffee fires. They held their sides when they discovered in the Capitol stands of mediaeval pikes and cutlasses with which the Georgians, minus firearms, had once thought to repel the Yankees. They held a mock session in the Georgia legislative chamber, repealed secession, voted the State back into the Union, and after comic speeches appointed a committee to kick Governor Brown and President Davis upon their official buttocks. Georgians burned with outrage when foragers quoted higher law, justice, and even Scripture as they emptied smokehouses. Bluecoats departing under burdens of hams would chirp in an owner's purple face, "Sufficient unto the meal is the evil thereof."

Along with the spirit of Hallowe'en glee and a sober, hard-headed realization of the campaign's punitive purpose, there went in some organizations a hunger for vengeance. Missouri regiments, before leaving Atlanta, had heard that General Price's invasion into their home regions had brought rape to their mothers, sisters, and wives. Also some of their comrades traveling home unarmed on sick leave had been massacred by guerrillas at Centralia, Missouri. And in general the bulk of the privates in all columns felt that while they would wait to vent their full hatred upon South Carolina, the mother of secession, it was only just that Georgia should be disciplined here and now. Almost daily they heard Georgians, mainly those of the poorer classes, beg them to be sure to punish their sister State. Colonel William D. Hamilton heard one rifled farmer say, "All I ask is that when you get to South Carolina you will treat them the same way." General Hazen observed that a typical remark of Georgians was, "Why don't you go over to South Carolina and serve them this way? They started it."

As early as the second day of the march, when the troops reached unravaged sweeps of Georgian farm lands, the foragers found it difficult to keep strictly within Sherman's directions. Here was the old question of Vicksburg again: How could a soldier seize meat, as ordered, when meat was inside a house that he was ordered not to enter? Captain Conyngham decided that "to draw a line between stealing and appropriating things that might be useful to the enemy would puzzle the nicest casuist."

Stragglers in the rear and on the fringes of the army began to set fire to buildings here and there; not many buildings, but enough to prompt the issuance of new warnings by division commanders. On November 9 Sherman had laid down the general principle that in the whole army only four men, other than himself, were to be intrusted with "the power to destroy mills, houses, cotton gins, etc." These men were the corps commanders and were to follow this rule:

> In districts and neighborhoods where the army is unmolested, no destruction of such property should be permitted; but should the inhabitants burn bridges, obstruct roads, or otherwise manifest local hostility, then army commanders should order and enforce a devastation more or less relentless, according to the measure of such hostility.

Supporting this order on November 17, Giles A. Smith directed that any soldier caught committing arson should be killed. Corse ordered the arrest of such offenders. Osterhaus attempted to place guards over dwellings along the route. Davis, catching two soldiers in a cottage door with women's dresses in their hands, made the fellows don the gowns and parade with Stolen placarded on their backs.

Violence, although the exception in the first week of the march and limited to stragglers, was commoner in the left wing than in the right. Major Hitchcock, riding at Sherman's elbow with the latter organization, wrote in his diary on November 20:

> I have observed closely as far as I could and repeatedly inquired. . . . I cannot learn of any outrage of any one, or the burning of any dwelling.

He had seen Sherman order the destruction of a cotton gin because its contents might help a Confederate army, and he had seen an old barn burn by apparent accident.

On the same day Osterhaus in the left wing was assessing each pillager a month's pay, and two days later Howard was declaring that arson and looting had become so common that "hereafter any officer or man discovered in pillaging a house or burning a building without proper authority will upon sufficient proof be shot." It was while the first division of the Seventeenth Corps bivouacked at Gordon, whence Howard issued this drastic order, that one of its soldiers was court-martialed for stealing a quilt from a dwelling. Sentenced to death, the man discovered at the last moment that Howard had commuted the decree to imprisonment in the Federal penitentiary on the hot and barren Dry Tortugas Islands, off Florida.

The Army of the Tennessee, from long intimacy with Sherman, felt that it was entitled to interpret his orders with liberality, and its notions soon spread to the right wing, where on November 23 Hitchcock heard Davis, in discussing the new devastation, say that "the army believed Sherman favored and desired it and that one man when arrested told his officer so."

The temper of the whole army grew worse when, as it reached Milledgeville on November 23, there stole into its boisterous camps a few haggard men who had escaped from Andersonville Prison and who wept now at sight of food and the flag. Colonel Kerr noted that the fugitives were emaciated and had "a wild-animal stare" in their eyes. Other prisoners from Andersonville had come to the army in the past, but none with the dramatic effect of these who arrived at the moment that the fat army was gormandizing—Thanksgiving Day! Men turned from feasts of turkey, chicken, all the delicacies that foragers had assembled, to behold the ragged newcomers. Colonel Kerr observed that the sight "sickened and infuriated the men who thought of them starving in the midst of plenty." An officer of the Seventieth Indiana wrote:

> An officer may instruct, command and threaten the men, but when foraging they think of the tens of thousands of their imprisoned comrades, slowly perishing with hunger in the midst of wealth untold, barns bursting with grain and food to feed a dozen armies, and they sweep with the besom of destruction. The war is with men and property, but women are always addressed with respect and children treated with tenderness. I gave orders to foragers and doubtless other regimental commanders did the same, to shoot down anything in the form of a man engaged in unsoldier-like deeds.

To the army at Milledgeville there also came stories of barbarities by Wheeler's cavalrymen. Kilpatrick reported to Sherman that after his skirmishes with Wheeler, the enemy had given captured Yankees the choice of being slaughtered or taking the oath of allegiance to the Confederacy. The rumor went through the camps that several of their comrades, captured in a brush near Macon, had had their throats cut. Two of these survived, so it was said, and had rejoined the army saying that their escape was only due to the fact that the "Rebs had sliced their throats too high up."

It angered the Federals to hear that a few days earlier Governor Brown had released some hundred convicts from the penitentiary on their promise that they would fight the Yankees. But of all the influences that developed at Milledgeville, the most tragic for Georgia was the discovery in its newspapers that Confederate editors and leaders, civic, military, and clerical, had been calling upon noncombatants to bushwhack the invading army. Having seen no newspapers since leaving Atlanta, the army and its general were both amused and incensed by what they now read. In black and white was the evidence that at the word of Sherman's eastward march the Confederate leaders had begun fluttering like mother birds at the approach of a plow, and their newspapers flapped like wings in the plowman's face.

Occupying the deserted home of Governor Brown in Milledgeville, Sherman saw by various Southern journals that on November 18 Jefferson Davis had advised Howell Cobb, the Georgia militia general and statesman, to put Negroes to blocking roads, and to secure from the Augusta arsenal special shells and bury them where they would explode at the pressure of marching men. Sherman saw that Beauregard at Corinth had wired the people of Georgia:

> Arise for the defense of your native soil! . . . Rally around your patriotic Governor and gallant soldiers. Obstruct and destroy all the roads in Sherman's front, flank, and rear, and his army will soon starve in your midst.

From Richmond, Senator Benjamin H. Hill and six Georgia Congressmen were telegraphing frantic words:

> Let every man fly to arms— Every citizen with his gun and every negro with his spade and ax, can do the work of a soldier. Remove your negroes, horses, cattle and provisions and burn what you cannot carry— Assail the invader. . . .

The Confederate Government, through James A. Seddon, Secretary of War, was endorsing the great bushwhacking campaign, and Robert E. Lee was writing Davis, "The population must turn out." The *Augusta Constitutionalist* was crying:

> The opportunity is ours. The hand of God is in it. . . . Let the invader find the desolation he would leave behind, staring him in the face. . . .

The *Savannah Daily Morning News* demanded that old and young attack the Yankees who were "sprawling all over the country . . . those who are not willing to surrender can be beautifully bushwhacked."

Brave though it might be, this clamor for civilian resistance was tragic folly, resulting in nothing but ruin for many Georgia buildings that would otherwise have escaped official condemnation. And while farmers could not obstruct enough roads to delay the army, they were prompted to work enough mischief to call forth Sherman's severity. The official appeals revealed too much hysteria to convince war-sick Georgians that they could gain anything by rising en masse, and human nature was too strong to allow farmers to destroy their own grain. For the most part, Georgians refused to resist the invaders and those who remained at home hoped to persuade the foragers to spare a part of their produce. Yet there were enough Georgians at work felling trees across roads, burning forage and bridges, to justify Sherman, in his opinion, in enforcing his orders for "a devastation more or less relentless." A man savage of heart would have found in the Milledgeville newspapers excuse for ordering not only wholesale destruction of property but also the imprisonment if not execution of citizens.

Before commencing his march to the Atlantic, Sherman had written Sheridan:

> I am satisfied, and have been all the time, that the problem of war consists in the awful fact that the present class of men who rule the South must be killed outright rather than in the conquest of territory.

That the letter had been written in wild mood was apparent from his past actions and it was doubly obvious now when, faced with almost universal clamor for noncombatant resistance, he refused to consider violence to the persons of Southern citizens. The *Richmond Enquirer*, citing on December 6 how Napoleon had shot Spanish peasants who had fired upon his men, revealed the Southern fear that Sherman might adopt the same course. But Sherman merely reissued his orders of November 9, directing that whenever obstructions were put in the army's path

> then the commanding officer of the troops present on the spot will deal harshly with the inhabitants near by, to show them that it is to their interest not to impede our movements.

Harshness, as he interpreted it, meant that "if the enemy burn forage and corn on our route, houses, barns and cotton gins must also be burned to keep them company."

Major Hitchcock saw the workings of Sherman's order on the day that the army marched out of Milledgeville, heading for Savannah, a hundred and seventy-five miles away. Finding a bridge in ashes at Buffalo Creek, Sherman ordered the destruction of a near-by house belonging to the farmer charged with the offense. Hitchcock, young, religious, and righteous, argued that the householder should be proved guilty before suffering punishment. "Well, let him look to his own people," Sherman answered. "If they find that their burning bridges only destroys their own citizens' houses, they'll stop it. . . . In war everything is right that prevents anything. If bridges are burned I have a right to burn all houses near. . . ."

As a lawyer, Hitchcock began to understand that an army in transit had no time to collect evidence, hold trials, or scatter its force by posting guards over houses. Sherman explained this to him one night after having refused earlier in the day an old woman's request for protection. "I'll have to harden my heart to these things," he said. "That poor woman today—how could I help her? There's no help for it. The soldiers will take all she has. Jeff Davis is responsible for all this." To another old woman Sherman sent back coffee and supplies because he feared she had been stripped of food.

Ever since leaving Atlanta, Hitchcock had shrunk from Sherman's psychology of war. Born in Alabama of parents who had hailed from the North, reared in Tennessee and Missouri, educated at Yale, and practicing law in St. Louis, the major had strong sympathy for the Southern people mixed with his devotion to the Union. In Milledgeville on November 23 he had written in his diary:

> I am bound to say I think Sherman lacking in enforcing discipline. Brilliant and daring, fertile, rapid and terrible, he does not seem to me to carry out things in this respect.

But Sherman's words at the Buffalo Creek bridge had opened his eyes, and that night he wrote that there was nothing to do but make war "so terrible that when peace comes it will *last*." His eyes opened wider on the following day when he heard Sherman vow to burn the town of Sandersville because the Union advance guard had been fired upon from street corners. But when Sherman learned that the riflemen had been Wheeler's regulars, he canceled the order except in the case of the courthouse, which had been fortified, and rode away saying to citizens, "I don't war on women and children." Hitchcock told his diary, "The General would be justified by laws of war in destroying the whole town."

To the major Sherman said that he hoped the Confederates would catch and kill Union stragglers; that for the first two years of war he himself had done as much as any man against pillaging; and that he had "personally beat and kicked men out of yards for merely going inside." He said that "he would not take the same trouble now"—regimental and company officers must enforce orders against looting; "I have been three years fighting stragglers and they are harder to conquer than the enemy."

At the end of two weeks at Sherman's side, Hitchcock recognized his leader's purpose as one that would

> produce among the people of Georgia a thorough conviction of the personal misery which attends war and of the utter helplessness and inability of their rulers to protect them.

And the youth, in his new, sad wisdom inscribed in his diary the belief that Sherman's way was the only path to victory.

> It is terrible to consume and destroy the sustenance of thousands of people, and most sad and distressing in itself to see and hear the terror and grief of these women and children. But personally they are protected and their dwellings are not destroyed. . . . It is mercy in the end.

He noted that Georgia women had been frightened cruelly by newspaper reports that Sherman's men were ravishers and by descriptions of a licentious ball that white officers and Negresses were said to have enjoyed in Milledgeville. This "Milledgeville myth" was widely republished across North and South until the *Richmond Whig* on January 6, 1865, officially put it to rest by reporting that Beauregard, visiting the Georgia capital after Sherman's departure, pronounced it pure fiction.

Those Southern newspapers which accused Sherman's men of rapine were strikingly deficient in citing anything like names or addresses of authorities for the charges. Union soldiers grew angry when in the *Macon Telegraph* of December 17 they read wholesale accusations that numbers of Southern women had fallen victim "to the lustful appetites of the hell-hounds" and

> that the cesspools of Northern infamy and corruption have been dredged to their vilest dregs in order to collect the infamous spawn of perdition sent out to despoil our country.

Sherman, wiser in the ways of war propaganda than his men, paid no heed to such ferocity as that which the *Telegraph* of the same date vented upon him in its insistence that his reputation "will be the fame of the ravisher, the incendiary and the thief" and that he owned a "hyena soul that lurks in the foul mass of corruption which has shaped itself into humanity."

Sherman knew of but two cases of rape among his soldiers in 1864-65; Hitchcock declared it—and murder—unknown during the campaigns. Cox thought rape "nearly unknown," and the testimony of many other responsible officers, as well as that of any number of private soldiers, supported this view. Many Southern scholars, examining the evidence one and two generations later, agreed with Cox's verdict. It was true that the fiery tongues of Southern women often provoked foragers to show their authority by rough language and to loot houses that might otherwise have gone unmolested. Stragglers were known to lock scolding women in closets, and to take jewelry from their persons, but the regularly detailed forager was characteristically amused by the spunk of Confederate girls and found amusement in teasing them. Sometimes soldiers lectured indignant housewives. Colonel William D. Hamilton of the Ninth Ohio Cavalry overheard such a reproof:

> You, in wild enthusiasm, urge young men to the battlefield where men are being killed by the thousand, while you stay at home and sing "The Bonnie Blue Flag"; but you set up a howl when you see the Yankees down here getting your chickens. Many of your young men have told us that they are tired of war and would quit, but you women would shame them and drive them back.

It was commonly believed in Sherman's army that the Confederacy would collapse if the women would stop prodding the men to further battle.

The Westerners never ceased to be amazed at finding how widely the Georgia population believed the myth that the Yankees killed Negroes and white male children. Upon setting fire to barns and corncribs foragers sometimes learned that small boys had been secreted therein. Then there would be hubbub, indeed, with disgusted soldiers plunging into the smoke to drag forth blubbering youngsters and with women sobbing that they had heard "you-uns killed our little boys."

As a matter of fact the soldiers were so friendly that officers had to be alert to keep them from adopting orphans. Charles E. Belknap, one of the marchers, knew of a squad of men who discovered in a wretched cabin two girls of five and three years "nearly starved and so dirty that it was thought they were darkies." Dressed in cotton grain bags with holes for arms and necks, the infants were shivering and "as shy as young partridges." Heating water, the men bathed and fed the infants, combed their hair, and coaxed their smiles. "Mamma gone," was all the available information concerning parents, and when none of the neighbors admitted knowing who the children were, the soldiers brought them to camp, dressed them in finery plundered from the aristocracy, and carried them on their backs during the long march. At night the babies slept in the arms of fathers who dreamed of their own children at home, and at the end of the campaign a lieutenant going back on sick leave took them North, where they were reared to maturity. Yet in regions outside the sixty-mile swath cut by the Federal marchers, there grew up a generation of Georgians who devoutly believed that Sherman's men were demons as insensate as any in mythology.

Federal officers who admitted with frank shame that outrages were committed agreed that the vast majority were perpetrated not by the regular foragers but by the stragglers who, as the march progressed, developed into a definite class—hobo soldiers or, as they were originally known, bummers. Separated from their commands and rarely reporting to superior officers, this class drifted parallel to the columns, a tatterdemalion, self-sufficient cloud of riders, mounted on captured horses. Living well and taking what they liked, they skirmished fearlessly with Wheeler's cavalrymen and kept themselves well informed on enemy movements. If interesting manoeuvers were seen, they conscientiously galloped into the columns and gave warning, doing it so often that the army believed Sherman tolerated them on this account. Free from supervision, they were occasionally cruel, choking aged planters to secure the secrets of hidden plate and jewelry, dancing on polished floors to the music of pianos played by gifted comrades, and before departing smashing the instrument with musket butts. It amused them to drag feather beds into open fields and scatter the contents like snow. They were known to frighten women, although convincing evidence of rapine among even so lawless a class was absent. Here and there vagrant Georgians, professing pro-Unionism, joined them for sport.

Often the bummers were confused with the bands of Southern freebooters, deserters, liberated convicts, and drifters who, posing as Wheeler's cavalry, raided the same countryside. That the latter were as destructive as Union foragers was widely charged by responsible Georgians, Governor Brown and Beauregard criticizing their depredations. In August Robert Toombs had written Vice President Stephens:

> I hope to God he [Wheeler] will never get back to Georgia. . . . His band consumes more than the whole army beside and will accelerate the evil day.

The *Charleston Mercury* of January 14 published a letter from a citizen to Seddon, Confederate Secretary of War, describing how Wheeler's men

> ride into camp with all sorts of plunder. Private houses are visited, carpets, blankets and other furniture they can lay their hands on are taken by force in the presence of their owners.

As the march progressed, Union bummers found their name appropriated by all foragers, the word growing in respectability until Sherman, at the end of the war, would speak jocularly of himself as an old bummer.

To prevent the killing of citizens as well as to conserve ammunition, foragers were forbidden to discharge their muskets except at armed assailants. Frank Blair ordered that his men be fined fifty cents for every cartridge expended unnecessarily. The universal order was that live stock be killed with axes or bayonets. Kilpatrick's orders read: ". . . let men catch and kill their hogs with sabers, a weapon that can be used equally as well to kill hogs as Rebels." It was Little Kil's thrift in powder that produced an olfactory horror on November 25, when after salvaging needed saddle and harness horses from a roundup he ordered the heads of the rest to be blanketed and then struck between the ears with axes. Soon five hundred horses were dead around the mansion where Kilpatrick made his headquarters and the owner, appearing on his veranda, threw up his hands with the cry, "My God, I'll have to move away!" Ammunition was frequently expended on hound dogs, for the soldiers detested them as the trackers and bayers of runaway Negroes and escaping Union prisoners.

The army, as it plowed onward, accumulated an extraordinary assortment of pets: lambs, raccoons, opossums, donkey colts, cats, nontrailing dogs, and hundreds of gamecocks. These roosters, riding on wagons, cannon, or the shoulders of the men, crowed lustily at each other and when night fell fought for the honor of companies and regiments.

Day and night, the army frolicked. Sherman at Milledgeville had officially reduced daily marches to ten miles so that railroads could be more thoroughly destroyed, and with leisure and food both so abundant, men grew fatter and more good-natured as they progressed. Understanding that they were headed for the Atlantic shore, the midland boys talked of the distant sea, which so few of them had seen. They reminded scholarly onlookers of those Grecian warriors who, after long years of inland campaignings, had approached the Mediterranean with cries of "*Thalassa! Thalassa!*"

Weary of turkey, chicken, lamb, and beefsteak, they dreamed of oysters awaiting them at the sea—oysters fried, stewed, and on the half-shell. To Ohio, Illinois, and Indiana boys, who had known only the tinned variety of oysters, the thought of fresh raw bivalves came with an adventurous glow. Early in the march they had eaten so many peanuts that many would never be able to look a goober in the face again as long as they lived. A sample menu of a meal in the camp of the Thirty-third Massachusetts was "Beefsteak, porksteak, broiled chicken, sweet potatoes, radishes, honey." When wagons were overflowing with food, soldiers sometimes marched with hams or quarters of fresh pork on their bayonets.

Knowledge that they were splitting as well as exhausting the Confederacy added to the manifold delights of the marchers. They were remarkably healthy, medical officers of the Army of the Tennessee, for instance, reporting that in the whole march less than 2 per cent, including wounded, were unfit for duty. Sherman was proving on a grand scale the truth of his earlier observation that men were healthier on the march than in camps. The zest of living off the country, the endless variety of food, the very knowledge that many regiments had no need to break open a single package of the food with which they had started from Atlanta, all served to make men sing and caper.

They looked at the herds of cattle with which they had set out from Atlanta, herds that had increased rather than shrunk in size. Sherman wrote Grant later that he had started with five thousand cattle and ended with ten thousand. Footsore soldiers rode captured horses in the rear of regiments. Sherman had ordered hundreds of horses shot to discourage laziness among the men, but every officer seemed to have three or four extra mounts.

Tirelessly Sherman roamed his camps seeing to it that the torch was put to those vehicles which he had condemned in his orders of November 23:

> All the useless wagons, ox-teams, etc., which encumber our trains should be destroyed . . . any wagon that delays the march or opens a gap in the column, no matter to whom it belongs . . .

Captain Conyngham heard an Irish private say: "When the war is over General Sherman will buy a coal mine in Pennsylvania, and occupy his spare time with smoking cigars and destroying and rebuilding railroads."

When night marches were necessary, riders galloped ahead to set rail fences afire on each side of the road, so that the men paraded under brilliant illumination. On the march they gabbled and joked, recited school recitations, and sang endlessly. They sneered at such sentiments as "We are coming, Father Abraham" and "Down with the traitor and up with the flag," saying that hymns of this type were for recruiting agents. More to their taste were comic songs: "Say, darkies, hab you seen Ol' Massa," "Benny Haven, O," or sentimental verses such as "We shall meet, but we shall miss him; there will be one vacant chair" and "We are sitting by the cottage door, brother." They enjoyed "John Brown's Body" and "The Battle Hymn of the Republic" for the matchless march time of the rhythm.

At night they washed clothes, played games with cards whose spots were almost indistinguishable, or sang with the brass bands which serenaded each other. Once men saw Sherman, sitting in the glow of his campfire, let his cigar go out while listening to a band playing "The Blue Juniata." Sherman, who could never associate names of songs with their melodies, sent an orderly to have "that tune played again." Other bands took it up, regiment after regiment sang from its bivouac, and soon it seemed that half the army was delivering an oratorio.

"Never do I recall any more agreeable sensation than the sight of our camps at night lit up by the fire of fragrant pine knots," said Sherman twenty-five years later. And to his men the memory of these bivouacs would come with nostalgia. To their deaths, which came soon or late, 62,000 men, generals and privates, would carry the thought of these marching days and feasting nights as life's highest tide.

44

A MAN DOWN SOUTH

TO the Northern populace, Sherman's seaward march was the most dramatic event of the war. The suspense was that of a crowd standing on a shore to await the reappearance of a diver. Would he come up, or would he drown? For thirty-three days there were nothing but rumors concerning him—rumors like bubbles rising to the surface. Even the erroneous descriptions of Sherman's progress in Southern newspapers stopped appearing after November 23, when Confederate editors were warned that their writings were the North's only source of information. Northern editors, grasping at straws of news, fired their readers "to look for glorious events." The glamour of exploration, adventure, and war centered around "the lost army."

The British *Army and Navy Gazette* declared:

> If Sherman has really left his army in the air and started off without a base to march from Georgia to South Carolina, he has done either one of the most brilliant or one of the most foolish things ever performed by a military leader. . . . The data on which he goes and the plan on which he acts must really place him among the great Generals or the very little ones.

The London Herald thought his campaign certain to result in either "the most tremendous disaster that ever befell an armed host" or "the very consummation of the success of sublime audacity." If he failed "he will become the scoff of mankind and the humiliation of the United

States"; if he succeeded his name would "be written upon the tablet of fame side by side with that of Napoleon and Hannibal. He will either be a Xerxes or a Xenophon."

At City Point, Virginia, where he sat facing Lee's army, Grant waited silently for his friend to "come out at salt water." If Sherman should be overwhelmed, the South might send up enough men to allow Lee to become the aggressor. Many thoughtful observers saw the ghost of Grant's future marching among Sherman's men. "Sherman is absorbing all attention," said a delegation of Philadelphians to Grant one day. "He is thundering away in the heart of the rebellion. You alone do nothing. We have come to implore you to wake up." Grant thrust a fresh cigar between his lips and walked to a match bowl that stood on the mantel. At one side sat his aide, T. S. Bowers, and General Lew Wallace. Bowers had told Wallace that whenever Grant

> was a little stumped and wants a moment to think, he always gets it by striking matches, pretending he can't get one to burn. Sometimes he spoils a bowlful, but when he has his idea clear . . . the match goes off . . . he turns and speaks.

Now while the Philadelphians stared, Grant wrecked match after match. At last there was a small blaze, and Bowers, nudging Wallace, whispered, "Listen, he's ready." Grant turned to the delegation and Wallace heard him say:

> I will take you into my confidence, provided you do not take the newspapers into your confidence. Sherman is acting by order and I am waiting on him. Just as soon as I hear he is at some one of the points designated on the seacoast I will take Richmond. Were I to move now without advices from Sherman, Lee would evacuate Richmond, taking his army somewhere South and I would have to follow him to keep him from jumping on Sherman. . . . I hope, gentlemen, you will report to your constituents how much obliged I am to General Lee for staying where he is, and be careful please to tell them that jealousy between General Sherman and me is impossible. Please smoke with me.

John Sherman waited anxiously in Washington. Once, when the papers published Southern claims that Cump had been repulsed, John asked Lincoln if it were true and if any one knew where his brother was heading.

"Oh, no," answered Lincoln, "I know the hole he went in at, but I can't tell you what hole he will come out of."

McClure, the Pennsylvania politician, thought Lincoln held "the firmest faith in Sherman as a commander." Once Lincoln electrified him by saying:

"McClure, wouldn't you like to hear something from Sherman?" McClure said that he would. "Well, I'll be hanged if I wouldn't myself," said Lincoln, laughing.

F. B. Carpenter, the painter who spent six months in the White House executing a portrait of the President, saw Lincoln upon one occasion drift off into preoccupation while shaking hands with visitors who passed him in a line. One of the callers, a friend of Lincoln, refused to pass on after receiving an absent-minded handshake, and spoke again, more loudly. Lincoln's mind came back to earth; he recognized his friend.

"How do you do?" he said, shaking the hand warmly. "How do you do? Excuse me for not noting you. I was thinking of a man down South."

The days wore on with no news from Sherman. December came. Lincoln wrote out the message that he would send to Congress on the sixth. After summarizing the military progress on all fronts, he wrote:

> The most remarkable feature of the military operations of the year is General Sherman's attempted march of 300 miles directly through the insurgent region. It tends to show a great increase of our relative strength that our General in Chief should feel able to confront and hold in check every active force of the enemy, and yet to detach a well-appointed large army to move on such an expedition. We must conclude that he feels our cause could, if need be, survive the loss of the whole detached force, while by the risk he takes a chance for the great advantage which would follow success. The result not yet being known, conjecture in regard to it is not here indulged.

But before the message went to Congress, the President ran his pen through that sentence beginning "We must conclude that he feels," and neither Congress nor the nation learned the extent of his doubts in Sherman's success. Perhaps the cancellation was done in kindness to Sherman. Perhaps it was done because on December 5 Northern newspapers were declaring, "from Southern sources that leave no room for doubt . . . Sherman has succeeded in reaching the seacoast with his entire army."

In another room in Washington sat Old Solitude, addressing the Supreme Court. He was so old, so heavy, that the justices did him the honor of inviting him to sit while delivering pleas. When Ewing heard men doubt Sherman's wisdom in making the march, he said laconically, "Cump will come out all right." John Sherman was writing Cump, "Mr. Ewing is the acknowledged Nestor of the Bar, and he has the great pride of a father in you."

In South Bend, Indiana, Ellen Sherman moved restlessly in the house she had rented near her children's schools at Notre Dame. Death was in her mind. Her mother had died the previous spring, her husband and three of her brothers were in the army, her youngest child, the baby, was ailing. Lung fever threatened it. As recently as August, she had written John Sherman that she wished to make a will,

> as the chances are that Cump and I may be taken from our children before many years. All that is in my name is a small farm in Illinois near St. Louis worth $1,000. I have $20,000 on interest and in government bonds, and $3,000 worth of property near Leavenworth.

Ellen reread the last letter Cump had written her before plunging into the depths of Georgia, a letter of lament for his lost boy Willy, his alter ego. In it he had said, "With Willy dies in me all real ambition." On December 4 the baby Charlie was buried in South Bend.

That night Sherman sat with his staff around a seven-foot stump that blazed like an enormous candle. He was telling Frank Blair that he would not attack the first of the earthworks, which his scouts had discovered in advance. There, fifty miles from Savannah, the enemy was preparing to make a stand. Sherman would flank them. Past his bivouac streamed a party of soldiers, walking home from work on the railroad. Hitchcock heard the rollicking note in their voices as they sang. They passed. From out of the distance came the music of a band playing "Thus far the Lord hath led me on." Religious officers, like Hitchcock and Howard, were glad to hear sacred music in these early days of December. A fresh clamor for vengeance had risen in the army on December 2 and 3 when troops had inspected the prison pen from which Confederates had hastily removed the inmates. General Geary summed up the emotions of his men when he reported that "the foul and fetid prison" had given "convincing proofs that the worst sufferings of our prisoners at Andersonville, at Americus and Millen were by no means exaggerated."

In the heat of war, Sherman had neither the time, the inclination, nor the opportunity to analyze the truth of prison horror tales—tales that were told with almost equal frequency about both Union and Confederate jailers. From Milledgeville he had sent General Kilpatrick riding hard to liberate the men in Millen's stockade, but the Confederate guards had been warned in time, and Kil had failed. Now on December 2, with his men cursing as they looked at the wretched "gopher holes" that their comrades had dug for themselves in the barren field of Millen's pen, Sherman ordered Kilpatrick to make "the most complete and perfect possible break of the railroad about Millen. Let it be more devilish than can be dreamed of."

The cavalry chief, crowing like a gamecock as the enemy fell back toward Savannah, sent a message to Colonel Atkins, one of his brigade commanders:

> Be bold. Times have wonderfully changed. One Yankee can run sixteen lousy Rebs. Isn't it funny? Keep your tailors, shoemakers, blacksmiths and farmers, poor cowardly devils from the North, constantly at work, and don't give the brave, chivalric and magnanimous sons of the sunny South a chance to steal, cook and eat ary a tater.

The soldiers pressed forward eagerly, some of them wearing white camellias in lapels of ragged coats, others dangling strings of long moss in their hands. Confederate cannon, up ahead, growled more in protest than in warning.

In the cold December nights Sherman kept his ears to the east. Before long some onshore wind would be bringing the sound of the sea. Hitchcock often awakened to see the general's shadow on the tent, "poking around the camp-fire . . . bare feet in slippers, red flannel drawers . . . woolen shirt, old dressing gown with blue cloth (½ cloak) cape." A significant proportion of Sherman's orders and letters were dated at or after midnight. He was always stirring before daylight, usually at three or four o'clock. He still liked to snatch cat naps in the grass, where the tramp of marching men rocked him to slumber. He wore low shoes and only one spur—a general without boots.

His sense of responsibility could not completely master his temper. Duties so heavy had improved his self-control, but there were times when he made hot-headed blunders. Hitchcock saw him grow swearing mad on December 8 when he came upon a lieutenant whose foot had been blown off by a torpedo that Confederates had buried in a country road. Hitchcock described the scene in his diary:

> Just as we came up a squad of rebel prisoners arrived under guard, whom Blair had ordered to be made to dig up the rest of the torpedoes. They were greatly alarmed—no wonder—and two of them begged Gen. S. very hard to be let off, but of course, to no purpose. He told them their people put these things there to assassinate our men instead of fighting them fair, and they must remove them; and if *they* got blown up he didn't care.

Hitchcock, Nichols, and many other officers wrote down their approval of Sherman's action. They understood the rules of war to specify that torpedoes were only in legitimate use when put in front of intrenchments or forts, which were visible warnings that defense was to be made. To plant explosives in public roads, far from fortifications, was regarded by the army as "cowardly murder." Six years after the event, Sherman would declare that it was no new thing to require prisoners to remove torpedoes buried by the enemy. Wellington did it in Spain, and history furnishes many similar instances. . . . Prisoners should be protected, but mercy is not a legitimate attribute of war. Men go to war to kill or to get killed if necessary and should expect no tenderness. . . .

But it was, I think, a much better show of tenderness for me to have the enemy do this work than to subject my own soldiers to so frightful a risk . . . they knew where the torpedoes were and could safely remove them while my men in hunting for them would be blown to pieces. The fact that every torpedo was safely removed showed my reasoning was right.

In March, 1862, General McClellan had forced Confederate prisoners to dig up mines at Yorktown, and Sheridan had done the same thing in March, 1864. Yet Sherman himself had ruled differently on June 3, 1864. At that time he had heard that Confederates were slipping in between his army and Chattanooga to plant torpedoes in his railroad, and he had written General Steedman to "order the point to be tested by a carload of prisoners, or citizens implicated, drawn by a long rope." But it had been clear to him that there was all the difference in the world between burying explosives before an army and behind it. He had phrased it:

I now decide that the use of the torpedo is justifiable in war, in advance of an army, so as to make his advance up a river or over a road more dangerous and difficult. But after the adversary has gained the country by fair warlike means then the case entirely changes.

Never did he attempt to reconcile this switch in his viewpoint occurring between June and December. He was evidently satisfied with the general sanction of his second policy by his generals. Yet war lawyers, international authorities, in later years held that Sherman, Sheridan, and McClellan had gone beyond the rules of war in forcing prisoners into such danger. Some experts agreed that the use of mines and torpedoes was "legitimate in all circumstances." The War Department, in General Order 100, issued on April 24, 1863, had specified that prisoners must be treated with humanity.

Sherman's act had two immediate results; it gave his enemies new proof of his severity, and it gave his men dramatic evidence that he was protecting them at every possible point. His officers saw him watch over their lives more than over his own. On December 10, while four corps, ranging abreast, came up to parapets that rose eight miles west of Savannah, Sherman and his staff pushed forward on foot to survey the field. Sherman's eyes, which his intimates thought hawklike, caught sight of enemy gunners pointing a cannon at the group. Ordering his aides to scatter, he pressed forward alone, exactly as he had done during the fighting at Arkansas Post. When the cannon ball came hurtling at him, he stepped quickly to one side, dodging it.

What he saw of the defenses convinced him that Savannah was too strong for a frontal attack. Hardee with 15,000 men and heavy cannon was awaiting him. He wanted to capture the city, although the main technical purpose of his march would be completed when he opened communication with the fleet at any point on the seacoast. His quickest avenue to the water front lay down the Ogeechee River, south of the city. Near its mouth, and fifteen miles from Savannah, stood Fort McAlister, and against these bastions Sherman sent the Fifteenth Corps in a fast march. Axmen dismantled houses, felled trees, and rebuilt the thousand-foot bridge that Hardee had burned, then came across it and formed for the charge.

To watch the sight, on December 13 Sherman, Charles Ewing, and several officers climbed to the top of a rice mill. Beyond the fort Sherman could now glimpse salt water—the sea at last, blue Ossabaw Sound. Couriers brought word that Negroes, while fishing in the Sound at night, had seen queer shooting stars in the sky. That meant rockets! The fleet was at hand!

As Sherman watched the Fifteenth Corps making ready at the edge of a forest, a voice shrieked in his ear, "A steamboat!" Black smokestacks and the Union flag were edging upstream. A signal flag in the prow spelled, "Who are you?"

"General Sherman," flashed back a wigwag flag on the rice-mill roof.

"Is Fort McAlister taken yet?" asked the ship.

"No, but it will be in a minute."

Charles Ewing saw Hazen's men, as if reading Sherman's signal, swarm out of the woods and walk toward the fort, which grew white with cannon smoke. From the rice mill, Captain Poe saw sharpshooters run ahead of the line, throw themselves on their bellies, and pick off enemy gunners. Suddenly Ewing saw the front line disappear from sight. Cump dropped his glasses as if unable to watch the failure of the assault. "No, by Heaven!" yelled some one beside Sherman. The charging men had merely passed across a depression in the terrain. Soon they were dancing on the ramparts, raising their flags and firing their muskets in the air.

"It's my old division," cried Sherman. "I knew they'd do it!"

They were, indeed, the same regiments he had commanded at the start of the Western war. Among them were hardened veterans of the

Fifty-third Ohio, who had run away through the peach blossoms on a Sunday morning in April, 1862. To Slocum, Sherman sent a message:

> Dear General; Take a good big drink, a long breath and then yell like the devil. The fort was carried at 4:30 P.M., the assault lasting but fifteen minutes.

In his ecstasy, he remembered a scene on a Georgia plantation a month before. He had been smoking before the fireplace, his supper eaten. Suddenly he had realized that an aged Negro was bending over him with a lighted candle and mumbling, "Well, well, and dis is Mr. Sherman! Dis nigger can't sleep tonight." Now, on the rice mill, Sherman pointed to the fort and cried, "This nigger'll have no sleep this night!" Nor did he. He visited Hazen in the fort, boarded the steamer in the river, returned to the fort, lay down to sleep, and was awakened by a messenger who said that General Foster was in the river on a steamer. Arising, he hurried down the stream in a yawl, scornful of mines. His eyes were dancing in the pale moonlight.

From the navy he received stirring news. Three of Howard's scouts, who had been sent down the Ogeechee on the ninth with dispatches to Washington, had made their way to Port Royal, South Carolina, and on the fifteenth Halleck was reading Howard's words, "We have met with perfect success thus far, troops in fine spirit and General Sherman near by."

Across the North there had been wild exuberance on the sixteenth. "He's made it!" householders called to each other on streets. "Sherman's at Savannah!" On country roads men stood up in buggies and shouted the news across snowy fields to corn-shuckers who threw red mittens at the sky.

Foster gave Sherman the Federal news. He had a full division of troops at Hilton Head, a few miles north of Savannah, as well as all the clothing, munitions, and coffee Sherman's men might need. Grant was still holding Lee at Richmond. Schofield had fought Hood at Franklin, killing or wounding 4,000 Confederates, and had drawn back to join Thomas at Nashville, and to await a finish struggle.

Next morning Foster took Sherman to Admiral Dahlgren's flagship, where, as Cump wrote Ellen, sailors "manned the yards and cheered, the highest honor at sea." In the admiral's cabin naval officers plied him with toasts, questions, and congratulations. He captured them as quickly as he had Admiral Porter on the Mississippi. They saw a landlubber whose habits were as bluff and direct as their own. They understood his march as well as their own voyages into distant seas. Immemorial kinship between sailors and landsmen who follow open roads!

The staccato voice of Sherman summarized his adventure—only two days of rain . . . good roads . . . a world of food . . . no fighting . . . "10,000 mules and horses captured" . . . the men had been "a little loose in foraging" and had "done some things they ought not to have done, yet, on the whole, they have supplied the wants of the army with as little violence as could be expected."

Sherman wrote telegrams and letters to Grant and Halleck and Meigs and Stanton. "I regard Savannah as good as gained." . . . "We have utterly destroyed over 200 miles of railroad." He urged that he be allowed to march straight north to Raleigh, destroying roads and resources, so that Lee must evacuate Richmond. He pointed to the damage done in Georgia:

> I estimate one hundred million dollars, at least twenty millions of which has inured to our advantage, and the remainder is simple waste and destruction. This may seem a hard species of warfare, but it brings the sad realities of war home to those who have been directly or indirectly instrumental in involving us in its attendant calamities.

He understood the economics and new principles of war which he had learned from Grant and perfected in Georgia. To Meigs he summed them up:

> My marches have demonstrated the great truth that armies even of vast magnitude are not tied down to bases. . . . More animals are lost to you whilst standing idle, hitched to their wagons, than during the long and seemingly hard marches into the interior. . . . I think I have personally aided your department more than any general officer in the service, by drawing liberally from the enemy, thereby injuring him financially and to the same extent helping ourselves.

A few hours after his return from the fleet to his army, Sherman saw his faithful mailman, Colonel A. H. Markland, appear with sacks of letters for the Army of the Tennessee. Sherman had sent him north from Atlanta to collect the mail and bring it to the coast, and as always Markland was on time. Now the practical colonel said, "Before leaving Washington, I was directed to take you by the hand wherever I met you and say to you for him [Lincoln], 'God bless you and the army under your command. Since cutting loose from Atlanta, my prayers and those of the nation have been for your success.' "

"I thank the President," said Sherman. "Say my army is all right." Then he sent a messenger to the signal station atop the rice mill to tell the army that the mail had come. Markland saw "a bewildering reception" as the sun went down—"a frantic sight, men snatching letters, whooping at this first touch with home."

From the ocean, which soldiers climbed trees and housetops to see, came wagons loaded with oysters. Troops stationed close to the water rushed into the surf looking for the bivalves. They pointed at sea gulls, at seaweed; they picked up shells, and stood shouting at the blue expanse. They ate like epicures. Captain Kerr noted a sample menu—"Oyster soup, oysters on the half shell, roast goose, fried oysters, rice, raisins, coffee and roast oysters."

It was a great war for Western farm boys.

PART THREE: THE PLATEAU

45

REPOSE OF THE TIGER

TWO days after the fall of Fort McAlister Sherman sat in his headquarters by the Ogeechee completing the plans that Northern newspapers described in the sentence, "Sherman is fastening a fatal girdle of veterans around Savannah." He expected to capture the city by Christmas and to start raiding northward through the Carolinas by New Year's Day.

A steamer docked in the river, and Grant's aide, Colonel Babcock, disembarked. Sherman met him outside the house. Babcock handed over a letter that Grant had written on the sixth. Sherman tore it open and read it through. Colonel Dayton, standing near, saw his chieftain "make that nervous motion of the left arm which characterized him when anything annoyed him. It seemed, for instance, as if he was pushing something away from him." "Come here, Dayton!" barked Sherman, and led the way into the house, closed the door, and began to swear and to exclaim, "Won't do it; I won't do anything of the kind!" Grant had upset Sherman's strategy for ending the war. He had written:

> I have concluded that the most important operation toward closing out the rebellion will be to close out Lee and his army. . . .
>
> My idea now is that you establish a base on the sea-coast, fortify and leave in it all your artillery and cavalry and enough infantry to protect them. . . . With the balance of your command come here by water with all dispatch. Select, yourself, the officer to leave in command, but you I want in person.

It was Grant's admission that he could not conquer Lee without Sherman and the Western army. With them he had had nothing but victory. When he had left them they had gone on irresistibly, while he after a series of costly frontal attacks and one brilliant manoeuver—the passage of the James—was still held in check by the resourceful Lee.

Sherman saw in the order the abandonment of his own scheme for ending the war, the policy of devastating property rather than life, and of reducing Southern morale rather than population—a policy that he described to Halleck on December 24:

> I attach more importance to these deep incisions into the enemy's country, because this war differs from European wars in this particular: we are not only fighting armies, but a hostile people, and must make old and young, rich and poor, feel the hard hand of war, as well as their organized armies. I know that this recent movement of mine through Georgia has had a wonderful effect in this respect. Thousands who have been deceived by their lying newspapers to believe that we were being whipped all the time now realize the truth, and have no appetite for the repetition of the same experience. To be sure, Jeff. Davis has his people under pretty good discipline, but I think faith in him is much shaken in Georgia, and before we have done with her South Carolina will not be quite so tempestuous.

Up in the Confederate capital the *Richmond Whig* a little later made a shrewd summary of Sherman's strategy when it said:

> Sherman is simply a great raider. His course is that of a bird in the air. He is conducting a novel military experiment and is testing the problem whether or not a great country can be conquered by raids.

Sherman had seen the moral effect of Atlanta's capture, and wished to shatter Georgia utterly by reducing its seaport as well. And on still another score he disapproved Grant's orders; the Western army, made up of farm boys and acclimated to life in the open air, would sicken and decline in effectiveness if cooped in transports for a sea voyage that would require a month, possibly two!

But when he had blown off steam to Dayton, Sherman set obediently to work to do as Grant wished. Collectıng steamers for the embarkation—it would require at least a hundred—he noted how slowly they arrived. This gave him a chance at Savannah. Perhaps he could capture the city before the fleet assembled. Otherwise he would be forced to leave Fort McAlister on the Ogeechee as the Union base. He attempted a quick stroke, sending Colonel Charles Ewing to Hardee on the seventeenth with a formal demand for the city's surrender, and adding:

> but should I be forced to resort to assault, or to the slower and surer process of starvation, I shall then feel justified in resorting to the harshest measures, and shall make little effort to restrain my army—burning to avenge the national wrong which they attach to Savannah and other large cities which have been so prominent in dragging our country into civil war.

To the demand he attached a copy of Hood's threat to take no prisoners; a paper sent to the Union garrison at Resaca two months before.

Sherman evidently had no copy of the insistence put upon the Federal garrison at Paducah by Forrest in March, 1864:

> If you surrender, you will be treated as prisoners of war, but if I have to storm your works, you may expect no quarter.

Like the Union commanders at Resaca and Paducah, Hardee refused to be intimidated, and rejected the demand with dignity. Indeed, officers in both armies had a fair understanding that such threats were merely bluff, and it was extremely unlikely that generals of Sherman's and Hood's standing meant what they said in such ultimatums. Veteran privates could not, in all probability, have been induced to massacre prisoners who were regularly enlisted, honorably arrayed—and white. Still, there was superb coolness in Hardee's defiance for, according to his report made to President Davis on December 21, he had only 9,089 men in the forts to oppose Sherman's 62,000.

That Sherman did not propose to waste blood in assaulting Savannah was apparent when, on receiving Hardee's refusal, he moved not to assault but to starve the defenders. Hardee's one remaining avenue for supplies was a wagon road on the far side of the city, reaching South Carolina by pontoon. To close this would compel Sherman to so scatter his forces that he would be late in embarking if transports should suddenly assemble in the river. Deciding to block the road by bringing down divisions from Foster's army at Hilton Head, Sherman steamed up the shore to make the arrangements. But before any move could be made, Hardee suddenly evacuated, on the night of the twentieth, and General Geary's blue division moved in. Savannah's mayor and aldermen, driving out to surrender the city, had their horses stolen by Confederate cavalry. Sherman, arriving in Savannah on the twenty-second, counted immense stores of ammunition among the spoils, 150 siege guns, and 25,000 bales of cotton. Subsequent inventory increased these to 250 cannon and 40,000 bales.

Chagrined at having lost the Confederate Army, as he had at Atlanta, Sherman found further irritation in the sight of a United States Treasury agent from Hilton Head already at work in the streets claiming property. Sharply Sherman warned him that the army was in charge and that the Treasury could have what the soldiers didn't need. The agent, A. G. Browne, deftly avoided a quarrel and suggested a happy thought that had not occurred to Sherman—a ship was on the point of sailing North. Why not send a telegram to Lincoln, presenting him with Savannah as a Christmas gift? Sherman heard Browne say, "The President particularly enjoys such pleasantry." The telegram, dropped off at a station en route, would reach Washington by the twenty-fourth or twenty-fifth. Sherman, taking Browne's advice, wrote Lincoln the message:

I beg to present you as a Christmas gift, the city of Savannah, with one hundred and fifty heavy guns and plenty of ammunition, also about twenty-five thousand bales of cotton.

This note would be republished countless times as an example of how intimate Sherman and Lincoln were during the war. However, it did strike home in the perplexed mind of Lincoln, who was full of gloom at the lack of victory on the Richmond front. Receiving the telegram on Christmas Eve, the President gave it to the North on Christmas morning. A week before he had issued the news that Thomas had finally crushed Hood at Nashville. Now he heard the Union States review the glorious concert of the Western armies, a concert more thrilling than that inspired by Chattanooga, when Grant had been the star of the West. On the day after Christmas, Lincoln wrote out his thanks to Sherman and sent it South by General Logan, who was departing to rejoin his Fifteenth Corps:

My Dear General Sherman:

Many, many thanks for your Christmas gift—the capture of Savannah.

When you were about to leave Atlanta for the Atlantic coast, I was *anxious*, if not fearful; but feeling you were the better judge, and remembering that "nothing risked nothing gained," I did not interfere. Now the undertaking being a success, the honor is all yours, for I believe none of us went further than to acquiesce. And taking the work of General Thomas into the count, as it should be taken, it is indeed a great success.

Not only does it afford the obvious and immediate military advantages, but in showing to the world that your army could be divided, putting the stronger part to an important new service, and yet leaving enough to vanquish the old opposing forces of the whole—Hood's army—it brings those who sat in darkness to see a great light.

But what next? I suppose it will be safe if I leave General Grant and yourself to decide.

Please make my grateful acknowledgments to your whole army, officers and men.

Yours very truly,

A. Lincoln.

It was the President's glad admission that since the coming of Grant and Sherman to power he had no more need to carry the military burden alone—planning campaigns, changing commanders, suffering the dread suspicion of this general's energy or that general's loyalty.

When Logan arrived with the letter, Sherman learned how nearly Thomas had come to disgrace at Nashville. For his finish fight with

Hood, Tom had taken so much time in recruiting his force that Grant had grown angry and, receiving no satisfactory answers to his demands for action, had sent Logan west to assume command of the Army of the Cumberland. Reaching the vicinity, Logan had discovered that Thomas had been waiting for a glare of ice to melt, and now that warm winds were blowing was preparing to advance through the mud. In generosity, Logan had kept Grant's order in his pocket—and himself in the background—so that Thomas might win and receive full credit for the victory.

From Grant's and Halleck's letters, Sherman learned that the Administration, however much relieved by Thomas's victory, was disappointed at his sloth in not hounding the remnants of Hood's army. Halleck was writing:

> Thomas is too slow for an effective pursuit. Moreover he will not live on the enemy. He is himself opposed to a winter campaign. . . . It is useless to talk of putting any of our armies into winter quarters . . . the financial condition of the country will not permit it. Those troops required for defense must move into the enemy's country and live on it.

Owing so much to Old Tom for the victory that justified his own march to the sea, Sherman would not join in criticizing him, but he was annoyed that Thomas had failed to obey his orders. Before they had parted in November Cump had told Tom to invade Alabama, once he had met and mastered Hood. Such action would prevent the remnants of Hood's army from coming to the Carolinas to face Sherman's northward raid. Now Sherman urged Grant to detach Schofield from Thomas's army and send him on a raid that would "tear out the heart of Alabama and prevent the farmers planting corn."

It was upon Halleck that Sherman concentrated his pleas for the abandonment of Grant's plan to ship the Western army north by steamer. One note ran:

> I think the time has come now when we should attempt the boldest moves, and my experience is, that they are easier of execution than the more timid ones. . . . I think our campaign of the last month, as well as every step I take from this point northward, is as much a direct attack upon Lee's army as though we are operating within the sound of his artillery.

Halleck needed no persuasions on this score. When Grant arrived at Washington on December 18 to hear the details of Thomas's victory, which had been won the previous day, he found Halleck arguing that Sherman should be allowed to make as his next move "another wide swath through the center of the Confederacy." Before night Grant wrote Sherman that the turn of affairs at Nashville, plus the news that it would take two months for the proposed sea voyage, had changed the situation. He might go ahead as he had planned. To Halleck Grant had already written:

> It is refreshing to see a commander, after a campaign of seven months' duration, ready for still further operations and without wanting any outfit or rest.

To listeners Grant praised Sherman steadily in spite of the growing demands that he give way to Sherman as general in chief. A bill was introduced in Congress to raise Sherman to Grant's rank of lieutenant general and divide control of the armies. Cump, hearing of this bill, fired a volley of ink at John:

> I will accept no commission that would tend to create a rivalry with Grant. I want him to hold what he has earned and got. I have all the rank I want. I would rather be an engineer of a railroad, than President of the United States. I have commanded a hundred thousand men in battle, and on the march, successfully and without confusion, and that is enough for reputation. Now, I want rest and peace, and they are only to be had through war.

He described for Ellen "the singular friendship of Grant, who is almost childlike in his love for me," and to Grant himself Sherman wrote:

> I doubt if men in Congress fully realize that you and I are honest in our professions of want of ambition. I know I feel none and today will gladly surrender any position and influence to any other who is better able to wield the power.

The day before Christmas, on receiving Grant's sanction for the Carolina raid, Sherman sent word that he would start "in about ten days." He had his plans ready: "I have thought them over so long and well that they appear as clear as daylight." He said that he had spared Augusta so that he could use it to feint against in his Carolina march. By threatening it and Charleston, he could lure the enemy into dividing their forces and opening a path straight to Columbia, the capital of South Carolina, and on to Raleigh, the capital of North Carolina. This plan would, he knew, disappoint Halleck, who had written him on the eighteenth:

> Should you capture Charleston, I hope that by *some accident* the place may be destroyed, and if a little salt should be sown upon its site, it may prevent the growth of future crops of nullification and secession.

For strategic and perhaps sentimental reasons Sherman did not wish to march against Charleston. In their inability to understand Sherman, who shared so many of their prejudices and valued personal friendships among them so highly, Southerners began to explain his avoidance of Augusta as romantic favoritism. They spread the legend that since 1844 he had always been in love with a belle of that city. And although there was no evidence to support this tale, it lived as late as two thirds of a century later. His strategic reasons for sparing Charleston he explained in a letter to Grant on December 24:

> Charleston is now a mere desolated wreck, and is hardly worth the time it would take to starve it out. . . . I would treat it as a point of little importance, after all its railroads leading into the interior have been destroyed or occupied by us.

He was tactful in writing Halleck:

> I will bear in mind your hint as to Charleston, and do not think "salt" will be necessary. When I move, the Fifteenth Corps will be on the right of the right wing, and their position will naturally bring them into Charleston first; and if you have watched the history of that corps, you will have remarked that they generally do their work pretty well. The truth is the whole army is burning with an insatiable desire to wreak vengeance upon South Carolina. I almost tremble at her fate, but feel that she deserves all that seems in store for her. . . . I look upon Columbia as quite as bad as Charleston and I doubt if we shall spare her public buildings as we did at Milledgeville.

There was something menacing in the kindliness and decorum with which the Westerners were conducting themselves in Savannah, as though they might be saving all their hatred for South Carolina, the mother of secession. Sherman wrote Grant that "notwithstanding the habits begotten during our rather vandalic march" the men's behavior in Savannah had "excited the wonder and admiration of all." He began to recede from his November belief that war would give democracy too much power. To Thomas Ewing he sent a description of his delight at discovering that warfare did not taint men "with the spirit of anarchy that threatened the stability of our government," and said:

> . . . when the war does end, we may safely rest the fabric of our government if necessary on the strong and safe base of a well-disciplined army of citizens.

Sherman found irony in the letters that the enemy generals, Hardee, Smith, and McLaws, left for him, asking his personal care for their families. These men had been spreading or sanctioning atrocity tales concerning him. However, he reasoned, they had done so "to arouse the drooping energies of the people"—an old war custom. The wife of

General A. P. Stewart, one of Hood's leading officers, came to him for special assistance. So did Mrs. Sarah Davenport, who won him with the statement that she had three sons with the Union, three with the South, and one son-in-law with Lee. As in Kentucky, Mississippi, upper Georgia, and on the seaward march, women crowded to ask his protection, so much so that his aides had to shield him. Southern mothers who quieted their children with tales of Sherman the ogre were those who had never laid eyes upon him. Throughout his lifetime women instinctively liked him, finding him easy to talk to. Perhaps every woman intuitively felt, as did those two who knew him best—Ellen and Theresa (Sissie) Ewing—that under his bristling, brusque manner was the sensitiveness and affection of a small boy. Two months after his arrival in Savannah, ladies in Charleston would tell a correspondent of the *London Times* how exemplary Sherman had been while living at Fort Moultrie. His reputation for "steadiness," they said, had been so universal that "no objection was ever made by ladies of Charleston to permitting their daughters to attend parties at which Lieutenant Sherman would be present." From Savannah, Cump wrote Ellen:

> There are some elegant people here whom I knew in better days, who do not seem ashamed to call on "the vandal chief." They regard us just as the Romans did the Goths, and the parallel is not unjust. Many of my stalwart men with red beards and huge frames look like giants.

Sherman's régime in Savannah was a repetition of his rule in Memphis rather than of that in Atlanta. He now allowed Episcopal churches to omit prayers for the President of the United States, saying to preachers who asked if they might pray for the Confederate President, "Yes, Jeff Davis and the devil both need it." He kept civil officers at their posts, and strengthened the hand of the mayor, Dr. Richard D. Arnold, the nationally famous health officer whom he had known before the war. He gave Arnold tons of rice to ship to Boston in exchange for meat and flour, and although the trade was never completed, he fostered the dispatch of ships laden with charitable gifts from citizens of Boston. He gave assistance in holding town meetings at which, under Arnold's gavel, resolutions were adopted urging Governor Brown to call a State convention for peace discussions. He heard citizens vote official thanks to his second in command, "the noble Geary," who as military governor had supplied citizens with firewood. Geary's experience as the first postmaster, first alcalde, first mayor, and judge of the first instance in San Francisco—also as one of the many governors of bleeding Kansas—had fitted him to govern Savannah wisely. At Sherman's direction he opened marketplaces for farmers, and nourished Union sentiment.

As news of this peace movement reached other sections of the South, editors began attacking Sherman and Arnold. "A dangerous bait to deaden the spirit of resistance in other places," the *Richmond Examiner* called Sherman's policy on January 7, 1865. "Sherman seems to have changed his character as completely as the serpent changes his skin with the approach of spring," said the *Richmond Dispatch* on January 7; "his repose, however, is the repose of the tiger. Let him taste blood once more and he will be as brutal as ever." To the *Macon Telegraph* of the twenty-third, he was a Delilah "lulling the South into a false and fatal security" prior to producing "his heartless Philistines to bind us hand and foot." The *Wilmington North Carolinian* of January 11 tried to halt rumors that Sherman was traveling incognito and alone in Columbia, arranging with Union sympathizers to "revolutionize North Carolina and deposit it safely in the bosom of Father Abraham."

As Sherman shook Southern morale, he strengthened Northern spirit. States, cities, clubs, commercial bodies, and the combined Senate and House thanked him. Young Henry Adams wrote home from London that Sherman had placed "our military position at the head of the nations. Even the *Times* is converted and gives us a long leader full of praise of Sherman." Ellen was writing John:

> Have you noticed how father dotes on Cump? The people of Ohio have made a move toward presenting Cump with a homestead, either a farm or a residence. If they really do, I hope Cump will not decline it. I shall give up if he does, as glory and éclat are very little comfort to me in my wanderings with my family.

Cump was relieved when the gift talk subsided. He had seen no way to pay taxes on so expensive a gift as a house. Howard, at this time, asked Sherman for a furlough to visit his home, and was answered, "I would give a million dollars, if I had it, to be with my children. Would you do more than that?" "I'll say no more," said Howard.

One day Sherman opened a newspaper to read that Charles Celestine, the baby he had never seen, was dead. A letter from Thomas Ewing, written on December 18, contained further details:

> My Dear Son:
>
> I am gratified beyond measure to know that you have successfully achieved your arduous undertaking. In all its details from beginning to end, summer, autumn and winter campaigns, it has not its parallel in history. The world is full of plaudits. What I esteem most worthy of commendation is the care you have taken to preserve your men.

You have lost your fine little boy Charles. He died two weeks ago of pneumonia or some other type of pulmonary disease. . . .

Thanking his father-in-law for such praise, Cump declared that he "would rather please and gratify you than all the world beside." He knew his men trusted him:

They will march to certain death if I order it, because they know and feel that night and day I labor to the end that not a life shall be lost in vain. . . . Every movement I have made in this war has been based on sound military principle, and the result proves the assertion.

He wrote words of comfort to Ellen concerning the baby:

All spoke of him as so bright and fair that I hoped he would be spared us to fill the great void in our hearts left by Willy. . . . I have seen death in such quantity and such forms that it no longer startles me.

He told her that the march from Atlanta still seemed more dream than reality—"Like one who has walked a narrow plank, I look back and wonder if I really did it." When he read his own fame in the papers he seemed to see beside him, staring at the columns, the specter of a small boy in a sergeant's uniform:

Oh, that Willy were living, how his eyes would brighten and his bosom swell with honest pride if he could hear and understand these things. . . .

On New Year's Eve loneliness drenched him. From his room in the huge mansion—Savannah's finest—where he lived with his staff, he could hear his officers laughing and clinking glasses in the dining-room. From outside came the gay shouts of his men as they feasted on turtle soup, broiled shad, and steamed oysters. Tomorrow there would be a banquet with officers comparing him to Hannibal, Caesar, Napoleon.

But tonight, as the great year of his life died, he wrote John that what he wanted most of all was

to slip out quietly and see more of my family which is growing up almost strangers to me. I have now lost Willy and the baby without even seeing him, and were it not for General Grant's confidence in me, I should insist upon a little rest. As it is I must go on.

46

INEVITABLE SAMBO

NEW YEAR'S DAY brought dispatches complicating Sherman's plans for the next campaign. In his mind he had foreseen a noble spectacle—two forces moving northward in unison. His own army, cutting railroads well inland, would doom the Confederate seaports to easy capture by Dahlgren's gunboats which were to parallel Sherman's progress. To Foster, who was to accompany Dahlgren, Sherman said, "I will shake the tree, and you must be quick to pick up the apples."

It was a plan economical of life and, as Dahlgren said in admiration, "grand in conception." Only one difficulty loomed. The city of Wilmington, defended by stout Fort Fisher, might be so well supplied as to require a siege from land and sea—and sieges went against Sherman's grain. True, an expedition from the north—an army under General Benjamin Butler and a fleet under Porter—was to attack Fort Fisher around Christmas time, but both Grant and Sherman expected it to fail through Butler's chronic incompetence as a militarist. Sherman had prophesied as much to Halleck.

It was the result of this assault that reached Sherman on January 1, an account of how Butler, after failing in a fantastic attempt to blow up the fort with a powder ship, had refused to charge with his soldiers even though Porter's guns had silenced defending batteries. Butler had announced grandiloquently that he would not waste the lives of his men—an evident thrust at his enemy Grant, who was generally criticized for having spilled so much blood fighting Lee.

"Fizzle—great fizzle!" said Sherman, while reading the account of this fiasco. "Knew it would be so. I shall have to go up there and do that job—eat 'em up as I go and take 'em backside." While he was saying this Halleck, in Washington, was writing him,

> Your anticipations . . . have proved so correct that your reputation as a prophet may soon equal that as a general. . . . Thank God, I had nothing to do with it, except to express the opinion that Butler's torpedo ship would have as much effect on the forts as if he should —— at them.

But soon Sherman was hearing that Grant had summarily removed Butler from command and had sent him home to Lowell, Massachusetts, replacing him with Major General A. H. Terry, who took the army back for a successful attack on Fort Fisher on January 15. Sherman wrote Porter:

> I am rejoiced that the current of events has carried Butler to Lowell where he should have stayed and confined his bellicose operations to the factory girls. . . . He has no blood on his skirts and judging from the past, it will be long before his blood stains anything. His solicitude for the blood of his men is as moonshine.

With his original plans now restored, Sherman awaited the arrival by boat of his last supplies before starting the campaign. While he waited, he received a confidential letter from Halleck. On December 30, Old Brains had written one of those tattling and shrewd messages that he so enjoyed:

> While almost every one is praising your great march . . . there is a certain class having now great influence with the President . . . who are decidedly disposed to make a point against you—I mean in regard to "Inevitable Sambo." They say that you have manifested an almost *criminal* dislike of the negro, and that you are not willing to carry out the wishes of the Government in regard to him, but repulse him with contempt. They say you might have brought with you to Savannah more than 50,000, thus stripping Georgia of that number of laborers and opening a road by which as many more could have escaped from their masters; but that, instead of this, you drove them from your ranks. . . . These I know are the views of some of the leading men in the Administration, and they now express dissatisfaction that you did not carry them out in your great raid.

Sherman did not know that the Abolitionists had been highly excited at newspaper descriptions of an "outrage" during the seaward march. General Jefferson C. Davis, it was charged, had taken up a pontoon bridge before a host of Negro refugees could cross, and had abandoned them to the vengeance of Wheeler's horsemen. Dramatic descriptions had been printed regarding the fury with which the enemy had driven the pitiful blackamoors into the river to drown. When in time the tale reached him, Sherman wrote Halleck:

> Of course that cock-and-bull story . . . is humbug. I turned nobody back. Jeff C. Davis . . . took up his pontoon bridge, not because he wanted to leave them, but because he wanted his bridge. He and Slocum tell me that they don't believe Wheeler killed one of them.

In his warning letter, Halleck did not specify who Sherman's high critics might be. Nor did Sherman appear to understand the zeal with which the Abolitionists were moving. He had evidently discussed politics very little with Frank Blair, who was at his elbow. Frank understood the political situation well. His brother Montgomery had been sacrificed to the Abolitionists and the Radicals the autumn before. The Blairs and Border State Moderates were believed by the bitter-enders to have influenced Lincoln in favor of gradual emancipation and against the policy of making the Negro a citizen and a voter. Senators Charles Sumner, Ben Wade, and Zachariah Chandler, Representative Thaddeus Stevens, and other determined Abolitionists were deciding that no Southern State should be readmitted to the Union until all freedmen were enfranchised. Otherwise, they said, the South when reinstated in the Union could combine with Northern Copperheads and by the ballot win the pro-slavery, States' rights victory that they had lost on the battlefield. Years later Sherman would describe his ignorance of this political campaign:

> I did not dream of such a result, then, and did not suppose that former slaves would be suddenly without preparation, manufactured into voters, equal to others, politically and socially.

On January 11 Sherman might have suspected who one of his critics could be. Secretary Stanton, with an entourage of officials, arrived on that day in Savannah, ostensibly to take charge of captured cotton, but in the opinion of his enemy, Secretary of the Navy Welles, "to pay court to Sherman when that officer was the favored general and supposed to have eclipsed Grant." It was far more likely that Stanton had come to study the problems that Sherman was creating by his reputed sympathy with the Southern civilians and institutions. Stanton was showing signs of drifting into the political camp of the Radicals—indeed, within four months, he would go over to them bag and baggage.

Sherman had been independent in his handling of some thirteen million dollars' worth of cotton found in Savannah, denying private traders the right to buy it, even refusing to honor permits for large amounts signed by the President himself. He insisted that the President would recall these permits if he could know what corruption would result from their exercise. Sherman wrote W. P. Fessenden, Chase's successor as Secretary of the Treasury, that he felt sympathy for "the small farmers that look to their parcels of cotton to exchange for food and clothing," and had opened a market for them in Savannah, stipulating that they buy with moneys received nothing but domestic necessities. At the market none but United States Treasury agents could buy, and the price was fixed at three fourths the value of cotton on the New York Exchange.

Sherman regarded cotton as a prize of war, but he was going to great lengths to adjust and reconcile the Georgians to peace and return to the Union. No such sympathy had he for English claims to part of the cotton in Savannah, and when Anthony Barclay, representing the British consul, appealed to him, Sherman pointed out the irony of English ships' smuggling cotton to the West Indies and paying for it with cannon and shells bearing the queen's portrait, munitions used by Confederates in killing Federal troops. "It would afford me great satisfaction," he told Barclay, "to conduct my army to Nassau and wipe out that nest of pirates." And the correspondent of the *New York Herald* had it that Sherman had added:

> I'd take picks and shovels and throw that cursed sand hill into the sea—and you may tell your government that, sir,—shovel it into the sea, and then I'd pay for it if necessary. Good day, sir.

The Captured and Abandoned Property Act, which Congress had passed in 1863, condemning property that could be "used for waging war," was, Sherman heard, to be extended to cover the real estate of secessionists, and this tendency offended his business and moral sense. He wrote Fessenden:

> . . . we can derive little revenue from the South, because no one will buy confiscated lands, and if we strip the inhabitants of personal property they at once fall back upon us with claims of inhumanity that cannot be disregarded.
>
> I think that General Grant and myself are as severe to secessionists as men could be, but each of us has been forced to feed the inhabitants of the conquered country after they have fallen helpless in our power. Without any clearly-defined rule, our practice has been harsh enough as long as resistance lasted, but the moment resistance has ceased, we could not see people hanging round our camps perish of hunger.

Sherman did not know how far the Radical Thaddeus Stevens was preparing to go in his demands for this confiscation of property—demands that would in time insist that the property of prostrate plantation-owners be divided among the Negroes and the poor whites, each Negro having "forty acres and a mule."

Sherman now saw Stanton take charge of the cotton, large amounts and small and, under the control of the Treasury, instead of that of the army, ship it north to be settled for at some future time.

It angered him to find Stanton so eager to question Negroes as to their opinion of the army's conduct. Sherman, on reaching the city, had broken out in rage against his old enemies the State recruiting agents, who had swarmed down from Hilton Head to tempt and coerce black men into blue uniform; they were at their bold work of breaking up Sherman's own pioneer corps again. When, by chance, he found a hundred wretched Negroes imprisoned, "waiting for the night to be conveyed to Hilton Head," he had set the poor fellows free and had scored the agents. His ideal of the dignity of the Federal cause was strengthening him more and more against the enlistment of Negro soldiers:

> I did not want them [the Confederates] to cast in our teeth what General Hood had done in Atlanta, that we had to call on their slaves to help us subdue them.

Within twenty-four hours after arriving, Stanton asked Sherman to summon colored leaders for questioning. To be tried, as it were, on the testimony of Negroes was as insulting to Sherman as to any Southern gentleman, but he quietly submitted, summoning some twenty black Methodist and Baptist preachers to his headquarters. There he heard the Negroes state, of their own free will, almost exactly the same truths he had given the Administration. The freedmen said,

> . . . every black man enlisted by a State agent leaves a white man at home . . . it don't strengthen the army . . . it would be far better for the State agents to stay at home and the enlistments be made for the United States under the direction of General Sherman.

At one point in the hearing Stanton asked Sherman to leave the room, since questions were to be asked concerning him. Later Sherman learned that Stanton had told the black clerics to say whether their race regarded Sherman as friendly or unfriendly. They answered, "friendly and courteous. . . . We have confidence in General Sherman and think what concerns us could not be in better hands." For fifty years afterward, Savannah Negroes could be heard dating everything from "the time when Tecumpsey was here."

His trial and vindication had awakened Sherman somewhat to current agitation among the Negro's political champions, and he wrote Halleck that Lincoln, having met States'-rights fanatics of the South, must face Abolitionist fanatics of the North. On the day of the hearing, he wrote Old Brains:

> But the nigger? Why, in God's name, can't sensible men let him alone. . . . Neither cotton, the negro, nor a single interest of class should govern us. But I fear if you are right that that power behind the throne is governing, somebody must meet it or we are again involved in war with another class of fanatics. . . .
>
> I know the fact that all natural emotions swing as the pendulum. These southrons pulled Sambo's pendulum so far over that the danger is it will,

on its return, jump its pivot. . . . They gather round me in crowds, and I can't find out whether I am Moses or Aaron, or which of the prophets; but surely I am rated as one of the congregation, and it is hard to tell in what sense I am most appreciated by Sambo—in saving him from his master or the new master that threatens him with a new species of slavery. I mean State recruiting agents.

Poor negro! Lo, the poor Indian! Of course sensible men understand such humbug, but some power must be invested in our Government to check these wild oscillations of public opinion. The South deserves all she has got for her injustice to the negro, but that is no reason why we should go to the other extreme.

Seemingly impressed by Sherman's knowledge of actual conditions, Stanton asked him to draw up suggestions for future policy. Quickly Sherman handed him a plan that was soon put into effect. The freedmen who wished it were colonized in abandoned fields and neighboring islands, and put to producing rice and cotton for their own benefit, secure from all white influence except that of a Government inspector. Young Negroes were encouraged, but not coerced, into enlistment and Federal officers, not State agents, handled the payment of bounties. The colonists, including the families of recruits who took up the plan, were given the temporary use of forty acres per family. In effect, Sherman had at last scotched the State agents, as was soon reported by the Federal inspectors, who said that the Negroes in Savannah were sleeping in the sun deaf to recruiting speeches. Enlistments were straggling at best.

On still another score Stanton saw how squarely Sherman was opposed to the bitter hopes of the Northern Radicals. Where the Sumner-Stevens bloc was preparing to go into legislative action, at the collapse of the Confederacy, with a program demanding that the prostrate States must revert to Territorial status before reëntering the Union, Sherman was believing that the States could regain their old status by simply grounding their arms. Northern Conservatives of the Lincoln-Welles-Blair-Thomas Ewing school of moderate thought were holding, or preparing to hold, the view that willful groups of citizens in these States had usurped local governments without altering the permanent and indestructible status of the States themselves. These conservatives and Sherman understood the war to be a clear-cut fight to save the Union—a fight in which the freeing of the slaves had been purely a military measure—and held that the war's great purpose should not be diverted into a squabble for sectional or commercial advantage.

To citizens of Liberty and Tatnall counties who wrote him concerning peace, he made answer on December 28:

> We are fellow countrymen and bound by every principle of honor and honesty to maintain and defend the Union given us by Washington and that is all I am at . . .

In and out of Sherman's office, during Stanton's presence there, came Georgians asking how their State could be readmitted to the Union. Encouraged in his old purpose of "creating a schism in Jeff. Davis's ranks," Sherman gained Stanton's approval of his letter written to these petitioners stating:

> My own opinion is that no negotiations are necessary, nor commissioners, nor conventions, nor any thing of the kind. Whenever the people of Georgia quit rebelling . . . elect members of Congress and Senators, and these go and take their seats, then the State of Georgia will have resumed her functions in the Union. . . . Georgia is not out of the Union, and therefore talk of "reconstruction" appears to me inappropriate.

To support his view, Sherman quoted to the Georgians the President's amnesty proclamation of December, 1863, offering "full pardon" to all Confederates except generals, high civil leaders, and persons who had resigned Federal posts to join the rebellion. Sherman quoted Lincoln's reaffirmation of this at the last assemblage of Congress. Stanton approved Sherman's reasoning. What Stanton did not do was to warn Sherman that Radicals were preparing to make trouble over a reconstruction clause in the '63 proclamation, a clause offering to readmit to the Union any Southern State that would, by the votes of one tenth of its legitimate suffrage-holders duly sworn to Federal loyalty, form a State government. One fifth of Louisiana's voters had accepted this invitation in February, 1864, but the Radicals, headed by Charles Sumner, were preparing to reject the chosen Senators and Congressmen because Louisiana had not made Negroes voters. A bitter tangle between Lincoln and Congress was looming, but Stanton allowed Sherman to face the complexities of civil matters without advice. Indeed, the Secretary encouraged the general "as a soldier and patriot" to end the war with speed because the Federal Government approached bankruptcy. Then Stanton hurried North.

Sherman turned to launch his campaign. He was anxious to escape the endless appeals of Southern women. Then too, city life, he admitted, had grown "tame and dull." Major Nichols, who said that the General "enjoys poverty of food," saw him apologize because canned fruit and jellies were served at headquarters during Stanton's visit. "This," he said, "is the consequence of coming into houses and cities. The only place to live, Mr. Secretary, is out of doors in the woods."

The army was growing bored with the tropical beauty of Savannah, surfeited with oysters. They honed again for the bright excitement of danger, the smell of the piny woods, the gamble of foraging. Recruits from the draft camps in the North filled up the regiments. Again the soldiers stripped for action. They were now seen to fit blankets tightly around their bodies and mark the excess material for scissoring. Each regiment had but one wall tent for headquarters; the officers must sleep under scanty "flies" like the men. Nichols thought Sherman's staff smaller than any brigadier's, and his servants and horses fewer than regulations specified. Old Sam was to be the general's favorite mount on the new campaign—a significant omen, for Sam was, said Nichols, "a horribly fast-walking horse."

The coming campaign would be, in Sherman's estimation, ten times more difficult, ten times more important, than the march to the sea. He wrote home that he would "dive again beneath the surface to turn up again in some mysterious place" and the chances were about even that he would be killed. That the secrecy, the mystery, and the independence of such adventures delighted his soul there could be no doubt.

In the country ahead, he expected to meet 40,000 Confederates—more than 30,000 already on hand under Beauregard, Hardee, and Bragg, and at least 10,000 more drifting east from Hood's shattered force. So strong an army made very respectable odds against 60,000 invaders, especially when the terrain was so favorable for defense. At this rainy season the eastern Carolinas were like a damp, sticky palm from which five river fingers reached across the upper clay country into the Allegheny Mountains. Between the fingers were webs of creeks, dismal swamps, and bayous.

That Sherman meant to cross the first of these river fingers in South Carolina, the Salkehatchie (commonly called the Salk), with its deep Whippy Swamp, was beyond the imagination of most Confederates. Hardee, cool and judicious, was sure Sherman would not attempt it. Joseph E. Johnston said, "My engineers reported that it was absolutely impossible for an army to march across lower portions of the State in winter."

But from his youthful hunting trips into the interior Sherman remembered where the marshy bottom lands blended with the clay of the upper country, and it was along this line that he proposed to march, once he had crossed the Salk. As for conquering that quagmire stream, he had no fears. He commanded men whose grandfathers had waded icy Wabash swamps with George Rogers Clark during the Revolution. The men themselves had worked draining slashes at home. They knew the trick of blazing trees for wagons to follow through forests. Lumbermen of Michigan, rail-splitters of Indiana and Missouri, formed the pioneer corps, 100 white men to every 75 Negroes—6,600 in all. Their skilled axes could cut, split, and lay—flat surface down—saplings so that roads could be corduroyed in record time.

By January 19 Sherman was moving. Two weeks earlier he had shipped the right wing by boat to Beaufort, a point in South Carolina halfway between Savannah and Charleston, and at Pocotaligo it seized the railroad. The left wing marched up the Savannah some twenty-five miles and waited for the swollen river to subside so that it might cross into South Carolina. The rains, which had been bad, continued. In some sections sentries stood their posts in boats.

Sherman gathered up the last loose ends. He told Foster, who was to rule Savannah, a secret. Schofield's whole corps had been brought to North Carolina's Neuse River by Grant, and Sherman had sent word for supplies to be assembled at New Berne, on that river. Schofield would march to Goldsboro with these supplies and meet Sherman's army. If any newspaper correspondents in Savannah discovered this, "don't risk them," said Sherman, "but imprison them till the time is past." To Grant Sherman wrote:

> I expect Davis will move Heaven and earth to catch me, for success to my column is fatal to his dream of empire. Richmond is not more vital to his cause than Columbia and the heart of South Carolina.

Sherman felt confident of mastering all opposition so long as Lee did not move south against him. If this happened Grant promised to follow with all speed. Major Nichols heard Sherman say:

> If Lee is a soldier of genius, he will seek to transfer his army from Richmond to Raleigh or Columbia; if he is a man simply of detail, he will remain where he is and his speedy defeat is sure. But I have little fear that he will be able to move, Grant holds him in a vice of iron.

It was a view more picturesquely put by Lincoln when he said, "Grant has the bear by the hind leg while Sherman takes off its hide."

47

HELL-HOLE OF SECESSION

IN the soft interlude after their happy march to the sea, Sherman's men might have forgotten some of their hatred for South Carolina had not the citizens of that State published such bold defiances. "Taunting messages," Sherman said they were, boasts "that when we should reach South Carolina, we would find a people less passive, who would fight us to the bitter end, daring us to come over, etc. . . ."

However defiant the South Carolinians might be in their public utterances, their governor, A. G. Magrath, was privately hopeless, writing President Davis on Christmas Day, "it is not an unwillingness to oppose the enemy, but a chilling apprehension of the futility of doing so which affects the people." The resentment of the Carolinas against the dominance of Virginia and Virginians in the war spoke out as Magrath begged Davis to abandon Richmond and concentrate in defense of Charleston:

> The force on the coast is not sufficient to make effectual resistance to General Sherman. If that is so, Charleston falls; if Charleston falls, Richmond follows. Richmond may fall and Charleston be saved, but Richmond cannot be saved if Charleston falls.

But Davis and Lee, electing to defend Richmond to the last, could send Magrath no effective aid, and South Carolina was unable to call home from Lee's army the brigades which had fought so stoutly there during the past three years. To further dismay the citizens, Southern newspapers republished widely an article which the *New York Times* had printed in July, 1863, promising that sooner or later Justice would "put on her terrible garments, her robes of hell fire" for the State that had begun secession and which had been "so habitually arrogant and domineering" toward the "greasy mechanics of the North."

Captain Conyngham in Savannah reported:

> Threatening words were heard from soldiers who prided themselves on "conservatism in house-burning" while in Georgia, and officers confessed their fears that the coming campaign would be a wicked one.

Sherman observed that his men were determined to visit upon South Carolina "the scourge of war in its worst form." He concluded that "we would not be able to restrain our men as we had done in Georgia. . . .

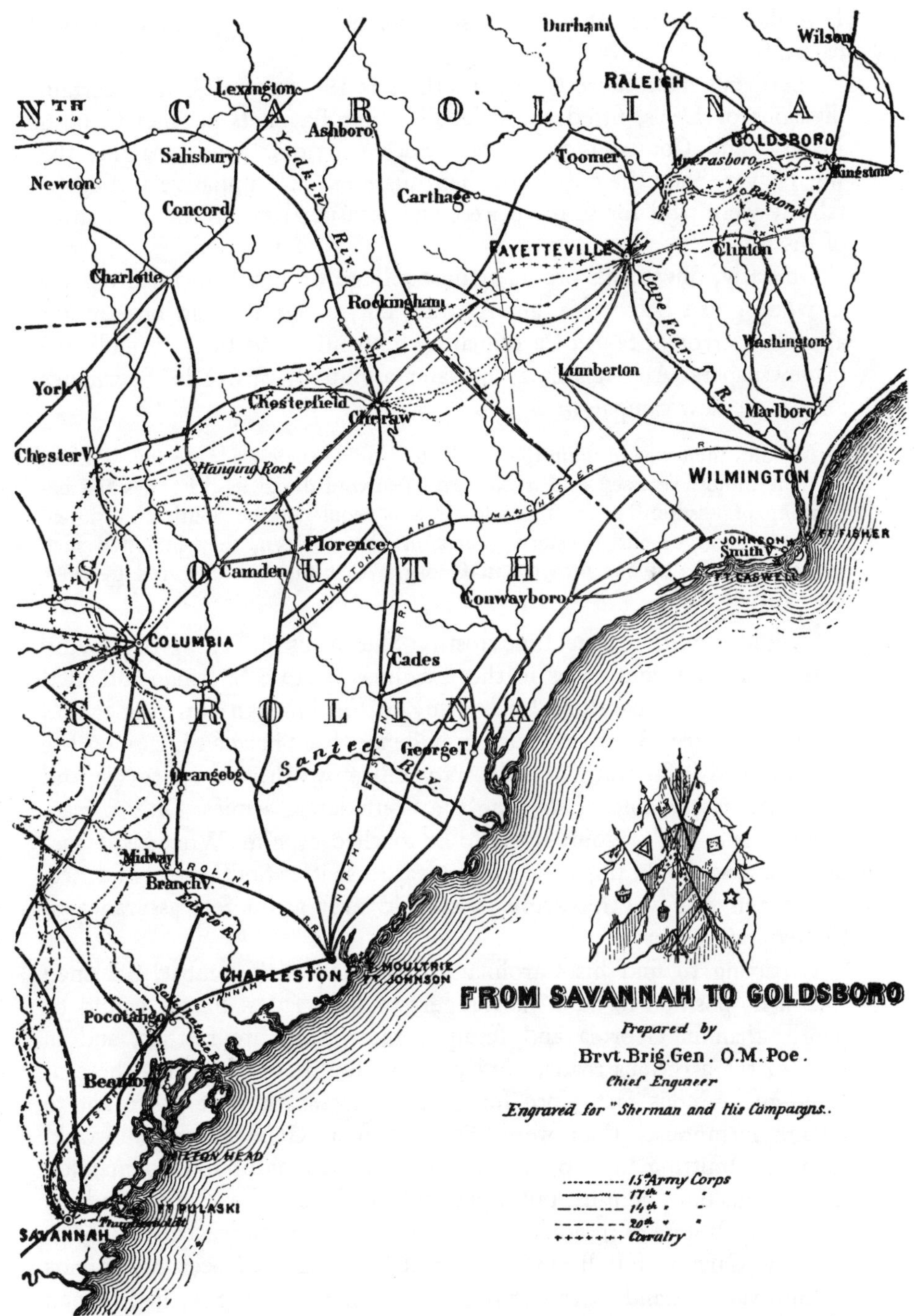
NTH CAROLINA
SOUTH CAROLINA
Durham
Wilson
Lexington
Raleigh
Ashboro
Goldsboro
Salisbury
Toomer
Kingston
Newton
Concord
Carthage
Fayetteville
Clinton
Charlotte
Rockingham
Cape Fear R.
Washington
Yadkin Riv.
Lumberton
York V.
Chesterfield
Cheraw
Marlboro
Chester V.
Hanging Rock
Wilmington
Florence
Ft. Johnson
Smith V.
Ft. Fisher
Ft. Caswell
Camden
Conwayboro
Columbia
Cades
George T.
Santee Riv.
Orangebg
Midway
Branch V.
Edisto R.
Charleston
Ft. Moultrie
Ft. Johnson
Pocotaligo
Beaufort
Hilton Head
Ft. Pulaski
Savannah
FROM SAVANNAH TO GOLDSBORO
Prepared by
Brvt. Brig. Gen. O.M. Poe.
Chief Engineer
Engraved for "Sherman and His Campaigns.
15th Army Corps
17th " "
14th " "
20th " "
Cavalry

I would not restrain the army lest its vigor and energy should be impaired."

Sherman's men, more than any others in the war unless it be certain divisions of Lee's, fitted the title Thinking Bayonets applied to both Federal and Confederate armies. "Such warriors," said Spaight, the war lawyer, "had the defects of their qualities . . . initiative and adaptability were paid for at the price of an occasional failure in the matter of discipline."

Officially, Sherman's orders against pillage were still in force exactly as when given before leaving Atlanta, but to repeat them now might allay the terror of South Carolinians who would read them republished in newspapers. And terror, as he later admitted, was to be Sherman's ally in the new campaign:

> My aim then was to whip the rebels, to humble their pride, to follow them to their inmost recesses, and make them fear and dread us. "Fear is the beginning of wisdom" . . . the soldiers and people of the South entertained an undue fear of our Western men and, like children, they invented such ghostlike stories of our prowess in Georgia, that they were scared by their own inventions.

Spaight would in due time justify Sherman's policy of destroying mills, granaries, and crops in the Carolinas because Sherman intended such wreckage to paralyze Lee's army in Virginia; an aim proper and legal in warfare. But there was no evidence that Sherman imagined the ruin of food in a swath of only sixty miles' width across Georgia and the Carolinas capable of starving the Confederate armies. Only a fraction of the South's resources would be touched by him. What his devastating course would do, as he saw it, was to shatter Southern confidence. No citizen who saw his army pass could ever again feel assurance of Confederate victory.

Expecting to find his Carolina march filled with combat, Sherman was in no position to bind his foragers to strict rules. Farms would be poorer than in Georgia and foragers must penetrate farther, and in view of the atrocious roads, must go mounted more often than heretofore—an ominous fact, since foragers on horseback were more apt to pillage farmhouses than were those on foot. General Hazen would soon be admitting that to collect the 7,000 pounds of food demanded daily by his unit, he must put 5 per cent of his total force in the saddle.

Sherman's state of mind at the start of the march was revealed to Mrs. Caroline Carson of Baltimore; she and her sister had been his friends on Sullivan's Island in the 1840's, and their relative, Sue, had owned

Lieutenant Sherman as "one of her standard beaux." On January 20 he wrote her:

> I will enter Carolina not as they say with a heart bent on desolation and destruction but to vindicate the just powers of a government which received terrible insults at the hands of the people of that State. Gladly will I try to temper the harsh acts of war with mercy towards them who by falsehood and treachery have been led step by step from the generous practice of hospitality to deeds of crime and violence. . . .
>
> I will take infinitely more delight in curing the wounds made by war than in inflicting them.

Two weeks later, as the left wing crossed the Savannah River, torpedoes exploded in roads, killing and wounding several soldiers. "Illegitimate warfare," Slocum pronounced it, and saw how his soldiers retaliated upon South Carolina. At the pontoon bridge near where the explosion had taken place, the Second Minnesota, waiting for Kilpatrick to cross, heard him say, "There'll be damn little for you infantrymen to destroy after I've passed through that hell-hole of secession." Chaplain Hight heard it whispered that Kilpatrick had filled his men's saddlebags with matches, and three days later Howard heard Sherman laugh at the way Kil had changed the name of a town from Barnwell to Burnwell. Colonel George A. Stone heard the Fifteenth Corps say, "Here is where treason began and, by God, here is where it shall end!"

By February 5 Sherman had moved Foster's men into Savannah, and was sweeping northwest between the Savannah and the Salkehatchie rivers in South Carolina. Frank Blair, on the right, marched within fifty miles of Charleston. Kilpatrick, spurring toward Augusta, convinced the enemy that that city was Sherman's goal. Bewildered, Hardee, Beauregard, and D. H. Hill tried to garrison both cities and at the same time to hold the marshy Salk. And, as in Georgia, Confederates were still debating where Sherman would strike when on the seventh he suddenly swung north and, scorning both citadels, plunged into the reputedly impassable swamps, cannon, wagons, and all. After the first skirmishes, Sherman wrote Grant, "I observe the enemy has some respect for my name." They had retired "when they heard that the attacking force belonged to my army. I will try to keep up that feeling which is a real power." Other men in the army observed that the Confederates were impressed when they discovered that their assailants were not Foster's Negro troops. Colonel Cassius Fairchild of the Sixteenth Wisconsin overheard an officer in opposition fortifications shout, "Look out, boys, you haven't got the damned niggers to fight now—this is Sherman's army!" Logan's men kept yelling, "You'd better get out, this is the Fifteenth Corps!"

Blair's Seventeenth Corps, especially Mower's division, challenged the Fifteenth's reputation. Silent, athletic Mower was soon said to have three successive sets of staff officers awaiting him in Heaven. He walked at the head of his men, breast-deep in water. Conyngham reported soldiers slipping on snakes and alligators among submerged tree-roots.

Joe Johnston, still without an active command, sat helpless at Lincolnton, North Carolina, watching Sherman disappear into the great morass. "The Salk is impassable," Hardee telegraphed him. Later Johnston told General Cox:

> But when I learned that Sherman's army was marching through the Salk swamps, making its own corduroy roads at the rate of a dozen miles a day and more, and bringing its artillery and wagons with it, I made up my mind that there had been no such army in existence since the days of Julius Caesar.

Hardee, in Charleston, shook his head in bewilderment. "I wouldn't have believed it if I hadn't seen it happen," he told Cox three months later.

Union officers stared at their men in admiration as the army drove onward. Every private was now a pioneer, splitting saplings for corduroy roads, laying pontoons, clearing entanglements. Corse, observing how his men carried fence rails for miles to build wagon roads, reported that they worked for hours waist-deep in ice-cold floods, "remaining thus exposed until they were brought from the water in a cramped and spasmodic condition." A prisoner told the One Hundred and Fourth Illinois, "If your army goes to hell, it will corduroy the road."

Skirmishers watched each other as they advanced against enemy sharpshooters, for a man when wounded would drown unless promptly shouldered. Sometimes regiments crossing mud flats halted at the edge of streams, took off their clothes, balanced garments on their heads, and stepped into the black water that came down from the wintry Alleghenies. Usually, however, they thrashed ahead without undressing, and on emerging, felt their torn clothing freeze stiff enough to rasp their flesh.

Once, in two days' time, Mower's division built a mile and a half of bridges, crossed sixteen streams, laid they knew not how much corduroy, and ended by capturing breastworks that Howard thought "the strongest I ever saw in my life . . . and defended by 2,000 men." These incomparable parapets lay behind the Edisto, second of the main rivers to be passed, and Mower came at them across pontoons and into sloughs—thousands of men, cartridge boxes tied around their necks, water to their armpits, the moon gleaming on muskets held high overhead. From their blue lips came Indian war whoops. It was madness, moon madness—and the Southerners retired.

Scholars in both armies thought of Hannibal's men forging over the Alps. Howard's wing was averaging 13.23 miles a day, accomplishing in mud and morass what other armies in the war averaged on good roads. Sherman's whole army, counting idle days in towns and reconnoitering days before breastworks, averaged ten miles a day, exactly what it had made on the sunny romp across dry roads in Georgia. Upon occasion the Army of the Tennessee waded twenty-five miles at a stretch.

Yet in the interminable wetness only 2 per cent of the men fell sick, exactly the proportion that had suffered when feet were dry in Georgia. John Moore, medical director, thought the strange immunity from disease due to novelty, enthusiasm, and freedom from the whores and saloons of large cities. Sherman believed open air and plain food responsible. "I have not heard a man cough or sneeze in three months," he said in April. He saw "wounds which in 1861 would have sent a man to the hospital for months" regarded in 1865 "as mere scratches, rather the subject of a joke than of sorrow." Now he heard men "exclaim on seeing a dead comrade borne to the rear, 'Well, Bill has turned up his toes to the daisies.' "

Of the 1,368 men wounded in the Carolinas, an unusual percentage recovered, particularly those with amputated limbs. Such patients, spending nights under tiny canvas strips and jolting by day in ambulances over horrible roads, fared better than did similar cases in city hospitals, Moore reported. No wounded were left behind. Helpless men still felt themselves part of the army. Foragers brought bedfast comrades fresh milk and preserves, amused them with gaudy lies, thrilled them with reports of surging victory. From rain-drenched ambulances lurching through the mud voices sang, "As we go marching on." Universally officers marked the unconquerable happiness of the wet, dirty marchers. Sherman said:

> It is impossible to conceive of a march involving more labor and exposure, yet I cannot recall an instance of bad temper. . . . I believe that this cheerfulness and harmony of action reflects upon all concerned quite as much real honor and fame as "battles gained" or "cities won."

In the flooded condition of the land—rain fell on twenty-eight of the first forty-five days—men often roosted in trees, Sherman among them. One stormy night he lay on a church pew, scorning a rug brought from the pulpit rostrum: "No, keep that for some of you young fellows who aren't well." Hitchcock saw him divide his luncheon with Carolina children, who, when he halted at houses, came to him instinctively. He scolded a young mother for bringing her small baby into the cold air when she ran from her door to ask protection.

Mud grew thinner in mid-February as the army came to high red ground on the rich farming lands near Columbia. Resistance, although continuous, was weak enough to give the four blue flanking columns no trouble. Governor A. G. Magrath's appeal to Carolinians to ambuscade the invaders was proving as futile as the call in Georgia. When the Twenty-ninth Missouri captured 120 militiamen, all old men or stripling boys, Hazen sent them home. Hazen described one haul of captives as

> venerable home-guards. I did not turn these old gentlemen over to the provost guard but gave them some tents near my headquarters. In the evening they all came over to my camp-fire and entertained me with an account of their novel war experiences. Each man had some peculiar and personal malady, an account of which figured largely in the conversation. In the morning I had a handsome walking stick cut for each, gave them a good breakfast and let them go. They thanked me pleasantly for the entertainment, liked the walking sticks, and did not see the joke.

Hitchcock, supported by many other soldiers, wrote, "Of all mean humbugs, South Carolina's chivalry is the meanest." He heard "more whining, more cowardly talk . . . more mean-spirited and abject submission to mere power . . . than in any other State of the South." Conyngham wrote:

> In Georgia we had to respect the high-toned feelings of the planters, for they yielded with a dignity that won our admiration. In Carolina, the inhabitants, with a fawning, cringing subserviency, hung around our camps, craving a bite to eat.

Political and social prejudice was blinding the Westerners to the fact that many thousands of South Carolina's young men had been killed during the past four years defending Richmond with a doggedness unexcelled by anything in the experiences of the Federal Army. The State had sent fully 45,000 men into the Confederate ranks.

For the first time the Westerners felt themselves in a foreign country. Never before had they seen people so poor, so shiftless, so ignorant, so resigned to peasantry, as these poor whites of South Carolina. Sex-starved soldiers hurrying toward factory towns recoiled at the sight of gaunt, slovenly, sallow women who were more abject than Negro slaves. Class hatred dawned upon many of the midland boys who had been reared in the sweet dream of democracy. They hated the "chivalry" and they hated the poor whites. In feudalism they saw none—or few—of their own pioneer middle class. South Carolina paid the price of strangeness.

From the start, the campaign was called the Smoky March. In spite of wet weather, fires licked at railroad cars, depots, ties, at bales of cotton and bins of cottonseed, at acres of pine trees, at barrels of resin, at factories, at public buildings—sometimes at whole towns. Rail fences smoldered when not too deep in water. Barns blazed after foragers had emptied them, and houses that farmers had deserted glowed on the horizon where bummers explored. Conyngham observed:

> In Georgia few houses were burned, here few escaped. . . . The middle of the finest day looked black and gloomy, dense smoke arose on all sides.

Sherman, riding at the head of first one column, then another, was too intent upon the army's safety, too content that his men were not harming women and children, to pry deeply into the conduct of his foragers. When General Wheeler, still hanging on the skirts of the army with his cavalry, offered to quit burning cotton if Sherman would "discontinue burning houses," Sherman replied, on February 8:

> I hope you will burn all cotton and save us the trouble. We don't want it and it has proven a curse to our country. All you don't burn I will. As to private houses occupied by peaceful families, my orders are not to molest or disturb them, and I think my orders are obeyed. Vacant houses, being of no use to anybody, I care little about, as the owners have thought them of no use to themselves. I don't want them destroyed but do not take much care to preserve them.

At the same time Sherman was ordering Kilpatrick to

> spare dwellings that are occupied and teach your men to be courteous to women; it goes a great way, but take all provisions and forage you need.

Howard heard Sherman tell Kil to signal the cavalry's position during raids by burning "a bridge or something" in order to "make a smoke like Indians do on the plains." Hitchcock noted his chieftain's anger when houses burst into flame near his camp.

One evident attempt at curbing depredations was made by Sherman at the end of the first week in February, for throughout the Army of the Tennessee, with which he was riding, there appeared simultaneous warnings. Corse limited foragers, all at once, to "the best disciplined men," and denunciations of pillage were issued by corps and division commanders. "Vandalism," said Conyngham, "though not encouraged, was seldom punished." He saw many officers working to prevent robbery, but he thought it impossible to check the bummers. A soldier of the

One Hundred and Third Illinois in the Fifteenth Corps wrote in his diary on February 7:

> I never saw so much destruction before. Orders are as strict as ever but our men understand they are in South Carolina and are making good their old threats.

Three weeks later he wrote:

> The stealing is awful . . . a Golden Christ had been stolen in Columbia and in an inspection on the 26th it was found in a Department Headquarters wagon. . . . Inspectors pounce down on wagons every day or two now. Everything imaginable is found. . . . The stuff is given to citizens or destroyed.

General Force declared that when inspectors suddenly swooped down upon the Seventeenth Corps as February ended, no loot was found in the baggage or blankets of the men—nothing but their own clothing and tobacco. He knew of a private drummed from camp for stealing a watch, and an officer arrested for failing to report promptly a robbery committed by one of his men. Investigating tirelessly, Howard discovered one instance where a forager struck a woman while stealing her gold watch, also a case in which an officer "had allowed his men to take rings off fingers of ladies in his presence." Howard's sworn testimony later was:

> I found one officer robbing a private house and stealing jewelry from a drawer; I had him instantly arrested and would like to have seen him hung.

Howard believed minor officers as scrupulous as their superiors, "unless they had been prisoners," when they were "particularly hard." Although it was said by South Carolinians that Sherman's men took special delight in shattering mirrors, it was not charged, as it had been in New Orleans, that Federals made a point of scribbling obscenities across the white shirt fronts and skirts of family portraits hanging on ancestral walls.

While the march was in progress a Dr. Anderson, Confederate surgeon, launched a legend that would find credence among certain Southerners for generations. He said that when the Federals marched away from Camden one of them accidentally left a letter on the street describing how the invaders divided their loot—Sherman receiving one fifth, the other generals one fifth, the colonels and lesser officers the same amount, and the common soldiers two fifths. This fiction probably developed from a condition Howard discovered; he said that most depredations had been the work of "a set of scoundrels who preceded and followed the army . . . a regularly organized banditti" numbering some two hundred, who divided their loot. Hitchcock confirmed this statement. Sherman, who took no plunder except a few rugs for saddle blankets, defended his army from the charge that its destructiveness was unprecedented. He declared:

> . . . the Duke of Wellington's private and official dispatches show that the French and English both plundered in France for food, fire-wood, etc., and that he excused if not condoned it, showing how impossible it was to prevent it.

Sherman had become so attached to his men that he could not bear to punish them. Again and again he threatened to send the Eighth Missouri to the rear, only to see them behave so courageously in battle that "I would have pardoned them for anything short of treason." He finally rationalized it thus:

> Fighting is the least and easiest part of war, but no General ever was or will be successful who quarrels with his men, who takes the part of citizens against the petty irregularities or who punishes them unduly for gathering fire-wood, using wells and springs of water and even taking sheep, chickens and food when their regular supplies are insufficient.

Furthermore, he believed that his hobo soldiers, ranging far afield, saved the army much bloodshed; exploring sometimes twenty miles in advance, they often menaced Southern intrenchments so confidently that defenders retired in the belief that Sherman's whole force was at hand. Howard, approaching railway fortifications on February 7 with his men in battle array, saw a bummer return from the front, swallow-tails flying over the rump of his ancient steed, and his voice bawling, "Hurry up, General, we've got the railroad!" The intrepid nomads had, indeed, expelled Confederate regulars.

The extent to which the independent foragers outstripped the cavalry in energy was confessed by Kilpatrick when he reported that "the infernal bummers . . . managed to plunder every hamlet and town before the cavalry came up." Robbery and violence became more frequent than in Georgia, but from the testimony of both officers and men it was evident that the average Federal saw no physical torture forced upon residents. Colonel Kerr declared the country was "stripped of farm buildings, farm animals, fences, property, and food of every description," but "I never heard of a case in which violence was offered to citizens." General Force knew of "no personal abuse of the people." The *Columbia Daily Phoenix* declared that the Eastern men in Sherman's army were "the biggest thieves" and that men from Indiana, Illinois, and Iowa showed more scruples in protecting houses. The Confederate, J. P. Austin, of the Ninth Kentucky Cavalry, thought the brutality of the men was largely confined to the foreign element in the army. The Western troops displayed a much higher standard of morals. . . . It was the dregs of the large cities and the scum of Europe who seemed utterly devoid of all the instincts of humanity—those who joined the Federal army for plunder and to gratify their inhuman lusts.

As in Georgia, charges of rape were vague and usually made in the form of such propaganda as Wade Hampton put forth in his letter-writing duel with Sherman and Kilpatrick late in February. Before 1861 Hampton had been a wealthy and aristocratic citizen of Columbia, mixing lightly in statecraft. As a volunteer officer he had risen to high command in Lee's army, and had been sent down from Virginia to organize his native State against Sherman. His many public announcements predicting swift success served perhaps to irritate him as the weeks wore on with himself and the whole Confederate force unable to check the invaders. Moreover, the mansions of both himself and his father, noble structures with Grecian pillars, costly waterworks, beautiful gardens, and upground wine cellars two stories high, had been destroyed.

Public and private vengeance were apparent in the actions of Hampton's command shortly after the ruin of his home. His men penned papers reading "Death to foragers" on the bodies of some eighteen Union soldiers, some of whom were found to have had their throats cut. Kilpatrick, storming to Sherman with this news, was ordered to "kill man for man" and to mark their bodies in the same manner. "It is petty nonsense," said Sherman, "for Wheeler and Beauregard and such vain heroes to talk of our warring against women and children." To Hampton Sherman sent an affirmation of his right to forage: "It is a war right as old as history"; in Europe armies levied supplies from civil authorities during invasions, but in Carolina, said Sherman,

I find no civil authorities . . . therefore must collect directly from the people. I have no doubt this is the occasion of much misbehavior on the part of our men, but I cannot permit an enemy to judge and punish with wholesale murder. Personally I regret the bitter feelings . . . but they were to be expected, and I simply allege that those who struck the first blow and made war inevitable ought not in fairness to reproach us for the natural consequences.

He wrote Kilpatrick:

I want the foragers to be regulated and systematized, so as not to degenerate into common robbers. . . . If our foragers commit excesses, punish them yourself, but never let an enemy judge between our men and the law.

He told Howard he would not protect foragers "when they enter dwellings and commit wanton waste" or when they took "such things as are not needed by our army." He said, "if the people resist our foragers I will not deem it wrong," but "the Confederate Army must not be supposed the champion of any people." Hampton, threatening to kill two Yankee prisoners for every Confederate executed, answered Sherman:

> Your line of march can be traced by the lurid light of burning houses, and in more than one household there is now an agony far more bitter than death. The Indian scalped his victims regardless of age or sex, but with all his barbarity, he always respected the persons of his female captives. Your soldiers, more savage than the Indian, insult those whose natural protectors are absent.

Believing that Hampton was as mistaken in his sex charges as Hood had been in talking of Negro allies, Sherman let the correspondence drop.

The range of food brought in by the smokehouse rangers was not as wide as in Georgia, but it was bountiful. The Thirty-third Massachusetts delighted in blankets full of peanuts. Regiments commonly demanded peach butter of their foragers and received it in great crocks. General Force knew of a Negro who said: "Dese Yankee soldiers hab noses like hound-dogs. Massa hide all his horses away out dar in de swamp. De soldiers held up dere noses and sniff and sniff, and Lord a' massy, went straight to de horses." Major Henry O. March saw one day a pagan bacchanal—a string of Negroes, in lieu of horses, pulling a wagon filled with rare wines and brandies and reeling bummers who were far gone in song. He watched foragers bring featherbeds to camp, sleep upon them, and abandon them in the morning. The Thirty-third Massachusetts noted how soldiers slept on cotton bales, then "burned their beds at daybreak." It chronicled how bummers dragged pianos from houses to secure wires for bails on coffee kettles, and to make kindling from the rosewood frames.

As when the opposing armies had moved through Georgia, civilians knew not which was more vandalic, the cavalry of Kilpatrick or that of Wheeler. The latter had grown more ruthless as they entered South Carolina. The majority of the men were from Kentucky and Tennessee—all of them in fact with the exception of those of five Georgia organizations, hailing from the Mississippi Valley. For South Carolina, as the mother of the war, they had a hatred almost as keen as that of the Federals of the Great Valley. Chaplain Bradley heard a Union soldier tell a South Carolina farmer, "You're unfortunate to be living in this State." The man answered: "That's just the way Wheeler's men talk. . . . They come to our homes saying, 'Shell out here, since you commenced this muss.' "

From all parts of the South could now be heard criticisms of the Confederacy for having relied too strongly upon cavalry in the beginning of the war. Both North and South were swinging to Sherman's early contention that romantic cavalry was antiquated in a war such as was being waged.

In an even more vital department Sherman's original conception of this struggle was being justified. Southern railroads had collapsed. General Hill, writing from Augusta on January 29, had declared, "There is the greatest inefficiency or basest treachery in our railroad department." Long before Sherman had begun to twist iron in Georgia, Southern railroads had deteriorated so badly that while Lee's army and the citizens of Richmond had been short of food, Georgia's granaries, at the other end of the open freight lines, had been overflowing. Having relied upon Northern mechanics to repair their railroads before the war, Southerners could not or would not develop enough artisans for the work, once the conflict had begun. Having scorned industrial labor and business efficiency as things beneath the dignity of proud agrarians, the Southerners had seen the railways sink into decay. Sherman had aided this decline by destroying the roundhouses in Atlanta and by closing the ore and coal fields of Georgia and Tennessee.

Too late the South was learning what Sherman had pointed out to Louisiana secessionists in the winter of 1860-61—that in all history no nation of mere agriculturalists ever made successful war against a nation of mechanics.

Too late the South was learning that bravery was not enough.

48

GOD ALMIGHTY STARTED WIND

"WE must all turn amphibious, for the country is half under water," Sherman had written to Slocum on February 9, and it was almost as some incredible monster of the marshes that he appeared to the Confederates when he came splashing out of the Edisto swamps and strode on firmer ground toward Columbia.

Cool heads in the South realized that with this latest demonstration of Federal power the Confederacy was nearing its end. Confederate commissioners, meeting President Lincoln on February 3 aboard a steamship in the James River, had learned that there could be no peace until the South acknowledged Federal supremacy. Lee had been made commander in chief of all the gray armies, and was preparing to reinstate Joe Johnston in the Carolina command even if that offended President Davis.

As early as January 21 the *Raleigh Progress* had begun to prepare North Carolinians for invasion. It said that South Carolina was whipped and would not check Sherman. And now, at the end of February's second week, it was plain to all that Beauregard had been tricked into remaining so long at Augusta that Columbia was defenseless.

How seriously Sherman's raids were impairing Southern morale was to be seen in the desperate eloquence with which on February 14 North Carolina's governor, Zebulon B. Vance, called upon his people to take new heart. His official paper denounced the "thousands and thousands, absent without leave" from the Confederate armies, who were now "lurking in the woods and swamps." He declared that over 400,000 names stood on the muster rolls, yet only a fraction of that number were in the ranks. It was not lack of food that was causing defeat:

> Hundreds of thousands of bushels of grain now rot at various depots of the South for want of transportation; and this transportation cannot be protected because these absent soldiers are not at the post of duty.

When Vance pointed out how relatively little Southern territory was held by the Federals—none in Georgia save Savannah—he was admitting the success of Sherman's contention that impressive demonstrations, awesome raids, would win the war. Vance's call was a confession that Sherman had been right in believing it wiser to subjugate territory by raiding it rather than by occupying it. Bravely Vance argued with his people to forget the disheartening ease with which Federals marched through the South. He spoke with words that sounded like bugle notes:

> Thank God, the Confederacy does not consist in brick and mortar, or particular spots of ground, however valuable they may be in a military point of view. Our nationality consists in our people. Liberty dwells in the hearts of her votaries, and the ragged barefooted soldiers, standing in the depths of the forest, or in the shadow of the mountain, can offer her sacrifices which will be as sweet and as acceptable as those offered in gorgeous temples in the midst of magnificent cities.

As Vance's people read his words, they learned that on February 15 Beauregard had ordered Hardee to abandon Charleston and bring his troops to a rendezvous north of Columbia. Union gunboats, paralleling Sherman's march, quickly seized the city, and a shout of elation came from the whole North. The popular as well as the military mind understood that the hated city's fall was due to Sherman's severance of its railroad communications at Columbia.

Confederates had no opportunity to defend Columbia for long; yet their cavalry attempted to defy the approaching Federal army—a gallant but foolish gesture. From a military point of view there was but one chance to delay Sherman as his men swarmed up to the Congaree River, which protected the city on the west. With the Congaree bridges destroyed, Sherman, if he was in a hurry, must cross higher up, choosing pontoon sites on the smaller Broad and Saluda rivers, which united above Columbia to form the larger stream. However, the Southern cavalrymen brought field batteries to the east bank of the Congaree and during the night of February 15 shelled Hazen's division in its bivouac. Sherman, leaping to the conclusion that Hampton was responsible for this, later declared that if the Confederate had fought at the upper crossing,

> where fifty men could have held us for five days, I would have honored him . . . but in firing into my camps as he did . . . he must have known that such an act would exasperate my troops, and was perfectly unjustifiable. . . . I never knew of such a mean act . . . not only bad warfare but very bad policy.

According to his own contention, Hampton did not assume command of the defense until the following day.

To add to the kindling anger of the Federals, many of their regiments slept in and around an abandoned prison pen that they called Camp Sorghum, where, as Captain George W. Pepper put it, 13,000 Union officers had been lately jailed in a space intended for 500. During the night ragged, wan refugees from this band, which had been hastily moved into Columbia, came into the Federal camps to recite their sufferings. They told how in past months bloodhounds had been set to catch and mangle them when they had tried to escape.

Hazen worked to still the vengeance of his men next morning when he moved opposite the city. Opening with his batteries on some cavalry in Columbia's streets, he directed his gunners not to shoot at military cadets who were digging frantically at trenches just across the river: "They were such young things—mere boys." Sherman, riding up, ordered Hazen to shell the railroad station, which was "full of corn which we must have." Crowds could be seen carrying bags away from it. When a few shots had scattered the civilians, Sherman ordered six cannon balls fired for moral effect at the new State House, which stood on an eminence. The skill of the artillerist, Captain Francis DeGress, a

European member of Sherman's army, was to be seen two thirds of a century later in six scars upon the Capitol's façade. After the sixth explosion Sherman ordered the bombardment to cease.

Early in the morning Sherman had ordered that nothing in Columbia excepting war materials and public buildings should be burned. But when news came to him that his bivouacs had been bombarded during the night, he decided to revoke his orders and give the whole city to the torch. His better judgment, however, won and in a few minutes he said to Howard, "I'll let my order stand as it is."

A day was spent in manoeuvering regiments toward the upper crossings and in selecting pontoon sites, and on the morning of the seventeenth Sherman was sitting watching the bridge-builders when a courier arrived announcing that Colonel George A. Stone, with a brigade of Iowa men, had crossed the stream and had received the mayor's surrender.

There was still time for Sherman to attempt to guarantee Columbia's safety, no matter how vengeful his men might be. He could have issued orders restricting the troops to the ranks when they should enter the city. But this would have been to insult his soldiers, for it was a tradition that the first force which marched into a captive town should police it, then scatter hunting food and fun. Sherman knew that much of his army's willingness to march barefoot on frozen clods in Tennessee, thirsty in the awful heat of Mississippi, and drenched in the cold rains of Carolina, had been due to their appreciation for his kindness in eliminating from their lives drills, reviews, inspections, and many details that irked other armies. When asked in later years why he had not kept his men in formation after they had entered Columbia, Sherman said, "I would not have done such a harshness to save the whole town; they were men and I was not going to treat them like slaves."

Sending Stone on into the city, Sherman at the same time dispatched a message of reassurance to a Roman Catholic convent whose Mother Superior had asked protection on the ground that she had once taught his daughter Minnie in Ohio. Stone's Iowans, entering the city, found cotton bales piled in the streets—many cut open and some burning. Citizens later swore that no cotton had been fired after the Confederates had left around daybreak. There was mystery about this as well as about many other details that ensued—the affair at Columbia becoming the most disputed chapter in Sherman's life and an event about which Southern and Northern prejudices would cluster for more than two generations to follow.

Hampton, who declared that he had not assumed command of the city until the night of the sixteenth, nevertheless issued an order on the fourteenth directing all citizens to place their cotton where it could be burned rather than let it fall into the enemy's hands. He, Beauregard, and several citizens insisted that this cotton, although piled in the center of wide streets, had never been fired by Confederate command. Yet Major Chambliss, a Confederate ordnance officer, later said that at 3 A.M. on the seventeenth—eight hours before the first Federals entered—the city was illuminated by burning cotton, and Sherman, Howard, and other officers stationed across the river at the time confirmed his statement. S. H. M. Byers, a Federal captain who had escaped from Camp Sorghum and taken refuge in the cabin of a friendly Columbian Negro, declared that from his refuge he saw Hampton's cavalrymen firing the cotton before their departure. Equally reputable citizens declared that all this was untrue. A reasonable explanation was that Negroes, escaped prisoners, town hoodlums, or Confederate deserters kindled the blaze shortly before Stone's troops entered.

Sherman and Howard, arriving some time before noon, found Stone's men—their muskets stacked—helping a local fire-engine company extinguish the fire. Sherman comforted the mayor, Dr. F. J. Goodwin, with the news that only public buildings and war property would be destroyed, and that this work would be put off until some succeeding day. Now the wind was too high; it was blowing loose cotton from the torn bales over the houses until, in Sherman's words, it resembled a Northern snowstorm. A mob filled the streets; Negroes preached, capered, sang. Escaped Federal prisoners exulted. Convicts had been loosed from jail in some unaccountable fashion. Drunken men were not uncommon. Sherman saw a soldier among these and said to Howard, "Look out, or you'll have hell to pay; you'd better go and see about it in person." Howard found many of Stone's soldiers maudlin. White citizens and black slaves had met incoming troops with buckets and bottles of whisky. At midday, when the main body of the Fifteenth Corps marched through town, Hazen saw white residents

> fraternizing with the soldiers and even treating them, very unwisely, to wines and liquors, which were passed along the lines in buckets and tin pans and in one instance in a large tin boiler. . . . Many of the men in the ranks were drunk.

Colonel Stone explained the condition of his brigade:

> The men had slept none the night before, and but little the night before that, and many of them had had no supper the night before, and none of them breakfast that morning, hence the speedy effect of the liquor. . . . I ordered all liquor destroyed and saw fifteen barrels destroyed within five minutes.

Soldiers breaking into one building found a citizen at work among forty barrels of whisky. The poor fellow was only attempting to destroy it, but the men, suspecting him of poisoning the liquid, forced him to take a drink from each barrel with "the consequence that he was drunk for a week."

As the Fifteenth Corps passed on to bivouac beyond the town—the Seventeenth Corps skirted it entirely—comparative quiet came during the afternoon. But doom was in the air. Captain Pepper had heard soldiers singing, as they crossed the pontoon bridge:

Hail Columbia, happy land,
If I don't burn you, I'll be damned.

Citizens declared afterward that soldiers told them, "You'll catch hell tonight," and that friendly bluecoats warned them to steal away. Members of the fraternal order of Masons were said to have been advised to leave by brethren in Federal uniforms.

Sherman took up his headquarters in a mansion. The inevitable rush of women began. They wanted guards for their homes. A Mrs. Campbell Bryce was told by him not to fear soldiers—"the poor fellows are hungry and want a chicken. Give them a chicken." But he wrote out her order and as he did so a small boy came pranking through the room, making excessive noises. Sherman smiled at Mrs. Bryce and said, "Children should be cashiered, don't you think so?" Mrs. Bryce thought him "respectful and kindly" and looking more like "a pedagogue than a great general."

In a lull, Sherman opened a paper that had been pressed into his hand by an escaped Union prisoner on the street. It was a song, entitled "Sherman's March to the Sea," written by "Adjutant Byers, Fifth Iowa Infantry; Arranged and Sung by the Prisoners in Columbia Prison." Beginning "Our campfires shone bright on the mountain," it recited in five verses and a chorus the glories of the march from "the wild hills of Resaca" to "fair Savannah." Highly pleased, Sherman ordered Byers to be brought to him as soon as the army should have resumed its progress.

The afternoon passed pleasantly. The mayor came to take him calling upon families Sherman had known at Charleston twenty years earlier. He visited the daughter of the Poyas family, which had entertained him in 1844 when he had dislocated his shoulder hunting deer. She told how, a few hours before, she had saved her henroosts by showing the soldiers a book in which Lieutenant Sherman had written his name, so long ago. Much impressed, the soldiers had given her a guard, an Iowa boy who was tending her baby for her in the back room that minute.

Goodwin escorted Sherman to the home of Harris Simmons, whose brother had been Sherman's friend in Charleston, and as they departed, the Reverend A. Toomer Porter, an Episcopal divine who had joined the party, asked Sherman to spare a college library of the town. It was safe, said Sherman, but added that if it had been put to better use the South Carolinians would have known too much of history to have started a war.

At sundown Sherman said to Goodwin, "Go home and rest assured that your city will be as safe in my hands as if you had controlled it"; then he went to headquarters and lay down to rest. At some time around seven o'clock he saw fire shadows on the wall—a building was burning; cotton always smoldered; these were flames. He sent aides to investigate. They reported guards in control of a fire that had caught in a structure near the spot where the cotton bales had smoked earlier in the day.

In the center of town Howard was doing what had never before been done in Sherman's army—he was removing the original guards from a captive town. A point of honor it had been to intrust a city to those who entered it first. But the drunken men must go. At 9 P.M. Colonel W. B. Woods's brigade marched in. As a man of character—he was later a justice of the United States Supreme Court—Woods was as sound a choice for provost marshal as existed in the Fifteenth Corps. He found fire blazing in three places and immediately began arresting drunken or lawless soldiers, clapping 370 under guard, killing two and wounding thirty. Yet so wild was the mêlée, with the mobs mingling with his troops, that he could not, as he told Hazen, "get enough men together to pull down buildings in the fire's path." He was distressed. Hazen, himself an admirer of South Carolina's aristocracy and a stickler for discipline, toiled diligently to halt the flames, which he said had been started in a hundred places. He saw soldiers fight fire as long as their officers stood over them, then vanish the moment commanders' backs were turned. The officers, he said, were helpless—"No one ordered it, and no one could have saved it." The high wind and the "sternly retributive" privates were too much for any general.

By eleven o'clock the fire had made such headway that Sherman went out to fight it. With so many of his generals at work, he had thought the situation sufficiently officered. But things were growing worse. He moved the Simmons family to his own headquarters. He put soldiers on rooftrees in bucket brigades. He ordered the arrest of a tipsy private and saw Colonel Dayton shoot the fellow down when he resisted. Several of his aides had faces, whiskers, and hands singed fighting fire. He saw Howard, Logan, Hazen, Woods, and their assistants toiling. Guards were placed over furniture in the center of streets.

Muskets blazed noiselessly in the roar of flames as Woods's soldiers fired at figures racing by, torch in hand. Villains threw turpentine on houses and struck matches. Some said they were Union soldiers, others that they were mainly vagrants, or convicts, or Negroes, or those liberated Union prisoners. Howard brought in Hazen's whole division, but it was only a sudden shift in the wind around 3:30 A.M. that saved the city from total destruction.

Sherman, going to bed at four o'clock, said that half the town had been spared. Mayor Goodwin, appealing to the citizens of Augusta for charity a little later, said, "Two-thirds of the city is in ashes." The Rev. Mr. Porter estimated that thirteen hundred houses had been burned and seven thousand women and children driven into the street. The Ursuline Convent, valued at a hundred and twelve thousand dollars, including a two-thousand-dollar painting by the old Italian master Correggio, was destroyed. Guards, it was said, had helped the incendiarists while the nuns, with sparks burning holes in their flying robes, had shepherded the children into a cemetery. Certain citizens suspected that the soldiers had learned that the Mother Superior, born Baptista Lynch, was the sister of the Charleston Bishop, Patrick N. Lynch, who had celebrated secession with cathedral rites in 1861, and who had been conspicuously orating for the Confederacy ever since.

Other citizens told how soldiers had asked the location of the church where the South Carolina delegates had first assembled in 1860 to vote disunion. An outbreak of contagious disease had driven the secessionists to adjourn to Charleston, but the Federals wished to burn the local "nest." The sexton of the guilty structure—a Baptist church—was said to have cleverly directed the torches to a Methodist church near by, thus saving his building.

Responsibility for the burning of Columbia was never determined. A committee of local citizens, appointed to take the testimony of eyewitnesses, reported that

> Columbia was burned by the soldiers of General Sherman; that the vast majority of incendiaries were sober; that for four hours they were seen with combustibles firing house after house without any affectation of concealment and without the slightest check from the officers.

Soldiers of the Eighty-fifth Illinois said, "If the Union men didn't burn Columbia, it was because the fire was accidentally started before they got around to what they considered a duty." With the exception of Hazen, who thought the cotton fire unimportant, most Federal officers—particularly Howard, the God-fearing—declared that the cotton, originally fired by retiring Confederates, was the cause.

Citizens of the town later insisted that during the terrible night and the succeeding day Sherman "attributed the fire to liquor and nothing else." They heard him blame State and Confederate army leaders for making "an evacuated city a depot of liquor for an army to occupy." He later declared that Mayor Goodwin explained to him that he had begged Confederate leaders to destroy all the liquor before departing, but that they had refused to make themselves thus liable for damages.

No matter how much Sherman blamed liquor at the time of the fire, subsequent reasoning convinced him that the cotton was responsible. His conclusions were reached on logic and circumstantial evidence rather than eyewitness testimony, for he had not seen the general conflagration start. He read Hampton's order promising to fire cotton; he saw the bales burning, and was assured by many around him that the retiring enemy had applied the torch; he was told by aides that the holocaust had begun near the spot where the cotton fire had apparently been extinguished. Therefore when he wrote out his report of the campaign on April 4 he declared:

> And without hesitation, I charge General Hampton with having burned his own city of Columbia not with malicious intent . . . but from folly and want of sense, in filling it with lint, cotton and tinder. Our officers and men on duty worked well to extinguish the flames; but others not on duty, including the officers who had long been imprisoned there, rescued by us, may have assisted in spreading the fire after it had once begun, and may have indulged in unconcealed joy to see the ruin of the capital of South Carolina.

Ten years later, in writing his *Memoirs,* he discussed this reference in his report, saying:

> I distinctly charged it to General Wade Hampton, and confess I did so pointedly, to shake the faith of his people in him, for he was in my opinion a braggart, and professed to be the special champion of the people.

Although it was apparent to most unbiased students that in this statement he meant to explain how he had stressed, not invented, the matter of Hampton's responsibility, various Columbians in their unrelenting hatred of him stoutly insisted that the wording was an admission that he had deliberately lied about Hampton in his report. That he sincerely believed Hampton and the cotton chiefly to blame was made clear in 1872 when, called to testify in a lawsuit regarding the fire, he swore:

. . . the fire was originated with the imprudent act of Wade Hampton in ripping open bales of cotton, piling it in the streets, burning it and then going away . . . that God Almighty started wind sufficient to carry that cotton wherever He would, and in some way or other that burning cotton was the origin of the fire . . . some soldiers after the fire originated may have been concerned in spreading it, but not concerned in starting it.

His testimony was taken in a suit that asked damages for privately owned cotton, on the ground that the Carolina city had been "wantonly fired by the army of General Sherman either under his orders or with his consent and permission." In an attempt to get an unprejudiced verdict the hearing was held before representatives of three governments, Italy, Great Britain, and the United States. Unanimously it was decided that the fire was due to neither "the intention or default of either the Federal or Confederate officers."

The climax of the trial came when the plaintiff's lawyers produced the letter in which Sherman had informed Halleck from Savannah that the Fifteenth Corps would be first into Charleston or Columbia and that they generally did "their work pretty well." Sherman's old fondness for language more violent than his actions had come thus to plague him. On the witness stand he explained that by "their work" he had meant the destruction of railroads, public buildings, and war material generally. Howard, summoned to testify, declared that the corps *did* give iron an extra twist such as no other organization gave. Sherman admitted that the corps was bitter against South Carolina, but he rose to protect their reputation, saying: "They were a very kind set of men, and I have known them frequently to share their rations with citizens." He told how at Orangeburg they had fed wounded enemies in a hospital and cared for orphans.

Counsel asked him if they were not noted "for the marks they left upon a country." Sherman, obviously sparring for time, asked what was meant by "marks." "Devastation," said the lawyer. The general was almost treed. Instinctively honest, he could not pretend that his men had been silk-gloved gentlemen. But the Fifteenth Corps was his own—his own shadow multiplied fifteen thousand times. So he side-stepped, barking fiercely, "They killed every Rebel within range of their guns and left their bodies to *mark* the ground!"

After that, the examination sagged and Sherman left the stand with a pointed thrust at the Confederacy; he declared that he had wanted to avoid the destruction of Columbia "so as to prevent the usual clamor where a city was burnt, as in Pennsylvania." With this reminder that Lee's men had burned Chambersburg, he notified his old enemies that the sword of criticism could cut two ways. The trial ended where Sherman left it when he threw back his red head and snapped at opposing counsel, "If I had made up my mind to burn Columbia, I would have burnt it with no more feeling than I would a common prairie dog village, but I did not do it!"

49

SPLENDID LEGS

FOR two days Sherman remained in the ruined city of Columbia, waiting for a cessation of the wind before destroying the Confederate arsenal and Treasury printing office. He did what he could to ease the pangs of the sufferers, giving them five hundred cattle for beef, and presenting his private allotment of the standard rations to families whom he knew. He sent Charles Ewing with the Mother Superior and the homeless schoolchildren to occupy the home of the Confederate General John S. Preston, brother-in-law of Wade Hampton. As the procession of white-clad little girls arrived at the mansion a few blocks from the charred center of town, they found its occupant, Logan, preparing to burn it; soldiers were rolling barrels of pitch into the cellar. In later years Columbians said Logan had "sworn mightily" when Ewing handed him Sherman's order, but that he set soldiers to removing the barrels.

Sherman left a hundred stands of muskets with the citizens when he marched northward on the nineteenth. With him went between two hundred and four hundred white refugees and many Negroes, the civilian train being guarded by the escaped officers from Camp Sorghum. Three weeks later, Sherman would guess the emigrants to number from twenty to thirty thousand. The presence of so many noncombatant dependents was one of his reasons for postponing the issuance of a nonforaging order he had planned to issue when the army reached North Carolina. He had told Frank Blair that in the next State the army would pay for all food. But in Cheraw, his last South Carolina stop, he saw a copy of the *New York Tribune* that betrayed the secret of his supply rendezvous at New Berne. This, he knew, would inform the enemy that he was striking at Goldsboro, not far from the port. To make this revelation more serious was the discovery that Joe Johnston was now commanding the opposition, and could, with this information, force the battle that Sherman had been eager to avoid. In the face of this threat, Sherman must continue foraging, since he could expect no Federal supplies until he met provision ships at crossings on the Cape Fear or Neuse rivers ahead. However, as the State line was passed on March 7 Sherman had his generals issue orders for the gentler treatment of North Carolinians, who had been the last Southerners to secede from the Union. His directions to Kilpatrick read:

In conversation with people, evince a determination to maintain the Union, but treat all other matters as beneath a soldier's notice. Give us a whole country with a Government and leave details to the lawyers.

Deal as moderately and fairly by North Carolinians as possible, and fan the flame of discord already subsisting between them and their proud cousins of South Carolina. There never was much love between them. Touch upon the chivalry of running away, always leaving their families for us to feed and protect, and then on purpose accusing us of all sorts of rudeness.

Guards now stood before plantation houses. One Westerner, Matthew L. Jamison, described how

ladies on porches looked at us floundering knee-deep in mud and torrents of rain. We glanced ruefully at them out of the shadow of our lowering, drenched hat rims.

But as the flames from buildings grew less frequent, smoke from burning forests grew heavier. North Carolina's turpentine forests blazed as bummers touched matches to congealed sap in notches on tree trunks. Colonel Hamilton wrote that "it looked like a fire in a cathedral; the smoke could hardly escape through the green canopy, and hung like a pall." Stretcher-bearer Benton saw weird beauty in the scene:

. . . in the endless blue columns swaying with the long, swinging step which became such a marked characteristic of the men who marched down to the sea; in the long bugle peal and rumbling artillery with chafing horses; in the glimmer of muskets and sabers; and all to be heard and seen only by glimpses under the smoke and muffled by the Niagara-like roar of the flames as they licked up turpentine and pitch. Now came rolling back from the depths of the pine forest, the chorus of thousands singing, "John Brown's body lies a-moldering" . . . at once a prophecy and a fulfillment.

The march became eerie, fantastic, awesome. A majestic horror rose on the sky as the army entered the State, vicious sheets of flame and evil smoke billowing from a turpentine factory, said to have been fired by Wade Hampton. The Fifty-third Ohio saw the smoke stand "as big as a mountain. It was awful. It rose four miles toward heaven, leaping and roaring like a bursting volcano." Benton saw the smoke at a distance of fifteen miles "like the approaching body of a tempest." The Fifty-third Ohio saw cavalry crossing a creek close to the conflagration—"and the water was so infernally hot from the heated air of that mighty cauldron that it took the hair off the horses' legs as they went through it on the double-quick." Colonel Hamilton saw burning barrels float downstream; it made him think of Dante's Inferno. On night marches soldiers carried pine knots ablaze, and set watchers to recalling tales of ragged pilgrims in religious processionals.

Inexpressible emotions were mounting in the army. Captain Byers, whom Sherman had attached to his staff as reward for having written the pleasing song, noted how the soldiers shouted at the sight of the general. Byers did not know how new this custom was. He heard staff officers halt at the sound of rolling cheers in the distance, and say, "Listen to them cheering Billy Sherman!" Veterans who had not stooped to anything so naïve in three years at last were becoming hero-worshipers. Sherman had brought them so far, kept them so healthy, shed so little of their blood! The magnitude of their tramping had begun to dawn upon them.

Where previously Sherman had grinned absent-mindedly at his jocular men, or waved to them a careless hand, he now stopped his horse and talked to soldiers. "He seemed to know the names of hundreds of his troops," said Byers, many other officers later verifying this as fact. Byers was amazed at Sherman's indifference to dress. "Once before breakfast Colonel Audenreid said, 'There's going to be a battle today sure. The General's there by the fire putting on a clean collar. The sign's dead sure.' " Before night a stiff skirmish was fought. Breakfast was always eaten before daylight. Byers saw Sherman remain in bed "but two hours many a night." Other soldiers said, "He seemed to need no more sleep than a bird."

More and more, in Southern eyes, he began to take on the qualities of some daemonic creature who coursed the blackening sky. "His failure will be grand, prodigious, equal to that of Phaëton when he attempted to drive the chariot of the sun," said the *Richmond Sentinel* on February 25. Such descriptions frightened as many readers as they encouraged. Despondency was spreading from the civilian population to the Confederate soldiers. On February 24 Lee wrote Vance that the despair of North Carolinians was threatening to break up his army in Virginia:

> Desertions are becoming very frequent and there is good reason to believe that they are occasioned to a considerable extent by letters written to the soldiers by their friends at home.

In the past two weeks several hundred North Carolina soldiers had left his ranks to go home, rifle in hand:

> It has been discovered that despondent persons represent to their friends in the army that our cause is hopeless, and that they had better provide for themselves.

Lee urged Vance to change public sentiment.

The Virginian had his back to the wall, for on the twenty-second Johnston had telegraphed him that the forces in Carolina were inadequate to check Sherman. Colonel Archer Anderson, adjutant to Johnston, said twenty-five years later that Lee's army in Virginia, living for months

> on less than one-third rations . . . was demoralized not by the enemy on its front [Grant], but by the enemy in Georgia and the Carolinas.

How well Sherman had applied the psychology of fear since leaving Savannah was stated by himself on March 15, in a letter to Major General Quincy A. Gillmore, commanding in South Carolina:

> All real good soldiers should now be marching.
>
> Do not let your command rest on its oars, but keep them going all the time, even if for no other purpose than to exhaust the enemy's country or compel him to defend it. The simple fact that a man's home has been visited by an enemy makes a soldier in Lee's or Johnston's army very, very anxious to get home to look after his family and property.

Through the Confederacy went the rumor that Sherman's Westerners, having conquered the South, would conquer the East and make their general dictator of the whole land. From its Richmond correspondent such views came to the *London Times* in an article written on March 4:

> The long arrest of Grant before Richmond will hardly be compensated by his capture of that city if Lee should eventually be forced to evacuate it, for it will be attributed more to the strategy of Sherman than to the coercion of Grant. Sherman, within a few weeks of this time, may, by possibility, be autocrat of this continent, but no conceivable concatenation of circumstances can, in my judgment, place the crown upon the head of Grant.

The Richmond critic, calling Sherman the ablest of Union generals, thought it very significant that he had refused to admit Negro soldiers to his army, and that at Savannah he had reputedly forbidden any junction between his own white Westerners and General Foster's army, which contained so many blacks:

> If in the Armageddon which now seems approaching General Sherman once gets the South down, it may be confidently predicted that his policies will be more in harmony with those of General Lee than those of President Lincoln. Mr. Lincoln has found him hitherto a very valuable friend—it is pos-

sible that before the end comes he will find him a still more dangerous enemy. During this war I have seen no man who seemed to me to possess so much of the temper of Cromwell as Sherman. . . . Vain, eager, enthusiastic, fanatical, at times gloomy and reticent, at others impulsive and talkative, by some regarded as half-mad when the fit is on him, General Sherman possesses a character which, unless I am mistaken, is of the stuff of which great and mysterious actors in history are often made.

Southern newspapers declared that Sherman was saying that slavery would exist no matter who won the war and that he some day expected to own a thousand chattels. The *New York Herald*, after studying the Southern press, said on March 3:

The idea that Sherman is irresistible is at this moment a great demoralizing influence through the South and is enough to shatter any power that can be put in front of him.

Helpless rage was visible in the *Richmond Examiner's* account, on March 29, of how 487 Yankee captives, shoeless, hatless, blackened by pine smoke, had been sent by Wade Hampton to prison in the Confederate capital. The prisoners were

scabs, scavengers and scum of creation. Never since the war began has such a crew of hell-born men, accursed and God-forsaken wretches polluted the air and defiled the highways of Richmond with the concentrated essence of all that is lecherous, hateful and despised. And these are part and parcel of that human fungi Johnston's noble army are confronting. . . . If he cannot successfully resist them, God help Richmond and her citizens.

Jealousy of the Western forces had been growing in the Army of the Potomac as the reports of Sherman's triumphs continued to arrive. Suspicion showed its head here and there quite naturally as Northern newspapers republished Southern accounts of outrages, sex orgies with Negresses, and wild rumors of devastation. Since December Western editors had been patronizing the Army of the Potomac, or, like the *Cincinnati Commercial*, taunting it. On December 12 that paper had asked whether the Eastern army would

now improve its last chance to do the work that has been before it throughout the war, or will it wait for the boys from the West, who have fought their way from Ohio to the ocean, to reap the long-awaited harvest of glory on the banks of the royal James?

It angered Eastern officers to read republication of the *Richmond Sentinel's* declaration of February 27:

The Yankees certainly think he [Sherman] is the first of their commanders, even the fires of Lieutenant-General Grant have paled before the splendor of Sherman's achievements. . . . Sherman is their hero . . . the idol of the hour . . . newspapers are filled with him. The populace babble of him.

And Sherman's first letters to reach the North, after his arrival at Fayetteville on March 12, crowed with a boyish pride in the Western army—a pride that unconsciously belittled the Army of the Potomac by comparison. To Stanton Sherman said, "There is now no place in the Confederacy safe against the army of the West"; and to Grant he wrote of how his force had conquered "roads that would have stopped travel to almost any other body of men I ever heard of." From Savannah Sherman had sent North descriptions of his "invincible army," and of how it had stormed forts that had long defied Eastern troops.

The speed with which the Westerners had covered the last stretch of country, ending at Fayetteville, had flushed Sherman with pride. Watching the One Hundred and Fourth Illinois tramp fifteen muddy miles in five hours, he said, "It's the damndest marching I ever saw." His bummers had dashed into Fayetteville hours ahead of the skirmishers and, driving Wade Hampton from his breakfast table, had actually attempted to wrest the city from whole regiments of cavalry. Repulsed, the hobo soldiers clung to the outskirts of the city until Hampton evacuated it on the twelfth.

Entering the city, Sherman scanned the river front. Several days before he had sent scouts through the country toward Wilmington to tell Terry of his progress and needs. Had they made it? A steamboat whistle answered from the river, the army set up a monstrous shout, and soon a Federal ship's captain was handing to the general letters from Terry. The campaign was moving like clockwork. The news was all good. Schofield was repairing the railroad from New Berne toward Goldsboro. Terry had troops ready to start marching for that city. Both forces on the seacoast had received Sherman's orders for the gigantic rendezvous at Goldsboro on the twentieth.

For two days Sherman remained at Fayetteville preparing for what he was sure would be the last campaign of the war. No uniforms or shoes had come up the river, but coffee and oats had arrived. Food was in the wagons. All the refugees were started down the river toward Wilmington.

The springtime was very beautiful. Lilacs and apple blossoms scented the air. Soldiers talked much about mocking birds. Only war property was destroyed in Fayetteville. One thing only marred the visit—an incident that Byers witnessed. To Sherman's headquarters in the city came, one day, a Southerner who explained to the staff that he had been Sherman's intimate at West Point. He would wait for the return of the general, who was riding about town. Sherman eventually arrived. The Southerner rushed forward. Sherman's face lit up, then suddenly froze with reproach and pathos; he said that they could not be friends; the Southerner had betrayed him, the old school, the country, by joining the Confederacy. "I will not punish you," said Sherman, "only go your way." Byers saw the caller depart "ashy white" while Sherman entered the house to sit down at the midday meal. Byers said:

> The staff never saw him under such emotion; the corners of his mouth twitched. He could scarcely eat . . . his hand trembled as he raised bread to his mouth. . . . There were tears in his eyes. He spoke as if he might not live through it all.

By the night of the fifteenth, however, Sherman had swung back to a gayer mood. His columns were marching on Goldsboro. He had warned his lieutenants to expect anything from Johnston. At two o'clock the next morning he was listening in the darkness and between times writing letters. He was happy at news that Sheridan might join him. Instead of resenting the prospect of dividing honors with the man who next to himself was the chief Union hero at the moment, he welcomed the idea. To Terry he wrote:

> I will make him a deed of gift of every horse in the State to be settled on the day of judgment. He will be a disturbing element in the grand and beautiful game of war, and if he reaches me, I'll make all North Carolina howl.

At two in the morning of a spring day he did not write of "horrid war," as he had done so often before and would do thereafter. "The grand and beautiful game of war," it was in this moment. Perhaps the artist in him had risen uppermost, moving the pen in that intoxicating hour of the night when the imagination is apt to take wing—the artist viewing his art as something above life and death. He had risked his reputation on a particular way of war, and success was at hand. He had imagined the long march and here it was certain of conclusion. He had brought conception and realization to a harmonious pitch.

Perhaps he was ironic when he wrote "the grand and beautiful game," but it is not likely. While writing in the night he was more apt to be poetic than to be grim. Perhaps he was yielding this once to the tragic fascination of war as a game—perhaps he was caught for an hour in the immemorial tragedy that develops when merciful men begin to like the business of devastation. Twenty-five years later he wrote, in remembering Carolina:

> To be at the head of a strong column of troops in the execution of some task that requires brain, is the highest pleasure of war—a grim one and terrible, but which leaves on the mind and memory the strongest mark.

All of Sherman's craft was needed as he pressed onward, feinting and manoeuvering to reach Raleigh or Goldsboro without a battle. He did not wish to fight Johnston at a time when the transportation of wounded would be a serious problem. When a brisk skirmish developed at Averasboro on the sixteenth, Sherman prevented it from developing into a battle. Flanking drove Hardee's troops back. By the eighteenth Sherman was within twenty-five miles of Goldsboro and thought that Johnston would abandon it without a fight, but on the night of the nineteenth when he was with the right wing helping it move through unmapped country, a courier arrived with word that Johnston's whole army was assailing Slocum's left wing at Bentonville.

On the moment Sherman sent the Fifteenth Corps on another of its old whiplash marches, a night-time rush that brought it to Slocum's side by dawn. Close behind it came the Seventeenth Corps, and the reënforcements enabled Slocum, who had at length stopped the Confederate rush, to take the offensive. But Sherman, having been told by Kilpatrick that Johnston had recently announced his strength at 40,000, evaded a pitched battle. He knew that Schofield and Terry were nearing Goldsboro. If he could wait for them to arrive, Johnston must retire peaceably.

But as he established quiet in his ranks, the pugnacious Mower, edging forward, spied a chance to turn Johnston's flank—and struck! Surprising the Confederates, he sliced through line after line, leading his men on foot, and was barely halted a few rods from a bridge that would have cut off Johnston's retreat. And it was Sherman who stopped him. Unaware of Mower's opportunity, and fearing that a general engagement would be brought on, Sherman recalled his charging soldiers, and the enemy trailed safely away.

It was Sherman's last chance, had he known it, to establish himself in history as a great battle leader. That he missed it did not annoy him, although years later he admitted that he had made a mistake in not throwing the full force of the army behind Mower at the crucial moment. And he liked to hint, in after years, that he might have fought it out then and there had he known that Johnston did not have the reputed strength of 40,000. But the fame and glory to be won in crucial battles did not tempt him. The old tradition of war as a test of chivalric prowess on a given battle ground had died with the rise of Sherman and Grant. And of Sherman it could be said he had never clearly won a battle, nor ever failed to win a campaign.

Howard was sure that Sherman's belief at the Battle of Bentonville "was that there had been enough blood shed already, and that Johnston would retire, leaving his objective, Goldsboro." Howard himself was grieving over spilled blood. The Confederate Stephen D. Lee had sent a note through the lines telling him that Hardee's sixteen-year-old son, Willie, had joined a Texas cavalry regiment a few hours before the fight, and after kissing his father farewell, had been killed in his first charge. Willie had been Howard's Sunday-school pupil at West Point, and for his sake Howard took great pains to protect friends and relatives of the Hardees in North Carolina.

As Sherman had foreseen, Johnston retired, opening the way to Goldsboro. On the edge of the town Sherman met Terry arriving from the seacoast, and when they entered the city on March 23, they found Schofield waiting with his Twenty-third Corps. The campaign was over, 80,000 assembled. Sherman looked back on four hundred and twenty-five blackened miles as "one of the longest and most important marches made by an organized army in a civilized country." Since July, 1863, when Sherman had begun his raids with the Meridian campaign, he had led his armies across twenty-five hundred miles. The legs of the Fifteenth Corps, which had followed him most faithfully, had walked as far as any emigrants passing from mid-Ohio to the gold fields of California.

As Sherman's men came into camp around Goldsboro, they heard that all foragers were to turn in their horses, and that bummers must rejoin original regiments. The hobo soldiers knew that their great days were done. Some of them drew rein on the edge of camp, brooded over the discipline that awaited them, listened for a time to the officers barking orders among the bivouacs, then whirled their horses' heads west and kept going until they found peace for their souls in the turmoil of cowboy life and Indian fights.

Sherman brought Schofield, Terry, Cox, and other newly arrived officers to see his tatterdemalions marching toward town. Ordering wagons from the road, he held a review. Laughing and cursing, the men made clumsy attempts to close files that had been open for months. General Force called it "a sorry sight." Colonel Kerr noted that "nearly every soldier had some token of the march on his bayonet from a pig to a potato." Sherman's generals told their guests anecdotes—one, often repeated, was of soldiers wading South River swamps hip-deep while a wag chirped, "I guess Uncle Billy's struck this stream endwise."

"They don't march very well, but they will fight," Sherman told Schofield. More than half were shoeless; some walked on blood-stained wrappings of old blankets. Trousers were torn, scanty, many of them nothing but breechclouts. Bare legs swung defiantly back and forth—calves knotted like professional dancers'. Colonel Hamilton, two days earlier, had stopped outside a hospital window through which surgeons tossed amputated arms and legs. In the grass Hamilton could distinguish the legs of infantrymen from cavalrymen—the former so thick, the latter so slim.

"Look at those poor fellows with bare legs," said Frank Blair, as the regiments, grinning in embarrassment, swung past the generals.

"Splendid legs! Splendid legs!" Force heard Sherman bark. "I'd give both of mine for any one of 'em."

But the review, Sherman realized, was a failure, and after two regiments had passed, he ended it. Reviews bored him exceedingly, the pretentiousness being too much for his patience. The correspondent of the *New York World*, watching him at a review in Goldsboro, wrote:

> Sherman acts as if he would rather be engaged in another kind of business . . . he seems all the while to be wishing it was over. While the troops are going by he must be carrying on a conversation or smoking or fidgeting in some way or other. . . . Very often he looks up just in time to snatch off his hat . . . and the way he puts that hat on again! With a jerk and drag and jam as if it were the most objectionable hat in the world and he was specially entitled to entertain an implacable grudge against it.

As he took up his residence in Goldsboro, Sherman wrote a response to congratulations sent him by Governor Frederick F. Low of California: "I do not believe a body of men ever existed who were inspired by nobler impulses or a holier cause than they who compose this army." He told Low that in California he had learned

> the art of making long journeys in safety, to endure privations with cheerfulness and to thrive under the most adverse circumstances, and these have enabled us to make strides in war which may seem gigantic to the uninitiated.

Then he sang a little with his pen:

> I bid you all be of good cheer, for there are plenty of brave men still left who are determined that the sun, as he daily reviews our continent from Chesapeake to San Francisco Bay, shall see a united people and not a bundle of quarreling factions.

50

MR. LINCOLN SPEAKS PRIVATELY

ON March 16 Adjutant Byers landed from a steamer at City Point and hurried to Grant's headquarters. Sewn in his coat lining was Sherman's letter to the chieftain, a letter written four days before when the Western army had reached Fayetteville, and announcing success. "Don't tell them we have been cutting any great swaths in the Carolinas," Sherman had said to Byers, "simply tell them the facts; tell them that the army is not lost but is well and still marching." While Byers ripped the message from his coat, Grant sat cross-legged on a camp stool, waiting, and when the general read his friend's words, Byers saw his face "glowing with silent satisfaction." All at once he called:

"Come in here, Ord," and Sherman's companion of young days in California entered. "Listen to this," said Grant, and read the letter aloud.

"Good! Good!" shouted Ord, dancing. "I was beginning to get afraid."

"Not I," said Grant, "not a bit. I knew my man. I knew General Sherman."

A few days later another Western emissary, Adjutant F. Y. Hedley of the Thirty-second Illinois, arrived in New York carrying Frank Blair's order to buy band instruments for the Seventeenth Corps. Knowing peace to be imminent, Blair wished to dress his legions for the grand review. Hedley, bronzed and rough, wandered through the lobbies of the Metropolitan Hotel late at night. He heard sleek Eastern officers ridiculing Sherman's army as undisciplined and coarse. He blazed out in hot retort. An old man with white hair hanging beneath a soldier's cap, and with a long cape concealing all sign of rank, approached Hedley. He said any one of Sherman's men should be his guest, and handed Hedley his card:

ROBERT ANDERSON
Major-General, U.S.A.

The hero of Fort Sumter, feeble for his sixty years, took Hedley to his home on Fifth Avenue and made the youth describe the famous marches. In return, Anderson related tales of the days when he and Sherman had been together at Fort Moultrie and Louisville. "He is one of my boys," said Anderson, when at the end of two days of conversation he saw the youth depart laden with messages to Sherman.

Then the frail old man—he had never been strong since his Kentucky experience in 1861—turned back to his pathetic pursuit, the translation of French books. One moment of reborn glory was coming to him, however. Orders were out for him to preside at a flag-raising over recaptured Sumter on April 14—the fourth anniversary of its surrender. He was to pull up the very flag he had pulled down.

From Sherman came a letter, regretting that he could not attend:

> It looks as a retribution decreed by Heaven itself. But the end is not yet . . . "mine not thine is vengeance, saith the Lord," and we poor sinners must let Him work out the drama to its close. I have not been in Charleston since we parted, then captain and lieutenant, in the spring of 1846, but I can see it in imagination almost as clearly as you behold it with your eyes and though I may be far away, you may think of me standing by your side. . . .

The religious note, so rare in Sherman's previous and subsequent letters, was evidently stressed to please a highly religious old man for whom Sherman felt affection.

In his letters to Ellen, Cump mixed a new assertiveness with tenderness. Success in the last year had refreshed the self-respect that had been well scotched in the husband during prewar years of failure. He knew that his wife, no matter how proud she might be of her warrior husband, was still prouder to be the daughter of Thomas Ewing. At odd times in his life he had perked up to give Ellen "her marching orders" or "to take the bit in my teeth," but with his recurring necessity to see her go home to Lancaster, he had never been able to establish himself in the rôle of masterful husband.

Now, as if to remind her that he was no longer the bruised and nervous mate whom she must soothe and protect, Cump wrote Ellen that his huge army held "a wonderful trust of my knowledge and attach much success to it. . . . The last march is by far the most important in conception and execution of any act of my life." He wrote that the soldiers "always said and felt that the Old Man would bring them out all right." He explained to her how, before leaving Savannah, he had arranged for supplies to meet him at Goldsboro and how when arriving there the loaded supply trains came thundering along from the ocean ninety-six miles away. Union officers escaping from Confederate captors in the vicinity had told him that the coincidence of the supplies and the army "made the Rebel officers swear that I was the Devil himself, a compliment," he pointed out to Ellen, "that you can appreciate." If his fame which filled the world contributed to her happiness and pleasure he hoped she would enjoy it. But the small ghost in the sergeant's uniform still marched with the general— "Oh, that Willy could hear and see."

From a distance, Cump attempted to rule the charitable activities with which Ellen busied herself. He learned that in St. Louis she had persuaded the departmental commander, Dodge, to help her free political prisoners. He sent Dodge word not to be swayed by friendship:

> You must not issue these orders and release these people simply because Mrs. Sherman requests you to do so. . . . I appreciate fully what you are doing, and why you do it, but, my dear General, you know you must cling to a soldier's duty.

Cump was perturbed when Ellen wrote him that she was planning to take part in a Sanitary Fair to be given at Chicago in May to raise soldiers' relief funds. She had written her father regarding it on February 13:

> I received a letter from Bishop Duggan of Chicago inviting me to preside at the Catholic table and expressing a wish that I could comply if possible as Catholics of the North need all we can do to relieve them from the stigma of disloyalty.

Republicans were accusing Irish Catholics, as Democrats opposed to Abolition, of leaning toward the Confederacy, and were whispering that the Papacy, like all other European thrones, sympathized with the aristocratic South. And because many Irish had been prominent among Copperheads, otherwise sensible Northerners were apt to forget the presence in the Federal army of so many thousands of Irish and German Catholics. It was not the religious phase that worried Cump. He wrote his objections:

> I don't approve of ladies selling things at a table. So far as superintending the management of such things, I don't object, but it merely looks unbecoming for a lady to stand behind a table to sell things. Still, do as you please.

Sherman's realization of how single-handed had been his achievement in the Carolinas came to him as he read Grant's messages on March 16 and 24, confessing that only now, when it was so late, had Thomas and Canby begun to carry out orders given earlier by Grant. Canby was at last starting to raid from Mobile into the interior. Thomas was starting Wilson's cavalry against the Confederate arsenal at Selma, and Stoneman's horsemen from Knoxville to join Sherman in North Carolina. But Thomas had not yet started on Grant's order that he move up through East Tennessee to catch Lee if the latter fled from Richmond to the mountains. Grant had concluded that a campaign was beyond the Rock of Chickamauga: "He never can make one there or elsewhere," he wrote Sherman.

Sherman's mind dwelt constantly on Grant's problem, and on March 24 he wrote his friend:

> I think I see pretty clearly how, in one more move, we can checkmate Lee, forcing him to unite Johnston with him in the defense of Richmond, or by leaving Richmond, to abandon the cause. I feel certain that if he leaves Richmond, Virginia leaves the Confederacy.

The following evening Sherman started for City Point, leaving Schofield in command, and saying in the presence of a *New York Herald* reporter at New Berne: "I'm going up to see Grant for five minutes and have it all chalked out for me and then come back and pitch in. I only want to see him for five minutes and won't be gone but two or three days."

A steamer landed him at City Point on the afternoon of March 27, and he hurried to the log house where Grant lived with his family and staff. The generals shook hands. It had been just a year since they had parted in Cincinnati. For an hour they talked. Then Grant remarked that President Lincoln was at the wharf on the steamer *River Queen*, having come down from Washington a few days before to visit the army. Grant suggested that they call upon him.

Four years had passed since Sherman had met Lincoln, and while time had eased much of the pain the President had given the soldier at their interview, Sherman still remembered how weak, how trivial, how like a pettifogging politician, Lincoln had seemed in those days of impending horror. Never had Sherman ceased to regard the President as a politician—now they met in the ship's cabin.

Ten years later Sherman described how the President "remembered me perfectly." Admiral Porter, who in after years insisted that he was present at the meeting, said that Lincoln could not recall ever having seen Sherman before, and was only able to remember the occasion when "the General reminded him of the circumstance. This was rather singular on the part of Mr. Lincoln, who was, I think, remarkable for remembering people." According to Sherman's memory, Porter did not accompany himself and Grant on this visit to Lincoln, but had come along when they returned for a second talk on the following day. However, he said that he was not sure, and in view of Porter's certainty and the fact that otherwise their accounts agreed, he would not challenge the admiral's statement. It was Porter's habit to make notes of interesting conversations immediately upon their conclusion and he had done so in this instance.

Lincoln began the first conference by asking Sherman to tell him about the great marches, and he laughed over stories of the bummers gleaning food. Sherman and Porter described in later years how often and how anxiously Lincoln returned to the subject of the army's safety, and to the fear that Johnston would escape capture. Porter heard Sherman answer:

> "I have him where he cannot move without breaking up his army, which once disbanded can never again be got together." Sherman energetically insisted that he could command his own terms and that Johnston would have to yield to his demands, but the President was very much decided about the matter and insisted that the surrender of Johnston's army must be obtained on any terms. . . . Sherman, as a subordinate officer, yielded his views to those of the President.

Strong as might be this claim of Porter's that Lincoln had ordered extension of "any terms" necessary for the capitulation of Johnston, it would receive further measure of substantiation from Gideon Welles, the Secretary of the Navy, who said:

> During the early months of 1865 he [Lincoln] frequently expressed his opinion that the condition of affairs in the rebel States was deplorable and did not conceal his apprehension that, unless immediately attended to, they would in consequence of their disturbed civil, social and industrial relations, be worse after the rebellion was suppressed.

Dramatically Sherman, after disapproving so many of Lincoln's acts across the past four years, was finding that the President's chief concern was now his own—his own old dread of anarchy. Sherman remembered in later years the President's statement in regard to this on the *River Queen:*

> Mr. Lincoln was full and frank in his conversation, assuring me that in his mind he was all ready for the civil reorganization of affairs at the South as soon as the war was over; and he distinctly authorized me to assure Governor Vance and the people of North Carolina that, as soon as the rebel armies laid down their arms, and resumed their civil pursuits, they would at once be guaranteed all their rights as citizens of a common country; and that to avoid anarchy the State governments then in existence, with their civil functionaries, would be recognized by him as the government *de facto* till Congress could provide others.

Sherman was finding that the President saw eye to eye with him in his desire to give prompt mercy and generosity to the enemy as soon as they laid down their arms. Porter said that Lincoln "was willing that the enemy should capitulate on the most favorable terms." Sherman heard the President declare that he wished "to restore all the men of both sections to their homes"; it must have recalled how often he himself had told Southerners what he would do for them if they would only abandon "rebellion," how he had told Hood, "I will this day make as much sacrifice for the peace and honor of the South as the best-born Southerner among you." Porter, listening to the President, thought that

> he wanted peace on almost any terms. . . . His heart was tenderness throughout, and as long as the rebels laid down their arms, he did not care how it was done.

That Lincoln should authorize him to deal with civil authorities in North Carolina did not seem strange to Sherman. In September, 1864, the President had encouraged him by telegraph to hold peace parleys with Governor Brown of Georgia and with Vice President Stephens of the Confederacy. At Savannah Stanton had sanctioned his civil negotiations with peace-hungry Georgians. In September, 1863, Lincoln had wanted to publish Sherman's letter written from the Big Black River, discussing in full the proper civil policy toward secessionists. The Administration had not objected to his Memphis program for encouraging Mississippi Rebels to recant, nor had it given anything but silent assent to his papers assuring Confederate populations that he considered their civil liberties as good as restored whenever they abandoned secession.

Sherman saw that the President agreed with him as to the war's purpose—the restoration of the Union, the compulsion of the South to obey the Federal laws, not the triumph of Northern States over their political and economic rivals, the Southern States, nor yet a moral crusade against slavery. War was merely a measure to reëstablish the supremacy of that general Government which had ruled East, South, and West—sections that were bound together by a common tongue, a similar ancestry, and by geography. In that war slavery had died an incidental death. Sherman believed that it, like the right of secession, would be dead on the day the Confederate armies surrendered.

Not yet did Sherman comprehend the magnitude nor the fury of the Republican Radical program, which, not halting with the emancipation of the slave, called for action either military or political until the Negro had been made a voter and a citizen equal to his late master and possessed of at least a part of his property.

Both Porter and Sherman were impressed by Lincoln's repeated wish that no more blood be shed. They heard him ask if it were not possible to avoid another fight. Grant and Sherman replied that they were afraid it would take "one more desperate and bloody battle." Sherman said, "We cannot control that event; this necessarily rests with our enemy."

"My God, my God," groaned Lincoln, "can't you spare more effusions of blood? We have had so much of it."

As a general who had characteristically manoeuvered to avoid battles, Sherman was beginning to understand this President whom he had so often criticized. At one point in the conversation, as Sherman remembered it, Lincoln said,

> in the most simple manner, "Sherman, do you know why I took a shine to Grant and you?"
>
> "I don't know, Mr. Lincoln, you have been extremely kind to me, far more than my deserts."
>
> "Well," said Lincoln, "you never found fault with me."

Perhaps Sherman argued to himself that all his objections to the President's policies had been impersonal and confidential.

For the first time Sherman heard the President tell one of those funny stories for which he had been so often praised or twitted in the newspapers. It came after Sherman had asked the President what was to be done with the Confederate armies, and had been told that he was expected to get them back to work on their farms. Then Sherman asked what was to be done with the leaders such as Jefferson Davis. He heard Lincoln say:

> As to Jeff. Davis, he was hardly at liberty to speak his mind fully, but intimated that he ought to clear out, "escape the country," only it would not do for him to say so openly. As usual, he illustrated his meaning by a story: "A man once had taken the total-abstinence pledge. When visiting a friend, he was invited to take a drink, but declined, on the score of his pledge; when his friend suggested lemonade, which was accepted. In preparing the lemonade, the friend pointed to the brandy-bottle, and said the lemonade would be more palatable if he were to pour in a little brandy; when his guest said, if he would do so 'unbeknown' to him, he would not object."

Grasping the point, Sherman filed it in his memory for future reference.

In the two conferences on board the presidential steamer, Lincoln captivated Sherman as he had done so many of the aristocrats and intellectuals who had disliked him personally in 1861. Everything connected with the meetings was gentle, soft, human—"good, long, social visits," Sherman called them. When he returned from the first, Mrs. Grant, over the supper table, asked her husband and Sherman if they had seen Mrs. Lincoln. Grant said they hadn't asked for her. "Well, you are a pretty pair!" exclaimed Mrs. Grant, and next day the two generals, like small boys obeying their mother, inquired about the President's lady, Lincoln replying that she sent her excuses for not receiving them—she was unwell.

During Sherman's stay with Grant, Meade called, accompanied by his aide, Colonel Theodore Lyman. The latter, arriving in the dawn, observed that Sherman had a very long neck and a very large skull with "a swelling 'fighting' back to his head"—a feature uncommon in most men so sparely built;

> and all his features express determination, particularly the mouth, which is wide and straight with lips shut tightly together . . . a very remarkable-looking man such as could not be grown out of America—the concentrated quintessence of Yankeedom . . . he believes in hard war. I heard him say "Columbia!—pretty much all burned; and burned *good!*"

At Grant's request, Sheridan called to see Sherman. The Irishman approached warily, fearing that "Sherman's zeal and powers of emphasis" would persuade Grant to send the cavalry down to join the Western army. Sheridan described his arrival:

> My entrance into the shanty suspended conversation only a moment and then Sherman without any prelude went on talking of the campaign, how he would come up through the Carolinas and hinting that I could join him.

Later it would appear that Sherman wanted large numbers of horsemen to round up the scattering bands of Confederate infantry, which he suspected would break off from the main force and turn into guerrillas. To this hint of Sherman's, Sheridan made strong dissent, growing so angry that Grant had to mollify him by confessing, a little later—and evidently in private—that the talk of sending him south was only a blind to deceive Lee. Sherman was most earnest and got Sheridan out of bed the next morning to renew the subject. He dropped it only when Sheridan began to show heat again.

Behind his grave silence, Grant was changing his wish to have Sherman assist in "closing out Lee." With the Army of Northern Virginia dwindling from desertion, Grant saw that it could be mastered by the Army of the Potomac alone. He began to see how he could force Lee out of his defenses and end him before the Western legions could arrive. Such a decision would have justified the suspicion of personal jealousy if made by a man less generous than Grant. But everything in the three-year relations between Grant and Sherman indicated that the former was candid in the explanation for his change of mind which he gave Lincoln—an explanation made soon after Sherman had returned to the Carolinas:

I told him that I had been very anxious to have the Eastern armies vanquish their old enemy. . . .

The Western armies had been in the main successful until they had conquered all the territory from the Mississippi River to the State of North Carolina, and were now almost ready to knock at the back door of Richmond, asking admittance. I said to him that if the Western armies should be even upon the field, operating against Richmond and Lee, the credit would be given to them for the capture by politicians and non-combatants from the section of country which those troops hailed from. . . .

Western congressmen might be throwing it up to the members of the East that . . . they were not able to capture an army, or to accomplish much . . . but had to wait until the Western armies had conquered all the territory south and west of them, and then come on to help them capture the only army they had been engaged with.

Mr. Lincoln said he saw that now, but had never thought of it before, because his anxiety was so great that he did not care where the aid came from, so the work was done.

To Sherman President Lincoln came as a revelation. He was touched by the tall statesman's face, so haggard with care, and by his arms and legs, which hung so heavily. Sherman's social nature responded warmly to the humor and conversational wizardry of the strange, lean giant. As Sherman left the *River Queen*, Carolina-bound, at noon on the twenty-eighth, Lincoln walked with him to the gangplank, talking to the last.

"I never saw him again," said Sherman afterward. "Of all the men I ever met, he seemed to possess more of the elements of greatness, combined with goodness, than any other."

51

SIC SEMPER TYRANNIS

A SWIFT steamer, the *Bat*, headed southward along the Atlantic shore during the afternoon of March 28. On its deck paced Cump Sherman with his brother John, whom he had invited to visit the army. None of the sailors who stared admiringly at them could know how dramatically time had reversed the characters of the two men. John, once the wild, bad boy of the Sherman family, was now watchdog of the nation's finance, chairman of the Senate committee on expenditures, a man already cold from the handling of money, public and private. Cump, the shy, gentle boy, had become a man whose name symbolized devastation.

The brothers were discussing Lincoln's plans for ending the war, the ideas Cump had listened to on the *River Queen*. John declared later that Cump had described these ideas "fully" and that "I did not at the time agree with the generous policy proposed by Mr. Lincoln."

To only one other individual did Cump indicate what the President had told him. At New Berne, as he hurried toward his army, he met Colonel Markland, that conscientious mailman and official keeper of secrets. Sitting beside Sherman while candlelight shone over the breakfast table, Markland asked what terms would be given Johnston when he surrendered. All other guests at the table were busy with general talk. Sherman quietly told Markland what he proposed to offer the defeated Confederates. Markland drank in the words, and in later years said:

> I regarded the conversation as one of the highest confidence and observed it as such. General Sherman did not say that President Lincoln suggested the terms. But I asked in the same connection and immediately after General Sherman had named the terms, "What will be done with President Davis and his cabinet?"
>
> General Sherman replied, "Said Mr. Lincoln, we will leave the door open; let them go! We don't want to be bothered with them in getting the government to running smoothly."
>
> I felt then that General Sherman had really given me the terms suggested by Mr. Lincoln to him.

To Schofield, Sherman telegraphed news of his return from a conference with the President and Grant, and added that from them he had received "a full understanding."

Arriving at headquarters on March 31, Sherman began preparing to move in harmony with Grant. At City Point it had been agreed that Grant should start at once to oust Lee from Richmond and Petersburg, and that Sherman should march on the tenth against Johnston. On the chance that Lee and Johnston might join and thus present a force of 60,000 men, Sherman re-formed his army into the three-wing formation that he had found so successful during the Atlanta campaign. Howard kept the Army of the Tennessee, Schofield took the center with the Army of the Ohio, and Slocum was given a new unit, the Army of Georgia—89,000 men in all.

Goldsboro rang with preparations, and roared with exultation as news came down from Virginia that on the twenty-ninth Grant had begun to cut the last of Lee's railroad communications. Lee's attack on the thirty-first had failed. Sheridan's counterattack, prompt and severe, had triumphed. On Lee's advice, President Davis had fled Richmond on April 2, entraining for Danville near the North Carolina boundary. Grant's army had come smashing into the capital. Lee and his hitherto invincible Army of Northern Virginia were trailing through hopeless nights toward Danville. If Lee reached that city, "you will have to take care of him," Grant wired Sherman on the third. Back flashed Sherman's answer:

> I am delighted and amazed at the result of your move, and Lee has lost in one day the reputation of three years, and you have established a reputation for perseverance and pluck that would make Wellington jump out of his coffin.

The turn of affairs drove from Sherman's mind all thought of interposing his army between Lee and Johnston, and he telegraphed Grant that it would now be wise to let the two Southern armies "come together, just as a billiard player would nurse the balls when he has them in a nice place." But Grant, either to prevent a bloody battle or to keep the Western army from dividing final honors with the Eastern force, hurried his legions to outfoot the Confederates in the race for Danville and, succeeding, forced Lee to surrender at Appomattox Courthouse on April 9.

"Glory to God and our country, and all honor to our comrades in arms, towards whom we are marching," announced Sherman to his men at 5 A.M. on April 12. Horsemen took the news through the drowsy camps, bellowing, "Lee's surrendered!" "Begod," cried an Irish private in the Eighty-fifth Illinois, "you're the man we've been lookin' for the last four years!" Many of the men who raised themselves from their blankets among the lilacs of North Carolina to hear that the war had ended, had as boys awakened one morning among the peach blossoms of Shiloh to hear that the war had begun for them. The cycle was complete in three years for the Western plowboys—three years, springtime to springtime.

All day on the twelfth the men reveled, even as the march went forward. They fired muskets in the air, they fired the blacksmiths' anvils. They howled and sang. Chaplain Hight, who had been drowned out by the tumult when attempting to hold prayer service in honor of Richmond's fall, now made no attempt to do anything religious on the twelfth.

Toward the shouting, capering army was coming a Confederate locomotive, with peace commissioners within and a seventeen-year-old soldier in gray sitting on the cowcatcher with a white flag in his hand. Behind the locomotive, from whose cab protruded apprehensive heads, was drama.

In the remnants of the Confederacy a struggle was going on at that moment between a few men who wished to continue the war and many men who thought it murderous to do so. Chief among the former was President Davis, who, with his Cabinet, had steamed as far as Greensboro, North Carolina, in his flight. Chief among the latter was Joe Johnston, flanked by Governor Vance of North Carolina and three ex-governors of the State, David L. Swain, William A. Graham, and Thomas Bragg.

On April 10, when rumors of Richmond's fall reached North Carolina, Swain left the village of Chapel Hill, where he was president of the State University, and hurried to Raleigh to advise Vance to make peace with Sherman, who was marching on them from Goldsboro. Vance was ready if Joe Johnston would surrender the army. He rode out to see Johnston, who was approaching Raleigh with his fast-dwindling ranks, and proposed that when the armed forces had evacuated the capital, he, as governor, should remain behind and make the best possible terms with Sherman for his State's capitulation. Johnston agreed that this was the right thing to do if it was certain that Richmond had gone down.

Returning to Raleigh, Vance and Swain telegraphed on the eleventh for William A. Graham to join them at once since the city "will not be held longer than tomorrow." As an old-line Whig, one-time United States Senator, Secretary of the Navy under Fillmore, and vice-presidential candidate with Scott in 1852, Graham shared the distrust that Swain, another ex-Whig, and Vance held for Davis. He voiced this antipathy to Vance soon after his arrival. Vance reported Graham's revelations as the latter had collected them on a recent trip to Richmond:

> . . . the whole of Congress had given up . . . had given up Davis as an incompetent and stubborn ass, and wanted peace made immediately and without regard to the Confederate authorities. This was especially the case, he said, with the cotton state fire-eaters, and though he did not say so, he led me to believe that the matter had been settled at Richmond . . . that the war was to be closed by the backing down of individual states, one by one, and that North Carolina not hampered . . . by false pride of opinion, was selected to lead the roll of infamy as she had been made to follow in the struggle for independence.

After listening to Graham's proposal, Vance declared that "if South Carolina or Alabama were whipped it was their duty to say so," and that the other States "were afraid of the odium of history." But to support Graham came Swain and a third ex-governor, Thomas Bragg, and at length Vance agreed to see Sherman. Graham and Swain drafted a note, which Vance signed, informing Sherman that the State capital surrendered and that mercy was bespoken for libraries, museums, records, and charitable institutions.

In the meantime Johnston, reaching the city, had been ordered by Davis to join him at Greensboro, seventy miles to the west. How much he knew of the civil peace plans was never a matter of record. Graham and Swain understood that he sanctioned them. He left Raleigh at midnight and the two ex-governors conferred with Hardee, second in command of the army. The fact that Hardee gave them prompt aid, writing out a safe-conduct and ordering up a locomotive to bear them to Sherman next morning, argued that he had the approval of Johnston.

Some time during this day, the eleventh of April, Johnston gave evidence that he was ready to end all bloodshed; he suspended orders for the execution of condemned prisoners. At eight o'clock on the morning of the twelfth he was in Greensboro preparing to enter Jefferson Davis's railroad-car headquarters, and to tell him that the war must be ended. At that hour Graham and Swain were preparing to mount their locomotive. On the streets of Raleigh certain army officers were declaring that such cowardly traitors ought to be hanged. The two humane old men, however, were not to be intimidated and at 10 A.M. started their journey. Somewhere along the line they would meet the Federals. The boy on the front of the engine, bearing a flag of truce, the locomotive crew, and a surgeon, Warren, were their only companions.

On the outskirts of the city Wade Hampton halted them. Angry at this attempt to end the war, which in his blind passion, he thought ought to continue indefinitely, Hampton tried to argue the commissioners from their course. But when they displayed Hardee's safe-conduct and insisted, he sent by courier to Sherman their request for a conference and included Vance's letter. Slowly their locomotive pulled ahead. It had gone a scant two miles when a courier arrived shouting that Hampton had just received an order from Johnston that they return to Raleigh. They were amazed. Later on they would learn that President Davis, not Johnston, had dictated this step. Some of "Davis's spies," presumably angry officers in Raleigh, had sent word of the move to Greensboro and stirred Davis to action.

Graham and Swain told the courier to go back and tell Hampton to make such orders in person or in writing. Soon Hampton galloped up and confirmed the news. He wrote out a note to Sherman canceling the request for a conference, but as he did so, carbines began popping near by and through the woods came his horsemen firing over their horses' tails at Kilpatrick's cavalry. Bullets sang. The two old men thought their day had come. Hampton and his men disappeared. Blue-coated invaders swarmed around the train.

Graham and Swain explained that they were noncombatants and asked to be allowed to return to Raleigh. The Yankees told them no; they were prisoners. They had no right, as civilians, to fly a flag of truce. Now there was only one man who could let them return, and he was Sherman. They would have to see him first! So it was that, as if by heaven's grace, the old men got what they wanted after all. Captured by their friends, rescued by their enemies, they came to Sherman, as he observed, "dreadfully excited" by their experiences.

They looked at the red-haired invader as Roman senators must have looked at Alaric. Cox, standing close by, saw that the delegation

> could scarcely believe its senses when they heard Sherman's earnest expressions of a desire to end the war at once and save the people from suffering and the country from devastation.

All day the commissioners talked with Sherman while around them flowed an army, whooping, shooting, prancing with exultation over the news that Lee had surrendered. Swain remarked that at the beginning of the war he and his host were engaged in similar pursuits.

"Yes," said Sherman; he knew Swain's position.

"Two or three of your boys were with me for a time," said Swain.

"Yes," answered the general, "and many more of yours have been with me during the war, who came, poor fellows, before they were men and when they ought to have remained with you, and they too frequently helped to fill my hospitals. I think, however, when they return they will do me the justice to tell you that I treated them kindly."

Swain asked for General Blair, saying that he had been his pupil in 1837. Sherman said that Blair was only two hours in the rear, and that since "I have been reading in a Raleigh paper terrible accounts of his proceedings I'll turn Frank over to you to answer for it in the morning." Before night Blair arrived and entertained Swain in his tent, while Sherman kept Graham with him until morning. The four men might have talked all night had not Sherman sent everybody to bed with the remark that the army got up at sunrise.

With the coming of the sun, the commissioners mounted their locomotive, bearing Sherman's invitation to Vance to remain with his State officers and keep the Government functioning. Graham and Swain steamed away with hope for their people high; Sherman was as humane as they!

Arriving in Raleigh after a journey of fourteen miles, they found Vance gone. He declared later that he had waited until midnight, then hearing that the locomotive had been captured by Federals, had decided that Sherman was imprisoning civil officers. Then, said he, "I rode out alone to join General Hoke's army." The Confederate Hoke, in later years, told J. G. DeRoulac Hamilton, the professor of history at Chapel Hill, that he had compelled Vance to leave the capital on the night of the twelfth when he retired with his force.

But Vance was not whipped. According to his own statement he struck off for Charlotte, where Davis had gone and

> where I informed him that I felt myself relieved from any further obligations to defer to his authority . . . and that I should henceforth manage for North Carolina.

He found Davis still hopeful; "he talked wildly about rallying scattered men around Johnston, etc. . . ."

Davis was, according to Vance, "a man of imperfectly constituted genius . . . and could absolutely *blind himself* to those things which his prejudices or hopes did not desire to see." Johnston, at his meetings with Davis at Greensboro on the twelfth and thirteenth, had come to the same conclusion. He had listened to the President boasting of new armies to be raised and fresh campaigns to be waged until, when prompted by brother generals and by Cabinet members, he had replied tartly that "it would be the greatest of human crimes for us to attempt to continue the war." Not unwilling to deflate the Executive who he thought had wronged him repeatedly, Johnston told Davis that the making of peace was "the only function of government still in his possession." When Davis, in exasperation, answered that the United States would not recognize him, Johnston held him firmly on the cruel pin and reminded him that it was traditional for military commanders to open negotiations. Why not let him make overtures to Sherman?

Cornered, Davis agreed, and wrote a letter to Sherman "proposing a meeting to arrange the terms of an armistice to enable the civil authorities to agree upon terms of peace." Signing it, Johnston sent it by courier to Sherman.

Then Johnston left to meet his army on the thirteenth at Hillsborough, where it had marched after leaving Raleigh the previous day. Over Johnston still hung Davis's order to arrest Graham, but the general found ways of evading the task. Between him and his President still gaped a chasm, and between him and Sherman, his old foe, now appeared the bridge of friendship. On the sixteenth admiration for

Sherman's military skill was seconded by realization of how kindly the Federal could be. On that date Johnston opened Sherman's reply to his note. "I really desire to save the people of North Carolina the damage they would sustain by the march of this army," said the Federal, in accepting the proposal of an armistice. Back to Greensboro went Johnston with this note, "supposing that the President was waiting to open negotiations." But Davis had gone, flying down the tracks to Charlotte, and Johnston turned back to handle alone the task of bringing peace to the South. He arranged with Sherman to meet on the seventeenth midway between their armies.

From Raleigh Sherman had wired Stanton on the fifteenth, "I will accept the same terms as General Grant gave General Lee and be careful not to complicate any points of civil policy." He had learned that Grant's terms had been most generous and had, in his opinion, gone far beyond Lincoln's amnesty offer of 1863. In that paper Lincoln had exempted from pardon all military men above the rank of colonel, and yet Grant had paroled Lee and other generals exactly like the officers of lower rank and the privates. As Sherman phrased it, Grant

> had extended the same principle to *all* officers . . . such a pardon I understood, would restore them all their rights of citizenship. . . . I was therefore willing to proceed with him [Johnston] upon the same principles.

Grant's "pardon" to the Confederates lay in a clause that he had written into the terms accepted by Lee—a guarantee that henceforth the surrendered officers and men were "not to be disturbed by United States authority so long as they observed their paroles and laws in force where they may reside." That this freed Confederates from either military or civil prosecution, for the time being at least, and morally pledged the Government to molest them no further was the construction put upon it by Sherman in North Carolina and by liberal, moderate men over the North. To Sherman it was plainly a fulfillment of Lincoln's wish that the Confederates be sent home at the earliest possible moment to resume peaceful industry.

With the conservative North Carolina leaders, Sherman continued to confer on friendly terms, and when on April 13 he learned that his soldiers had stolen Graham's horses and carriage, he sent the admired old gentleman a note:

> I can well appreciate how you must take these acts of war and will not even offer an apology but rather refer to them to illustrate how rapidly men's ideas of property degenerate during war.

Nine days later he wrote Graham that the Federal Army wished to be the friend of the farmers and the working class of North Carolina as well as the actual patrons of churches, colleges, asylums and all institutions of Learning and Charity.

Toward Raleigh, Sherman directed a policy that he felt to be Lincolnian. Private property was carefully spared. A soldier of the One Hundred and Third Illinois wrote, "Discipline was now so good that the men didn't know themselves and took out their mischief in frightening Negroes." Sherman toured the city preserving order. One trip took him through an insane asylum where when a patient demanded freedom he tried to quiet the fellow with the advice that he put his trust in God, "who rules the world." But the patient, whom Major Nichols described as having a keen, gray Yankee eye, said, "When it comes to the question of power, it strikes me that for a man who has been walking about over the country whipping these cursed Rebels, you have a damned sight more power than anybody I know of." Sherman passed on—out-talked for once.

The great morning of April 17 came. Sherman and his staff mounted a train that would take them to within five miles of the place appointed for his meeting with Johnston. As the signal was given for the train to start, a telegrapher came running; would the general wait? An important cipher dispatch was arriving over the wire. Sherman held the train. Thirty minutes later the man dashed up with the message decoded. It was from Stanton and was dated at ten minutes past noon on April 15. Sherman read:

President Lincoln was murdered about 10 o'clock last night in his private box at Ford's Theatre in this city, by an assassin who shot him through the head by a pistol ball. About the same hour Mr. Seward's house was entered by another assassin who stabbed the Secretary in several places, but it is thought he may possibly recover; but his son Frederick will probably die of wounds received from the assassin. The assassin of the President leaped from the box brandishing a dagger, exclaiming, "*Sic semper tyrannis!*" and that now Virginia was revenged.

Mr. Lincoln fell senseless from his seat and continued in that state until twenty-two minutes after 7 o'clock at which time he breathed his last. General Grant was published to be at the theatre, but fortunately did not go. Vice-President Johnson now becomes President, and will take the oath of office and assume the duties today. I have no time to add more than to say that I find evidence that an assassin is also on your track, and I beseech you to be more heedful than Mr. Lincoln was of such knowledge.

Folding the paper and thrusting it in his pocket, Sherman quietly asked the operator if any one else had seen it, and when the man answered, "No," he commanded, "Then don't reveal the contents by word or look till I come back."

The train was started. Sherman sat alone with the secret while his staff talked gayly of the approaching surrender. Sherman was afraid

> that some foolish man or woman in Raleigh might say something or do something that would madden our men, and that a fate worse than that of Columbia would befall the place. . . . Mr. Lincoln was particularly endeared to our soldiers.

He kept the secret while they alighted at a station, mounted horses, and jogged on until they met Johnston in the road. He said nothing of it to his gray-bearded adversary as they shook hands, eyeing each other with the curiosity of men who, without having met, know each other far better than intimates around them. Johnston was quiet, as became a general who had that very day noted that of the 73,260 men on his muster rolls only 14,770 were present.

Quickly the two leaders found a small frame house, asked Bennett, the farmer owner, if they might use it a few hours, and entered while the man and his wife withdrew to another building. Then when they were alone Sherman handed over Stanton's telegram. Always he remembered how perspiration "came out in large drops" on Johnston's forehead and how the Confederate said that "Mr. Lincoln was the best friend they had" and that the assassination was "the greatest possible calamity to the South."

Instinctively the opponents were agreed on many points. They both saw that further fighting would be "the highest possible crime" and would do nothing but breed guerrillas, for whom both held particular abhorrence. Sherman explained that he could not agree to an armistice, which would permit rival governments to confer; all he could do would be to receive Johnston's surrender on the Grant-Lee terms. This was enough to have ended the conference if Johnston had been bound by President Davis's orders. Davis had only proposed an armistice as a means of opening civil negotiations. But Johnston, inwardly declaring himself as free from Davis as had Vance, took the bull by the horns. He stepped forward as the representative of the Confederacy. He proposed that he and Sherman then and there "make one job of it," settle "the fate of all armies to the Rio Grande."

"*To the Rio Grande*"—the phrase kindled in Sherman's mind like a fire on an altar. It radiated to the very core of his religious belief in unity—one act of sweeping harmony! Perhaps the memory of past frustrations was fuel to the blaze. Here was his chance to show the world, his famous father-in-law, and his wife how, in all justice and merit, he could handle limitless tasks. Quite possibly, he thought, "Lincoln is dead. I will make his kind of a peace."

Dazzling though dreams might be, Sherman behaved sensibly. He told Johnston that no peace of such scope could be made without ratification from Washington. And, asked he, could Johnston deliver "all armies to the Rio Grande"? Johnston said that John C. Breckinridge, Confederate Secretary of War, was at hand, and "his orders will be obeyed anywhere." Pressing home his points, Johnston shrewdly continued—Napoleon had once proposed just such a peace to a defeated army, saying "if his overtures should save the life of one man, he would value the civic crown so won above any honor merely military." Johnston saw Sherman's "color heighten" and heard him say:

> . . . to put an end to further devastation and bloodshed, and restore the Union, and with it the prosperity of the country, were to him the objects of ambition. He regarded joint resolutions of Congress and proclamations by the President . . . as proving that the restoration of the Union was the object of the war. A long conversation with Mr. Lincoln at City Point but a short time before impressed upon him that the President then so considered it.

The sun was going down when the generals parted "in extreme cordiality" to meet the following day at the same place and hour. And as they emerged from the shabby little house with a great war dying on their hands, they saw in the yard those two cockerel cavalrymen, Kilpatrick and Hampton, scraping their spurs around each other and squabbling about a recent skirmish in which the former, after losing his trousers to the latter in a nocturnal surprise, had chased his enemies from the field, his own legs clad in comic drawers, gripping the bare back of his horse. Then he had returned to his headquarters and the lovely lady—not his wife—from whose bed he had sprung when Hampton's men had rung pistol butts upon the chamber door.

52

I AM NOT STONE

KNOWING that one word from himself would send his army out to burn and kill in a mob attempt to revenge Lincoln's death, Sherman moved cautiously in his announcement of the tragedy. Upon his return to Raleigh he sent the news confidentially to Lincoln's friend Frank

Blair, then cleared the streets, ordering all soldiers to their camps. When the men were regimented, he sent them a bulletin exonerating the Confederate Army from complicity in the assassination and charging it to the general spirit of rebellion. For hours he and his generals watched the men closely, noting that they wept, or were stunned, or stood gritting their teeth and demanding that the armistice be ended so that there might be one last savage battle.

From all accounts that came to him Sherman supposed Lincoln's assassin, Booth, to be one of those undisciplined Southern youths who had been recognized by Bragg and himself to be anarchical in 1859-60, and whom Sherman himself had described in September, 1863, as "young bloods . . . the most dangerous set of men that this war has turned loose upon the world." On April 22, 1865, he wrote Ellen concerning them: "Such men as Wade Hampton, Forrest, William Wirt Adams, etc., never will work and nothing is left for them but death or highway robbery." In due time Sherman, and the world, would learn that Lincoln's murderer had no connection with "chivalry" as Southern cavalry represented that waning institution, but on April 19 Wade Hampton was opening himself to suspicion by the freedom with which he wrote Jefferson Davis his opposition to Johnston's negotiations:

> No suffering which can be inflicted by the passage over our country of the Yankee armies can equal what would fall on us if we return to the Union. . . . We shall live under a base and vulgar tyranny . . . I shall never take the oath of allegiance.

Hampton's rash speeches did him the injustice to make him seem at this time a kindred soul to the Booth who had shouted, "Thus always to tyrants!" Hampton was urging officers and men to follow him to Texas, where they might persuade the Hapsburg emperor Maximilian to establish a protectorate over that State. Sherman was writing:

> There is great danger that the Confederate armies will dissolve and fill the whole land with robbers and assassins. . . . The assassination of Mr. Lincoln shows one of the elements in the rebel armies which will be almost as difficult to deal with as the main armies. . . . I don't want Johnston's army to break up.

To him in Raleigh came petitions from North Carolinians asking for protection against Confederate soldiers—chiefly paroled men from Lee's army—who were wandering through the country. Swain wrote him that Wheeler's men were "denuding" the land and that women and children would soon starve—"delay of a few days only may render it impossible to plant corn." Vance, angry because Davis had denied him the right to sit with Johnston at the table across from Sherman, denounced Confederate soldiers who, "with the sanction of their officers," carried on "the most complete and outrageous robbery of private citizens." Logan and Blair, supported by almost all other Federal generals, urged Sherman to accept practically any terms so that the army could escape another long march after Johnston.

Sherman began to recede from his decision to inject no questions of civil policy into the negotiations. The most obvious of all the new forces that pushed him toward such a decision came from columns of Northern newspapers which arrived in Raleigh four to five days after publication. The *New York Herald* of April 7 announced, "President Lincoln is earnestly engaged in Richmond in settling upon some just and generous proffer of pardon to the Rebel rank and file." The *Richmond Whig* of April 8 revealed that Lincoln had met Judge J. A. P. Campbell, Confederate Assistant Secretary of State, in Richmond and had given him terms for Virginia's pacification. The *New York Times* stated on the tenth that Lincoln would allow the Virginia legislature to assemble. The *Herald* of the twelfth said Virginia leaders had left Richmond to bring the legislators from Lynchburg to the capital. That same day the *Whig* published a call from Campbell assuring legislators protection by the Federal army.

By April 18 Sherman understood that Lincoln's action meant that "State authorities are recognized and invited to resume their lawful functions." Such a step fitted perfectly into the picture that Lincoln had given Sherman on the *River Queen*, and also it dovetailed with what Stanton had said in Savannah about the weakness of Federal finances. Sherman saw that millions would be saved by allowing the Southern States, after surrender, to maintain their own civil officers and thus free the Federal Government from the expense of military occupation.

On the eighteenth Sherman set off for his second conference with Johnston, determined, as he afterward described his attitude, "to manifest real respect for his [Lincoln's] memory by following after his death that policy, which, if living, I felt certain he would have approved."

Through the same morning Johnston was riding with Breckinridge at his side. For hours the two men had been closeted with John H. Reagan, Postmaster-General, discussing terms. Beauregard had contributed the suggestion that Sherman allow the army to march home under arms and be mustered from service at various State capitals. Reaching the Bennett farmhouse, Johnston entered alone.

"Are the States to be dissevered, and the people denied representation in Congress?" he asked Sherman. Was it true that the whites of the South were to become "the slaves of the people of the North"?

"Of course not," snapped Sherman. "We desire that you shall regain your position as citizens of the United States, free and equal to us in all respects and with representation upon the condition of submission to the lawful authority of the United States. . . ."

"By the way, Cump," said Johnston, "Breckinridge is with me . . . a better lawyer than any of us. Why not ask him in?"

"No, no," answered Sherman. "We don't recognize any civil government among you fellows, Joe." But when Johnston proposed bringing in Breckinridge under his status as a major general, Sherman consented and the huge Kentuckian entered, heavy and dull because, as Johnston later put it, he had gone for days without his quota of whisky. To temper his craving, Breckinridge was chewing tobacco vigorously and it was to him a voice from heaven that announced, soon after his arrival:

"Gentlemen, it occurred to me perhaps you were not overstocked with liquor, and I procured some medical stores." Breckinridge looked up to see Sherman drawing a bottle from his saddlebags and asking, "Will you join me before we begin work?"

A beatific light shone in the Kentuckian's face; he tossed his quid into the fireplace, rinsed his mouth with water, and when his turn came poured out what Johnston thought "a tremendous drink." Downing it, he sat back "with an air of content, took a fresh chew of tobacco," and stroked his mustache. Thenceforth he shone, Johnston marveling at the ease with which he quoted laws of war, laws governing rebellions, and laws of nations:

> . . . in a manner so resourceful, cogent, persuasive and learned that, at one stage of the proceedings, General Sherman . . . pushed back his chair and exclaimed, "See here, gentlemen, who is doing this surrendering anyhow? If this thing goes on, you'll have me sending an apology to Jeff Davis."

When the two Confederates tried to make terms for Davis's personal surrender, Sherman was deaf, as Lincoln would have wished. Sherman would consider a people but not an individual. His frame of mind in these days was made clear in a letter to Rawlins:

> The South is broken and ruined and appeals to our pity. To ride the people down with persecutions and military exactions would be like slashing away at the crew of a sinking ship.

And a few hours after the conference with Johnston and Breckinridge he wrote Grant:

I know that all men of substance South want peace, and I do not believe they will resort to war again during this century. I have no doubt that they will, in the future, be perfectly subordinate to the laws of the United States.

Having repeatedly told Southerners during the past four years that he would risk everything for them once they had lain down their arms, Sherman was now prepared to prove his words. How far his Government would support him he did not know, but he told Johnston and Breckinridge that

Lincoln in letters and telegrams had encouraged me by all the words which could be used in general terms, to believe, not only in his willingness, but in his desires that I should make terms with civil authorities, governors and legislatures even as far back as 1863.

In the midst of the negotiations, a courier arrived with a set of terms written out by Reagan back in Greensboro, but Sherman discarded them as "too general and verbose." Taking a pen, he decided to write

some general propositions, meaning little or meaning much, according to the construction of the parties—what I would term "glittering generalities" —and send them to Washington, which I could do in four days. That would enable the new President to give me a clew to his policy . . . and to define to me what I might promise, simply to cover the pride of the Southern men. . . .

At one point Sherman arose and, with a far-away look in his eyes, took the whisky from his saddlebags again. Breckinridge made ready, tossing his tobacco cud into the fireplace and stroking his mustache. But Sherman, wrapped in thought, poured out but one drink, returned the bottle to the bag, and sipped his liquor at the window, staring out at the Carolina sunshine. When he returned to his writing, the mournful Breckinridge returned to his tobacco plug.

In time Sherman handed the completed paper across the table saying, "That's the best I can do." The Confederates began to read:

1. The contending armies now in the field to maintain the *statu quo* until notice is given by the commanding general of any one to its opponent, and reasonable time—say, forty-eight hours,—allowed.

2. The Confederate armies now in existence to be disbanded and conducted to their several State capitals, there to deposit their arms and public property in the State Arsenal; and each officer and man to execute and file an agreement to cease from acts of war, and to abide the action of the State and Federal authority. The number of arms and munitions of war to be reported to the Chief of Ordnance at Washington City, subject to the future

action of the Congress of the United States, and, in the mean time, to be used solely to maintain peace and order within the borders of the States respectively.

3. The recognition by the Executive of the United States, of the several State governments, on their officers and Legislatures taking the oaths prescribed by the Constitution of the United States, and, where conflicting State governments have resulted from the war, the legitimacy of all shall be submitted to the Supreme Court of the United States.

4. The reëstablishment of all the Federal Courts in the several States with powers as defined by the Constitution of the United States and of the States respectively.

5. The people and inhabitants of all the States to be guaranteed, so far as the Executive can, their political rights and franchises, as well as their rights of person and property, as defined by the Constitution of the United States and of the States respectively.

6. The Executive authority of the Government of the United States not to disturb any of the people by reason of the late war, so long as they live in peace and quiet, abstain from acts of armed hostility, and obey the laws in existence at the place of their residence.

7. In general terms—the war to cease; a general amnesty, so far as the Executive of the United States can command, on condition of the disbandment of the Confederate armies, the distribution of the arms, and the resumption of peaceful pursuits by the officers and men hitherto composing said armies.

Not being fully empowered by our respective principals to fulfill these terms, we individually and officially pledge ourselves to promptly obtain the necessary authority, and to carry out the above program.

The agreement contained no mention of slavery, Johnston admitting that the institution was dead and buried, a view in which all Southerners with whom Sherman had lately talked agreed most emphatically. Reagan, when the paper was shown him a little later, wrote President Davis:

[It] contains no direct reference to the question of slavery, requires no concession from us in regard to it, and leaves it subject to the Constitution and the laws of the United States and of the several States just as it was before the war.

At the time, however, it was certain that a Constitutional amendment, the Thirteenth, abolishing slavery forever in the United States, would be ratified by enough States to put it speedily into effect. Passed by the United States Senate in April, 1864, it had been adopted by the House of Representatives on January 31, 1865, and was agreed by friend and enemy to be certain of success in the vote of the various States.

Passing over the subject, Sherman and Johnston signed the agreement, then parted in even stronger friendship than at their previous conferences. Johnston asked Breckinridge, as they rode away, "What do you think of Sherman?" "He is a bright man and a man of great force," said the Kentuckian; then, raising his voice in sudden passion, "General Johnston, General Sherman is a hog! Yes, sir, a hog! Did you see him take that drink by himself?" Johnston protested that Sherman was, really, "a royal good fellow, but the most absent-minded man in the world." "Ah," said Breckinridge, "no Kentucky gentleman would ever have taken away that bottle. He knew we needed it." When John S. Wise, years later, told Sherman the story as Johnston had originally given it, Sherman laughed and said, "I don't remember it, but if Joe Johnston told it, it's so. Those fellows hustled me that day; I was sorry for the drink I did give them."

Late in the night of the eighteenth Sherman finished letters explaining to Grant and Halleck his reasons for making the agreement as it stood. He urged them to help secure President Johnson's signature to it. "Influence him not to vary the terms at all," he asked Halleck, "for I have considered everything." He wrote Ellen, "I can hardly realize it, but I can see no slip." The next day, when Major Hitchcock started for Washington with the papers, Sherman announced to his army that the agreement "when formally ratified, will make peace from the Potomac to the Rio Grande." His announcement added, "The General hopes and believes that in a very few days it will be his good fortune to conduct you to your homes."

On the twentieth New York newspapers arrived, containing praises of Lincoln for his leniency in Virginia. The *Herald* of the twelfth lauded the President's shrewdness and sagacity:

> . . . he not only pardons the leading rebels of Virginia, from the governor down, but he invites them, with their late rebel Legislature to meet. . . .
>
> In this connection we may say that the recent interview between the President and Judge Campbell related to the restoration of peace in all the States, not to Virginia alone. . . .

Evidently Sherman did not see the *New York Tribune* of the fourteenth, with its announcement that General Weitzel, the officer in charge of Richmond, had been removed from his post and that "Secretary Stanton is strongly adverse to permitting the Rebel Legislature in Virginia to assemble at Richmond under the auspices of the Government." To Johnston on the twenty-first Sherman wrote:

> By the action of General Weitzel in relation to the Virginia Legislature I feel certain we will have no trouble on the score of recognizing existing

State Governments. It may be, however, the lawyers will want us to define more minutely what is meant by the guaranty of rights of persons and property. It may be construed into a compact for us to undo the past as to the rights of slaves and leases of plantations on the Mississippi. . . . I wish you would talk to the best men you have on these points, and, if possible, let us, in the final convention, make these points so clear as to leave no room for angry controversy. I believe, if the South would simply and publicly declare what we all feel and know, *that slavery is dead*, that you would inaugurate an era of peace and prosperity that would soon efface the ravages of the past four years of war.

Peace seemed sure. Instead of confiscating locomotives, Sherman now offered to borrow or rent them from Raleigh owners. He used Johnston's telegraph lines to halt the devastation of his cavalry under Wilson in Georgia and Stoneman in western North Carolina. In so doing, he confessed to Johnston on the twenty-third, "I have almost exceeded the bounds of prudence and only did so on my absolute faith in your personal character." He was embarrassed at sending Johnston messages in the Federal secret cipher to be relayed to Stoneman and Wilson, and in explaining their contents to Johnston he placed his foe in a position to work out the code had the Confederate cared to do so. Obviously the generals expected to fight no more.

Admiration for Johnston and liking for the Confederate soldiers intensified Sherman's contempt for the stay-at-home Southerners who professed Union sympathy. When S. L. Fremont, a Wilmington friend of other days, asked favors on the ground that he had been personally loyal throughout the war, Sherman answered:

I will be frank and honest with you. Simple, passive submission to events by a man in the prime of life is not all that is due to society in times of revolution. Had the Northern men residing at the South spoken out manfully and truly at the outset the active secessionists could not have carried the masses of men as they did . . . and in consequence we mourn the loss of such men as John F. Reynolds, McPherson and thousands of noble gentlemen, any one of whom was worth all the slaves of the South and half of the white population thrown in.

He would prefer to forgive all this, but he could not—"I am not made of stone." Always he remembered the horrors—"desolation from the Ohio to the Gulf and mourning in every household."

For three days Sherman and Johnston waited for their governments to pass upon the agreement. On the twenty-second Jefferson Davis read the opinions of his Cabinet members, urging him to sign. They agreed with George Davis, Attorney-General, who wrote:

Taken as a whole the convention amounts to this; that the States of the Confederacy shall reënter the old Union upon the same footing on which they stood before seceding from it.

On the twenty-third, Sherman read New York newspapers that seemed to blanket the sun. Promptly he sent Johnston a telegram:

General Ord at Richmond has recalled the permission given for the Virginia Legislature, and I fear much the assassination of the President will give such a bias to the popular mind, which, in connection with the desire of our politicians, may thwart our purpose of recognizing "existing local governments." But it does seem to me there must be good sense enough left on this continent to give order and shape to the now disjointed elements of Government.

Some time on the following day, Stephen R. Mallory, Confederate Secretary of the Navy, added his persuasions to those of other cabinet members, and Davis notified Johnston that he would sign the agreement.

The evening of the twenty-third brought Sherman a telegram stating that Hitchcock was at the mouth of the river and would come to camp by train during the night. Not a word as to what decision he carried. At 6 A.M. the next morning the messenger alighted from the railroad coach, followed by other officers, among whom was a short man, who always walked with a queer, stumbling stride that seemed ready to tip him on to his nose in the dirt.

It was Grant!

53

SHERMAN HAS FATALLY BLUNDERED

GRANT'S arrival at Raleigh was the culmination of a series of events that were unknown to Sherman, and indeed only partially understood in the North for what they were—a wrestle between Lincoln and the Radicals for the body of the prostrate South.

The particular chain of circumstances that came to a focus on Sherman's and Johnston's peace terms had begun on March 3, 1865. On that day Grant, facing the Confederates around Richmond, had learned that Lee was suggesting to President Davis a conference of generals at which peace might be discussed. Relaying this information to Washington, Grant received an answer that, though signed by Stanton, had been dictated by Lincoln:

> The President directs me to say to you that he wishes you to have no conference with General Lee, unless it be for the capitulation of Lee's army or on solely minor and purely military matters.
>
> He instructs me to say that you are not to decide, discuss or confer upon any political questions. Such questions the President holds in his own hands and will submit them to no military conference or conventions.

No copy of this had been sent to Sherman, although communication with him was open after March 16. Nor had Lincoln mentioned it during those long meetings on the *River Queen* on the twenty-seventh and the twenty-eighth. In fact, in those discussions Lincoln had taken a very different stand; he had authorized Sherman to hold specific conferences with North Carolina officials regarding political questions. And a week after Sherman had departed Lincoln journeyed to Richmond, which Grant had just captured, and offered Virginians substantially the same terms that he had instructed Sherman to give North Carolinians.

He told Judge Campbell, self-constituted spokesman for his State, that if Virginia would withdraw her troops from the field there would be no hangings and there would be cancellation of all incompleted and proposed confiscations of property. Campbell heard the President say that he did not want action by the loyal Virginia legislature—a shadowy organization that functioned only where the blue armies ruled. Lincoln said that "it had but a small margin and he was not disposed to increase it . . . he wanted the very legislature which had been sitting 'up yonder'—pointing to the capitol—to come together and to vote to restore Virginia to the Union and to recall her soldiers from the field." Campbell later said that Lincoln "never for a moment spoke of the legislature except as a public corporate body."

Apparently the President was holding the same view he had given Sherman—recognizing State governments "as the government de facto till Congress could provide others." When Campbell agreed to call the legislature, Lincoln wrote out an order for General Weitzel, commanding in Richmond, to allow the assemblage "of the gentlemen who have acted as the legislature." Then Lincoln returned to Washington, where on the evening of April 9 he received news of Lee's surrender. Although this removed one of the principal purposes of the meeting, he made no move to cancel it. And judging from the popular exultation over the Appomattox surrender, the public seemed willing that the President should have his own merciful way with the South.

But amid the roaring celebrations of victory there was ominous whispering among the Radicals. Ever since the outbreak of the war, these proponents of a strong, punitive peace, with citizenship for ex-slaves, had been insisting that sooner or later Lee and other high Confederates must be tried for treason and hanged as an object lesson to future generations. It made them furious, therefore, to discover that Grant's terms to Lee had placed the chief officers of the Army of Northern Virginia beyond the reach of vengeance, at least for the time being. Vice President Johnson, proverbially ferocious toward enemy leaders, asked Lincoln when Lee could be tried for treason and was told that the parole signed by Grant could not be violated. As did almost all officials, newspaper men, and observers in Washington, the Radicals believed that Lincoln had been the real author of the terms given by Grant. The *New York Tribune* reporter, after circulating among the Republican politicians of Washington on the tenth, telegraphed his Abolitionist editor:

> While all rejoice at the prospect of a speedy termination of the war, there are many who are chagrined at the virtual pardon extended Lee and his chief officers.
>
> The bribe of unconditional forgiveness offered by Lincoln to the Rebels has already established a split in our party—the opposition is forming here hourly. Ben Butler in a big speech made from Willard's steps fully expressed the popular dissatisfaction. The other speakers who followed, demanded punishment for the Rebel commanders and leaders and offered forgiveness only to the rank and file.

With the masses viewing Grant and Lincoln as heroes, the Radicals found that "popular dissatisfaction" did not develop. Where they found Lincoln's peace plans more vulnerable was in connection with his Virginia move. When he revealed this action to the Cabinet on April 11, Welles, Secretary of the Navy, saw that "the subject caused general surprise and, on the part of some, dissatisfaction and irritation." The three most Radical of the secretaries, Stanton, James Speed, Attorney-General, and William Dennison, Postmaster-General, attacked the offer so strongly that Lincoln confessed to Welles that they were "annoying him greatly." By nine the following morning he telegraphed Weitzel to withdraw the offer "if there were no signs of the Legislature coming together." At 3 P.M. Weitzel answered that "it is common talk that they will come together," and that the passports had gone out to them.

In confidence, Lincoln asked Welles, whom he knew to be as lenient as himself, what he thought of the matter, and was told that the plan savored too strongly of "recognizing" a rebellious body. Lincoln answered that he had not thought of acknowledging the legislators "like a real assemblage." He had higher aims: "Courts must be reëstablished as soon as possible, there must be law and order or society should be broken up, the disbanded armies would turn into robber bands." But Lincoln told Welles, "as we had all taken a different view, he had perhaps made a mistake and was ready to correct it if he had."

As though to answer his necessity for finding an excuse to revoke the order, there came to him a paper sent Stanton by Dana—the copy of a letter in which Campbell had invited five Virginia leaders to consider Lincoln's proposal. In it Campbell had assumed that Lincoln would recognize the legislature. The President discussed this with Stanton, who, according to his own account, spoke against "allowing Rebel legislatures to assemble or Rebel authorities to have any participation whatever in the business of reorganization." Thereupon Lincoln, at 6 P.M. on the twelfth, telegraphed Weitzel a cancellation of the permit; the legislature must not meet because Campbell had erred:

> He assumes, as appears to me, that I have called the insurgent legislature of Virginia together, as the rightful legislature of the States. . . . I have done no such thing. I spoke of them not as the legislature, but as the gentlemen who have acted as the legislature. . . . I did this on purpose to exclude the assumption that I was recognizing them as the rightful body.

But no word of this vital shift in policy was sent Sherman. And, in an allied matter the Virginia incident had results that could have given Sherman helpful hints as to the Radical opposition which Lincoln's schemes of mercy were meeting.

Dana, in Richmond, wired his chieftain, Stanton, that Campbell had contaminated Weitzel and persuaded him to allow Richmond clergymen to omit prayers for the President of the United States. When Stanton rebuked Weitzel for this, the latter answered that Lincoln, while in Richmond, had told him "to make concessions in small matters." At the same time Dana telegraphed Stanton that Weitzel's action had been "in a great measure the result of the President's directions to let them down easy." After Stanton, still hounding Weitzel, had forbidden him to see Campbell again, Weitzel countered with a wire asking for permission to reveal something that Lincoln had said to him in confidence at Richmond.

At this suggestion that he had been keeping Stanton in ignorance of things said to generals at the front, Lincoln took action, telegraphing Weitzel on the twelfth:

> I do not remember hearing prayers spoken of while I was in Richmond, but I have no doubt you have acted in what appeared to you to be the spirit and temper manifested by me there.

Weitzel answered:

> You spoke of not pressing little points. You said you would not order me, but if you were in my place you would not press them.

At six o'clock that night Stanton was reading a telegram from Dana, stating that General Ord had transferred Weitzel from Richmond to the field. No attempt was ever made by Stanton to reply to Weitzel's observation that the War Department had not made such prompt and harsh demands upon preachers when Union armies had occupied New Orleans, Savannah, Charleston, and Norfolk. In all probability Stanton had demoted Weitzel for showing too much sympathy with Lincoln's dangerous ailment—mercy. It was probable, too, that Lincoln never knew of Weitzel's transfer—the act was accomplished quietly as a detail of internal army administration.

The revocation of the permit and the removal of Weitzel came too late on the twelfth to prevent the publication in morning newspapers of Weitzel's call to the legislators, and this was read in Richmond by five Radicals who were visiting the city as members of the Joint Congressional Committee on the Conduct of the War. These five men, Senators Ben Wade, Zachariah Chandler, and Representatives Daniel W. Gooch, George W. Julian, and Benjamin F. Loan, were fresh from an emotional examination of Union soldiers recently brought North from Confederate prison pens. And from the sight of such piteously emaciated creatures Wade had been seen by Julian to rush "sobbing like a child." They were also offended by the unfortunately pompous manners of paroled Confederate officers on the streets of Richmond.

The five Radicals were in no mood to applaud Weitzel's call as they read it in newspapers. "We were all thunderstruck," said Julian, "and sympathized with the hot indignation and wrathful words of the chairman [Wade] . . . we were thoroughly disgusted by this display of misguided magnanimity." Back to Washington came the committeemen, certain that Lincoln in "weakness" was tossing away all that the armies had won. Arriving on the fourteenth, they discovered that three days earlier Lincoln had made a speech for his lenient program. To a crowd of serenaders he had indicated that he would not insist upon Southern States' awarding the vote to all Negroes as a price of readmission to the Union; he would consider it enough if the franchise was merely given those black men who were unusually intelligent or who had worn Federal soldiers' uniforms. This, in the minds of Radicals, was neither just to the great mass of Negroes nor wise politics. It would keep the Republican party from capturing the Southern States through votes of freedmen.

On the day that the Radical committeemen spread their anger through Washington, Lincoln was sitting in the White House telling Grant that he was wrong to worry over lack of news from Sherman. Favorable word would come, Lincoln felt sure; he had had, last night, the strange dream that always came to him before important events:

> I have no doubt that a battle has taken place or is about to be fought and Johnston will be beaten. . . . It must relate to Sherman; my thoughts are in that direction, and I know of no other very important event which is likely just now to occur.

It was that same day that Sherman read Johnston's first proposal of a truce and a discussion of surrender.

Lincoln was murdered that evening, and Stanton, taking control of the Government, assumed that the crime had been plotted by the Confederacy. Feeding the newspapers reports that gave this—not unnatural—color to the crime, he saw public opinion swerve from belief in Lincolnian mercy to faith in Radical vengeance. In the maelstrom of hysteria that swept the North, moderate, conservative men deserted the dead President's policy of gentleness for the more satisfactory revenge promised by the Radicals. Republican leaders, caucusing on the fifteenth, were found by Congressman Julian to be almost unanimous in believing "that the accession of Johnson to the Presidency would prove a godsend to the country." Johnson's past diatribes against Southern aristocrats now gave him the appearance of the Radical of Radicals. In particular did the five bitter-enders on the War Investigating Committee rejoice; not long before Johnson had served with them on their body, and they now rushed to steel him to vengeance. On the sixteenth Wade led them to see the new Executive, and said, "Johnson, we have faith in you. By the gods, there will be no trouble now in running the government!" Julian heard Johnson reply, most satisfactorily, that treason, like rape, must be punished, and that "traitors must be impoverished."

To aid in the conversion of the populace to the belief that the South was innately "hellish," came Lincoln's funeral, with services beginning in Washington on the eighteenth amid stupendous crowds, wild grief and clergymen calling upon the God of Vengeance to punish traitors and

> the treason that has deluged our land with blood and desolated our country and bereaved our homes and filled them with widows and orphans and which has at last culminated in the assassination of the nation's chosen ruler.

At dawn on April 21 Lincoln's funeral train, swathed in black, was departing on its monstrous trip of two weeks and sixteen hundred miles through morbid and suffocating crowds. At 4 P.M. Major Hitchcock arrived with Sherman's agreement, which proposed for the South Lincolnian forgiveness.

That night at eight o'clock Stanton asked Grant to read Sherman's memorandum aloud to the hastily assembled President and Cabinet. As Grant concluded Stanton broke out in excited condemnation of the agreement. Welles observed that Speed, "prompted by Stanton who seemed frantic . . . expressed his fears that Sherman at the head of his victorious legions had designs upon the government." In the stampede every one agreed that the President must not approve Sherman's action. It was decided that Grant, who was silent amid the denunciations of his friend, must immediately inform General Sherman that his course was disapproved.

Next day Welles was surprised to learn that during the night Grant had started in person for Raleigh. Some time after the adjournment of the night meeting Stanton, either with or without the President's sanction, had decided that Sherman was not to be trusted with knowledge that his agreement had been rejected. Grant was steaming South with stealth and secrecy. Ben Butler, hanging on Stanton's coat tails in these days, understood that the Administration had wind of some desperate agreement reached between Sherman and his generals, a pact to enforce at all costs the agreement with Johnston. Butler said that the Cabinet knew

> a paper had been circulated among the commanders making a closer union on the subject. They further knew the obstinacy of Sherman in sustaining his opinions, and they feared him. Indeed, they looked upon it as almost treasonable intent.

Apparently this tale of secret cabal was merely Stanton's hysterical interpretation of the news that on April 14 Sherman's officers, while waiting in Raleigh, had decided to form the Society of the Army of the Tennessee, a social organization for reunions after the war.

On April 21, with Grant on the Atlantic, there came to Stanton's nervous hands an inflammatory telegram from Halleck, who since the seventeenth had been in charge of Virginia and such portions of North Carolina as were not occupied by Sherman's army. Halleck had been listening to fanciful tales told by Richmond bankers. His telegram read:

> It is stated here by respectable parties that the amount of specie taken south by Jeff. Davis and his partisans is very large. . . . They hope, it is said, to make terms with General Sherman or some other Southern commander by which they will be permitted with their effects, including this

gold plunder, to go to Mexico or Europe. Johnston's negotiations look to this end. Would it not be well to put Sherman and all other commanding generals on their guard in this respect?

Stanton's jumping nerves behaved now like dervishes. He associated the news with an innocent item in the letter that Hitchcock had brought Halleck from Sherman. Addressed to Old Brains as chief of staff at the War Department, the letter had been opened, properly enough, by Stanton. It had stated at one point: "Johnston informed me that General Stoneman had been at Salisbury, and was now at Statesville. I have sent him orders to come to me."

The map showed Stanton that Salisbury stood some fifty miles southwest of Greensboro on the railroad over which Jefferson Davis was fleeing. Stanton leaped to the conclusion that if Stoneman left the railroad he could not catch the fugitive. In his disordered state of mind he did not note that Stoneman was not now at Salisbury, but at Statesville, twenty-five miles west, and that if the cavalry had obeyed Sherman's orders, it necessarily moved toward Raleigh, a course that lay across the railroad and directly upon, not away from, Davis's path.

Ignoring or concealing Sherman's plain statement of fact, on the twenty-second Stanton wired Halleck that Sherman's "order to Stoneman will allow Jeff. Davis to escape with his plunder," and a little later Stanton fed the newspapers the story that Sherman's orders "will probably open the way for Davis to escape to Mexico or Europe."

As a matter of fact, Sherman's telegram to Stoneman was written in utter indifference to Davis's flight; he merely sought to halt the cavalry's devastation and to bring it to Raleigh, where it could be fed. As it happened, Stoneman did not receive the order, having started with his staff to Knoxville while his cavalry raided southwestward in ignorance of either Sherman's wishes or Davis's whereabouts.

On April 22, Stanton decided to make a public statement regarding Sherman. His reason for doing this, he declared later, was that there had come to his notice the special field orders with which Sherman, on the nineteenth, had notified his troops of peace "in a very few days." Stanton declared that unless the Government published its reason for rejecting Sherman's agreement, the army might be disturbed. An erratic mixture of truths, half-truths, and falsehoods it was that Stanton gave the New York newspapers for publication on April 24. It implied that Sherman had willfully disobeyed Lincoln's order of March 3 directing Grant to hold no conferences with the enemy on political questions—the order Sherman had in reality never seen. Then Stanton quoted Halleck's wire of the twenty-second concerning Davis's flight with the gold, and from this he deleted the last sentence, which proved that Halleck had no doubts as to Sherman's honesty—the sentence reading, "Would it not be well to put Sherman and all other commanding generals on their guard?" Not content with thus smirching Sherman with the suspicion of bribery, Stanton strengthened his fictitious case by adding statements concerning Sherman's orders to Stoneman.

Then Stanton catalogued other errors of Sherman's in the agreement—the general had practically acknowledged the Rebel government; he had arranged to let the Rebels keep their arms "which might be used as soon as the armies of the United States were disbanded . . . to conquer and subdue the loyal States"; he had made it possible for slavery to be reëstablished; he had endangered the status of the new State of West Virginia; he had "practically abolished the confiscation laws and relieved the Rebels of every degree, who had slaughtered our people, from all pains and penalties for their crimes"; he had given the South terms that even Lincoln had refused.

Concerning the last of these charges, Grant knew its complete falsity, for he had accompanied Lincoln at the meeting with Confederate envoys in early February and had heard the President's two proposals:

> One being that the Union should be preserved and the other that slavery should be abolished; and if they were ready to concede these two points he was almost ready to sign his name to a blank piece of paper and permit them to fill out the balance of the terms upon which we would live together.

Stanton's broadside appeared in newspapers whose columns, banded in heavy mourning, gave long accounts of the crazed displays of grief with which New York City was receiving Lincoln's funeral cortège. Across the North rose a howl scarcely less pained than that which Georgia had so recently uttered during Sherman's passage. In one day Sherman was toppled from a hero's pedestal into the dust. Radical politicians telegraphed Stanton congratulations, Senator Sprague of Rhode Island wired, "Loyal men deplore and are outraged by Sherman's agreement with Johnston. He should be promptly removed." The *New York Herald* declared:

> Sherman's splendid military career is ended, he will retire under a cloud. . . . Was he caught napping or was he too eager for the laurels of the peacemaker? . . . Sherman has fatally blundered, for, with a few unlucky strokes of his pen, he has blurred all the triumphs of his sword.

The *New Haven Journal* of April 27 insinuated that Sherman had been an accomplice in the plot to assassinate Lincoln and had juggled his cavalry so that Davis might escape. The *Chicago Tribune* declared on April 24:

> Sherman has been completely over-reached and outwitted by Joe Johnston. . . . We cannot account for Sherman's signature on this astounding memorandum, except on the hypothesis of stark insanity. . . . He has given the great weight of his name and prestige to the pestilent dogmas which plunged the country into war. . . . We will not charge that he has been wilfully untrue to his country. . . .

But, the *Tribune* continued, men who knew Sherman informed it that he had determined to put himself at the head of the proslavery party in the reunited country, a combination of Southern reactionists and Northern Copperheads.

As denunciations of Sherman poured into Washington, the Cabinet met on April 25, and at the conclusion of the gathering, a *New York Tribune* reporter, still close to Stanton, telegraphed his editor:

> It is stated that the significant Richmond letter in the *London Times* of April 5th was read and discussed in cabinet meeting today. It is now known to the government that the news of the President's assassination had reached General Sherman several hours prior to his settling upon the terms of capitulation.

This indicated that Stanton was whispering that Sherman was trying to make himself Lincoln's successor. The *London Times* article, written on March 4 and published a month later, had arrived in America to set editorial columns buzzing. The writer of the article had suggested that "in the approaching Armageddon," Sherman might make himself "dictator," and that Sherman was "half-mad when the fit was on him." Reading this, men remembered Sherman's reputed insanity in 1861; they remembered how both Democrats and Republicans had talked of nominating him for the Presidency less than a year before. Was he now planning a short cut to that office? Stanton could easily have recalled how Sherman, only six months earlier, had written the Administration that if politics ruled army promotions it was time "to change front on Washington." Earlier in the war Sherman had described himself "almost a monarchist"; his contempt for democracy was well known.

Old World history was full of professional armies marching home from heroic campaigns of pillage and conquest to overthrow civil rulers and enthrone idolized generals. Napoleon had been gone but fifty years. The Western men had been away from home so long, had appeared and disappeared in the South so mysteriously and independently, had devastated so much and become so irresistible, that the East, for all its pride in victory, felt that there was something strange about them. Easterners had read reprints of many Southern accounts of their "barbarism"; it could recall how the Northwest, home of the majority of Sherman's men, had but lately fermented with revolt, and how for years it had damned both the Abolitionists of New England and the capitalists of Wall Street. Could it be that the Western agrarian soldiers would take it into their heads to make a clean sweep of the whole Atlantic coast, subjugating the East as they had South Carolina? Welles believed that Stanton held "a mortal fear of the generals and the armies."

At the Cabinet meeting on the twenty-fifth Welles noted how Speed came "strongly charged" by Stanton to say that there was little doubt but that Sherman was plotting to make himself dictator. "Suppose," said Speed, "he should arrest Grant . . ."

As if in answer, Stanton opened a telegram from Grant, dispatched three hours after his arrival at Sherman's headquarters. He handed out for publication what purported to be a copy of this telegram. His bulletin read:

MAJ.-GENERAL DIX:—

A dispatch has just been received by this Department from General Grant dated Raleigh, 9 A.M., April 24th. He says, "I reached here this morning and delivered to General Sherman the reply to his negotiation with Johnston. Word was immediately sent to Johnston terminating the truce and information that civil matters could not be entertained in any convention between army commanders."

EDWIN M. STANTON,
Sec. of War.

The depths to which Stanton would go to ruin Sherman's reputation became visible in later years when the full copy of Grant's telegram was found. Stanton had deliberately cut from its contents those portions which made plain to the world Sherman's reasons for making the agreement with Johnston. The complete telegram read:

I reached here this morning and delivered to General Sherman the reply to his negotiations with Johnston. He was not surprised but rather expected the rejection. Word was immediately sent to Johnston terminating the truce and information that civil matters could not be entertained in any convention between army commanders. General Sherman has been guided in his negotiations with Johnston entirely by what he thought was precedent authorized by the President. He had before him the terms given by me to Lee's army and the call of the rebel legislature of Virginia as authorized by General Weitzel as he supposed with the sanction of the President and myself. At the time of the agreement General Sherman did not know of the withdrawal of authority of the meeting of the legislature. The moment he learned through the papers that authority for the meeting had been withdrawn he communicated the fact to Johnston as having bearing on the negotiations . . .

The reply Stanton sent to Grant on the twenty-fifth was brutally indifferent to the explanations made for Sherman:

Your dispatch received. The arrangement between Sherman and Johnston meets with universal disapprobation. No one of any class or shade of opinion approves it. I have not known as much surprise and discontent at anything that has happened during the war. . . . The hope of the country is that you repair the misfortune occasioned by Sherman's negotiations.

In all probability Grant pocketed this telegram, keeping it from Sherman's sight. Grant had arrived at Raleigh stealthily, had darted inside Sherman's headquarters, and had remained there, asking that neither the Federal nor Confederate armies be advised of his arrival. Sometimes Grant could have for the feelings of friends the delicacy of a nurse for a patient. He now wanted to remain hidden so that no one would imagine he had superseded his friend. He merely told Sherman that the agreement was disallowed, told him to offer capitulation and nothing more. He had Sherman send notification to Johnston, and when the latter asked for another conference at noon on the twenty-sixth, Grant told his friend to handle everything. Sherman asked him to come along and meet Johnston. Grant wouldn't think of it. He wanted Sherman to salvage what honor was left.

54

HORRID DEFORMITIES

SHERMAN received the rejection of his memorandum with a calmness that was surprising. Undoubtedly Grant's steadying influence—like a hand always on his shoulder—had much to do with this. Grant had seen from the first that, with the North in its present state of mind, Sherman's terms could not be approved, and his descriptions of the situation in Washington confirmed what Sherman had gathered from the latest New York newspapers that had reached Raleigh. To Stanton, Sherman wrote apologetically and frankly on the twenty-fifth:

I admit my folly in embracing in a military convention any civil matters but unfortunately such is the nature of our situation that they seem inextricably united, and I understood from you at Savannah that the financial state of the country demanded military success and would warrant a little bending to policy. . . .

I still believe that the General Government of the United States has made a mistake but that is none of my business; mine is a different task. . . .

It was obvious in this letter that Grant had told Sherman nothing of the wild charges and suspicions Stanton had leveled against him in the night meeting of the Cabinet that Grant had attended.

Grant, as soon as Sherman and Johnston had met on the twenty-sixth and signed a new set of terms—as generous, simple, and almost as brief as those Grant had given Lee—returned to Washington. He had seen enough, for all his care to keep inconspicuous, to make him share Sherman's sympathy for the people of North Carolina. From Raleigh he had written his wife:

. . . suffering coming to the South will be beyond comprehension. People who talk of further retaliation and punishment, except of political leaders, either do not conceive the suffering endured already, or they are heartless or unfeeling.

Only one change did Grant make in the articles that Sherman brought back from the final meeting with Johnston; he reversed the signatures so that his friend's name might come first when the paper was published. Sherman had graciously given Johnston the honor. Personal affection for Johnston, coupled with pity for the South, prompted Sherman to interpret the terms with increasing liberality in the days that followed. He gave ten days' rations to all surrendered soldiers and loaned them "enough farm animals to insure a crop." His special field orders were to "encourage the inhabitants to renew their peaceful pursuits and to restore the relations of friendship among our fellow-citizens and countrymen." And he wrote Johnston:

Now that the war is over, I am as willing to risk my person and reputation as heretofore to heal the wounds made by the past war, and I think my feeling is shared by the whole army.

Johnston's habitual lack of emotion was melting. On April 28 he wrote Sherman more warmly than he had perhaps ever written to a brother officer of the Confederacy:

The enlarged patriotism exhibited in your orders reconciles me to what I have previously regarded as the misfortune of my life, that of having you to encounter in the field. The enlightened and humane policy you have adopted will certainly be accepted.

As if to show the South how firm was his faith in its honor, Sherman quietly allowed Johnston's men to retain one seventh of their muskets as they started home with their paroles. Guerrillas might need quelling.

With Schofield ready to complete the final details of the surrender, Sherman prepared for a quick trip to Savannah, where he could arrange for the feeding of Wilson's cavalry in central Georgia. He would return by boat to Richmond, there to meet his four corps, which he enjoined to make a "model march."

In upon his pacific mood there came, on April 28, the New York newspapers of the twenty-fourth with Stanton's broadside shrieking its catalogue of accusations. Here was an attack worse than the charge of insanity in 1861. Carl Schurz saw Sherman, amid a dozen generals, pacing the floor

> like a caged lion, talking to the whole room with a furious invective which made us all stare. He lashed Stanton as a mean, scheming, vindictive politician who made it his business to rob military men of their credit earned by exposing their lives. . . . He berated the people, who blamed him for what he had done, as a mass of fools, not worth fighting for. . . . He railed at the press which had become the engine of vilification.

Seizing a pen, Sherman sent Grant a categorical denial of Stanton's charges, and accused the Secretary of violating the secrecy of military communications and of inviting "the dogs of the press to be let loose upon me." He was particularly incensed by the absurd declaration that by his orders to Stoneman he had enabled Davis to escape. "Even now," he wrote, "I don't know that Mr. Stanton wants Davis caught." He was almost frantic at the charge of insubordination made against him by the *New York Times*, and declared to Grant:

> I have never in my life questioned or disobeyed an order, though many and many a time I have risked my life, health and reputation in obeying orders or even hints to execute plans and purposes not to my liking. . . .
>
> It is true that non-combatants, men who sleep in comfort and security while we watch on the distant lines, are better able to judge than we poor soldiers, who rarely see a newspaper, hardly can hear from our families, or stop long enough to draw our pay. I envy not the task of reconstruction, and am delighted that the Secretary of War has relieved me of it. . . .

He wrote Grant in disgust at the disposition of politicians to put new burdens upon the prostrate South; the army had, he thought, done all that was proper in that regard:

> although as an honest man and soldier, I invite them to go back [to Nashville] and follow my path, for they will see some things and hear some things that may disturb their philosophy.

In a postscript he demanded that this letter, answering Stanton, be published.

Bitter against politicians, newspapers, and erratic democracy, suffering from the laceration of his feelings, he felt now as if his only friends were the soldiers, blue and gray, and the Southern people. He wrote Ellen that the politicians were keeping the war going: "They may fight it out, I won't."

A week later he would be writing Chief Justice Chase that he knew the Southern people well:

> I have no fear of them armed or disarmed . . . and, in war, would not hesitate to mingle with them and lead them to battle against a national foe. But we must deal with them in frankness and candor, and not with doubt, hesitancy and prevarication.

At 3 A.M. on the twenty-ninth he was writing Rawlins:

> The South is broken and ruined and appeals to our pity. To ride the people down with persecutions and military exactions would be like slashing away at the crew of a sinking ship. . . .
>
> If he [Stanton] wants to hunt down Jeff. Davis . . . let him use sheriffs, bailiffs and catch-thieves and not hint that I should march heavy columns of infantry hundreds of miles on a fool's errand. The idea of Jeff. Davis running about the country with tons of gold is ridiculous. I doubt not he is a beggar and who will say that if we catch him he will be punished. The very men who now howl the loudest will be the first to intercede. . . .
>
> We must if possible, save our country from anarchy. I doubt not efforts will be made to sow dissension between Grant and myself on a false supposition that we have political aspirations or after killing me off by libels, he will be the next to be assailed. I can keep away from Washington and I confide in his good sense to save him.

When he reached Savannah, Sherman spread food and kindliness across Georgia's devastated regions. On May 13 three judges of Thomas County wrote one of his lieutenants, General Edward M. McCook:

> The generous spirit evinced by the order of General Sherman and so cordially adopted by you, has had a happy effect upon the whole people of our State, and will convince them that you and your colaborers have a humane and Christian feeling for them, which will be properly appreciated.

Wilson, carrying out Sherman's orders, by May 24 was issuing two hundred and fifty bushels of corn daily to civilians, although the amount endangered the rations of his own men; and by mid-June he was ladling out in Atlanta forty-five thousand pounds of meal and ten thousand pounds of flour a week. So generous was the distribution of food that Thomas, ruling the district from Nashville after Sherman had gone North, ordered Wilson not to issue it in "such extravagant and extensive proportions as heretofore."

Leaving Savannah on May 2, Sherman halted overnight at Hilton Head, where New York newspapers of the twenty-eighth were awaiting him. The hue and cry was still loud against him. George Bancroft, the historian, had singled him out for criticism in the funeral oration delivered over Lincoln's body in New York City; the orator said that he had "usurped more than the power of the executive, and has revived slavery and given security and political power to traitors from the Chesapeake to the Rio Grande."

Here and there a rare note of apology was being made for Sherman. Horace Greeley's heart was beginning to speak. In the *New York Tribune* he was ridiculing the *London Times's* hints as to Sherman's ambition for the dictatorship, and he was dismissing Stanton's charges concerning the Sherman-Stoneman incident as "flapdaddle." Sherman, according to Greeley, might have been "unwise but not treasonable."

Then Sherman opened the *New York Times*. Its columns were like fists beating on his face. It reported that men in Washington were asking, "Has Sherman gone mad?" On another page was a more deadly blow—Halleck, who had rescued him in '62, had now joined Stanton. Here was proof! Old Brains had, according to published orders, directed Thomas and Wilson to disregard Sherman's truce while negotiations were under way in North Carolina. He had sent large sections of the Army of the Potomac through southern Virginia to cut off Johnston's retreat. And Stanton had telegraphed Thomas to "obey no orders from Sherman" and to send cavalry after Jefferson Davis.

That the War Department should have commanded his own subordinates to ignore him was almost beyond Sherman's power of endurance. He knew that with the return of Grant to Washington all these orders and movements would have stopped, but his own honor must be avenged. On the twenty-eighth he had written Rawlins that in time he would express his resentment of Stanton's gross outrage, and on May 4 he wrote Schofield concerning "Halleck's perfidious order . . . I will attend to him in time."

It would be weeks before he learned what had really happened in the Stanton-Halleck affair. On April 22 Grant, steaming south to join Sherman, had stopped at a station to wire Halleck at Richmond:

> The truce entered into by General Sherman will be ended as soon as I reach Raleigh. Move Sheridan with his cavalry toward Greensboro as soon as possible. I think it well to send one corps of infantry also . . . The in-

fantry need not go farther than Danville unless they receive orders hereafter . . .

It was plain that Grant meant to have horsemen available for juncture with Sherman if Johnston refused the new demands for surrender, but Halleck, interpreting the order awkwardly—to say the least—wired Sheridan:

> Pay no attention to the Sherman and Johnston truce. It has been disapproved by the President. Try to cut off Jeff. Davis's specie.

He also telegraphed General Meade and General Wright in lower Virginia to "disregard any truce or orders from Sherman." Sheridan halted at Danville, but a detachment of Wright's infantry entered Greensboro on the evening of April 29, when Sherman's men were idle in distant camps. Wright telegraphed an assistant:

> Dear Webb; Give it circulation among the newspaper reporters that the advance of the Army of the Potomac occupied Greensboro ahead of the forces of General Sherman. It is the best joke of the war. . . .

Whatever friction might have arisen at a meeting between Wright's soldiers and Sherman's with a truce still in effect was obviated by Halleck, who on learning during the twenty-eighth that Johnston had surrendered, halted all forward movements.

Studiously the Secretary of War ignored Sherman in his furious chase, through early May, after Jefferson Davis. His secret-service operatives, inventing evidence to link Davis with the assassination of Lincoln, kept Stanton in mental tumult. On May 2 President Johnson offered a hundred thousand dollars for Davis's arrest as a party to the murder. Stanton and Halleck professed to believe that Davis was carrying as much as thirteen or fifteen million dollars in bullion, a figure that made Sherman scoff; he estimated that if the fugitive had but six millions in gold—the minimum estimate—it would require fifteen six-mule teams to pull it, and Davis was flitting rapidly.

Poor Davis had brought from Richmond only five hundred thousand dollars and of this sum two hundred and thirty thousand was later returned to the Richmond banks; thirty-seven thousand of it was distributed to Johnston's army. Each of 32,174 men received $1.17. To make even this pitiful payment Johnston had been forced to defy Davis, who asked that the money be forwarded to him.

On May 10 Davis was captured while fleeing through the dawn dressed in his wife's raincoat and shawl. To the last he believed that Johnston had purposely exposed him to this fate by denying him the proper cavalry escort. Johnston's position was that the cavalrymen were in honor bound to surrender to Sherman like the rest of the army, and not to go trailing off protecting an Executive who ran away.

As the war ended Johnston and Sherman stood in the proverbial shoes of peacemakers—each blamed by civilian superiors for interference. Johnston told Schofield and Cox, as the final details were adjusted, that the Federals

> treated the people around them as they would have done those of Ohio or New York . . . inspired in them a kindlier feeling to the people of the North and Government of the United States than that existing ten years before!

Sherman, steaming northward on the *Russia*, through the night of May 5, was thinking that it might be best to quit the army and America! Writing to Schofield, he spoke freely concerning the Northern Radicals:

> Their minds are so absorbed with the horrid deformities of a few assassins and Southern politicians that they overlook the wants and necessities of the great masses. . . . It makes me sick to contemplate the fact, but I am powerless for good and must let events drift as best they may.

Then he turned to the writing of a paper that he expected would force Stanton to demand his resignation. But as he did so a storm came sweeping down the coast and the *Russia* lay for two days in harbor at Morehead City. Beside it lay the *Wayonda*, bearing Salmon P. Chase on the first leg of his tour of the South, where he would collect evidence that Negroes should vote. Sherman and the Chief Justice saw much of each other, and Sherman, after talking over his proposed blast against Stanton, sent a copy of it to the *Wayonda* with a note which described it:

> . . . an order I make to my troops to counteract the effect of the insult so wantonly and unjustly and so publicly inflicted on me by the Secretary of War.
>
> Of course this will soon lead to the closing of my military career and I assure you this, I can have no aspiration to civil favors but will shun them with disgust. Indeed, I have not yet thought whither I will cast my fortunes but probably to some foreign land if, in my judgment, events are drifting further into another civil and anarchical war.

Chase went to work to kill the order. He wrote Sherman soothingly how the President and Stanton had changed their minds when they found out what Sherman's motives had been. He could see nothing but evil resulting from the order:

> I earnestly hope you will let reason and reflection do the work of your vindication and put the order at least in abeyance . . . you are a native of Ohio—a State which has received me by adoption and has favored me

beyond my desert. Your honor and repute are therefore especially dear to me. Besides this, your brother was one of my most able and efficient supporters in my whole difficult financial administration; and my gratitude to him in some sort extends itself to you. So you must excuse my solicitude not forgetting that it is that of one who is a good deal older than you are, and has a very large experience if not so varied as your own.

The Chief Justice won his case; Sherman neither issued nor preserved the order.

Fresh from long talks with Chase, in which the latter explained many of the puzzling actions of the past three weeks, Cump wrote Ellen on the eighth and tenth with new insight:

A breach must be made between Grant and Sherman, or certain cliques in Washington, who have a nice thing, are gone up. . . .

. . . heaven and earth will be moved to kill us. . . . Washington is as corrupt as hell, made so by the looseness and extravagance of war. I will avoid it as a pest house. . . .

Stanton wants to kill me because I do not favor the scheme of declaring the negroes of the South, now free, to be loyal voters whereby politicians may manufacture just so much more pliable electioneering material.

In Washington Secretary Welles was writing in his diary:

We were all imposed upon by Stanton for a purpose. He and the Radicals were opposed to the mild policy of President Lincoln on which Sherman acted, and which Stanton opposed and was determined to defeat.

Friends of Stanton told Thomas Ewing that the Secretary had been "thrown from his balance" by the assassination of Lincoln. Old Solitude observed also, "It was thought by a few sagacious observers that Stanton had sought cause against Sherman ever since the fall of Atlanta—jealousy." George C. Gorham, one of Stanton's biographers, believed that the Secretary had been stirred to anger by Sherman's sweeping boast that his terms would bring "peace from the Potomac to the Rio Grande." Various other observers concluded that Stanton's motive had been to smirch Sherman so that he could not be advanced as an anti-Radical candidate for President in 1868. Stanton had received from John Sherman a letter written April 27 admitting that he "was distressed beyond measure" by Cump's terms to Johnston and that they were "inadmissible." John had begged that mercy be shown his brother:

The most that can be said about him is that he granted the rebels too liberal terms. The same may be said, but to a less degree, of Mr. Lincoln and General Grant in their arrangement with Lee. . . .

He [General Sherman] thought the disbanding of their armies the end

> of the war, while we know that to arm them with the elective franchise and state organization is to renew the war.

John had shown Stanton that he was at the moment a Radical:

> There should now be literally no terms granted. We should not only brand the leading rebels with infamy but the whole rebellion should wear the badge of the penitentiary, so that, for this generation at least, no man who has taken part in it would dare to justify or palliate it.

How far the brothers had been swept apart by the revolutionary times was apparent in every line of the letters that Cump wrote on board the *Russia* and sent to Chase on the *Wayonda*. Chase had written him that "sound policy and impartial justice" required giving the Negro the vote even if it meant the occupation of the South by Federal armies as a police force. Sherman answered that such a course would "produce new war . . . more bloody and destructive than the last." He said that the Federal armies would not support such a step. He attacked the Radicals' program for keeping the Southern States out of the Union until they had fulfilled the stipulations specified. He said that the Constitution guaranteed each State "a republican form of government" and that it must be observed. He asked the Chief Justice to look at the storm which on the sixth was still raging in the harbor:

> . . . is it not better to be quiet at anchor till these whitecap breakers look less angry and the southwest wind shifts? I think all old sailors will answer yes . . . don't you think it better first to get the ship of State in some order that it may be handled and guided?
>
> If now we go outside the Constitution for a means of change we rather justify the rebels in their late attempt.

The soldier, with the courage of his own irony, lectured the nation's leading lawgiver on the virtues of clinging to the American system of effecting changes calmly and with order through the proper legal instruments:

> . . . the tribunal before which all conflicts must come at last, the Supreme Court, before whose decrees I and all soldiers of my school bend with the veneration of religion, is now surely safe to us on "the vexed questions" which led to one war and now threatens another. In it I hope is the "anchor of safety."

With this parting shot—as forceful and penetrating as those which he had fired at Hood during their correspondence eight months before—Sherman ended the exchange. Next day the southwest wind shifted and Chase steamed south and Sherman north over calming seas. On the evening of the eighth Sherman came ashore at Fortress Monroe, ready to entrain for Richmond, where his army was arriving. A telegram was handed him; it was from Halleck in Richmond:

> When you arrive here come directly to my headquarters, I have a room for you and will have rooms elsewhere for your staff.

Sherman answered:

> After your dispatch to the Secretary of War of April 26th I cannot have any friendly intercourse with you. I will come to City Point tomorrow and march with my troops and I prefer we should not meet.

55

THE CUD OF BITTER FANCY

JOINING his men outside Richmond on May 9, Sherman found them cursing the Army of the Potomac, Halleck, Stanton, and the East; many men were demanding that they be allowed to use muskets to ease their anger. Trouble had begun at Raleigh, where the men had burned newspapers containing Stanton's broadside against their chieftain. On April 30 a private of the Thirtieth Illinois had written in his diary his faith in Sherman: "I won't believe he has made a mistake until I know all about it. It can't be. . . . I'd rather fight under him than Grant and if he were Mahomet we'd be devoted Mussulmen."

The men had fraternized with paroled Confederates around campfires as they had marched northward, but they had glared belligerently at Army of the Potomac cavalrymen whom they met. They said they would have fought such fellows to preserve their armistice; fighting Easterners would not be half-bad, anyway.

The northward march had been pacific, with guards standing outside houses. The last march of Sherman's men was like their first in Kentucky so far as the sanctity of chickens and green apples was concerned. Perhaps the sudden restraint made the Westerners angry, too. They poured up to the camp ground opposite Richmond to find that Halleck, inside the walls, would not let them enter to view the historic capital of their enemies. General Force saw "guards posted across roads to prevent any member of Sherman's army from going into the city." Colonel O. L. Jackson saw men of the Fifteenth Corps "pelting Halleck's guards with stones" and heard it said that "Logan looked on and laughed." Soldiers begged their officers to let them shoot their way into town. One squad of the Eighty-fifth Indiana tossed the provost guard into the river and whooped on into the city. Sherman, working hard to quiet the boys, listened to their demand that he permit them to revenge the insult Halleck had given him. He wrote Ellen, "Ord, Merritt, Crook and all the big men of Halleck's army have been to see me and share with me the disgust at their [Stanton's and Halleck's] base betrayal of my confidence."

When Halleck ordered the Fourteenth Corps to enter the city so that he might review it, Sherman canceled the plan and wrote Old Brains that he had lain awake all night trying to understand the "deadly malignity" that his former friend had shown. He said that he would march his army through Richmond when Grant ordered it "and I beg you to keep slightly perdu," since if the Western men saw Halleck, they might revenge their leader. "If loss of life or violence result . . . you must attribute it to the true cause—a public insult to a brother officer." Eight years later Sherman wrote Halleck's widow:

> The feeling of my army was so high that it was with difficulty I could prevent riot and collision and I actually feared my men would insult the General, and it was for this reason that I advised him to remain indoors during our passage. . . .
>
> My warning against bloodshed was not ill timed, for at the bridge when my men were refused passage it required some pains to prevent them from using their firearms to open the way.

In bitter mood Sherman, on the ninth and tenth, wrote his official report of the negotiations with Johnston, and into it put the declaration that when Halleck had sought to violate the armistice "he knew I was bound in honor to *defend* and *maintain* my own truce and pledge of faith even at the cost of many lives." Frankly Sherman went on record as having been ready to fight fellow Federals rather than break his word to a Confederate.

On May 11, after Grant had given the necessary orders, Sherman marched his men through Richmond, whose streets were lined with citizens, Negroes, and well-dressed Eastern soldiers. The Twelfth Wisconsin heard the Army of the Potomac spectators talk about "Sherman's Greasers" because "we looked like Mexicans, dark with pitchpine smoke." Easterners said that the West had never had to handle Lee; Sherman's men sneered at Richmond's defenses and said they were weaker than Atlanta's. Men in the Twelfth Wisconsin decided, "The West felt superior in wits, courage and independence."

Flags and sentries told the marchers where Halleck had his headquarters. The Wisconsin regiment saw "a splendidly built and equipped guard, very spick and span" before the door, and as the men passed "a ragged, dirty Westerner, with the devil-may-care swing, sauntered out of the ranks, stared impudently at him, then shot a stream of tobacco juice all over his well blacked shoes."

At noon on the twelfth Sherman loosed his wrath in a letter to Logan:

> The manner of your welcome was a part of a grand game to insult us—us who have marched 1,000 miles through a hostile country in mid-winter to help them. We did help them and what has been our reward?
>
> Your men were denied admission to the city, when Halleck had invited all citizens (rebels of course) to come and go without passes. If the American people sanction this kind of courtesy to old and tried troops, where is the honor, satisfaction and glory of serving them in constancy and faith? If such be the welcome the East gives to the West, we can but let them make war and fight it out themselves.

Here a wave of homesickness made Sherman sing:

> I know where is a land and people who will not treat us thus—the West, the Valley of the Mississippi, the heart and soul of the future strength of America, and I for one will go there. . . .
>
> Chew the cud of bitter fancy as you ride along, and when events draw to a conclusion we can step into the ring. Men who are now fierce and would have the Army of the Potomac violate my truce and attack our enemy discomfited, disheartened and surrounded, will sooner or later find foes, face to face, of different metal. Though my voice is still peace, I am not for such peace as makes me subject to insult by former friends, now perfidious enemies.

When he arrived, on May 17, at the camp prepared for him at Alexandria, it was manifested to him that the long-hated "grannies of New England" had succeeded in imposing their Abolitionism on the country anew. The principal agitators now at work for Negro suffrage were Charles Sumner and Wendell Phillips of Massachusetts; Thaddeus Stevens of Pennsylvania, Vermonter by birth; and Chase, born in New Hampshire. Friends of the Negroes had named General Howard, Maine-born, to head the Freedmen's Bureau that was attempting to adjust ex-slaves to their new condition. Sherman, learning of this appointment, sat down and wrote Howard a warning against allowing himself and his bureau to be used by politicians whose interest was not humanitarian but "to manufacture available votes." He begged Howard, "Don't let the foul airs of Washington poison your thought toward your old comrades in arms." He reminded his friend that all but a few Northern States still denied the Negro a vote:

. . . if we attempt to force the negro on the South as a voter . . . we begin a new revolution in which the Northwest may take a different side from what we did when we were fighting to vindicate our Constitution . . . and if the "theorists" of New England impose this new condition on us I dread the result. The West will not submit to the taxation necessary . . . to enforce the rights of negroes.

From his tent, soon after arriving, he sent word to Rawlins to

let some newspaper know that the vandal, Sherman, is encamped near the canal bridge . . . where his friends, if any, can find him. Though in disgrace, he is untamed and unconquered.

That the Ewings feared a return of the cerebral excitement Sherman had developed in 1861 was obvious in an entry Hugh made in his diary on May 20:

The threats of Gen. Sherman against the authorities, that we heard on the streets this morning, made it necessary that he be counseled, and I found John Sherman in Willard's barbershop in the chair, took him to Charles Sherman's room, where the Shermans and Gen. Tom [Ewing] and myself held a consultation over his condition, and had John go to his camp and quiet him. . . . Sherman's officers are loud in denunciation of Halleck and Stanton.

Grant, sending for Sherman on the twentieth, soothed him materially, and on the same day President Johnson and all the Cabinet except Stanton welcomed him with honor. All assured him that they now understood his Johnston terms and that none of them had known of Stanton's broadside until it appeared in the papers. Howard and Grant suggested a reconciliation with Stanton, but Sherman refused; he was planning to strike back at Stanton when his time came to testify before Wade's Committee on the Conduct of the War, which was holding sessions in the Capitol.

On May 21 he sent his friend General Van Vliet, stationed in New York, a letter:

Dear Van:

. . . I am now getting ready for the review of Wednesday, after which I am to go before the war investigating committee, when for the first time, I will be at liberty to tell my story in public.

Don't be impatient, for you will be amazed when the truth is narrated—how base Stanton and Halleck have acted toward me. They thought they had me down, and when I was far away on public business under their own orders, they sought the opportunity to ruin me by means of the excitement naturally arising from the assassination of the President, who stood in the way of fulfillment of their projects, and whose views and policy I was strictly, literally following.

But in less than twenty-four hours something made Sherman abandon his intention of placing upon Lincoln the responsibility for the terms given Johnston. Unexpectedly called before the committee on the twenty-second, he walked into a room over which presided the hard face of Ben Wade and which was packed with Wade's fellow Radicals. There could be no doubt that Sherman, after having spent a week with well-informed leaders in Washington, understood very clearly how eager the committee was to prove Lincoln's whole policy of mercy a colossal error. Daily the Radicals were urging Andrew Johnson to scorn his predecessor's attitude toward the South. If now they could establish that the Sherman-Johnston agreement—admittedly a mistake, in public estimation—had been dictated by Lincoln, they would take a long step toward convincing the new President, and the world in general, that the dead Executive had been incapable of handling reconstruction.

Under Wade's questioning Sherman, on the witness stand, told fully all that happened between Johnston and himself. He took special pains to denounce Stanton and Halleck but avoided all mention of Lincoln until, near the end of his narrative, he said that when inviting Vance to continue in control of North Carolina:

I did so because President Lincoln had encouraged me to a similar course with the Governor of Georgia when I was at Atlanta. . . . Had President Lincoln lived, I know he would have sustained me.

Then he read into the record his official report of the surrender, establishing how he had been guided by Lincoln's amnesty proclamation of 1863, by Grant's terms to Lee, and by the invitation to the Virginia legislature to assemble. But not a word did the report contain of his conversation with Lincoln on the *River Queen* in March.

Ben Wade was not to be denied. He was sure that such conversations had been held, and he was determined that Sherman should not evade the matter. He asked:

"Did you have, near Fortress Monroe, a conference with President Lincoln, and if so, about what time?" Sherman admitted that he had and gave the dates. Wade came to the point: "In those conferences was any arrangement made with you and General Grant, or either of you, in regard to the manner of arranging business with the Confederacy in regard to the terms of peace?"

"Nothing definite," answered Sherman; "it was simply a matter of general conversation, nothing specific and definite."

The answer would remain one of the riddles of Sherman's life. He would never explain why on the twenty-first he wrote a friend that he had been "strictly, literally following" Lincoln's views and policy and yet on the twenty-second stated something very different. Ten years after the occasion, when writing his *Memoirs*, he declared that Lincoln's conversation had been "full and frank" in its authorization of at least temporary recognition of a Southern State government, and in its wish that he use extraordinary means to get the "Rebels" to their homes and normality.

There could be no question that Sherman was concealing much from the committee. Colonel Markland had evidence of it. Markland came rushing to Sherman's camp at Alexandria asking to be allowed to tell the truth. He said that from the moment he had read the Sherman-Johnston agreement in a newspaper, he had recognized it as substantially that which on March 30 Sherman, fresh from talks with Lincoln, had declared himself ready to offer. Markland wanted to tell this significant fact to the world. But, as he later admitted, "General Sherman was in no mood to take up the subject and very clearly intimated to me that I should be silent concerning it." Whenever, in years to come, Markland importuned Sherman to let him speak, Sherman would always say no.

The most likely explanation of Sherman's decision to throw a wall of silence about Lincoln's words lay in his lifelong habit of refusing to throw off on other men. It was his way to shoulder responsibility, and it would have been utterly characteristic for him to have concluded that it would be unmanly to assign to Lincoln the authorship of a course so universally damned by enemies of the dead man.

That Sherman was telling the truth to Van Vliet and in his *Memoirs* was attested not only by Markland and John Sherman, but also by Gideon Welles, who wrote in his diary that "from many talks with Mr. Lincoln after his return from Richmond, I came to the conclusion that Sherman in his terms to Johnston had acted under instruction from President Lincoln." Admiral Porter declared that Sherman's terms to Johnston were "exactly in accordance with Mr. Lincoln's wishes . . . Mr. Lincoln did, in fact, arrange the (so considered) liberal terms offered General Joe Johnston."

Grant's continued silence upon the subject of the conferences with Lincoln indicated that he had a special reason for keeping back something. The one inkling that the inquisitive Welles found as to Grant's views came in the spring of 1869, when a newspaper, *Wilkes' Spirit of the Times*, openly asserted that Lincoln had dictated terms to Sherman. Welles understood from sources in Washington that Grant had supplied the facts for the article. The *New York Tribune* of April 10, 1869, declared that there could now be no doubt that Mr. Lincoln had "substantially arranged" the terms, and that if he had lived he would "have taken on his own shoulders the responsibility of having dictated" them. It quoted *Wilkes' Spirit of the Times's* laudation of Sherman for having borne in silence "undeserved obloquy." On the following day Sherman wrote the *Tribune* that he understood

> Mr. Wilkes' original article was compiled by him after a railroad conversation with Admiral Porter.
>
> . . . I repeat that according to my memory, Mr. Lincoln did not expressly name any specific terms of surrender, but he was in that kindly and gentle frame of mind that would have induced him to approve fully what I did.

Among all the shifting sands of the situation, with Radical politicians attempting to prove Lincoln a fool and the public irresistibly elevating the dead President to godhood, Sherman and Grant behaved like men who had either promised Lincoln secrecy as to his instructions on the *River Queen* or had resolved after his death not to make him responsible for mooted actions.

In his desire to place Confederates outside of Radical vengeance, Lincoln might well have asked Grant and Sherman to keep his plans secret. It would have been characteristic of him to have instructed them to go beyond the proffer of simple surrender if necessary to gain quick peace, and to have asked that this intention be confidential. Grant, as it happened, found Lee willing to accept the first offer of terms; Sherman was forced to go further.

That Lincoln had privately given Grant the form of parole which the latter extended to the Confederates was generally accepted at the time by Radicals, Moderates, Democrats, and the newspaper men of Washington. The *New York World* declared confidently on May 27 that the parole had been made under Lincoln's "specific orders." For two months there was dispute over the meaning of this parole, and in particular about the phrase "not to be disturbed by United States authority." Radicals insisted that the words freed Confederates from nothing but military prosecution and left them free to be tried for treason in civil courts. The *National Republican*, accepted as Stanton's mouthpiece, insisted that at the moment Lee and his men were exchanged "they become ordinary citizens and are amenable to civil authorities." Democrats and Moderate Republicans agreed with the *New York World*, which said on May 27 that the clause was

> an arrangement which not merely has a military scope and settles the status of the rebel soldiers as prisoners of war, but has also a civil scope and pledges

their future status as citizens though guilty of past treason—pledges their future security as citizens so long as they obey the laws.

Attorney-General Speed, keeping close to Stanton, decided that the Radicals were right—Lincoln had had no authority to delegate the pardoning power to a general, and Lee could not be relieved by military arrangement from responsibility to the civil law. On May 31 Judge J. R. Underwood of the United States District Court at Norfolk, Virginia, charged a grand jury to examine Lee's case with a view to indictment for treason. Lee informed Grant of this on June 13, and three days later Grant was warning the Administration that the parole, having been approved by Lincoln, could not be broken without "bad faith." He asked that all indictments be quashed and further prosecution abandoned. To support Grant came public opinion, many Radicals questioning Speed's interpretation; and the Radical *Chicago Tribune* admitted that although Lee deserved hanging, the parole must be regarded "as amnesty" and that if he were executed it would be in violation of the clause that gave him protection from prosecution by United States authority. The *Philadelphia Public Ledger* called the indictment nonsensical, because "the Government is pledged not to molest Lee." In the end the courts and most vengeful Radicals desisted; Lee went free, and legal or illegal, the parole had done its work.

No result so sane was apparent to Sherman in late May. One of the few men he saw to be strong enough to resist the tide of vengeance was his brother-in-law, General Tom Ewing, who since the twelfth of May had been defending three of the persons accused of complicity in the murder of Lincoln. Representing Dr. Samuel A. Mudd, Samuel Arnold, and Edward Spangler, Tom was bitterly criticized by Radicals as he walked the streets of Washington. Yet his motives could not be impugned. He had fought for free soil in Kansas, he had become a Federal brigadier general in March, 1863, a major general in September, 1864, after a heroic defense of Pilot Knob, Missouri; he was the son of Old Solitude, who had been trusted by Lincoln and was now trusted by Andrew Johnson. His brother Hugh was a major general, his younger brother Charles had been made a brigadier general on March 8. He was a disturbing element to the Radicals, who planned a quick verdict of guilty against the eight prisoners accused of conspiring to assassinate Lincoln. And in the end he saved his three clients from the noose that claimed four of the remaining five.

The Ewings were gathering in Washington for the grand review. Ellen was coming with her father and her son Tommy. She had written Cump on April 26 her lack of sympathy with his terms of surrender:

But my opinion of you is unaltered, and, my heart not having been set on popular favor, I care nothing for the clamor they have raised. I *know* your motive was pure. I know you would not allow your army to be in the slightest imperiled by this armistice, and however much I differ from you, I honor and respect you for the heart that could prompt such terms.

After all his military triumphs, Cump was still in the shadow of his father-in-law—still the dear, impulsive brother over whom Ellen must always be watching.

56

HAPPIEST MOMENT OF MY LIFE

IT was May 23, 1865. Sherman sat in a wooden stand before the White House. Close by sat President Johnson and his Cabinet, and around them governors, senators, notables, and ladies. Crowds jammed Pennsylvania Avenue, roofs, windows. From a distance came the blare of bands, shouts. The Army of the Potomac was being reviewed. The East was having its day. Tomorrow would come Sherman's day and the West's. Into view swung General Meade. The crowd shrieked, "Gettysburg!" Here came George Armstrong Custer—a brigadier general at twenty-six—the Eastern army's most romantic figure. Female voices squealed. The *New York World* reporter jotted down his description:

fair and ruddy complexion—a sunrise of golden hair which ripples upon his blue shoulders—on his left arm hangs a wreath of evergreens—scarlet kerchief—white gauntlets.

An overwrought woman threw a wreath. Custer snatched at it. His horse bolted. The crowd shrieked, "A runaway!" The *World* man saw Custer's hat blow off; "in the sunshine his locks, unskeined, stream a foot behind him . . . it is like the charge of a Sioux chieftain." (Prophetic simile; in eleven years Custer would be dead under a charge of Sioux warriors.) Sherman watched Custer disappear—"he was not reviewed at all." (Prophetic dramatization of the end of cavalry as a major arm of war.)

Sherman was critical of Eastern troops, noting that many "turned their eyes around like country gawks to look at the big people on the stand." They did not march well, because of the faulty music from two civilian orchestras—"pampered and well-fed bands that are taught to play the very latest operas." He resolved to eliminate that music tomorrow, and have his own men march to their own regimental bands. Come what might, his army *must* outmarch the Easterners.

Meade walked up onto the stand. Sherman said to him, "I'm afraid my poor tatterdemalion corps will make a poor appearance tomorrow when contrasted with yours." Meade said the people would make allowances. Comparisons were in the generals' minds. Six years later Meade said that his Army of the Potomac had suffered 60 per cent of the Union casualties of the whole war.

That night Sherman ordered his officers, "Be careful about your intervals and your tactics. I will give plenty of time to go to the Capitol and see everything afterward, but let them keep their eyes fifteen feet to the front and march by in the old customary way." Many men had new uniforms, but rags were still common. The *World* man noted many bare feet. Hazen was still making vain efforts to have the Fifteenth Corps cut its hair. Sherman was going to let the East see his army as it had lived, for better or for worse.

Through the night he moved in from Virginia, closer to the city, and at break of day bugles blew and the *World* reporter wrote:

> . . . directly all sorts of colors, over a wild monotony of columns, began to sway to and fro, up and down, and like the uncoiling of a tremendous python, the Army of Sherman winds into Washington.

The Fifteenth Corps led the way. For a little while it paused behind the Capitol, snickering to see Uncle Billy ride past, "dressed up after dingy carelessness for years." His horse wore wreaths on its neck. Young ladies were thrusting roses in lapels and down gun barrels, or bringing ice water from tubs on street corners. Springtime flirtations danced up and down the waiting lines. Sherman eyed his men anxiously. Had he any right to expect them, after all those reckless years and miles, to march like bandbox soldiers?

He would not ride alone. Howard would be seen at his side. In Carolina he had said that if he were killed Howard must take command and end the campaign. Now Howard, although transferred to the Freedmen's Bureau, was entitled to ride at the head of the Army of the Tennessee, but Sherman had asked him, out of respect for Logan's disappointment at Atlanta, to let the Illinois soldier have that honor.

The Capitol was blooming with flags. The morning was bright and soft. A cannon boomed. Nine o'clock! Sherman shook a spur; his horse stepped forward, drumsticks made the air flutter like flying canister or wild-geese wings. Bands blared into "The Star-spangled Banner." Around the corner of the Capitol the Westerners came.

Stage fright stuck in plowboys' throats. The roofs and trees were black with people. Pennsylvania Avenue stretched like a long, long river between human banks. White handkerchiefs waved like apple blossoms in an Indiana wind. Boys' eyes caught blurred sights of signs spanning the avenue—"Hail to the Western Heroes" . . . "Hail, Champions of Belmont, Donelson, Shiloh, Vicksburg, Chattanooga, Atlanta, Savannah, Bentonville—Pride of the Nation."

Cheers crashed against the blushing faces of the marchers. Their lips twitched and their eyes fell in self-consciousness. Many of them wished they were back among the swamps of Carolina—even among the bullets of Vicksburg. J. W. Anderson, Company G, Nineteenth Illinois, heard people pray as his regiment swept by; he noted sobbing women hold up babies to see the soldiers. Mourning still hung on buildings—mourning for Lincoln. Crape draped all flags. Now and then curious cheers welled up from the marching men, wild cries arising from the excitement and from comprehending at last the tremendous miles behind them.

Sherman, riding ahead, his old slouch hat in hand—the sun on his red hair—was listening to the tread of his men. Sometimes in sudden hushes he could hear one footfall behind him. The hushes came when ambulances rolled by with bloodstained stretchers fastened on their sides. Gales of laughter followed hushes, as at the end of the corps came Negro refugees of both sexes and all ages, leading or riding mules, walking beside wagons filled with tents and kettles surmounted by turkeys and pet raccoons. Pigs grunted from end gates here and there. Gamecocks rode cannon, crowing. Ragamuffin Negroes bearing Revolutionary blunderbusses grinned at guffawing spectators.

Sherman hoped, as perhaps he had never hoped anything in his lifetime, that his men were marching well. They sounded all right, but he couldn't be sure in the roaring current of noise. They *must* show the East that they were not "an undisciplined mob." Sherman neared the White House, where the test would come. Ellen would be in the stand, with Tommy and Old Solitude; Willy's eyes would not be there to shine. Cold eyes of elegant society people would be leveled.

Sherman's horse walked up the avenue slope before the Treasury Building. In a minute it would swing to the right and come into view of the stand. Behind him he heard the tumult growing louder. Were his wild young fellows behaving? He dared not look back; he had ordered everybody to hold eyes front.

He was on the crest of the rise now. He could hold his nerves no longer. He spun in the saddle and looked. A blissful thrill ran to his finger tips. His legions were coming in line, every man locked in steady formation—formal for perhaps the first and the last time in their lives. "They have swung into it," said Sherman to himself. Long afterwards he said, "I believe it was the happiest and most satisfactory moment of my life."

He turned back to the front and led the way up the avenue before the Treasury and the White House. Some one called to him to look at a window. From it peered a face that Charles A. Dana described as "one of the most horrible spectacles that the human eye ever beheld"—the face of Secretary Seward recovering from a series of injuries: a jaw broken in a carriage runaway, a face and throat scarred by a would-be assassin on April 14. Bands of steel and rubber, clamps on top of his head and under his chin, made him hideous, but not to Sherman, who had been looking at wounded men across four years. Sherman waved his hat, Seward waved a wan hand. Sherman fixed his hat on his head, whipped out his sword, and rode past the stand, saluting the President. The *World* man wrote:

> . . . the acclamation given Sherman was without precedent . . . greater than the day before . . . the whole assemblage raised and waved and shouted as if he had been the personal friend of each and every one of them. . . . Sherman was the idol of the day.

Ellen, standing with Mrs. Grant, looked for Cump past black silk hats that waved and white handkerchiefs that flew. It would be her first sight of him in eighteen months. There he was on a "shining bay"—his saber was flashing in front of his face . . . his beard was getting terribly grizzled . . . his hair was cut closer than usual, thank the Lord . . . he was very thin . . . he was gone.

The whole army was thin. Carl Schurz, in the stand, felt his heart leap as the Westerners wheeled into view—"nothing but bone and muscle and skin under their tattered battle-flags." Their flags were thin, too, from winds and bullets—many were nothing but shreds of faded red and white and blue. Cheers drowned the bands. The street in front of the stand was ankle-deep in flowers—worn heels, bare heels, kept step among the roses.

Cheers for Howard with the empty sleeve . . . for Logan with the black hair . . . For Hazen, very handsome . . . for Mother Bickerdyke riding an army horse side-saddle, a sunbonnet on her head, a calico dress on her capable body. The *New York Tribune* reporter saw officers of the Fifteenth Corps shout something unintelligible in the uproar, and the men without turning their heads, their eyes still front, relax their imperturbable faces and break into wild yells, tearing off their hats with free·hands and waving them in air—their eyes still front.

They were cheering the President and Grant. Boys of the Twelfth Wisconsin said, "We couldn't look at the reviewing stand. If Lincoln had been there I'm afraid our line would have broken up."

Almost all the spectators, it seemed, noted that the Westerners took a more springy stride than had the Easterners the day before, a step guessed at from two to four inches longer—a proud, rolling, swinging step. One old man in the stand thrilled as he saw it; Tom Corwin, who at seventy-one had been remembering how, so long ago, he had sat beside the deathbed of Judge Sherman. Who would have thought then that the judge's boy Cump would march so far in history? Eloquence came from Corwin as the river of Westerners rolled by.

"They march like the lords of the world," he said.

Another Ohio pioneer sat glowing in the stand, the Methodist Episcopal Bishop Edward R. Ames, remorseless traveler of the wilderness, itinerant preacher, missionary to the Indians, criss-crosser of the continent, understanding, now, those "splendid legs." Beside him sat the German ambassador, who said as the Fifteenth Corps passed: "An army like that could whip all Europe." As the Twentieth Corps went by he said: "An army like that could whip the world"; and when the Fourteenth Corps had gone, ending the parade, he said to Ames, "An army like that could whip the devil."

It was commonly agreed that Sherman's men were taller, leaner, than Easterners; their beards were longer and more shaggy—more of them wore beards, more of the beards were yellow and red. It was also agreed that the Westerners were more obviously the symbol of democracy, the private soldiers apparently hailing from the same social strata as their officers. Spectators had difficulty distinguishing officers from the men, whereas such differences had been plain in the Army of the Potomac. Many observers noted how completely the Eastern regiments in Sherman's Twentieth Corps had taken on the characteristics of their Western comrades—"they walked like Westerners."

The East had shown better clothing, more paper collars, superior discipline; the West had marched far better. Western boys had older faces. The *New York World* man thought Sherman's soldiers "hardier, knottier, weirder." He concluded that the army of the East had been composed of "citizens, the West of pioneers." Charles A. Page of the *New York Tribune* declared the Westerners' "faces were more intelligent, self-reliant and determined."

To Washingtonians, Sherman's army had the variety and strangeness of a foreign caravan—blackamoors, mules, swaying wagons, signalmen carrying sixteen-foot staffs with small flags that looked to the *New York World* man like "talismanic banners, emblems of a grander Masonry than the world is worthy of." Excited onlookers spoke of the Crusaders—a word that no member of the army, so far as later research would reveal, had ever applied to themselves.

Once he had passed the reviewing stand, Sherman left the line of march and with his staff entered the White House grounds, where he dismounted and hurried to enter the tier of seats. He found Ellen, Tommy and the Salt-Boiler and embraced them, then hurried to shake hands with President Johnson. Grant was next, then Stanton.

The time had come to repay insult with insult. The Secretary of War held out his hand, but Sherman ignored it. Elbridge J. Copp, a telegrapher in the War Department, saw the incident plainly; "Sherman's face was scarlet and his red hair seemed to stand on end." A buzz of surprise eddied through the stand, whispers flew. Sherman sat down to watch his men go by.

Charles A. Dana, admirer of Sherman and assistant to Stanton, thought that the affair had been carefully plotted. He said that the Blairs, who had been working to persuade President Johnson to desert the Radicals and swing back to Lincolnian gentleness toward the South, had been conniving to oust Stanton from office. Dana declared that for some days before the review Cump's brother Charles "had been very active in stirring up a quarrel" and, with the Blairs and other anti-Radical politicians, had gathered on the stand to humiliate Stanton publicly. In all likelihood General Sherman had not been acting in concert with any one. For a month he had planned to insult Stanton, and this had been his first opportunity.

As the last pickaninny-laden mule disappeared, the notables came down from the stand. Copp, the telegrapher, saw throngs pump Sherman's hand and shower bouquets upon him:

> At first he was affable, then he grew less cordial as the crowds crushed in. He pushed down the steps, step by step, and refused proffered hands, finally exclaiming, "Damn you, get out of the way, damn you!"

That night when serenaders called him out from John Sherman's house—next door to Stanton's—he said he wouldn't make a speech because he might get excited and say things better left unsaid. The *World* man heard him add:

> For when I speak, I speak to the point and when I act in earnest I act to the point. If a man minds his own business I let him alone, but if he crosses my path, he must get out of the way. I want peace and freedom for every man to go where he pleases, to California or to any other portion of our country without restriction.

From the crowd came a voice referring to gossip that the army was to help Mexico drive out Emperor Maximilian:

"How about going to Mexico, General?"

"You can go there if you like and you can go to hell if you want to!" barked Sherman, and he went indoors.

For days and nights he was busy with complaints that his Westerners were fighting with Eastern soldiers in saloons, stealing horses and buggies—the Eighty-fifth Illinois played such a prank upon Washington's chief of police—capturing horse cars, kicking off conductors, collecting fares, refusing to make change, and carrying passengers beyond their stops. He heard of one group who refused to alight at the end of the line. "End, hell!" they bellowed. "We paid to be hauled out to camp, five cents to be hauled out to camp, and we're not going to be swindled." And, said Sherman in later years, "Do you know, those boys seized the reins and drove that car right up on the road to camp a mile beyond the end of the track? Fortunately the road was smooth and hard and the poor horses were able to pull it."

Grant wrote him that General Augur, policing Washington, complained that Western and Eastern troops whenever they met "are sure to fight" and that Sherman's men exhibited "deep feeling, especially when in a little liquor, on account of the difficulties between yourself and Secretary Stanton." Augur described how Western officers jumped on bars, gave "three groans for Mr. Stanton, then get down and take another drink." Sherman rode the streets after midnight calming his men. Soon Dana was writing General Wilson that Grant had been forced to put the Potomac River between the Westerners and the Easterners, on account of the fist-fighting.

> I have heard of one or two men who have been killed and one or two who have been seriously wounded. Sherman's men are pretty troublesome to the farmers and other quiet people where they are.

Hazen thought the Army of the Tennessee was ordered to Louisville for demobilization with unseemly haste. He admitted that the boys were still free with "reckless appropriation of other people's property" and that "an amount of investigation and police-court work was done daily which very soon made it necessary to send the Army of the Tennessee away, so that our expected long rest at Washington was reduced to a few days."

While they prepared to depart, Sherman found himself the center of a political fight, with Democrats planning to run him for President in 1868 on the strength of his hostility to Stanton. The *New York World* of May 30 charged that "the two organs of Stanton in New York," the *Herald* and the *Times,* were dramatizing Sherman's insult to the Secretary in an attempt to make Stanton a presidential candidate. On the twenty-eighth Sherman wrote Grant that if his retaliation to Stanton

> at all incommodes the President or endangers public harmony all you have to do is to say so and leave me time to seek civil employment and I will make room. . . . I would like Mr. Johnson to read this letter, and to believe me that the newspaper gossip of my having Presidential aspirations is absurd and offensive to me, and I would check it if I knew how. . . .
>
> To accuse me of giving aid and comfort to copperheads is an insult. I do not believe in the sincerity of any able-bodied man who has not fought in this war, much less in the copperheads who opposed the war or threw obstacles in the way of its successful prosecution.

John was now working with Cump to force the publication of the general's report of the Johnston negotiations. John wrote an unsigned article in the *Washington Chronicle* of May 25 charging Stanton with malice; "General Sherman's agreement breathed the spirit of the dead President, but it came one week too late or one month too early."

Colonel S. M. Bowman, who was writing a book to be called *Sherman and His Campaigns,* gave to the newspapers on May 25 a letter sent him by Sherman on the nineteenth declaring:

> I dare the War Department to publish my official letters and reports. I assert that my official reports have been purposely suppressed while all the power of the press has been malignantly turned against me.

A few days later the report was published.

On May 30 Sherman wrote his farewell address to his men. As the soldiers read it, they were sad. They rejoiced, of course, at the prospect of seeing home folks, yet army comrades now seemed closer than relatives. They had prayed and sung about the happy day when "the cruel war is over." They had longed to be done with stinking death. But that had been in days when peace was far away. Now it was here, and it was not what they had expected. It was hard to say good-by to boys with whom they had walked, fought, bled, and stolen chickens.

All at once they knew that the sun would not rise on danger in Ohio, and that in the twilights of Indiana would come the boom of frogs—not Joe Johnston's cannon. There would be fireflies and not sharpshooters blazing in the long grass of Missouri. Soon they would be hunting work instead of hens. All too quickly now their iron legs would be following plows and harrows round and round a narrow field —their feet would be boxed in by inviolate fences or frame villages that never changed. Never again would they move with the equinoxes, sweating in the Southern sun. Life's supreme sweetness was ending, not beginning. "Our work is done," they read in Uncle Billy's farewell. Their eyes ran down the printed page regretfully. They caught sentences that recounted their triumphs—he was reminding them that success in the past was due to hard work and discipline and that the same work and discipline were equally important in the future:

> . . . our favored country is so grand, so expansive, so diversified in climate, soil and productions, that every man may find a home and occupation suited to his taste . . . none should yield to the natural impatience sure to result from our past life of excitement and adventure. You will be invited to seek new adventures abroad; do not yield to the temptation, for it will lead only to death and disappointment . . . farewell . . . you have been good soldiers . . . you will make good citizens. . . .

To the men the paper read like a lament, until near the end:

> If, unfortunately, new war should rise in our country, "Sherman's army" will be the first to buckle on its old armor, and come forth to defend and maintain the Government of our inheritance.

"New war?" Occasionally boys wondered vaguely about this as the railroad trains hauled them westward. War with whom? Certainly not with the South. The West need never go there again. With France over Mexico? Not likely.

No, if war came it would be with those damned Easterners in the paper collars!

57

LEAR ROARING AT THE STORM

THE Western army's arrival at Washington had come at a psychological moment in the career of President Johnson. In the four weeks that had passed since Lincoln's death Johnson had been slowly recovering his poise. New and awful responsibility tempered the tongue that had demanded punishment and impoverishment of Southern "traitors." Radicals were still confident that the President would stand with them on the platform of vengeance, which they had all mounted beside Lincoln's corpse, but Moderates were beginning to see signs that the President was quietly veering back toward Lincoln's general ideas of a kindly reconstruction. Grant, returning from North Carolina, had thrown his influence toward tolerance.

Then, in mid-May, Sherman and his 65,000 men had come like emissaries from the dead Lincoln. Their reputation as the chief wreckers of the South heightened the effectiveness of their anti-Radical words. Their faces, black from the smoke of devastation, were the faces of Radicals, but their voices were the voice of Lincoln. At the review Johnson had seen that the public had discounted Stanton's broadside against Sherman. It had cheered him strenuously, crazily, in spite of the fact that he was fresh from a campaign in which he had turned back Negro refugees, opposed Negro soldiers, and tried to allow "Rebel" State governments to continue in office. In all but a few Radical newspapers, Johnson had seen reflected the enthusiasm of the press for Sherman as a hero.

He had seen Sherman openly, confidently, insult Stanton, and during the nights that followed there had come through the White House windows the sound of Westerners jeering Stanton in the barrooms of the capital. From Sherman, and from both Frank Blair and Logan—chief voices of the Western volunteers—Johnson learned that the army had not gone to war either to wipe out State organizations or to give Negroes control of the South. From Schofield, commanding other Western troops in North Carolina, Johnson received strong arguments in favor of quick restoration of civil government based on white franchise.

Before and after the review Sherman was received by the President often and with "marked courtesy and warmth." He was sufficiently close to the throne to have an inkling of Johnson's first public departure from the Radical program. On May 28 Sherman wrote Schofield:

> I have reason to believe Mr. Johnson is not going as far as Mr. Chase in imposing negro votes on the Southern or any States. I have never heard a negro ask for that, and I think it would be his ruin. . . . Besides it is not the province even of our Congress, much less the Executive, to impose conditions on the voters in "organized States." That is clearly reserved to them. . . .
>
> I think I see already signs that events are sweeping all to the very conclusion I jumped to in my terms. . . . The people of this country are subject to the Constitution, and even they cannot disregard it without revolution, the very thing we have been fighting against.

On the following day Johnson announced his first plan of reconstruction; the extension of amnesty on the scale previously offered by Lincoln, the appointment of a provisional governor for North Carolina, and the permission to all citizens who could now qualify under North Carolina's prewar laws and who would take the oath of allegiance, that they might vote for delegates to a State convention. The Negro was ignored.

While the Radicals growled in their homes, the general public approved. Recovering from the convulsions produced by Lincoln's death and funeral, the Northern masses had begun to realize how unpalatable Negro suffrage might be. But Republicans of the mental cast of John Sherman—strong party men yet sympathetic with Johnson—had begun to see practical difficulties confronting this Lincolnian scheme. John agreed with Cump that the Negroes were unprepared for the ballot. Yet they were free and soon to become citizens. Before the war, in representation a Negro had counted as three fifths of a white man. Southern representation in Congress had been determined by adding to the white population three fifths of the slaves. When a Negro became five fifths of a white person, this representation would be increased. And who, asked John, would exercise this new power? "Shall the Rebels do so? If yes, will they not now in effect restore slavery?"

Cump stood steadfast on the platform that the South was done with slavery and that if "ex-Rebels" did rule their own States, the country would not be endangered. He told Schofield that if "Northern politicians are going to divide again . . . and enable the minority of the South . . . to govern both, it is our fault not theirs."

He apparently sensed something suspicious when in late May a committee of New-Yorkers arrived in Washington inviting him, with Johnson and Grant, to attend a monster mass meeting in Cooper Institute on June 7 "to express approval of the measures of the government in enforcing the national authority." He declined to make the appearance, although he was to be in New York as late as June 5. His excuse was that he had a previous engagement at the Sanitary Fair in Chicago. Perhaps Thomas Ewing's astuteness aided him in side-stepping this invitation, for Ewing distrusted Chase, and the New York committee was made up of Chase's political henchmen. The *New York Herald* later described the mass meeting as an attempt of the Chase political machine to steal a march upon the Moderates and to dictate to the President a Radical policy "under the pretense of endorsing him."

There was something of defiance in the words with which Sherman declined the invitation. He declared himself ready to support law and order, "but at the same time we should aim to escape the reaction to the opposite extreme, so common to violent revolutions."

Grant made similar efforts to avoid the committee, but in the end was sent to the meeting, with Blair and Logan, to represent the President. He sat upon the stand, consumed with diffidence, while Chase's henchmen read resolutions accusing the South of Lincoln's murder, demanding punishment for "traitors," votes for Negroes, and "loyal" control of the South. It was a thoroughgoing Radical set of resolutions, but the crowds in Cooper Institute adopted them heedlessly, indeed shouting, "Grant! Grant!" while the vengeful paper was being read and adopted. Although Grant would not speak at all, and although Blair and Logan declared themselves against the spirit of the resolution, all three were henceforth entangled, more or less, in the political brambles that Sherman had skirted.

While they worried, Sherman moved through unending ovations. New York gave him enthusiastic banquets and receptions, Wall Street brokers vied with bootblacks in running after him in the streets. William Scott, the cousin-in-law who had stared at Sherman in 1836 "as at an untamed animal," now threw open his mansion on Twenty-third Street for a reception and basked in Sherman's reflected glory. On June 5 Cump took Ellen and Tommy to West Point, where at Cozzen's Hotel he was embraced by General Scott, who "almost kissed him." The ancient warrior quavered, "I thank God you have lived to see this day and that I, too, have lived to see it." Cadets stared at Sherman and almost burst with pride when he shook their hands "as though they were men," and in the words of one of them, Charles King, "began at once with tales of how they did things in his time, as though his subsequent times were of no account compared with the old days in the corps."

King noted how carelessly Sherman treated invitations and flattery, "but what an eye he had for pretty girls!" Sherman's career as a social lion had begun. Speedily it became the fashion for young women to shower him with public kisses, and in time orators at meetings of the Society of the Tennessee would refer to him as "the great American soldier who whipped every foeman who stood before him and kissed every girl that he met." At forty-five he was still so slender and virile as to be physically attractive to women, and moreover his prematurely wrinkled face and well-grizzled beard gave him a patriarchal glamour that made caresses innocent. As he would grow older the kissing would, if anything, increase. Thomas B. Bryan, the Chicago civic leader, attending a White House reception in the early 1870's, saw how Sherman

> amused himself and everybody else by his frolicsome snatching of kisses from young women, whose ringing laugh attested their willing tribute to his age and distinction . . . If all the fair of our land had but one pair of lips and Sherman were anywhere within reach, terrific would be the concussion.

When in his sixties he addressed a throng at Indianapolis, there was much humorous comment among the admiring populace as to the number of girls and women he had publicly kissed during his visit.

The fury of this admiration struck him in 1865 when he reached the Sanitary Fair in Chicago, where buttons, autographs, kisses, and photographs were torn from him. With Minnie, now a tall girl of fourteen, upon his arm and with Tommy trotting beside him, he toured bazaars. Behind one counter stood Ellen "selling things," as he had asked her not to do. Cheers called him to speak at the fair, in restaurants, in lobbies, and from his opera box, which he occupied nightly. At the fair on June 9 he talked of peace to the crowds:

> You gentlemen know what you must do. Instead of destroying you must build up; instead of insulting you must conciliate; instead of destroying you must encourage those who are willing to aid us in building up this diversified land . . . all parties have prejudices and we must respect them and they must respect ours.

That night soldiers serenading him at his hotel heard him speak against Radical plans for letting the Negro enjoy complete political and civil freedom:

> The Government will require to institute some system of labor in order that the lands of the South may be cultivated. . . .
>
> Negroes are not fitted for the exercise of the franchise . . . not fitted to take part in the legislation of the country.

By the thirteenth, the *Chicago Tribune*, awakening to the damage his words had done its own Radical attempts to sway the midlands, attacked his stand, and when Grant joined him at the fair the *Tribune* praised the hero of Appomattox for not joining Sherman in attacks on Negro suffrage. This fired the *Times*, Democratic rival of the *Tribune*, to magnify Sherman diligently, and to point out his perfect qualifications as the Democratic party's presidential candidate in 1868.

On the seventeenth, Sherman departed for South Bend, where he visited the younger children in school and where, as he rode up to the convent, he laughed to see a large Confederate flag break from an upstairs window. Several little Southern girls had stolen time from class to stitch together a banner with which to defy the "ravisher" of their homeland. Sherman soothed the horrified nuns and thought it fine of the little girls. He passed on to St. Louis, Mansfield, Lancaster. All Fairfield County—and beyond—was at the station to meet him on June 24. His words were heard in fragments far back in the large crowd:

> . . . It is nearly thirty years since I left here as a boy. . . . Trust the Constitution. . . . Let each State take care of its own local interests and

affairs. . . . You all know that I have lived much at the South, and I say that though we have had bitter and fierce enemies in war, we must meet this people again in peace. The bad men among them will separate from those who ask for peace and order.

Six days later he was in Cincinnati, speaking from a hotel balcony, and was receiving what the *Enquirer* called "the largest [local] ovation that has been paid to any distinguished man during the war." He told the crowd:

We have the best country on earth. Our history in the past is beautiful, and her future is in our keeping. . . . For fifty years to come, at least, I never want to hear a word about war in America. . . . I am for peace now.

On July 4 he was in Louisville, to attend the barbecue and banquet that celebrated the final mustering out of his army. For two weeks the saloon-keepers and grocers of the city had been complaining at the freedom with which "Sherman's bummers" stole liquor, vegetables, and cans of sardines. The *Louisville Journal* of June 17 described such antics as "all very well during war time in the South but not among friends."

Men of the Fifty-fifth Ohio heard Sherman tell the Twentieth Corps good-by. A horribly hot day . . . Sherman standing on a hill . . . soldiers at his feet . . . like a blue lake. His voice was low but it carried far. He thanked the men, spoke of their dead, said that at first he had feared that Eastern regiments among them could not stand the shock of war as it was fought in the West, "but after Peach Tree Creek he relied upon them as much as upon the Fifteenth Corps, and he could say no more than that." He asked the men to equal in civil life their wartime records. He gave them his blessing and a last farewell, came down from the hill—and the blue lake flowed away. That night at the banquet the *Cincinnati Enquirer* reporter jotted down Sherman's words:

I think that the interest of the whole country demands that when troubles arise, they should be determined by the courts of law and not by the force of the musket.

Returning to Lancaster, he found official orders awarding him his favorite of the military divisions—the Mississippi—stretching from Ohio's eastern border to the Rockies and from Texas to Canada. And as he prepared to move to St. Louis, his new headquarters, the Republican *Albany Journal* declared that Democratic managers "intend to give Sherman McClellan's place as he is an enemy of the Administration." It guessed that he might run for Governor of Ohio, "so that no matter if he won or lost he would be in a position to run for President in 1868." At the same time Duff Green, astute and ancient Democrat, wrote President Johnson:

> If you identify yourself with the ultra-Abolitionists in their warfare on the South, then Democracy will rally on Sherman, and aided as he will be by his brother's influence in Ohio, he will carry the Conservative Whigs and organize the Northwest and South against New England.

Sherman's answer to this swelling chorus came on July 20 in St. Louis. A few days earlier General Dodge had brought to him stories that Union men of the city were much disturbed because he had been wining and dining with the old pro-Confederate aristocracy of the town.

"They are going to give me a dinner in a few days," Sherman had said, "and, General, don't worry; I will settle that question there." His words at the banquet in the Lindell Hotel were remembered by Dodge:

> . . . since the war was over he did not feel that it was necessary for him to refuse any attentions, no matter from whence they came, but when it came to the question between loyal men and rebels, every one knew where his heart was . . . and that it was only the clemency of the government that saved them from receiving their just dues long before this time. . . .
>
> Let us all go to work and do what seems honest and just to restore our country to its former prosperity—to its *physical* prosperity. As to its political prosperity he knew nothing of it and cared far less.

In following weeks Sherman refused to join in the Northern revulsion against the South's revival of the "black codes." State conventions or legislative assemblies adopted modification of slavery laws in an effort to keep the freedmen subservient and busy at agricultural tasks. Necessary though some legislation might be, the codes sounded to even conservative Northerners like an attempt to retain slavery by subterfuge. In general the codes fined Negroes if they did not work, charged them almost prohibitive license fees if they sought to practice mechanical trades, and apprenticed minors to white employers who held the right to whip them if insubordinate and to recapture them if they ran away. In some quarters Negroes were forbidden to preach, teach, or hold property.

Cump wrote John that for some time to come "the State governments must be controlled by the same class of whites as went into Rebellion against us. . . . I would have used it and had it subservient to the uses of Government." And on November 4, when newspapers were quoting Johnson as having announced that the Executive had no right to dictate to any State, North or South, the character of its voters, Cump was writing John: "You observe that Mr. Johnson is drifting toward my terms to Johnston. He cannot help it, for there is no other solution."

In September he had told John in a letter, "You may look for outbreaks in Ohio quicker than in Georgia or Mississippi," and on November 25, when Radicals were protesting against allowing Southern representatives to sit in the coming Congress, Cump was pressing John to welcome the new members. One by one the Southern States had repealed secession, abolished slavery, and voted to return to their former stations.

When, on February 19, 1866, President Johnson vetoed the Freedmen's Bureau Bill by which Congress, yielding to Radical determination, had decreed that Federal agents could imprison or fine Southern whites who discriminated against blacks, Cump declared to John, "as I am a man of peace, I go for Johnson and the Veto."

It was depressing to find the fruits of the war dissipated and to discover that New England, represented by Charles Sumner, was still as sectional as Jefferson Davis had been. "It will be a pity," said Sherman, "if the great mass of our people have to go on fighting forever to demonstrate the fallacy of extreme opinions." Exactly as in days when Bleeding Kansas had been an issue, Cump begged John to indulge the South until time could bring its beneficent wisdom—"Whenever State legislatures and people oppress the Negro, they cut their own throats, for the Negro cannot again be enslaved."

For all his resolution to keep away from politics, Sherman could not refrain from pushing his moderate views on all the Congressmen and Senators whom he met in St. Louis or in his travels over his division. He publicly endorsed General Cox for Governor of Ohio, knowing him to be anti-Radical, able, honest, and intellectually penetrating. But from the bitter and abusive struggle that developed in 1866 between Johnson and the Radicals, Sherman drew back. As much as he approved Johnson's reconstruction policy, there was a headlong ferocity about the President that repelled him. John Sherman, who had made manful efforts to keep the Republicans from driving Johnson into the Democratic camp, in July, 1866, began to advise Cump to "avoid all expressions of political opinions." The political feud was to be murderous. John edged away from Johnson when the latter vetoed a Civil Rights Bill that would have given Negroes most of the social and civil privileges—practically all except the ballot and intermarriage. Passing this bill over the President's veto, Congress drew up the Fourteenth Amendment to the Constitution and started it on its way toward ratification by the States. Since this amendment made Negroes citizens, Southern States turned down their thumbs, although tolerant Northerners thought this a mistake as long as the amendment did not compel Negro suffrage.

Sherman, traveling much over his enormous military division, was congratulating himself on escape from the political shambles. In the autumn of 1866 he was at a fort in the Southwest enjoying himself—and an ancient Apache—when newspapers began hinting mysteriously that he was to be called to Washington. The Apache was interesting. Every day he asked Sherman for an old cannon that lay in the fort's junk heap. Finally the general let him take it, with the stipulation that he would never use it to kill soldiers. "Humph!" grunted the old Indian. "Cannon kill cowboys; kill soldiers with club!"

Returning to St. Louis, he found newspapers hinting that he had written a letter endorsing Johnson in the latter's quarrel with Congress. Apparently the President was seeking to inform the public that Sherman was behind him. This news annoyed Sherman. The letter he felt to be private property. He had written it in February, 1866, while in Washington on army business. Preparing to leave the city, he had been unable to say good-by to the President, and in sending a note of apology he had wished Johnson success "in his professed desire to accomplish . . . the restoration of Civil Government all over the land." In the summer Johnson had telegraphed to ask to be allowed to publish the letter, but Sherman had begged off on the ground that he wished "to avoid controversy." Now hints of the letter had been made public, also there were rumors that Sherman was to be called to Washington. Cump wrote John that he would resist anything that took him East. "I must keep clear of politics in all its phases, for I must serve any administration that arises."

But soon orders came to report at the capital, and on arriving there Sherman speedily gathered from conversations with Grant and other friends that the President was planning to get rid of Stanton and to make Sherman Secretary of War, "on the theory," as Cump told John, "that I would be more friendly to him than Grant." Sherman also came later to believe that at the time Stanton had wished to remove Grant from Washington in order to scotch the latter's growing boom for the Republican presidential nomination.

Whatever the motives might be, Johnson had asked Grant to escort to Mexico the new minister, Lewis D. Campbell. Johnson told Sherman that Grant's prestige would be useful in establishing Campbell with Juarez, the President recently elected by the Mexican people in their effort to be rid of the European Maximilian, whose Latin empire was expiring. Grant refused to be thus buried from sight for what might be a long period; also, he had genuinely important duties of army reformation that he could not afford to leave.

Sherman took Grant's objections to the President, and warned the latter not to start a quarrel with the head of the army. To solve the difficulty Sherman proposed that he take Grant's place on the journey. And when the President agreed, Sherman sailed away satisfied that the trip, while of no account, had at least given him the chance to prevent a breach between the Executive and the army. Sailing early in November, the mission came to a farcical end in early December when, after a vain search for Juarez up and down the coast, Sherman came home, leaving Campbell to follow soon afterward. More than ever Sherman regarded Mexico as his pet symbol for anarchy.

Coming home by way of New Orleans, he was pleased to find himself not unpopular with Southerners. Stopping to visit Jackson, Mississippi, which he had twice burned, he wrote John that the people "met me in the most friendly spirit." Contrasted with the Radicals, Sherman was in Southern eyes a very different man than he had seemed in 1863-64. Recognizing this fact, John asked Cump to use his influence with Southerners to procure the vote for the Negro as a means of ending the political warfare—"Three years ago they hated you and Johnson most of all men; now your advice goes farther than any two men of the nation."

But Cump skillfully avoided the temptation to assume this hopeless rôle of peacemaker. The President, lacking the poise to handle opponents tactfully, had been drawn into harmful exchanges of abuse by hecklers during a stump-speaking tour in the fall of 1866, and had further antagonized new blocs of conservative Republicans by discharging from office "loyal" men—some of them ex-soldiers. Striking back at the President, on March 2, 1867, Congress passed over his veto the Tenure of Civil Office Bill, which forbade the discharge or replacement of civil officeholders without the consent of the Senate. On the same day it made law another bill that had been vetoed by Johnson, an act placing the late Confederate States under military law and giving the army power over local affairs. Tales of outrages upon Negroes and loyal whites in the South had inflamed the North. Stories of the whippings inflicted upon blacks and carpet-baggers—white exploiters from the North—by a secret society of Southerners, the Ku Klux Klan, had given Thaddeus Stevens, author of the Military Reconstruction Bill, the votes necessary to its passage. Also, the failure of Southern States to ratify the Fourteenth Amendment, making the Negro a citizen although not a voter, had turned fresh armies of Northerners to the support of the Radicals.

Through the summer of 1867 the situation grew more vicious. On August 5 Johnson, deciding to defy the strict interpretation of the law regarding tenure of civil office, asked Stanton to resign, and when he refused, the President named Grant Secretary of War *ad interim*. A little later in the month Johnson, over Grant's protests, removed Sheridan from command at New Orleans. Sheridan had been delighting the Radicals with his reports of horrors perpetrated by Southern whites upon freedmen and loyalists.

Sherman, called to Washington in January, 1868, to recodify army regulations, learned from Grant, who was next door in the War Office, how confused the army was. He believed Grant when the latter told him that it was only to protect the army that he had accepted the War Secretaryship. On January 11 Grant came to Sherman with another perplexity. The Senate was soon to vote on the question of Johnson's right to remove Stanton. Grant, studying the Tenure of Civil Office law, had just discovered that if he held the office in the face of an adverse vote by the Senate, he would be liable to a fine of $10,000 and five years' imprisonment. At Sherman's insistence Grant took the matter immediately to the President, and on the following day he sent Sherman to propose the appointment of Governor Cox as Secretary of War.

About this suggestion Johnson was so noncommittal that Sherman decided he had some definite alternative plan in mind, and he departed. On the night of the thirteenth, after the Senate had voted Stanton the rightful holder of the office, Grant had his resignation delivered to Johnson, and the next morning he quit his desk shortly before Stanton marched in. On that day the *National Intelligencer*, Administration organ, proclaimed Grant's "duplicity" in not having retained the office, as he had previously promised, until the President could anticipate any move by Stanton or the Radicals. Grant's answer was that at the time he had made this promise he had not known of the legal penalties attached to such retention, and that even so he had sent Sherman to Johnson on the thirteenth with word that he hoped Cox would be given his place. Such action had made clear his wish to retire.

Sherman accompanied Grant to the White House on the fourteenth to protest against the *Intelligencer's* attack, and heard the President disclaim knowledge of it and insist that he was Grant's friend. In the end Sherman heard "both parties profess to be satisfied," although he wrote Ellen that "the mutual explanations are full and *partially satisfactory*." He made no secret of his approval of Grant's refusal to run the risk of fine and imprisonment. "The whole matter," he wrote Ellen, "is resolved into a war between parties and neither care nor seem to care a damn for the service of the country."

The situation grew worse as Stanton and Johnson, "two strong, stubborn and willful men," locked horns. The army's predicament became apparent as Johnson refused to issue an order requested by Grant that would inform it whose orders it must obey. The President, summoning Grant before the Cabinet, cross-examined him, as might a prosecutor, upon his course in surrendering the office to Stanton. Grant's explanation was put down by the hostile secretaries as full of falsehoods and confessions of "duplicity," but to persons better informed on Grant's character these reports were not convincing. Grant's habits of silence, his unfamiliarity with politics, and his well-known bashfulness in the face of even a friendly audience, had not prepared him to put up an accurate self-defense when assailed by a prosecutor such as Johnson, who had been trained in rough and ready debate.

Although John Sherman voiced the general view of level-headed men when he said that Grant had not been harmed by the exchange of denunciations, it was at last becoming apparent that Cump had been right in 1864 when he had predicted that Grant could not stand up against the politicians of the capital. Grant was now becoming bewildered.

On January 24, 1868, Grant sent Johnson a request that he put in writing verbal orders, given by the President on the nineteenth, that bade the army to disregard Stanton's commands. The next day Johnson sent for Sherman and asked him to become Secretary of War. Sherman did not seem to suspect that this might be what Johnson had had in mind when he had failed to name Cox. To the President Sherman said that he doubted if the Executive had the power to oust Stanton or to name a successor, but that he would ask Thomas Ewing's advice.

Letters from both himself and Ewing came to Johnson on the twenty-seventh, refusing compliance. On the twenty-ninth, and again on the thirty-first, Johnson stubbornly insisted that Sherman accept. By that time Ewing had told Johnson, "I cannot advise Sherman to take the place, and he is not willing to do it"; also, that it would be wise to let Stanton remain in office to become "a stench in the nostrils" of the Radicals. Sherman had written Johnson on the twenty-fifth:

> For eleven years I have been tossed about so much that I really do want to rest, study and make the acquaintance of my family. I do not think, since 1857, I have averaged thirty days out of three hundred and sixty-five at home.

He thought he had made himself clear, but when Johnson had persisted on the thirty-first, Sherman wrote him a letter to end all further offers:

To bring me to Washington would put three heads to an army, yourself, General Grant and myself . . . would ruin the army, and would be fatal to one or both of us.

He hated the "spies and slanderers" of the capital, but in the end it was obviously loyalty to Grant that was the most insurmountable barrier against acceptance. He recounted for Johnson how the war had gone better in the West than in the East, because in the former "there was no political capital near enough to poison our minds and kindle into life that craving itching for fame which has killed more good men than bullets." He recounted the times he had seen Grant ignore slander, criticism, and abuse:

. . . and yet I never saw him more troubled than since he has been in Washington, and been compelled to read himself a "sneak and deceiver" based on reports of four of the Cabinet, and apparently with your knowledge. If this political atmosphere can disturb the equanimity of one so guarded and so prudent as he is, what will be the result with one so careless, so outspoken as I am? Therefore with my consent, Washington never.

With that rebuke, he was off for St. Louis, where now six children awaited him; the youngest, Philemon Tecumseh, was born on January 9, 1867, at a time when Cump had written John, "My pay is now about $1,070 a month. . . . I can barely get along and could not live here except that I received a house as a present." All the negotiables he had were "about $11,000 worth of bonds presented me by Ohio." In August, 1867, he had felt unable to send Minnie to school in New York because the schools were "so extravagant and fashionable."

Sherman had spent scarcely more than a week with his family when, on the evening of February 13, he was faced with almost the same situation that had confronted him in 1861. Then, a telegram from Montgomery Blair had offered him the prospect of becoming virtually Secretary of War; now, a wire from Grant ordered him back to Washington. On the twelfth the President had moved boldly to attach Sherman to his cause. He had created a new military division, that of the Atlantic, and had taken steps to promote Sherman to Grant's rank. In July, 1866, when Grant had been elevated to the highest possible position, that of full general, Sherman had stepped up into Grant's vacated rank, that of lieutenant general. Now Johnson planned to make Sherman brevet general, a post that, as Sherman wrote Grant, would make him a go-between, a buffer, between Johnson, Stanton, and Grant: "I would be there with naked, informal, and sinecure duties. . . . I object to the false position I would occupy as between you and the President."

He confessed to his friend that he suspected the Ewings of having told Johnson of Ellen's wish to live in Washington, near her father and brothers. It was true that Ellen was unhappy in St. Louis, as unhappy as she had been in California, Kansas, in every place that kept her out of touch with her idolized father. And as in every home that her husband had selected, so in St. Louis she thought the place unhealthful for the children. But Cump wrote Grant now, "I know better what is to our common interest and prefer to judge of the proprieties myself." He was evidently trying to be firm with his wife.

Once more he felt himself "hedged around." He thought of resigning and seeking work on the railroad or in some college, "but hard times and an expensive family have brought me back to staring the proposition square in the face." As he had done in 1861, he declined the appointment offered by the President on the ground that he could not afford to break up his home and move on the promise of impermanent employment. He wrote Johnson that he was not financially prepared to resign, "but I shall proceed to arrange for it as rapidly as possible, so that when the time does come (as it surely will if this plan is carried into effect) I may act promptly."

In the same mail that carried this letter East went an explanation to the Salt-Boiler, a statement that he could not seem to be put in opposition to Grant. He thought, also, that Johnson was presuming. Because Sherman had approved his plan of reconstruction, he thought "that I will go with him to the death." Thoughts of poor Johnson, blundering in a good cause, stirred Cump to prose poetry:

> He never heeds any advice. He attempts to govern after he has lost the means to govern. He is like a General fighting without an army—he is like Lear roaring at the wild storm, bareheaded and helpless.

Cump wrote Ewing his old trust in time:

> . . . if all hands would stop talking and writing, and let the sun shine and the rains fall for two or three years, we would be nearer reconstruction than we are likely to be with the three and four hundred statesmen trying to legislate amid the prejudices begotten for four centuries.

To Grant he voiced the same philosophy:

> My opinion is, the country is being doctored to death, and if President and Congress would go to sleep like Rip Van Winkle, the country would go on under natural influences and recover far faster than under their joint and several treatment.

Upon receiving Sherman's virtual ultimatum, Johnson dropped direct overtures and named Adjutant General Lorenzo Thomas as temporary

Secretary of War. But he was still determined to secure Sherman's influence. His chance lay in bringing the Ewings closer to the Administration. In 1866 he had named Hugh minister to the Hague, and now in March, 1868, he offered General Tom the appointment of permanent Secretary of War. Tom's father blocked this on the ground that Johnson was doomed to failure and that close association with him would injure the young man's career. Then Johnson sent the name of Old Solitude, himself, to the Senate for confirmation in the office. Ewing's former partner, Henry Stanbery, was already Johnson's Attorney General and, with other Cabinet members, was certain Ewing, for all his seventy-nine years, was the best man for the task. The Salt-Boiler, feeling that his own career was finished both in politics and at the bar, acquiesced, but before the Senate could act either favorably or unfavorably, political warfare intervened. The Radicals, declaring that Johnson had violated the Tenure of Civil Office law, impeached him on March 5 and, bringing the trial to a vote on May 16, failed by only one voice.

Two days before the all-important vote, Cump wrote John, "The Ewings are all down on me for my difficulty with the President." It was again the deadly parallel with his ordeal in 1861 when, after refusing high offers in Lincoln's first army, he had written Boyd, "My family and friends are almost cold to me and say that I have failed at the critical moment of my life."

But from this second domestic storm Sherman had new friends to rescue him—angels unawares, red angels in war paint on the Western plains. He had an engagement to powwow with a murderous Sioux named Sitting Bull at Fort Laramie when the willows would be green and the wild colts and buffalo calves nuzzling their mothers' udders in arroyos of the Rockies.

58

NO HONORABLE MAN WILL BE TOLERATED

FROM the tangles of reconstruction, which were almost as vicious and not so clean as actual warfare, Sherman had turned in relief to the West, where two tasks waited for a patriot—pacification of the Indians and completion of the transcontinental railroad. To him, both tasks were essentially the same. When the railroad should join its half that was inching east from California to its half that was edging west from Lawrence, Kansas, settlers would pour into the wilds and conquer redskins far more quickly than could squads of soldiers. The railway, too, would end old feuds between Mormons and "gentiles" in Utah.

Let the East, the South, and the midlands keep up their traditional hostilities; Sherman would work on the plains for an orderly and harmonious nation! His first act on assuming command of the Division of the Mississippi was to throw the resources of the army behind the railroad-builders. Time and again he used his prestige to fight off politicians and business men who, for local gain, sought to turn the right of way from its true course. In February, 1866, he journeyed to Washington to persuade the President to create new military departments for the better protection of railroad workmen. During the summer and autumn of 1865, he inspected the construction each month. "Every time they build a section," he said, "I'll be on hand to look at it and see that it is properly built."

Endless encouragement and advice he gave General Grenville M. Dodge, who had resigned from the army to become chief engineer of the railroad. It delighted him to see how many of his former officers held executive posts with the line. Riding past section hands, he heard voices hail him as Uncle Billy. Hundreds of discharged veterans—still in blue uniforms—were laying rails. Sherman laughed with them, recalling how recently he had taught them to twist iron in Georgia. Seeing them made him feel like the godfather of the Union Pacific. Indeed, Dodge said later that no other man had accomplished so much for the road.

"I think this subject as important as Reconstruction," Cump wrote John, urging that the railroad be not forgotten in the excitements of political strife between Congress and the Executive. It angered him in 1867 to find that the dispatch of so many troops South in the military occupation of that region, dangerously lessened the guards on the railroad.

For two years he flitted westward from St. Louis whenever possible, to scout his immense division and to direct small campaigns against the savages. He saw no fighting. He saw merely the Indian summer of his life as a campaigner—one last mild return of the hardships that in four strenuous years had become delights. Again he could eat camp fare, roll in a blanket, then, when all but the pickets were asleep, he could rise and stand by the dying bivouac fire, listening. Only the maniac coyotes spoke to him. Only the white fluff from river-bottom willows rode past him in the moonshine—riding winds that had come a long way across the plains and that were going a long way. In the autumn of 1866 he longed for brush and paint—as he had at Kenesaw—to capture the quaking aspens turning gold on high frost-nipped Rockies and to fix the rich colors in the verdure carpets at his feet. He rode across oceans of grass while cavalry scouts on the hills watched for hostile braves. General Rusling, accompanying Sherman on this tour, wrote:

> . . . he acted like a boy turned loose—threw off reserve—asked 1,000 questions of everybody—never at a loss for a story or joke—a comic twinkle in his eye—a toss of his head—a serio-comic twitch to his wrinkled features—with a long stride he paced up and down constantly, never weary—a prodigious smoker and talker—stretched in blankets before the fire in the shadow of mountains, he talked the night half away.

His talk was most often of his own men, of Alexander's, Caesar's, Napoleon's—he talked of Grant's genius at Vicksburg.

Visiting the southwestern corner of his division, he refreshed his dislike of Mexicans. Twelve years later he told General Lew Wallace that the United States ought to declare war on Old Mexico and make it take back New Mexico.

For two years, after the war's end, he felt himself, as he had in the Civil War, to be the bringer of the law, the stern apostle of national authority. It is likely that in his zeal to protect the transcontinental railroads he pressed his troops harder against the red men than he would have done had there been no section gangs on the plains. But to him the problem was essentially that of the late war; insurgents must be taught that time and logic and irresistible resources were all against them, and that their losses would increase in proportion as they continued their resistance to the Federal Government.

He had entered upon his Western duties with sympathy for the Indians, writing Grant on August 24, 1866, that they were "pure beggars and poor devils more to be pitied than dreaded." Boiling his own coffee on fire made from buffalo chips, he noted how the gradual disappearance of the fuel, due to the extermination of the bison, was making life hard for the savages. And although he encouraged irrigation on the plains and assisted the white settlers, he quickly understood how many of the Indian outbreaks were provoked by the farmers in the expectation of selling their hay and corn at high prices to the soldiers who arrived to quell the rioters. On September 21, 1866, he wrote Grant that the settlers wanted the troops "to kill all the Indians" but "I will not permit them to be warred against as long as they are not banded together in parties large enough to carry on war." Nine days later he was advising Grant that he had ridden great distances "without a single soldier" to guard him, yet was beset by farmers wailing for protection. He counted the names of able-bodied settlers on petitions that asked him to import soldiers, and saw that they outnumbered troops in nearest army posts. Contempt rose in him and he wrote Grant, "God only knows when, and I don't see how, we can make a decent excuse for an Indian war." In his letter of the 21st he grew sarcastic:

> I learn that General Pope has collected at . . . Fort Stanton all the Navajoes, 8,000 in number, who are held as prisoners of war and have to be fed as such. . . . I think we would better send them to the Fifth Avenue Hotel to board at the cost of the United States. . . . This whole subject of maintenance of the Indians who won't work and must be fed or turned loose is one that should be solved at Washington and not thrown on us.

A massacre of soldiers by Indians, under circumstances which Sherman regarded as treacherous, prompted him to inform Grant on December 28th, "We must act with vindictive earnestness against the Sioux, even to their extermination, men, women and children." As always, his bite did not measure up to his bark, but his violent words were thrown back at him by Eastern humanitarians in the succeeding decade. Six years later his old-time Abolitionist enemy, Wendell Phillips, was telling newspaper reporters that "Sherman is for exterminating Indians." Sherman answered hotly, branding the accusation "a most impudent fabrication throughout" and denying that he had ever "favored wanton destruction of human life in any instance." His only policy, he said, had been to compel Indians to remain on their reservations. On January 23, 1868, he wrote Dodge:

> We had to bear the blame of precipitating an Indian war, because we tried to protect the roads and stage lines, and that was used as an argument why the military should not be used for a purpose antagonistic to the Indian nation.

In September, 1867, he gave the Indians the philosophy that he had given the Confederacy in his "Prepare them for my coming" letter of 1864. Heading the peace commission that the Administration sent to confer with all tribes, he met hundreds of redskins at Fort Laramie on September 16 and 17—Cheyennes, Ogallalas, and Brûlés arriving behind their chieftains Big Mouth, Man That Walks Under the Ground, Pawnee Killer, Spotted Tail, Cut Nose, Turkey Foot, Man Afraid of His Horses, Whistler, and Cold Face. He received them with friendly smiles. Colonel W. H. Wolcott, of his escort, was thoughtful; he rolled up his trousers and showed the Indians an artificial leg, won in the Civil War. Big Mouth and Spotted Tail felt it with wonder and reverence.

Among the correspondents who thronged the powwow was an English traveler, Henry M. Stanley, due in four years to rescue Livingstone in Africa. Stanley saw two large wigwams converted into one and filled with chieftains of both races, each of whom took three whiffs at the pipe of peace. He heard the Indians, in fine oratory, recite their wrongs and describe how in the growing scarcity of game they could not supply their families unless they were given the ammunition that Sherman had denied them. They were incensed because white miners and railroaders were trespassing on their reservation in the Powder River country.

Stanley listened, in admiration, to Sherman's answer. Sherman warned the savages that white men were taking all the good land:

> If you don't choose your homes now it will be too late next year. . . . You can see for yourselves that travel across the country has increased so much that the slow ox wagons will not answer the white man. We will build iron roads, and you cannot stop the locomotives any more than you can stop the sun or moon. . . . Our people East hardly think of what you call war out here, but if they make up their minds to fight they will come out as thick as the herd of buffaloes, and if you continue fighting you will all be killed.
>
> We now offer you this, choose your homes and live like white men and we will help you. . . . We are doing more for you than we do for white men from over the sea.
>
> This commission is not only a peace commission but a war commission also. We will be kind to you if you keep the peace, but if you won't listen to reason we are ordered to make war upon you in a different manner from what we have done before.

The Commission, while at first only partially successful, began work which eventually settled all Indians on reservations, and although the task required occasional raids and slaughter which shocked professional charity workers in the distant East, the West persisted in declaring Sherman's régime not severe enough. By 1872 Sherman was speaking with pride of how he had settled on their reservations the Navajoes, Cheyennes, Kiowas, Arapahoes and Comanches.

His sympathy for the savages forced him, in 1868, to reverse his opinion that the Indian problem should not be thrown upon the army. On July 8 he was writing his brother John that white civilian agents, who had been put in charge of provisioning the tribes, were corrupt and neglectful. Everything should be in the hands of the Army. And when Grant, in 1869, awarded the care of the Indians to the various churches, Sherman wrote one of his critics, the Reverend Henry Ward Beecher:

> Opposition, diversity and rivalry among churches, as among merchants, stimulates activity. Now each tribe or subdivision of a tribe is let out to some special denomination which has a monopoly of the business. The result is Protestant Indians are in the spiritual custody of Catholic priests and vice

versa, Catholic Indians . . . are turned over body and soul to the Methodists or Episcopalians exclusively. . . .

In a business sense this is not fair or honest. But our Christian friends raise the cry that soldiers are men without religion and therefore incompetent to judge of such matters. This may be so, but we soldiers point back to a hundred years of such history and ask a comparison of results with the self-professed Christians.

At the coming of Sheridan to the West in 1867, Sherman gave over the active anti-Indian campaigns to this energetic subordinate. And the completion of the Union Pacific Railroad on May 10, 1869, ended Sherman's personal concern for military pressure in the region. On that date he opened a telegram that had come to him in Washington from Dodge at Promontory Utah:

The tracks of the Union and Central Pacific Railroads were joined today . . . 2,500 miles west of the Atlantic and 790 miles east of the Pacific Oceans.

Your continuous active aid, with that of the Army, has made you a part of us and enabled us to complete our work in so short a time. I congratulate you for all you have done for us.

The next day Sherman answered:

In common with millions, I sat yesterday and heard the mystic taps of the telegraphic batteries and heard the nailing of the last spike in the great Pacific road. Indeed, am I its friend? Yes. Yet I am to be a part of it, for as early as 1854 I was vice-president of the effort begun in San Francisco. . . . All honor to you . . . and the thousands of brave fellows who have wrought out this glorious problem.

Across the remainder of his life Sherman would glow when he thought of the railroad. In old age he said:

I firmly believe that the Civil War trained the men who built that great national highway, and General Dodge could call on any body of men to "fall in," "deploy as skirmishers," and fight the marauding Indians just as they had learned to fight the rebels down at Atlanta.

He took pride, some six years later, when he found Corse building railroads near Chicago, although the strange little man would soon abandon his work for the dubious joys of a political career in Massachusetts. In 1886 Corse would become postmaster of Boston and would be pointed out as the hero of Allatoona with increasing frequency as the country learned Philip Paul Bliss's religious hymn "Hold the Fort" inspired by the message Sherman had wigwagged to the abattoir-fort in 1864. No one dared twit the postmaster because his famous cheekbone and ear were not missing, as his immortal signals had indicated in more strenuous times.

The mystic taps of the telegraph were poignant in Sherman's ears in the springtime of 1869—because they reached him in Washington, where at last he had been pinioned. Early in the spring of 1868 he had seen the handwriting on the wall. His friend Grant had finally decided to accept the Republican nomination for the Presidency. Ambition and the urgings of his staff, of his wife, and seemingly of three fourths of the North had determined Grant. He would run on a ticket dominated by Radicals. Probably at no time in 1868 had Sherman resumed his early pleas to Grant to avoid politics. He saw irresistible forces at work. The worst of it was that when Grant should be elected, as he was certain to be, Sherman would naturally become head of the army. That meant Washington and hell.

Grant was viewing the Presidency without the alarm that had once been his. Now that his mind was made up, he seemed to regard the most difficult of offices as something that self-confidence could conquer. And this faith of Grant's was a thing for which Sherman was indirectly responsible—Sherman and the dead McPherson. In war, Grant had started with belief in eventual victory. He had imparted it, in a way, to Sherman. Then, as the war had gone on, Grant had found most of the officers about him—especially Sherman and McPherson—selfless and utterly loyal. He had never come to know the officers of the Army of the Potomac as well as his Westerners, but they had on the whole served him faithfully. In 1868 he apparently expected that as President he could find supporters and aides as true and honest as those he had found in the camps of Mississippi.

For a time after his overwhelming election in November, Grant seemed to Sherman likely to carry his wisdom from the field into the Presidency. One day, as the two friends rode down Pennsylvania Avenue in Washington, Grant said, "Sherman, what special hobby do you intend to adopt?" He explained that "all men had their special weakness or vanity, and that it was wiser to choose one's own than to leave the newspapers to affix one less acceptable." He had chosen horses, "so that when any one tried to pump him he would turn the conversation on his horse." The remark illuminated a statement of Ben Wade's to the effect that he could make nothing of Grant, "for whenever I talked politics he talked horses." Sherman told Grant that when it came to hobbies he would stick to theatres and balls, "for I was always fond of seeing young people happy." Although he never essayed the waltz or anything more aesthetic than the cotillion, soon after the war's end Sherman found himself—the king of marchers—celebrated in newspapers as the lion of the dance.

Three weeks after Grant's inauguration, Sherman learned that as President his friend was not the executive he had been in war. Between 1861 and 1865 Grant and Sherman had agreed that red tape had made army administration faulty and that it must be cleared away. The system was wasteful in that it made bureaucrats and staff officers at the War Department independent of the head of the army. Bureaus reporting direct to the Secretary of War hampered the general of the army and made him almost unimportant. Temperamentally Sherman was opposed to staff councils, to councils of war and conferences. A genius, capable of almost incredible feats of single-handed administration, he scoffed at the laborious systems of complicated business as things of inefficiency.

In December, 1868, Grant had told Sherman that when he became President he would correct these clumsy abuses and put the bureaus under the general in chief, not the Secretary of War. True to his word, President Grant, four days after inauguration, had General Schofield, the hold-over Secretary of War, issue such orders. But General Rawlins, when appointed to the Secretaryship, rescinded the orders, and on March 26, 1869, returned to the old system of red tape. Dying from tuberculosis, Rawlins was putty in the hands of the bureaucrats, who objected violently to the simplicity and directness of the plan of Grant and Sherman.

When Sherman demanded Grant's reasons for this abandonment of their reform, the President squirmed. He explained that there was doubt if it was legal. Sherman answered that this question had been previously threshed out. "Rawlins feels badly about it," Grant said; "it worries him and he is not well." Sherman answered that Rawlins should "acquiesce in what he knew was your fixed purpose, and what was done before he entered the War Department."

"Yes, it would ordinarily be so," said Grant, "but I don't like to give him pain now; so, Sherman, you'll have to publish the rescinding order."

"But, Grant, it's your own order that you revoke, not mine, and think how it will look to the whole world!"

"Well," grumbled Grant, "if it's my own order, I can rescind it, can't I?"

Sherman rose in anger, bowed stiffly, said, "Yes, Mr. President, you have the power to revoke your own order; you shall be obeyed. Good morning, sir."

Grant hastened to have Rawlins mollify Sherman by sending all organization orders through the general's rather than the Secretary's office, and the rift slowly closed.

Sherman was busy in those days acting as peacemaker. Old Tom had had his feelings hurt again. Grant had named Sheridan to take Sherman's vacated rank of lieutenant general. Thomas, whom Sherman saw daily, said that he had always been discriminated against, kept in obscure posts South or West. He would not come with Sherman to talk to Grant. The latter would not change his decision; he said that on a fine construction of rank Sheridan's commission gave him preference and that, furthermore, Sheridan was better fitted than Thomas to deal with Indians, who needed aggressive handling. However, Grant told Sherman to favor Tom in all possible ways. When Cump offered Tom his preference of the remaining divisions, the Virginian chose the Pacific.

Soon after arriving at San Francisco, Thomas was given a dinner by Halleck, who, with his proverbial fondness for talebearing, told his guest a hitherto secret story—the story of how, before the Battle of Nashville, Grant had sent Logan to take command of the Army of the Cumberland. Old Brains might as readily have sunk a knife in Thomas's heart. And when, on March 28, 1870, the Rock of Chickamauga was found dead from heart failure, his body lay across a half-written letter in which he was defending his conduct in the great victory over Hood. Through the army reunions in years to come Sherman spoke often of Thomas's virtues, repeating, "He was my best friend." Once in 1879 while addressing veterans and civilians in Washington, Sherman risked a prophecy while discussing a monument to Thomas:

> The day is coming, gentlemen of Virginia, of North Carolina, of South Carolina, of Alabama when you and your fellow citizens will be making pilgrimages to this magnificent monument . . . and [you will] say that there was the man, who under the tumult and excitement of the times stood true and firm to his country, and *he* is the hero . . . brave George Thomas will become the idol of the South. I predict it, gentlemen. I won't be alive then. . . .

To General Force, Sherman once wrote concerning Thomas:

> We recited together four years in the same section, served as lieutenants in the same regiment ten years. . . . Thomas leaned on me, and never to the hour of his death did he have reason to believe that his memory was less precious to me than my own. Never since the world began did such absolute confidence exist between commander and commanded, and among the many mistakes I made I trace some to his earnest and vehement advice.

Memories of the most striking surrender of Sherman to Thomas came to the former's mind on March 29, 1870, as the news of the latter's death was arriving in Washington. On that day John A. Logan was on his feet in the House of Representatives revenging himself for the "injustice" that Sherman had done him after the Battle of Atlanta. Logan would not know for years to come that it had been Thomas who had influenced Sherman to deny him command of the Army of the Tennessee after McPherson's death. Logan still blamed Sherman, and "the West Point clique."

As a leading Congressman, Logan had swung rapidly to the Radical viewpoint and had been prominent in the impeachment of Johnson. In the spring of 1865 he had spurned Sherman's suggestion that he remain in the army. Volunteers could never get justice in an army dominated by caste, he said, and had gone about organizing into national scope a small veterans' fraternal order, the Grand Army of the Republic. By 1870 he was making this body felt and was beginning the work that would turn pensions into a political issue.

While a fellow critic, Negley, introduced into the Senate a resolution to investigate West Point with a view to discontinuing so "snobbish" an institution, Logan launched a bill in the House to effect drastic deflation in the army, curtailing its power, reducing its personnel, and trimming its salaries. In particular the bill slashed Sherman's pay from a total (including expenses) of $18,700 to $12,000. Logan, effective orator that he was, scored pointedly when he all but wept in comparing with this the vice president's salary of only $8,000 and in describing the lot of "the poor shot-to-pieces privates" who roamed the land penniless. He struck boldly at Sherman's entertainments, his travels, and his sociability.

This attack touched Sherman in a tender point. Before leaving St. Louis he had feared that his income would not meet social requirements in Washington. "Ellen and the children have so much churchgoing" and schools were so costly. He wrote John in December, 1868, "My expenses are increasing. . . . A growing family has no limit in their desires and call for money." His natural warmth toward his family made him indulgent; he was happiest when his children were happy, yet when he faced the bills he gave startled roars of anger—then the storm passed. While he complained of expense, he quietly gave money to needy soldiers. When friends collected a thousand dollars in the spring of 1868 to have his portrait painted by the Chicago artist, G. P. A. Healy, Sherman noted that the artist "could not afford it," so "I gave him a commission to paint Ellen for $500."

He had been frightened when in the autumn of 1868 Grant admitted that no general could live on his pay at the capital. On November 30, Sherman wrote:

Grant lived beyond his salary but had more than $100,000 donated by his friends in New York. I declined an effort on the part of General Butterfield to attempt same for me because it would have left me under obligations to favor him as Grant has actually done. He has been kept in New York ever since the war closed to the detriment of other officers who had superior claims.

On January 15, 1869, Cump was writing John:

Grant wrote me last week that some New York gentlemen had approached him and offered him $65,000 for his house and lot to be presented to me and to know how it would suit me. He answered that the price was much more than he asked but he could throw in the furniture and that would make the thing more complete. . . . I of course promptly replied that it would suit me to a T, and more especially would it suit Ellen and the family who want a big house.

Although rumor had it that the house had been given Grant by admirers, Sherman was to write John on March 10, 1876, that Grant had bought it "of his brother-in-law, Corbin, for $30,000 on a ten-year credit." By the time Sherman reached the capital to take up his office as general in chief, the mansion was his. He wrote John on February 21, 1869:

Dan Butterfield claims to have been largely instrumental in it, but I should prefer that he should not be the chief party. . . . I will not let such influence move me. I prefer that Scott, Aspinwall, Stewart, Williams, etc., should be the donors.

William Scott, the wealthy New York husband of his cousin Miss Hoyt, had been instrumental in raising the fund among Manhattan and Boston friends of Sherman, and in their hands Sherman felt himself free from any obligations that might complicate his official position. Judged by later standards, he had sacrificed dignity in accepting even so unencumbered a gift, but in his time testimonials of the sort were generally regarded as quite the proper thing.

The cost of living up to so expensive a mansion soon irritated Sherman. On May 11, 1869, he complained to John that a carriage had cost him fifteen hundred dollars and harness three hundred. He took pride in one saddle horse that he pointed out to a friend, Major Henry O. March, saying, "Kil stole him for me up in Georgia."

It was Sherman's letter to the Military Committee of the House of Representatives, defending his entertainments, that Logan read into the record on March 29, 1870.

After replying at length to Logan's charge that the army was overstaffed, overgeneraled, and overpaid, Sherman pointed out that "death is already doing his work among our veterans" and that mortality among ex-soldiers was "at least double what is the case with civilians of like age and condition who stayed at home." Time, he said, would soon kill off enough officers to bring the army down to the desired standard. Sherman then launched into a defense of his living costs, declaring that he had spent

> every cent and more, too, of the pay allowed me.
>
> I have endeavored to entertain my friends, come from what quarter they might, and have given some dinners and some receptions, and hope to do so again at my expense, not the people's. If my pay is reduced I may not be able to do it to the same extent hereafter but never will I receive the courtesies and hospitalities of others unless I can reciprocate them. . . .
>
> I claim that I have earned my past and present pay; that during the war when I commanded more men than the Duke of Wellington had in Spain, my pay as brigadier and major general was less than his private secretary's, and was so small that, though I lived on a soldier's rations, my pay was not more than enough to maintain my family in Ohio.
>
> I did not complain of it then, nor do I now; but I believe that my present pay is not wholly for present work, but is in great part for past services. . . . What money will pay Meade for Gettysburg? What Sheridan for Winchester? . . . What Thomas for Chickamauga, Chattanooga or Nashville? What American would tear these pages from our national history for the few dollars saved from their pay during their short lives?

Supported by his former lieutenant, General Slocum, who was now a Democratic Congressman from New York, Sherman kept Logan's bill from carrying out all its intended reductions. His own pay was reduced to $13,500 salary, $3,000 for rent and horses, $16,500 total. A little later Sherman discussed this subject with a reporter of the *St. Louis Globe-Democrat:*

> I outlived the amount by several thousand. I had to keep open house all the time. My family rarely had any rest from entertaining people, most of them utter strangers in whom we could feel no interest. Besides everybody considered themselves privileged to practice extortion upon any person who holds a prominent place in Washington. Gas companies, markets, always charged me exorbitant prices simply because I was General of the Army.

On July 27, 1870, he was writing his brother John that Logan's bill had so reduced his army influence that he was considering handing in his resignation and seeking some other business in St. Louis; "it will not be long before we will all be turned out to grass, or what is worse lopped off little by little to reduce us and our offices to ridicule." On August 5 he was writing John:

Our country is bound to be governed by its meanest people and soon no honorable man will be tolerated. The extension of the franchise don't elevate the ignorant but pulls down the educated.

That Grant had not moved to prevent the pay cut disappointed Sherman, but it was worse to note Grant's pliability in the hands of politicians. On October 23 he wrote John:

I have observed with great concern that General Grant is moved by the urgent demands or remonstrances of men who care no more for him, and who would as gladly sacrifice him. . . . Ben Butler, Logan and men of that stripe. . . . A great many of our old friends have come to me, or have written to me to know the cause and holding me responsible for not telling him the exact truth. I have ventured to do so more than once, but without success, and henceforth I shall not thrust my advice where it is not needed. I saw him yesterday, and he seems to be unconscious that he is losing the confidence of some of the best men of our country.

It outraged Sherman to note that Simon Cameron, the Pennsylvania politician who had treated him badly in Kentucky in 1861, had enough power in the autumn of 1870 to influence Grant against General Cox, who was Secretary of the Interior. In his letter of October 23 Cump declared:

Whilst the cabinet was in Session last Friday it was announced that Cameron was stricken with paralysis whilst en route from Washington to Harrisburg. . . . I wish he had been disabled before he came here and instigated Grant to break with General Cox. The latter was in my judgment the most honest and outspoken member of the Cabinet, and about the only one in that body that could talk strongly and rationally. I know from him that the President "went back" on him in certain matters that had been agreed on between them, just as he went back on me when I was doing just what he asked me to do, before he was installed as President and *after*. As soon as Congress repealed the clause compelling the residence of the General at Washington, I asked his consent to go to St. Louis, but he asked me in writing to remain, but he has stripped my office of certain powers which he exercised as General and which he then deemed essential, and has forced some unjust appointments.

Still I want to stand by him, for as his term draws to a close, he will have a hard time, and I don't want you to abandon him, unless self-respect compels you and then the more outspoken you are the better.

Irritations, differences, disappointments, could not break the bonds that had been welded in four years of war. Whenever Sherman came upon Grant's failures as a civil executive, there would always rise the majestic, thrilling picture of Grant at Vicksburg. Fifteen years after these difficulties of 1870, Sherman wrote President Charles W. Eliot of Harvard an estimate of Grant—particularly in regard to the current tale that Grant had refused to listen to smutty stories. Legend had it that when a staff officer had once prefaced such an anecdote with the remark, "I believe there are no ladies present," Grant had said, "No, but there are gentlemen here," and had silenced the recital. Sherman wrote:

> Grant was not the saint and perfect man described by . . . panegyrists, but had some human infirmities and weaknesses which would have clouded any public character of less strength. He played poker . . . all through his presidential career for money. Instead of getting up and leaving when stories were told involving obscenity with wit—such as George Derby and Jim Nye [Senator from Nevada] were famous for—he stayed and encouraged them by his hearty laughter and enjoyment.
>
> He did not have about him near his person officers of refinement and culture; his staff at Shiloh was inferior—Rawlins, Lagow, Hillyer, etc., and when he was at the White House he had as his intimates men I could not have tolerated, the very men who Iago-like, excited his suspicions against his friends—Washburn, Bristow, Wilson, etc. . . .
>
> His love for his children was an amiable weakness, not only pardonable, but attracting the love of all who did not suffer the consequences. I know too much of things behind the curtain to go further than I have gone, and therefore want to stop right there.

To Grant on November 27, 1872, Sherman wrote concerning the President's son Fred:

> I fear from what Mrs. Grant said here yesterday that she has set her heart on my appointing Fred an aide on my staff. . . . I think it best for Fred to serve with his regiment until he has done some act to make him prominent, or until he has gained real experience. When I have a vacancy I will appoint him; but meantime I would like Mrs. Grant to understand how I am situated, for I would like above all things to do her some special act of kindness to demonstrate my great respect.

An army regulation forbade the appointment of any officer to staff duty outside his own regiment until he had served with it three years. Grant understood this and did not press Sherman to take his son. Sherman wrote his brother on March 10, 1876:

> But Mrs. Grant was unwilling to wait so long, and Sheridan told me he had put him on his staff to reconcile Mrs. Grant's difficulty with me. . . .
>
> I know that Gen. Grant feels as I do on this subject—but he may have some reserved thought that I, knowing Mrs. Grant's feelings for her children, ought to have suffered in this matter for his peace in his family.

When, in the autumn of 1872, he discovered that one of his own nephews, a paymaster in the army, was accused of "mingling his private with public funds," Sherman wrote the youth, "as head of the army I would be the first to prosecute the case were it not already in progress." And on the same day, September 19, he wrote Paymaster-General Alvord:

> Neither my brother, Senator Sherman . . . nor myself . . . wish him to receive any favor because he is the son of our beloved sister . . . but, on the contrary, hold that his relationship to us by blood, should subject him to even a higher test of responsibility than otherwise. . . . I hereby approve of the course you were bound to pursue, viz.; to cause his arrest and to submit the facts to the Judge Advocate General for proceedings.

Though he rejoiced to hear that the difficulty had been solved without going to trial and the case had been dismissed, he kept rigidly aloof during the investigation.

Sherman was offended by the new Secretary of War, General W. W. Belknap, whom Grant had appointed from civil life after Rawlins's death. Sherman himself had recommended the Iowa politician for the post. He remembered how as a colonel in the Army of the Tennessee the huge tawny fellow had tossed the Confederate Colonel Lampley over his head during the Battle of Atlanta. Furthermore, the man had delivered a speech of impressive patriotism at a reunion of veterans in Chicago on December 15, 1868. But in the War Office, Belknap sided with the bureaucrats. In 1869 he ousted a sutler at Fort Laramie and appointed a man whom the soldiers thought suspicious. Sherman promptly restored the former sutler and held to his point of authority. Belknap countered by aiding Logan and other volunteer veterans in Congress to pass a law in 1870 that took jurisdiction from the general in chief and gave it back to the Secretary of War. Then he appointed his own man.

Little by little Congress and Belknap stripped Sherman of power. Over Sherman's protests Grant and his Secretary of War eliminated one military division in the West, where public resentment, assuming that Sherman was responsible, denounced the general at length. Cump explained this to his brother John:

> . . . it was the sole act of the President after he knew the full outcry the knowledge of it would cause. Grant has simply let down this pressure and now allows his understoppers to throw off on me. This is eminently mean—but he has done it more than once, merely saying that he cannot prevent the misconstructions of newspaper reporters.

Then, in August, 1871, there came to Sherman a chance to flee Washington. Admiral Alden invited him to visit Europe; Alden was sailing on navy business. In early November Sherman was off.

59

KETTLE FIRES FLICKER OUT

SHERMAN hurried to the boat from the funeral of Thomas Ewing at Lancaster. Old Solitude had died on October 26, 1871, within two months of his eighty-second birthday. After the first blow, it had taken death two years to chop him down. On October 22, 1869, he slipped from his chair while addressing the Supreme Court, and lay insensible on the floor. Scrambling down from their seats, the black-robed justices lifted him on to a bench, and summoned physicians and his children. Ellen and Cump were among the first to arrive—the newspapers chronicling Sherman's tears. Physicians said that Ewing's trouble was "nervous exhaustion." All night he lay in the judges' chambers, and in time he grew well enough to be taken to Lancaster. There, with the families of Philemon, Hugh, and Theresa around him—shoals of grandchildren at his feet—he grew a little stronger.

From his windows he saw dead leaves whirl down Main Street, snow cover the Kettle Hills, young corn shine on Fairfield loam, and summer sleep again on Standing Stone. With the first frosts of 1870-71 he was strong enough to return to his Washington office and to labor there at the law. But with the spring he came home. Through the summer he took long, slow rides in his carriage through country roads. One day when April was at the full he told his carriageman to drive him to Athens County. It had been fifty-five years since he had seen his boyhood home. He drifted down through processionals of trees. Strange, friendly people came to the carriage wheel to tell how their grandparents had helped him with the Coonskin Library, or how their fathers had seen him come home with his black hands from the salines. More important now than wars and Presidents and Senators were the sweet wild plums that had grown over yonder so long ago and the Indian village where he had played with the naked boys. He looked at old sites, then jogged back to Lancaster. When the cornleaves grew yellow in the distance he left his house no longer, but sat by his study window.

A few years earlier he had distributed his estate, approximately a hundred thousand dollars, among his children. He thought mostly of them now—and their religion. He had a lilac bush cut down because it stood between his window and the little church to which he had given some three thousand dollars at various times. His children and his grandchildren went in at the church door. He wanted to accept their faith. Ever since marrying, he had admired the peace faith brought Roman Catholics. Archbishop Purcell later told how he had urged the evangel upon Ewing:

> More than once at the earnest request of Mrs. Ewing and his daughter, Mrs. Sherman, I availed myself of what I regarded as auspicious occasions to urge him to embrace that saving faith to which I had often heard him render unmistakable testimonies. His answer was, "Not now."

Two or three years before his attack, Old Solitude had been approached by his wife's kinswoman from South Bend, Sister Angela, and had told her, "My family could not be more anxious for me to have the faith than I myself am to possess it. I pray for it daily."

Ellen, who divided her time between Lancaster and Washington, was also praying for it daily. If it should come, she could worship at one altar the two dominant loves of her life—her father and her church. Priests came and went with their gentle persuasions. On October 13 Sherman, returning from Lancaster to his office, wrote Blaine that "Mr. Ewing's life is now flickering in its socket, so that at any moment the dread notice may come." Agonizing pains were attacking the old man. The Hocking Valley, and all that he owned of it both physically and spiritually, grew faint in his mind. At last the Salt-Boiler gave up his life work of putting two and two together and, as though recognizing that logic and faith had after all nothing to do with each other, he asked for the sacrament of the Holy Eucharist. Archbishop Purcell arrived, and gave him baptism, communion, and extreme unction. For a few more days the kettle fires burned on, lower and lower, until on October 26 they flickered out.

At the burial there was a mixture of grief and reverential rejoicing. Many Catholics were overloud, in days that followed, with their talk of "the victory." Many Protestants were overeager to hand around a clipping from the *Methodist Advocate* that criticized Ewing's funeral:

> It may not be generally known that the occasion was employed to eulogize the Romish Church to the shameful neglect if not positive insult of the memory of the distinguished citizen over whose senseless body mummeries were performed and statements made that in any rational hour of his former life he would have spurned with contempt.

Religious tolerance was passing from the Middle West; it had gone down under the storm of war passions. The war had, in spite of the feelings of Sherman's army, linked the old Northwest to New England and to the latter's habit of forcing its beliefs on other sections—the evangelism of the Puritans. The West had conquered everything in the South except Virginia, and as an ironical result had lost its own identity.

Ellen Sherman fought Protestant criticism; she published testimony of clerics and relatives in an attempt to show that her father had always tended toward Catholicism, and in July, 1873—the year she issued her book, *Memorial of Thomas Ewing*—she had Hugh ask Cump to testify that her father had "died in the Church." On the fifteenth Cump evaded —"It struck me as something out of my line entirely for the fact was evidenced at the time . . . it would sit awkwardly on my pen." What Cump could and did give was a testimonial to Ewing's unfaltering patriotism during the war and his zeal for a postwar peace that would be constitutional.

Ellen was working on her book during the ten months that Cump spent abroad in 1871-72. Eleanor, the daughter of Philemon Ewing, was with her Aunt Ellen in Washington during the spring of 1872, and in later years recalled it:

> Uncle Cump was traveling abroad, and such an odd tour, not going first to England as was the custom, but first through the continent, then even to Egypt, saving England for the last, as he explained, so that he might be equal to those Englishmen when they mentioned their travels abroad. As most Britishers had been abroad, he would not appear at a disadvantage.

Landing in Spain, Sherman passed by train, boat, and carriage through the Riviera, Italy, Turkey, Egypt, Russia, Germany, France, and the British Isles. Traveling as a private citizen, he asked for no formal attention, yet he was pleased when it came. The President of France, King Victor Emmanuel of Italy, and the nobility in general gave him dinners or receptions. At Stamboul the Turkish minister held an army review for him and at Constantinople the Sultan gave him a luxurious yacht trip into the Black Sea. A magnificent banquet raged until the royal steamer docked, then with many salaams a courtier presented Sherman with something on a silver platter. It was a bill for the entertainment—six hundred dollars, which Sherman paid with seeming pleasure.

He toured Russia on the arms of Grand Dukes. Berlin was the one capital that did not honor him, a failure, according to his aide Colonel Audenreid, due to a diplomatic blunder by Ambassador Bancroft. Court attachés notified Sherman that he could meet the Kaiser by attending a review to be given Italian royalty. Sherman asked if the Emperor had expressed a desire to see him and when Bancroft said that he had not, Sherman refused to attend. Germans said Bancroft had not notified the court that the general was coming to Berlin.

Whenever the railroad train stopped, in his nine months' tour, Sherman popped off and conversed with bystanders, whether he understood their language or not. Somehow he managed to learn and to remember the names of almost all towns through which he passed. "His memory for names was phenomenal," said S. H. M. Byers, whom he visited at Zurich, Switzerland. Sherman had been friendly with Byers ever since the latter had presented him with the song "Sherman's March to the Sea" at Columbia in 1864, and now that Byers was consul general to Switzerland and Italy, Sherman was glad to stop with an army comrade and rest. Byers led the general to his home and seated him where he could see the fairyland of Lake Zurich and the Alps spread at his feet. Bluntly Sherman announced:

> It's not more beautiful than the lakes near Madison, Wisconsin. I think of them when I see this. I like American scenery better than any of it. It's the real native thing in our country. Man has done nothing there. Here in Europe so much is artificial.

First of all he wanted to get his directions straight—"North must be right over there." Then he guessed the height and distance of mountains. Byers said they were twenty miles away. No, said Sherman, they were thirty—"I never miss distance." But he had missed these. After dinner, wines, and cigars, he took a second look at the view and said he guessed the Alps beat Wisconsin after all. He climbed into a loft and scrambled around on top of a wine press studying it. He went into the fields and took hold of the strange scythes used by peasant harvesters. He spent some time describing an American mowing machine to a peasant who understood nothing of what he said. During supper he ridiculed American tourists:

> Tourists is the right word for them. They are not observing travelers at all. An American girl rode in the car with me through the most interesting part of Spain and read a paper-backed novel all the way. I never go to a place but I know all about it, its topography, geography and history. A thousand times my old habit of observing has afterward been of use to me.

Swiss cadets visited him, big-eyed in their admiration. Army officers banqueted him, and on a lake trip produced a map of his Atlanta campaign and demonstrated that they knew his every move. He traced for them his march to the sea, and in departing, the officers wrung Byers's hand, saying, "I'll never forget this day." Byers wrote later:

I never saw a man so run after by women in my life. When he was leaving a train at Bern a whole crowd of women, old and young, pretty and ugly, children and all, kissed him.

After a week spent in festivities and in attempting to force Mrs. Byers to give him just a cot in the hall as became a soldier, instead of a large bed in the front salon, he was off in the rain for St. Gotthard's Pass, saying, "Weather never holds me back. If it's raining when I start it's almost sure to clear up on the way and when I most need it."

Music from the street interrupted his letter-writing at a hotel in Dublin:

It was that old air, "Marching Through Georgia." Here was an end to my quietness. It was evident that some one had found me out. I got up, put on an old uniform coat and sat down and waited. The band came nearer and it was all I could do to keep my feet still. I waited for the band to stop. . . .

Well, they went prancing past the hotel and down the street, the music fading away in the distance. There was something wrong here, evidently. I took off my uniform, put on another suit of clothes and went to interview the proprietor. . . .

"Good-morning," I said. "I heard a band on the street a few minutes ago. Anything of special importance going on here today?"

"A band? Oh, yes; they're bound for a picnic." . . .

"Do you remember what they were playing? It sounded to me like an American march."

"Humph! It was an old Irish air. All the bands in Dublin play it as a march."

As he neared the time for his return to America, the world of strife swam back upon Sherman. Newspapers told him that Grant, renominated by the Republicans, was to be opposed by Horace Greeley, upon whom the Democrats and liberal Republicans had united in demands for reform. From Paris, Cump wrote John:

Grant, who never was a Republican, is your candidate; and Greeley, who never was a Democrat, but quite the reverse, is the Democratic candidate.

To Ellen, Cump wrote from Vienna that Grant, who had started out to be his own master, had now allowed himself to be so surrounded by flatterers that "he cannot know the whole truth," but that even so he was better than Greeley, "who has no stability at all" and who would be "the worst President any country ever had."

Arriving home on September 22, 1872, to find Grant certain of reëlection, Sherman discovered that forward-looking men, in search of an "Andy Jackson type," were already considering himself for the

MARCHING THROUGH GEORGIA.

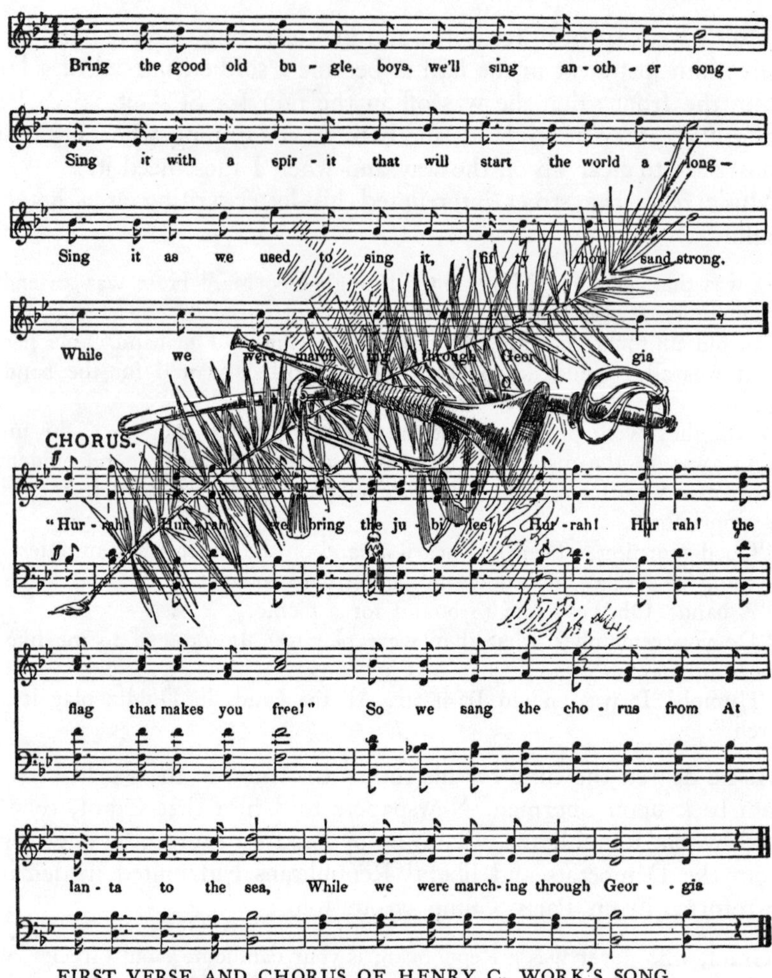
Bring the good old bu - gle, boys, we'll sing an - oth - er song—
Sing it with a spir - it that will start the world a - long—
Sing it as we used to sing it, fif - ty thou - sand strong,
While we were march - ing through Geor - gia
CHORUS.
"Hur - rah! Hur - rah! we bring the ju - bi - lee! Hur - rah! Hur rah! the
flag that makes you free!" So we sang the cho - rus from At
lan - ta to the sea, While we were march - ing through Geor - gia

FIRST VERSE AND CHORUS OF HENRY C. WORK'S SONG

In illustrated booklets, as well as sheet music, it sold widely throughout the Northern States during the twenty years subsequent to the Civil War.

Presidency four years hence. On November 14 he wrote James S. Rollins that he would decline it "if nominated or elected." He fully understood just how unprecedented was such a statement. It was a national axiom that "no American was big enough to turn down the Presidency," and it was universally believed that no man had ever done so, on pain of being branded unpatriotic. Yet Sherman wrote Rollins, "You may argue that none before has done such an act, then, if the case arises, I must be the first of a series."

His antipathy toward politicians was not lessened by discovering that in his absence Belknap and the bureaucrats had usurped still more of his duties. Also taxes had risen on Washington real estate until his home, on which he had paid four hundred dollars yearly, now cost him fifteen hundred. He ran a partition through its middle and rented half of it.

When Minnie married Lieutenant Thomas W. Fitch of the Navy on October 1, 1874, Sherman made a bold move. He took his family back to St. Louis and made that city the headquarters of the army. Grant allowed him to do it, even though his going made gossips say that Sherman was too honest to stand the corruption of the Administration. The move was not without precedent, General Scott having lived long in New York while head of the army. Scarcely had Minnie's bridal veil fluttered out the door before Sherman was on a westward train. He sold the white-elephant mansion. He was happy in the removal to St. Louis, but later he wrote:

> I realized that it was a farce, and it did not need a prophet to foretell it would end in tragedy. We made ourselves very comfortable, made pleasant excursions into the interior, had a large correspondence, and escaped the mortification of being slighted by men in Washington who were using their temporary power for selfish ends.

With duties so slight, he completed the writing of his *Memoirs*, which he had begun early in 1874. He worked diligently among his war papers and in the forty-four volumes of his letter book that he had preserved. On August 8, 1874, he had written Byers:

> No one who was an actor in the Grand Drama of the Civil War seems willing to risk its history. . . . All histories thus far, of which Draper's is the best, are based for facts on the newspaper reports, which were necessarily hasty and imperfect. . . . I have some notes of my own part in manuscript and copies of all my reports and letters but am unwilling to have them printed lest it should involve me in personal controversies.

But in the remoteness of St. Louis, his fear of strife faded, and by March, 1875, he had the manuscript in the hands of D. Appleton &

Co., the New York publishers. It appeared in two volumes, minus portrait (probably at Sherman's insistence). No more than six chapters were given to his life before the Civil War, while eighteen were devoted to the conflict itself. Brusque, direct, candid, at times blunt, the book dealt in none of the sugared oratory and fulsome laudations so common since the end of the war. In it were no heroes and no villains. It was, as his foreword declared, addressed to his comrades in arms "not as history but as recollection of events."

It fell with a splash into the sea of veterans. It became the book of the year, the first soldier's reminiscences of first-rank importance—and so full of frank opinions as to beget hot criticism. Many officers of the Army of the Cumberland charged that the book undervalued their force in favor of the Army of the Tennessee. H. V. Boynton, who had served in the former army under Buell and Thomas and who was now Washington correspondent of the *Cincinnati Gazette*, that ancient enemy of Sherman's, rushed to Grant with sensational stories of how Sherman's book denied the general in chief his due. Grant grew angry, but when he got hold of the book, he calmed. He admitted to Sherman that he had been "bothered" until he read the volumes; then he had seen that Sherman had treated him justly. He would change nothing except some of Sherman's references to Blair and Logan, who had been criticized for paying so much attention to politics.

But Boynton persisted, and before the year was out published a volume *Sherman's Historical Raid; The Memoirs in the Light of the Record*. It declared Sherman to be

> intensely egotistical, unreliable and cruelly unjust to nearly all his distinguished associates. Our erratic General thrusts his pen recklessly through reputations which are as dear to the country as his own.

Boynton catalogued and attacked, by citing official records, Sherman's assignment to Halleck of Grant's achievement in the West at the start of the war, Sherman's failure to give Buell credit for saving himself and Grant at Shiloh, Sherman's neglect in not crediting Grant with the authorship of the march to the sea, and many other matters. He sought to show that Sherman had belittled Thomas, Buell, Rosecrans, Logan, Blair, Hooker, and Stanton; "he repeatedly loads failures for which he was responsible now upon Thomas, now upon Schofield, now upon McPherson." Also he charged that Sherman had surrounded with darkness his own failures in all his pitched battles from Shiloh to Bentonville.

Investigating the motives behind Boynton's attacks, Sherman concluded that they had been inspired by his old enemies, the bureaucrats of the War Department, among whom was Colonel Babcock, once of Grant's staff. On May 14, 1886, Cump summarized the matter for John:

I know he [Boynton] was paid $600 Government money and supplied with hired clerks to copy the extracts of official reports. . . . Babcock was the main spirit and his motive was to prevent my influence in cutting the wings of the Staff Corps in Washington who are inimical to the Real Army which does the work.

In January, 1880, Sherman told a reporter of the *Cleveland Leader* that Boynton would "do anything for money," and would "slander his own mother for a thousand dollars." When Boynton, threatening libel, asked Sherman if he was correctly quoted in the *Leader's* issue of January 15, Sherman wrote him, "This is a hard thing to say of any man, but I believe it of you." The interview was correct.

On March 8, 1876, the *New York Herald* was printing a conversation of a reporter with Sherman in St. Louis:

"Have attacks upon your Memoirs annoyed you?"

"Not at all. They amuse me and frequently, I am glad to say, serve a good purpose of calling attention to real defects which will be corrected. . . . Friends urged me to publish them. I expected severe criticism and got it. No writer ever gets justice from his contemporaries and outside of this I knew I was liable to err and only pretended to give things as they looked through my glasses. . . . Possibly I colored things unconsciously in favor of the Army of the Tennessee. I had this army so organized there was no red tape.

That Sherman should have issued the book while still head of the army seemed to many friends rash, and in private Sherman seemed at times to agree. He wrote Colonel Bowman, "I am sick and tired of it, actually ashamed of having risked such a thing," and he wrote to another of his defenders, Col. C. W. Moulton, "This matter worries me more than I can explain." General Cox defended the *Memoirs* in a review written for *The Nation*, and Moulton put out a pamphlet attacking Boynton's book. But Sherman, stung by the charge that he had been unjust to men he cared for, McPherson and Thomas and Schofield, decided to revise the *Memoirs*. He asked Cox, Bowman, Moulton, and Henry Hitchcock, all lawyers as well as friends, to help him, but at conferences they could not agree as to what the changes should be. Sherman wrote Bowman, "If we can't agree I don't see how the general public will"; but they compromised on a preface and a supplement that would mollify friends of the supposedly damaged generals. John and Ellen both opposed any material alterations, Ellen writing Bowman:

. . . it is mortifying that the General wishes to alter and in that way condemn himself . . . he cannot have the heart to humiliate his family and take pride (just and honorable pride) out of my life by printing them. With preface and supplement as proposed, the book would be to me a source of profound humiliation, and a copy of it should never remain where I can have control. . . . I warn you, my dear friend, not to be hasty in acquiescing in the publication.

The idea perished before such opposition. Ten years later Sherman wrote a chapter on his life from birth to the Mexican War, another chapter headed "After the War." Inserting one at the beginning of his book and the other at the end, he reissued the *Memoirs* through Charles L. Webster & Co., the firm of his friend Samuel L. Clemens. He made a few inconspicuous changes in the original text but in effect stood to his guns.

Reviving the pangs that Sherman had caused during the war, the *Memoirs* halted the progress of what promised to be Southern friendship for the general. Up to 1875 Southerners apparently regarded him as a friend, in contrast to the dominant Radicals of the North. Old scores had been evened by his sympathy for the South during the Johnston surrender and reconstruction. He had made it no secret that he regarded the Fifteenth Amendment, which made the Negro a voter, as a mistake equivalent to the earlier "pro-black" legislation. To John Sherman, to James G. Blaine, and to many others he deplored the stupidity of Republicans in antagonizing instead of wooing "the young Confederates who realized that they had been misled by their selfish leaders." He had been kind to the Louisiana seminary, sending it, at Boyd's request, books and a portrait of himself. On January 6, 1885, Sherman wrote:

I interceded and aided Gov. Thomas O. Moore to regain possession of his plantation . . . on the express ground that under the pressure brought to bear upon him from Washington he could hardly help acting as he did in 1861. I also renewed my correspondence with Bragg, tried all I could to help him regain his property . . . also to aid him in his declared purpose to become connected with the management of the Opelousas Railroad.

He exchanged visits and letters with Joe Johnston, tried to obtain Federal appointments for him, saw that he received governmental publications on the war; and in February, 1876, he recommended Bragg for appointment to the staff of Egypt's Khedive. Each of his three or four trips through the South had been pleasant, that of 1869 having been "in every sense agreeable . . . I never received more marked attention by all classes and not a word or look reached me that was not most respectful and gratifying." In 1870 while in New Orleans he had a long and pleasant talk with Hood, who in business and parenthood was proving as precipitate as in war. Hood had organized a commission business and life insurance company both of which would subsequently crash, and was conducting a domestic campaign which, at the time of his death nine years later, would have resulted in thirteen children including two sets of twins.

With the appearance of the *Memoirs,* Jefferson Davis, who had been living quietly at home since release from confinement, came into print with denunciations. Sherman's accounts of the last year of the war had disparaged him, particularly in his differences with Joe Johnston, and in reading them Davis felt his hatred of Johnston extending itself to Sherman. Davis now assailed both men, and branded Sherman's depopulation of Atlanta as the most inhuman act "since Alva's atrocious cruelties in the Netherlands." Beauregard also appeared in print attacking Sherman for compelling prisoners to unearth torpedoes.

Sherman gave newspaper reporters his justification for all alleged "cruelties" and on March 8, 1876, the *New York Herald* carried his words:

> I feel kindly toward all Southern Generals. I think people of the West and North cherish no bad feelings except toward Jeff. Davis. He did no worse than anybody else but people seem bound to have somebody to hate. For instance the Southern people hate Butler.

But his *Memoirs* were working at that moment to place Sherman on Butler's pedestal of infamy in Southern minds. Sherman had written of the Confederacy with the same unsentimental candor and frankness that he had applied to his fellow Federals, and his unequivocal words opened old sores. His accounts of his gigantic raids seemed heartless to Southerners. His words reminded them of all the terror and destruction he had but lately spread through their land. It was humanly impossible for the South, grieving for the "lost cause," suffering from financial and spiritual collapse, and writhing under Radical oppression, to read Sherman's book as he had intended it to be read—a lesson to Americans to obey the Constitution and the Federal laws. Most Southerners who read it were so angry by the time they came to the end of the book that they failed to appreciate the lengths to which Sherman had gone to defend them in 1865.

Northern orators intensified Southern emotion by speaking of Sherman's army as having gone through the South "like the plow of God." There was a triumphal jeer in the words Henry C. Work had written for his song "Marching Through Georgia," and the Northern fondness for the song, and for remembering the march itself, fanned Southern hatred of Sherman.

Postwar bitterness survived among civilians rather than among ex-soldiers. Southern noncombatants fixed upon Sherman as their pariah because he had been the one Federal to traverse their interior conspicuously. In many places they preserved blackened chimneys as monuments to the Sherman Torch. In time it seemed almost forgotten that his swaths had touched but relatively little of Southern territory and that his devastation, severe as it was, could not be charged with more than a fractional portion of the Southern poverty that existed after the war. From the standpoint of drama it was easier to blame Sherman's army than to realize that poverty was principally attributable to reconstruction, the stupendous war debts, and the economic difficulty of changing from a system of slave labor to one of free labor. Sixty-six years after the war, there were to be found instances of Southerners accusing Sherman's soldiers of outrages committed by Federal troops totally outside his jurisdiction—stories that reflected the enormity of the shock he had given the South during his campaigns.

There was irony in the fact that as a general thing Grant did not share the hatred given Sherman by the South. Much was made of Grant's generosity in restoring their horses to Lee's men at Appomattox; little or nothing was remembered of the far more elaborate attempt of Sherman to restore to Southern civilians their State governments, or of his even more extensive award to Johnston's men of food and horses, plus one seventh of their arms.

One factor in this discrimination against Sherman lay in the fact that Grant had fought principally on the border, while Sherman had fought in the interior. Little was ever said of the devastation during the Vicksburg campaign, in which Sherman had inherited from Grant the principle of "living off the country," as Grant, in turn, had inherited it from Halleck, and all of them, perhaps, from Bragg.

In the later and more spectacular years of the war Grant had won his victories by steady, remorseless slaughter. Sherman had won by avoiding bloodshed and by destroying property instead. Northerners hated the Confederate raider Morgan, who had only burned their buildings, far more than they hated Lee, who had killed bluecoats by tens of thousands. Both sections came to praise if not revere those enemies who had destroyed human life and to execrate those enemies who had destroyed barns.

60

I WILL NOT SERVE IF ELECTED

IF Sherman's *Memoirs* made him a devil in Southern eyes, they made him a prophet in the Northern view, reminding readers as they did how many of his predictions in 1861 had come true. In them was apparent his scorn of faction and his trust in the Constitution rather than in sectional powers. Even Republicans but lately Radical opened their eyes as they read his story of his attempts at reconciling the South in the spring of 1865. Such a story read very differently in 1875 than it would have in 1865. After ten years of Radical reconstruction, the Northern masses were beginning to sicken of vengeance. It had proved expensive, destroying Southern markets for Northern manufactured goods. Negro suffrage had been a comic failure.

Corruption in the Republican Administration was also sickening voters, who, while refusing to believe Grant contaminated, felt his incapacity for controlling the grafters. The author of the *Memoirs* stood forth as fiercely honest and, if hot-headed, competent to enforce virtue.

Through the late months of 1875 a new demand arose for Sherman to accept the Presidency. Newspapers discussed his probable stand on an issue that had agitated the last gubernatorial election in Ohio—the question of the propriety of forcing Catholics to pay taxes in support of public schools while they were financing their own parochial schools. On December 29 Cump wrote John:

> I am almost made to laugh that my name should be thought of for the Presidency and still more that it should be complicated with the Catholic Institution. I have been doubly taxed all my life for schools. If I had now what I have paid for school taxes, besides being forced to pay school bills to Catholic schools, I would have capital enough to set up some business. . . . I have always favored common schools but schools have grown to be uncommon—too costly in buildings, professors. . . . In these common schools, schools of religion should be excluded, but I doubt the wisdom of a constitutional amendment. . . . The Pope, now in a Catholic state, is powerless, and the Bishops, priests, etc., all over the world are losing their political power. The only way they differ from Protestants is in their combined action.
>
> I am not a Catholic and could not be because they exact a blind obedience and subordination that is entirely foreign to my nature. Ellen is so by inheritance and it is so deep seated it can never be eradicated, and she will work like a beaver to spread the faith.

A few days after sending this letter, Sherman read the *New York Herald's* call for him to become the Republican nominee. Rutherford B. Hayes, the leading candidate, in winning his third election as Ohio's governor, had taken a stand for religious freedom, but also one for taxation of all citizens to keep up common schools. He might be injured on this account. The Democrats were certain to be dangerous with their exposé of Republican scandals. Their candidate—Samuel J. Tilden, the reformer—would be strong. There was need of a powerful, unquestionably honest nominee on the Republican ticket.

Sherman wrote a letter to the *Herald* declining; he stated flatly, "My wife and family are strong Catholics, but I am not; that, however, is nobody's business"; he said he believed in common schools, thought them "in some quarters, extravagant," but that the question should be kept out of politics.

In March of that year, 1875, there suddenly developed a situation that dramatized Sherman's honesty as compared with that of so many of Grant's henchmen. Secretary Belknap resigned from office, confessing that he had sold army sutlerships for personal gain. His slip had come in that very branch which, in 1869, Sherman had wanted taken from political patronage. The *St. Louis Globe-Democrat* quickly had a reporter at Sherman's home for an interview. Deftly Sherman sidestepped the chance to make personal capital at Belknap's expense. He avoided discussing corruption; he would not point up his own recent differences with the soiled minister. Instead he spoke chivalrously of Belknap's war record, and blamed the general condition of politics—just such an attitude as he had always taken in protecting his soldiers when they failed during the war:

> His downfall was due to the vicious organization of Washington society and the ridiculous extravagance of the first social circles. Very few Cabinet officers are able to live within their means, none can begin to live within their salaries. . . . Now Belknap got $8,000 a year and had no outside resources. His wife was fashionable and ambitious. . . . I left Washington because my salary would not support me and because I did not consider society there a proper place in which to rear a family.

The scandal forced Sherman to move his headquarters to Washington. Grant, appointing Judge Alphonso Taft to the War Office, corrected almost all the matters that had driven Sherman away. Still protesting that he did not want to go, Sherman went, and was happy. Grant was now closer to him than he had been in the past six years. Sherman's relations with Secretaries of War through the next eight years were pleasant; he took pride in the efficiency with which the army was managed despite its decline in numbers; he was glad when experts praised the school of instruction he founded in Kansas.

Only once in these Washington years did trouble shake the general. The election of 1876 was deadlocked—Republican Hayes against Democrat Tilden. John Eaton, United States commissioner of education, noted how the news was received in the Executive Mansion.

> Sherman, with usual impetuosity, was pacing the room, lamenting with some profanity the fate of the Nation and especially of the army should the Democrats—otherwise the rebels—assume control, but Grant was perfectly calm and serene.

The result hinged on the votes of Southern States, in three of which there was a contest, with both Republicans and Democrats insisting that they had won the electors. Not until March, 1877, was the question finally decided by a commission, in favor of Hayes. In the meantime threats of violence were not uncommon, as each party swore to protect itself from being cheated. Sherman brought troops into the city and prepared to shoot down any one who made trouble, be they Republican or Democrat. He told Byers:

> If civil war breaks out, it will be a thousand times worse than the other war. It will be the fighting of neighbor against neighbor, friend against friend. . . . It is only a question of time until the politicians ruin us. Partisanship is a curse. These men are not howling for the country's good but for their own political advantage and the people are too big fools to see it. We are liable to smash into a thousand pieces every time we have an election.

But the storm went around. Hayes was seated without turmoil, and with his coming the heyday of a hero's life began for Sherman. Mrs. Hayes admired Sherman no less than did her husband. In her gentle hands the general who opposed professional moralists and religious reformers was very pliable. The First Lady soon had Sherman singing hymns regularly in the choruses that she organized among official guests; more marvelous than that, she got him to issue an order to the army to drink less because she wished it. When at home, Sherman liked to tilt his chair on flagstones in his front yard and to call in friends who came by under the gas lamps. John, now Secretary of the Treasury, and Blaine, Republican leader in the Senate, often sat with him. Living in a rented house, he could now make ends meet and considerably more. Colonel Edward Bouton, visiting him to recall their Shiloh days, heard him say that he "gave one-third of his pay each month to soldiers and charity." Bouton observed that "he educated several poor boys, sons of comrades."

One day Sherman met Mrs. Bickerdyke on the streets of the capital.

The old lady had followed the discharged soldiers West, and had operated an eating-house along the new railroad. Now she was in danger of losing it through debt. Sherman took her case to the railroad magnates and obtained an extension of time on her mortgage.

In 1885 Blanche McCook, born a few months after her father died at the Battle of Kenesaw Mountain, asked Sherman to help secure for herself or her stepfather the position of postmaster at East Portland, Oregon. Sherman immediately wrote the Postmaster-General:

> McCook was my law partner and *I* caused his death. . . . Since the creation, no intelligent man on earth has sacrificed his life, and all that was dear, for his Government with better grace than Gen'l Dan McCook, and this Government, be it Democratic or Republican, will deserve eternal damnation if it closes its ears to the appeals of the widows and orphans. . . . When the children of my old war associates appeal to me, my heart goes out and I cease to be a reasonable being.

Byers, while visiting Sherman, was amazed to see how often the maid answering the doorbell, reported, "It's a soldier."

"Let him in," was Sherman's invariable command. He kept charge accounts at clothing stores and boot shops for penniless veterans and gave the men written orders for supplies. He often purchased railroad tickets for them.

Once, when he was in St. Louis, a caller asked for $26.50 with which to reach his Ohio home. He described accurately enough his regiment and service under Sherman until he related how good he had felt at the grand review. Then Sherman interrupted: "Yes, I left your regiment at Raleigh with Kilpatrick." The veteran thought for some minutes, then smiled and said:

> Uncle Billy, it wasn't *all* a lie; I confess I lied some, but I was in truth a lieutenant in the —th Ohio Cavalry, and have since the war been out on the plains as a teamster, and have told the story so often that I believed it myself; the story is true up to Raleigh, but after that it is fiction.

Sherman saw that he got the ticket to Ohio.

In each of his homes after the war, Sherman had a study of his own in the basement. At the head of the stairway leading to it was a sign, GENERAL SHERMAN'S OFFICE—a sign whose lettering seemed "unnecessarily large and emphatic," as though a warning to his wife and children. So thought a French boy who played with the Sherman children in Washington, and who grew up to be the French statesman Marquis de Chambrun.

In his sanctum Sherman read and wrote letters, filed papers, and thumbed through his favorite authors: Burns, Scott, and Dickens. He told Byers that he read some of Dickens's novels each year, over and over. Safe in his lair, he read or worked until well past midnight. From it Ellen had difficulty in extracting him for breakfast. The surest method was not to allow the morning newspapers to be delivered at his "office" but to have them on the breakfast table. He ate no lunch, and he was out to dinner a good half of the time he was in Washington. Ellen rarely accompanied him to these social events. She had a study upstairs, an office of her own where she toiled on her religious and charitable work. The death of her father, the growth of her children into adolescence and maturity, the settlement of her husband into relative routine, all allowed her to draw more and more into religion. Always an efficient housekeeper, she now found herself able, with sufficient servants, to be free for Catholic charities. Her attitude toward Cump was still motherly and sisterly—he was her boy, not a hero.

It was her sister Theresa's young son, Sherman Steele, who saw his Aunt Ellen and Uncle Cump in a revealing scene:

> Once at the age of eight, I was sitting in the General's study staring at him as he read a newspaper. He grew restless under my steady gaze and said, "What are you thinking of?"
>
> "I was just thinking that I guessed you are the greatest general that ever lived."
>
> "What made you think that?"
>
> "Well, if you hadn't gone through Georgia, I guess Grant would be there at Richmond fighting yet."
>
> The General called, "Ellen!" as Aunt Ellen passed through the hall visiting bedrooms with towels preparatory for the night.
>
> She came in and he repeated what I had said. She ran her hands through his dark-brown hair and down into his snow-white beard, saying, "Oh, we all think that."

Once Sherman put Theresa's boy on a St. Louis cable car in front of his house on Garrison Avenue, paid his fare, and told him to make the circuit and see the town. Then he went into the house waving goodby. Fascinated by the ride, the boy made the circuit several times without considering home. Eventually he saw from the window the Sherman house with the general fuming at the gate and scanning the windows of passing street cars. Catching the boy's eye, Sherman motioned for him to alight. Then he turned and shouted back at the house: "Here he is, Ellen! Didn't I tell you he would be all right?" Together the general and the little boy entered the door sheepishly, and the youth saw certain signs that the conqueror of the Confederacy had been suffering defeat at Ellen's hands for his carelessness in intrusting a nephew to the perils of the cable cars which took curves at a speed that allowed few passengers to keep their seats or their feet. Indeed, but a few days previous the General, dressed for a banquet, had been thrown from a car platform into the mud.

Ellen had grown stouter with the passing years and her heart was not strong. Rachel and Lizzie were the daughters who accompanied him at times. In Washington in 1880 Ellie, the gayest of his children, married a navy lieutenant, Alexander M. Thackara. She and Minnie brought their families home often on visits; by 1888 Minnie's children numbered six and Ellie's four.

Byers, who visited the household in Washington, said of Ellen:

> Probably no woman in America spent more time and money doing good. She was extremely bright and kind in her ways. Army officers all liked her and her house stood open to every friend.

Under this incomparable blessing of having a wife who would welcome his friends, Sherman made relatively little of her dogmatism on religion. He spoke tenderly of her to Byers one morning in his study after breakfast:

> Don't talk religion with her though. . . . As for myself it makes no difference. Why, I guess I don't believe in anything, so in this room talk as you please.

Although she did not, as announced, receive the order of the Golden Rose from a Pope, Ellen was known to Catholics all over the world. The Empress Eugénie, in Byers's knowledge, knew Mrs. Sherman's work intimately. Her refusal to allow Cump much authority in the education of the children was to her merely a part of her devotion to her church. Sometimes he would say nothing after her declarations had wounded his feelings, and would take his wounds to Theresa Steele for healing. As a baby Sissie had wound herself around his heart and as a woman, for all her devotion to Ellen, she was sympathetic with him and knew the soothing words that brought comfort. His emotion for Sissie he recorded on September 13, 1888, when on visiting her home in Ohio he was asked to write in the family autograph album. He protested that he wasn't worthy; the album had been awesome in his youth, a volume to be opened only for the Daniel Websters and Henry Clays. Sissie answered that he now ranked with any of the great names which, at Thomas Ewing's request, had been inscribed there long before. At last, Sherman yielded. He wrote:

> Dear Theresa:
>
> A mere glance at this precious album recalls sad and pleasant memories of your grand old father and most loving mother, when you were a baby and I a conceited young officer. May you long survive me and cherish in a corner

of your heart a small spot for a brother who has known and loved you since you were a baby.

A niece of Ellen's, visiting the household soon after the war, knew of a storm that had swept over her uncle with painful effect:

One day the General came in to dinner full of spirits, sparkling and happy.

"I was talking to Grant today," he said. "He's going to send Fred to such and such a preparatory school and I'll have Tom go there, too; so Grant's boy and mine can be together. Later on, they can go to West Point together. That will be splendid.

"And Senator Blank wants Ellie and Rachel to go to such and such a school with his little girls . . ."

Aunt Ellen broke in—

"Cump, tomorrow morning at 8 o'clock Tom's going to Georgetown to the Jesuit College and tomorrow morning the girls are going to the Sisters' school around the corner—or tomorrow morning at ten o'clock I'll take them all back to my father."

The General was terribly hurt, got up and left the table. He was mum for several days. But by the end of the week Aunt Ellen said he was reconciled to it and was helping Tom with his lessons as though nothing had happened. He was tremendously loving with his family, very close to them and affectionate.

Sherman saw himself in his son Tom. The slender, sandy-haired boy had taken Willy's place. A relative of Ellen's put it:

He was wrapped up in Tom, whom he expected to be an engineer, a lawyer or a soldier. Cump, his younger son, was a normal promising boy but not so like his father as Tom.

From the Jesuits' school in Georgetown, Sherman sent Tom through a scientific course at Yale University, then through the Law School of Washington University in St. Louis. In the spring of 1878, at twenty-one, Tom emerged ready, as his father thought, for a professional career. Instead the youth announced that he was going to enter the priesthood. Rachel told a cousin, "Tom nearly broke Papa's heart." Cump carried his grief to John with such emphasis that the latter interceded. He told Tom that he would educate six boys for the priesthood if only the youth would give up his idea. But Tom, supported by his mother, clung to his decision. His own suffering was apparent in a letter written June 1 to a kinsman. He penned it on the eve of sailing for England to take up his religious studies:

My father, as you know, is not a Catholic, and therefore the step I am taking seems as startling and as strange to him as, I have no doubt, it does to you. . . . I go without his approval, sanction or consent; in fact, in direct opposition to his best wishes in my behalf. For he had formed other plans for me, which are now defeated, and had other hopes and expectations in my regard, which are necessarily dashed to the ground. . . .

Feeling painfully aware that I have grieved and disappointed my father, I beg my friends and his, one and all, of whatever religion they may be, to spare him inquiries or comments of any sort.

Eleven years after this blow, Sherman told a nephew: "I can't get over Tom. Why should they have taken my splendid boy? They could have brought over thirty priests from Italy in his place." Although newspapers reported that Sherman refused to attend the ordination of his son, there could be no question that, at least shortly thereafter, he was as affectionate and intimate with the boy as before.

Angela, daughter of Philemon Ewing, remembered a visit to the general's:

Rachel said, "Oh, Angela, I think it is so nice to hear you say 'Father' and 'Mother'; we always say 'Papa' and 'Mamma.' I think I'll change after this." The next morning at breakfast, Rachel said, "Oh, Father," and the General laid down his knife and fork and looked at her so hurt and pained, saying, "What have I done to make you call me 'Father'?" Rachel never tried it again.

Young Sherman Steele noted the general's habits at the table:

Moderate in his appetite, he ate without paying much attention to the food. Once when visiting there, my mother, Theresa, was handed a cup of coffee in which Aunt Ellen had put too much sugar. When she noted this, Aunt Ellen said, "Oh, pass it to Cump. He won't know the difference."

The General heard his name used and spoke up, "What's that, Ellen? What's that?"

Aunt Ellen said, "I was just saying to Sissie that you didn't mind whether there was sugar in your coffee or not."

"All right, all right," he said and drank it down. He really never noticed if there be one spoonful or ten.

He left all household details to his wife, always turning his Army vouchers over to her to cash. He urged her to use his pay as she saw fit.

Although in time Sherman came to joke about his wife's passion for parochial schools—he said once during an address at a "last day" of a common school, "I don't know anything about public schools, but my wife says she would as lief send her children to the saloon on the corner"—it was unquestionable that his family's religion was a factor in determining him to decline nominations for Presidency of the United States. Particularly did this factor become important in 1884, when he resisted one of the most determined efforts ever made by an American political party to draft a reluctant man for the post.

The insistence began, in an increasing flood of letters, after November 1, 1883, when Sherman retired from the army. Under a law passed June 30, 1882, retirement was compulsory at the age of sixty-four, and although Congressmen and Senators volunteered to exempt Sherman from the law he refused because he considered it right for officers of lower rank to be freed from labor at the specified age—and a general must obey the laws that bound his underlings. Furthermore he realized, he said, that "no man could know when his own mental powers began to decline." Generosity also prompted him. Sheridan, his successor, was nine years younger and ought to have his chance at the honored post. To give Sheridan time to prepare for his organizational requests of Congress at the coming March session, Sherman retired on November 1, four months ahead of schedule, and, with the praise of President Arthur, Congress, the press and civic bodies in his ears, moved to St. Louis. His pay would continue in full.

Before leaving he had been urged by his former aid, Willard Warner, to accept the Presidency because "the people are ripe for such an administration of honesty and straight-forward, blunt, soldierly ways" as Sherman, like William Henry Harrison, might give: "We'll have 1840 all over again." Sherman had answered:

"No, I wouldn't take it if elected. It killed Harrison, Taylor, Lincoln, Garfield, and it will kill Arthur."

In Cincinnati, Judge Joseph B. Foraker remembered how as a lieutenant on the field of Bentonville he had heard Sherman silence generals who predicted the Presidency for him. Sherman had said:

"No; the American people are so exacting in their demands that no man can afford to give them service except when duty requires." His voice had sounded "like the rattle of musketry."

When Mrs. J. B. Henderson, a friend and neighbor of Sherman's in St. Louis, joined her husband in begging Sherman to accept the Republican nomination in 1884, Sherman wrote her that he would not; "Washington ruined Grant's children," and if he himself were to be elected, his wife's zeal for her church would keep "the White House full of priests." He declined to listen to John, who called on him to "acquiesce." His friend Blaine, the leading candidate for the nomination, began to despair of victory as strength developed behind President Arthur and Senator Logan. On May 25, the eve of the convention at Chicago, Blaine wrote Sherman:

> . . . it is more than possible, it is indeed not improbable, that you may be nominated. If so you must stand your hand. . . . If it comes to you it

will come as the ground-swell of popular demand, and you can no more refuse than you could have refused to obey an order when you were a lieutenant. . . . It would in such an event injure your great fame as much to decline it as it would for you to seek it.

In several letters Sherman declined Blaine's assistance; and in one said that he would resist even if it gave "offense to the convention which construes itself the people . . . whose mandate was the voice of God." He stated bluntly that he thought the voice of God had nothing to do with a political matter. He still held to the dream that politics was beneath the notice of the ideal soldier. His greater fondness for the Society of the Army of the Tennessee than for the enormously larger Grand Army of the Republic was partially due to the former's freedom from the latter's activity in politics. When G.A.R. posts in their characteristic zeal for the Republican party threatened discourtesy to national officials who had been Democrats or peace advocates during the war, Sherman publicly rebuked them as "bigots." His enrollment in the G.A.R. was merely that of a member in the lowest organizational rank, and his excuse for refusing high office was that he had his own title while many a veteran private could by securing election gain the coveted prefix of general or colonel and so secure the recognition denied him in the Sixties.

On May 28, 1884, he wrote Blaine that soldiers were not schooled in the practices of government and that "our experience since 1865 demonstrates the truth of this." To accept would mean "a sacrifice of judgment, of inclination and of self-interest." He was in no man's debt, had simple tastes,

and would account myself a fool, a madman, an ass, to embark anew, at sixty-five years of age, in a career that may, at any moment, become tempest-tossed by the perfidy, the defalcation, the dishonesty, or neglect of any one of a hundred thousand subordinates utterly unknown to the President of the United States, not to say the eternal worriment by a vast host of impecunious friends and old military subordinates. Even as it is, I am tortured by the charitable appeals of poor distressed pensioners, but as President these would be multiplied beyond human endurance.

He explained to Blaine that in St. Louis he and his family were happy. There "Catholicism is held in respect and veneration and . . . my children will naturally grow up in contact with an industrious and frugal people." He reminded Blaine of his knowledge of the Sherman family's characteristics and asked him to "understand, without any explanation from me, how their thoughts and feelings should and ought to influence my action." But he added:

I will not even throw off on them the responsibility. I will not, in any event, entertain or accept a nomination . . . for reasons personal to myself.

He declared that he had earned the right to do what he pleased:

In every man's life there occurs an epoch when he must choose his own career, and when he may not throw the responsibility, or tamely place his destiny in the hands of friends. Mine occurred in Louisiana when, in 1861, alone in the midst of a people blinded by supposed wrongs, I resolved to stand by the Union as long as a fragment of it survived to which to cling.

The convention assembled at Chicago. On June 3 Sherman read a telegram from Henderson, who was a delegate, announcing that the drift could not be halted. He must prepare. Sherman answered, "Please decline any nomination for me in language strong but courteous." A deadlock seemed certain. On June 5 Henderson again rushed to the telegraph office. Sherman's son Tom saw the reception of this wire:

I was at his side in his library on Garrison Avenue when he received the telegram . . . "Your name is the only one we can agree upon, you will have to put aside your prejudices and accept the Presidency."

Without taking his cigar from his mouth, without changing his expression, while I stood there trembling by his side, my father wrote the answer, "I will not accept if nominated and will not serve if elected."

He tossed it over to me to be handed to the messenger and then went on with the conversation he had been engaged in. In that moment I thought my father a great man.

To Philemon Ewing, Sherman discussed the offer:

It's simply absurd. I wouldn't think of it for the fortieth part of a second. I lead a peaceful life here and if I ran for President I'd wake up some morning and find all over the newspapers that I'd poisoned my grandmother.

Now you know I never saw my mother's mother, but the newspapers would say I killed her and *prove* it.

61

DEATH WALKED WITH ME

THE last twenty-five years of Sherman's life were, in a way, one long chicken dinner. He became America's favorite toastmaster, and Chauncey M. Depew, his chief rival for that honor, declared after having studied him "at hundreds of public dinners" that any one must admit that

Sherman was "the readiest and most original talker in the United States." Depew added:

> I don't believe that he ever made the slightest preparation, but he absorbed, apparently while thinking and while carrying on a miscellaneous conversation with those about him, the spirit of the occasion, and his speech, when finished, seemed to be as much of a surprise to himself as it was to the audience. . . . Once I was with him from ten o'clock in the morning until six in the afternoon and he talked without cessation for the whole period. . . . I only regretted that the day was limited. . . . He always ought to have been accompanied by a stenographer.

To Ellen, Cump was the image of a man rushing out the front door, bag in hand, depot-bound, and hurling back over his shoulder imprecations against the committees that were killing him with their demands for speeches. This was the last time he'd accept! A few days later the little drama would be repeated. By 1885 he was receiving an average of one definite invitation a day, and in addition more general requests for attendance at functions. Solicitations for speeches came from all over the North and the West. He protested, complained, denounced, but he reveled in so national a demand. Characteristic of his declinations was one he sent on April 25, 1885, to the secretary of a county fair at Rockford, Illinois:

> I have a family of six children and seven grandchildren. Now the question is, Shall I abandon them, take to the road and consume all my time . . . ? Were you to see my mail for any three days in succession you would exclaim, "For God's sake allow an old soldier some little rest."

He never thought to ask fees for speeches, or to appear where admissions were charged. His duty—as well as private pleasure—was to travel the land and instruct the younger generation in loyalty and obedience to the law. During the 1870's and '80's he was seen and heard by more people than any other American of his time. He enjoyed speaking, but hated hand-shaking, once complaining to John that eager crowds had cost him a finger nail and almost a finger. At a reunion of the Grand Army of the Republic in Milwaukee he jammed his hands in his pockets when the crowd rushed him at the end of a parade.

"Get out!" he barked. "This is no place to shake hands. Come down to the hotel. I'll hire a man to shake hands for me."

At the veterans' reunions, which he attended regularly—usually many of them each summer—he preferred to march with the men in a common soldier's blouse, merely adorned by four silver stars, to joining the generals on horseback. At celebrations given for him he frequently asked that "Marching Through Georgia" be omitted from the music. But this request was rarely heeded. His nephew, Sherman Steele, while traveling with him heard him curse softly—but proudly—one morning because Pullman porters had assembled at an end of the car during the night to sing that war song.

He stormed against ostentation and against the practice of making banquets so elaborate that twenty-five dollars was frequently charged for each plate. He protested against French words on menus and against "these mixed-up French concoctions which are only chicken hashed up with some kind of sauce and called a croquette or something of the kind." His cigars were so cheap that his secretary, James Madison Barrett, thought them "vile." Barrett saw him "always eat a good big dinner at home before attending a banquet." His son-in-law, Thackara, declared that the general "never drank more than one glass of sherry during a public dinner no matter how long the program lasted." Thackera saw him come home in this cold sobriety from one banquet accompanied by several younger men who were sick from champagne. The general had failed to notice his companions' condition, and opening a cupboard, took out a brandy bottle saying, "Now we'll have a drink." The younger men collapsed.

Honors failed to impress him. Neither self-satisfaction, patience, nor repose ever came to him. When sitting upon the rostrum at Yale University in 1876 to receive the degree of LL.D. and to see his son Tom graduate, he grew weary with the long academic addresses and tiptoed into the open air. Faculty members stole out to bring him back. There he sat on a bench, with a Negro vagrant; he had felt the need of a smoke, he said, and thought it no harm to leave, since he was disturbing nobody. He and the Negro had smoked his cigars and the black man had given him some very interesting memoirs of a recent incarceration in the New Haven workhouse.

According to his son Tom, he never aspired to but one elective office: the presidency of the Society of the Army of the Tennessee, a post that he held from 1869 to 1891. Sitting at the head of its sessions, he could hear more plainly than at any other time the never-ending music that the war played in his memory. In the chair he was again the Sherman of '64; he disregarded parliamentary rules as freely as he had military red tape, and treated society members as tyrannically and genially as he had staff officers in the army. He made motions, rushed them through, declared them carried almost before the "Ayes" could be heard. He humbled would-be orators—"Yes, Major, speak but a few words, we know all about it," "Now don't make a speech, Colonel, let's vote." On entering a hall he would shout at soldiers who applauded him, "Stop that foolishness, and let's get down to business!" He warned visitors, "Now while we're carrying out this program, we want quiet. We like to have visitors here but they must understand that this is a society meeting and we're not to be interrupted by applause from outsiders." Once at a meeting in St. Louis, a young "society" man called, "Several of us would like to hear from Mr. Blank," naming a prominent civilian. Sherman thundered, "Sit down, young man; we're willing you and your friends should stay here and listen, but this is our meeting and we propose to run it!"

At banquets his fashion was to arise and address the musicians, "When the program calls for music, give a soft strain, not a whole tune; make it a loop between speeches." Then, to the waiting orators, "Each speaker is to speak as long as he holds his audience." Then, to the guests, "A good hearty laugh and marked applause are all right, but don't drawl it out into a long giggle or into a noise. Let it be short and emphatic." At a gigantic reunion banquet in Chicago he called out:

"Can you hear in the middle of the hall?"

"No!"

"All right, read it in the papers tomorrow!"

Toward women he was gracious. They were attracted by his fire and bluntness. And men were not angered by his autocracy. They all "spoiled" him shamelessly.

At soldiers' reunions, in the freemasonry of veteranship, he would occasionally speak of Southerners with a severity that he avoided when addressing the general public. To veterans in St. Louis, in 1867, he spoke of the war's devastation, and added:

> How any Southern gentleman can still boast of "the lost cause" or speak of it in language other than that of shame and sorrow passes my understanding.

He addressed the Society of the Army of the Potomac in 1876 from a Philadelphia stage that had been turned into an imitation bivouac with tents, artillery, cannon balls and stacked muskets.

"Let us live and forget," he said, "provided they do the same. But if they will not"—he jerked his head toward the munitions—"Boys, there are the things." When the roof had ceased to shake from the resulting applause, he went on: "I see you understand your business. But I'm out of practice now and I'm going to live a peaceable life from now on."

In 1879 he wrote E. P. Howell of the *Atlanta Constitution* a long, friendly and apparently non-ironic testimonial as to the remarkable healthfulness of northern Georgia. He urged Howell to help Atlanta catch up in progress and growth to those Western cities which were "less favored in climate and location"—cities like San Francisco and Chicago. The chief reason for Atlanta's sloth, as he saw it, was her refusal to welcome immigrants as did Western cities. He advised Atlanta to "let up somewhat on the favorite hobby of 'carpet-baggers.'" He had seen carpet-baggers develop every city from Chicago to the Pacific; many of the carpet-baggers in the West were from the South, too! Open the doors, he told Howell, and let Atlanta go on to its destiny as one of the great cities of the whole continent, "an end which I desire quite as much as you do." He warned Georgians that

> if any part of a community clings to distinctions founded on past conditions, it will grow less and less with time and finally disappear. Any attempts to build up an aristocracy or a privileged class at the South on the fact that their fathers or grandfathers once owned slaves will result in a ridiculous failure and subject the authors to the laughter of mankind. . . . I am certain it will not be attempted in Georgia.

Characteristically, he reminded audiences that war was wasteful and that glory was a delusion. Once he told a crowd:

> I think we understand what military fame is—to be killed on the field of battle and have our names spelled wrong in the newspapers.

On 1878's Memorial Day he made an audience in New York's Booth Theatre roar with fervor when he said, "We saved the Union from absolute annihilation"; but he sobered it quickly by denouncing the current habit of orators and writers to employ military terms in describing political campaigns. They should not talk of "lines of battle" in civil contests; it was "dangerous to familiarize young people with the idea of war." He added:

> War is usually made by civilians bold and defiant in the beginning but when the storm comes they generally go below. Of the 500,000 brave fellows whose graves we strew with flowers, not one in a thousand had the remotest connection with the causes of the war which led them to their untimely death.

On August 11, 1880, at Columbus, Ohio, he told five thousand G.A.R. veterans, and unnumbered masses of civilians, that war was hell. It was raining when he, with other notables, escorted President Hayes to a speakers' stand in the fair grounds. When the President had finished a short speech under an umbrella, from the sea of faces of old soldiers, came shouts of "Sherman! Speech! Uncle Billy!" He stepped forward. The faces grew quiet. The rain pattered on the wide campaign hats of the veterans. They heard him say:

> Fellow soldiers: My speech is not written, nor has been even thought of by me. It delights my soul to look on you and see so many of the good old

boys left yet. They are not afraid of rain; we have stood it many a time.

I came as part escort to the President, and not for the purpose of speaking to you, but simply to look on and let the boys look at Old Billy again. We are to each other all in all as man and wife, and every soldier here today knows that Uncle Billy loves him as his own flesh and blood. . . .

The war now is away back in the past and you can tell what books cannot. When you talk you come down to the practical realities just as they happened. You all know this is not soldiering here.

There is many a boy here today who looks on war as all glory, but, boys, it is all hell. You can bear this warning voice to generations yet to come. I look upon war with horror, but if it has to come I am here.

Nobody in the crowd realized that Sherman had said anything immortal. No telegraphers were busy that night informing the world that Sherman had said that war is all hell. The *Ohio State Journal* put the general's speech in among its other items of the day's festivities. But his words, shortened to "War is hell," gradually spread over the world to become one of the most widely known statements by an American. Where or when he had said it was forgotten. Years later, he could never remember having said it at all; he supposed he might have. It was certainly what he thought; but he guessed it was just a popularization of the phrase he had written during the Civil War struggle: "War is cruelty and you cannot refine it."

In the comradeship of reunions he forgave old enemies. Logan, speaking at a birthday dinner to Sherman in 1883, buried the hatchet with laudations of his old commander. Sherman embraced him and wept a little. Next day he sent Logan an impulsive letter beginning, "This is a rainy Sunday, a good day to clear up old scores," and reciting to Logan for the first time his reasons for not having put him in McPherson's shoes after the Battle of Atlanta. Logan replied in ardent friendship, revealing what Sherman had not known, that Lincoln had secretly sent Logan home after the fall of Atlanta to electioneer for the Republican ticket. This freed him from the suspicion that he had left the army for his own political profit.

Frank Blair died in St. Louis on July 8, 1875, aged fifty-four, his end perhaps hastened by political disappointments. He had followed the cause of liberalism after the war, despite Sherman's frequent urgings that he remain in the army and avoid politics. He had been the unsuccessful Democratic nominee for the vice-presidency in 1868, and had been defeated for reëlection as Missouri's Senator in 1874. Sherman spoke when Blair's monument was dedicated, and wrote privately: "He was noble and intelligent as a soldier but as a politician he was erratic and unstable. He admitted this many and many a time to me." When

GENERAL W. T. SHERMAN.

There was a continued demand to see and hear General Sherman, and he was introduced at the conclusion of President Hayes's address. After the demonstration had subsided, the General said:

FELLOW-SOLDIERS—My speech is not written, nor has been even thought of by me. It delights my soul to look on you and see so many of the good old boys left yet. They are not afraid of rain; we have stood it many a time. I came as part escort to the President, and not for the purpose of speaking to you, but simply to look on and let the boys look at old Billy again. We are to each other all in all as man and wife, and every soldier here to-day knows that Uncle Billy loves him as his own flesh and blood. Could I command the language I would like to speak to you an hour; there are others here who can and we will give echo and say amen to their expressions. The war now is away back in the past and you can tell what books can not. When you talk you come down to the practical realities just as they happened. You all know this is not soldiering here. There is many a boy here to-day who looks on war as all glory, but, boys, it is all hell. You can bear this warning voice to generations yet to come. I look upon war with horror, but if it has to come I am here. (This last remark was received with long applause and a hurrah by the audience.) We have a little war on hand to-day to make homes for the people who are coming to our shores; it is being fought and your sympathy is needed. I wish to again congratulate you. Those who were at the rear in the war would have been gone from here covered with umbrellas before now. The country is now peaceful and long may it so remain. To you soldiers they owe the debt of gratitude.

PHOTOSTAT OF SHERMAN'S "WAR-IS-HELL" SPEECH AS PUBLISHED IN THE "OHIO STATE JOURNAL" OF AUGUST 12, 1880

Halleck died at his army post, Louisville, in 1872, Sherman wrote his widow a friendly letter. On March 1, 1886, Sherman wrote concerning Stanton, who had died in 1869:

> We were good friends for years before his death. . . . Stanton had some magnificent qualities which I have ever recognized and applauded, but he had others which brought him into conflict with his best friends.

Through the winter of 1884 and the spring of 1885 Grant sat dying in a chair at his home, Mount McGregor, New York. Cancer at the base of his tongue was destroying him and he knew it. He was racing with Death, trying to finish his *Memoirs* before his last strength faded. By their sale, his friend and publisher Mark Twain assured him, he could provide for his family. He had gone bankrupt in May, 1884, betrayed by two partners whom he had trusted as much as he had any of the similarly fraudulent supporters of his Presidency.

It had been war that had made him, and in his literary return to it twenty years later he found himself again. As he wrote of the conflict, bewilderment left him. Again he was the master, writing swiftly, concisely, without loss of words or need for an eraser. News of his illness aroused enormous public sympathy. Sherman came to see him again and again, and on December 24, 1884, wrote Ellen, "Grant says my visits have done him more good than all the doctors." On March 17, 1885, when newspapers announced that Grant was sinking, Sherman wrote his friend's son Fred:

> I am older than your father and of a shorter-lived race than he, therefore never dreamed of outliving him. . . . I wish to be . . . a willing witness to the great qualities which made him the conspicuous figure of our eventful epoch.

Never before had the illness of an American affected such multitudes. Offers of help almost snowed under the Mount McGregor cottage. Congress on March 4 placed Grant on a general's salary. His old opponent General Buckner, the man who had made the "unconditional surrender," vainly tried to give him money. It seemed that the whole North, with many Southerners in addition, was striving emotionally to show that no one, even amid all the corruption that had dogged his civil career, had ever doubted his personal honor. Magazine editors, learning in April that his death was expected hourly, bombarded Sherman with offers for articles regarding Grant's career. Refusing, Sherman told his brother "as to money in this connection the very thought is revolting."

On April 18 Cump wrote John that the evening papers were reporting Grant so much better "that he talks about going to California this summer—that is better than a first-class funeral even in Washington." But on June 16 Grant was worse and Sherman wrote his friend Postmaster-General William F. Vilas:

> I aim to be content with what I have; but he aimed to rival the millionaires who would have given their all to have won any of his battles. . . . Man is allotted only a measure of vital force—that exhausted, he dies. No one can comprehend the waste of this force in Grant's case, night and day, when he realized that he had committed the fatal mistake of placing his war fame in a banking venture as part of its capital. . . . You need not fear that I will make *that* mistake—I may commit others.

Grant's manuscript was finished on the nineteenth of July, and his life on the twenty-third. Sherman would not speak at his funeral and, after delivering an address in Chicago upon his friend's virtues, told John, "I feel embarrassed in speaking of him lest I say too much." The eulogies of orators, none of whom knew Grant as he knew him, angered Sherman, and on September 15 he confessed to John, "I actually wish I had imitated Grant's example of silence, which was purely the result of his will power." It was idle, he told friends, for any living man to attempt to evaluate Grant's place in history. "It will be a thousand years before his character is fully appreciated."

The fervor of wartime emotions might have been coloring Sherman's view in 1866 when he had told General Rusling:

> Grant is the greatest soldier of our time if not all time . . . he fixes in his mind what is the true objective and abandons all minor ones . . . he dismisses all possibility of defeat. He believes in himself and in victory. . . . If his plan goes wrong he is never disconcerted but promptly devises a new one and is sure to win in the end.

But time had had its chance to let Sherman weigh Grant in 1885 when, after many disappointments in his friend as President, he spoke calmly to the Society of the Army of the Tennessee:

> Grant more nearly impersonated the American character of 1861-5 than any other living man. Therefore he will stand as the typical hero of the great Civil War in America.

To the Society of the Army of the Potomac in 1881 Sherman spoke on the question of Grant's "butchery" of his own men in conducting the Richmond campaign:

> I wish to say publicly that I approve of General Grant's movements from Washington to Richmond by land instead of by water. War is an awful

game and demands death and destruction. A certain amount of killing had to be done, and the banks of the Rapidan and Mattapony were as good a place as those of the James and Appomattox.

He was offended when Grant's family allowed the dead chieftain to be entombed in a huge mausoleum in New York. Sherman thought he should have been buried simply and modestly, as became his character, in St. Louis. Thackara heard Sherman say, "No mausoleum for me! I don't want my body taken over the country like General Grant's and then deposited on the banks of the Hudson where there is no one to take care of anything." In his service as chairman of a committee to erect a memorial to Grant, he discovered that patriots who talked most of donations gave the least. For himself, as he wrote Mark Twain, "I subscribed $100 for a good old-fashioned tombstone and release all my friends from subscriptions."

Clemens, knowing Sherman's eagerness to see Grant's *Memoirs,* sent him an advance copy, even at the risk of involving his publishing house in legal complications by anticipating publication dates. Fred Grant had told Sherman that in the book his father had shown how in his later years he had come to realize that Sherman "had been his most loyal friend throughout his military career." Sherman found Grant's story of the war all he had hoped and more; it supported his own *Memoirs* on most of the points disputed by critics.

Mark Twain's rise as a publisher had interested Sherman, and in October, 1885, he had sent him three hundred foolscap pages filled with a narrative of his European tour. "I do not need the money," he wrote, "but my grandchildren and old soldier dependents and beggars do . . . give me your honest opinion." Clemens did so on October 5, advising him not to publish it, since it was but the framework of a book, and would compare badly with the *Memoirs:*

> . . . a skeleton is valuable, but it must have meat on it and the muscle and the beating heart and the blood in its veins before it can march. . . . Your "Memoirs" are rich in incident, anecdote, fact, history; it is a book which is all food . . . it is *fat;* there is no lean . . . its interest is unflagging and absorbing; it is a model narrative and will last as long as the language lasts. If I had read my own books half as many times as I have read those "Memoirs," I should be a wiser and better man than I am.

Sherman accepted the verdict graciously, gave Clemens the right to issue a new edition of the *Memoirs* and saw the volume sold very successfully along with Grant's.

Although his income was more than ample, Cump wrote John frequently about the burden of his expenses. He said that he had given

Ellie "about $12,000, her share of my estate," when she had married Thackara, and had maintained for more than a year in his St. Louis home Minnie, her children, and her husband Fitch, who had suffered financial reverses. He let off to John some private grumblings about the costliness of this plan, yet when Fitch, launching a factory, moved his family to Pittsburgh in the spring of 1885, Sherman felt almost insulted and on April 1 informed John:

> I confess that this move of Minnie and her children will change the aspect of St. Louis . . . I will soon be isolated—but I deem it best to end my days here. Grant's fate confirms me in the wisdom of this conclusion.

He wrangled endlessly with the St. Louis authorities over taxes. A neighbor protested to F. W. Mott, the water commissioner, that General Sherman was wasting water sprinkling the street in front of his house. When Mott sent Sherman a bill, the latter refused to pay it, and the newspapers resounded with his roars. An ex-war-correspondent, Joseph B. McCullaugh, plagued Sherman constantly with barbed paragraphs in the *St. Louis Globe-Democrat.* By November 28, 1885, Cump informed John that water and gas cost more than in Washington, "and in addition all my neighbors throw off on me the poor soldiers drifting about as beggars," and on December 11 he added:

> I can maintain this establishment unless half my family continues to go away. Next year I must allow for Cump to go to Yale and his mother clings to him so that I fear she must go along—that would leave me with Lizzie and Rachel in this expensive city. I may in this event go to New York to some hotel for a couple of years . . . I will not live again in Washington.

On January 19, 1886, he informed John that his son's education was the reason for the final decision:

> I know Ellen well enough to conclude she will be at New Haven or on the road half her time trusting to Providence or the Church for means . . . we shall be in New York next September. . . . My neighbors and friends will make a big fuss over this and I am very fond of some of them, though Turner, Lucas, Patterson . . . etc., etc., are dead and gone—and I also claim that the State of Missouri has no claim to my gratitude because the State by her Constitution disfranchises all Army officers classifying them as "paupers and idiots" yet taxing me nearly if not quite double my neighbors. I sometimes suspect that they tax me specially for being a fool to come to live with them.

He had been asked by the President of the Chicago Board of Trade, "Why do you live in such an old, played-out town as St. Louis?" His nephew, Sherman Steele, said later, "St. Louis simply got too slow for him."

In the autumn of 1886 the move was made, with his St. Louis properties rented to give him an annual income of some $6,000. Departing, he wrote John, "My chief regret will be to part with my horses." In New York, soon afterwards, he told army veterans:

> I sought refuge in the city of St. Louis; I found but little peace there. But I read, I think in Dr. Johnson, that peace and quiet can only be had in a great city or in the forest and I therefore sought it in New York.

The metropolis instantly lionized him. Appraiser Cooper of the city saw him "take out an engagement book and give a man a date six weeks in advance."

He spoke harshly of public men who made promises with no intention of keeping them. He appeared at every function for which he had accepted an invitation, even if it were only for a few minutes and acceptance had been much against his wish. Sometimes when neither his private secretary nor engagement book were handy, he would dress for a social affair, come downstairs, and stand about unable to remember where he was scheduled to appear. Ellen would tell him never mind; just stand at the window until he saw his greatest crony, Van Vliet, come along the sidewalk, then go out and fall in. The chances were a thousand to one that the two would be attending the same function. Two days after his seventieth birthday he wrote a soldier friend:

> Here in this great city I am subjected to dangers greater than those of the march or battlefield, or, as Chauncey Depew said a few evenings ago after Howard, Schofield and Slocum had boasted of following me to Atlanta, Savannah and Raleigh midst danger and triumph—he had followed me for an equal if not longer time through these campaigns of New York dinners.

Even at the risk of antagonizing correspondents he answered all letters, his secretary assisting. Once a Dutch immigrant boy, Edward Bok, wrote him a request to send the sentence, "The pen is mightier than the sword," for his autograph collection. Sherman sent the boy a long, stern letter:

> I prefer not to make scraps of sentimental writing. When I write anything I want it to be real and connected in form, as for instance in your quotation from Lord Lytton's play of "Richelieu," "the pen is mightier than the sword." Lord Lytton would never have put his signature to so naked a sentiment. Surely I will not. In the text there was a prefix or qualification:
>
> "Beneath the rule of men entirely great
> The pen is mightier than the sword."

He told young Bok that Washington, and Lincoln, who was a master of the pen, had both been forced to resort to "flaming swords":

> No, I cannot subscribe to your sentiment. . . . Rather in the providence of God, there is a time for all things, a time when the sword may cut the Gordian knot and set free the principles of right and justice, bound up in the meshes of hatred, revenge and tyranny that the pens of mighty men like Clay, Webster, Crittenden and Lincoln were unable to disentangle.

Several nights each week Sherman rode the elevated trains down to the Union League Club in New York to spend hours conversing with friends. He disliked to ride in carriages, because in them he was lonely. He preferred to walk or to flit about the city in common carriers, where he could talk to and observe people. He became the most noted of New York's theatrical first-nighters, and attended all the most important back-stage suppers and theatrical dinners. He shed patriarchal radiance and wit, and accepted actresses' kisses as a father might. He called all actors "his children." In 1880 he had written, "Let the statesmen, the moralist and the preacher surpass Shakespeare before they attempt to criticize the stage." He helped organize the Players' Club, one of the city's most successful organizations. He fussed at late dinners because they made him late at the theatre, yet he could not sit through a five-act play, and usually saw three acts one night, two the next.

Funerals of generals kept him traveling—Burnside, Kilpatrick, Logan, Hancock, Sheridan: He wept at Sheridan's. Little Kil, at the war's end, had found the army too tame and had resigned to become President Johnson's minister to Chili. Too turbulent, he had been recalled by President Grant and had taken to the lecture platform. Orating for the Republicans in 1868, the Democrats in 1872, the Republicans in 1880, defeated for Congress in New Jersey at the '80 elections, he had been sent to Chili as minister again when death struck him in 1881. At the time he had been quarreling bitterly with the minister to Peru, Stephen A. Hurlbut, Sherman's old lieutenant in Mississippi battle days. From the ill-fitting world of diplomacy he was laid at last under the cemetery flag at West Point where he could sleep easily. In March, 1887, Sherman flamed when the British military critic, Lord Wolseley, published in *Macmillan's Magazine* the statement that Lee, who had died in 1870, had "towered above all men on either side in that struggle." Quickly Sherman wrote an answer, in the *North American Review,* declaring that the British were still judging military matters by antiquated standards. Lee, he said, had fought "like a gallant knight, as he was," but was lacking in military greatness:

He never rose to the grand problem which involved a continent and future generations. His Virginia was to him the world. Though familiar with the geography of the interior of this great continent, he stood like a stone wall to defend Virginia . . . stood at the front porch battling with the flames whilst the kitchen and house were burning, sure in the end to consume the whole.

He cited Lee's two attempts to assume "the bold offensive" and how he had each time failed:

As an aggressive soldier Lee was not a success, and in war that is the true and proper test. . . . Grant's strategy embraced a continent; Lee's a small State. Grant's "logistics" were to supply and transport armies thousands of miles, where Lee was limited to hundreds.

Between the two men, said Sherman, there was no comparison; furthermore Thomas,

in all the attributes of manhood was the peer of General Lee—as good, if not a better soldier, of equal intelligence, the same kind heart. . . . Nashville was the only battle of our war which annihilated an army. . . . England and even some of our Eastern States . . . still see only the war in Virginia. The Civil War was concluded when Vicksburg, Chattanooga and Atlanta fell. After these it only remained to dispose of Lee's army, which was promptly and scientifically done.

He concluded by taunting Wolseley with absurdity in upholding the justice of the Southern cause when "Ireland today has many times the cause to rebel against England which the South had in 1861."

When in 1887 John Sherman thought that Mexico and Canada might well be annexed to the United States; Cump was unalterably opposed. The imperialism that was beginning to rise in the country found in him an opponent.

The brothers were as affectionate toward each other in their old age as in their younger days. It was still a question as to whether Cump wrote more often to John than to Ellen when apart from them. He still gave each his complete confidence. As a capitalist and as a statesman devoted to capitalism—the evangel of industrial prosperity—John had linked his name to the financial legislation and policies of the Republican party and was continually suggested by powerful commercial interests as the proper man to be President. For this honor John was ever ready, yet the call never came. Cump wondered that John should hold this ambition and wrote Ellen on August 8, 1887, that the Presidency "would kill any man of sensibility in a year." John in his turn declared that he could not endure for three months the strain Cump underwent in attending reunions and banquets, invitations to which in

1887 came at the rate of twenty a week. Cump declared that calls from the 4,000 G.A.R. posts would drive him to take refuge in the Rocky Mountains. He told the Society of the Army of the Potomac in his 68th year, "I was turned out to grass but nobody will let me stay there . . . just mark me dead. . . . Let me alone and I will have some peace the rest of my days." In his 69th year he wrote Ellen that he was refusing to attend burials of generals—"will attend my own funeral, but must be excused from others."

On November 28, 1888, nine weeks after writing this, Cump was called upstairs to the bed of Ellen, who was dying. His nephew Tom Ewing, son of General Tom, described it:

> General Sherman would not admit that it was serious and used to say to her that her father was troubled in the same way for years and that she was in no danger, but finally she had to be confined to her bed all the time in the care of her nurse.
>
> The General was seated in his office when the nurse came to the head of the stairs and called to him that Mrs. Sherman was dying. Though he had known she was in danger, I think this was the first moment when he realized the imminence of her death. He ran upstairs calling out, "Wait for me, Ellen, no one ever loved you as I love you"; if she was alive when he reached her bedside it was only for a moment.

It was days before the shock struck the general with full force. At first he was busy comforting his children. James Madison Barrett, his private secretary, in later years recalled the scene:

> The daughters were inconsolable till the General said, "Now, girls, remember it is just as natural to die as to be born."
>
> While Mrs. Sherman was lying in her coffin, Will Ewing, one of General Tom's sons, and I sat up with the body one night. All at once we heard a terrible noise and we hurried into the room thinking that the casket had fallen, but it was a bust of Thomas Ewing, Mrs. Sherman's father, that had toppled from its pedestal onto the floor. General Sherman and the children came running down stairs.

The activities of the funeral warded off the shock for a few days more. There was the long trip to St. Louis, where Ellen was buried beside Willy and the baby Charles. On Willy's tombstone was an inscription, "Our little sergeant; From the First Battalion, 13th U. S. Infantry. In his breast there was no guile."

But when he reached New York again and walked into the lonely house, the blow fell. He had bought a new house, No. 75 West Seventy-first Street, and had occupied it only a few months before Ellen's death. Now it mocked him. He wrote the *New York Herald* a note of thanks for public sympathy:

I expected to be the first to go, as I am much older and have been more severely tried, but it was not to be. But I expect to resume my place at her side one day.

Only his children knew of the spiritual depths to which he sank. They wrote:

His physical depression was such that an alarming illness followed. . . . One day one of his sons found him sitting speechless in his little basement office . . . he only pointed to his throat which the asthma, his lifelong enemy, had almost completely closed. He had not even taken sufficient heed to summon a physician. On another occasion a gust of air had extinguished the gas-light in his office, and he was breathing the poisonous vapor without caring to stir, unconscious or not caring that death hung in the poisoned air and was stealing upon him.

But his old resilience was apparent within four weeks, and with Rachel and Lizzie caring for his comfort and needs as Ellen had, he returned to his former way of life. As he neared seventy he found that he could no more remain quiet than he could when he was thirty. His circle of friends, already enormous, widened. He made friends with Whitelaw Reid, who had succeeded Greeley as editor of the *Tribune*, and the two men forgot their Shiloh quarrel. It was Reid who attempted to persuade him to sit for the sculptor St. Gaudens:

. . . after the old veteran had profanely refused to be pestered with damned sculptors, Stanford White came to me in despair about it and I tackled the old gentleman through his daughter Rachel and afterwards in person the next time he came to my house. He swore a little and finally consented.

Reid later summarized Sherman—"He never acknowledged an error and never repeated it."

With age, Sherman's passion against sectionalism grew more intense. For more than a decade he had ceased to talk of the Mississippi Valley as the seat of coming empire. On that topic his prophecies had not come true. The war, by splitting the agrarians into rival political parties, had let the manufacturing interests of the East determine the destiny of the nation. Industry and capital and the railroads had centered on the Northeastern seaboard. The wealth of New York did not impress him, but the city's social life, its power, answered best to the demands of his imagination. To radiate from that city, and to feel himself, as he said, welcome in all parts of the nation, was bliss.

He had written Ellen in 1883:

The whole Western world recognizes the truth that since the close of the Civil War I have so used my power and office to encourage the growth and development of the great West, giving me a hold on their respect and affection worth more than gold. . . . Every day I am reminded of little things done, of words spoken which have borne fruit. I honestly believe in this way I have done more good for our country and for the human race than I did in the Civil War.

To him, in 1888, it seemed that the Ohio Society of New York was too exuberant with State pride, and, when called upon to speak at its banquet, he began:

My young friends from Ohio, whilst you bear your honored state in memory, honored memory, never reflect upon others. There were good men born long before there were in Ohio. There are a great many good men born in States out of Ohio. . : . I hope you will bear in mind that you are citizens of a greater country, the United States of America.

And returning to address the society two years later, he was heard by Ohio's governor, William McKinley, to say:

The world takes count of what men do, not what they say; not where they live, but how they live. . . . I have sometimes thought that we attach more importance to the place of our birth than it is really entitled to.

Once in his seventieth year his mind seemed to weaken and to drift from its anchor of realism into sentimentalism and romance. An unnatural dreaminess came into his words as he addressed the Society of the Army of the Tennessee at Cincinnati:

Now my friends, there is nothing in life more beautiful than the soldier. A knight errant with steel casque, lance in hand, has always commanded the admiration of men and women. The modern soldier is his legitimate successor and you, my comrades, were not hirelings; you never were, but knight errants transformed into modern soldiers, as good as they were and better.

Now the truth is we fought the holiest fight ever fought on God's earth.

The old man had forgotten that he, Grant, and the Westerners had triumphed largely because they had approached the war with a psychology diametrically opposed to the feudal traditions of chivalry.

Then, as he talked on, he came out of his romantic dream: his common sense asserted itself:

We made our credit better than England's. . . . The South should not complain, because they deliberately put their slaves in the balance and lost them. They bet on the wrong card and lost.

In July, 1890, Sherman was as keen, as disciplinary, as he had ever been—and perhaps more realistically eloquent. On the third he was speaking to the Potomac veterans at Portland, Maine. Rising after orators had extolled the city's virtues, he said:

Remember that this country extends over the whole continent and is not confined to one part. You people of Portland should look westward 3,000 miles to another Portland. . . . I won't say more beautiful and yet I would be prepared to argue that question with any one, for I have never seen a sight more beautiful than Mount Hood. . . .

You people should be proud of such a namesake for it is growing like the great West and it will overshadow this Portland. But I don't want it to happen. I want all parts of the country to be alike and equal. . . .

We cannot see far ahead but the art of war should be kept pure and simple and at the base . . . love and devotion to our country . . . not to any State because you happen to be born there but to the whole United States.

For the Easterners he summed up the meaning of the phrase "grand strategy," which military experts were applying to his contributions in the war:

What is grand strategy? Common sense applied to the art of war. You have got to do something. . . . You can't go around asking corporals and sergeants. You must make it out in your own mind.

That night after his speech he learned that the Portland citizens were much offended by his comparison of their city to the Oregonian Portland, and when he was called upon at another session of the convention next day, he pretended that he had only tried "to stir things up—a good thing at meetings—makes 'em more interesting." But he added:

I don't intend to mar an occasion like this with anything but feelings of mutual respect and love. . . . Whether Portland, Oregon, or Portland, Maine, is the more beautiful city makes no difference, they both belong to us.

Then he turned lyric with thrilling effect—threw back his shoulders, raised his stubby white beard, and pointed to the flag:

And what is the emblem of that power that binds our hearts? It is over your heads, now, gentlemen! . . .

I have seen it on the high seas. I have seen it come out of the water; first a little fluttering something . . . little by little it comes over the horizon, more and more your glasses tell you that there is red, and there are white and blue. . . .

Yes, my friends, on the vast plains of the West I have seen the same thing. As you approach one of those little military posts . . . there is the flag . . . and you feel at home. . . .

You and I have seen it on the battlefield, and when you have recognized it coming to your aid when we needed aid, oh, how beautiful it was.

On his seventieth birthday, he invited sixteen guests to his home—among them his brother John, Schofield, Slocum, Howard, Tom Ewing, Chauncey M. Depew, Fred Grant, Joseph Choate. He was so gay, so quick, so sharp, that Howard said:

"Sherman will never die."

"My body will die," he answered. He made a little speech to his guests:

> I am too old to hope for many returns of the day. . . . Death seems to come nowadays without almost any warning, but many a man has sprung up in readiness when I have had the trumpets sounded, and I am still a soldier. When Gabriel sounds his trumpet I shall be ready.

Asthma was troubling him. He drew the design for his tombstone, wrote his epitaph—"William Tecumseh Sherman. General U.S.A. Born at Lancaster, O., Feb. 8, 1820. Died at —— —— —. Faithful and Honorable." He ordered that there be a simple military funeral, no exhibition of his body in various cities, no "lying in state," no tombs, mausoleums, or vaults, just a grave beside Ellen's. His niece Eleanor Ewing recalled that he said at this time:

"When I come home these nights, I feel as if Death walked with me and laid his hand upon my shoulder."

What he thought of the hereafter was known only to a few. The clergyman DeWitt Talmage kept a letter Sherman had written him shortly after Ellen's death:

> . . . all my children inherit their mother's faith, and she would have given anything if I would have simply said Amen; but it was simply impossible.
>
> But I am sure that you know that the God who created the minnow and who has molded the rose and the carnation, giving each its sweet fragrance, will provide for those mortal men who strive to do right in the world which He, himself, has stocked with birds, animals and men—at all events I will trust Him with absolute confidence.

In his seventy-first year he still believed that there were cosmic harmonies to be heard if men would listen. He wrote a Southern editor:

> Mathematically the whole is greater than a part, and is worthy of more respect and affection. Instead of boasting of the spot where one is born by an accident over which he has no control, I should suppose the boast would be of the former, that is, every American should be proud of his whole country rather than a part.
>
> How much more sublime the thought that you live at the root of a tree whose branches reach the beautiful fields of Western New York and the

majestic cañons of the Yellowstone, and that with every draught of water you take the outflow of the pure lakes of Minnesota and the drippings of the dews of the Allegheny and the Rocky Mountains.

On February 4, 1891, he gave a box party to army friends at the Casino Theatre in New York, and came home through severe weather to awaken next morning with a cold. He rose, wrote a letter to the Grant Monument committee charging them to remind him in May when the memorial in Chicago would be ready—he wanted to be there—then, against his children's protests, he attended a wedding. The church was chilly. Facial erysipelas developed on the seventh. The next day, his seventy-first birthday, two physicians were called, and the following morning telegrams were sent Minnie, Ellie, and a cable to Tom, who was attending a Jesuit seminary on the Island of Jersey. Tom caught the *Majestic* in England.

On the twelfth the nation knew that Sherman's illness was serious. The Western Union gave its wires free to the family. John Sherman and General Tom Ewing were at the bedside. At 11 A.M. the newspaper men, massed at the door, learned that the general was sinking, and that Roman Catholic priests, who had been coming and going during the past two days, had given him extreme unction. But at 1 P.M. John Sherman telegraphed President Harrison that there was now a chance of recovery. At 1:30 the general crept out of bed and sat in a chair, saying, "Tom, I want to see Tom."

The next day the *New York Times* charged that a priest had been spirited into the house in John Sherman's absence and had given the last rites of the Church to an unconscious man. It declared that John "has never been even lukewarm toward the Roman Catholic Church," that the general had in maturity maintained silent disapproval toward the priesthood, and that he had been outspoken on the subject since "its members crossed his path and persuaded the one of whom he was very fond and for whom he had planned an active public life to become one of their number."

John answered the *Times* immediately, declaring it in error when it insinuated "that advantage was taken of my absence to introduce a Catholic priest into General Sherman's chamber." John declared that while his brother was not a Catholic, he was "too human a man to deny to his children the consolation of their religion," and he added:

> He was insensible, but if he had been in the full exercise of his faculties he would not have denied them. Certainly if I had been present I would have assented to and reverently shared in an appeal to the Almighty for a life here and hereafter of my brother.

The children felt that since their father had been baptized as a boy, he should be given the last rites of the Church even if he had never called himself a Catholic. A priest at the Church of the Blessed Sacrament, from which Father Byrnes had come to give Sherman the death rites, told the *Tribune:*

> Extreme unction is not administered to a person who positively rejects the Catholic Church. It is not withheld, however, from those who profess a leaning toward our Church. . . . I cannot positively say that General Sherman has joined the church but I know Father Taylor visited him just a week ago and talked with him about it. The General spoke of his son who has been in Rome at the Church of the Propaganda and said he was satisfied to have him in the Catholic Church although there were certain doctrines which he himself did not agree to. He said to Father Taylor that he intended looking more deeply into those activities.

Although the erysipelas disappeared on the thirteenth, asthma killed Sherman at ten minutes before two o'clock in the afternoon of February 14. Although he had been able to talk on the thirteenth, it was unlikely that he knew that controversy was raging about him exactly as it had about Old Solitude at the latter's death. He passed with contention clinging to him and with John defending him—his immemorial situation.

For five days his body waited for Tom to arrive. On the eighteenth thousands viewed his remains, old soldiers weeping, mumbling things about Atlanta and Shiloh. He had asked that none but the family view his face when he was dead, but it was felt that so many veterans should not be denied. Undertakers dressed him in his general's uniform with its yellow sash across his breast. Seven tapers in a brass candelabrum threw soft light on the nose that still curved like a cutlass. In the past decade his face had lost many of its seams. Except for the whitening of his beard, he looked almost younger than at forty. On the coffin lay his soldier's cap and sword. A bunch of violets was beside them. While the public streamed past, a woman arranged flowers bearing names from all quarters of the North and West—some from Europe. She was the widow of Little Kil. Heavy booms jingled the saber on the casket lid. Workmen were exploding dynamite in a foundation near by.

Father Tom arrived at 1:30 A.M. on the nineteenth and was taken by his sisters to the casket. "Move the lights closer, I can't see the face," he said. A soldier guard shifted his musket and held the candelabrum nearer. Tom sobbed, yet later in the day he read the funeral service with a clear voice. At the final service fifty choir boys sang "Pie Jesu." Outside on the streets hawkers were shouting, "General Sherman's photograph!" New York was in mourning, flags at half-mast on buildings and ships. G.A.R. members, many of them Sherman's veterans, were in line, uniformed and armed. Behind them were regiments of the National Guard, West Point's cadet corps—30,000 soldiers or ex-soldiers in all. Schofield, Howard, Slocum, Dodge, Corse, were with the family.

The hearse, an artillery caisson, stood at the door. Close to it was a horse bearing the general's saddle, with his boots reversed in the stirrups. Behind waited blocks of carriages—carriages for President Harrison, ex-President Hayes, ex-President Cleveland, the Cabinet, Congressmen, Senators, Governors, mayors, friends. Crowds jammed the sidewalks along the route between the house and the ferry where the casket was to cross to the funeral train that would bear it directly to St. Louis. Sherman's wishes against being exhibited in Washington or any other city were to be obeyed. All eyes were now on the crape-draped door of Sherman's home.

At last one-armed Howard strode out and in a voice as clear at it had been in Carolina, shot an order to the soldiers. They stiffened, their musket butts crashed on the pavement. Out came six sergeants with the coffin on their shoulders, their eyes on the steps down which they came gingerly. A flag covered the casket.

The day was raw and cold. Bareheaded stood the honorary pall-bearers. One was seen by Thackara to bend toward the oldest of the group, a man who had celebrated his eighty-second birthday twelve days earlier. He said:

"General, please put on your hat; you might get sick."

Joe Johnston turned. "If I were in his place and he were standing here in mine, he would not put on his hat." From this last meeting with Sherman, Johnston would not retreat. In his breast as he went home were the seeds of the pneumonia that killed him ten days later.

The coffin was on the caisson. The drums rolled, the fifes began to whine the "Dead March," the banners to wave. Many of these last were only tattered remnants close to the pole, nothing more—battle flags. One band played "Marching Through Georgia," transposed into dirge tempo. Bells tolled all over the city; that of the Scottish Rite Cathedral had only rung once before for a non-Mason—Grant.

The procession—a cavalcade whose trappings and colors exhausted the newspaper writers—wound through packed, hushed streets. In the funeral car, swathed in crape the general's saddle, bridle, boots, and spurs were laid at the foot of the catafalque. His picture was fixed on the engine headlight, and below it, as the train pushed West, his saber swung in the wind.

At crossroads along the route squads of veterans wearing slouch campaign hats held up their old flags as the locomotive came in view. They raised army muskets and volleyed over the passing cars—a blank salute into the sky. Then lowering their empty guns, they watched the train disappear. In towns children sang and waved little flags edged with black. In cities where the train halted, ex-soldiers passed through the car, looking at the coffin, which was not opened.

Another vast processional in St. Louis. Father Tom read the service of the dead at the cemetery where the high ceremonies of Catholicism were performed. "It's a comfort to the children," said John Sherman to General Howard when the latter asked him why the full rites were given a man who had never practiced the religion. David French Boyd wiped his eyes beside the bier, as he thought of seminary days. His hero was gone. Veterans fired three blasts of musket fire over the grave. A bugle blew "Taps." The crowd went away. The general was alone by his Mississippi.

In time stonemasons came and set up the monument Sherman had designed for himself—a simple shaft with draped stone banners on its face and, between them, the insignia he had drawn in 1868 to symbolize the unity of his armies—at the top the swift arrow, badge of Blair's Seventeenth Corps; hanging from it the shield of Schofield's Twenty-third; on the shield the star of Slocum's Twentieth; dangling below, the acorn of Davis's Fourteenth; but standing out at the very heart of the design, the badge of the Fifteenth Corps—a cartridge-box bearing the words that a ragged private had hurled one cold marching day in Tennessee. "Forty Rounds!"

BIBLIOGRAPHY

GENERAL SOURCES

Blaine, J. G., *Twenty Years of Congress,* Norwich, Conn., 1887.
Bok, Edward, *The Americanization of Edward Bok,* N. Y., 1920.
Boyd (D. F.), mss. in possession of Walter L. Fleming, Nashville, Tenn.
Carpenter, F. B., *Six Months in the White House,* N. Y., 1866.
Carr, C. E., *My Day and Generation,* Chicago, 1908.
Cortissoz, Royal, *Life of Whitelaw Reid,* N. Y., 1921, 2 vols.
Ganoe, W. A., *The United States Army,* N. Y., 1924.
Graham, A. A., comp., *History of Fairfield and Perry Counties,* Chicago, 1883.
Hale Papers (E. J.), mss. in possession of North Carolina Historical Commission, Raleigh.
Hamilton, Gail, *James G. Blaine,* Norwich, Conn., 1895.
Hay, John, *Letters of John Hay and Extracts from Diary,* printed but not published, Washington, D. C., 1908, 3 vols.
History of the Ohio Society of New York, ed. by Committee on Publication, N. Y., 1906.
Howe, Henry, *Historical Collections of Ohio,* Norwalk, O., 1889, 2 vols.
Lay Papers (Bishop Henry C.), mss. in possession of University of North Carolina.
McMaster, J. B., *History of the People of the United States,* N. Y., 1891, 8 vols.
Milton, G. F., *The Age of Hate,* N. Y., 1930.
Morrow, Josiah, *Life and Speeches of Thomas Corwin,* Cincinnati, 1896.
Morse, C. F., *Letters,* privately printed, 1898.
Osborn, Hartwell, *Trials and Triumphs,* Chicago, 1904.
Rhodes, J. F., *History of the United States,* N. Y., 1920, 8 vols.
Riddle, A. G., *Life of Benjamin F. Wade,* Cleveland, 1886.
Schurz, Carl, *Reminiscences,* Garden City, N. Y., 1917, 3 vols.
Southern Historical Society, *Papers,* Richmond, 1876-1920, 43 vols.
Spaight, J. M., *War Rights on Land,* London, 1911.
Stanley, H. M., *My Early Travels and Adventures in America and Asia,* London, 1895.
Swain, D. L., mss. Letters and Papers in possession of North Carolina Historical Commission, Raleigh.
Vance, Z. B., Letters, Papers, and Letter-books, in possession of North Carolina Historical Commission, Raleigh.
Villard, Henry, *Memoirs,* Boston, 1904.
Walker, C. M., *History of Athens County, Ohio,* Cincinnati, 1869.
Wiseman, C. M. L., *Centennial History of Lancaster,* Lancaster, O., 1898.
Worth Papers (Jonathan), ed. by J. G. DeR. Hamilton, in North Carolina Historical Commission Publications, Vol. 1, 1909.

WEST POINT

Cullum, G. W., *Biographical Register of Officers and Cadets of the United States Military Academy,* Boston, 1891.
Farley, J. P., *West Point in the Early Sixties,* Troy, N. Y., 1902.
Official Register of the Officers and Cadets of the United States Military Academy, ed. by B. J. D. Irwin, N. Y., 3 pamphlets, 1819-40; 1841-60; 1861-78.
Park, Roswell, *Sketch of the History of West Point,* Phila., 1840.

THE CIVIL WAR

Alexander, E. P., *Military Memoirs of a Confederate,* N. Y., 1907.
Austin, J. P., *The Blue and the Gray,* Atlanta, 1899.
Battles and Leaders of the Civil War, N. Y., 1884, 4 vols.
Beatty, John, *The Citizen-Soldier,* Cincinnati, 1879.
Belknap, C. E., *The War of the Sixties,* N. Y., 1912.
Benton, C. E., *As Seen from the Ranks,* N. Y., 1902.
Bradley, Chaplain G. S., *Notes of an Army Chaplain,* Milwaukee, 1865.
Bricker, William, *A Drummer-Boy's Diary,* St. Paul, 1889.
Brooks, U. R., *Stories of the Confederacy,* Columbus, S. C., 1912.
Byers, S. H. M., *With Fire and Sword,* N. Y., 1911.
Cist, H. M., *The Army of the Cumberland,* N. Y., 1882.
Cobb Papers (Howell), in possession of Miss Mary L. Irwin, Athens, Ga.
Copp, Elbridge, *Reminiscences,* Nashua, N. H., 1911.
Cox, J. D., *Atlanta,* N. Y., 1882.
—— *Reminiscences,* N. Y., 1900, 2 vols.
Cycle of Adams Letters, A, ed. by E. C. Ford, Boston, 1920.
Dana, C. A., *Recollections of the Civil War,* N. Y., 1913.
Davis, Jefferson, *Rise and Fall of the Confederate Government,* N. Y., 1881.
Force, M. F., *Personal Recollections of Vicksburg Campaign,* pamphlet, Cincinnati, 1885.
Freemantle, A. J. L., *Three Months in the Southern States,* Edinburgh, 1863.
French, S. G., *Two Wars,* Nashville, 1901.
Graham (William A.), Letters and Papers, in possession of North Carolina Historical Commission, Raleigh.
Gordon, J. B., *Reminiscences,* N. Y., 1905.
Hamilton, W. D., *Recollections of a Cavalryman,* Columbus, O., 1915.
Hamilton, J. G. DeR., *Reconstruction in North Carolina,* N. Y., 1914.
Hazen, W. B., *Narrative of Military Service,* Boston, 1885.
Hood, J. B., *Advance and Retreat,* New Orleans, 1880.
Howard, C. H., "Capture of Savannah," in *Military Essays and Recollections,* Chicago, 1907, 4 vols.
Jackson, O. L., *The Colonel's Diary,* Sharon, Pa., 1922.
Jamison, M. L., *Recollections,* Kansas City, Mo., 1911.
Johnston, J. E., *Narrative of Military Operations and Recollections,* N. Y., 1874.
Kellogg, F. S., *Mother Bickerdyke,* Chicago, 1907.
Kellogg, J. J., *The Vicksburg Campaign,* pamphlet, Washington, Ia., 1913.
Keyes, E. D., *Fifty Years' Observation of Men and Events,* N. Y., 1885.
King, Charles, *A Boy's Recollections of Our Great Generals,* Loyal Legion Wisconsin Commandery, Papers, Vol. 3, Milwaukee, 1903.
Knox, T. W., *Campfire and Cottonfield,* N. Y., 1865.
Lieber, Francis, *Instructions for the Government of Armies of the United States in the Field,* United States War Department General Order 100, Apr. 24, 1863, pamphlet.
Livermore, T. L., *Numbers and Losses in the Civil War,* Boston, 1900.
Lloyd, E. M., *History of Infantry,* N. Y., 1908.
Lusk, W. T., *War Letters,* privately printed, 1911.
Lyman, Theodore, *Meade's Headquarters,* Boston, 1922.
March, H. O., *The Carolinas,* Loyal Legion, Massachusetts Commandery, Papers, No. 2.
Military Essays and Recollections, Chicago, 1899, 3 vols.
Moore, Frank, *Women in the War,* Hartford, Conn., 1866.
Moore, James, *Kilpatrick and Our Cavalry,* N. Y., 1865.
Nisbet, J. C., *Four Years on the Firing Line,* Chattanooga, 1914.
Official Records of the War of the Rebellion, Washington, 1880-1901, 128 vols.
Page, C. A., *Letters of a War Correspondent,* Boston, 1899.
Porter, D. D., *Incidents and Anecdotes of the Civil War,* N. Y., 1886.
Richardson, A. D., *The Secret Service,* Hartford, Conn., 1865.
Rusling, *Men and Things I Saw* (N. Y.), 1899.
Sherman, W. T., "The Grand Strategy of the War of the Rebellion," in *Century Magazine,* February, 1888.
Society of the Army of the Cumberland, *Reports of the Meetings,* Cincinnati, 30 vols.
Society of the Army of the Potomac, *Reports of the Meetings,* 1880-1915, N. Y.. 4 vols.

Society of the Army of the Tennessee, *Reports of the Proceedings,* Cincinnati, 27 vols.
Sparks from the Camp Fire, Phila., 1899.
Speed, Thomas, *The Union Cause in Kentucky,* N. Y., 1907.
Spencer, C. P., *The Last Ninety Days of the War,* N. Y., 1866.
Stewart, N. B., *Dan McCook's Regiment,* Alliance, O., 1900.
Stillwell, Leander, *The Story of a Common Soldier,* Kansas City, Mo., 1920.
Taylor, B. F., *In Camp and Field,* Chicago, 1875.
Taylor, J. T., *Reminiscences,* Loyal Legion, Kansas Commandery, Papers, April, 1892.
Terrell, W. H. H., *Indiana in the Civil War,* Indianapolis, 1869.
Toombs, Robert, Letters to Alexander H. Stephens, in American Historical Association, *Reports,* 1911.
Townsend, E. D., *Anecdotes of the Civil War,* N. Y., 1884.
Tregevant, D. H., *The Burning of Columbia,* pamphlet, Columbia, S. C., 1886.
Underwood, J. L., *The Women of the Confederacy,* N. Y., 1906.
Victor, O. J., *Incidents and Anecdotes of the War,* Torrey, N. Y., 1862.
Welles, Gideon, *Diary,* Boston, 1911, 3 vols.
Who Burnt Columbia?, pamphlet (containing testimony of Sherman and Howard), Charleston, S. C., 1873.
Wilkie, F. B., *Pen and Powder,* Boston, 1888.
Wilson, J. H., *Under the Old Flag,* N. Y., 1912.
Woodford, Stewart L., "The Story of Fort Sumter," in *Personal Recollections of the Rebellion,* Loyal Legion, New York Commandery, 1891, 4 vols.

REGIMENTAL HISTORIES

Note: Exact titles are not given, except when they are unusual.

Seventh Illinois, by D. L. Ambrose, Springfield, Ill., 1868.
Tenth Illinois, *Memoirs of War,* by Ephraim Wilson, Cleveland, 1893.
Nineteenth Illinois, by J. H. Haynie, Chicago, 1912.
Thirty-fourth Illinois, by E. W. Payne, Clinton, Ia., 1902.
Thirty-sixth Illinois, by L. G. Bennett, Aurora, Ill., 1876.
Fifty-fifth Illinois, Clinton, Mass., 1887.
Fifty-ninth Illinois, by D. Lathrop, Indianapolis, 1865.
Eighty-fifth Illinois, by H. J. Aten, Hiawatha, Kan., 1901.
One Hundred and Third Illinois, C. W. Willis, Washington, 1906.
One Hundred and Fourth Illinois, by W. W. Calkins, Chicago, 1895.
Battery 1, First Illinois Artillery, *Events of the Civil War,* by Edward Bouton, privately printed.
Sixth Indiana, by C. G. Briant, Indianapolis, 1891.
Thirty-first Indiana, by J. T. Smith, Cincinnati, 1900.
Thirty-third Indiana, by J. R. McBride, Indianapolis, 1900.
Thirty-eighth Indiana, by H. F. Perry, Palo Alto, Cal., 1906.
Fifty-first Indiana, by W. D. Hartpence, Cincinnati, 1894.
Fifty-eighth Indiana, by J. J. Hight, Princeton, Ind., 1895.
Seventy-second Indiana, by S. Vater, Lafayette, Ind., 1882.
Eighty-third Indiana, by Joseph Grecian, Cincinnati, 1865.
Fifth Maine, by G. W. Bicknell, Portland, 1871.
First Massachusets, by W. H. Cudworth, Boston, 1866.
Thirty-third Massachusetts, by A. B. Underwood, Boston, 1881.
Fourth Minnesota, by A. L. Brown, St. Paul, 1892.
Missouri Engineer Regiments, by W. A. Neal, Chicago, 1889.
Sixty-ninth New York, *Last Days of the,* by T. F. Meagher, N. Y., 1861.
Seventy-first New York, by Henry Whittemore, 1886.
Seventy-ninth New York Highlanders, by William Todd, Albany, 1886.
Fifteenth Ohio, by Alexis Cope, Columbus, 1916.
Fifty-second Ohio, by J. T. Holmes, Columbus, 1898.
Fifty-third Ohio, by J. K. Duke, Portsmouth, O., 1900.
Seventy-fourth Ohio, by I. S. Owens, Xenia, O., 1872.
Eighty-first Ohio Volunteers, *The Corporal's Story,* by Charles Wright, Phila., 1887.
Eighty-sixth Ohio, by J. N. Ashburn, Cleveland, 1909.
First Rhode Island, by Augustus Woodburt, Providence, 1862.
Company E, Twelfth Wisconsin, privately printed, 1893.

SHILOH

Colby (Enoch), mss., in possession of Chicago Historical Society.
James, A. P., "Shiloh," in American Historical Association, *Reports*, Vol. 1, 1919.
Jordan, Thomas, "Shiloh," in Southern Historical Society, *Papers*, Vol. 8.
Sherman, W. T., "Shiloh," S. A. T., *Reports*, speech April 6, 1881.

SHERMAN'S MARCH TO THE SEA

Boynton, H. B., *Sherman's Historical Raid*, Cincinnati, 1875.
Byers, S. H. M., "The March to the Sea," *North American Review*, September, 1887.
Connolly, J. A., *Major Connolly's Letters*, Illinois State Historical Library, Publication No. 35.
Conyngham, D. P., *Sherman's March through the South*, N. Y., 1865.
Force, M. F., *Marching across the Carolinas*, Loyal Legion, Ohio Commandery, Papers, 1883.
Fuller, J. F., "March to the Sea," S. A. T., *Reports* (1883 reunion).
Hedley, F. Y., *Marching through Georgia*, Chicago, 1890.
Hitchcock, Henry, *Marching with Sherman*, New Haven, Conn., 1927.
Hopkins, C. A., "March to the Sea," Soldiers' and Sailors' Historical Society of Rhode Island, *Personal Narratives*, Third Series, Providence, 1885-87.
Kerr, C. D., "Sherman's Marches," in *Glimpses of the Nation's Struggle*, St. Paul, 1887, 2 vols.
Nichols, G. W., *The Story of the Great March*, N. Y., 1865.
Oakey, Daniel, "Marching through Georgia and the Carolinas," *Century Magazine*, October, 1887.
Slocum, H. W., "Sherman's March," *Century Magazine*, October, 1887.

BIOGRAPHIES

Bragg, Braxton. Seitz, D. C., *Braxton Bragg*, Columbus, S. C., 1924.
Butler, Benjamin F. Butler, B. F., *Ben Butler's Book*, Boston, 1882.
Campbell, John Archibald. Connor, H. S., *John Archibald Campbell*, Boston, 1920.
Chase, Salmon P. Schuckers, J. W., *Life of Salmon P. Chase*, N. Y., 1874.
Dana, Charles A. Wilson, J. H., *Life of Charles A. Dana*, N. Y., 1907.
Davis, Jefferson. Dodd, W. E., *Jefferson Davis*, Phila., 1907.
Grant, Ulysses S. Badeau, Adam, *Grant in Peace*, Hartford, Conn., 1887.
——— *Military History of U. S. Grant*, N. Y., 1881.
—— Church, W. C., *Ulysses S. Grant*, Garden City, N. Y., 1926.
—— Conger, A. L., *The Rise of U. S. Grant*, N. Y., 1930.
—— Coolidge, L. A., *Ulysses S. Grant*, Boston, 1917.
—— Dana, C. A., and Wilson, J. H., *Ulysses S. Grant*, Springfield, Mass., 1909.
—— Eaton, John, *Grant, Lincoln and the Freedmen*, N. Y., 1907.
—— Fuller, J. F. C., *The Generalship of Ulysses S. Grant*, N. Y., 1929.
—— Headley, J. T., *Grant and Sherman*, N. Y., 1865.
—— Grant, U. S., *Personal Memoirs*, Hartford, Conn., 1885.
Howard, O. O. *Autobiography*, N. Y., 1907.
Johnson, Andrew. Welles, Gideon, "Andrew Johnson," *Galaxy Magazine*, Vol. 13.
Johnston, Albert Sidney. Johnston, W. P., *Albert Sidney Johnston*, N. Y., 1878.
Lee, Robert E. Long, A. L., *Memoirs of Robert E. Lee*, N. Y., 1887.
Lincoln, Abraham. Eaton, John, *Grant, Lincoln and the Freedmen*, N. Y., 1907.
—— McClure, A. K., *Abraham Lincoln and Men of War Times*, Phila., 1892.
—— Nicolay, J. G., and Hay, John, *Complete Works of Abraham Lincoln*, N. Y., 1905, 12 vols.
—— Welles, Gideon, "Abraham Lincoln," *Galaxy Magazine*, Vols. 22-24; 41.
Logan, John A. Dawson, G., *Life and Services of General John A. Logan*, Chicago, 1888.
McClellan, George B. *McClellan's Own Story*, N. Y., 1887.
Polk, Leonidas. Polk, W. M., *Life of Leonidas Polk*, N. Y., 1915.
Rawlins, John A. Wilson, J. H., *Life of John A. Rawlins*, N. Y., 1916.
Schofield, John M. Schofield, J. M., *Forty-six Years in the Army*, N. Y., 1897.
Sheridan, Philip H. Hergesheimer, Joseph, *Sheridan*, Boston, 1931.
—— *Personal Memoirs*, N. Y., 1892.
Slocum, Henry W. Slocum, C. E., *Life of Henry W. Slocum*, Toledo, O., 1913.
Smith, Thomas Kilby. Smith, W. G., *Memoir of Thomas Kilby Smith*, N. Y., 1898.
Stanton, Edwin M. Gorham, G. C., *Life of Edwin M. Stanton*, Boston, 1899.
Thomas, George H. Coppee, Henry, *Life of General George H. Thomas*, N. Y., 1893.

—— Piatt, Don, and Boynton, H. V., *General George H. Thomas,* Cincinnati, 1891.
Wallace, Lew. *Autobiography,* N. Y., 1906.
Wheeler, Joseph. Du Bose, J. W., *General Joseph Wheeler,* N. Y., 1912.

SHERMAN AND HIS FAMILY

Thomas Ewing and Sons

Browning, O. H., *Diary* [includes reports of many conversations with Ewing], Illinois State Historical Library Collections, Vol. 20.
Ewing, Thomas, Ewing Papers, in Library of Congress.
—— "Thomas Ewing," in *Bench and Bar of Ohio,* Chicago, 1897.
—— *Autobiography,* pamphlet, Columbus, O., 1912.
—— *Thomas Ewing to Benjamin Stanton,* pamphlet, Columbus, O., 1862.
—— *Memorial of Thomas Ewing,* by Ellen Sherman, N. Y., 1873.
Ewing, Hugh, *Autobiography of a Tramp,* and *Journal,* mss. in possession of Mrs. Udell Ewing Gault, Milford Center, O.
Ewing, General Thomas, Jr., *Address at the Centennial Celebration at Marietta, Ohio, July 5, 1888,* pamphlet.
—— "Speech," May 9, 1892, in *History of the Ohio Society of New York,* N. Y., 1906.
—— "The Struggle for Freedom in Kansas," *Cosmopolitan Magazine,* May, 1894.

John Sherman

Burton, T. E., *John Sherman,* Boston, 1906.
Hinman, W. F., *The Story of the Sherman Brigade,* Alliance, O., 1897.
Sherman, John. *Recollections,* N. Y., 1895.

William Tecumseh Sherman

Audenreid, J. C., "General Sherman in Europe," *Harper's Monthly,* July, September, and October, 1873.
Bowman, S. M., and Irwin R. B., *Sherman and His Campaigns,* N. Y., 1865.
Byers, S. H. M., *Twenty Years in Europe,* N. Y., 1900.
—— "Sherman's Attack at the Tunnel," in *Battles and Leaders,* Vol. 3.
Dodge, G. M., *Personal Recollections of Lincoln, Grant and Sherman,* Council Bluffs, Ia., 1914.
—— *Transcontinental Railways,* S. A. T., *Reports,* 1889.
Fleming, W. L., ed., *General Sherman as a College President,* Cleveland, 1912.
Force, M. F., *General Sherman,* N. Y., 1899.
Halstead, Murat, "Recollections and Letters of General Sherman," *Independent,* June 15-22, 1899.
Hart, Liddell, *Sherman, Soldier, Realist, American,* N. Y., 1929.
Headley, J. T., *Grant and Sherman,* N. Y., 1865.
Headley, P. C., *Life of General Sherman,* N. Y., 1865.
Jenney, W. L., "Reminiscences," in *Military Essays and Recollections,* Vols. 3-4.
Johnson, W. F., *Life of General W. T. Sherman,* Edgewood Publishing Co., 1891.
Keim, Randolph, *Sherman: A Memorial in Art, Oratory and Literature,* Washington, 1904.
Lee, S. D., "Sherman's Meridian Expedition," Southern Historical Society, *Papers,* Vol. 9.
Life and Reminiscences of General W. T. Sherman, by Distinguished Men of His Time, Lenox Publishing Co., 1891.
Markland, A. H., "Recollections of Sherman," S. A. T. *Reports,* 1885.
Marshall, W. L., *Sherman;* Speech, Nov. 8, 1892, Loyal Legion, Minnesota Commandery, Papers.
Shanks, W. G. F., "Recollections of Sherman," *Harper's Monthly,* Vol 30.
Sherman, P. T., *General Sherman in the Last Year of the Civil War,* pamphlet, privately printed, 1908.
Sherman, W. T., "General Sherman in Russia; Extracts from His Diary," *Century Magazine,* March, 1899.
—— *Home Letters,* ed. by M. A. DeW. Howe, N. Y., 1909.
—— *Memoirs,* N. Y., 1875, 2 vols.; Webster, N. Y., 1891, 1 vol.
—— *The Sherman Letters,* ed. by Rachel Sherman Thorndike, N. Y., 1894.
—— Sherman Letter-book, mss. in Library of Congress, 44 vols.
"Sherman's Campaigns in Mississippi in 1864," in Southern Historical Society, *Papers,* Vol. 9.

"Sherman's Method of Making War," Southern Historical Society, *Papers,* Vol. 13.
Smalley, E. V., "General Sherman," *Century Magazine,* Vol. 5.
Wise, John A., *The End of an Era,* Boston, 1899.

PARTICULAR SOURCES

Out of regard for the presumable wishes of the average reader, footnotes have been eliminated from the text of this volume and instead under chapter headings, in the sequence that follows, there have been grouped particular sources for various incidents whose genesis is not apparent in the text.

All references to letters between W. T. and John Sherman are from *The Sherman Letters* collected by Rachel Sherman Thorndike or from the Sherman Letter-book deposited by the Hon. Thomas Ewing in the Manuscript Division of the Library of Congress. Correspondence between W. T. and Ellen Sherman is from *The Home Letters of General Sherman* or from the Sherman Letter-book or the Ewing Papers, the last of which have also been deposited by Mr. Ewing at the Library of Congress. Ellen Sherman's letters to John are to be found in the Sherman Letter-book. All correspondence between Thomas Ewing and Sherman is located in the Ewing Papers and the Sherman Letter-book with the exception of a very few included in *The Home Letters.* Correspondence between members of the Ewing family is from the Ewing Papers or the private collection (at Yonkers, New York) of the Hon. Thomas Ewing, who is for the purpose of distinction referred to hereafter in the notes as Thomas Ewing, III. Grateful acknowledgment is made to Charles Scribner's Sons for permission to quote from *The Home Letters.*

Correspondence between army officers and government officials of both United States and Confederate forces is from the *Official Records of the War of the Rebellion,* which, although voluminous, are published in chronological and well-indexed form under groupings by military campaigns. These are referred to in the notes as O.R. They include the Sherman-Grant correspondence from 1861 to 1865 inclusive. Subsequent references to Sherman-Grant letters are taken from the Sherman Letter-book.

The reader is requested to assume that textual references to the observations of certain individuals, such, for example, as General Howard, Carl Schurz, Colonel Kerr, General Hazen, General Cox, indicate that the material has been taken from the books or articles written by them and so scheduled under General Sources. Likewise the observations of various regiments are from their respective regimental histories as listed in General Sources.

CHAPTERS 1-4

Thomas Ewing's *Autobiography* and *Memorial of Thomas Ewing;* histories of Lancaster and Fairfield and Athens counties; *Bench and Bar of Ohio; General Thomas Ewing's Address; Sherman's Memoirs;* John Sherman's *Recollections.* The last-named contains the statement of the Protestant baptism of Charles R. Sherman's children.

CHAPTER 5: THE REDHEAD CLIMBS THE HILL

Thomas Ewing's statement as to his informal adoption of Tecumseh Sherman, letter to Ellen Sherman, Feb. 13, 1865, Ewing Papers. Added details, also an account of Tecumseh Sherman's baptism into the Roman Catholic Church, were given the author by Thomas Ewing's grandchildren—Thomas Ewing, III; Mrs. E. M. Brown; Sister Philemon, St. Joseph's Hospital, Chicago; Sherman Steele; and the late George W. Ewing. Sherman's description of the religion of Thomas and Maria Ewing, *The Americanization of Edward Bok.* Thomas Ewing on Sherman's boyhood character, *New York Tribune,* Feb. 14, 1891. Hugh Ewing's statements, *Autobiography of a Tramp.* Incidents of Sherman's youth, letters of Mrs. E. M. Brown to author. Description of Aunt Beecher, *Autobiography of a Tramp.* Thomas Ewing's letter to his wife, Dec. 8, 1831, collection of Thomas Ewing, III.

CHAPTER 6: WASHINGTON

John Sherman's statements, his *Recollections.* Sherman on the Wizard of the North, *New York Tribune,* Feb. 12, 1891. Philip H. Sheridan's youth, *Autobiography of a Tramp.* "Old Solitude" nickname, Halstead's *Recollections.* Sherman's trip to Washington, his *Memoirs.*

CHAPTER 7: WEST POINT

Works on the United States Military Academy, as cited in general sources; Cox's *Reminiscences;* Polk's *Life of Leonidas Polk.* Sherman on Thomas's boyhood, S. A. C. Reports, Sherman speech, 1872 reunion.

CHAPTER 8: ELLEN

S. A. French on Grant, his *Two Wars.* Rosecrans on Sherman, Marshall's *Sherman, Speech.* Blaine on Lancaster, Halstead's "Recollections." Ewing's sons' trip to Columbus, Hamilton's *James G. Blaine.* Beecher's death, *Autobiography of a Tramp.* Sherman's letter to Maria Ewing, collection of Thomas Ewing, III.

CHAPTER 9: THE ENCHANTRESS, THE SOUTH

Life in Florida, Sherman's *Memoirs.* Theresa Ewing on Sherman's engagement, statement of Sherman Steele. Sherman on "pretty girl" incident, Sherman Letter-book. Keyes on Sherman and Thomas, Keyes's *Fifty Years.* Sherman, Hugh Ewing, and West Point, *Autobiography of a Tramp.* Bragg-Stewart quarrel, Sherman in *North American Review,* October, 1888.

CHAPTER 10: WITHOUT SMELLING GUNPOWDER

General narrative, Sherman's *Memoirs.* Letter of resignation, Sherman Letter-book. Thomas Ewing and "Ohio wants no sugar plums," statement of the late George W. Ewing. Sherman and Corwin, Johnson's *Sherman.* Henry Clay at Sherman's wedding, letter of Mrs. E. M. Brown to author. Sherman and belle of Monterey, Gertrude Atherton's *Adventures of a Novelist,* N. Y., 1932, p. 189; Sunset Magazine, April, 1916.

CHAPTER 11: THE JONAH OF BANKING

Ewing and $100,000 lawsuit, statements of Thomas Ewing, III, and Sherman Steele. Sherman and personal creditors, Sherman Letter-book; Ewing Papers. Sherman on meeting with Grant, Church's *Ulysses S. Grant.*

CHAPTER 12: DEAD COCK IN THE PIT

Sherman to Cooper, Sherman Letter-book. Sherman to Lucas, Barnard, Alden, Bowie, Buckner, etc., *ibid.* Thomas Ewing, Jr., in Kansas, Ewing's "Struggle for Freedom" and statements of Thomas Ewing, III. Sherman's case in court, his *Memoirs;* Marshall's *Sherman; Speech.*

CHAPTER 13: SOLITUDE AND BANISHMENT

Sherman's business accounts, Sherman Letter-book and collection of Thomas Ewing, III. Sherman-Buell correspondence, Sherman Letter-book. Correspondence with Bragg, Graham, Thomas Ewing, Jr., Minnie Sherman, Fleming's *General Sherman as a College President.* Graham to Moore, *ibid.*

CHAPTER 14-15: WE DESERVE A MONARCH; EACH TO OUR OWN SHIP

Statements of Boyd, the correspondence of Boyd and Sherman, Sherman to Minnie, Bragg to Sherman, Fleming's *General Sherman as a College President.* Sherman on Buell at the War Department, his *Memoirs.* Boyd on Sherman at the reception of South Carolina's secession, Boyd mss. Sherman and Mrs. Bragg, his *Memoirs.* Sherman on Bragg's position in the war, *North American Review,* October, 1888. Sherman to Moore on slavery, his *Memoirs.* Thomas Ewing receives Taylor's version of Bragg's exploit, Browning's *Diary.*

CHAPTER 16: A CHIP ON THE WHIRLING TIDE

Sherman's meeting with Lincoln, his *Memoirs;* John Sherman to A. K. McClure, McClure's *Lincoln and Men of War Times;* Sherman to Boyd, Fleming's *General Sherman as a College President.* Family and business details, Sherman Letter-book; Ewing Papers. Lincoln's comment on the Blairs, John Hay's *Diary.* Toombs on Fort Sumter, Rhodes's *History of the United States,* Vol. 3. Sherman on "war, pestilence and death," statement by Thomas Ewing, III, to author. Sherman to Cameron, Sherman Letter-book. Sherman at St. Louis bloodshed, his *Memoirs.* Sherman-Boyd correspondence, Fleming, *op. cit.*

CHAPTER 17-18: SICKENING CONFUSION; NO MAN CAN SAVE THE COUNTRY

General narrative, Sherman's *Memoirs.* Turner's action, W. T. to John, Sherman Letter-book. Sherman and McDowell conversation, statement of Thomas Ewing, III.

Sherman on Washington sentiment, Halstead's "Recollections." Description of regiments before and during Battle of Bull Run, histories of First Rhode Island, Sixty-ninth New York, Seventy-first New York, Fifth Maine; Victor's *Incidents and Anecdotes of War;* "Ireland and Fontenoy," Lusk's *War Letters;* Lieutenant Cummings's statement made to author in Chicago, 1929. Lincoln's visit, Sherman's *Memoirs.* Northern men and foreigners form rank and file of U. S. Army, statement of U. S. Senator J. W. Nesmith, Jan. 15, 1863, *Congressional Globe.*

CHAPTER 19: I AM TO BE SACRIFICED

General narrative, Sherman's *Memoirs;* O. R. Rousseau on "bloodshed," Richardson's *The Secret Service.* Sergeant's cigar, Shanks's "Recollections." "Old Pills," *ibid.* Sherman and the stovepipe hat, *Battles and Leaders,* Vol. 1, p. 380. Army rations, faulty weapons, Indiana parades and experience of Sergeant William Shaw, McBride's history of the Thirty-third Indiana; Cox's *Reminiscences.* General Dumont, history of the Seventy-second Indiana. Rousseau on the Constitution, Victor's *Incidents and Anecdotes.* Sherman and reporter with Ewing letter, Halstead's "Recollections." Villard's observations, his *Memoirs.* Sherman imprisons reporter, Shanks's "Recollections." Pawnee Indians, *ibid.* Sherman and Cameron, Sherman's *Memoirs.* "Victory or damned badly wounded," W. W. Belknap to Loyal Legion, Iowa Commandery. Blankets and recruit roommates, Kellogg's *War Experiences.*

CHAPTER 20: A LETTER TO LINCOLN

Sherman and Mrs. Ingraham, Shanks's "Recollections." Sherman to Kentucky ladies, *ibid.* Richardson's quotation, his *The Secret Service.* "Sanctified rifles," history of the Fifty-fifth Illinois. Conversation of Sherman and his wife, letter of Mrs. E. M. Brown to author. Ellen to John, Sherman Letter-book. Halstead on "insanity," his "Recollections." Anecdote of Darby, S. A. T. *Reports,* Belknap to the 1885 reunion. Ellen to Lincoln, Sherman Letter-book.

CHAPTER 21: UNCONDITIONAL SURRENDER GRANT

Halleck-Sherman conference, Sherman's *Memoirs.* Grant on Sherman, Grant's *Personal Memoirs.* Sherman, Hazen, Buckner, Hazen's *Narrative.* C. F. Smith on trenches, Grant's *Personal Memoirs;* Richardson's *The Secret Service.* C. F. Adams on trenches, Adams in Cortissoz's *Life of Whitelaw Reid,* Vol. 2, p. 337.

CHAPTER 22: SHILOH, BLOODY SHILOH!

Sherman's wound, Bouton's *Events of the Civil War;* Headley's *Life of Sherman;* Smith's *Memoir of Thomas Smith;* Grant's *Personal Memoirs;* Richardson's *The Secret Service.* Quotations of Confederates, Jordan in Southern Historical Society, *Papers;* Dubose's *General Joseph Wheeler;* O. R. Statement of Major Whitfield, history of the Fifty-fifth Illinois. "Johnnies thicker than Spanish needles," Wallace's *Autobiography.* Grant on fugitives, his *Personal Memoirs.* John Day quoted, *New York Tribune,* Sept. 26, 1903. Sherman on horrors, S. A. P. speech and the *Reports,* discussion, 1887 reunion. Charging lines shake like loose rope, Jackson's *The Colonel's Diary.* Anecdotes of Waterhouse's Battery, Colby mss. Sherman to Fry, Sherman Letter-book, Sept. 3, 1884. Anecdote of J. Ammen, Beatty's *The Citizen-Soldier.* Sherman meets Rousseau's Brigade, Shanks's "Recollections." Beauregard and Bragg sleep in Sherman's tent, S. A. T., *Reports,* Sherman at the 1881 reunion. Sherman quoted, "Take regiment back to Ohio," Wallace's *Autobiography.* Sherman's loss of horses, J. T. Taylor's *Reminiscences.* Lieut. Stevenson and gully of blood, Stevenson in *American History Told by Contemporaries,* edited by A. B. Hart, N. Y., 1901, Vol. 4.

CHAPTER 23: AS SMART AS TOWN FOLKS

Anecdote of Sherman and the sutler's cheese, S. A. T., *Reports,* Sherman at the 1881 reunion. Woodpeckers to feed Sherman's children, Carr's *My Day and Generation.* Sherman persuades Grant to remain, Sherman's *Memoirs.* Jeff Thompson's poem, Richardson's *The Secret Service.* Data on Sibley tents, Brown's history of the Fourth Minnesota. Rosecrans and pup tents, Beatty's *The Citizen-Soldier.* Shell through tent door, *ibid.* Rousseau and Nelson on Sherman, Headley's *Life of Sherman.* Sherman befriends Sheridan, Sherman's *Memoirs.* Norton's comment on Sherman's literary ability, Fiske's *The Mississippi Valley in the Civil War.* Officers sell beer, Beatty's *The Citizen-Soldier.*

CHAPTER 24: WE CAN MAKE WAR TERRIBLE

Sherman's Memphis administration, O. R., Vol. 17, Part 2. Anecdote of Sherman and slaveholder, "set machine running again," Richardson's *The Secret Service.*

CHAPTER 25: THE VULTURES ARE LOOSE

Conversations involving Porter, Porter's *Incidents and Anecdotes.* Knox incident, Sherman's *Memoirs;* Shanks's "Recollections"; S. A. T., *Reports,* A. H. Markland letter, to the 1885 reunion; S. A. P., *Reports,* speech of Slocum at the 1891 reunion; Knox's *Campfire and Cottonfield;* Wilkie's *Pen and Powder;* O. R., Vol. 17, Part 2. Thomas Ewing to Browning, Browning's *Diary.* Chickasaw expedition, Sherman's *Memoirs;* Grant's *Personal Memoirs;* G. W. Morgan in *Battles and Leaders,* Vol. 3; Welles's *Diary.* McClernand's actions and correspondence, O. R., Vol. 17, Part 2; Coolidge's *Ulysses S. Grant;* Grant's *Personal Memoirs;* Nicolay and Hay's *Abraham Lincoln; Battles and Leaders,* Vol. 3, p. 450; Wilson's *Under the Old Flag;* Wilson's *Life of Rawlins;* Terrell's *Indiana in the Civil War* contains letters of O. P. Morton to Lincoln describing sentiment of Northwest on need for Vicksburg's capture.

CHAPTER 26: I TREMBLE FOR THE RESULT

Plague of gnats, Force's *Personal Recollections.* W. P. Mellen on Grant, Shuckers's *Life of Chase;* Medill to Colfax, Rhodes's *History of the United States,* Vol. 4, p. 222. Lincoln on Grant's lack of friends, Helen Nicolay's *Personal Traits of Lincoln,* N. Y., 1912. Sherman on river during passage of batteries, his *Memoirs* and *Home Letters;* Porter's *Incidents and Anecdotes.* Sherman congratulates Grant on campaign, Rusling's *Men and Things.*

CHAPTER 27: THIS FELLOW MC CLERNAND

Sherman and Davis's book, Sherman's *Memoirs.* McClernand and Wilson, Wilson's *Life of Rawlins;* Wilson's *Under the Old Flag.* Hugh Ewing and the wooden bridge, statement to author by the late George W. Ewing, son of Hugh Ewing. Orion P. Howe incident, history of the Fifty-fifth Illinois. Pemberton on end of career, S. H. Lockett in *Battles and Leaders,* Vol. 3. Military movements, Sherman's *Memoirs;* Grant's *Personal Memoirs;* Johnston's *Narrative;* "Vicksburg Campaign" in *Battles and Leaders,* Vol. 3. J. E. Griffith's feat, Belknap's *The War of the Sixties.* Rawlins to Grant on drinking, Piatt and Boynton's *George H. Thomas.*

CHAPTER 28: MANY SOLDIERS

Military movements and Lockett reference, the same as in Chapter 27. Irishman hit by clod, history of the Twelfth Wisconsin. Sherman-Boyd incident, Marshall's *Sherman; Speech,* "Many soldiers" letter, O. R., Vol. 24, Part 3.

CHAPTER 29: THEY CRY ALOUD FOR MERCY

Jenney quotations, his *Reminiscences.* Markland on McPherson, S. A. T., *Reports,* Markland's letter to the 1885 reunion. Markland on the United States mails, *ibid.* Sherman on Vicksburg's fall as justifying end of war, Dodge's *Personal Recollections.* Anecdote of baby named for Sherman, history of the Fifty-fifth Illinois. Sherman and Grant on private property and Negroes, O. R., Vol. 30, Part 3.

CHAPTER 30: BLOWS THICK AND FAST

Fight at Colliersville, Jenney's *Reminiscences;* Duke's history of the Fifty-third Ohio; Sherman's *Memoirs.*

CHAPTER 31: VISIBLE INTERPOSITION OF GOD

Sherman to Hurlbut, O. R., Vol. 31, Part 1. Sherman to Chase, *ibid.* Battle of Chattanooga, articles by Grant, Byers, W. F. Smith, J. F. Fullerton, in *Battles and Leaders,* Vol. 3; Sherman's *Memoirs.* Sherman on "greedy rascals," O. R., Vol. 31, Part 3. Sherman on "quicker you build railroads quicker you eat," S. A. C., *Reports,* 1903 reunion, p. 101. Anecdotes of pickets, Gordon's *Reminiscences;* Grant's *Personal Memoirs.* Anecdote of Sherman and Thomas and Bragg's letter, Sherman to J. A. Garfield, July 28, 1870, Sherman Letter-book. Sherman to Smith, "I can do it," Wilson's *Under the Old Flag.* Taunts between Western and Eastern troops, history of the Fifty-fifth Illinois; *New York Herald,* Apr. 18, 1864. Dana on "lamentable blunder," O. R., Vol. 31, Part 2. Thomas on Orchard Knob as cemetery, Piatt and Boynton's

General George H. Thomas. Eclipse of moon, Connolly's *Letters;* report of Maj. Gen. P. R. Cleburne, O. R., Vol. 31, Part 2, p. 749. Byers on Sherman at river, *Battles and Leaders,* Vol. 3. Sherman's conversation with Hugh Ewing, Shanks's "Recollections." Sherman on Grant, "I thought the old man daft," Rusling's *Men and Things*. Dispute as to Bragg's reënforcement of right wing, Howard's *Autobiography;* Hazen's *Narrative;* Alexander's *Military Memoirs;* Sherman's *Memoirs;* Grant's *Personal Memoirs*. Sheridan and whisky flask, Dana's *Recollections;* Taylor's *In Camp and Field*. Men throw haversacks in air, Bennett's history of the Thirty-sixth Illinois. Sheridan and Hazen quarrel, *ibid*. Howard and the dying soldier, Underwood's history of the Thirty-third Massachusetts. Chaplain Stewart and the moon, Stewart's *Dan McCook's Regiment*. Confederates quoted, "We could see too much," Nisbet's *Four Years*.

CHAPTER 32: PREPARE THEM FOR MY COMING

Sherman on "twelve thousand of our fellow-soldiers," his *Memoirs*. Soldiers and molasses barrels, Nisbet's *Four Years*. "Gander dances," etc., Underwood's history of the Thirty-third Massachusetts. Negro on sleeping in sunshine, Stewart's *Dan McCook's Regiment*. Savior in stable, Wilson's *Memoirs of War*. Sherman in Nashville, Dodge's *Personal Recollections*. Hooker to Chase, O. R., Vol. 32, Part 2. Sherman's Memphis speech, *Sherman Letters; Home Letters;* Sherman to Halleck, Jan. 29, 1864, in O. R. S. D. Lee on Meridian, Southern Historical Society, *Papers,* Vol. 8. Polk quoted, letter of Dec. 23, 1863, in O. R.

CHAPTER 33: THE MAN ON HORSEBACK

Sherman on infantry waiting for cavalry, and "infantry can always whip cavalry," Sherman's letters to Buckland and Steedman in O. R., Vol. 32, Part 2. Farm boys avoid cavalry, Piatt and Boynton's *General George H. Thomas*. Meigs on ruin of horses, in O. R., Vol. 23, Part 2, letter to Rosecrans. Sooy Smith's loss of horses, letter of Sherman, Apr. 9, 1864, in O. R., Vol. 32, Part 3. Cox on cavalry, his *Reminiscences*. Long on Stuart, Long's *Memoirs of R. E. Lee*. Major McClellan on Stuart and Lee, letter of Gen. T. T. Munford, C. S. A., July 22, 1915, to Mrs. C. H. Hyde, Lookout Mountain, Tenn., in possession of Mrs. Hyde. Sherman on "prudence and caution" of cavalry, letter of July 7, 1864, in O. R., Vol. 38, Part 5. Grant on Wheeler, letter to Sherman in O. R., Vol. 32, Part 2. Sherman on Wheeler and Hampton, letter to Grant, Mar. 24, 1865, in O. R. Hill on cavalry, in O. R., Vol. 41, Part 2. Vance on cavalry, Hamilton's *Reconstruction in North Carolina*. Sergeant Sleeper on cavalry, in O. R., Vol. 32, Part 2. Major Ewing on cavalry, in O. R., Vol. 38, Part 5. *Richmond Examiner* on cavalry, Oct. 19, 1864. Sherman to Thomas on spies, in O. R., Vol. 32, Part 3. Sherman on "beginning of end," S. A. T., *Reports,* Sherman at the 1889 reunion. R. E. Lee opposes repeating rifles, Lloyd's *History of Infantry*.

CHAPTER 34: THE BEAUTY OF TIME

Sherman on McPherson's marriage, in O. R., Vol. 32, Part 3; S. A. T., *Reports,* Willard Warner at the 1891 reunion. Sherman on Logan-Thomas quarrel, in O. R., Vol. 32, Part 3; Sherman's *Memoirs;* correspondence of Sherman and Logan in Dawson's *Life of Logan*. Sherman and Hovey dispute, Cox's *Reminiscences*. Hazen on the Army of Tennessee, Hazen's *Narrative*. Sherman and Davis on Howard's piety, Schurz's *Reminiscences*. McClellan on Sunday observances, Howard's *Autobiography*. Sherman on food of horses and men, in O. R., Vol. 32, Part 3, letter of Apr. 25. Sherman to Lincoln on food for East Tennessee, in O. R., Vol. 38, Part 4. Sherman on conduct of railroad and on appeals to Guthrie, in O. R., Vol. 32, Part 3. Sherman on Fort Pillow, etc., *ibid*. Hickenlooper on Sherman's clerical preparation, S. A. T., Hickenlooper at the 1891 reunion. Anecdote of Dr. Mary Walker, history of the Fifty-second Ohio. Grant on Sherman, "He bones all the time," Howard's *Autobiography*. Forrest's faulty spelling, Appleton's *Cyclopedia of American Biography*. Sherman's letter to Dana on "beautiful harmony in life" during peace, Dana's *Recollections*.

CHAPTER 35: TERRIBLE DOOR OF DEATH

Sherman quoted, "I've got Joe Johnston dead," Du Bose's *General Joseph Wheeler*. Soldiers wonder if Sherman must march all night, Bricker's *Drummer-Boy's Diary*. Baptism of Hood and Johnston, Du Bose, *op. cit*. Death of Polk, *ibid*. Schofield on character of men, his *Forty-six Years*. Sherman on telegraph operators, his *Memoirs,* 4th ed., Chapter 25. Sherman loses facial twitching, Benton's *As Seen from the Ranks*. Sherman on "Now what is Johnston's game?" Cox's *Reminiscences*. Adventure of the Rev. E. P. Smith, Howard's *Autobiography*. Mrs. Bickerdyke anecdotes, Kellogg's *Mother Bickerdyke;* Moore's *Women in the War;* S. A. T., *Reports,* speeches regarding her at the 1886 and 1901 reunions.

CHAPTER 36: BIG INDIAN WAR

Sherman on youthful explorations around Kenesaw, Byers's *Twenty Years in Europe.* Sherman on temperance, Howard's *Autobiography.* Blair's men and apples, Hedley's *Marching through Georgia.* Sherman and Lessoffski, S. A. T., *Reports,* Sherman at the 1867 reunion. Description of Dilger, Hinman's *Story of the Sherman Brigade;* Bradley's *Notes of an Army Chaplain;* Cope's history of the Fifteenth Ohio. Sherman on battles fighting themselves, Hedley's *Marching Through Georgia.* Sherman's later views on Forrest and Sturgis, P. T. Sherman to author.

CHAPTER 37: WITH BOOTS ON

Sherman and the Kenesaw peach orchard, Smalley in *Century Magazine,* Vol. 5. Dan McCook at battle, Appleton's Cyclopedia of American Biography. Sherman's "trumpeters," S. A. T., *Reports,* Admiral J. L. Worden at the 1873 reunion. Johnston on Federal engineers bathing with Confederate pickets, dispatch of July 11, in O. R., Vol. 38, Part 5. Anecdote, "Rob cradle and grave," history of the Seventy-second Indiana. Howell Cobb on invaders, Cobb Papers. Sherman bathing in river, Payne's history of the Thirty-fourth Illinois. Kentucky colonel on Hood's poker traits, Hedley's *Marching through Georgia.* Johnston-Davis correspondence, O. R., Vol. 35, Part 5. Sherman's tribute to the Army of the Tennessee, S. A. T., *Reports,* Sherman's speech at the 1867 reunion. Schofield on McPherson's marriage, Schofield's *Forty-six Years.* Sherman and McPherson, Sherman's *Memoirs.* W. W. Belknap at battle, S. A. T., *Reports,* M. D. Leggett at the 1883 reunion. Sherman and "close shaving," Conyngham's *Sherman's March.* Sherman teases soldier, *ibid.* Sherman to Warner, S. A. T., *Reports,* Warner at the 1891 reunion. Thompson's letter to Sherman on McPherson's death, S. A. T., *Reports,* Sherman's letter to the 1878 reunion. Comparison of mortality in armies of respective generals, computed from Livermore's *Numbers and Losses.*

CHAPTER 38: CHANGE FRONT ON WASHINGTON

Military movements based on memoirs of Sherman, Cox, Howard, Johnston, Hood; Force's *General Sherman;* Dawson's *Life of Logan;* Cox's *Atlanta;* O. R., Vol. 35, Part 5. Conversation of Dodge and Sherman, S. A. T., *Reports,* Dodge to the 1889 reunion. Sherman-Thomas conversation regarding the Army of the Tennessee commander, Dawson's *Life of Logan;* Sherman's *Memoirs;* Cox's *Reminiscences.* Hovey-Osterhaus incident, in O. R., Vol. 38, Part 5; Cox's *Reminiscences.* Sherman and the seidlitz powder, *Sparks from the Camp Fire.* Negro soldiers and bayonet, A. R. Abbott in *Military Essays,* Vol. 3. Sherman to Spooner, in O. R., Vol. 38, Part 5. New England manufacturers' lobby for Negro recruiting bill, Halleck to Sherman, O. R., Vol. 38, Part 5, p. 857. Sherman on Kentucky guerrillas, in O. R., Vol. 39, Part 2.

CHAPTER 39: GLORIOUS LAUGHTER

"Enough for another killing," Cox's *Atlanta.* Shell-Anna anecdote, Dawson's *Life of Logan.* Sherman's "nose like a cutlass," Hedley's *Marching through Georgia.* Sherman on food and health of men, his *Memoirs,* 4th ed., Chapter 25. Soldiers and beans, etc., Bricker's *Drummer-Boy's Diary.* Kilpatrick's character, Moore's *Kilpatrick;* Wilson's *Under the Old Flag.* Johnston on "Sherman's one mistake," Lay Papers. Hood fooled by Sherman, T. B. Roy in Southern Historical Society, *Papers,* Vol. 8. C. F. Adams, Jr., on Sherman, *A Cycle of Adams Letters.*

CHAPTER 40: WAR IS WAR

Sherman and Bishop Lay, Lay Papers. C. F. Adams, Jr., on Sherman's letter, *A Cycle of Adams Letters.* Lincoln to Sherman, Sept. 14, 1864, Nicolay and Hay's *Complete Works of . . . Lincoln.*

CHAPTER 41: I CAN MAKE GEORGIA HOWL

References to Hitchcock, Hitchcock's *Marching with Sherman.* Howell Cobb on demoralization, Cobb Papers. Sherman's decision to "apply the rod," his speech in St. Louis, 1865, quoted in Dodge's *Personal Reminiscences.* Vance letter, Vance Papers. Sherman's negotiation for Georgia's surrender, Austin's *The Blue and the Gray;* Sherman's *Memoirs.* Toombs to Stephens, American Historical Association, *Reports,* Vol. 2, 1911. Sherman to Wilson on Grant's character, Wilson's *Under the Old Flag.* Battle of Allatoona, in O. R., Vol. 39, Part 3; Brown's history of the Fourth Minnesota; Ambrose's history of the Seventh Illinois; article of G. W. Hill, Rhode Island Soldiers' and Sailors' Historical Society, 4th Series, No. 13; French's *Two Wars;* S. A. T., *Reports,* Warner at the 1891 reunion.

CHAPTER 42: THE ANGEL OF THE LORD

"Sherman has big head," S. A. T., *Reports,* Gen. R. A. Alger at the 1887 reunion. W. P. Howard's report on Atlanta destruction, *Macon Telegraph,* Dec. 10, 1864. Northwesterners "damn the Negro," Spencer's *Last Ninety Days.* Sherman on Wisconsin's superiority, his *Memoirs,* 4th ed., Chapter 25. German regiments, Capt. William Vocke in *Military Essays.* "God has put hook in Sherman's nose," Rhodes's *History of the United States,* Vol. 5.

CHAPTER 43: THE BESOM OF DESTRUCTION

Sherman on "old West Point notion" of pillage, his letter to J. B. Fry, Sept. 3, 1884, in Sherman Letter-book. Vengeance of Missouri regiments, Neal's history of the Missouri Engineer Regiments. Federals smash pianos, Underwood's history of the Thirty-third Massachusetts. Toombs to Stephens, American Historical Association, *Reports,* Vol. 2, 1911. Report of Medical Director, Army of the Tennessee, D. L. Huntington in O. R., Vol. 44. Sherman listens to band, Headley's *Life of Sherman.* "Lincoln gimlets," Underwood, *op. cit.* Confederates quoted on resistance, in O. R., Vol. 44. Sherman on rape, his deposition in *Who Burnt Columbia?*

CHAPTER 44: A MAN DOWN SOUTH

Delegation of Philadelphians and Grant, Wallace's *Autobiography.* John Sherman and Lincoln, McClure's *Abraham Lincoln.* Carpenter's observations, his *Six Months in the White House.* Lincoln on Sherman in message to Congress; original mss. of message, showing correction, in possession of Oliver R. Barrett. Sherman on "devilish" destruction, Jackson's *The Colonel's Diary.* Wellington and torpedoes, Sherman quoted in *Life and Reminiscences of Sherman, by Distinguished Men.* Sherman to Steedman, Bowman's *Sherman and His Campaigns.* Sherman at Fort McAlister, Howard's "Capture of Savannah." Markland and Sherman, S. A. T., *Reports,* Markland to the 1885 reunion. McClellan on torpedoes, *McClellan's Own Story.* Sheridan and torpedoes, Hergesheimer's *Sheridan,* p. 184.

CHAPTER 45: REPOSE OF THE TIGER

Sherman to Dayton, Johnson's *Sherman,* p. 584. Sherman's Christmas telegram to Lincoln, Sherman's *Memoirs.* Sherman protects wives of Confederates, *ibid.;* statement to author of William Harden, president of the Savannah Historical Society. Mayor's horses stolen, *idem. London Times,* article of Apr. 5, 1865, reprinted in *Chicago Tribune,* Apr. 25, 1865. Sherman on prayers for Jeff Davis and the devil, Calkins's history of the One Hundred and Fourth Illinois. Henry Adams on Sherman, *A Cycle of Adams Letters.* Sherman on his children, Howard's *Autobiography.*

CHAPTER 46: INEVITABLE SAMBO

Butler's "fizzle," Headley's *Life of Sherman.* Sherman to Halleck on Jeff C. Davis's repulse of Negroes, in O. R., Vol. 47, Part 2, letter of Jan. 12, 1865. Sherman on his own ignorance of plans for Negro votes, his *Memoirs,* Vol. 2, p. 245. Sherman's letter to Georgians, "My opinion is no negotiation necessary," Bowman's *Sherman and His Campaigns,* p. 326. Stanton sanctions policy, Sherman's *Memoirs.* Sherman's testimony before Committee on the Conduct of the War, reprinted in Nichols's *The Story of the Great March.* J. E. Johnston on impossibility of Sherman's march, Force's *Marching Across the Carolinas.* Sherman to Foster, "I will shake tree, you pick up the apples," quoted by S. L. Woodford in *Personal Recollections of Rebellion,* Vol. 1.

CHAPTER 47: HELL-HOLE OF SECESSION

Sherman on "taunting messages" and Southerners "scared by their own inventions," his *Memoirs.* Sherman to Mrs. Carson, letter in possession of Professor Yates Snowden, University of South Carolina. Surgeon John Moore on wounds, his report on Carolina campaign in O. R. Mower's three sets of staff officers in heaven, Underwood's history of the Thirty-third Massachusetts. Johnston on Sherman's and Caesar's armies, S. A. T., *Reports,* speech of J. D. Cox at the 1881 reunion. Sherman on absence of coughs, *Home Letters.* Sherman on wounds and soldiers' attitude toward death, *Memoirs,* 4th ed., Chapter 25. Dr. Anderson and legend of organized theft, E. J.

Hale letter to Mrs. Cornelia Spencer, Hale Papers. Sherman takes rug, his *Memoirs*. Sherman on Wellington's plunder, S. A. T., *Reports,* Sherman at the 1881 reunion. Sherman on Eighth Missouri plunder, *ibid.* Sherman and Hampton correspondence, in O. R., Vol. 47, Part 1.

CHAPTER 48: GOD ALMIGHTY STARTED WIND

Vance's call, in O. R. Sherman on Hampton's bombardment near Columbia, Sherman's testimony in *Who Burnt Columbia?* Reference to Major Chambliss, in O. R., Vol. 53, p. 1050. Colonel Stone on drunkenness, in O. R., Vol. 47, Part 1. Account of fire, Sherman's *Memoirs;* Hazen's *Narrative;* pamphlet collection of the University of South Carolina; *Report of the Committee to Collect Testimony,* Bryan Printing Co., Columbia, 1903. Hampton's order to burn cotton, Tregevant's *The Burning of Columbia.* Ruse of Baptist sexton, told to author as folk tale by Professor D. D. Wallace, Wofford College, Spartansburg, S. C.

CHAPTER 49: SPLENDID LEGS

Sherman to Blair on payment for food in North Carolina, in O. R., Vol. 47, Part 2. Col. Archer Anderson on Sherman's demoralization of Lee's army, Anderson's speech, May 29, 1890, quoted in Spaight's *War Rights on Land.* Lee to Vance, O. R., Vol. 47, Part 2. *London Times* article on Sherman quoted in *Chicago Tribune,* Apr. 25, 1865, and *New York World,* Apr. 27, 1865. Sherman on "highest pleasure of war," his *Memoirs,* 4th ed., Chapter 25. Death of Willie Hardee, Howard's *Autobiography.* "Splendid legs" incident, Force's *Marching Across the Carolinas;* Sherman to Low, in O. R., Vol. 47, Part 3.

CHAPTER 50: MR. LINCOLN SPEAKS PRIVATELY

Porter's account of meeting on *River Queen,* mss. by Porter, in possession of the Chicago Historical Society. Lincoln authorizes Sherman to deal with Vance, Sherman's *Memoirs.* Lincoln quoted, "My God, my God," and, "Do you know why I took a shine to Grant and you?" S. A. T., *Reports,* Sherman to the 1887 reunion. Lincoln "unbeknown" anecdote, Sherman's *Memoirs.* Mrs. Grant quoted, *ibid.* Lyman on Sherman, Lyman's *Meade's Headquarters.* Sheridan's visit, Sheridan's *Personal Memoirs.* Grant quoted on reasons for wishing victory without help from West, his *Personal Memoirs.* Sherman on Lincoln's greatness, Sherman's *Memoirs.*

CHAPTER 51: SIC SEMPER TYRANNIS

John Sherman on W. T. Sherman's talk with him aboard the *Bat,* McClure's *Abraham Lincoln,* p. 220. Markland on talk with Sherman at New Berne, S. A. T., *Reports,* Markland to the 1885 reunion. Actions of J. E. Johnston, Vance, Graham, Swain, in peace negotiations, Swain Papers; Vance Papers; Hale Papers; Worth Papers; Graham Letters; letter collections of Mrs. Cornelia Spencer; pamphlet and newspaper clipping collections of Fred A. Olds, custodian of the Museum of the North Carolina Historical Commission; Spencer's *Last Ninety Days;* Sherman's *Memoirs.* General Hoke to Professor Hamilton on Vance, statement of Hamilton to author. Sherman's receipt of news of Lincoln's death, Sherman's *Memoirs.* Sherman-Johnston conference, Johnston's *Narrative;* Sherman's *Memoirs;* Sherman's testimony before Committee on the Conduct of the War as reprinted in Nichols's *The Story of the Great March.* Kilpatrick's loss of trousers to Hampton, Du Bose's *General Joseph Wheeler.*

CHAPTER 52: I AM NOT STONE

Swain and Vance on Confederate depredations, in O. R., Vol. 47, Part 3. Johnston-Sherman conference, Sherman's *Memoirs;* Johnston's *Narrative.* Johnston-Sherman-Breckinridge anecdotes, Wise's *The End of an Era.* Sherman to S. L. Fremont, in O. R., Vol. 47, Part 3.

CHAPTER 53: SHERMAN HAS FATALLY BLUNDERED

Campbell on conferences with Lincoln, Connor's *John Archibald Campbell.* Correspondence on Weitzel incident, in O. R., Vol. 46, Part 3. Butler on paper circulated among Sherman's officers, *Ben Butler's Book.* Stanton's excuse for attacking Sherman-Johnston terms, Gorham's *Life of Stanton;* Gorham to McClure in McClure's *Abraham Lincoln.* Grant on Lincoln's February peace terms, his *Personal Memoirs.* Stanton's mutilation of telegrams, comparison of original messages in O. R., Vol. 47, Part 3, with newspaper publication on obvious dates.

CHAPTER 54: HORRID DEFORMITIES

Johnston to Sherman on the latter's "enlarged patriotism," transcript from copy of original made by Fred A. Olds, custodian of the Museum of the North Carolina Historical Commission. Wilson feeds Southern civilians, in O. R., Vol. 49, Part 2. Thomas curtails feeding, *ibid.* Davis's specie consists of $500,000, Dodd's *Jefferson Davis.* Correspondence of Sherman and Chase at Morehead City, in O. R., Vol. 47, Part 3; Schuckers's *Life of Chase.* Thomas Ewing on Stanton's motives, Ewing to S. M. Bowman, Dec. 1, 1865, Ewing Papers. John Sherman to Stanton on "rebellion should wear the badge of the penitentiary," Gorham's *Life of Stanton.*

CHAPTER 55: THE CUD OF BITTER FANCY

Sherman to Halleck's widow, letter of May 16, 1873, Sherman Letter-book. Westerners compare Richmond's defenses with Atlanta's, Aten's history of the Eighty-fifth Illinois. Hugh Ewing's comment on Sherman, May 20, 1865, mss. in possession of Mrs. Udell Ewing Gault. Sherman to Van Vliet, in O. R., Vol. 47, Part 3. Sherman examined by Senator Ben Wade, Sherman's testimony before the Committee on the Conduct of the War, in Nichols's *The Story of the Great March.* Markland asks Sherman for permission to "tell the truth," S. A. T., *Reports,* Markland's letter to the 1885 reunion. Porter quoted on Sherman's terms as "exactly in accordance with Mr. Lincoln's wishes," Porter to Healey, mss. in possession of the Chicago Historical Society.

CHAPTER 56: HAPPIEST MOMENT OF MY LIFE

Sherman on Eastern "gawks" and "pampered bands," the S. A. P., *Reports,* Sherman to the 1890 reunion. Conversation with Meade, *ibid.,* Meade on losses of the Army of the Potomac, *ibid.,* Meade to the 1871 reunion. Hazen and haircuts of the Fifteenth Corps, Hazen's *Narrative.* Sherman "dressed up after dingy carelessness," Hedley's *Marching through Georgia.* Girls supply ice water, Jackson's *The Colonel's Diary.* Sherman on "the happiest moment of my life," speech of Dodge in Keim's *Sherman; A Memorial,* p. 54. Dana's description of Seward, Wilson's *Life of Dana.* Tom Corwin on "lords of the world," *New York Times,* May 27, 1865. German ambassador on army corps, Stewart's *Dan McCook's Regiment.* Dana on Charles Sherman's attempts to "stir up quarrel," Wilson, *op. cit.* Sherman on soldiers and street car, Carr's *My Day and Generation.*

CHAPTER 57: LEAR ROARING AT THE STORM

Johnson's return to Lincoln's policy, summary from Johnson's correspondence in Milton's *The Age of Hate.* Ewing distrusts Chase, Browning's *Diary.* Sherman's letter declining invitation to New York meeting, *New York World,* June 8, 1865. Description of meeting, *New York Herald,* June 9, 1865. Sherman in New York, *New York World,* June 2, 1865. Sherman meets General Scott, *New York Herald,* June 6, 1865. T. B. Bryan on Sherman's kissing of girls, in *Military Essays,* Vol. 3. Sherman kissing girls at Indianapolis, statement to author of Evangeline E. Lewis, Pendleton, Ind. Sherman at Chicago Sanitary Fair, *Chicago Tribune,* June 9-17, 1865; *Chicago Times, idem.* Sherman's speech at Lancaster, Bowman's *Sherman and His Campaigns.* Duff Green to President Johnson, Milton's *The Age of Hate.* Sherman's speech at St. Louis, Dodge's *Personal Recollections.* Sherman urges moderate views on Congressmen and Senators, Johnson Papers, quoted in Milton's *The Age of Hate,* p. 287. Sherman and Indian discuss cannon, *Life and Reminiscences of Sherman, by Distinguished Men,* p. 98. Sherman, Grant, and Stanton in tenure-of-office difficulty, Sherman's *Memoirs; Sherman Letters; Home Letters.* Sherman's correspondence with Grant, Sherman's *Memoirs.* Sherman to Ewing on Johnson, *Home Letters.*

CHAPTER 58: NO HONORABLE MAN WILL BE TOLERATED

Sherman to Grant on Indians, Senate Executive Document No. 13, Fortieth Congress, 1st Session; House Executive Document No. 23, Thirty-ninth Congress, 2nd Session. Sherman's speech to Indians, Stanley's *My Early Travels.* Sherman to Henry Ward Beecher, Mar. 7, 1879, Sherman Letter-book. Sherman on Civil War training for railroad men, Dodge's *Personal Recollections.* Sherman and Grant on hobbies, Sherman's *Memoirs.* Sherman's prophecy on Thomas's fame in the South, S. A. C., *Reports,* 1879 reunion. Logan and Sherman in Congressional battle over army appropriation bill, *Congressional Globe,* February-April, 1870. Sherman on Healy's portraits, letter to John, Sherman Letter-book. Sherman's Nov. 30 letter on Grant, *ibid.* Sherman to John and to C. W. Eliot, *ibid.* Sherman's letter on Grant as "not a saint," Sept. 12, 1885, *ibid.* Sherman to Grant, Nov. 27, 1872, Sherman Letter-book. Sherman to Paymaster General Alvord, *ibid.*

CHAPTER 59: KETTLE FIRES FLICKER OUT

Description of Thomas Ewing's last illness, statements to author of Thomas Ewing, III; *Memorial of Thomas Ewing*. Archbishop Purcell's statement, *ibid.* Ewing to Sister Angela, *ibid.* Sherman to Blaine on Ewing's illness, Sherman Letter-book. *Methodist Advocate* quoted in *Memorial of Thomas Ewing*. Eleanor Ewing's comment on Sherman's European trip, letter of Mrs. E. M. Brown to author. Byers on Sherman in Europe, Byers's *Twenty Years in Europe*. Sherman on "Marching Through Georgia" in Dublin, *Life and Reminiscences of Sherman, by Distinguished Men*. Sherman to John, Sherman Letter-book. Sherman to J. S. Rollins, *ibid.* Sherman to Byers, Aug. 8, 1874, Byers, *op. cit.* Sherman to Boynton, Sherman Letter-book. Sherman to Bowman and Moulton on concern over *Memoirs*, letters quoted by Jared W. Young in *Booksellers and Print Dealers Weekly*, Dec. 8, 1927. Ellen Sherman to Bowman, *ibid.* Sherman's letter of Jan. 6, 1885, on help to Southerners, Sherman Letter-book. Sherman tries to help J. E. Johnston secure Federal appointment, statement of Secretary of the Interior John W. Noble to Sherman Steele; Steele to author.

CHAPTER 60: I WILL NOT SERVE IF ELECTED

All correspondence of W. T. and John Sherman, Sherman Letter-book. Sherman on Belknap's downfall, *New York Herald*, Mar. 7, 1876. Eaton quoted, Eaton's *Grant, Lincoln and Freedmen*. Sherman to Byers, Byers's *Twenty Years in Europe*. Sherman aids Mrs. Bickerdyke, S. A. T., *Reports*, Sherman's speech at the 1871 reunion. Sherman to Postmaster General, Sherman Letter-book. Anecdote of Sherman and veteran who "lied," *Life and Reminiscences of Sherman, by Distinguished Men*, pp. 462-63. Observation of the Marquis de Chambrun, the marquis to author. Statement of Sherman Steele made to author. Sherman's relatives quoted, statements to author. Tom Sherman's letter regarding his father and religion, *Life and Reminiscences of Sherman, by Distinguished Men*, p. 249. Sherman's reasons for declining retention in office, his *Memoirs;* statement of Thomas Ewing, III, to author. Sherman to Mrs. Henderson, Mrs. Henderson's statement to J. G. DeR. Hamilton; Professor Hamilton to author. Blaine to Sherman on the Presidency, *Life and Reminiscences of Sherman, by Distinguished Men*. Sherman refuses G. A. R. office, Thomas Ewing, III, to author. Sherman to Blaine, "In every man's life," etc., Sherman in *North American Review*, November, 1888. Henderson's telegrams to Sherman, Sherman's *Memoirs*, 4th ed., Chap. 27, written by Sherman's children. Tom Sherman quoted, S. A. T., *Reports*, speech in 1892. Sherman to Philemon Ewing on the Presidency, statement to author by Sister Philemon, daughter of Philemon Ewing.

CHAPTER 61: DEATH WALKED WITH ME

Depew on Sherman, *Life and Reminiscences of Sherman, by Distinguished Men*. Sherman to Rockford County Fair, Sherman Letter-book. Statements of James Madison Barrett, made to author. Anecdote of Thackara and Sherman after banquet, Thackara's statement to author. Sherman at Yale, Johnson's *Sherman*, p. 550. Sherman's method of conducting Society meeting, Hedley's *Marching through Georgia*. Sherman at banquets, S. A. T., *Reports*, reunions. Sherman to E. P. Howell, Johnson's *Life of Sherman*, p. 557. Sherman on "I think we understand what fame is," S. A. T., *Reports*, speech at the 1885 reunion. Sherman's "War is all hell" speech, *Ohio State Journal*, Aug. 12, 1880. Sherman and Logan "bury hatchet," Dawson's *Life of Logan*. Sherman on reconciliation with Stanton, Sherman Letter-book. Sherman to Fred Grant, *ibid.* Sherman to W. F. Vilas, *ibid.* Sherman to John, *ibid.* Sherman to Thackara, *Chicago Journal's* account of Sherman's funeral. Sherman and Mark Twain, Sherman Letter-book. Sherman plagued by J. B. McCullaugh, *Chicago Tribune*, Feb. 11, 1891. Sherman to a friend on dangers of New York banquets greater than battlefield, mss. dated Feb. 12, 1890, in possession of Oliver R. Barrett. Sherman to Bok, *The Americanization of Edward Bok*. Sherman's physical depression after his wife's death, Sherman's *Memoirs*, 4th ed., Chapter 27, written by his children. Sherman poses for St. Gaudens, Cortissoz's *Life of Whitelaw Reid*, Vol. 2, p. 379. Sherman's speeches to Ohio Society, *History of the Ohio Society of New York*. Description of Sherman at death of Ellen, statement to author by Thomas Ewing, III; statements to author by James Madison Barrett. Sherman to the Rev. DeWitt Talmage, *The Americanization of Edward Bok*. Letter of Sherman to Southern editor, speech of William McKinley, 1894, quoted in *History of the Ohio Society of New York*. Sherman's death and funeral, newspapers of the time.

INDEX

NOTE: The names of unimportant persons before and after the Civil War, and of unimportant places, are not in this index. Military titles of *officers* are omitted; (C.W.) indicates a Union officer in the Civil War, (C.W., C.S.), a Confederate officer.